Bank Guarantees in International Trade

Bank Guarantees in International Trade

The Law and Practice of Independent
(First Demand) Guarantees and
Standby Letters of Credit in Civil Law
and Common Law Jurisdictions

Third revised edition

By
Roeland Bertrams

ICC Publishing S.A.
Paris – New York

A C.I.P. catalogue record for this book is available from the Library of Congress.

ISBN 90 411 2243 5

Published by:
Kluwer Law International
P.O. Box 85889
2508 CN The Hague
The Netherlands

Sold and distributed in North, Central and South America by:
Aspen Publishers, Inc.
7201 McKinney Circle
Frederick, MD 21704
USA

Sold and distributed in all other countries by:
Extenza-Turpin Distribution Services
Stratton Business Park
Pegasus Drive
Biggleswade
Bedfordshire SG18 8QB
United Kingdom

ICC Uniform Rules for Demand Guarantees
ICC Publication No. 458 (E) – ISBN 92.842.1094.1
Published in its official English version by the International Chamber of Commerce.
Copyright © 1992 – International Chamber of Commerce (ICC), Paris.

International Standby Practices – ISP 98
ICC Publication No. 590 (E) – ISBN 92.842.1247.2 Published in its official English version by the International Chamber of Commerce
Copyright © 1998 – The Institute of International Banking Law & Practice, Inc.

Printed on acid-free paper

© 2004 Kluwer Law International

All rights reserved. No part of this publication may be reproduced, stored in a retrieval system, or transmitted in any form or by any means, mechanical, photocopying, recording or otherwise, without prior written permission of the publishers.

Permission to use this content must be obtained from the copyright owner. Please apply to: Kluwer Law International, Rights and Permissions Department, P.O. Box 85889, 2508 CN The Hague, The Netherlands. E-mail: permissions@kluwerlaw.com.
Website: www.kluwerlaw.com

TABLE OF CONTENTS

Preface	vii
Detailed Table of Contents	ix
Abbreviations	xxvii
Text	1-466
Uniform Rules for Demand Guarantees (URDG)	467
International Standby Practices (ISP98)	475
Uncitral Convention on Independent Guarantees and Stand-by Letters of Credit	505
Table of Cases	517
Bibliography	537
Index	549
About this book and its author	561

PREFACE TO THE THIRD EDITION

The first edition of this book on independent bank guarantees and standby letters of credit was published in 1990 and a second revised edition appeared in 1996. With an interval of eight years, a third edition was long overdue. Here it is. The entire text has been thoroughly revised, updated and amended in the light of new developments in the law and changing patterns in practice. This also resulted in the deletion of several (sub)paragraphs and the addition of a significant number of new (sub)paragraphs. All new case law as from 1995 until approximately 2002/2003 in The Netherlands, Germany, England, France and Belgium as well as new case law from certain other European countries and the United States has been taken into account. Legal writing throughout the period from these jurisdictions has also been incorporated into this third edition. Much attention has been paid to the new International Standby Practices (ISP98) which were promulgated in 1998, and the UNCITRAL Convention on independent guarantees and stand-by letters of credit which entered into force, albeit in a small number of countries, in 2000. A third important development on the level of uniform law was the entry into force in 1998 of the Uniform Act on Securities of the 15 West African Member States of the OHADA; the chapter on independent guarantees was directly derived from the 1992 ICC Uniform Rules for Demand Guarantees (URDG).

As I wrote in the preface of the first and second edition, this book is not a one-man operation. Many persons and institutions have greatly contributed in different ways to this third edition. Again I have had the good fortune to maintain invaluable as well as congenial contacts with the banking community. I would especially like to mention Mr. E. Onderstal, Mr. J.A. Hol, Mr. J.P. Vaes, Mr. R. Zijlemaker, Ms. P.R.M. Vernooij and Mr. L.W. Mooij of ABN-AMRO, Mr. F. Gambrosier, Mr. H.J. Gostelie, Ms. F. Vosslamber and Mr. R. van den Bosch of ING Bank, Mr. R.W.H.A. Verhoeven and Mr. P.H. Kuypers of Fortis Bank. The library and information desk of the London, Paris, New York, Frankfurt, Amsterdam and Brussels office of Clifford Chance, solicitors, have been most helpful in tracing case law, legal publications and other materials from their jurisdiction. I am also grateful to the Amsterdam office of Clifford Chance which gave me (some) time to work on the project. Several of my collegues at the Law Faculty of the Free University (*Vrije Universiteit*) of Amsterdam gave me much appreciated academic support. Many others gave technical assistance. In particular, I would like to mention Steve Lambley who did a great job on editorial work.

Roeland Bertrams

Amsterdam, December 2003

DETAILED TABLE OF CONTENTS

CHAPTER 1. INTRODUCTION 1
   1-1 General 1
   1-2 Terminology. Guarantee = independent guarantee 4
   1-3 The origins of the American standby letter of credit 5
   1-4 The American standby letter of credit is similar to the European
   independent guarantee 7
   1-5 Issuers of guarantees 8
   1-6 Countries and regions covered in this study. Practice 9
   1-7 Method. Uniformity of the law 9

CHAPTER 2. OVERVIEW 11
2.1   Independence 11
2.2   Functions 13
2.3   Structure and terminology 15
      2-3 Guarantee as a multi-party relationship. Interdependence 15
      2-4 Direct guarantee 15
      2-5 Direct guarantee and advising bank 16
      2-6 Indirect guarantee. First/instructing bank and second/issuing bank .. 18
      2-7 The American standby letter of credit as a counter-guarantee 19
      2-8 Confirmed guarantee 21
      2-9 Personal security for reimbursement by the account party 21
      2-10 Syndicated guarantees 24
      2-11 Back-to-back guarantees 25
      2-11a Loans and risk participation through guarantees 25
      2-11b Transfer of credit risk by the bank 25
2.4   Sources of law 25
      2-12 The UNCITRAL Convention on independent guarantees and
      stand-by letters of credit 25
      2-13 Developments in uniform law. URCG and URDG of the
      International Chamber of Commerce; ISP98 28
      2-14 Main features of the URDG and ISP98 31
      2-15 Standby letters of credit and the UCP and UCC 33
      2-16 The ICC Uniform Rules for Contract Bonds (URCB) 34
      2-17 National laws and regulations 35
      2-18 Case law and legal writing 36

CHAPTER 3. TYPES OF GUARANTEE 37
3.1 General 37
3.2 Tender guarantees 38
3.3 Performance guarantees 39
3.4 Maintenance (or warranty) guarantees 40
3.5 Repayment (or advance payment) guarantees 41
3.6 Retention guarantees 42
3.7 Payment guarantees and standby letters of credit 42
3.8 Customs guarantees. EC repayment guarantees 44
3.9 Judicial guarantees 44
3.10 Other types 45
3.11 Autonomous guarantees. The German Garantievertrag. Indemnity 45

CHAPTER 4. CONDITIONS OF PAYMENT (PAYMENT MECHANISM) ... 47
4.1 Introduction. Main types. Documentary nature 47
4.2 Payment on first demand 48
    4-2 General 48
    4-3 'On simple demand'. Statement of default; prior notice of default and grace period 49
    4-3a Art. 20(a) URDG and statement of default 50
    4-4 Reversal of risks 51
    4-5 Words and phrases. Construction of the instrument 52
    4-6 Origins 53
    4-7 'First justified demand' 53
    4-8 'In the event of default'. Effektivklauseln 53
4.3 Payment upon submission of third-party documents 54
    4-9 Terminology and nature 54
    4-10 Documents to be submitted by the beneficiary 55
    4-11 Documents to be submitted by the account party 56
    4-12 Evaluation 57
4.4 Payment upon submission of an arbitral or court decision 58
    4-13 General 58
    4-14 Comparison with suretyship. Advantages for banks 58
    4-15 Miscellaneous 59
    4-16 Some variants and additional clauses 60
4.5 Suretyship payable on first demand. Conclusive evidence clauses 61
    4-17 'Suretyship' payable on first demand. France, the Netherlands and Belgium 61
    4-18 Suretyship payable on first demand. Germany 62

4-19 Germany. Differences between a suretyship payable on first demand and a first demand guarantee 63
4-20 Conclusive evidence clauses. United Kingdom 64

CHAPTER 5. LEGAL NATURE 67
5-1 Subsumptions and comparisons with traditional concepts 67
5-2 Contract *sui generis* 68
5-3 Independent guarantees compared with documentary credits and suretyship 68
5-4 Domestic first demand guarantees 70

CHAPTER 6. PARTIES TO THE UNDERLYING RELATIONSHIP 71
6.1 Allocation of risks 71
    6-1 From the viewpoint of the beneficiary 71
    6-2 First demand guarantee from the viewpoint of the account party, 'pay first, argue later' 73
    6-3 Recovery after payment 75
    6-4 First demand guarantee and risk evaluation 75
6.2 Negotiations 76
    6-5 General 76
    6-6 Direct/indirect guarantees 77
    6-7 Protective clauses in the guarantee and counter-balancing provisions in the underlying contract 79
    6-8 Issuance of the guarantee as a condition precedent and principal obligation 79
    6-9 Even-handedness of a first demand guarantee; contractual relationship as a whole 80

CHAPTER 7. ROLE AND POSITION OF THE BANK 83
7.1 Issuing guarantees as a financial service 83
7.2 The bank's interest in independence 85
7.3 The bank's interest in the terms and conditions of the guarantee; documents 87
7.4 Factors influencing (non-)acceptance of the request 88

CHAPTER 8. DRAFTING AND CLAUSES 91
8.1 Interests of the parties; documentary nature 91
8.2 Drafting of the text, patterns and development 91
    8-2 Drafting 91
    8-3 Patterns and development 93

8.3	Reference to the underlying relationship; consideration	94
	8-4 Reference to the underlying relationship	94
	8-5 Consideration	95
8.4	Beneficiary. Creditor's bank as beneficiary	95
8.5	Conditions precedent	96
	8-7 Introduction	96
	8-8 Performance guarantees	96
	8-9 Standby letters of credit (payment guarantees)	97
	8-10 Repayment, retention and maintenance guarantees	97
8.6	Period of validity	98
	8-11 Introduction	98
	8-12 Expiry date – calendar date, expiry event, or a combination	98
	8-13 Extension clause	100
	8-14 Commencement date	101
	8-15 Return of the guarantee document	101
	8-16 Guarantees payable upon a court or arbitral decision; absence of expiry date; continuing guarantee	102
8.7	Amount, currency	104
8.8	Reduction and increase of the maximum amount	105
8.9	Amendments to the secured contract	106
8.10	Grace period	106
8.11	Time of payment; interest	106
8.12	Assignment; pledge; transfer	107
8.13	Set-off	108
8.14	Non-recourse or subordination clause	108
8.15	Jurisdiction, applicable law	109

CHAPTER 9. RELATIONSHIP BETWEEN ACCOUNT PARTY – FIRST INSTRUCTING BANK – SECOND ISSUING BANK. INTRODUCTION AND STRUCTURE ... 111

9-1 Direct guarantee ... 111
9-2 Direct guarantee and advising bank ... 111
9-3 Indirect guarantee ... 112
9-4 The American standby letter of credit as counter-guarantee ... 113
9-5 Relationship between account party – first instructing bank – second issuing bank and the guarantee. Independence from mandate ... 114

CHAPTER 10. RELATIONSHIP ACCOUNT PARTY – BANK. DIRECT GUARANTEE ... 115

10.1 Introduction ... 115
10.2 Legal nature ... 116
    10-2 Mandate ... 116
    10-3 Account party – bank and documentary credit ... 117
    10-4 Main features: instructions, duty of examination, reimbursement, duty of care ... 117
10.3 Counter-guarantee ... 118
    10-5 Counter-guarantee by the account party ... 118
    10-6 Instructions and counter-guarantee by a party other than the principal debtor; affiliated company ... 121
10.4 Security for reimbursement ... 122
    10-7 Security ... 122
    10-8 Release and prolongation ... 122
10.5 Commission ... 123
10.6 Incidental expenses, litigation and costs ... 123
    10-10 Incidental expenses ... 123
    10-11 Litigation and costs. Risks ... 123
10.7 Instructions by the account party. Adherence to the instructions. Review and acceptance by the bank ... 126
    10-12 The principle of strict compliance, direct guarantees ... 126
    10-13 Indirect guarantees ... 128
    10-14 Review by the bank. Duty of bank and account party in general ... 129
    10-15 Imprecise and incomplete instructions ... 130
    10-16 Advice to the account party ... 133
    10-17 Acceptance and refusal by the bank ... 134
10.8 Duty of examination with respect to compliance with the terms and conditions of the guarantee ... 135
    10-18 Introduction. Relationship bank-beneficiary and bank-account party ... 135
    10-19 Compliance with all positive conditions, fulfilment of negative conditions ... 136
    10-20 Formal compliance ... 137
    10-21 Strict compliance ... 138
    10-22 Relaxation of the principle of strict compliance? Substantial compliance ... 140
    10-23 Inconsistencies ... 143
    10-24 Reasonable care, discretion ... 144
    10-25 Reasonable care, discretion. Third-party documents ... 145

		10-26 Reasonable care, discretion. Non-documentary conditions of payment. Effektivklauseln 147

             10-26 Reasonable care, discretion. Non-documentary conditions of payment. Effektivklauseln 147

             10-27 Limitations of liability, notification to account party 149

10.9   Bank's duty of notification of the demand for payment 150

             10-28 Significance of notification... 150

             10-29 Opinions differ, the law at present, notice injunctions 150

             10-30 Arguments pro and contra a duty of notification 152

             10-31 Art. 17 and 21 URDG, Rule 3.10 ISP98: notification and transmission of documents 154

10.10 Recourse of the bank against the account party. Special risks 154

10.11 Subrogation 156

CHAPTER 11. RELATIONSHIP ACCOUNT PARTY – FIRST INSTRUCTING BANK – SECOND ISSUING BANK. INDIRECT GUARANTEE. COUNTER-GUARANTEE 159

11.1   Account party – first instructing bank – second issuing bank. General . 159

       11.1.1 Introduction. Structure and terminology 159

       11.1.2 First instructing bank – second issuing bank. Legal nature. Mandate 159

       11.1.3 Various aspects 160

       11.1.4 Instructions for the issuance of the primary guarantee. Advice . 161

             11-4 Instructions and adherence; imprecise instructions 161

             11-5 Errors in the transmission of the instructions. Issuing bank's failure to carry out the instructions. Arts. 12, 14 and 15 URDG 162

             11-6 Advice with respect to local practices 163

       11.1.5 Second issuing bank's duty of examination with respect to compliance 164

11.2   The counter-guarantee 164

       11.2.1 General 164

       11.2.2 Legal nature and effect of counter-guarantees 166

             11-9 Introduction. The issue of independence between the primary guarantee and counter-guarantee 166

             11-10 The view that the counter-guarantee is independent of the primary guarantee and operates as an ordinary independent guarantee 168

             11-11 The view that the counter-guarantee is independent of the mandate and operates as an ordinary independent guarantee. Germany 171

Contents   xv

    11-12 The counter-guarantee is independent of the underlying relationship 172
    11-13 The view of this study. The counter-guarantee is an independent indemnity and operates as an ordinary independent guarantee, subject to certain limitations. Summary 172
    11-14 The independent nature of counter-guarantees and its limits in case law. Introduction 176
    11-15 Cases decided on the basis of independence. Fulfilment of the terms of the primary guarantee not considered. No evidence of fault by the issuing bank 176
    11-16 Cases decided on the basis of independence. Fulfilment of the terms of the primary guarantee considered. No evidence of fault by the issuing bank. 179
    11-17 Cases decided on the basis of independence. Terms of the primary guarantee not fulfilled. Claim under the counter-guarantee rejected. 180
    11-18 Other cases. Fulfilment of the terms of the primary guarantee considered. No evidence of fault by the issuing bank. 181
    11-19 Other cases. Terms of the primary guarantee not fulfilled. Claim under the counter-guarantee rejected. 182
    11-20 The limits and exception to the independence of counter-guarantees in relation to the primary guarantee. Conclusions in respect of case law. 183
11.3 The instructing bank owes no general duty to the account party to investigate fulfilment of the terms of the primary guarantee 184
    11-21 Introduction 184
    11-22 No general duty 184
    11-23 Banking practice 185
    11-24 Limited duty to assist the account party 186
    11-25 If the counter-guarantee prescribes a statement from the issuing bank and the transmission of documents. Art. 20(b) and 21 URDG 187
11.4 Clauses in the counter-guarantee 188
    11-26 Clauses relating to payment 188
    11-27 Duration, expiry date 190
    11-28 Amount and currency, transfer 191
    11-29 Choice of law, jurisdiction 191
    11-30 Garnishment ('Kuwaiti') clauses 191
11.5 Instructing bank's duty to inform the account party of the content of the counter-guarantee 193

CHAPTER 12. OTHER ASPECTS OF THE BANK GUARANTEE 195
12.1 The principle of independence re-examined 195
    12.1.1 Recapitulation 195
        12-1 Introduction 195
        12-2 Between bank and beneficiary 195
        12-3 Between account party and bank, indirect guarantee and counter-guarantee 196
        12-4 Between parties to the underlying relationship 196
    12.1.2 Independence and functional interdependence 196
        12-5 Synthesis instead of antithesis 196
        12-6 Antithesis instead of synthesis 197
    12.1.3 Independence as an abstract concept and as a matter of construction. Relativeness and evolution 200
12.2 Formation 201
    12-8 Unilateral engagement or consensual contract. Formation 201
    12-9 Arguments 204
    12-10 Rejection, counter-proposals 205
    12-11 Requirements as to form 206
    12-12 Transmission, authenticity, authority, operative instrument 207
    12-13 Commencement, taking effect 208
    12-14 Amendments, irrevocability 208
    12-15 Guarantees issued by private individuals and non-financial institutions. Duty to advise guarantor 208
    12-15a German Act on General Terms and Conditions. Invalidity of suretyship and guarantee payable on first demand 210
12.3 Construction 210
    12.3.1 Independent guarantee or accessory suretyship. Introduction ... 210
    12.3.2 Suggestions for some general guidelines 211
        12-17 Introduction 211
        12-18 When does the issue of construction arise? 212
        12-19 Finding the intention of parties 212
        12-20 Full and entire text as primary source 213
        12-21 Drafting technique in historical perspective, weighing of terms and phrases. 'Effektivklauseln' 214
        12-22 Specification of the means of proof; documentary proof; statements by beneficiary 216
        12-23 Reference to the underlying relationship 217
        12-24 Reference to international usage 218
        12-25 To what terms have parties agreed 219
        12-26 Resort to general (statutory) rules for construction; presumptions 220

	12.3.3	Miscellaneous aspects	222
		12-27 Special rules for banks?	222
		12-28 Special rules for domestic cases and for 'guarantees' issued by private individuals or non-financial institutions?	223
		12-29 Procedural aspects	225
	12.3.4	Overview of case law	226
		12-30 Introduction	226
		12-31 'First demand' clause. Held: suretyship.	226
		12-32 No 'first demand' clause. Held: first demand guarantee	227
		12-33 Payment on 'first justified demand'	228
		12-34 Held: independent (first demand) guarantee	229
		12-35 Held: first demand suretyship. Germany	230
		12-36 Held: suretyship	231
	12.3.5	Construction of terms and clauses in independent guarantees and counter-indemnities	231
		12-37 Independent guarantees	231
		12-37a Indemnity ('counter-guarantee') by instructing bank to issuing bank in the case of an indirect guarantee	234
12.4	Period of validity. Law and practice		235
	12.4.1	Significance of expiry date. The risk of the 'perpetual' (counter-)guarantee	235
	12.4.2	Extension clauses	236
	12.4.3	'Extend or pay' requests	236
		12-40 Practice and motives	236
		12-41 Legal position	237
		12-42 Tender guarantees, 'extend or withdraw' requests	239
		12-43 Account party and bank. Who is to decide? Art. 26 URDG	240
		12-44 Indirect guarantee, extension of counter-guarantee	241
		12-45 Counter-guarantee, absence of 'extend or pay' request from the beneficiary	243
	12.4.4	'Hold for value' requests	244
		12-46 Practice and motives	244
		12-47 Legal characterisation	244
		12-48 Implications	245
	12.4.5	Enforceability of expiry dates	246
		12-49 General trend towards enforceability	246
		12-50 Assimilation to accessory guarantees. Statute of Limitation	248
		12-51 Enforceability of expiry date uncertain. Syria	249
		12-52/53 Expiry date enforceable	250

	12.4.6	(Non-)Return of the guarantee document. (No) statement of discharge	252
		12-54 Return of the guarantee document. Statement of discharge. Legal significance	252
		12-55 Return by mistake. Avoidance of payment	252
		12-56 Non-return of the guarantee document. Reasons	253
		12-57 Non-return of the guarantee document. Legal significance	254
		12-58 No statement of discharge in respect of the counter-guarantee. Primary guarantee expired	254
		12-59 Initiatives by the account party and instructing bank if the (counter-)guarantee document has not been returned or if no discharge has been given	255
	12.4.7	Release of security furnished by the account party, unblocking of the credit facility, release of the duty to pay commission. Discharge of the account party's liability	256
		12-60 Introduction	256
		12-61 Direct guarantees	257
		12-62 Indirect guarantees	258
		12-63 Indirect guarantees. Counter-guarantee contains expiry date	259
		12-64 Indirect guarantees. Counter-guarantee valid until discharge. Release of security, unblocking of the credit facility	259
		12-65 Indirect guarantees. Counter-guarantee valid until discharge. Release of the duty to pay commission	260
		12-66 Discharge of account party's liability	261
12.5	Assignment. Pledge		262
	12.5.1	Meaning and significance of assignment	262
	12.5.2	Contractual assignment	262
	12.5.3	Effect of contractual assignment. Position of assignee	263
		12-69 General	263
		12-70 Case law	265
	12.5.4	Strengthening the position of the assignee; special provisions; irrevocable power of attorney?	267
	12.5.5	Assignment by operation of law	268
	12.5.6	The effect of transfer of the secured contract; lease contracts	270
	12.5.7	Pledge of the guarantee	272
12.6	Transfer		272
		12-75 Transfer and documentary credits; back-to-back credits	272

Contents

| | 12-76 Transfer and guarantees; back-to-back guarantees .... 273 |
| | 12-77 Fraudulent trading schemes .... 274 |

CHAPTER 13. THE DEMAND FOR PAYMENT 277
13.1 General aspects 277
       13-1 Percentages and their significance for the account party 277
       13-2 Bank's examination with respect to compliance with the
       terms and conditions of the guarantee. Summary 278
       13-3 Direct and indirect guarantees. Applicable law 279
13.2 Call on the guarantee 279
      13.2.1 The call 279
              13-4 The guarantee must have been called 279
              13-5 Who is entitled to call; identity of the person calling the
              guarantee; change of status; agency and power of attorney 280
              13-6 Addressee and place of the call 283
              13-7 Formal requirements 284
              13-8 Has a proper request for payment been made? 285
      13.2.2 The call must relate to the secured contract and/or obligation ... 286
              13-9 General 286
              13-10 Position of beneficiary, bank and account party 286
      13.2.3 Call on a first demand guarantee 288
              13-11 Simple demand guarantees 288
              13-12 Statement of default and other statements by the
              beneficiary 288
              13-13 Ambiguous texts and statements; 'Effektivklauseln';
              guarantees payable on 'first justified demand' 290
              13-13a Documents from the account party 291
      13.2.4 Call on a guarantee requiring submission of third-party
             documents 292
              13-14 Documents to be tendered by the beneficiary 292
              13-15 Documents to be tendered by the account party 293
      13.2.5 Call on guarantee requiring submission of an arbitral or
             court decision 294
              13-16 General 294
              13-17 Validity of the arbitral or court decision 295
      13.2.6 Other conditions and clauses 296
              13-18 Conditions precedent 296
              13-19 Clauses limiting or terminating the right to payment 297
              13-20 Repayment guarantees and advance payment 297
              13-21 Reduction clauses 298

13.2.7 Period of validity 300
    13-22 Call must be made on or before the expiry date or before the expiry event 300
    13-23 Significance and effect of expiry dates; independence and relationship with underlying contract; submission of statements and documents; discharge of restraining orders 302
    13-24 Special problems. 'Extend or pay' requests, ambiguous requirement as to statements by the beneficiary 305
    13-25 Commencement date 307
    13-26 Expiry event 307
13.2.8 Amount and currency 310
    13-27 Amount, partial and successive drawings 310
    13-28 Currency 311
13.2.9 Period of examination. Time of payment 311
13.2.10 Interest and damages for late payment 312
13.2.11 Procedures on non-compliance. Notice of dishonour.
    13-31 Preclusion rule 314
13.2.12 Bank's defences 316
    13-32 General. Judgment in summary proceedings and other procedural aspects 316
    13-33 Set-off with bank's own counter-claims 318
    13-34 Set-off with the bank's own counter-claims in the case of indirect guarantees 322
    13-35 Set-off with counter-claims derived from the underlying relationship; assigned counter-claims 322
    13-36 Set-off between banks 322

13.3 Call on the counter-guarantee 323
    13-37 General 323
    13-38 Statement from the issuing bank concerning the primary guarantee. Transmission of documents. Art. 20(b) and 21 URDG 324
    13-39 Period of validity 324
    13-40 Is a call or actual payment under the primary guarantee a prerequisite? 328
    13-41 Date for determining the rate of exchange 329

13.4 The effect of UN embargoes 330
13.5 Non-compliance and restraining orders 331
13.6 Recovery after payment. Final settlement 331

CHAPTER 14. THE CONCEPT OF FRAUD		335
14.1	Introduction	335
	14-1 Significance	335
	14-2 Procedural background	336
14.2	Plan of discussion	337
14.3	Comparative overview	337
	14.3.1 Introduction	337
	14.3.2 The Netherlands	338
	14-5 Case law	338
	14-6 Legal writing	339
	14.3.3 Germany	340
	14-7 Legal writing	340
	14-8 Case law	341
	14.3.4 France	342
	14-9 Case law	342
	14-10 Legal writing	344
	14.3.5 Belgium	344
	14-11 Case law	344
	14-12 Legal writing	345
	14.3.6 England	345
	14.3.7 United States of America	349
	14.3.8. Summary of the comparative overview, UNCITRAL Convention	353
14.4	Fraud and evidence of fraud. Some reflections	357
	14-18 Fraud in relation to the nature and purpose of first demand guarantees	357
	14-19 Evidence of fraud	358
	14-20 The notion 'fraud'	360
14.5	Overview of possible types of fraud	360
	14.5.1 Introduction	360
	14.5.2 Lack of authority	361
	14.5.3 Mistake, misrepresentation, economic duress, undue influence	362
	14.5.4 Conditions precedent	362
	14-24 General	362
	14-25 Condition precedent and breach of contract by the beneficiary	363
	14.5.5 Completion of the secured contract or obligation	363
	14-26 General	363
	14-27 Completion of the secured contract or obligation established	364

14-28 Completion of the secured contract or obligation not established 368
14-29 Account party not liable for defects 369
14-30 Lapse of contractual warranty period 369
14-31 Account party complies with the terms of a documentary credit 370
14-32 Non-payment by the beneficiary 370
14-33 Completion not yet due 371
14.5.6 Material breach of contract by the beneficiary 371
14-34 General 371
14-35 Material breach of contract not established 372
14-36 Material breach of contract established 372
14-37 Beneficiary's failure to furnish a documentary credit 373
14-38 Beneficiary makes performance by the account party impossible 374
14.5.7 *Force majeure* 375
14-39 *Force majeure* not established 375
14-40 *Force majeure* established 375
14-41 Government measures, embargoes 376
14-42 Evaluation 377
14.5.8 Violation of public order; illegality 378
14.5.9 Termination, cancellation and avoidance of the secured contract 381
14.5.10 Beneficiary's cause of action is time-barred 382
14.5.11 The amount claimed is excessive; damages already assessed and/or paid; payment already made 383
14.5.12 The call does not relate to the secured contract or obligation, or is inspired by improper motives 384
14.5.13 Liquid counterclaims against beneficiary, set-off 385
14.5.14 Court or arbitral decision 386
14.5.15 Tender guarantees 387
14.5.16 Repayment, retention and maintenance guarantees 388
14.5.17 Beneficiary's statement is false. Third-party document is forged 390
14.5.18 Conclusion 391
14.5.19 Fraud: distinction between guarantees and documentary credits? 391
14.6 Fraud and summary judgment. Direct and indirect guarantees 393

Contents   xxiii

CHAPTER 15. FRAUD AND THE POSITION OF THE BANK. BANK'S LIABILITY IN 'AFTER-PAYMENT' CASES 395

15.1 Direct Guarantee 395
    15-2 *If* fraud is evident to the bank, it is liable to the account party when it pays under the guarantee 395
    15-2 Distinction between 'before-' and 'after-payment' cases. Extent of the bank's duty and potential liability 396
    15-3 Bank's knowledge of the beneficiary's fraud. The test 399
    15-4 Appraisal and suggestions for an alternative set of rules 400
15.2 Indirect guarantee 402
    15-5 Issuing bank's liability 402
    15-6 Instructing bank's liability 402
15.3 Banking practice 403

CHAPTER 16. FRAUD AND RESTRAINING ORDERS 405

16.1 Introduction 405
    16-1 General 405
16.2 Applications for restraining orders against the beneficiary, direct guarantee 406
16.3 Applications for restraining orders against the bank, direct guarantee. Must the beneficiary's fraud be evident to the bank? Cause of action. Are restraining orders against the bank permissible? 407
    16-3 Introduction 407
    16-4 England 408
    16-5 Germany 411
    16-6 The Netherlands 414
    16-7 France and Belgium 414
    16-8 United States of America 415
    16-8a UNCITRAL Convention 416
    16-9 Summary and evaluation 416
    16-10 Applications for restraining orders against beneficiary and bank is the better procedure 419
16.4 Applications for restraining orders in respect of indirect guarantees and counter-guarantees 420
    16.4.1 General 420
        16-11 Restraining orders against instructing and/or issuing bank and/or beneficiary. Cause of action 420
        16-12 Beneficiary's fraud and foreign applicable law 421

16.4.2 Restraining orders against the instructing and/or issuing bank in 'after-payment' cases 423
16-13 Fraud by the issuing bank. Issuing bank's knowledge of beneficiary's fraud 423
16-14 Issuing bank's knowledge of the beneficiary's fraud. The test 426
16-15 Identification 427
16.4.3 Restraining orders against the instructing and/or issuing bank and/or beneficiary in 'before-payment' cases 428
16-16 Introduction 428
16-17 Applications for orders restraining the issuing bank from paying under the primary guarantee and for orders restraining the beneficiary from demanding or receiving payment under the primary guarantee 429
16-18 Applications for orders restraining the instructing bank from paying under the counter-guarantee and for orders restraining the issuing bank from demanding or receiving payment under the counter-guarantee 430
16-19 The limited effect of restraining orders. Non-recognition and contrary decisions by the foreign court 431
16.4.4 The limited effect of restraining orders. Inter-bank relationship. Recourse against account party 432
16.5 Other Aspects Concerning Restraining Orders 433
16-21 Restraining orders and the commercial viability of guarantees ... 433
16-22 Hardship for the account party to litigate in the beneficiary's country 434
16-23 Restraining orders and the reputation of the bank 434
16-24 Bank's duty to defer payment if the account party applies for restraining orders? 435

CHAPTER 17. CONSERVATORY ATTACHMENT AND THE U.K. FREEZING (MAREVA) INJUNCTION 437

17-1 Introduction 437
17-2 Conservatory attachment is incompatible with the agreement between account party and beneficiary in the event of non-established fraud 437
17-3 Conservatory attachment in the event of established fraud 439
17-4 Conservatory attachment and counterclaims ex secured contract. Set-off 441
17-5 Conservatory attachment and counterclaims ex other contracts. Set-off 442

17-6 Conservatory attachment in respect of the beneficiary's accounts after payment 443
17-7 Conservatory attachment and indirect guarantees 445
17-8 Conservatory attachment does not prohibit the bank from paying into a blocked account and from debiting the account party's accounts 445
17-9 The U.K. freezing (Mareva) injunction 446

CHAPTER 18. JURISDICTION AND APPLICABLE LAW 449
18.1 Jurisdiction 449
    18-1 Introduction 449
    18-2 Proceedings between the parties to the (counter-)guarantee 449
    18-3 Proceedings initiated by the account party. Direct guarantee 450
    18-4 Proceedings initiated by the account party. Indirect guarantee 451
18.2 Applicable law 451
    18-5 (In)significance of private international law 451
    18-6 General rules of private international law. 1980 Rome Convention 453
    18-7 Relationship account party/bank 454
    18-8 Relationship bank/beneficiary 454
    18-9 Relationship instructing bank/issuing bank in the case of indirect guarantees 455
    18-10 Public mandatory law 457

CHAPTER 19. BANK GUARANTEES AND CONSTRUCTION CONTRACTS 459
19-1 First demand guarantees as financing instruments 459
19-2 Disputes revolve on the payment scheme. Call as *ultimum remedium* 460
19-3 Joint ventures 461
19-4 Subguarantees from subcontractors. Subguarantees distinguished from counter-guarantees 463
19-5 Subguarantees and clauses; special risks 465

ABBREVIATIONS

AA	Ars Aequi
All ER	All England Law Reports
Banking L.J.	Banking Law Journal
Bb	Nieuwsbrief Bedrijfsjuridische Berichten
BFLR	Banking and Financial Law Review
BRH	Belgische Rechtspraak Handelszaken (=JCB)
Bus. Law.	Business Lawyer
CISG	UN Convention on Contracts for the International Sale of Goods (Vienna 1980)
D.	Recueil Dalloz Sirey
D.-CDA	Receuil Dalloz, Cahier Droit des Affaires
DB	Der Betrieb
DCI	Documentary Credits Insight
DPCI	Droit et Pratique du Commerce International
FIDIC	Federation Internationale des Ingenieurs-Conseils, Conditions of Contract for Works of Civil Engineering Construction, 1999
Harvard Int. L.R.	Harvard International Law Review
HLR	Harvard Law Review
IBL	International Banking Law
IBLJ	International Business Law Journal (= RDAI)
ICC	International Chamber of Commerce
ICLR	International Construction Law Review
IFLR	International Financial Law Review
IPRax	Praxis des Internationalen Privat- und Verfahrensrecht
JBL	Journal of Business Law
JCB	Jurisprudence Commerciale Belge (=BRH)
JCP	Juris-classeur Périodique (La Semaine Jurdique)
JDI	Journal du droit international (Clunet)
JIBFL	(Butterworth's) Journal of International Banking and Financial Law
JIBL	Journal of International Banking Law
JLMB	Jurisprudence de Liege, Mons et Bruxelles
JMLC	Journal of Maritime Law and Commerce
JOR	Jurisprudentie Onderneming & Recht
JT	Journal des Tribunaux
Jur. Liège	Jurisprudence Liège
KG	Kort Geding
KGK	Kort Geding Kort

Lloyd's Rep.	Lloyd's Law Reports
LMCLQ	Lloyd's Maritime and Commercial Law Quarterly
Meed	Middle East Economic Digest
NJ	Nederlandse Jurisprudentie
NJB	Nederlands Juristenblad
NJW	Neue juristische Wochenschrift
NTBR	Nederlands Tijdschrift Burgerlijk recht
OHADA	Organisation pour l'Harmonisation de Droit des Affaires en Afrique
Q.B.	(Law reports) Queen's Bench Division
R.N.B.	Revue du Notariat Belge
RDC	Revue Droit Commercial Belge (=TBH)
Rev. Banque	Revue de la Banque (Bank- en Financiewezen)
RPDB	Répertoire Pratique du Droit Belge
Rev. Reg. Dr.	Revue Régionale de Droit
RDAI	Revue de Droit des Affaires Internationales (= IBLJ)
RGDC	Revue Générale de Droit Civil Belge
RIW	Recht der internationalen Wirtschaft
RTDC	Revue trimestielle droit commercial
RW	Rechtskundig Weekblad
S & S	Schip en Schade
SAMA	Saudi Arabian Monetary Agency
TBBR	Tijdschrift voor Belgisch Burgerlijk Recht
TBH	Tijdschrift Belgisch Handelsrecht (=RDC)
TPR	Tijdschrift voor Privaatrecht
TVVS	Tijdschrift voor Verenigingen, Vennootschappen en Stichtingen
UCC	United States Uniform Commercial Code
UCC LJ	Uniform Commercial Code Law Journal
UCP	Uniform Customs and Practice for Documentary Credits (1993 edition), ICC Publication no. 500
Uncitral Convention	United Nations Convention on Independent Guarantees and Stand-by Letters of Credit, 1995
URCG	Uniform Rules for Contract Guarantees, ICC Publication no. 325 (1978)
URCB	Uniform Rules for Contract Bonds, IIC Publication no. 524.
URDG	Uniform Rules for Demand Guarantees, ICC Publication no. 458
WLR	Weekly Law Reports
WM	Wertpapier-Mitteilungen
WPNR	Weekblad voor Privaatrecht, Notariaat en Registratie
ZGR	Zeitschrift für Unternehmungs und Gesellschaftsrecht
ZHR	Zeitschrift für das gesamte Handelsrecht und Wirtschaftsrecht
ZIP	Zeitschrift für Wirtschaftsrecht und Insolvenzpraxis

CHAPTER 1
INTRODUCTION

GENERAL

1-1 Independent bank guarantees and their American equivalent, standby letters of credit, are a relatively new legal phenomenon. It seems that they first appeared in the American domestic market sometime in the mid-1960s,[1] while according to bankers they began to be used in some appreciable measure in respect of international transactions during the early 1970s. The increasing wealth in the oilproducing countries of the Middle East in this period enabled these countries to conclude major contracts with Western firms for large-scale projects, such as infrastructure improvements (roads, airports, harbour facilities), public works (housing, hospitals, communication networks, power stations), industrial and agricultural projects, and national defence. It is to these developments that the origins and the early demand for independent bank guarantees and especially those payable on first demand can probably be traced.

At present, the use of independent bank guarantees is widespread and the total volume has expanded dramatically.[2] One may safely assume that major transactions today do not take place without some kind of guarantee support, while their frequency in smaller

---

[1] See Harfield, 4 U.C.C.L.J., p. 251 (1972), Verkuil, 25 Stan. L. Rev., pp. 716, 717 (1973), Wiley, 20 Bus. Law. pp. 495, 496 (1965), Note, 66 Yale L.J., p. 902 (1957).

[2] According to an estimate by the Drafting Committee of the revised Art. 5 of the U.S. Uniform Commercial Code the total of outstanding standby letters of credit amounted to US$ 250 billion in 1995, and US$ 500 billion worldwide, while the outstanding amount of standbys exceeded that of commercial letters of credit by 5:1. According to Dan Taylor, Vice-Chairman of the ICC Banking Commission and a member of the ISP98 Drafting Group, the outstanding amount of standbys in 1998 amounted to US$ 750 billion (DCI Autumn 1998, p. 14). The individual amounts of guarantees can be colossal too. In the *American Bell v. Islamic Republic of Iran* case, 474 F. Supp. 420 (S.D.N.Y. 1979), an amount of US$ 30.2 million was at stake, while the *GTE International Inc. v. Manufacturers Hanover Trust* case, No. 3525/79 (Sup. Ct., 29 March 1979), involved two guarantees, one of US$ 72.9 million and the other of US$ 31.4 million. The guarantee in *LG Duisberg, 27 November 1987*, WM 1988, p. 1483, amounted to DEM 70 million (approx. e 35 million), that in *Muduroglu Ltd. v. Ziraat Bankasi*, [1986] 1 Q.B. 1225, to US$ 36 million, that in *Paris, 2 March 1990*, D. 1990 Somm. p. 209, to FRF 145 million (approx. e 25 million), and in *Gulf Bank v. Mitsubishi Heavy Industries*, [1994] 2 Lloyd's Rep. 145, a guarantee was issued for the amount of £ 55 million.

deals depends on a number of factors. Moreover, bank guarantees are increasingly used in domestic contracts too. The growth is partly due to the fact that bank guarantees can be employed to back up all kinds of transactions, both non-financial (such as contracts of sale, leases and construction contracts), and financial transactions, such as loans and overdraft facilities, participation in joint ventures, bond issues, reinsurance and other financial commitments). In addition, bank guarantees can provide security to both the party which is entitled to payment (such as the seller, contractor, lender, lessor, etc.) and the party which is entitled to receive goods or services (such as the buyer, employer, lessee, etc.).

In international trade, risk is becoming a factor of increasing significance and concern. Transactions tend to grow and investments in projects are becoming larger. Projects nowadays are often complex, comprehensive and large-scale. A particular feature of trade today is its global expansion. For example, a British and Dutch construction firm may set up a joint venture, in which other companies also agree to take a financial interest, for the construction of an airport and ancillary facilities in Saudi Arabia, employing Turkish and South Korean subcontractors and procuring technical equipment from French and German suppliers. As a result of their size and complexity, the realisation of many of these transactions often takes a considerable period of time and a wide range of events may impede completion. Some types of contract are intended as long-term deals. All these and other factors increase the risk of non-performance, with large amounts at stake, while the scope for assessing and mitigating the risks involved are limited.

As far as international trade is concerned, the risk of non-payment has been accommodated by such devices as documentary credits and banks accepting or guaranteeing (avalising) bills of exchange. These techniques have been known for a long time. However, matters were different with respect to the risk of non-performance of obligations other than payment. Traditional means of security, such as the accessory guarantee or suretyship, are cumbersome and disadvantageous to the creditor because the accessory guarantor can invoke every defence which the principal debtor could raise. This often forces the creditor to initiate legal proceedings, which entail further inconvenience and risk. Banks are not very keen to act as accessory guarantors as it is difficult for them to determine in which situations they should proceed to payment and because they may become involved in disputes between the parties to the underlying relationship. In order to avoid these drawbacks, the independent guarantee was invented, issued by reliable and financially sound institutions such as banks. This new breed operates in much the same way as documentary credits (or letters of credit). As a matter of fact, the American variant, namely the standby letter of credit, is directly derived from the traditional letter of credit which is used as a means of payment in sale transactions and which is also called a commercial letter of credit. The modern type of independent guarantee shares many of the characteristics of documentary credits or commercial letters of credit, notably the rule of independence, the principle that payment is to be made if and only if the conditions of payment as stated in the guarantee, which are ordinarily of a documentary nature, have been fulfilled, and the rule of strict compli-

Introduction

ance. Accordingly, if the terms and conditions of the guarantee are met the bank must pay and it cannot invoke defences derived from the underlying contract. Unlike documentary credits, guarantees serve as a security device – they assure financial compensation in the event of non-performance by the principal debtor.

Independent guarantees and standby letters of credit may secure both non-monetary and monetary obligations. As far as crossborder transactions are concerned, guarantees and standby credits are frequently issued as security for default in connection with contracts for the supply of goods, construction and shipbuilding contracts, large-scale service contracts and technology transfers, mergers and acquisitions, especially in relation to representations, and warranties and environmental contractual guarantees given by the vendor of the shares. They are also used to secure financial obligations such as those resulting from loans, leases, mergers and acquisitions and financial participation in joint ventures, bond issues, commercial paper and other financial transactions, payment obligations pursuant to, for example, a contract of sale, or contingent tax debts. Domestically, guarantees are employed to back up the same types of transaction, especially in connection with financial transactions and payment obligations.[3]

The structure of independent guarantees allows for different payment mechanisms. The type which has attracted the greatest attention is the guarantee payable upon first demand, which is sometimes also referred to as an 'unconditional guarantee'. It entitles the beneficiary to receive payment from the bank without any proof or corroboration of the principal debtor/exporter's default. This type is common in certain trade branches and regions, and in certain circumstances, but its growth is primarily occasioned by the fact that international trade tends to take place in a buyer's market. Where the bargaining power of the exporter is stronger, that party might be able to negotiate a guarantee which is payable only if the creditor/importer produces third-party documents attesting non-performance or even a judicial or arbitral award affirming the creditor's right to payment.

It was not until the Iranian revolution of 1979-1980, when large numbers of guarantees and standby letters of credit in favour of Iranian Government agencies and banks were called and when Western firms in many countries rushed to the courts attempting to prevent payment, that this new breed of independent guarantee began to attract the attention of lawyers and the courts. This period marked the beginning of the development of the law in this new area, although some exploratory legal writing and a few court decisions had already paved the way.

---

[3] See further Dolan, 1.06, for an extensive description of the dazzling variety of transactions served by standby letters of credit in the American domestic and crossborder markets.

TERMINOLOGY. GUARANTEE = INDEPENDENT GUARANTEE

1-2 Both terminologically and conceptually the entire area of guarantees is, or at least was, marked by confusion, uncertainty and inconsistency. The adoption of English and American terminology by Continental banking practice also added to the confusion. In this study the term guarantee means independent guarantee, as opposed to the accessory or conditional guarantee. The perhaps best known type of independent guarantee is the so-called '(first) demand guarantee', but it should be noted that there are independent guarantees with different types of payment mechanism (see Chapter 4). When put in inverted commas ('guarantee'), the term is used in a neutral sense and includes both the independent and the accessory (or co-extensive or conditional) type of personal security.

The modern independent guarantee originated from practice, and the concept, as it functions today, was unknown in law. Practice drew and elaborated on the related, and also familiar and well-established type of personal security, namely the accessory type which is known as 'suretyship' (*borgtocht, Bürgschaft, cautionnement*), although commercial and banking practice also employed the term guarantee when in fact meaning the accessory type of security. This accounts for the terminological and conceptual confusion.[4] After some initial confusion, Continental law now reserves the term guarantee for the concept of independent guarantee, while the term suretyship refers to the accessory type, but practice continues to use the term 'guarantee' indiscriminately. American law and practice have been and are more consistent in this respect. The term guaranty or guarantee expresses that the obligation of the guarantor is co-extensive with or accessory to that of the principal debtor. This was one of the reasons why another term, namely the standby letter of credit, came to be used when parties envisaged the independent type of security. This concept is equivalent to the Continental independent guarantee.[5] English law and practice do not principally distinguish between the two concepts. Traditionally the term guarantee ordinarily denotes the accessory (or 'conditional') type of security and as a rule of construction, guarantees were presumed to be co-extensive with the underlying relationship. The term 'suretyship', which unequivocally denotes the accessory type, appears to have become obsolete and is, at any rate, used infrequently. At present, the notion of guarantee has possibly a neutral meaning while the specific nature of the security is to be gathered from the terms and conditions of each individual instrument. The term 'letter of credit' to describe an independent guarantee is also found. In many other countries and regions, a clear distinction in concept and terminology is still lacking.

As a result of the prevailing uncertainty, several other terms are used which express independence. Thus, in English and American legal language the obligation of the

---

[4] See further Chapter 12.1.3, Chapter 8.2, No. 8-3 and Chapter 12.3, Nos. 12-16 and 12-21.
[5] See further Nos. 1-3 and 1-4.

Introduction 5

independent guarantor is often described as 'primary' as opposed to the 'secondary' obligation of the surety. The term 'autonomous' is also often used. Other adjectives which purport to express independence are 'irrevocable', 'abstract' or 'unconditional', or the instrument may state that the guarantor pays the debt as his own debt. These terms and phrases are rather confusing and they are often inadequate.[6] Moreover, it is a misconception to assert categorically or assume that independent guarantees are always payable on demand without any evidence of default. Although this is indeed the prevailing type of independent guarantee, there are other payment mechanisms, such as payment upon the submission of third-party documents or a court or arbitral decision.[7]

This study avoids the term 'bond'. It has no defined meaning in law and it may refer to any kind of financial undertaking. The term 'performance bond' is especially precarious. In the United States, Canada and England performance bonds (also called 'surety bonds') are typically issued by specialised insurance and bonding companies, in connection with construction contracts. They assure the employer that in the event of default by the construction firm the project will be completed, for example by another contractor or that the employer will receive financial compensation. These performance bonds are a hybrid form of security and they cannot be circumscribed in terms of independence or co-extensiveness. They are never payable on demand and they always require (some) evidence of default, while the degree of (non-)co-extensiveness and (non-)likeness with the contract of suretyship entirely depends on the terms and conditions of the bond.[8] The rights and obligations of both parties are contained in instruments which tend to be rather lengthy and detailed, and which are, because of their archaic eighteenth-century English language, difficult to comprehend.[9]

THE ORIGINS OF THE AMERICAN STANDBY LETTER OF CREDIT

1-3 The term standby letter of credit is of American making. Two factors contributed to its emergence and use. The National Bank Act of 3 June 1864 (as amended) sets out

---

6   Rule 1.10(a) ISP98, therefore, dissuades the use of terms such as 'unconditional', 'abstract', 'absolute' and 'primary'.

7   See Chapter 4.

8   See Dolan, § 1.05, for the differences between performance bonds and standby letters of credit/independent guarantees.

9   See *Trafalgar House Construction (Regions) Ltd v. General Surety and Guarantee Co. Ltd.*, [1995] 3 All ER 737. The Association of British Insurers has meanwhile revised the standard text for performance bonds with a view to clear and modern language. The traditional language is sometimes still employed, but with the addition of clauses whereby the guarantor undertakes to pay upon first demand to be accompanied by a statement of default which is conclusive evidence that the amount is due, see, e.g., *Balfour Beatty Civil Engeneering v. Technical & General Guarantee*, [1999] 68 Con. LR 180.

the activities in which banks are authorised to engage. As a result it has generally been assumed that banks lacked the power to answer for the debts of others. The issuing of guarantees was considered to be *ultra vires* and was believed to be the sole province of insurance and bonding companies. In order to circumvent this prohibition, American banks resorted to such devices as the indorsing of bills of exchange and the issuance of letters of credit although these techniques undeniably served the purpose of guaranteeing potential debts of their customers. This practice became gradually well-established and remained largely unopposed. This being so, a second question arose – what type of guarantees could banks issue?[10] As is the case in the United Kingdom, the term guarantee (or guaranty) is generally taken to mean the accessory or secondary type of security, thus a contract of suretyship. It remained a well-established rule that banks were not permitted to engage in the business of issuing this kind of security, for two reasons. First, if a bank were to act as a surety, it would have to assess the chances that the principal debtor will default and, secondly, after undertaking the secondary guarantee, it would have to determine whether default had occurred, both being investigations for which banks are ill equipped. It was different, however, where the bank's liability was to be determined solely by reference to the terms of its undertaking to pay, in particular where the tender of certain documents was the event triggering payment without reference to the terms of the underlying transaction, and if the decision to issue the undertaking depended on the usual investigation of the account party's creditworthiness. The power of American banks to issue letters of credit *and* 'other independent undertakings' to pay against documents without factual investigation into the underlying transaction was finally recognised in the final revised Interpretive Ruling 7.1016 of the Comptroller of the Currency of 9 February 1996 (as revised on 1 January 2000). Accordingly, while the use of language too closely aligned to the underlying relationship, and the term guarantee in particular, continue to be suspect, the power of American banks to act as independent guarantors is now well established. This may truly be characterised as a triumph of substance over semantics.

In order to distinguish the traditional letter of credit, serving as a means of payment in sale transactions in the ordinary execution of the transaction, from this new breed of letters of credit, serving as security for default, and in order to emphasise the independent and documentary nature of the undertaking, banks introduced the term 'standby letter of credit'.[11] The traditional letter of credit came to be referred to as a commercial letter of credit. As has been pointed out above, the bank's undertaking to effect payment must depend on the presentation of documents as specified in the standby letter

---

[10] For a detailed analysis of these developments, see Dolan, § 12.03.

[11] According to the abovementioned Ruling, American banks are also allowed to issue such undertakings in the form of independent bank guarantees as envisaged in, e.g., the UNCITRAL Convention.

of credit without the need for investigating factual matters, especially default in the underlying transaction. In the case of first demand standby letters of credit, the presentation of a written unilateral statement from the beneficiary to the effect that the principal debtor has defaulted on his obligations meets this requirement. Arts. 5-101 – 5-117 of the U.S. Uniform Commercial Code, dealing with letters of credit, govern both the traditional letter of credit (or commercial letter of credit) and the standby letter of credit.

The term and technique of standby letters of credit are also used by non-American banks when issuing guarantees in favour of U.S. companies, as well as in countries in Latin America and the Far East which are influenced by American banking practices.

THE AMERICAN STANDBY LETTER OF CREDIT IS SIMILAR TO THE EUROPEAN INDEPENDENT GUARANTEE

1-4 There is a widespread belief that American standby letters of credit are different from the European independent guarantee. This is a fallacy. As is apparent from the above description, its function, i.e. the furnishing of security, and its mechanics, notably the rule of independence and the documentary nature of the conditions of payment, are the same as those of the European independent guarantee. They can be used for the same purposes (see Chapter 3), and they may contain the same conditions of payment (payment mechanism) (see Chapter 4). Accordingly, the American standby letter of credit and the European independent guarantee represent conceptually and legally the same device.[12] All one could say is that there are some minor differences which relate to practice and terminology. For example, whereas European guarantees were used first in connection with crossborder transactions, the standby letter of credit originates

---

[12] *Cf.* Dolan, § 2.03(2), Wunnicke/Wunnicke/Turner, § 2.08(B), Kozolchyk, 11 Univ. Pennsylvania Jo. International Business Law, pp. 7-69 (1989), Goode, p. 16, and in 1992 Lloyd's Mar. & Com. L.Q, p. 193. In *OLG Frankfurt a.M., March 18 1997*, RIW 1998, p. 477, *Csarnikow-Rionda v. Standard Bank London*, [1999] 2 Lloyd's Rep. 187 and *Kvaerner John Brown v. Midland Bank plc*, [1998] CLC 446, 449, it was expressly observed that standby letters of credit and independent (first demand) guarantees are governed by the same rules and principles. See also *Turkiye Is bankasi v. Bank of China*, [1998] Lloyd's Rep. 250. In *American National Bank & Trust v. Hamilton Industries International*, 583 F. Supp. 164 (N.D. Ill. 1984), the court expressly ruled that a documentary guarantee letter was a letter of credit for the purposes of Art. 5 of the Uniform Commercial Code. It is worth noting that the 1995 UNCITRAL Convention covers both the independent guarantee and the standby letter of credit (see Chapter 2, No. 2-12), and that, according to the Final Interpretative Ruling 7.7016 of the Comptroller of the Currency, American banks are allowed to issue security both in the form of standby letters of credit and independent bank guarantees (see No. 1-3).

from the domestic market;[13] guarantees were initially used primarily in support of non-financial obligations, while the utilisation of standby letters of credit was at first confined to securing financial obligations. Moreover, because of its origins, the technique of the standby letter of credit is more closely aligned to the commercial letter of credit than is the guarantee. Accordingly, the textual format tends to show some differences with that of guarantees, the practice of confirmation of the standby by a second bank is more widespread and there are some variants in the method of payment which do not exist in the case of guarantees.

In conclusion, apart from these practical differences the function and mechanics of standby letters of credit are indisputably the same as those of independent guarantees. This study, therefore, ordinarily refers to the term guarantee only, which includes the American standby letter of credit.[14]

ISSUERS OF GUARANTEES

1-5 Independent guarantees are typically issued by banks, which explains the term 'bank guarantee', although not every 'guarantee' issued by a bank is necessarily an independent guarantee. Insurance companies in the United States and Canada occasionally furnish the same service, as do specialised bonding companies in the building industry on the Continent. Certain export credit insurance companies, such as Gerling NCM, are also engaged in the business of issuing independent guarantess. In principle, guarantees can be issued by any institution, individual or legal entity.[15] They are frequently provided by a parent or finance company in favour of banks or other lenders in connection with credit facilities and loans granted to subsidiaries or affiliated companies. From the viewpoint of the creditor, guarantees issued by entities other than a bank or insurance company are less safe, not only because their financial position could be uncertain, but also and especially because they are ordinarily commercially and financially tied up with the principal debtor. This may cause these guarantors to resist or frustrate the beneficiary's demand for payment.[16] Creditors, therefore, tend to insist on a guarantee issued by a bank or similar institution of proper standing.

---

[13] See Dolan, § 1.06, for an overview of the variety of domestic transactions backed up by standby credits.

[14] Standby letters of credit are also used as a purely financial credit instrument which does not secure performance under an underlying transaction. These are called 'direct pay' or 'financial' standby letters of credit under which the borrower can draw in certain specified events.

[15] But see Chapter 12.2, No. 12-15.

[16] See, for example, *OLG Hamm, 24 June 1986*, WM 1986, p. 1503.

Introduction 9

COUNTRIES AND REGIONS COVERED IN THIS STUDY. PRACTICE

1-6 This study is based on case law and legal writing from the Netherlands, Germany, France, Belgium and England. In order to ensure reliability, all case law in the field of independent guarantees as from 1977 has been reviewed on the basis of the original reports as cited. As far as the United States is concerned a major part of the prolific legal writing on the subject has been taken into account. With a few exceptions, representations concerning American case law are not derived from the original reports, but from the extensive analyses in American legal writing. In addition, some Swiss, Austrian and Italian decisions have been included. These have been taken from the reports as cited.

Considerable attention has also been paid to the way guarantees function in actual practice and to the numerous practical aspects and issues to which they give rise. Since guarantees are nothing but a creation of practice in international trade, and as the law in this area can be nothing but a response to what it finds in practice, any attempt to understand, to map or to develop the law must start with the bare roots. To this end intensive contacts over a number of years have been maintained with the leading Dutch banks – in particular with the departments dealing with guarantees and the legal departments – with the Dutch export credit insurance company (Gerling NCM), which is actively involved in the guarantee business, and with Dutch construction firms and organisations. Much energy has been spent in researching a huge number of files, which provided insight into 'the daily life' of the world of guarantees and the practices, difficulties and peculiarities in a great number of countries and regions. Legal opinions from local lawyers and circular letters from foreign banks have especially been an invaluable source of information. This is particularly relevant in relation to countries in the Middle East and North Africa. I have, of course, also drawn from my own experience as solicitor, with a mainly international practice.

METHOD. UNIFORMITY OF THE LAW

1-7 Although this book covers case law and legal writing from a number of countries, it is not a comparative study and no particular system of national law has been taken as a point of reference. The phenomenon of the independent guarantee as it is encountered in practice has been the point of departure. Several factors account for this approach. The modern guarantee and notably the guarantee payable on first demand is a product of international trade in response to the changing needs for a more suitable and convenient security instrument in the light of changing trade patterns, the increasing significance of risk and risk avoidance as a factor, a shift in bargaining power, the demand for new and versatile financing instruments, and the need for intermediation by banks. These modern guarantees developed autonomously and independently of national law with its traditional concepts, categories, principles and its domestic peculiarities. As independent guarantees are born and bred in a transnational setting, the law on such guarantees is and should also be developed on a transnational level, taking the phenomenon of the guarantee as it functions in international trade as the point of reference. It is true that, in the absence of generally adopted international conventions, the law on independent guarantees is necessarily national law and has developed in national courts. But it is equally true that, from the beginning, there has been a general awareness that guarantees are an international phenemenon and that national law should be finely attuned to developments elsewhere. Indeed, case law and legal writing in the various countries have drawn on developments from elsewhere. In fact, a significant degree of uniform law across jurisdictional boundaries has spontaneously emerged.[17] This is also borne out by the fact that the role of private international law is relatively unimportant.[18] On the other hand, there are many areas which continue to give rise to controversies and where the law is unsettled and inconsistent. However, these uncertainties in the law do not run along national boundaries, but tend to occur in all jurisdictions equally. Accordingly, in respect of these areas, too, the law in the various countries cannot be said to differ. The significant degree of uniform law also enhances the confidence which the business community across the world has in respect of crossborder independent guarantees as reliable security instruments, as the risk of greatly diverging local law peculiarities is small.

It is quite a different matter that certain divergent regional patterns in actual practice can be discerned, such as in relation to the requirements in respect of the terms and conditions of the guarantee and counter-guarantee, the guarantee format and the way banks and beneficiaries handle guarantees. This means that guarantees issued in a certain region may give rise to problems, difficulties and legal issues which are less relevant to guarantees issued in other regions. This does not necessarily imply that the judicial response to these differences also varies from country to country. In conclusion, in accordance with the origins and functioning of independent guarantees, the law in the countries covered in this study and, no doubt, in many other countries has, of its own accord, developed along uniform patterns.

---

[17] *Cf.* Cabrillac/Mouly, No. 396-1.
[18] See Chapter 18.2, No. 18-5.

CHAPTER 2
OVERVIEW

2.1 INDEPENDENCE

2-1 An essential feature of guarantees, as this term is used in this study, is their independence (or autonomy) from the principal contract.[1] Although the purpose of a guarantee is to indemnify the creditor/beneficiary for losses resulting from the principal debtor's default in the underlying relationship, the beneficiary's right to claim payment under the guarantee is to be determined solely by reference to the terms and conditions as specified in the guarantee, and the bank cannot invoke defences derived from the principal contract, *cf.* Art. 2 (b) URDG, Rule 1.06 and 2.01(a) ISP98 and Art. 2 UNCITRAL Convention. The question whether or not the principal debtor has failed to comply with his obligations and whether or not the creditor/beneficiary is entitled to payment as measured by the underlying relationship, is not a relevant issue between bank and beneficiary. Accordingly, once the terms and conditions of the guarantee are met, the beneficiary/creditor is entitled to claim payment and he need not show default in any other way than that prescribed by the terms of the guarantee.

One must, however, bear in mind that as far as the principal debtor/account party and creditor/beneficiary are concerned the true significance of the principle of independence depends entirely on the particular type of conditions of payment. For example, if the guarantee is payable on first demand, the beneficiary is entitled to payment forthwith without any condition or requirement other than making the demand for payment. Accordingly, the bank must proceed to payment and the principal debtor/account party must reimburse the bank, without the slightest item of substantive evidence concerning the principal debtor's default. First demand guarantees are, therefore, markedly different from the traditional suretyship (or accessory guarantee). On the other hand, if the guarantee is payable on submission of a judicial or arbitral award establishing the principal debtor's breach of contract, the principle of independence is of little practical significance and the actual difference between that type of guarantee and suretyship is negligible. The relationship between independence and the selected payment mechanism is examined in Chapter 4.

The rule of independence is limited by the exception of fraud. As a matter of fact, the earliest decisions on guarantees recognised both the independent nature of guaran-

---

[1] See Chapter 1, No. 1-2 for the terminology used in this study (guarantee means 'independent guarantee', as opposed to the 'accessory guarantee').

tees, in particular of first demand guarantees, and the exception in the case of fraud.[2] The scope of the concept of fraud and especially the actual application of the juridical patterns which have evolved over time to actual cases, is examined in Chapters 14-16.

As far as banks are concerned, the principle of independence carries a significant advantage. When the guarantee is triggered by a call from the beneficiary, the bank's role is mainly confined to verifying whether the terms and conditions of the guarantee have been complied with. This task is facilitated by the fact that the conditions of payment are usually framed in a documentary fashion, for instance the submission of a written demand for payment, often to be accompanied by a formal and unilateral statement from the beneficiary concerning the principal debtor's default (first demand guarantee), or the presentation of third-party documents testifying non-performance or performance of the principal contract, or the submission of a judicial or arbitral award. As in documentary credits, the bank, both in its relationship with the beneficiary and in its relationship with the principal debtor/account party, is merely expected to compare the documents tendered with the documents prescribed in the guarantee. The bank does not, therefore, become involved in the rights and obligations as they exist on the basis of the underlying relationship and it need not concern itself with any disputes between account party and beneficiary.

The term independence is also used in another context, denoting the independence between the contract of guarantee and the mandate relationship between bank and principal debtor/account party, which involves the latter's instruction to the bank to issue the guarantee for his account. Accordingly, the bank cannot invoke defences which it might have against the principal debtor/account party.[3] Chapter 12.1 contains some further reflections on the principle of independence.

---

[2] See, for early examples, the Netherlands: *CA Amsterdam, 30 March 1972*, NJ 1973, 188; *Rb Amsterdam, 18 December 1980*, S & S 1981, 135; *Rb Amsterdam, 19 March 1981*, KG 1981, 30; *Rb Amsterdam, 14 May 1981*, KG 1981, 71. Germany: *LG Frankfurt a.M., 11 December 1979*, NJW 1981, p. 56; *LG Braunschweig, 22 May 1980*, RIW 1981, p. 789; *OLG Saarbrücken, 23 January 1981*, RIW 1981, p. 338; *BGH, 12 March 1984 (ll ZR 198/82)*, NJW 1984, p. 2030. France: *Riom, 14 May 1980*, D. 1981 J. p. 336; *Trib. com. Paris, 24 March 1981, and 5 May 1981*, D. 1981 J. p. 482; *Trib. com. Paris, 12 February 1982*, D. 1982 J. p. 504. Belgium: *Trib. com. Brussels, 15 January 1980*, JCB 1980, p. 147; *Trib. com. Brussels, 23 December 1980*, Rev. Banque 1981, p. 627; *Trib. com. Brussels, 11 March 1981*, BRH 1981, p. 361; *Brussels, 18 December 1981*, Rev. Banque 1982, p. 99. United Kingdom: *R.D. Harbottle (Mercantile) Ltd. v. Nat. Westminster Bank Ltd.*, [1977] 2 All E.R. 862; *Edward Owen Engineering Ltd. v. Barclays Bank Int. Ltd.*, [1978] 1 All E.R. 976; *Howe Richardson Scale v. Polimex-Cekop*, [1978] 1 Lloyd's Rep. 161.

[3] See further Chapter 9, No. 9-5.

2.2 FUNCTIONS

2-2 Bank guarantees have several functions, which vary in accordance with the point of reference. Their paramount function is the furnishing of security for either financial obligations, namely payment of the agreed amounts, or non-financial obligations, namely payment of damages. This purpose is achieved by assuring the creditor/beneficiary financial compensation in the event of default by the principal debtor/account party. However, in contrast to the traditional suretyship, the beneficiary's entitlement to payment under an independent guarantee is defined solely by the terms and conditions as specified in the guarantee.

By agreeing to issue a guarantee, the bank assumes an obligation of its own to the beneficiary, but for the risk and account of the principal debtor. Should the bank be obligated to effect payment, it is entitled to immediate recourse against the principal debtor. The bank, thus, accepts a credit risk, which is ordinarily limited by requiring security for reimbursement, and it does not act as an insurer.[4]

In a broader sense and especially when viewed from the principal debtor/account party's and creditor/beneficiary's stance, a bank guarantee represents an allocation of risks between these parties.[5] The extent of this allocation of risks depends on the type of conditions of payment. A first demand guarantee, which is in many situations the prevailing type of guarantee in international trade, is characterised by a complete reversal of risks. As noted in No. 2-1, the beneficiary is entitled to payment forthwith and without any proof of default, while the bank, with a view to its reputation as a reliable institution and because of its right to immediate reimbursement from the account party, will ordinarily honour its obligation without haggling. Thus, it is quite possible that the beneficiary is entitled to payment under the guarantee, because he has made a demand for payment in the manner prescribed in the guarantee, while he might not have a claim against the account party as measured by the underlying relationship or where his claim is disputed. Should the account party indeed be of the opinion that he has correctly performed the contract, he might attempt to recover the amount paid under the guarantee from the beneficiary ('pay first, argue later'), but will then be confronted by grave difficulties. Such attempts ordinarily entail initiating proceedings, often in the beneficiary's country, with all the attendant risks, including the burden of proof, costs and other uncertainties and vagaries which attend such proceedings. Should the account party be able to secure judgment or an arbitral award, he then runs the risk that the award cannot be enforced, for example because the beneficiary is insolvent, or because the beneficiary is a State agency which enjoys immunity, or because of currency exchange restrictions. In many cases, actual recovery of the amounts paid under

---

[4] See further Chapter 7 for the role and position of the bank.

[5] See Chapter 6 for a more detailed analysis. For the functions of first demand standby letters of credit and independent guarantees in general, see also Dolan, § 3.07.

the guarantee will prove to be illusory. Conversely, a beneficiary enjoying the advantages of a first demand guarantee encounters none of these risks and difficulties which he would have had to face in the absence of such a guarantee.

Another benefit for the beneficiary of a first demand guarantee is that he receives immediate payment when he is of the opinion that the principal debtor defaulted, without the need of having to establish his case first and regardless of the account party's objections. It is the precise purpose of a first demand guarantee to put the beneficiary in possession of the funds pending the final resolution of their dispute. This is known as the 'liquidity' (or 'cash' or 'prompt payment') function of first demand guarantees.

A further very important function of first demand guarantees is that they enable the beneficiary to put pressure on the principal debtor/account party to complete the contract to his satisfaction by threatening to call the guarantee. This constant threat certainly constitutes a forceful incentive for the principal debtor to perform his obligations promptly and satisfactorily. In view of the fact that the percentage of actual calls for payment is very small, one could justifiably argue that the prime function of first demand guarantees is to secure performance, rather than to secure financial compensation for non-performance. The actual exercise by the beneficiary of his legal rights must be regarded as an *ultimum remedium*.

In contrast, independent guarantees which prescribe the submission of a court judgment or an arbitral award, merely dispose of the execution risk. Their function is much the same as that of the traditional suretyship (or accessory guarantee), since the beneficiary must prove the principal debtor's default in such proceedings. Guarantees requiring the submission of third-party documents relating to the principal debtor's default carry many of the same advantages as first demand guarantees, but to a lesser extent. Their usefulness for the creditor/beneficiary and the precise extent of the reallocation of risks depend on the nature of the third-party documents which have to be submitted.[6]

First demand guarantees are also used as financing instruments. They facilitate the readjustment of the burden of financing the contract or project by protecting the importer or employer against the risks which arise from his making advance and interim payments to the exporter.[7] Another function of bank guarantees, and especially of first demand guarantees, is that they give the importer/beneficiary a fair indication of the exporter/principal debtor's financial standing and ability to perform. A contracting party whose bank is not prepared to issue a guarantee is not likely to be a trustworthy partner.

---

[6] See Chapter 4.3.

[7] See further Chapter 19, No. 19-1.

2.3 STRUCTURE AND TERMINOLOGY

Guarantee as a multi-party relationship. Interdependence

2-3 A guarantee is a contract between two parties, namely the guarantor/bank and the beneficiary, and it is independent of the underlying relationship, However, in order to understand the mechanics of these instruments, the applicable rules of law and the quintessence of most disputes to which they may give rise, it is essential to be aware that a guarantee is not just a two-party relationship between guarantor and beneficiary. It forms part of and is embedded in a multi-party relationship which, apart from the guarantee itself, consists of the underlying relationship between principal debtor (account party) and creditor (beneficiary) and the relationship between principal debtor (account party) and bank. A guarantee cannot come into existence without these two other contracts.[8] Although distinct, these three relationships are intrinsically linked to one and another and they affect each other. In many situations the guarantee structure of interdependent relationships is even more complex, for example in the case of an indirect guarantee or where the bank seeks assurances for reimbursement in the form of a counter-guarantee.

Direct guarantee

2-4 The basis of a guarantee is always a contractual relationship between principal debtor and creditor, which is either a contract that has been definitely concluded or a relationship in its pre-contractual phase as is the case with tender guarantees. This relationship is referred to as the principal or underlying relationship or contract.

The underlying contract contains a clause or understanding that one of the parties is to provide a guarantee in favour of the other in order to secure proper performance of his obligations. In the context of guarantees, the former is called the principal debtor while the latter is called the creditor. The agreement may be explicit and detailed in respect of the precise terms and conditions of the guarantee and its wording or, at this stage, it may be quite vague and obscure.

Implementing the agreement with the creditor, the principal debtor instructs his bank to issue the guarantee with terms and conditions as specified by him. The bank charges a commission for this service. Should the bank be called on to effect payment in accordance with the terms and conditions of the guarantee, the principal debtor is then obliged to reimburse the bank. The bank's recourse is often contained in a separate document, the counter-guarantee. In his relationship with the bank, the principal

---

[8] This is only different if a standby letter of credit is issued by the bank for its own account, as American banks do in case of a 'direct pay' or 'financial' standby letter of credit. In that event, the standby letter of credit operates as a credit instrument.

debtor is called the customer, principal or account party. This last-mentioned term aptly illustrates that although the bank assumes an obligation of its own towards the beneficiary, it acts for the risk and account of the principal debtor. The relationship between account party and bank is regarded as a contract of mandate.

Pursuant to the instructions from its customer the bank then issues the guarantee in favour of the creditor. In his relationship with the bank, the creditor is called the beneficiary. The guarantee specifies the terms and conditions under which the bank is to effect payment. It should be noted that these terms and conditions stem from the instructions by the bank's customer and these, in turn, are fixed by the agreement between the parties to the principal contract. The bank's role in determining the terms and conditions of the guarantee is small.

Diagram 1 shows how a contract of guarantee comes into being and how the three contracts are linked with each other.

Diagram 2 shows the various payment flows. Fulfilment of the terms and conditions of the guarantee results in payment by the bank and this triggers the claim for reimbursement by the account party. The ultimate effect, intended and anticipated by all parties concerned, is that the creditor/beneficiary is indemnified for the loss which he has suffered as a result of the principal debtor/account party's default and that the compensation has been paid by the latter as the one responsible for the non-performance of the contract. Diagrams 1 and 2 clearly show the interdependence between the three seperate legal relationships.

Direct guarantee and advising bank

2-5 Direct guarantees are ordinarily issued by the account party's own bank or by another bank in the account party's country. When the beneficiary is situated abroad, a second bank in the beneficiary's country is sometimes requested to act as advising bank for the sake of convenience.[9] Its role is confined to the notification and transmission of the guarantee as well as the transmission of communications from the beneficiary to the bank. In contrast to documentary credits, advising banks in the case of guarantees are very rarely designated as paying banks. The advising bank does not assume any obligations towards the beneficiary as far as the guarantee is concerned, but it may owe a general duty of care towards the beneficiary. This duty especially entails check-

---

[9] Those banks that are authorised to issue guarantees directly in favour of Saudi Arabian beneficiaries must issue the guarantee through a local advising bank. Under local law and regulations, the Saudi Arabian advising bank is entrusted, *inter alia*, with the task of ensuring that the guarantee complies with the terms and conditions as defined by the Saudi Arabian Monetary Agency (SAMA).

Overview

Diagram 1

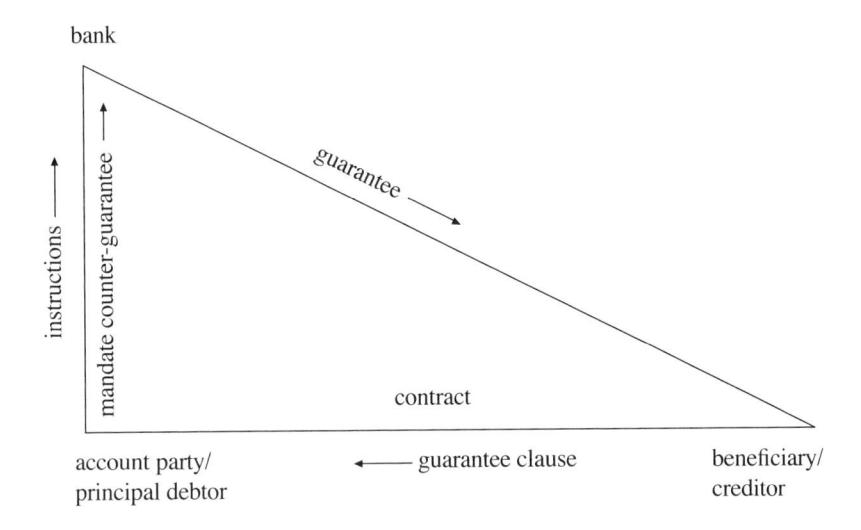

```
                    bank
                    /|\
                   / | \
                  /  |  \
                 /   |   \
                /    |    \  guarantee →
               /     |     \
    instructions ↑   |      \
              /  mandate     \
             /  counter-      \
            /   guarantee ↑    \
           /      |              \
          /       |               \
         /_____|_____\
    account party/    contract    beneficiary/
    principal debtor              creditor
              ← guarantee clause
```

Diagram 2

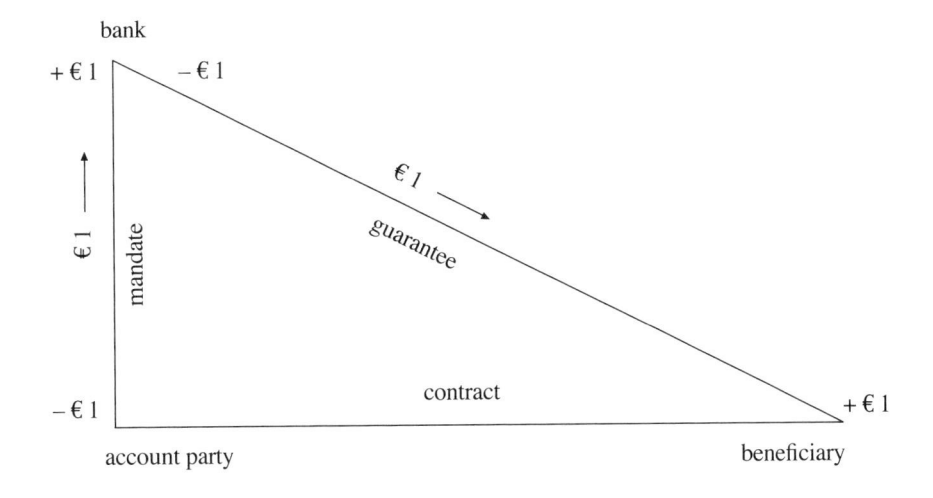

```
              bank
    + € 1    /|  − € 1
            / |
           /  |
      ↑   /   |      € 1 →
     € 1 /    |       guarantee
        / mandate
       /      |
      /       |         contract
   − € 1 ─────────────────── + € 1
   account party          beneficiary
```

ing the authenticity of the guarantee it advises.[10] Apart from this, the interposition of an advising bank does not alter the legal structure of a direct guarantee.

Indirect guarantee. First/instructing bank and second/issuing bank

2-6 Beneficiaries frequently stipulate for the issuance of a guarantee by a bank in their own country since this has many advantages.[11] In this event, the principal debtor/account party requests his bank to instruct a bank in the beneficiary's country to issue the guarantee. In accordance with the prevailing terminology, the first-mentioned bank is called the first or instructing bank while the last-mentioned bank is called the second or issuing bank. Taking the beneficiary as the point of reference, French legal writing and case law refer, however, to the first-mentioned bank as the second bank and to the last-mentioned bank as the first bank.

It is important to note that it is only the second bank that issues the guarantee while the first bank merely acts as instructing bank without any contractual relationship with the beneficiary. The beneficiary can never claim payment from the instructing bank. The relationship between instructing and issuing banks is similar to the relationship between principal debtor/account party and bank in the case of a direct guarantee. The obligation to indemnify the issuing bank is often contained in a counter-guarantee. Accordingly, if the second issuing bank is called on to effect payment to the beneficiary pursuant to the terms of the guarantee, it will be reimbursed by the first instructing bank, and the first instructing bank will take recourse against the principal debtor/account party. Thus, the ultimate effect as far as the payment flows are concerned is the same as that of a direct guarantee. The adjective 'indirect' relates to the structure consisting of two links, namely instructions, mandate and counter-guarantee between the account party and the first bank, and instructions, mandate and counter-guarantee between the first instructing bank and the second issuing bank. The guarantee issued by the second bank in favour of the beneficiary is usually referred to as the 'primary' guarantee in order to distinguish it clearly from the counter-guarantee issued by the first instructing bank in favour of the second issuing bank.

In German and American legal language the term 'indirect guarantee' (or 'indirect standby letter of credit') is sometimes used to mean the counter-guarantee furnished by the instructing bank in favour of the issuing bank. This is not the way the term is used in this study.

---

[10] See, for example, *Trib. com. Antwerp, 25 September 1987*, TBH 1989, p. 100, where it was stated that the advising bank owes a duty to ascertain the authenticity of the messages received from the issuing bank. The advising bank was held liable for forged communications. See also Rule 2.05(a) ISP98 and Goode, p. 11.

[11] See Chapter 6.2, No. 6-6.

Diagram 3

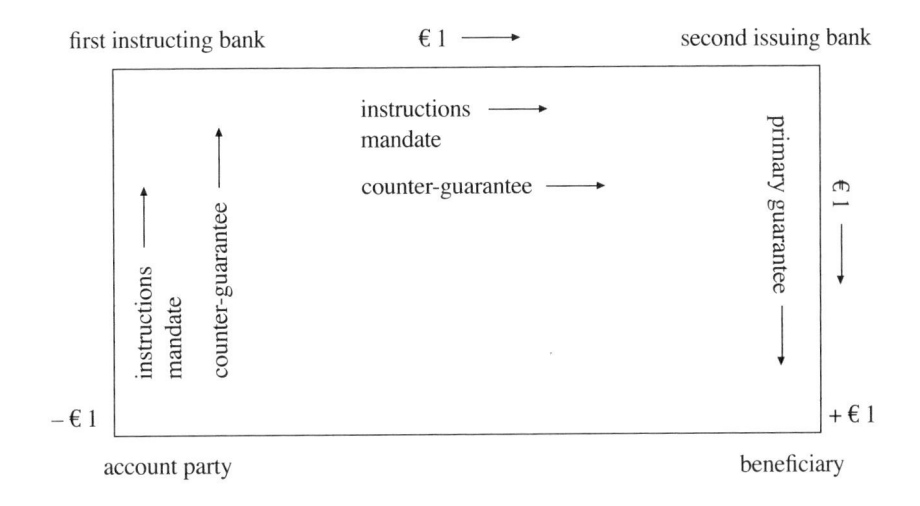

```
first instructing bank          € 1 ──▶          second issuing bank
         ┌─────────────────────────────────────────────────────┐
         │              instructions ──▶                        │
         │              mandate                                 │
         │    ↑                                        │        │
         │    │   │      counter-guarantee ──▶         │        │
         │    │   │                                    │        │  € 1
         │   ins  c-g                              primary      │   │
         │   tru  gua                              guarantee    │   ▼
         │   cti  ran                                  │        │
         │   ons  tee                                  │        │
         │   man                                       ▼        │
         │   date                                               │
  -€ 1   └─────────────────────────────────────────────────────┘  +€ 1
         account party                              beneficiary
```

The American standby letter of credit as a counter-guarantee

2-7 Indirect guarantees issued on behalf of U.S. exporters in favour of Iranian beneficiaries at the time of the Iranian revolution had a different structure from the one described in No. 6-6. This variant was, however, not limited to guarantees supporting transactions with that country and it is occasionally still being employed. In this situation the U.S. exporter turns directly to the bank in the beneficiary's country with the request to issue the guarantee. The foreign bank is usually prepared to do so only if an American bank gives an undertaking assuring prompt reimbursement. This undertaking is called a standby letter of credit. The idea is that in the event of payment by the issuing bank, it can take immediate recourse against the American bank while that bank will seek reimbursement from the U.S. exporter. The foreign issuing bank is not expected to try to obtain repayment from the U.S. exporter first. Consequently, in this situation the standby letter of credit operates as a counter-guarantee and the structure, while different in form, functions in substance in the same manner as an indirect guarantee (see Diagram 4).

The term standby letter of credit is also used in two different meanings. American terminology refers to a guarantee, i.e. the contract of (independent) guarantee between bank and beneficiary, as a standby letter of credit in order to avoid confusion with the

Diagram 4

```
U.S. bank          standby letter of credit ──▶    issuing bank

    ↑    ↑                                              │
    │    │                                         guarantee
instructions  counter-guarantee    instructions ↗        │
                                                         ↓

account party/          contract              beneficiary/
U.S. exporter                                 importer
```

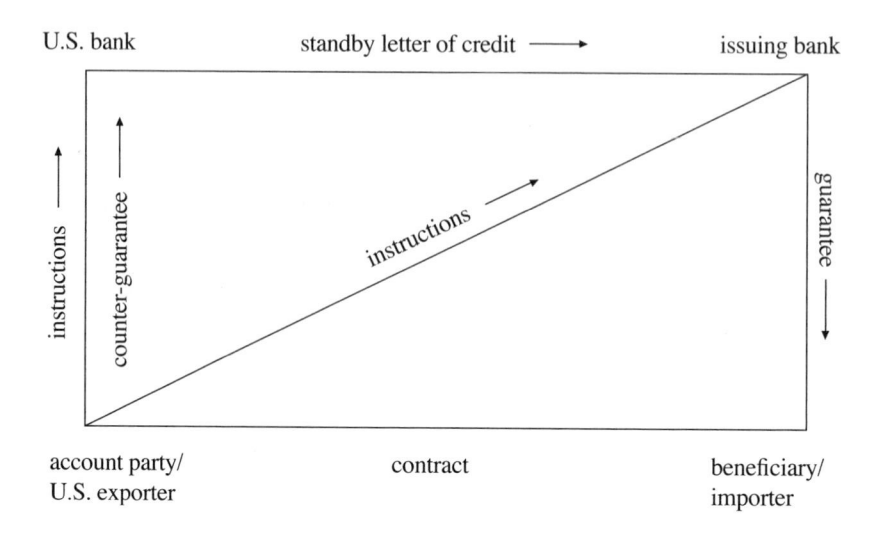

Diagram 5

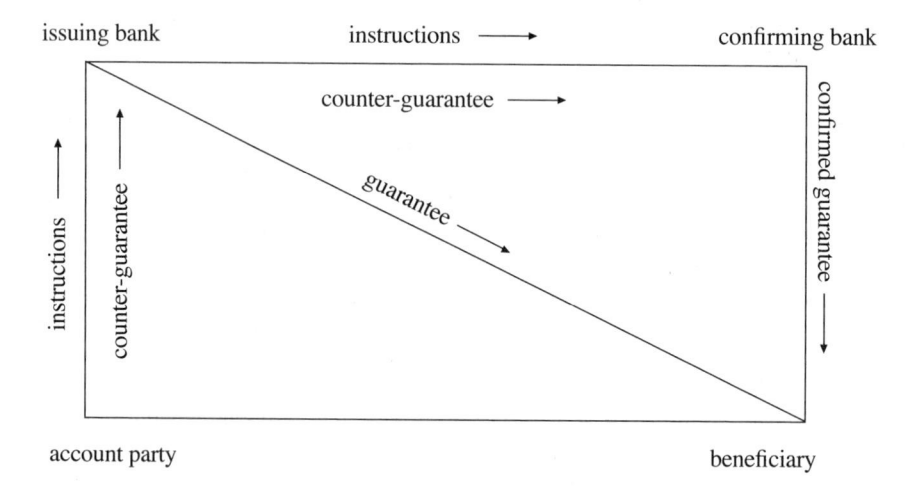

```
issuing bank        instructions ──▶         confirming bank
                    counter-guarantee ──▶

    ↑    ↑                                              │
    │    │                                         confirmed
instructions  counter-guarantee    guarantee ↘    guarantee
                                                         ↓

account party                                 beneficiary
```

Overview

American concept of guarantee (or guaranty) which is the accessory type of security.[12] The term is further used as a synonym for a particular type of guarantee, namely the payment guarantee, which is a variant of a documentary credit.[13]

Confirmed guarantee

2-8 In documentary credits, the credit is often issued by a bank in the buyer's country while a bank in the seller's country adds its confirmation. In this event, the seller can tender the documents and ask for payment from the confirming bank in his own country, and could also look to the buyer's bank, should this prove to be necessary (see Diagram 5). Although quite feasible, this technique is rarely used in case of guarantees, no doubt because the actual advantages of having a second foreign bank which is also bound by the guarantee is small.[14] Incidentally, it is most unusual for sellers in the case of a confirmed documentary credit to turn to the first bank. However, the technique of confirmation is regularly used in the case of the American standby letter of credit.[15]

Personal security for reimbursement by the account party

2-9 It may happen that the bank, either the issuing bank in the case of a direct guarantee or the first instructing bank in the case of an indirect guarantee, does not wish to rely on the creditworthiness of the account party/principal debtor, but insists on assurances for prompt reimbursement by another institution. This might be another bank or financial institution, an export credit insurance company or a company affiliated to the account party. The security is usually made available in the form of a counter-guarantee operating in the same way as a counter-guarantee in the case of indirect guarantees. Thus, if the bank is obligated to effect payment under its own (counter-)guarantee, it is entitled to seek immediate recourse against the institution which furnished the counter-guarantee. Whether that institution will look for reimbursement from the principal debtor, and under what conditions, will depend on the nature of their relationship. Where the principal debtor's business requires the issue of guarantees on a regular

---

[12] See Chapter 1, Nos. 1-3 and 1-4.

[13] See Chapter 3.7.

[14] Owing to the general equating of guarantees with documentary credits, English legal language sometimes refers to indirect guarantees as confirmed guarantees. This is incorrect since the first instructing bank does not issue the guarantee and the beneficiary cannot turn to that bank for payment.

[15] See Rules 1.09 and 1.11 ISP98. The UNCITRAL Convention also provides for confirmed guarantees, see Art. 6(e).

Diagram 6

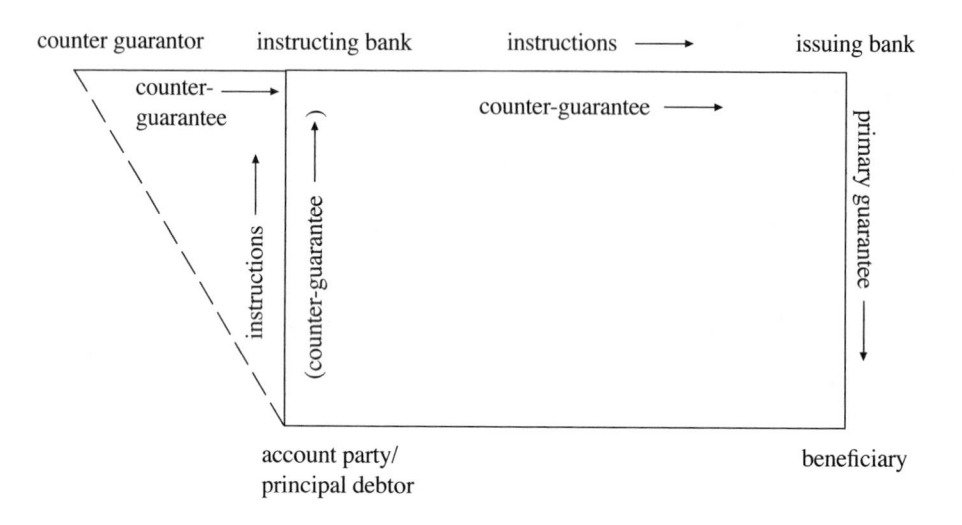

Diagram 7

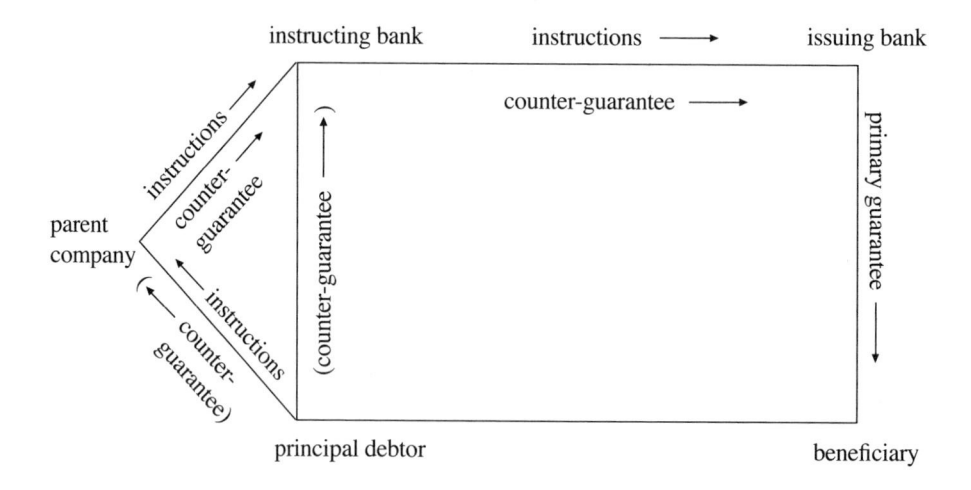

Diagram 8

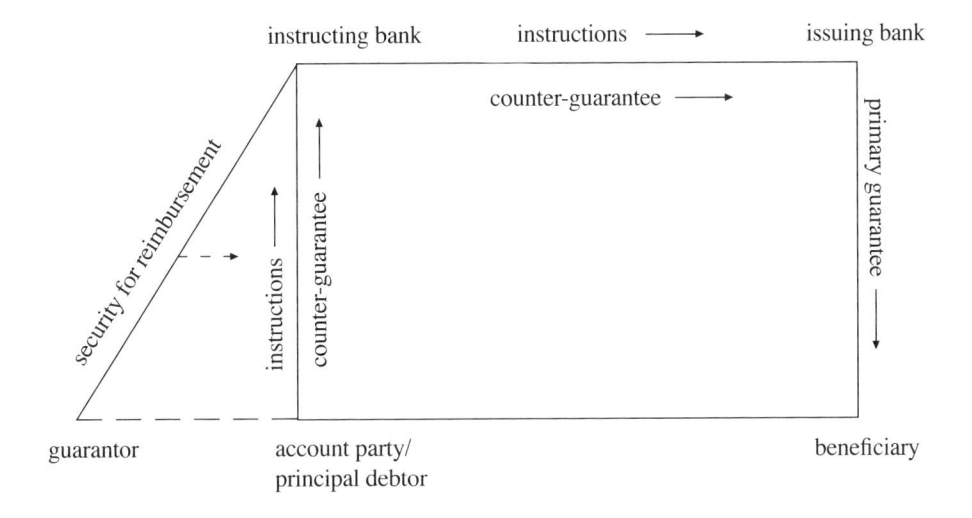

```
          instructing bank    instructions ──►    issuing bank
                    ┌─────────────────────────────────────────┐
                   /         counter-guarantee ──►            │
                  /     ▲                                     │ p
        s       /       │                                     │ r
         e     /    i   c                                     │ i
          c   /     n   o                                     │ m
           u /      s   u                                     │ a
            r       t   n                                     │ r
         f  i       r   t                                     │ y
         o  t       u   e                                     │
         r  y ──►   c   r                                     │ g
                    t   -                                     │ u
            f       i   g                                     │ a
            o       o   u                                     │ r
            r       n   a                                     │ a
                    s   r                                     │ n
            r           a                                     │ t
            e           n                                     │ e
            i           t                                     │
            m           e                                     │ ──►
            b           e                                     │ │
            u                                                 │ ▼
            r                                                 │
            s  ─ ─ ─ ─ ─                                      │
            e                                                 │
            m                                                 │
            e                                                 │
            n                                                 │
            t                                                 │
                └─────────────────────────────────────────────┘
        guarantor    account party/                    beneficiary
                     principal debtor
```

basis, the bank may request the relevant institution to furnish a master counter-guarantee covering the guarantees which the bank may issue from time to time on behalf of the principal debtor. Such a master counter-guarantee is often given for an indefinite period of time, but it can be terminated upon giving notice to the bank. In that event the principal debtor shall have to procure a fresh counter-guarantee by another institution. If the instructions from the principal debtor so provide or if he has also furnished a counter-guarantee, the bank may of course also turn to him for reimbursement (see Diagram 6).

It may also be the case that the instructions to the bank for the issuance of an (indirect) guarantee do not originate from the principal debtor in the underlying transaction, but, for example, from its parent or affiliated company. This structure will be employed when there is no existing business relationship between the principal debtor and bank or where the bank prefers to deal with the parent or affiliated company only, on which it relies for reimbursement. In the absence of a counter-guarantee from the principal debtor, the bank will have no contractual claim for reimbursement by the principal debtor, but otherwise the structure is much the same as the one described above (see Diagram 7).

The security can also be couched in the form of an (accessory) suretyship (see Diagram 8). In that event, the bank must first seek reimbursement from the principal debtor and it will only be able to turn to the guarantor if the principal debtor does not pay. The guarantor thus acts as a true accessory guarantor (surety), since it does not directly

Diagram 9

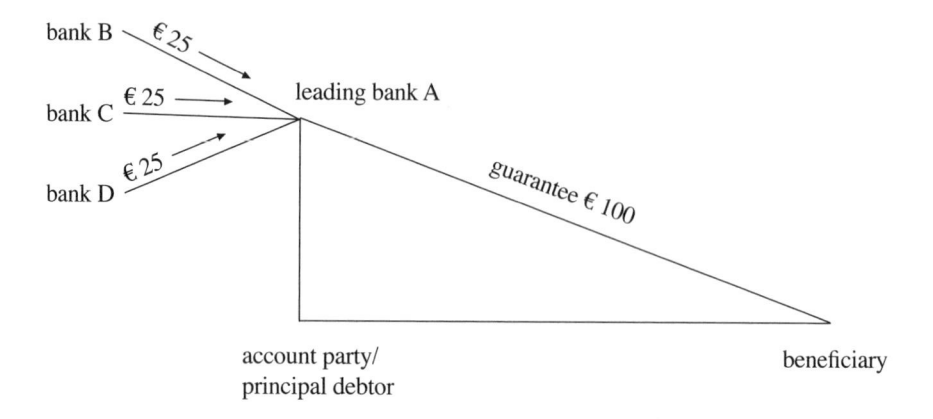

```
bank B  €25 ↘
bank C  €25 → leading bank A
bank D  €25 ↗         ╲
                       ╲ guarantee €100
                        ╲
          account party/              beneficiary
          principal debtor
```

indemnify the bank in the event of payment but it guarantees reimbursement by the principal debtor. If the security is furnished in the form of suretyship, the guarantor is entitled to invoke any defences which the principal debtor might have against the bank. It is obvious that banks generally have a strong preference for security in the form of a counter-guarantee as described in Diagram 7.

Syndicated guarantees

2-10 Where, in view of the colossal size of the exposure, the risk is too great to be borne by one bank, a spreading of risk can be achieved by syndicating the guarantee. The usual technique, which is ordinarily preferred by the beneficiary, is that one bank – the so-called leading bank – issues the guarantee for the full amount and this is backed up by counter-guarantees from the participating banks. Upon payment the leading bank then takes recourse against those banks which are each liable for their agreed percentage (see Diagram 9). Syndication occurs especially in the case of guarantees involving huge amounts.[16]

The technique of syndication is also used when a construction project is to be carried out by a joint venture consisting of a number of contractors.[17]

---

[16] See for this subject especially Kronfol, JBL 1984, pp. 13-20; ICLR 1984, pp. 230-233.

[17] See further Chapter 19.

Back-to-back guarantees

2-11 The flow of trade in products from the original supplier to the end buyer often takes place through a number of intermediary buyers/sellers. The risk of non-payment or non-performance in respect of each link in the chain of contracts can be covered by a payment and performance guarantee. The procurement of a guarantee from the preceding link in the chain constitutes the financial basis for the issuance of a guarantee in favour of the next link. It is, of course, important that the terms of the guarantee are synchronised (see Diagrams 10 and 11).

It should be noted that back-to-back guarantees are independent of each other. The fact that one of them can be called does not necessarily mean that the others can also be called.[18]

Loans and risk participation through guarantees

2-11a Diagram 12 shows a structure whereby the leading bank provides the entire loan of € 100 and banks A, B and C each participate in the risk for € 25. This technique allows the leading bank to furnish loans for larger amounts than it could do without the risk participation by other banks.

Transfer of credit risk by the bank

2-11b If the bank wants to be released of the credit risk of the guarantee without the agreement or involvement of the beneficiary, this can be accomplished in a contractual sense by obtaining a counter-guarantee from another bank which then assumes the credit risk. The account party should ensure that its counter-guarantee in favour of the issuing bank is cancelled when it furnishes a new counter-guarantee to the other bank (see Diagram 13).

2.4 SOURCES OF LAW

The UNCITRAL Convention on independent guarantees and stand-by letters of credit

2-12 At one time an UNCITRAL working commission was set up in order to investigate whether it would be useful and feasible to work towards the creation of an interna-

---

[18] See *Trib. com. Paris, 14 December 1990*, D. 1991 Somm. p. 201.

Diagram 10

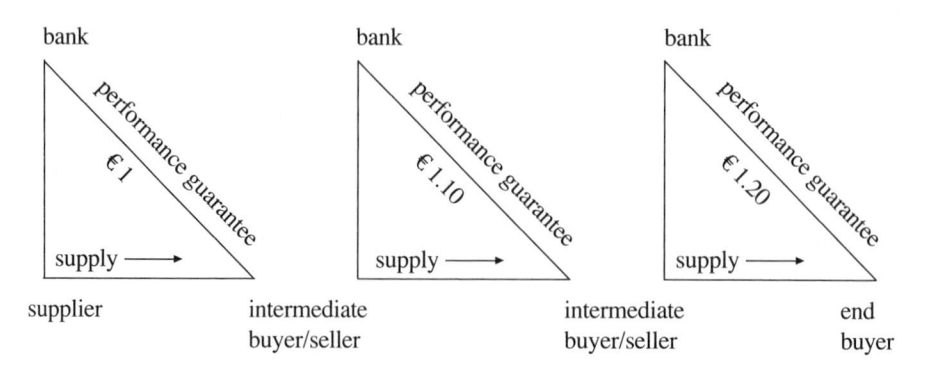

```
bank                          bank                          bank
 |\                            |\                            |\
 | \ performance guarantee     | \ performance guarantee     | \ performance guarantee
 |€1\                          |€1.10\                       |€1.20\
 |___\                         |___\                         |___\
 supply →                      supply →                      supply →
supplier      intermediate           intermediate          end
              buyer/seller           buyer/seller          buyer
```

Diagram 11

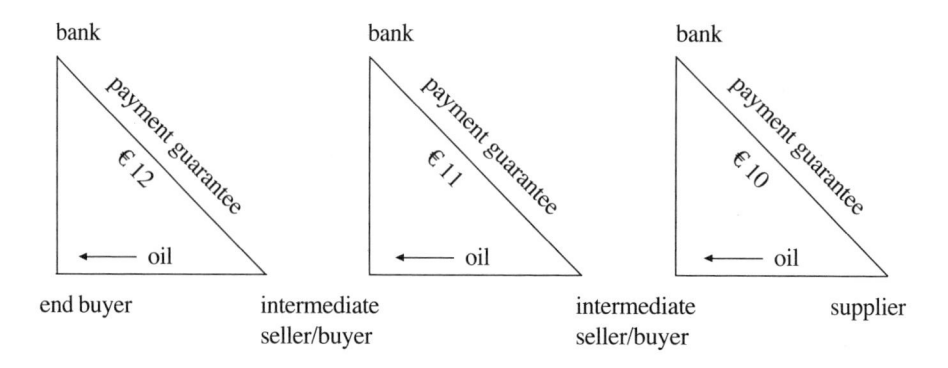

```
bank                          bank                          bank
 |\                            |\                            |\
 | \ payment guarantee         | \ payment guarantee         | \ payment guarantee
 |€12\                         |€11\                         |€10\
 |___\                         |___\                         |___\
 ← oil                         ← oil                         ← oil
end buyer    intermediate            intermediate          supplier
             seller/buyer            seller/buyer
```

tional set of rules for guarantees.[19] Some suggestions for tentative drafts were circulated but these efforts were eventually taken over and pursued by the International Chamber of Commerce, see No. 2-13 below.

---

[19] Project for 'Guarantees and Securities as Related to International Payments', Document A/LN 9/37 of 6 February 1970.

Overview

Diagram 12

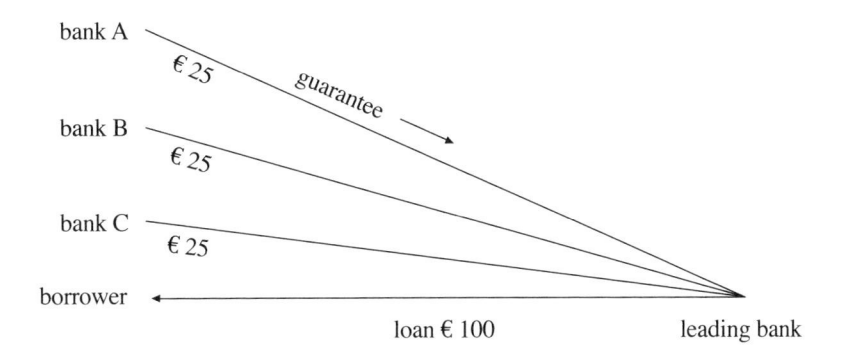

bank A
€ 25 guarantee
bank B
€ 25
bank C
€ 25
borrower
loan € 100   leading bank

Diagram 13

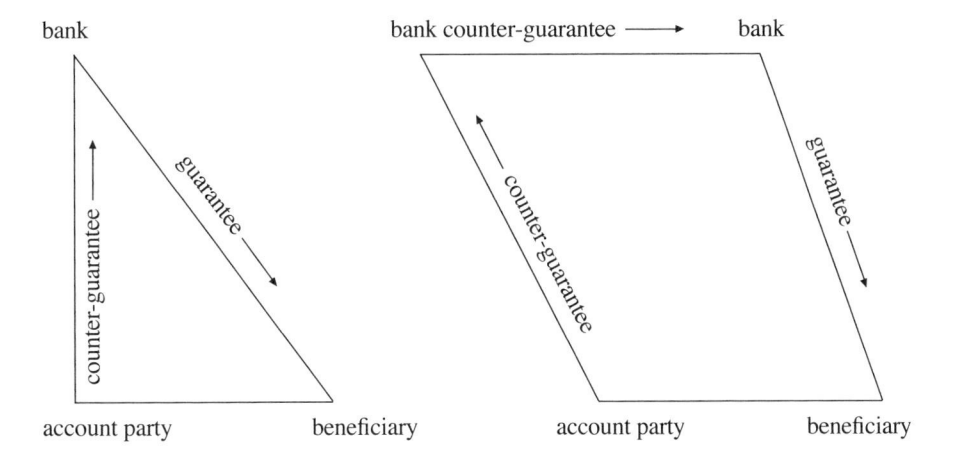

bank
counter-guarantee guarantee
account party   beneficiary

bank counter-guarantee → bank
counter-guarantee guarantee
account party   beneficiary

In 1988, the UNCITRAL took a renewed interest in independent guarantees and many sessions of the Working Group on International Contract Practices were devoted to working towards a Convention on independent guarantees and standby letters of credit. By 1995 these sessions had resulted in a final text of the UN Convention on independent guarantees and stand-by letters of credit (the 'UNCITRAL Convention').[20] The Convention entered into force on 1 January 2000 for Ecuador, El Salvador, Kuwait, Panama and Tunisia, and on 1 February 2003 for Belarus. It would appear that this Convention is especially useful for countries with immature independent guarantee regimes.[21]

Developments in uniform law. URCG and URDG of the International Chamber of Commerce; ISP98

2-13 *URCG*

In 1978 the International Chamber of Commerce (ICC) introduced the Uniform Rules for Contract Guarantees (URCG), ICC Publication No. 325. Apart from creating uniformity, the URCG aimed at encouraging more equitable practices in the area of guarantees, especially by reducing the opportunities for abuse. It was, therefore, considered desirable that the URCG should not provide for first demand guarantees payable without any evidence of default. Because of the strong bargaining position of importers, this explains why the URCG have largely remained unacceptable. Another factor which contributed to their ill fate is that the URCG are rather general, imprecise, fragmentary and conceptually fragile.

URDG

The limited success of the 1978 URCG prompted the ICC to work on a new set of uniform rules. The idea was that the inclusion of first demand guarantees, as well as a more comprehensive and detailed body of rules, would promote wider adoption in practice. The ICC Joint Working Party on 'Contractual Guarantees', consisting of the ICC Commission on Banking Technique and Practice and the Commission on International Commercial Practice, was entrusted with the task of preparing draft proposals. The UNCITRAL Working Group on International Contract Practices also contributed by reviewing the ICC drafts and making several recommendations for changes and

---

[20] See the Appendix. The text accompanied by a short Explanatory Note has been published as document V.96-87187-December 1996-5,100.

[21] *Cf.* Dolan, J.F., 'The UN Convention on International Independent Undertakings: Do States with Mature Letter-of-Credit Law Regimes need it?', in The 1999 Annual Survey of Letter of Credit Law & Practice, p. 97

improvements. A major difficulty in formulating uniform rules continued to be reconciling the conflicting interests of banks, exporters and industrialised countries, which tend to be at the account party end of guarantee deals, and importers and developing countries, which are typically at the beneficiary's end. This was one of the reasons why the project took considerably more time than initially envisaged.[22] The Uniform Rules for Demand Guarantees (URDG) were eventually completed by a smaller Drafting Group and endorsed by the ICC's Executive Board in December 1991. They were published as ICC Publication No. 458 in April 1992.[23] Meanwhile, official and comprehensive commentaries have appeared which provide a detailed explanation of the URDG.[24]

The success of the URDG will ultimately depend on the extent to which the international business community is prepared to adopt them in practice. Regrettably, at this stage the URDG have not yet gained wide acceptance. The precise reasons for this rather luke-warm reception remain somewhat obscure. One motive appears to be the fear that the URDG might conflict with the standard guarantee texts which banks employ or the particular provisions which banks and beneficiaries wish to include or exclude. This fear is unfounded since the URDG themselves do not contain guarantee texts or specific provisions.[25] Moreover, any of the Rules can be excluded or modified by contractual clauses in the guarantee as agreed by the parties thereto. Certain banks in some countries raise the objection that the prototype of payment condition is a written demand for payment supported by a specific statement of default, Art. 20(a) URDG, whereas these banks are used to issue 'simple demand' guarantees not requiring such a statement. It is noted, however, that the difference between these two types of demand

---

[22] One of the most acute controversies related to Art. 20, which provided at one time that the beneficiary must submit a statement concerning the account party's default in support of his demand for payment. This Article caused great tribulation, since a considerable percentage of guarantees do not require the submission of such a statement ('simple demand guarantees'). In view of the ongoing difficulties, sometimes on completely opposing grounds, the Joint Working Party decided to delete Art. 20. The two ICC Commissions requested the Joint Working Party to reconsider this decision, which eventually resulted in a reinstatement of Art. 20, while allowing for the possibility of its exclusion.

[23] See the Appendix.

[24] Roy Goode, 'Guide to the ICC Uniform Rules for Demand Guarantees', ICC Publication No. 510 (1992) and Georges Affaki, 'A User's Handbook to the URDG', ICC Publication No. 631 (2001). See for other comments: Goode, LMCLQ 1992, pp. 190-206; Vasseur, RDAI 1992, pp. 239-294; Martin and Delierneux, RDC 1993, pp. 228-328; Bertrams, TVVS 1993, pp. 95-100; Pabbruwe, WPNR 1993, pp. 921-925; von Westphalen, DB 1992, pp. 2017-2021, and RIW 1992, pp. 961-965; Hasse WM 1993, pp. 1985-1993, and Lipton, JIBL 1993, pp. 402-409.

[25] The ICC has, however, prepared standard texts (see the Appendix).

guarantees is small,²⁶ and that demand guarantees requiring a statement of default are increasingly becoming common practice. A third reason for the luke-warm reception of the URDG by banks appears to be that, according to them, the market – i.e. account parties and especially beneficiaries – does not ask for the incorporation of the Rules.²⁷

In any event, it would be unfortunate if the URDG were not to become widely accepted. But regardless of their global acceptance, it may well be that, in view of their authoritative source and the way they have come into existence, the URDG will affect developments in the law anyway. This is illustrated in *Trib. com. Brussels, 15 December 1992*, where the court resolved one of the issues by express reference to the Rules, although the guarantee had not been made subject to the URDG.²⁸ The URDG had also a direct impact on the chapter on independent guarantees in the Uniform Act on Securities which entered into force in 1998 in the 15 West African Member States of the OHADA.

ISP98

Taking the view that the American standby letter of credit represents unique features which require coverage seperately and distinctly from independent guarantees, the American Institute of International Banking Law & Practice adopted in 1998 a new set of uniform rules known as International Standby Practices (ISP98). The ISP98 are also published as ICC Publication No. 590. A detailed commentary on the rules ('The Official Commentary on the International Standby Practices') has been written by Professor James E. Byrnes, the chairman of the ISP Working Group.²⁹ Bearing in mind that the American standby letter of credit is functionally the same type of security as the independent guarantee,³⁰ it has been doubted whether there was any real need for a seperate

---

26 See Chapter 4.2, No. 4-3a. Moreover, Art. 20(c) allows parties to exclude the requirement of a statement of default.

27 If they do, banks appear willing to comply with their request.

28 RDC 1993, p. 1055. The issue concerned the expiry provision which referred to an expiry date and an expiry event, and which was resolved on the basis of Art. 22 URDG. See also *Trib. com. Namur, 12 September 1994*, RDC 1995, p. 68, for references to the URDG, although the guarantee was not made subject to the URDG. See further *OLG Karlsruhe, 21 July 1992*, WM 1992, p. 2095, where the court decided one of the issues on the basis of Art. 16 (d/c) of the 1983 UCP version which had not been declared applicable.

29 The most important Rules of ISP98 are also discussed in Chapter 6 of Wunnicke/Wunnicke/Turner. See also Dolan, § 4.09.

30 See Chapter 1, No. 1-4.

set of rules.³¹ This may be true, but the ultimate answer depends on the point of reference. In the absence of any other uniform rules, American banks used to routinely incorporate the UCP in standby credits, although it is commonly accepted that the UCP are not appropriate for standby credits. From this perspective the ISP98 are to be welcomed as they are specifically and exclusively drafted for standby credits. The ISP98 contain a vast number of rules and subrules (most of them with further subdivisions) which, taken together, are exceptionally complex and detailed and which contrast with the concise provisions of the URDG. In addition, several provisions of the ISP98 would surprise the commercial parties and/or are rather peculiar, while some of them display a certain bias in favour of the banks.³² Beneficiaries and account parties, but also banks, which are not sufficiently familiar with the ISP98 should, therefore, be cautious with accepting them. Nonetheless, the ISP98 contain many useful provisions, certainly when contrasted with the UCP if used in relation to standby credits.

Main features of the URDG and ISP98

2-14 The main features of the URDG and ISP98 can be summarised as follows.

Contractual nature

The URDG and ISP98 do not have the force of law, but are of a contractual nature and thus require the explicit or implicit consent of the parties. This is ordinarily achieved by virtue of an incorporation (or reference) clause in the guarantee or standby document, see Art. 1 URDG and Rule 1.01 ISP98. The contractual nature of the URDG and ISP98 also plays a part at a secondary level. Even if they are made applicable to the guarantee or standby, parties remain free to exclude or modify any of the Rules, although it would seem inappropriate to amend them too drastically.

While, as mentioned, the URDG do not have force of law, the majority of the URDG contain general principles which constitute the core of the concept of the independent

---

31 It is significant that the ICC only endorsed the ISP98 by what should be described as 'acceptance by abstention'(32 votes for, 9 against and 46 abstentions). See for critical comments Taylor, 'Were the new ISP Rules on standbys fairly adopted and will they be useful?, DCI, Vol. 4 No. 4, p. 14; Affaki, 'How do the ISP rules fit in with other uniform rules?, DCI, Winter 1999, 3; Nielsen, 'Internationale Bankgarantie, Akkreditiv and anglo-amerikanisches Standby nach Inkrafttreten der ISP98', WM 1999, pp. 2005-2020, 2049-2063. Interestingly, the ISP98 Commentary No. 3 on Rule 1.01 states that independent guarantees can also be made subject to the ISP98, and Goode, URDG Guide, p. 16, confirms that standby letters of credit are capable of falling within the URDG.

32 *Cf.* Dolan, § 4.09, § 4.09[5][i]. See also Wunnicke/Wunnicke/Turner, § 6.10.

guarantee and form part of established law. Other, more specific issues may be influenced by the URDG too.[33]

Independence

A basic feature of the modern guarantee and standby is its independence from the underlying relationship. This means that the payment obligation of the guarantor is solely determined by reference to the conditions of payment as specified in the guarantee, regardless of any defences under the underlying relationship. This notion of independence is clearly expressed in Art. 2(b) URDG and Rule 1.06 (a and c) ISP98.

Documentary conditions

Banks cannot properly function if they are compelled to investigate and verify facts. They can only deal with documents. Under the URDG and ISP98 regime, conditions of payment which relate to facts should, therefore, be converted to conditions requiring the presentation of documents which relate to these facts. The bank's duty is then confined to checking whether the documents tendered are in conformity with the documents prescribed in the guarantee or standby, which is the kind of operation banks are very familiar with. The documentary nature of the conditions of payment is emphasised in Art. 2(b) URDG and Rule 1.06(a/d) ISP98 and restated in several other articles for its practical implications.

Formal examination

Associated with the principle of independence and the documentary nature of the conditions of payment is the rule that, in its relationship with both the account party and the beneficiary, the bank is merely concerned with the question whether the documents tendered appear *on their face* to conform with the documents required by the guarantee or standby (see Art. 2(b) and especially Art. 9 URDG and Rule 4.01(b) ISP98). Accordingly, if, for example, the guarantee or standby requires a statement of default from the beneficiary concerning the account party's default and the beneficiary does indeed submit such a statement, the bank need not and may not investigate the veracity of this statement.[34]

---

[33] See, e.g., *Trib. com. Brussels*, RDC 1993, p. 1055, mentioned in No. 2-13.
[34] See further Chapter 10.8, No. 10-20.

URDG and ISP98 are not exhaustive

While the URDG and especially ISP98 provide a comprehensive set of uniform rules, they are of course not exhaustive in the sense that they provide an answer to each and every question. The issue of fraud has been completely left out, since it was felt that this was not a matter of contract law.

Transnational/national use

Since one of the objectives of formulating the URDG and ISP98 was to provide a uniform set of rules, they are primarily intended for use in connection with cross-border transactions and guarantees or standbys with parties established in different countries. There is, however, no reason why they should not also be applied in respect of domestic transactions.[35] This is consistent with the fact that national law also does not distinguish between transnational and national guarantees and standbys.[36]

All payment mechanisms

It is perhaps unfortunate that the ICC 1992 uniform Rules are called the Uniform Rules for *Demand* Guarantees. Demand (or first demand) guarantees are commonly understood to refer to independent guarantees which do not require any kind of real evidence concerning the account party's default.[37] Contrary to what its name suggests, the URDG do, however, also relate to guarantees with different payment mechanisms which require real or substantive documentary proof of default, such as a certificate by an architect or engineer, or a judgment or arbitral award,[38] as is expressly stated in Art. 2(a) URDG. Rules 4.19 and 4.20 ISP98 also allow for standbys with such different payment mechanisms. Apart from this, both the URDG and ISP98 permit the insertion of all kinds of other terms and conditions, provided they are formulated in a documentary fashion.

Standby letters of credit and the UCP and UCC

2-15 One of the changes in the 1983 version of the Uniform Customs and Practice for Documentary Credits (UCP), and maintained in the current 1993 version, ICC Publications No. 500, concerned the inclusion of standby letters of credit. Banks in the

---

35 Rule 1.01(b) ISP98 expressly provides for the use of ISP98 for domestic standbys.
36 See also Chapter 5, No. 5-5.
37 See Chapter 4.2.
38 See Chapter 4.3 and 4.4.

United States and in some other countries which are influenced by American banking practices, regularly refer to the UCP when issuing standby letters of credit. This can be explained by the fact that the standby is a derivative of the traditional (commercial) letter of credit and by the desire to dispel any doubt as to its independent and documentary nature and possibly by the fact that a suitable uniform set of rules other than the UCP did not exist until recently. Because of their different nature, Art. 1 UCP provides that 'these articles apply to documentary credits, including, *to the extent to which they may be applicable*, standby letters of credit'. In fact, the larger part of the UCP, notably the provisions of Parts D and E and several other provisions, do not apply to standby letters of credit or are inappropriate, whilst other issues which are vital in a standby context, are not addressed at all in the UCP.[39] It may be expected that, with the publication of ISP98, standby letters of credit will no longer be made subject to the UCP.

As far as the United States is concerned, all 50 states have adopted Art. 5 of the Uniform Commercial Code (UCC). This Article deals with letters of credit and it encompasses both the traditional (commercial) letter of credit (documentary credit) and the standby letter of credit. The text of Art. 5 was revised in 1995.

The ICC Uniform Rules for Contract Bonds (URCB)

2-16 During the preparations of the URDG some representatives, especially those from the Scandinavian countries and Japan, expressed concern about the desirability of simple first demand guarantees requiring no evidence of the principal debtor's default and the attendant risk of abuse by the beneficiary. This concern was shared by the insurance industry, active in the business of bonds, and the construction industry, which tends to be on the principal debtor's side. It was felt that there was some need for a security device whereby the guarantor's liability is accessory to that of the principal debtor and based upon established default. The ICC Commission on Insurance, in cooperation with representatives from the construction industry, was requested to draw up rules which were finally adopted in April 1993 and which became effective on 1 January 1994, ICC Publication No. 524 (Uniform Rules for Contract Bonds, URCB). Obviously, these Rules only apply to bonds to which they are stated to apply. The key provisions are Art. 3(b) and (d), which provide that the guarantor's liability under the bond is accessory and arises upon default, and that all defences of the principal debtor against the beneficiary under the underlying contract are also available to the guarantor. In case of dispute, Art. 7(j) states that default is deemed to be established upon the issue of a certificate of default by the guarantor, or, if the bond so provides, upon the issue of a certificate of default by a third party, which could be, for example, an independent engineer or a pre-arbitral referee of the ICC, or upon final judgment or arbitral award. As is peculiar to bonds, the guarantor may elect to complete the underlying contract instead of paying the bond amount (Art. 2 definition of 'bond').

---

[39] *Cf.*, e.g., Dolan, § 4.09, Wunnicke/Wunnicke/Turner, § 6.01.

Unfortunately, the URCB are difficult to comprehend. Their structure and language follow those of the traditional common law performance bonds, the language of which has been described as archaic.[40] Although Art. 7 describes in detail certain technicalities with respect to the submission of claims, the URCB do not clearly state when and in which circumstances the beneficiary is entitled to payment, or they do so in a negative way (Art. 7(i): 'a claim shall not be honoured unless …'). Because of their different nature, this type of security and the URCB fall outside the scope of this study.

National laws and regulations

2-17 In most countries, no specific legislation exists on independent guarantees, while only a very few countries have some statutory provisions of a general nature.[41] The 15 OHADA countries in West Africa have adopted uniform legislation, several provisions of which have been directly derived from the URDG.[42]

Countries in the Middle East, particularly Saudi Arabia and Iraq, and in North Africa have promulgated mandatory regulations concerning independent guarantees and it is important to have a clear view of the legal nature and effect of these regulations, which, incidentally, are by no means peculiar to these regions.[43] These regulations contain mandatory instructions, directed to their national entities, typically government departments and agencies or State-controlled companies operating in the public sector, and they specify in which circumstances these entities are to insist on the procurement of guarantees when inviting tenders or awarding contracts to foreign companies. They usually also prescribe the guarantee format, for example an indirect guarantee

---

[40] *Trafalgar House Construction (Regions) Ltd v. General Surety and Guarantee Co. Ltd.*, [1995] 3 All ER 737.

[41] Arts. 665-674 of the 1964 International Trade Code of the Czech Republic; Art. 1087 of the 1978 Law of Obligations of Yugoslavia expressly mentions first demand guarantees; Arts. 331-336 Law of Commerce of Bahrain, No. 7/1987; Arts. 382-387 Commercial Code of Kuwait of 1980; Arts. 287-293 Commercial Code of Iraq, No. 30/1984; Arts. 1497-1503 Civil Code of Yemen, No. 8/1988.

[42] The OHADA (*Organisation pour L'Harmonisation de Droit des Affaires en Afrique*) adopted the Uniform Act on Securities which entered into force in all 15 Member States on 1 January 1998. Arts. 31-38 of this Act provide statutory rules for independent guarantees, reprinted in Affaki, No. 209. The Member States are: Benin, Burkina Faso, Cameroon, Central Africa, Comoros, Congo, Ivory Coast, Gabon, Equatorial Guinea, Guinea Bissau, Mali, Niger, Senegal, Chad and Togo.

[43] There is a certain tendency among some writers to attribute undue significance to these regulations by suggesting that they represent a comprehensive body of law which applies regardless of the contractually agreed terms and conditions, and which some way or other becomes automatically part of the contract of guarantee. These suggestions are misleading, if not incorrect, *cf.* El Hakim, Tours, pp. 386, 387 notes 10 and 11.

issued by a local bank, the conditions of payment, typically payment on first demand, and other terms, such as the amount payable expressed as a percentage of the contract value and the period within which the guarantee must be made available. The national entities which are subject to these regulations are sometimes required to employ approved standard texts. In short, the effect of the regulations is that these national entities are obligated to procure guarantees which meet the standards set forth in the regulations and that foreign exporters and contractors have virtually no option but to furnish guarantees which comply with the requirements.

Banks are ordinarily also subject to government regulations dealing with their power to issue guarantees and licenses for so doing, the maximum exposure, accounting and other procedures. In some countries in the Middle East and North Africa, for instance Syria, Saudi Arabia and Algeria, banks are required to employ standard or approved texts for guarantees and counter-guarantees, either by virtue of State regulations or as a matter of practice.

As far as Saudi Arabia is concerned, the Saudi Arabian Monetary Agency (SAMA) is empowered by virtue of Art. 16(4) of the Banking Control Law to issue binding circulars, with the approval of the Minister of Finance and National Economy. In respect of the public sector, it has promulgated mandatory rules governing bank guarantees and the exact texts of those guarantees.[44] SAMA is also the appropriate authority for interpreting the standard SAMA guarantee instruments and for defining and reviewing customary law and banking practices.

Case law and legal writing

2-18 Apart from the URDG, ISP98 and the UNCITRAL Convention, the most important sources of law are case law and legal writing. Since 1977 there has been a steady flow of case law. The Iranian revolution of 1979-1980 in particular sparked off the first major bulk of litigation in a great number of countries, and this period can be characterised as the formative phase of the law on independent guarantees, as shaped by the courts. The end of the Iranian revolution did not by any means herald a period of tranquillity. On the contrary, the body of case law continues to grow and guarantees must prominently figure among those contracts which are exceptionally litigation prone.

Apart from its authority as a source of law which varies from country to country, legal writing on the Continent has greatly contributed to the creation of a framework for the development and formulation of the general principles of law. This is especially true for the initial phase when the law consisted of little more than a few scattered judicial decisions.

---

[44] The current version is the 1991 Circular No 7821/MA/251. The standard texts are in practice increasingly used in the private sector too.

CHAPTER 3
TYPES OF GUARANTEE

3.1 GENERAL

3-1 The variety of risks which attend the conclusion and execution of contracts or which result from advance and interim payments by the importer or employer to the exporter or construction company has engendered different types of guarantee, although they basically serve the same overall purpose, namely protection against non-performance.

It is usual to distinguish between two main types of guarantee: guarantees which provide security for financial obligations and guarantees which provide security for non-financial obligations. The first type secures financial obligations such as those of the buyer in respect of the purchase price arising from a contract of sale, or those of the employer for the payment of installments in connection with a construction contract, or those of the borrower for payment of principal sum and interest arising from credit facilities (see Nos. 3-3 – 3-7). The second type of guarantees provides security for non-financial obligations such as those of the seller for the delivery of goods, or those of the construction firm for the completion of the project. This second main type can be subdivided into several other subtypes, such as tender, performance and maintenance guarantees, which correspond with the successive phases of the lifetime of a contract, while others, such as repayment and retention guarantees, relate to payments made by the importer/beneficiary to the exporter/account party (see Nos. 3-2 – 3-6). Whether just one, several or all types of guarantee are needed depends on the circumstances of the case. It should also be noted that some types can be used for more than one purpose. For example, a performance guarantee ordinarily also covers the risk of defects during the maintenance period after delivery of the goods or after provisional acceptance in construction contracts, and a repayment guarantee might also be used for the same purpose as a performance guarantee. Accordingly, the ambit and purpose of a guarantee should not be gathered from its label, but must be derived by reference to the risk description, if explicitly expressed, as it appears from the text of the guarantee, the other terms and conditions, especially the validity period and reduction mechanism, and the absence or presence of other types of guarantee. At any rate, the exporter/account party should be careful to avoid situations in which several guarantees cover the same risk simultaneously.

3.2 TENDER GUARANTEES

3-2 Construction contracts and major contracts for the supply of capital goods are often, especially in the public sector, awarded through tender procedures. The conditions or regulations governing the invitation for tenders invariably require bidders to furnish a tender guarantee (or bid bond or guarantee for preliminary deposit) for a certain percentage, which ordinarily ranges from one to five per cent of the project value. The tender documentation often fixes the text of the guarantee and the guarantee format, i.e. a direct or indirect guarantee. Tender guarantees are typically payable on first demand.

The purpose of a tender guarantee is to ensure that the bidder does not withdraw or alter his tender before adjudication and that he will accept and sign the contract if and when awarded to him. The tender regulations regularly require bidders also to furnish a performance guarantee within a certain period after adjudication.[1] It is not unusual to require that the tender must be accompanied by a letter of commitment or a binding letter of intent to this effect from a bank. The employer or buyer/beneficiary is entitled to call the tender guarantee when the bidder fails to fulfil said obligations stemming from his submitting a tender.[2] Payment serves as compensation for the loss of time and expenditure incurred as a result of the employer having to re-examine the tenders submitted by other contractors. In a broader sense, requirements in respect of tender guarantees and letters of commitment are aimed at ensuring that only serious, reputable and financially sound contractors respond to the invitation for tenders, which greatly facilitates the procedures and evaluation of the various bids.

Tender guarantees usually contain a fixed expiry date which corresponds with the expected date of adjudication. However, the guarantee or the rules for submitting tenders may allow the beneficiary to have the validity period extended or they may provide for a 'extend or withdraw' mechanism.[3] Extensions of the validity period are a constant cause of concern, and bidders should provide for this contingency in their tender, especially in respect of the computation and indexation of the contract value. It is noted that tenders which are stated to be valid for a limited period of time are often unacceptable.

By their nature, tender guarantees cease to be capable of fulfilling their function and they cannot be called once the contract has been awarded to another bidder. Tender guarantees sometimes state explicitly that they must be returned to the unsuccessful bidder.

---

[1] In the Middle East tender guarantees are often referred to as the 'initial' guarantee and performance guarantees as the 'final' guarantee.

[2] *Cf. Paris, 13 December 1984*, D. 1985 I.R. p. 239, upheld by *Cass., 10 March 1987*, D. 1987 Somm. p. 172, von Westphalen, p. 38, in respect of the beneficiary's right to call the tender guarantee when the bidder fails to furnish the required performance guarantee.

[3] See further Chapter 12.4.3, No. 12-42.

In Europe tender guarantees are often replaced by a letter of commitment or a binding letter of intent only. In such an instrument the bank irrevocably undertakes to issue a performance guarantee in accordance with the requirements as stated in the tender documentation if and when the employer awards the contract to the contractor. These letters provide the same degree of protection to the employer as a tender guarantee, because upon adjudication of the contract to the contractor the bank will issue the performance guarantee which can be called by the employer at once, if the contractor fails to sign the contract or does not complete the contract. The advantage for the contractor is that the costs may be reduced, but the disadvantage is that the maximum amount of the performance guarantee tends to be higher than that of a tender guarantee.

3.3 PERFORMANCE GUARANTEES

3-3 Apart from judicial guarantees (see No. 3-9), performance guarantees are the type used most frequently. They can be characterised as the counterpart of a documentary credit. A documentary credit assures payment in anticipation of proper performance by the seller, as evidenced by the tender of the documents specified in the credit. In contrast, a performance guarantee assures payment to the importer or employer in the event that the exporter or contractor has not, not timely, not completely or not properly fulfilled his obligations from the underlying contract. As a matter of fact, many contracts for sale provide for the issuance of two security instruments: a documentary credit in favour of the seller and a performance guarantee in favour of the buyer.

The percentage of the contract value covered by the guarantee, as expressed in the maximum amount, varies. It usually ranges from five to ten per cent, but this could be higher depending on the payments made by the beneficiary to the account party pursuant to the underlying contract. In most situations a buyer could obtain the same benefits as those accruing from a first demand guarantee by withholding part of the contract price as security for proper performance. However, as sellers usually prefer to receive the full contract price at once, this security can be replaced by a performance guarantee. This underscores that performance guarantees could also operate as financing instruments. If, especially in relation to construction contracts, the account party (contractor) is assured of payment as the performance of the contract progresses, the maximum amount of the performance guarantee may also increase. Cases have been known whereby the maximum amount of the guarantee increases with an amount equal to the sums paid by the beneficiary in accordance with the underlying contract.

The text of performance guarantees nearly always describes the object of the guarantee in general wording, namely cover by means of compensation in the event of non-performance by the account party. The ambit of performance guarantees thus extends not only to the delivery of, for example, equipment, but includes the installation, contractual warranty obligations during the warranty period and all other obligations which form part of the principal contract, unless clearly stated otherwise.[4] Should the warranty obligations and other obligations after delivery or initial or provisional completion be extensive, or should they run for a considerable period of time, it can be advisable to arrange for multiple performance guarantees, each covering a segment of the entire contract. This technique is especially useful in the case of turnkey and product-in-hand contracts, which could encompass the actual putting into operation of the plant, staffing, training and monitoring of management, transfer of technology and know-how, and the marketing of products. A separate guarantee covering the warranty period is often called a maintenance (or warranty) guarantee, but such a guarantee serves the same purpose as a performance guarantee (see No. 3-4). In the event of multiple guarantees it is vital for the account party to ensure that these guarantees do not run simultaneously. This can be accomplished by an accurate risk description and by clauses stipulating that the successive guarantees do not enter into force until the release of the preceeding guarantee. The advantage of multiple guarantees is that the maximum exposure under each of the guarantees is smaller, but the total costs for the account party can be higher. A similar arrangement, but one which is riskier for the exporter, can be achieved by one performance guarantee covering the entire project, but allowing for a reduction of the maximum amount upon completion of the successive stages.

3.4 MAINTENANCE (OR WARRANTY) GUARANTEES

3-4 It is possible that, in addition to a performance guarantee, a maintenance (or warranty) guarantee is issued in order to ensure that the exporter or construction firm remedies any defects which become apparent after delivery of the goods or after provisional or substantial completion of the plant. This type of guarantee thus covers the maintenance or warranty period during which the exporter continues to be responsible for the adequate functioning of the equipment or works, but otherwise serves the same purpose as a performance guarantee. The maximum amount tends to be considerably lower than that of performance guarantees. Since they basically cover the same risk, maintenance and performance guarantees should ordinarily not run simultaneously, but this is merely a rule of thumb. It might well be different if the value of the guarantees, especially that of the maintenance guarantee, is small, if no certificate of (provisional) acceptance has been issued and if the beneficiary has paid the full contract price.

---

[4] German authors, such as Von Westphalen, p. 39, Zahn/Ehrlich/Neumann, 9/52/56, Dohm, No. 20, and Nielsen, ZHR 1983, p. 149, take the view that performance guarantees do not encompass defects which become apparent during the warranty period, and that these should be covered by a separate warranty (or maintenance) guarantee. This may be peculiar to German domestic trade, but otherwise the texts of crossborder performance guarantees lend no support at all to this view.

Maintenance guarantees are especially used in connection with construction contracts and for a specific purpose. They can be furnished in order to persuade the employer to release the last installment(s) of the contract price, which he would otherwise have withheld as security for repairs or supplemental works by the contractor during the maintenance period. In this situation also, the guarantee is utilised as a financing instrument. The amount payable under the guarantee then equals the amounts of the released instalments and it is typically payable on demand without any evidence of default.

3.5 REPAYMENT (OR ADVANCE PAYMENT) GUARANTEES

3-5 In most major contracts the exporter or contractor negotiates for advance payments, which ordinarily range from five to thirty per cent of the contract value, in order to be able to finance the transaction, especially in the initial phase of execution. In turn, the importer or employer will require a repayment (or advance payment) guarantee assuring repayment of the down-payment in the event of non-performance. They are issued for the full amount of the advances.

The specific risk covered by a repayment guarantee is ordinarily described in general terms, namely non-performance. Accordingly, the text of most repayment guarantees does not indicate whether the beneficiary can only call the guarantee in the event that the exporter has failed to apply the advance payment to certain specific activities to be carried out in the early stages of execution, such as the purchase or manufacture of equipment, the preparing of drawings and designs or (successive) shipments of materials and equipment, or whether the guarantee can be called if the exporter has failed to carry out the contract up to the amount for which he received advance payments, or whether the beneficiary is justified in calling the guarantee if the contract has not been completed. In the last-mentioned event the repayment guarantee operates as a variant of a performance guarantee and might run simultaneously since a performance guarantee does not secure repayment of the down-payment. It is submitted that a repayment guarantee can be called for the full amount and for the same reasons as in the case of a performance guarantee, namely non-performance of the principal contract, and without any restrictions save those which are explicitly mentioned in the text of the guarantee. This proposition accords with the basic rule of guarantees that they can be called, provided that the terms and conditions as specified in the text are met. It also accords with the fact that importers are ordinarily not interested in the way the down-payment is applied as long as the contract is properly performed.

Repayment guarantees often contain a reduction clause. Reduction clauses typically provide for a reduction of the maximum amount upon evidence of progressive performance, for example the tender of shipping documents evidencing the (successive) dispatch of equipment or materials. The maximum amount is ordinarily reduced to zero when goods have been shipped or when works have been carried out up to the value of the advance payment. The repayment guarantee then ceases to have effect, and completion of the entire transaction will, thereafter, be secured by a performance guarantee. Insertion of a reduction mechanism clearly reveals that parties intended the repayment guarantee to ensure execution of the initial stages or parts of the contract only.

The object of a repayment guarantee is broader than that of a performance guarantee. It can also be called, for example, when the contract is cancelled by mutual consent, if the contract has not entered into force, if the contract cannot be executed because of *force majeure* or if the contract turns out to be void, invalid or unenforceable. This is because repayment guarantees envisage primarily a refund of advance payments which have been made in anticipation of execution of the contract and which can be viewed as a loan, whereas performance guarantees secure compensation for losses other than the advance payment which result from breach of contract.

It is advisable that the repayment guarantee explicitly stipulates that it does not take effect until the down-payment has been received.

3.6 RETENTION GUARANTEES

3-6 Construction contracts usually provide for interim payments upon certificates from the engineer, which testify completion of a certain amount of work or a certain stage of the project. These interim payments as the work progresses enable the contractor to finance his operations. The employer is ordinarily entitled to retain a percentage of the instalments, normally between five and ten per cent, as security for defects which may become apparent at a later stage. Contractors and employers often agree to the release of the so-called retention moneys so that the contractor receives the full amount of the interim payment at once, in return for a retention (or withholding) guarantee. Retention guarantees are a further example of guarantees being used as financing instruments. They tend to be payable on first demand. Their purpose is similar to repayment and maintenance guarantees in that they ensure a refund of payments made by the employer, and they resemble performance guarantees by indemnifying the employer if the contractor fails to complete the project. Unlike repayment guarantees containing a reduction mechanism, the maximum amount payable under a retention guarantee may increase in accordance with the successive releases of the retention money.

3.7 PAYMENT GUARANTEES AND STANDBY LETTERS OF CREDIT

3-7 As noted in No. 3-1, a guarantee can also be used as security for a payment obligation, such as in connection with a contract of sale, a take-over, a lease, a construction contract, loan, bond issue or any other financial commitment. These guarantees are called payment guarantees, but the term standby letter of credit is also prevalent and is not confined to American banking practice. In this situation the term standby letter of credit has a specific meaning.

Payment guarantees and standby letters of credit are often used as credit enhancement tools for notes, bonds and other types of commercial paper. The security for redemption and payment of interest provided by a reliable bank enables the issuer to market their paper more easily and at lower rates of interest.

In recent years there has been a growing demand for payment guarantees (or standby letters of credit) assuring payment in sale transactions, in lieu of the traditional letter of credit. The difference is that utilisation and payment under the traditional documentary credit take place in the ordinary course of events as contemplated by all parties concerned, whereas the beneficiary of a payment guarantee is expected to seek payment from the buyer/account party first. He can only call the guarantee if the buyer fails to pay. In other words, the traditional letter of credit serves primarily as a means of payment in the contemplated execution of the transaction, while a payment guarantee or standby letter of credit serves as security for payment in the event of the buyer's default. If issued in the form of a standby letter of credit, it can be made subject to the UCP, but incorporation of the URDG or ISP98 is equally possible.

The most important reason for the increasing demand for payment guarantees or standby letters of credit in support of sale transactions is that the total costs thereof are lower than those in the case of a documentary credit. It is ordinarily sufficient for the exporter, who supplies a particular buyer on a regular basis, to have the benefit of just one standby covering the amount of any shipments that have not yet been paid, whereas a traditional letter of credit would have to be issued for each individual shipment or there must be a revolving credit. Another reason is that the bank charges are lower, because the utilisation of the standby is the exception rather than the rule and because the documents, which have to be examined by the bank, tend to be less extensive. They are ordinarily payable on demand accompanied by the seller's statement that the buyer has failed to pay the contract price and sometimes (a copy of) the invoice. In view of the lower rates, banks are reluctant to agree to the inclusion of other conditions, such as the tender of (copies of) the bill of lading, insurance documents, quality certificates and certificates of origin. Banks take the view that if the buyer wishes these documentary conditions to be included he must apply for an ordinary documentary credit. In any event, the usual format of standby letters of credit exposes the buyer to greater risks than is the case with a traditional letter of credit, because, as mentioned, the required documentation which the seller has to present is ordinarily less comprehensive.

Another explanation for the growing demand for payment guarantees is that many exporters who are willing to agree to payment by the importer on open account on, say, 30, 60 or 90 days are increasingly experiencing difficulties in obtaining credit for their own operations. A payment guarantee issued in favour of the exporter could solve this problem, since on the strength thereof banks will be more inclined to finance the exporter and possibly at lower rates, while the exporter could then continue to give credit to the importer.

Payment guarantees may contain a payment mechanism other than payment on first demand without any proof of default. They could, for example, stipulate for payment on condition that the beneficiary submits invoices endorsed by a specified third party. This technique is not uncommon in construction contracts where payment under the guarantee requires the beneficiary/construction firm to present invoices endorsed by the engineer. Such endorsement confirms that the construction firm has properly carried out works and that payment is, therefore, due. The stipulated endorsement, thus, serves as a protection for the account party/employer.

3.8 CUSTOMS GUARANTEES. EC REPAYMENT GUARANTEES

3-8 If a bank's client is exhibiting goods at an exhibition in another country or if a contractor needs to import building equipment temporarily for a project, payment of import duties can be avoided by an undertaking to re-export the goods or equipment, backed up by a customs guarantee. The tax exemption is withdrawn and the guarantee can be called if the goods have not left the country by the end of the expected period of use. Within the countries of the European Community, customs guarantees are also used to allow goods in transit to travel without clearance and without paying taxes and duties except in the country of destination. These guarantees are issued in favour of the customs and excise agencies in the country of destination and they can be called if the goods are not cleared within a certain period of time.[5]

Exporters of agricultural produce in the EC may be required, in lieu of making cash deposits, to put up guarantees assuring repayment of subsidies or advance payments in connection with export transactions or the purchase of intervention commodities by EC authorities. These guarantees can be called if the exporter fails to comply with the relevant EC regulations.

3.9 JUDICIAL GUARANTEES

3-9 On the Continent it is not uncommmon for plaintiffs to apply for conservatory attachment orders in respect of the defendant's assets, such as real property or bank accounts, when commencing proceedings. The purpose of these measures is to ensure that the plaintiff will be in a position to enforce a future judgment in his favour by seizing the defendant's assets at the commencement of the proceedings. The English Mareva injunction ('freezing' order) serves a similar purpose. Conservatory attachment orders hamper the defendant in his business activities since he loses the power of dealing and disposing of the attached goods. Defendants, therefore, usually offer to furnish a guarantee against discharge of the conservatory attachment. For the sake of convenience, these guarantees can be called judicial guarantees. By their nature these

---

[5] *Trib. com. Paris, 7 October 1988*, D. 1989 Somm. p. 145, and *Cass. 19 May 1992*, D. 1993 Somm. p. 103 provide examples of a call on a customs guarantee.

judicial guarantees are payable upon submission of an arbitral award or court judgment affirming the plaintiff/beneficiary's right to payment of a certain amount by the defendant/account party or upon the latter's acknowledgement of default. The maximum amount payable under the guarantee usually corresponds with the amount of the asserted claim or with the value of the goods that have been attached. The amount can also be fixed by the court when the defendant applies for discharge. The underlying dispute can be of any kind, such as non-performance of contractual obligations or tort. Unlike the guarantees discussed above, judicial guarantees are not furnished until an actual dispute has arisen.

3.10 OTHER TYPES

3-10 Due to their flexibility, bank guarantees can be utilised to cover all kinds of risks, in addition to those mentioned above. For example, a guarantee could secure payment of liquidated damages pursuant to a penalty clause in the underlying contract or it may secure representations and warranties made by a seller of shares in a company in connection with a take-over. Guarantees are also frequently used in connection with missing or defective documents relating to the sale and shipment of goods. For example, a buyer who is not yet in possession of the relevant documents, such as the bill of lading or delivery order, might be able to persuade the carrier or warehouse owner to release the goods in return for a bank guarantee. A bank which has issued a documentary credit, but refuses to accept the documents on account of some defects, might be prepared to make payment if the beneficiary/seller puts up a bank guarantee. These guarantees are usually payable on first demand.

3.11 AUTONOMOUS GUARANTEES. THE GERMAN *GARANTIEVERTRAG*. INDEMNITY

3-11 German law, and especially German doctrine, has developed an overall concept of guarantee, the *Garantievertrag*, which is typified by the rule of independence, in contradistinction to the accessory suretyship. Although this concept has a broad and general character, it has been applied especially to situations where an underlying relationship is lacking, or where the beneficiary of the *Garantievertrag* is not also a creditor in the underlying relationship or where the guarantor acts for his own account: for example, a promise by local government, inspired by a desire to attract business activities, to compensate investors for possible losses, or a guarantee by the engineer in favour of the employer to the effect that the total costs and expenditures of a construction project will not exceed a certain amount or hold harmless clauses. The guarantor in a *Garantievertrag* indemnifies the beneficiary if a certain 'result' (*Erfolg, Leistung, Zustand* or *Umstand*) occurs, or if a certain 'result' does not take place, and he is also answerable for 'atypical risks'.[6] These guarantees are exclusively two-party relationships and their independent nature goes without saying. They can be labelled as autonomous guarantees. Their factual context is entirely different from the modern bank guarantee, which operates in a multi-party relationship whereby the beneficiary is the creditor in the underlying relationship and whereby, pursuant to a guarantee clause in the principal contract, the principal debtor requests the bank to issue a guarantee for his account and risk. The modern bank guarantee is occasionally said to be a species of the general concept of *Garantievertrag*. Given the significant differences in factual setting, this subsumption does not appear to be helpful. The modern bank guarantee and the autonomous guarantee clearly envisage distinct forms of security in distinct situations.[7]

The English notion of 'indemnity' is similar, but does not entirely cover the German *Garantievertrag*. The idea of an autonomous guarantee is also known in the Netherlands, France and Belgium. Due to its manifold manifestations, legal writing in these countries has refrained from developing an overall concept.

---

[6] *BGH, 28 October 1954*, WM 1955, p. 265; *BGH, 5 May 1960*, NJW 1960, p. 1567; *BGH, 21 February 1968*, WM 1968, p. 680.

[7] *Cf.* von Westphalen, pp. 49-51.

CHAPTER 4
CONDITIONS OF PAYMENT (PAYMENT MECHANISM)

4.1 INTRODUCTION. MAIN TYPES. DOCUMENTARY NATURE

4-1 Apart from the specifically agreed upon terms and conditions, the rights and obligations of parties and more specifically the conditions of payment under a contract of suretyship are fixed by the co-extensiveness principle. By virtue of this principle the underlying relationship is transposed, as it were, to the relationship between surety and beneficiary/creditor, and the content and extent of the surety's liability, both as a matter of substance and as a matter of evidence, are determined by the principal debtor's liability towards the creditor according to the underlying relationship. This is the characteristic pattern of the suretyship as fixed by law. It is only when parties want to depart from this pattern and when they wish to fix the surety's liability in another manner that they need to insert specific clauses in order to modify the co-extensiveness principle.[1]

The independent guarantee shows a reverse pattern. The principle of independence tells us how the bank's obligations and the beneficiary's rights are *not* to be determined, and that the characteristic pattern, as fixed by law, is that of separation of guarantee and principal contract. It does not, however, provide any positive clue in respect of the question of when and in what circumstances the guarantor is obligated to proceed to payment, and when and in what circumstances the beneficiary is entitled to receive payment. This function is performed by the conditions of payment, also known as the payment mechanism. They specify the kind of evidence concerning the principal debtor's default upon which the bank is to pay, or, as is the case in first demand guarantees, they provide that no such evidence is required and that the demand for payment suffices. The payment mechanism must, therefore, be agreed upon in each individual case and it has to be explicitly inserted into the text of the instrument.

The conditions of payment form the heart of the guarantee. They determine the actual benefits for the beneficiary/creditor and the risk exposure for the account party/principal debtor. For example, it is the clause which states that payment will be made on the beneficiary's first demand without any proof of default (Chapter 4.2) that renders this particular guarantee totally different from the traditional suretyship (or accessory guarantee). On the other hand, a guarantee payable upon submission of an arbitral or court decision (Chapter 4.4) hardly differs in substance from the contract of suretyship,

---

[1] See Chapter 4.5.

while a guarantee requiring the submission of third-party documents (Chapter 4.3) occupies a middle position. In conclusion, statements to the effect that the independent guarantee and the accessory suretyship are fundamentally different are quite correct, but solely emphasising the contradistinction between independence and co-extensiveness can, however, be equally misleading, because it ignores the pivotal role of the particular payment mechanism.

While different as regards the degree of proof of default, the three above-mentioned conditions of payment share a common characteristic, namely their documentary nature. All three require the submission of documents and the bank's duty is confined to examining whether these documents comply with the documents prescribed in the guarantee. It is this documentary nature of the conditions of payment which enables the bank to perform its function.

It is commonly assumed that independent guarantees and first demand guarantees are synonymous. This is incorrect. A first demand guarantee is a particular type of independent guarantee which relates to the payment mechanism, while guarantees which contain one of the two other mechanisms are also independent guarantees.

4.2 PAYMENT ON FIRST DEMAND

General

4-2 In international trade, payment on the beneficiary's first demand is probably the prevailing type of payment mechanism. If the guarantee provides for this mechanism the beneficiary is entitled to payment without any condition other than submitting the request for payment. He need not adduce any evidence or corroboration concerning the principal debtor's default or his entitlement to compensation according to the underlying relationship. Further, the beneficiary is entitled to claim the full amount of the guarantee without proof or specification of the size of his loss. In its turn, the bank is not permitted to ask for any evidence or to enquire into these matters. At any rate, any queries and doubts on the part of the bank do not exonerate the bank from the obligation to proceed to payment forthwith when the beneficiary demands it. In short, the beneficiary's substantive entitlement to compensation according to the underlying relationship is not an issue which can be addressed as far as the contract of guarantee is concerned. That issue can be raised by the account party after payment by the bank. Accordingly, it is quite possible that the beneficiary is fully entitled to receive payment pursuant to the terms of the guarantee, while in subsequent proceedings between account party and beneficiary it turns out that the beneficiary had no right to compensation as adjudged by the principal contract, or to a lower amount. The only factor that matters is that the beneficiary at the time he requests payment meets the conditions of payment as specified in the guarantee, which, in the case of a first demand guarantee, is simply the request itself. These remarkable features are mind-boggling indeed and it is quite understandable that it took some time and effort for the legal community and judiciary to accept fully the validity and enforceabilty of guarantees with this particular payment mechanism.[2]

In English legal language first demand guarantees are sometimes referred to as 'unconditional' guarantees.

'On simple demand'. Statement of default; prior notice of default and grace period

4-3 First demand guarantees are known in two variants. The so-called simple demand guarantee requires no more than the beneficiary's written demand for payment. This variant used to be prevalent in the Middle East. At present, in most regions, including the Middle East, the Far East, Latin America and Africa, the vast majority of first demand guarantees stipulate that the beneficiary must also submit a statement concerning the account party's default, for example, a statement to the effect that the bidder has refused to sign the contract and/or has failed to furnish a performance guarantee (tender guarantee), or that the contractor has failed to complete the project (performance guarantee), or that the importer has not paid the purchase price (payment guarantee). These statements of default merely entail a formal, unilateral declaration from the beneficiary, which need not be accompanied by further corroboration.[3] In its relationship with the beneficiary, the bank is not permitted to enquire into the veracity of the beneficiary's statement while in its relationship with the account party the bank owes no duty in this respect. In English legal language, clauses requiring a statement of default are commonly referred to as 'conclusive evidence' clauses. This label aptly conveys that the beneficiary's statement in respect of the principal debtor's default is to be treated as conclusive evidence as far as the guarantee is concerned.[4] Inclusion of the

---

2   Kerr, J., in *Harbottle (Mercantile) Ltd. v. Nat. Westminster Bank*, [1977] 2 All ER 862,865: 'Performance guarantees in such unqualified terms seem astonishing, but I am told that they are by no means unusual, particularly in transactions with customers in the Middle East.' See also *LG Frankfurt a.M., October 16 1962*, NJW 1963, p. 450, which must be one of the earliest cases in this field, and *Bache & Co v. Banque Vernes et Commerciale de Paris SA*, [1973] 2 Lloyd's Rep. 437, where the courts were persuaded by expert evidence to acknowledge the validity of first demand guarantees. With a view to the apparent lack of a *causa* the enforceability of first demand guarantees has long been a controversial issue in Belgian and French legal writing and case law, see further Chapter 12.1, No. 12-6.

3   French and German legal writing sometimes equates a first demand guarantee with a simple demand guarantee and refers to a demand guarantee requiring a statement of default as a documentary guarantee. As in other countries, in this study the term 'first demand guarantee' comprises both variants, the common denominator being that no evidence of default is required. This is just a matter of terminology.

4   See also Chapter 4.5, No. 4-20.

aforementioned clauses could, nonetheless, ameliorate the account party's position as it may prompt the beneficiary to exercise a greater degree of restraint when considering a call on the guarantee. They force the beneficiary to make his position known. This is particularly true when the clause requires the beneficiary to specify the nature of the principal debtor's breach of contract, and he might feel inhibited to submit such a statement when he knows it to be untrue. Nonetheless, however valuable such a clause could be, it mainly brings the account party some tactical and psychological advantages.

A first demand guarantee may also require the beneficiary, when making a request for payment, to enclose a copy of a formal notice of default addressed to the account party. Such a clause will then often also provide that no demand for payment can be made until a specified number of days has elapsed from the date of the notice. This grace period serves at least two purposes. It enables the account party to try to settle the dispute with the beneficiary, for example by remedying the defects, or to agree on an extended period for performance. This may lead to the beneficiary revoking the demand for payment, whilst reserving the right to lodge a claim in the future. For the account party it has also the advantage that he will be advised in time of an imminent call on the guarantee. This is particularly important if the account party considers a call unjustified and wishes to attempt to prevent payment through a restraining order. On his side, the beneficiary should be careful to issue the notice of default in time so as not to allow the validity period of the guarantee to lapse.

Art. 20(a) URDG and statement of default

4-3a If the guarantee has been made subject to the URDG, the payment mechanism is as provided for in Art. 20(a) of these Rules. This article states that the demand for payment must be in writing and that it must be supported by a written declaration stating (i) that the account party (principal) is in breach of his obligations under the underlying contract(s) or, in the case of a tender guarantee, the tender conditions; and (ii) the respect in which the account party (principal) is in breach.[5] Art. 20(a) thus requires the beneficiary to submit a statement of default and, importantly, one which contains an indication of the nature of the account party's default. While being one of the most controversial provisions of the URDG, it was ultimately felt that this particular requirement was important in order to accommodate the conflicting interests of the beneficiary, who needs rapid payment without any real evidence of default, and the account party, who needs some kind of safeguard against frivolous and capricious calls. However, as stated in No. 4-3, the degree of protection remains limited.

---

5   Art. 34(1) of the OHADA's Uniform Act on Securities contains the same provision.

With respect to the requirement under (ii), Art. 20(a) envisages only the most general description of the account party's breach.[6] Indeed, any construction to the effect that a more specific and detailed statement of default is required would be unacceptable since it would give rise to grave difficulties and uncertainties both for the beneficiary and for the bank. Thus, the requirement under (ii) hardly alters or adds anything to what the beneficiary is expected to declare in a general statement of default as discussed in No. 4-3, when the URDG do not apply.

The requirement in respect of the specification of the nature of default as contained in Art. 20(a) has been criticised, because it might come as an unpleasant surprise for the beneficiary if the guarantee, which has been made subject to the URDG, does not itself mention this requirement, which means that he may not expect this particular condition of payment.[7] In order to avoid this kind of surprise, it is highly advisable that guarantees to which the URDG apply clearly incorporate the requirements of Art. 20(a) into the text of the guarantee itself, as has been done in the model texts prepared by the ICC.

If the guarantee has been made subject to the URDG, but the beneficiary (or bank) is not prepared to accept the requirement in respect of the statement of default, Art. 20(a) can be excluded, but this has to be done by means of a specific clause in the guarantee, see Art. 20(c).

Reversal of risks

4-4 A first demand guarantee, whether one on simple demand or one requiring the submission of a statement of default, brings about a complete reallocation of risks, with the beneficiary enjoying a very strong and advantageous position and the account party occupying a correspondingly weak and disadvantageous position.[8] The beneficiary has the power to call the guarantee and to receive payment forthwith at any moment he is of the opinion that the account party has defaulted on his obligations. The right to immediate payment without proof of default or the amount of loss also underlines the liquidity function of this type of guarantee. As it is so easy for the beneficiary to encash the guarantee and as the account party/principal debtor is aware of this, first demand guarantees enable the beneficiary to put severe pressure on the principal debtor to

---

6   Affaki, No. 101 (with examples), Goode, p. 93, See also Bertrams, TVVS 1993, p. 98, Hasse, WM 1993, p. 1993.

7   For this reason Von Westphalen, RIW 1992, p. 963, DB 1992, p. 2020, argues that Art. 20(a) is not enforceable in view of para. 3 of the German AGBG (Unfair Contract Terms Act), which deals with 'unexpected' clauses in general terms and conditions. See also Hasse, WM 1993, p. 1992.

8   See further Chapter 6.

perform the contract to his complete satisfaction. Moreover, it is commonly recognised that beneficiaries could take unfair advantage of their position, while it is very difficult for the account party to prevent fraudulent practices.[9] American vernacular aptly refers to first demand guarantees as 'suicide letters of credit'.

Although the beneficiary need not adduce any evidence concerning the principal debtor's default, it is wrong to proceed to such general statements that these guarantees are entirely unconditional and that the bank must always pay when the demand is made. Nearly all first demand guarantees contain clauses which qualify the beneficiary's right to payment, notably clauses in respect of the validity period. They may also contain clauses of another nature, such as conditions precedent or a reduction clause.

Words and phrases. Construction of the instrument

4-5 The term 'first demand guarantee' relates to a legal concept, namely an independent guarantee whereby the beneficiary is entitled to payment without any proof of default or the amount of loss. In order to be a first demand guarantee, it is not necessary that the instrument states explicitly that payment is to be made upon the beneficiary's first demand. There are several other words and phrases which convey the same notion. Conversely, a 'guarantee' instrument may contain the phrase 'payment on first demand' and yet not be considered a first demand guarantee in the sense described in Nos. 4-2 – 4-4.[10] It is ultimately how the particular wording of the text is construed that determines whether or not the instrument amounts to a first demand guarantee.[11]

The following phrases, which can frequently be found in guarantee instruments, are generally taken to mean that payment is to be made on demand in the sense described in Nos. 4-2 – 4-4 above: payment will be made 'without any objection', 'regardless of any objection', 'despite any objection by … (account party/principal debtor)', 'upon simple request', 'on demand and without notice or any condition or restriction', 'payment without proof or justification', or 'no opposition, objection or recourse to arbitration or to the courts … shall be taken into consideration'. Other formulations include: 'payment will be made upon the contractor's default as determined by you at your absolute discretion', 'we guarantee payment on your request whether or not any amount is due on the … contract'. Guarantees issued by British banks often state: 'your demand (or statement) shall be accepted as conclusive evidence of liability'.

---

[9] See further Chapters 14-16.

[10] Particularly in English law documents, the phrase payment 'on demand' frequently occurs in security instruments which unmistakably embody a traditional accessory suretyship.

[11] See in general Chapter 12.3.

Origins

4-6 The device of guarantees payable on first demand originates from the former practice of exporters and contractors having to place a cash deposit (or 'earnest' money) which could immediately be seized by the importer or employer in the event of default. This technique was found cumbersome. It necessitated exporters and contractors raising funds which remained tied up for a considerable period of time, and this adversely affected their liquidity position. 'Legal engineers' then conceived the idea of first demand guarantees as a substitute for cash deposits, thus avoiding these disadvantages while preserving the favourable position of the importer or employer.

It is generally believed that the concept of first demand guarantees was originally devised in the Middle East. This is true if the volume of the first demand guarantee business is taken as a yardstick. A similar evolution occurred during the same period, if not earlier, in some Western European countries where cash deposits in favour of Government departments and tax authorities came to be replaced by the same device. However, these instruments continued to be referred to as suretyship payable on first demand. A comparable development took place in the United Kingdom in the form of 'conclusive evidence' clauses,[12] and in the domestic market of the United States in the form of standby letters of credit.

'First *justified* demand'

4-7 Guarantee instruments sometimes state that they are payable on 'first *justified* demand'. The question of whether these instruments amount to proper first demand guarantees or to something else, and what meaning is to be given to the adjective 'justified' is a matter of construction. In the absence of clear indications to the contrary, case law treats these 'guarantees' as independent guarantees requiring the submission of a statement of default along the lines of Art. 20(a) URDG.[13]

'In the event of default'. *Effektivklauseln*

4-8 Many guarantee instruments state that they are payable on first demand and also contain phrases such as: payment will be made 'in the event of the principal debtor's default' or 'should the principal debtor fail to comply with the terms and conditions of the ... contract'. German law refers to these clauses as *Effektivklauseln*. The combination of both types of phrases appears to be contradictory as the latter type has strong suretyship (or conditional guarantee) connotations. The legal effect of such instruments is also a matter of construction. It is the view of this study that once it is found

---

[12] See Chapter 4.5, Nos. 4-17 and 4-20.
[13] See further Chapter 12.3, No. 12-33.

that, in the final analysis, the instrument is to be taken as a first demand guarantee, the beneficiary need not adduce any evidence whatsoever concerning the event described in the *Effektivklausel*. Such clauses are merely an expression of the purpose of the guarantee.[14]

4.3 PAYMENT UPON SUBMISSION OF THIRD-PARTY DOCUMENTS

Terminology and nature

4-9 A second type of payment mechanism involves the submission of documents from a third party as a condition of payment. These guarantees are sometimes referred to as 'documentary' guarantees, but this term is somewhat misleading since all independent guarantees are documentary in nature in the sense that they require the submission of a document (a written demand for payment, whether or not supported by a statement of default, or third-party documents, or an arbitral or court decision). There are two variants. The usual type provides for payment upon submission by the beneficiary of certain documents which attest to non-performance of the principal contract. But there are also guarantees which state that they are payable – usually on the beneficiary's first demand – unless the account party tenders certain documents which affirm the performance of the contract.

Guarantees requiring the submission of third-party documents are sometimes called conditional guarantees, in contrast to first demand guarantees, which are then referred to as unconditional guarantees.[15] The adjectives 'conditional' and 'unconditional' do not, however, have a clearly defined meaning and, in the context of guarantees, they lack distinguishing features.[16] These terms should be avoided. Moreover, first demand guarantees are also conditional, namely upon the beneficiary's demand for payment, which may have to be accompanied by a statement of default, while they may also contain other terms and conditions which have to be met. To add to the confusion, conditional guarantees are sometimes equated with guarantees which require the submission of an arbitral or court decision, or with traditional suretyship or with bonds as envisaged in the URCB. On the other hand, the American standby letter of credit is occasionally likened to a documentary guarantee, because it always entails the presentation of a document. It is noted that the standby letter of credit as used in American

---

[14] See further Chapter 10.8, No. 10-26, Chapter 12.3, No. 12-21, Chapter 13.2.3, No. 13-13.

[15] This is common in Anglo-American terminology. See also, for example, Dubisson, DPCI 1977, p. 423, Stumpf, RIW 1979, p. 1, Horn, NJW 1980, p. 2153, Trost, RIW 1981, p. 659, von Mettenheim, RIW 1981, p. 581, and further Dohm, no 41.

[16] Cf. Nielsen, ZHR 1983, p. 151.

practice is the functional equivalent of the European independent guarantee,[17] and may, depending on its terms, relate to any of the three types of payment mechanism and their corresponding types of document.

In practice, many guarantee instruments state that they are payable on first demand, provided that the beneficiary submits the prescribed third-party documents. Such an instrument should not be construed as a first demand guarantee proper, in the sense described in No. 2-4, in the light of the requirement to present third-party documents evidencing the account party's default.[18] Its presence might have to be attributed to force of habit or thoughtless drafting or possibly to the attempt to emphasise the independent nature of the undertaking.

By definition, guarantees payable upon submission of third-party documents are independent guarantees and they can be made subject to the URDG or ISP98. Consequently, the beneficiary is entitled to payment forthwith if he submits the documents prescribed by the guarantee. He need not adduce any other evidence of the principal debtor's default. In its relationship with the beneficiary, the bank is not entitled to require any other proof and it cannot invoke defences derived from the underlying relationship, while in its relationship with the account party the bank has no duty to ask for further evidence. The bank's right as well as duty to ascertain compliance with the conditions of payment is confined to the formal examination of the documents tendered in the light of the documents prescribed.[19] As far as the payment mechanism is concerned, this type of guarantee is very similar to a documentary credit, although the kinds of documents are quite different.

Documents to be submitted by the beneficiary

4-10 Several types of third-party documents are suitable for inclusion as conditions of payment. For example, a tender guarantee could stipulate a statement from a notary public indicating that the employer/beneficiary has accepted the contractor's bid and that the latter has failed to sign the contract. A repayment guarantee in favour of the buyer could require a statement from a bank, which has issued a documentary credit, that the seller has not tendered the shipping documents, or not in time. A performance guarantee could call for certificates from an independent surveyor or claim assessor, or from the engineer in the case of a construction contract which affirm defects or non-performance of the principal contract. In the case of a payment guarantee, the beneficiary might have to present third-party documents relating to performance on his part. For example, a seller/beneficiary may be required to submit (copies of) the shipping and

---

[17] See Chapter 1, No. 41-.

[18] See further Chapter 12.3, No. 12-22.

[19] See further Chapter 10.8, No. 10-18, Chapter 13.1, No. 13-2, and Chapter 13.2.4.

other documents drawn up by certain third parties, or a building firm/beneficiary in the case of a construction contract may have to submit invoices endorsed by the engineer, with a statement that the invoice which was due and payable has remained unpaid.

The significance of guarantees payable upon submission of third-party documents is that the beneficiary is compelled to furnish some evidence of non-performance on the part of the account party, or, in respect of payment guarantees, some evidence that he has performed the contract and that payment is, therefore, due. The intrinsic value of the evidence depends on the nature of the documents, but whatever their nature, submission of the correct documents does not conclusively show that the principal debtor/account party is liable to the creditor/beneficiary according to the underlying relationship, just as tender of the correct documents under a documentary credit does not necessarily prove that the seller is discharged from all liabilities under the contract of sale. For example, a statement by the engineer to the effect that the project has not been completed in accordance with the specifications of the construction contract is primarily a statement of a technical nature. It does not in itself prove that the contractor is liable in law, for it is possible that the contractor was entitled to suspend or rescind the contract because of non-payment by the employer/beneficiary, or because the latter failed to perform other obligations pursuant to the terms of the contract. Non-performance could also have been brought about by *force majeure*. Accordingly, there is always the possibility that the beneficiary is entitled to payment under the terms and conditions of the guarantee, while not entitled to compensation according to the principal contract, and that, after payment, the account party has a right to obtain recovery from the beneficiary.

The reverse situation is possible too: the beneficiary is unable to procure the correct documents, or is not able to do so in time, while he is in fact entitled to damages because of the principal debtor's default. One must bear in mind that the kind of documents which can be prescribed by the guarantee are diverse and not standardised, unlike the documents under a documentary credit. Moreover, third-party agencies might not be so familiar with the release of these different types of documents. This payment mechanism, therefore, entails some risks for the beneficiary. This is especially true if the guarantee exactly prescribes the contents and wording of the document. In order to avoid this risk it is advisable for the beneficiary to insist on a provision which allows the submission of a court or arbitral decision as a substitute document.

Documents to be submitted by the account party

4-11 Using this technique the beneficiary need not produce any evidence of the account party/principal debtor's default, but his right to payment ceases to the extent and in the manner specified in the guarantee if the account party presents the third-party documents mentioned in the guarantee instrument. The documents ordinarily affirm performance of (part of) the contract, but otherwise they are of the same nature as those described in No. 4-10.

This variant is common in repayment guarantees containing a reduction mechanism, but can also be found in performance guarantees. In the latter case it is advisable for the beneficiary to ensure that his right to payment under the guarantee does not cease altogether, but, for example, is reduced to a lower amount. The reason for this is that submission by the account party of the prescribed documents does not conclusively evidence that he has fully performed the contract. It is also important that the guarantee specifies the period within which the account party must submit the documents.

Evaluation

4-12 Compared with first demand instruments, guarantees requiring the submission of third-party documents obviously accommodate the interests of the account party better, since no payment will be made without at least some kind of evidence concerning non-performance and because the risk of abuse is considerably reduced. They are correspondingly less advantageous for the beneficiary. In particular, he is no longer in a position to call the guarantee any time he is of the opinion that the account party is in default. This also affects his power to virtually force the account party to perform the contract to his personal satisfaction and to continually exact extensions by means of the 'extend or pay' practice. Whether parties will agree to this type of guarantee rather than to a first demand guarantee will depend on bargaining strength and all the terms and conditions of the contract. Nonetheless, there are indications of a rising need for guarantees payable upon submission of third-party documents.

Banks tend to prefer issuing first demand guarantees to guarantees of this type, claiming that examination of the documents in relation to the latter is more complex and riskier. To some extent this might be true, but it is no reason for general anxiety. The task of ascertaining compliance with the terms of a guarantee payable upon submission of third-party documents is, in principle, no more difficult than in the case of documentary credits, provided that the bank has made sure that the guarantee clearly specifies the nature of the documents, the (type of) issuing agency and other relevant particulars. Moreover, the bank's interests are accommodated by the rule that its liability towards the account party is confined to a duty to exercise reasonable care and by a certain degree of discretion.[20] The argument that there is a risk of becoming involved in disputes between account party and beneficiary is certainly spurious. Because of the rule of independence the bank is solely concerned with the examination of formal compliance with the terms and conditions of the guarantee.

---

[20] See Chapter 10.8, No. 10-24.

4.4 PAYMENT UPON SUBMISSION OF AN ARBITRAL OR COURT DECISION

General

4-13 A third type of payment mechanism involves the submission by the beneficiary of an arbitral or court decision which affirms the principal debtor's liability to the creditor/beneficiary as a condition of payment. The decision is reached in the main proceedings between the parties just-mentioned and these proceedings encompass a full review of the facts and law pertaining to the underlying relationship. The bank is not a party to the proceedings. It is not the award itself, but the presentation by the beneficiary of the decision which triggers off the bank's payment obligation. This type can also be made subject to the URDG and ISP98.

Submission of an arbitral or court decision is the common type of payment mechanism in the case of judicial guarantees, which are furnished in order to have a conservatory attachment order (freezing order) lifted. This type is also quite common in domestic situations, especially in relation to construction works either in the public or private sector. In these cases the guarantee often provides for payment on the beneficiary's first demand without any evidence of default, unless the account party serves notice within a certain period of time that it challenges the demand and initiates judicial or arbitral proceedings as provided for in the underlying contract.

As far as international trade is concerned this type of guarantee is believed to be rare. This is certainly true in respect of guarantees issued in favour of beneficiaries in the Middle East and North Africa. No such certainty can be said to exist in respect of trade within Europe. One must bear in mind that these guarantees are often equated with traditional suretyship or at least not recognised or classified as independent guarantees. As is the case with guarantees payable upon submission of third-party documents, the chances of parties agreeing on this type of payment mechanism depend on their bargaining power and the terms of the contract as a whole. Mutual confidence and the assessment of risks by the beneficiary are additional factors.

Comparison with suretyship. Advantages for banks

4-14 Since the beneficiary is only entitled to payment upon full proof of the account party's liability, as embodied in the arbitral or judicial decision, this type of guarantee is in substance very similar to a traditional accessory suretyship as far as the beneficiary and account party are concerned. The significance of the principle of independence is, in some respects, severely eroded, since any defences relating to the underlying relationship, which the bank could plead, will, no doubt, already have been raised by the principal debtor in the main proceedings and will have been considered by arbitrators or the court. It is, nonetheless, important to distinguish conceptually between the two security devices.[21] In the case of this type of guarantee, the bank must pay, and must only pay if the beneficiary tenders a judicial or arbitral award as specified in the guarantee instrument. The bank's role is thus confined to verification of the document tendered and it does not become involved in disputes between the parties in the underlying relationship. This follows from the rule of independence, and it is this rule which protects the bank, especially in its relationship with its customer. Banks, therefore, very much prefer issuing this type of guarantee to acting as a traditional surety. Moreover, this type of guarantee is not likely to be subject to the peculiarities and unexpected pitfalls of national laws of suretyship which vary from country to country. Guarantees requiring submission of an arbitral or court decision can, therefore, be regarded as the modern substitute for the the traditional suretyship (or accessory guarantee).

Miscellaneous

4-15 One aspect which needs to be considered when drafting the text is the question of whether and in what manner the instrument should specify criteria which the decision must meet.[22] In general, the more requirements that are set, the more difficult the position of the beneficiary becomes, while the bank's position is generally facilitated by an exact description of the criteria. For example, the guarantee could state that a decision of a particular court or arbitrators must be submitted. In this event it is vital for the beneficiary that the specification tallies with the relevant provisions of the main contract. The guarantee could also address the issue of the contents of the decision, the effect of appeal proceedings and whether the decision must be final. The absence of any specification may well cause difficulties when the beneficiary calls the guarantee.[23]

Guarantees requiring submission of a judicial or arbitral award do not ordinarily contain an expiry date for a number of reasons, but especially because litigation between principal debtor and creditor could be protracted while the latter lacks the power to exact an extension of the validity period by means of an 'extend or pay' demand. The beneficiary's interests can, however, also be accommodated by a clause which allows him to obtain an extension upon simple request. On the other hand, many of these guarantees require the beneficiary to institute proceedings within a certain period of time after the issue of the guarantee and to submit a request for payment within a certain period of time after the delivery of the judgment. Such guarantees may, how-

---

[21] In the same vein von Westphalen, p. 104, Eisemann, Rev. Arbitrage 1972, pp. 379-405, Tondeau de Marsac, DPCI 1980, p. 157, Vasseur, Tours, p. 357,364, von Marschall. p. 37. Contra: Dubisson, DPCI 1977, pp. 441, 446-449, Poullet, DPCI 1979, pp. 394, 416, Gavalda and Stoufflet, RTDC 1980, p. 13.

[22] See also von Westphalen, p. 105.

[23] See Chapter 13.2.5.

ever, also provide that the call must be made within a certain period (e.g. 6 months after the projected date for completion of the underlying contract) but that payment will only be made after submission of the award, which may occur after the expiry date. This structure has the advantage of providing greater certainty and releasing the bank (and account party) from its liability if no call has been made on or before the expiry date.

Some variants and additional clauses

4-16 One of the drawbacks of a guarantee payable upon submission of an arbitral award or court decision is that the proceedings between account party and beneficiary can be protracted, with the result that the beneficiary does not receive compensation until a considerable period of time later. There is, however, an alternative. Parties to the underlying relationship could appoint a third party, in whom they both have full confidence, and entrust him with the decision of whether the creditor/beneficiary is entitled to payment. The guarantee, then, provides that it is payable upon first demand by this third party.[24] Whether or not payment is final between account party and beneficiary depends on their arrangements as set out in the principal contract.

Most guarantees of the type examined in Chapter 4.4 contain an alternative payment mechanism, namely a statement by the principal debtor/account party to the effect that the guarantee amount is indeed due and payable. This alternative allows for payment under the guarantee where the principal debtor's liability is admitted, so that unnecessary litigation can be avoided.

In most jurisdictions it is not possible to commence or continue proceedings against a defendant (principal debtor) who has been declared bankrupt. In such a situation a beneficiary would never be able to comply with the conditions of payment, at a time when he needs recourse to the guarantee most. In order to provide for this contingency most guarantees of this type allow the beneficiary to have the principal debtor's liability determined in proceedings against the bank in the event of the principal debtor's bankruptcy or to submit the receiver's acknowledgement of the debt as the document triggering payment.

---

[24] This technique is used in the Netherlands in connection with the sale and conveyance of real estate whereby the notary public is designated as the one who is authorised to call the guarantee if he is of the opinion that the buyer is in default.

4.5 SURETYSHIP PAYABLE ON fiRST DEMAND. CONCLUSIVE EVIDENCE CLAUSES

'Suretyship' payable on first demand. France, the Netherlands and Belgium

4-17 For several decades, France and the Netherlands have had security devices bearing the label 'suretyship', which provide for immediate payment upon the beneficiary's first demand without any evidence of the principal debtor's default and without challenge by the 'surety'. These instruments came to be used as a substitute for cash deposits, especially in connection with construction contracts in the public sector and contingent tax debts. In these sectors, the title 'suretyship' payable on first demand continues to be used. The aforementioned instruments pose a problem: do they constitute an (independent) guarantee payable on first demand or should they be viewed as a suretyship, and, if so, what legal effects are to be attributed to this kind of suretyship?

As far as France is concerned the validity of this peculiar type of 'suretyship' has been recognised, but the legal effects were held to be the same as those of first demand guarantees.[25] As a matter of fact, in two more recent cases it was observed that the description 'suretyship' in a security instrument which provided for payment upon first demand without any evidence of default was incorrect, and that the instrument in fact constituted a first demand guarantee, provided that other terms and conditions also pointed to that type of security.[26] There is no Dutch case law in respect of a 'suretyship' payable on first demand.[27] Certain Dutch bonding companies active in the construction industry occasionally issue bonds which use the term 'suretyship' but also provide for payment upon first demand. This may still also happen in relation to security in favour of the Dutch tax authorities. It is generally believed that the continued use of the term 'suretyship' is to be attributed to stubbornness and bureaucratic conditions and that the legal effect of these bonds are the same as those of independent guarantees payable on first demand.

In conclusion, French and Dutch law do not recognise a 'suretyship' payable on first demand as a truly existing, distinct legal concept. Eventually, such instruments are either construed as an ordinary accessory suretyship (thus denying effect to the 'pay-

---

[25] *Cass., 14 January 1963*, Rev. Banque 1963, p. 199, *Paris, 8 December 1977/22 June 1978*, D. 1979 J. p. 259. See further Wattiez, pp. 72, 133.

[26] *Poitiers, 13 March 1985*, D. 1988 Somm. p. 241, *Trib. com. Paris, 7 October 1988*, D. 1989 Somm. p. 145. See also Chapter 12.3.4.

[27] There is, however, the very early case of *CA The Hague, 5 March 1922*, NJ 1924, p. 1262. The Court of Appeal did not consider the clause 'payment on first demand', and, at any rate, it did not accord any particular effect to the phrase.

ment on first demand' phrase) or as a proper first demand guarantee (thus denying effect to the title of 'suretyship').[28]

Owing to certain recent decisions the situation in Belgium is somewhat confusing. Ordinarily, in case of ambiguity Belgian courts construe the security instrument either as an ordinary accessory suretyship or as an independent first demand guarantee in the same way as French and Dutch courts do. In 1994 the Belgian Supreme Court rejected the possibility of an accessory suretyship which is payable on first demand without raising any defences from the underlying contract as incompatible with the nature of a suretyship.[29] In two subsequent decisions, *Trib. com. Charleroi, April 23 1997*,[30] and *Trib. com. Brussels, February 11 1999*,[31] the courts seem, however, to have construed the instrument as a suretyship payable on first demand – a distinct, hybrid type of security. According to these two decisions, the effect is that the surety must pay first without being allowed to raise defences from the underlying relationship and without the beneficiary having to prove his claim, albeit that the surety is allowed, after payment, to recover the amount paid from the beneficiary if he is able to prove that the beneficiary was not entitled to payment according to the underlying relationship. However, in both cases the courts did in fact treat the security as an ordinary and traditional suretyship by requiring the beneficiary to prove his claim before payment by the surety (*Charleroi* case) and by permitting the surety to raise defences from the underlying relationship before payment (*Brussels* case). Belgian authors have expressed considerable doubts both as to the existence of a suretyship payable on first demand as a seperate legal phenomenon and to the usefulness thereof.[32]

Suretyship payable on first demand. Germany

14-18 Instruments which bear the label 'suretyship' and which keep referring to that term in the text of the instrument, but which also state that they are payable on the beneficiary's first demand without any further evidence of default, are a common phe-

---

[28] See further Chapter 12.3.4.

[29] RW 1995/1996, p. 323.

[30] JLMB 1998, p. 1073.

[31] RDC 2000, p. 725.

[32] In his comments on the 1994 decision of the Belgian Supreme Court, RW 1995/1996, p. 323, Dirix observes that, while the existence of the hybrid 'suretyship payable on first demand' in the German law sense (see Nos. 18-19) is theoretically conceivable, emphasises that such phenemenon is only confusing and serves no practical purpose. According to him, this notion should best be abandoned. This conclusion is shared by Van Reensbeeck in his thorough analysis 'De borgtocht op eerste verzoek. Een geldige rechtsfiguur?', TBBR pp. 173-194.

nomenon today in Germany. These instruments are especially prevalent in connection with domestic construction contracts and are by no means confined to the public sector. Case law has consistently and explicitly held that such instruments constitute an accessory suretyship and not an independent guarantee. However, in view of the first demand clause, case law has consistently pronounced that the purpose and legal effects of a first demand suretyship are the same as those of a first demand guarantee.[33] Accordingly, the beneficiary is entitled to immediate payment without proof of the account party's breach of contract and the bank cannot invoke defences derived from the underlying relationship. The bank's duty to the account party is confined to ascertaining formal compliance with the terms, i.e. the request for payment and the beneficiary's statement of default, if prescribed. The fraud exception is governed by the same stringent criteria as those which apply to first demand guarantees. Nonetheless, case law and legal writing explicitly recognise and emphasise the existence of two distinct legal concepts.

Germany. Differences between a suretyship payable on first demand and a first demand guarantee

4-19 While, as mentioned in No. 4-18, German law recognises that the key elements of a suretyship payable on first demand are the same as those of a guarantee payable on first demand, it also attributes two different features to a suretyship payable on first demand.

– German case law and legal writing emphasise that, because of the accessory nature of a suretyship payable on first demand, the surety is entitled to recover the amount

---

[33] See for example *BGH, 2 May 1979*, NJW 1979, p. 1500, *BGH, 24 November 1983*, WM 1984, p. 44, *BGH, 31 January 1985*, WM 1985, p. 511, *BGH, 11 December 1986*, WM 1987, p. 367, *BGH, 26 February 1987*, NJW 1987, p. 2075, *BGH 21 April 1988*, WM 1988, p. 934, *BGH, 9 March 1989*, NJW 1989, p. 1606, *BGH, 13 July 1989*, WM 1989, p. 1496, *BGH, 5 July 1990*, WM 1990, p. 1410, *BGH, 28 October 1993*, WM 1994, p. 106, *BGH, 14 December 1995*, WM 1996, p. 193, *BGH, 17 October 1996*, WM 1996, p. 2228, BGH, *23 January 1997*, WM 1997, p. 656 (because of their similarities the court did not need to decide whether the 'guarantee' was a first demand suretyship or a first demand guarantee), *OLG Düsseldorff, 9 August 2001*, WM 2001, p. 2294 (enumerating a series of key features which apply to a first demand suretyship and a first demand guarantee alike). See also the case law cited in No. 4-19. See for legal writing especially Schmidt, WM 1999, pp. 308-313 (with further references), and Bydlynski, WM 1990, p. 1401, and further von Westphalen, pp. 59-78, Staudinger/Horn, Nos. 24-37, Canaris, no 1148a, Mülbert, pp. 39-42, Horn, NJW 1980, p. 2153 *et seq.*, p. 2159.

Because of their similarity this study treats the independent guarantee payable on first demand and the accessory suretyship payable on first demand alike, except when certain differences (see No. 4-19) are relevant.

from the beneficiary after payment if in subsequent proceedings it appears that the beneficiary was not entitled to payment according to the underlying contract, whereas the independent guarantor cannot recover the amounts paid.[34] Accordingly, the accessory nature of this type of security is only temporarily suspended, namely until after payment. It should be noted, however, that the surety's right to recovery from the beneficiary is ordinarily of little practical significance as he is entitled to immediate reimbursement by the account party.[35] If the surety is a bank, as is usually the case, it is not likely to engage in protracted, costly and hazardous proceedings against the beneficiary if it can recover the amount paid from the account party quickly, for example by debiting its account.

– A second difference relates to the burden of proof in proceedings initiated by the surety for recovery from the beneficiary after payment. In *BGH, March 9 1989*, the Supreme Court ruled that in such proceedings it is incumbent upon the beneficiary to show that he was entitled to payment according to the underlying relationship. The ruling that the burden of proof lies with the beneficiary, not with the surety, was founded on the argument that initial payment by the surety did not amount to an admission of (final) indebtedness.[36] It should be noted, however, that payment in the case of a first demand guarantee for the account of the account party does not amount to an admission of indebtedness either ('pay first, argue later'), but it has never been in doubt that in proceedings for recovery the burden of proof lies with the account party, not with the beneficiary.[37]

Conclusive evidence clauses. United Kingdom

4-20 Clauses which oblige the 'guarantor' to pay immediately following a statement of default from the beneficiary have been regular practice in the United Kingdom for

---

[34] See especially *BGH, 23 January 1997*, WM 1997, p. 656, *BGH, 2 April 1998*, WM 1998, p. 1062, *BGH, 10 November 1998*, WM 1998, p. 2522, *BGH, 25 February 1999*, WM 1999, p. 895.

[35] See especially, *BGH, 17 January 1989*, NJW 1989, p. 1480, and *Kammergericht, 20 November 1986*, NJW 1987, p. 1774. It is revealing that in the case first mentioned the German Supreme Court declined to take a position as regards the nature of the first demand instrument (suretyship or guarantee), since it was immaterial to the decision: the bank was entitled to immediate reimbursement in both cases.

[36] NJW 1989, p. 1606, and the comments of Bydlinski, WM 1990, pp. 1401-1405. See also *BGH, 23 January 1997*, WM 1997, p. 656, and *BGH, 12 July 2001*, WM 2001, p. 2078, and Staudinger/Horn, No. 33. Canaris, No. 1148a, takes a contrary view. It is noted that to the extent that Belgian law acknowledges a suretyship payable on first demand, it is common ground that the burden of proof rests with the surety, see No. 4-17.

[37] See Chapter 13.6.

some decades. They can be found in crossborder as well as domestic transactions, both in the commercial and private sector. These clauses are known as 'conclusive evidence' clauses, since the beneficiary's statement that the principal debtor has defaulted on his obligations is considered conclusive evidence for the purposes of the contract of security. It should be noted that conclusive evidence clauses are often inserted in instruments which, apart from these clauses, bear great resemblance to traditional accessory guarantee (= suretyship) instruments.

It is established law that these clauses are valid and enforceable and that such instruments operate in the same way as first demand guarantees.[38] The question of whether these instruments are to be considered as an accessory suretyship or as an independent guarantee has not been regarded as relevant. Insertion of a conclusive evidence clause, in lieu of a 'payment on first demand' clause, continues to be a common technique for British banks and bonding companies to express that payment is to be made forthwith without any further evidence of default, in the same way as a first demand guarantee.

---

[38] See especially *Bache & Co. v. Banque Vernes et Commerciale de Paris*, [1973] 2 Lloyd's Rep. 437, *State Trading Corporation of India v. ED & F Man (Sugar)*, [1981] Com LR 235, *Balfour Beatty Civil Engineering v. Technical & General Guarantee*, [1999] Con. LR 180. See further Collins and Livingstone, JBL 1974, pp. 212, 215, Ryder, JBL 1974, p. 233.

CHAPTER 5
LEGAL NATURE

SUBSUMPTIONS AND COMPARISONS WITH TRADITIONAL CONCEPTS

5-1 Especially in the early period of legal writing, Continental authors would draw comparisons with or, as the case may be, fit the modern independent bank guarantee into existing traditional concepts, particularly those which are recognised in statutory provisions of national civil codes. Concepts which have been mentioned include delegation (*Anweisung*), aval and bankers' acceptances of bills of exchange, third-party stipulations, the *porte-fort*, indemnities, the German *abstraktes Schuldversprechen* and the German *Garantievertrag*. These efforts can be explained by the Continental tradition which, compared with the Common Law tradition, is marked by a more dogmatic approach and by a certain propensity to subsume new phenomena under existing and familiar categories, concepts and general principles, in order to get to grips with the novelty. Another motive could have been to enhance the process of recognition of guarantees, in particular first demand guarantees, as valid and enforceable contracts. This was especially relevant in Belgium and France where, at one time, the validity of first demand guarantees was called into question because of the apparent lack of a *causa*.[1]

Apart from the question of whether subsumptions under any of the above-mentioned categories are correct, the difficulty is that these concepts represent such general canons that they can afford little guidance.[2] At most one could arrive at knowledge which one already possessed, namely that a guarantee is independent of the underlying relationship and that there are other concepts which share the same feature. At any rate, doctrine does not attach any specific legal consequences to subsumption under the above-mentioned categories.

One has also attempted to define the legal nature of the independent guarantee by distinguishing this type of security from the accessory suretyship with the aid of juxtapositions such as primary/secondary, unconditional/conditional, automatic/non-automatic, abstract/causal, etcetera. One may, however, doubt whether these juxtapositions are correct and/or provide clear insight into their divergent legal nature.

---

[1] See in general Cabrillac/Mouly, Nos. 417-436-1.

[2] In relation to independent guarantees Aden, RIW 1981, pp. 439,440, aptly refers to '*ideologischer Typenzwang*' (ideological obsession with juridical categories). Zahn/Ehrlich/Neumann, No. 9/6, also advise against subsumption under traditional national categories, while Stoufflet, Garantie Bancaire Internationale, No. 23, refers to the irrelevance of subsuming the independent guarantee under traditional concepts.

In any event, it is worth noting that the drafters of the 1978 URCG, the 1992 URDG, the ISP98 and the UNCITRAL Convention on independent guarantees and stand-by letters of credit have deliberately refrained from expressing any opinion as to the legal nature of independent guarantees being impracticable. They have confined themselves just to giving a general description in which the key characteristic of independence features prominently.

CONTRACT *SUI GENERIS*

5-2 Notwithstanding occasional subsumptions under such open-ended concepts as delegation, the German *abstraktes Schuldversprechen* and the German *Garantievertrag*, at present case law and doctrine view the modern independent bank guarantee, as employed in domestic and international trade and which forms part of a multi-party relationship, as a contract *sui generis*.[3]

Recognition of this fact is important in that one is dissuaded from attempting to resolve issues pertaining to the modern independent guarantee by reference to other concepts. These should be resolved on the basis of the specific nature, mechanics and purpose of these guarantees.[4] The fact that the modern guarantee is a new phenomenon also implies that patterns in respect of notions such as, for example, the construction of the contract, set-off, assignment, conservatory attachment (freezing orders) and the principle of good faith, as they have evolved in other contexts, cannot be transposed mechanically to the independent guarantee.[5] The awareness that the guarantee, notably the first demand guarantee, is a novel technique, which originates from and is used especially in international trade, also enhances the readiness to be aware of developments in other countries.

INDEPENDENT GUARANTEES COMPARED WITH DOCUMENTARY CREDITS AND SURETYSHIP

5-3 If insight into the nature of the independent guarantee can be furthered by comparing it with other concepts, it is by comparison with the documentary credit[6] and suretyship (= accessory guarantee).

---

[3] See, for example, Pabbruwe, p. 4, Mijnssen, p. 11, Zahn/ Ehrlich/Neumann, 9/7, Canaris, No. 1106, Poullet, thesis No. 320, Tours, p. 156. In *Cass., December 12 1984*, D. 1985 J. p. 269, the Cour de Cassation held that a first demand guarantee does not amount to delegation.

[4] Cf. White and Summers, Uniform Commercial Code, p. 715: 'In short, a letter of credit is a letter of credit. As Bishop Butler once said: 'Everything is what it is and not another thing'.

[5] Cf. Dolan, 4 Banking & Finance L.R., pp. 244, 261-265.

[6] Cf. Mijnssen, p. 20, von Westphalen, p. 106-108, Zahn/ Ehrlich/Neumann, 9/15, Bontoux, Banque 1982, pp. 171-174.

Legal Nature

Independent guarantees and documentary credits (or letters of credit) share many significant features, such as the commercial context – often in an international setting – their structure and mechanics, the way they come into existence, the fact that the bank's customer is the account party and hence a truly interested party, risk allocation, and their purpose, namely the furnishing of security. On a legal level, they are both characterised by the principle of independence, the requirement that the beneficiary, when demanding payment, must strictly comply with the terms and conditions of the instrument, the formal nature of examination by the bank and the comparatively small impact of the principle of good faith, although the fraud exception is recognised in respect of both devices.

In view of their similarities, independent guarantees and standby letters of credit are treated in much the same way as documentary credits in American and English law in particular.[7] Nonetheless, one must be careful not to adopt each and every rule relating to letters of credit mechanically and without reflection. Apart from this, the issues which arise in the context of guarantees tend to be quite different from those in the case of documentary credits.

There are also a number of significant differences.[8] A documentary credit is a means of payment of the purchase price and actual payment occurs in the ordinary course of events, in contemplation of performance as envisaged by all parties concerned, whereas a guarantee provides secondary security and contemplates payment of compensation in the unexpected event of non-performance of the principal contract. From the account party's viewpoint this difference is critical. In the case of a documentary credit, actual payment serves his interests too, since he will thereby obtain the goods which he intended to obtain. In contrast, payment by the bank pursuant to a valid call under the guarantee merely results in the account party's duty to reimburse the bank without any corresponding advantage and he might, therefore, challenge the payment by the bank. This is rarely the case in documentary credits. A second difference is that the nature of the documents to be tendered under a documentary credit is quite different from that in the case of a guarantee. In the case of a documentary credit, the documents tendered by the beneficiary/seller represent and/or relate to the merchandise and have an intrinsic commercial value, whereas any documents presented under a guarantee relate to the account party's non-performance and do not have any intrinsic value. Further, a documentary credit is 'self-executing' – the credit, which the bank extends to its customer/buyer, can be repaid from the proceeds of the goods – and the bank has a security interest in the documents which represent the

---

[7] Article 5 of the UCC covers both the traditional letter of credit (=documentary credit) and the standby letter of credit. See further Roskill, L.J. in *Howe Richardson Scale v. Polimex-Cekop*, [1978] 1 Lloyd's Rep. 161, Kerr, J., and Denning, M.R., in *Edward Owen Engineering v. Barclays Bank Int. Ltd.*, [1978] 1 All E.R. 976, 981, 982, Donaldson, L.J., in *Intraco Ltd. v. Notis Shipping Corporation Ltd.*, [1981] 2 Lloyd's Rep. 256, Ackner, L.J., in *United Trading Corp. v. Allied Arab Bank*, [1985] 2 Lloyd's Rep. 554, 558, 561.

[8] Cf. Dolan, 1.04, Cabrillac/Mouly, No. 424.

merchandise. This is not the case with guarantees and the credit risk for the bank is, therefore, much greater, the more so as a call under the guarantee might signal financial or technical weakness on the part of the bank's customer.

The independent guarantee and suretyship (= accessory guarantee) share a significant characteristic in that they both provide security to the beneficiary in respect of non-performance by the account party in the underlying transaction. The difference is that the payment obligation of the guarantor is by definition independent of that of the account party/principal debtor, whereas the payment obligation of the surety is co-extensive. In accordance with the principle of co-extensiveness, the surety is entitled to invoke the defences which the principal debtor might have against the beneficiary and the latter must fully prove his claim as measured by the underlying transaction in case of a dispute. Pursuant to the principle of independence, the guarantor cannot invoke defences derived from the underlying transaction and his payment obligation is solely defined by the terms of the guarantee. Whether or not this abstract difference also amounts to a substantive difference depends on the selected payment mechanism of the guarantee, for example payment of first demand without any evidence of default or payment upon submission of a judicial or arbitral decision.[9]

DOMESTIC FIRST DEMAND GUARANTEES

5-4 While the advantages of a first demand guarantee for the beneficiary and the risk exposure of the account party are especially apparent in crossborder transactions, its utility is substantial in domestic settings too. This explains why first demand guarantees are by no means unusual in domestic transactions. When the parties to the underlying relationship have agreed upon such a guarantee, it should be governed by the same rules as those which apply to first demand guarantees issued in support of crossborder transactions. Indeed, case law, which has dealt with numerous domestic first demand guarantees, does not distinguish between the two situations.[10] Also, the URDG and ISP98 apply to both crossborder and domestic guarantees.

---

[9] See Chapter 4.1, No. 4-1 *et seq.*

[10] See, for example, *BGH, 10 November 1998*, WM 1998, p. 2522, *BGH, 10 October 2000*, WM 2000, p. 2334, *Rb Haarlem, 21 November 1986*, KG 1987, 57, *Rb Amsterdam, 7 March 1985*, KG 1985, 87, *Rb Amsterdam, 10 January 1997*, KG 1997, 44, *Rb Alkmaar, 3 December 1998*, KG 1999, 2, *Rb Utrecht, 22 January 1998*, JOR 2000,40, *Rb Leeuwarden, 10 January 2001*, KGk 2001, 1567, *Cass., 20 December 1982*, D. 1983 J. p. 365, *Cass., 7 October 1997*, JCP Éd. E, p. 226, Antwerp, *15 October 1985*, TBH 1986, p. 646, *Potton Homes Ltd. v. Coleman Contractors Ltd.*, [1984] 28 Build. L.R., 19, *Balfour Beatty Civil Engineering v. Technical & General Guarantee*, [1999] Con. LR 180. See also the German case law concerning first demand suretyship, mentioned in Chapter 4.5, No. 4-18, which is virtually the same as a first demand guarantee. See also Mattout, No. 197, with further references.

CHAPTER 6
PARTIES TO THE UNDERLYING RELATIONSHIP

6.1 ALLOCATION OF RISKS

From the viewpoint of the beneficiary

6-1 The independent guarantee, as a contract between bank and beneficiary, is a product of the underlying relationship. When parties to the underlying relationship agree that a guarantee will be furnished, they agree to a certain allocation of risks with respect to the realisation of claims concerning breach of contract. The way this allocation operates can best be illustrated by contrasting the situation where no guarantee has been furnished with the situation where a guarantee has been issued.

Take a contract for the supply of machinery between a seller, located in continent X, and a buyer, located in continent Y, providing for full payment through a documentary credit. Upon tender of the documents, the seller receives full payment from the bank, but for the buyer's account. Should the buyer find the machinery defective, he will then face some formidable obstacles on his way to obtaining proper compensation. If the seller disputes the claim, the buyer will be forced to embark on a protracted, costly and particularly uncertain expedition. First, there is judgment risk. The claimant/buyer may lose the case on some procedural issues or because he is unable to prove his claim to the court's satisfaction or because the court takes a different view as regards the merits of the case. Proceedings might have to take place in the defendant/seller's country and the buyer may find that the administration of justice there is slow, inadequate and malfunctioning or that the local courts are not free from bias, especially when government agencies or state-controlled companies are concerned. Should the final judgment eventually be given in his favour, he then faces execution risk. If the judgment has been obtained in a jurisdiction where the seller has no assets, there is a considerable risk that the judgment is not enforceable in a country where the seller does have assets. He may have to start all over again. There could also be exchange control regulations which prevent the transfer of money to the buyer's country, and worse, the seller may have become insolvent in the meantime.

Apart from judgment and execution risks, there are some other factors that render the position of the claimant most precarious. The costs of litigation tend to be huge. They have to be advanced and even if all other hurdles described above are overcome, experience shows that only a fraction of these costs are compensated. In the face of all these risks, obstacles and uncertainties the buyer may well decide to abandon legal action and cut his losses. Under favourable conditions, he might perhaps be able to settle for a fraction of his claim. Finally, there is the liquidity problem. The buyer will have to raise funds to remedy the consequences of the breach of contract by the seller at the time of the breach. A future judgment for interest does not always make up for the real costs of financing alternative measures and it in no way abates the difficulties when they arise. Being out of pocket until actual recovery is likely to have a severely adverse impact on his (financial) ability to enter into other transactions.

The combination of these risks, obstacles and difficulties explains why commercial practice considers a right to damages, which is an abstract notion and which does not even become crystallised in law until its final pronouncement in court, of small significance. What matters is the actual and immediate possession of compensation. This wisdom is reflected in the time-honoured expression 'the law is where the money is'.

A complete reversal of the allocation of risks is brought about by a guarantee payable upon first demand. If such a guarantee is issued in favour of the buyer, it entitles him to claim damages up to the maximum amount of the guarantee immediately, without the need to prove default or the amount of his loss in any way. This right has substance too, for a bank will ordinarily not haggle with the beneficiary but proceed to actual payment for fear of damaging its reputation. The risks of obstructions and delays will be even smaller if the guarantee has been issued by a bank in the buyer's own country. In short, as a result of a first demand guarantee the buyer encounters none of the risks and other disadvantages described above. Furthermore, the guarantee is not only a means of easily obtaining immediate compensation in the case of non-performance, as determined by the beneficiary, but also and perhaps foremost a very effective means of putting acute pressure on the other party to perform the contract properly, which is what the beneficiary desires to achieve above all. Indeed, these means are so effective that the phrase 'proper performance' should be understood to mean 'proper performance *to the complete satisfaction of the beneficiary*'.

Guarantees requiring the submission of third-party documents evidencing non-performance carry many of the same advantages but to a lesser extent. The crucial difference is, of course, that the beneficiary is not in a position to call the guarantee at will, since he has to produce some kind of evidence of default as specified in the guarantee. There remains the risk that the beneficiary, while having a valid claim, is unable to obtain the correct documents. The need for third-party evidence also reduces the possibilities of threatening to call the guarantee as a means of putting pressure on the other party. This also accounts for the fact that beneficiaries have a strong preference for first demand guarantees.

The advantages of guarantees stipulating the submission of an arbitral or judicial decision are mainly confined to the removal of execution risks. They do not confer any advantages on the beneficiary that he would not have had with a traditional accessory suretyship.

First demand guarantee from the viewpoint of the account party, 'pay first, argue later'

6-2 The quintessence of the reallocation of risks from the creditor (beneficiary) to the principal debtor (account party) by virtue of an agreement in respect of a first demand guarantee is fittingly conveyed in the universally adopted expression 'pay first, argue later'. In *Itek Corporation v. First National Bank* it has been formulated this way: 'Parties to a contract may use a letter of credit (in the instant case a first demand guarantee, R.B.) in order to make certain that contractual disputes wend their way toward resolution with money in the beneficiary's pocket rather than in the pocket of the (other, R.B.) contracting party'.[1] Similarly, *Rb Leeuwarden, 10 January 2001*, observed that the purpose of a first demand guarantee is 'to ensure, in case of a dispute between the parties to the underlying transaction, payment of damages by the account party to the beneficiary without any evidence of default, and that after such payment the parties may negotiate or litigate about the question of final indebtedness, if any'.[2] In *BGH, 12 July 2001*, the German Supreme Court described the purpose of a first demand guarantee as putting the beneficiary 'in the money' pending the final resolution of the dispute.[3]

An agreement by the parties to the underlying relationship with respect to a first demand guarantee signifies agreement that, whenever the creditor (beneficiary) considers that the principal debtor (account party) has committed a breach of contract and while that breach may be disputed by the principal debtor, payment by way of compensation is to be made forthwith pending and until final resolution of the dispute, amicably or by arbitral or judicial decision. By opting for a construction whereby the creditor first receives compensation for breach of contract, but without the need of proof or judicial determination thereof, the parties have accomplished what they in-

---

[1] 730 F 2d 19, 24 (1st. Cir. 1984). See for explicit mention of the principle of 'pay first, argue later' in case law, e.g., *E-Systems v. Islamic Republic of Iran*, 491 F. Supp. 1294 (N.D. Tex. 1980), *ICC (Geneva), No. 3316 (1979)*, J.D.I. 1980, p. 970, *BGH, 12 March 1984 (ll ZR 198/82)*, NJW 1984, p. 2030, *BGH, 28 October 1993*, WM 1994, p. 106, OLG *Stuttgart, 15 January 1979*, RIW 1980, p. 729, *OLG Frankfurt a.M., 3 March 1983*, WM 1983, p. 575, *OLG Frankfurt a.M., 26 June 1984*, RIW 1985, p.407, *OLG Frankfurt a.M., 27 April 1987*, WM 1988, p. 1480, *Trib. com. Brussels, 15 January 1980*, JCB 1980, p. 147, *Trib. com. Brussels, 11 March 1981*, BRH 1981, p. 361, *Brussels, 25 February 1982*, JCB 1982, p. 349, *Ghent, 25 February 1988*, TBH 1989, p. 40, *Brussels, 26 June 1992*, RDC 1994, p. 51, *Trib. com. Liege, 7 April 1995*, RDC 1996, p. 1063, *Trib. com. Kortrijk, 21 October 1996*, RW 1996/1997, p. 1447, Rb *Rotterdam, 16 March 1993*, KG 1993, 222, *Rb Leeuwarden, 4 July 1997, KGK 1998, 1454*.

[2] KGK 2001, 1567.

[3] WM 2001, p. 2078. German case law repeatedly emphasises the liquidity function ('cash in hand') of first demand guarantees.

tended to accomplish, namely a reversal of risks. For, after payment, it is now the principal debtor (account party) who encounters the formidable risks and difficulties attending the realisation of a claim for repayment.[4] Accordingly, the explanation and legal justification of the phenomenon 'pay first, argue later' is the contemplated reallocation of risks. Payment is not founded on a provisional admission by the principal debtor of default, nor on a presumption or (provisional) assumption of default.

The creditor in the underlying relationship will not be satisfied with the principal debtor's undertaking 'to pay first and argue later' alone. Such an undertaking on its own does indeed confer substantial rights on the creditor, but if the principal debtor stalls on his obligation 'to pay first', which he is quite likely to do, the creditor will still be forced to go to court and seek enforcement of his rights. In order to avert this risk, the creditor insists that the implementation of the agreement that payment will be made first is transferred to a neutral, reliable third party – the bank.[5] The bank, having undertaken this obligation in its own name, will, ordinarily, not stall for fear of impairing its reputation and because it will be paying for the account of the principal debtor. In this way the creditor is assured of the least possible gap between a right to payment and actual, immediate payment.

The view that the agreement 'pay first, argue later' as contained in the guarantee is primarily and essentially a product of the underlying relationship and affects the position of the parties to that relationship may perhaps not be commonplace. In particular, it is not yet a commonly accepted idea that a first demand guarantee, while indisputably a contract between bank and beneficiary only, is primarily and essentially a vehicle ensuring the realisation of the contemplated reallocation of risks as between principal debtor and creditor. At least, it has not yet been put this way.[6] The view that a first demand guarantee reflects, the risk assumption of the principal debtor and that it brings about a reversal of procedural risks is, however, widely acknowledged.[7]

In order to dispel any possible queries, this study does not in any way deny or question the principle of independence, on the contrary. The above observations are only intended to provide a true understanding of the principle of independence in a

---

[4] Cf. Dolan, § 3.07 [4][5], referring to the shifting of litigation costs and forum.

[5] Cf. Dolan, § 3.07[2], referring to the substituting of credit by the bank 'analogous to collateral'.

[6] But see *Geneva, 12 September 1985*, D. 1986 I.R. p. 165: 'In respect of guarantees the true parties are the parties to the underlying relationship. The bank is merely an intermediary mandatee charged with the implementation of one of the modalities of the principal contract'.

[7] Acceptance of a more comprehensive notion of reallocation of risks, though primarily related to documentary credits, can be found in American legal writing, see, for example, Dolan, 1.05, White & Summers, ' 18-7, p. 631, Harfield, 4 UCCLJ (1972), p. 257, Note, Minnesota L.R. 1979, pp. 489, 490, and Driscoll, Virginia J.I.L. 1980, pp. 472-474.

first demand guarantee as a risk reallocation device between the parties to the underlying relationship.

Recovery after payment

6-3 After payment under the guarantee for his account the principal debtor may try to recover the amount paid from the beneficiary and, if necessary, initiate proceedings before courts or arbitrators as provided in the principal contract, if he is of the opinion that he was not in default or that the actual loss sustained by the beneficiary was less than the amount paid under the guarantee. The burden of proof lies with the account party/principal debtor. The entitlement to recovery after payment under the guarantee directly derives from their 'pay first, argue later' agreement as discussed in No. 6-2.[8] It should be noted that the actual chances of recovery are determined by such factors as described in Nos. 6-1 and 6-2, but they are often small. A settlement out of court for part of the (asserted) claim for recovery is often the most which the principal debtor/ account party can hope to achieve. In many situations the possibilities of recovery are considerably enhanced if the principal contract provides that disputes are to be settled by arbitration in a neutral country.

First demand guarantee and risk evaluation

6-4 As has been observed in No. 6-2, the principal debtor, by agreeing to a first demand guarantee, accepts the risk that payment under the guarantee will be made, while no payment is due as measured by the principal contract and that the chances of actual recovery are often doubtful for the reasons mentioned in Nos. 6-1 and 6-2. The magnitude of the risk assumption could also be assessed from a different angle, namely the likelihood of the beneficiary calling the guarantee or perhaps one should say his readiness to do so.

The breakdown of a contract, in fact, may be caused by a great number of reasons, often in combination. Apart from default of the principal debtor/account party, the contract may not be completed, for example, due to non-performance by subcontractors of the principal debtor or non-performance by the beneficiary himself, unexpected obstacles in the case of construction contracts, natural disasters, political and social instability, war, second thoughts by the beneficiary concerning the feasibility and profitability of the project or his ability to finance the project. Non-completion could occur as a result of government measures such as embargoes, expulsion of the workforce or currency exchange restrictions. All these events increase the chances of a call on the guarantee and the principal debtor will have to assess the likelihood of these events in advance. With a view to the ease with which the beneficiary can collect under

---

[8] The specific issues relating to recovery by the account party are examined in Chapter 13.6.

a first demand guarantee and the grave difficulties which the account party will encounter when attempting to obtain stop-payment orders, particularly in the case of an indirect guarantee, it offers little solace to suggest that in some of the examples mentioned above the beneficiary might perhaps not be entitled to utilise the guarantee.

There is no denying that the possibility of abuse of a first demand guarantee by the beneficiary does exist. However, while the question of whether and when that possibility has in fact materialised arouses vehement differences of opinion time and again, the true answer will ordinarily remain concealed, even apart from the fact that the meaning of the notion of fraud itself is still a subject of on-going controversy. Estimates of the percentage of fraudulent calls are therefore futile. They are also unreliable, since they can only be based on a minute percentage of the total number of guarantees and they will inevitably be coloured by the position of the estimator.

It must also be borne in mind that under normal conditions certain constraints will inhibit the beneficiary from calling the guarantee for trivial reasons or where his claim for compensation lacks any substance at all. Collecting under the guarantee in these circumstances will assuredly result in a definite breakdown of the contract and the beneficiary may find himself left with a half-completed project of little value. Chances of doing further business with the other contracting party will no doubt be lost and he could even experience difficulties in doing business with any other partners.

Nonetheless, an assessment of the beneficiary's integrity remains important. The status of the beneficiary, i.e. a private company or a state agency, could also be a factor that determines the risk rate, but the one is not necessarily more or less risky than the other. Trade organisations and banks, which are often in a position to discern certain patterns, could provide useful information. Should the evaluation turn out to be unfavourable, exporters are likely to elect not to do business at all. Anticipated bad faith not only spells disaster as far as the first demand guarantee is concerned, but also in respect of the entire execution of the contract.

Other factors to be taken into account for a proper risk assessment include the account party's performance ability in all its aspects, the country risk and the reputation of foreign issuing banks in the case of indirect guarantees. Trade organisations and banks can advise account parties in this respect too.

6.2 NEGOTIATIONS

General

6-5 It is often said that the issuance of a first demand guarantee and its precise terms and conditions are non-negotiable. General statements in this respect are not very helpful and may even be misleading. General and perfunctory references to mandatory state regulations should also be looked upon with circumspection. Such regulations might in fact not exist at all or they might not be applicable to the case at hand. If they do apply, their ambit and effect tend to be exaggerated.⁹ Apart from the impact of such regulations, it is an empirical fact that, when negotiating for a contract, many exporters/account parties direct their efforts towards getting the deal so much that they hardly bother about the implications of the required guarantee. It should be stressed, however, that, even if the furnishing of a first demand guarantee is unavoidable, it remains important to pay proper attention to the various terms and clauses of the guarantee, such as provisions concerning the expiry date, the maximum amount and other clauses examined in Chapter 8. Carelessness in this respect could wipe out any profit expectation that the exporter might otherwise have.

As far as the scope for negotiation is concerned, it is useful to distinguish between guarantees in favour of state departments or state enterprises and guarantees in favour of private companies.

Most countries, not only in the Middle East and North Africa, but also in the West, have state regulations concerning guarantees directed at state agencies. They typically specify which agencies are subject to the regulations and to what kind of contracts, i.e. the nature as well as the amount of the contract, they relate. One can safely say that public works operating under a public tender system are subject to regulations. Usually – and invariably in the Middle East and North Africa – they prescribe first demand guarantees, while the precise text of the guarantee is ordinarily fixed too. In other cases one must examine the specific regulation in question. To the extent that they are applicable, state agencies are bound by these regulations and they will not be prepared to depart from them. The inflexible nature of bureaucracy is also believed to be a factor which accounts for the fact that even points of detail and the drafting of the text are rarely open to discussion.

State regulations do not apply to private companies. Here the scope for negotiation is entirely determined by the relative bargaining strength of the contracting parties.

Parties to the underlying contract should bear in mind that whatever terms and conditions, as well as text, they may agree upon, these must also be acceptable to the bank.¹⁰ Banks ordinarily prefer to use their own standard forms so that the format of the text is more or less fixed, while leaving the selection of the type of clauses and the implementation thereof to the account party and beneficiary.

Direct/indirect guarantees

6-6 A major subject for consideration will be whether the guarantee is to be framed in a direct or indirect way.

An indirect structure whereby the primary guarantee is issued by a bank in his home country is clearly advantageous to the beneficiary on several counts. The primary guar-

---

9   See also Chapter 2.4, No. 2-17.
10 See also Chapter 7, No. 7-3.

antee will be governed by local law and practice and this is particularly important with respect to the validity period of the guarantee. The risk of currency exchange restrictions is also eliminated. The issuing bank could be the house bank of the beneficiary and, if not, he is at least in a better position to assess its reliability and financial standing. Contacts with the bank run more smoothly and any possible problems can be resolved more easily than would be the case with a foreign bank. A very important factor is that the bank will naturally be inclined to pay more heed to the interests of the beneficiary than to those of the account party abroad, with whom it has no contractual relationship. This manifests itself especially when disagreements between account party and beneficiary ensue following a call on the guarantee. The beneficiary's bank is more likely to proceed to timely payment than is the account party's bank in the case of a direct guarantee. In direct guarantees, banks might postpone payment for a while to make further inquiries with the beneficiary, something which at the same time allows the account party to take legal action designed to forestall payment.

From the viewpoint of the account party, indirect guarantees present several significant drawbacks. The risks to which he is exposed are determined not merely by the terms of the primary guarantee but also by the terms of the counter-guarantee, which his bank furnishes to the foreign, issuing bank. The terms for reimbursement by the instructing bank to the issuing bank for the account of the account party are often broader and less restrictive than those of the primary guarantee.[11] A second disadvantage is that the account party is to pay charges to both the instructing and issuing bank during the validity period of the counter-guarantee. This is particularly burdensome if the counter-guarantee states that it remains in force until discharge, which also has other adverse implications.[12] Finally, it is virtually impossible to obtain a stop-payment injunction on the basis of fraud.[13]

As far as state agencies are concerned, indirect guarantees are predominant in the Middle East,[14] North Africa, Latin America and the Indian subcontinent. In other regions, indirect guarantees are probably more common than direct guarantees. As far as the private sector is concerned, both types occur. Although it is true that indirect guarantees are more common in the Middle East and North Africa, any generalisation with respect to any region proffers unsafe guidance for an individual case.

---

[11] See Chapter 11.4.

[12] See Chapter 12.4.7, Nos. 12-62/65.

[13] See Chapter 16.4.

[14] In Saudi Arabia certain foreign approved banks are permitted to issue direct guarantees in favour of state agencies if advised, but not necessarily confirmed, by a local Saudi bank. Under certain circumstances Bahrain also permits foreign approved banks to issue direct guarantees in favour of Bahrain Government agencies.

Protective clauses in the guarantee and counter-balancing provisions in the underlying contract

6-7 Should the issuance of a first demand guarantee turn out to be inevitable, there will often still be room for negotiating protective clauses. Reduction clauses in repayment guarantees, for example, are very common, both in the private and public sector. The insertion of other clauses regularly proves to be possible too, depending on the sector and bargaining power. Some of these clauses will be examined in Chapter 8.

Attention should also be paid to the inclusion in the principal contract of protective clauses which curb the beneficiary's resort to calling the guarantee. Although such clauses do not ordinarily affect the guarantee as such, they will be useful in subsequent proceedings after payment when the exporter/account party seeks recovery. As noted in No. 6-3 above, a clause providing for arbitration or court proceedings in a neutral country might turn out to be vital. A provision requiring the importer/beneficiary to put up an (accessory) guarantee assuring repayment in the event of a judicial or arbitral award in favour of the exporter/account party improves the latter's position greatly of course, but it will be difficult to negotiate for such terms.

It is vital for the exporter who has to furnish a first demand performance guarantee to counter-balance the ensuing risks by negotiating for favourable payment terms and security for payment. If not, he runs the double risk of a call on the guarantee for his account and non-payment of the contract price. The interplay between the contractual terms for payment to the exporter and first demand guarantees in favour of the importer are especially relevant for construction contracts.

Issuance of the guarantee as a condition precedent and principal obligation

6-8 When parties to the underlying relationship have agreed that the principal debtor is to furnish a guarantee payable under certain terms and conditions, that agreement constitutes a condition precedent in the sense that the obligations of the other party are suspended until the issuance of the guarantee. That agreement is also considered a principal agreement in the sense that if the guarantee has not been issued in time, the other party is ordinarily entitled to repudiate the contract and he may even be entitled to damages.[15] Specification of the final date of issuance is, therefore, important. If that date has not been fixed, the principal debtor is allowed a reasonable period of time.

Sometimes problems occur as a result of the fact that parties, while having agreed that 'a guarantee' is to be furnished, have failed to express themselves sufficiently clearly as regards the precise terms and conditions of payment. This often fails to

---

15 Mijnssen, p. 22, Bannier, in Hague-Zagreb Essays 6, p. 76, von Westphalen, p. 392, Canaris, No. 1151. See also *Gyllenhammar v. Sour Brodogradevna Industrya*, [1989] 2 Lloyd's Rep. 403, where it was the principal debtor who pleaded that the contract had not come into force.

emerge until the bank has been requested to draft the guarantee. Evidently, these matters have to be clarified first and the above-mentioned remedies to the other party will, of course, not be available in this situation.

Even-handedness of a first demand guarantee; contractual relationship as a whole

6-9 It has been suggested that guarantees prescribing documentary proof of default from impartial third parties or an arbitral or court decision better serve the mutual interests of parties than do first demand guarantees. The former type would constitute a fair equilibrium with regard to the legitimate interests of parties by eliminating the possibility of fraud while still ensuring compensation to which the creditor is entitled, whereas the latter type would give rise to strained relations, increased costs and the blocking of funds.[16] This may all be true from the viewpoint of the principal debtor, but it is unlikely that creditors will feel the same way. It must be borne in mind that the catalogue of risks revolving around breach of contract and described in Nos. 6-1 and 6-2 is inherent in international transactions and that these risks must fall somewhere. There is no sound argument for the proposition that it is only appropriate that the risks should principally lie with the creditor, rather than with the principal debtor. Accordingly, general statements on the even-handedness of the first type of guarantee and allusions to the immanent unfairness of the first demand guarantee are out of place. It is not surprising that the ICC, conscious of the realities of the prevailing market conditions, decided in favour of payment on first demand as the protype payment mechanism in the 1992 URDG.

One should also be careful not to be unduly overwhelmed by the recurrent, if correct, references to the possibility of abuse. No doubt there will be cases of fraud – if only one knew for sure when such cases occur – and other sharp practices. These incidents, the frequency of which is unknown, do not warrant a general denunciation of the concept of first demand guarantees. Every type of contract is liable to be used for fraudulent purposes, the consequences of which cannot always be undone by law. The numerous incidents of forged documents have never been cause for questioning the utility of documentary credits.

If one is inclined to give an opinion on the (dis)equilibrium brought about by the various types of guarantees, one should have regard to the contractual relationship as a whole, and especially the terms of payment to the exporter and the security for the importer in respect of proper performance. If the importer is willing to (co-)finance the transaction, it is only reasonable that he should insist on a first demand guarantee in

---

[16] Introduction and Comments to Article 9 of the 1978 URCG, Eisemann, Rev. Arbitrage 1972, pp. 390-391, Matray, Rev. Banque 1974, pp. 280-288, Beckers, IFLR October 1982, pp. 32-33, Stumpf/Ullrich, RIW 1984, p. 845.

order to counterbalance the risks which result from this financial construction. A few examples may illustrate the point.[17] A buyer or an employer in a construction contract cannot be expected to agree to advance payments or to the release of retention moneys if repayment is not assured by guarantees payable on first demand. If the exporter is not prepared to put up these guarantees, he can only blame himself for the ensuing difficulties of having to finance the entire transaction on his own. When a seller has the benefit of a documentary credit covering the full contract price, he is assured of immediate and full payment. The buyer, however, cannot be certain that all the terms and warranties of the contract of sale have been and will be complied with. If one were to assess such conditions as causing a disequilibrium, one could say that this could be remedied by a first demand guarantee in favour of the buyer for, say, 5% to 20% of the contract price. It would be different if the documentary credit only covered, say, 80% per cent or if payment is to be made after delivery on open account without any security in favour of the seller. In this situation, the withholding of 20% of the contract price or the unsecured future payment of the full contract price ordinarily provides the buyer with sufficient security for non-performance by the seller, and an additional first demand guarantee in favour of the buyer would not be justified. On the other hand, a buyer in continent X, who has had unfavourable experiences in the past with a seller in continent Y, could hardly be criticised for insisting on a first demand guarantee. In construction contracts, interim payments are ordinarily due upon presentation of certificates for work done, issued by the engineer. The employer is thus assured that no payments will be made unless the work is done, but he still faces the risk that certain defects only surface at a later stage or that the project will not be completed.

In conclusion, the wide range of factors that affect the equilibrium of a contract, each of which is very difficult to gauge, alone and in relation to other factors, renders any general judgment as to the even-handedness of a first demand guarantee virtually impossible. While the parties to the contract will ordinarily be the best judges, one should at least take into account the contractual relationship as a whole and the surrounding circumstances. At any rate, contentions by a principal debtor/account party that a first demand guarantee should not be enforced because of its unfairness, because of unequal bargaining powers or because it has been exacted by means of undue influence are to be dismissed.[18] Parties entering the international business arena cannot successfully invoke defences of this kind.

It has often been hinted that first demand guarantees may in effect operate as a discount for the beneficiary on the contract price and that the exporter will be wise to

---

17 See also Chapter 19, No. 19-1.
18 Cf. *Rb Amsterdam, 19 March 1981*, KG 1981, 30. See also *BGH, 24 November 1983*, WM 1984, p. 44.

take that into account when quoting the contract price.[19] There are, however, no clear indications that quotations are increased by the amount of the guarantee, in full or partially, to any significant extent. Fierce competition and the difficulties of concealing price mark-ups often leave little room for such practices. Should it occur, however, it would signify the collapse of first demand guarantees as useful security devices.

---

[19] See for such statements in case law, for example, Denning M.R. in *Edward Owen Engineering Ltd. v. Barclays Bank Int. Ltd.*, [1978] Q.B., 159, 170, Kerr J. in *R.D. Harbottle (Mercantile) Ltd. v. Nat. Westminster Bank Ltd.*, [1978] Q.B., 146, 150.

CHAPTER 7
ROLE AND POSITION OF THE BANK

7.1 ISSUING GUARANTEES AS A FINANCIAL SERVICE

7-1 Some of the basic features and rules of law pertaining to the bank as guarantor can be more readily comprehended if one looks at the facts surrounding the position of banks, both in general and in the context of a multi-party guarantee.

The business of banks is to render financial services. One of their services is issuing independent guarantees and standby letters of credit. Banks are not insurers. When taking on payment commitments under a guarantee or standby letters of credit they do not envisage guarding the beneficiary from certain misfortunes. Nor do they intend to assume the economic risk of payment, which insurers do assume. They accept a credit risk, namely the risk of not being reimbursed by their customer. To a large extent banks are in control of this risk. By insisting on adequate collateral security the credit risk can be reduced considerably. From the bank's point of view, their part in the guarantee transaction consists in effecting payment if certain terms and conditions specified in the guarantee are satisfied, and in procuring immediate reimbursement, which often requires no more than debiting the account of the customer.[1] The economic risk of payment under a guarantee or standby letter of credit lies with the customer/principal debtor. That is why the latter is called the account party.

When banks agree to play a part in the multi-party relationship involving the issuance of a guarantee, they agree to provide a financial service not a legal service, for which, in general, they would lack the specialised skill and experience. Accordingly, their participation cannot and does not extend to the determination of legal issues between account party and beneficiary in case of disputes. Moreover, any such involvement would entail the risk of the bank finding itself entangled in an insoluble conflict of interests, as the bank stands in a contractual relationship – with its ensuing duties – with both the account party and beneficiary. The bank may not and cannot be made a

---

[1] This may be contrasted with the contract of suretyship. Traditionally the surety has a special relationship with the principal debtor (family, holding subsidiary company, business relationship), which induces him to act as a surety. He is well aware of the financially precarious situation of the principal debtor, which is precisely the reason why the creditor has stipulated a surety. The risk of not being reimbursed may be so considerable that the surety effectively accepts the economic risk. In contrast, the solvency of the principal debtor is only one of the factors for the creditor to insist on a first demand or documentary guarantee, see Chapter 6.1, No. 6-1.

referee on matters that divide the parties to the principal contract.[2] These considerations lie at the bottom of the bank's own legitimate interest in the principle of independence and in maintaining a neutral position.

The service of furnishing guarantees is a low cost facility, particularly when compared with the services rendered by bonding companies.[3] The relatively modest remuneration is based on the assumption that the bank's task is confined to duties which can be performed quickly, easily and almost mechanically. The work must be capable of being carried out by the middle ranks of the bank from behind their desks. This provides another explanation as to why banks have a legitimate interest in the principle of independence and more specifically in having their payment obligations determined on the basis of documents, i.e. matching the documents tendered against the documents prescribed in the guarantee. This is what they are paid for. They are not expected to go beyond the documents and to assess the beneficiary's right of payment on the basis of the underlying relationship, which would implicate the bank in intricate legal issues. In addition, the size of the commission fee also accounts for the fact that several kinds of risks which attend the issuance of guarantees and standby letters of credit are allocated to the customer, rather than to the bank.

There is yet another avenue to the allocation of risks. It is the customer who has chosen to deal with a particular beneficiary. The selection of the terms and conditions and the type of guarantee, i.e. a direct or indirect guarantee or a guarantee payable on first demand or upon a court decision, is also a matter of agreement between the account party/principal debtor and beneficiary/creditor. They represent a shift of advantages and risks, typically in favour of the creditor and to the detriment of the principal debtor, which the latter is prepared to accept as the price for gaining the contract. This allocation between principal debtor and creditor is not affected by the interposition of the bank. It is important to recognise that the bank is merely called in as a neutral and reliable intermediary entrusted with the task of ensuring proper and smooth implementation of the agreed allocation of risks. This is accomplished by the bank assuming the obligations pursuant to the terms and conditions of the guarantee in its own name.[4] The allocation of risks is preserved by the principal debtor´s obligation to repay the

---

[2] This principle, which also applies to documentary credits, is universally acknowledged, see, for example, von Westphalen, p. 28, Dohm, No. 54 and DPCI 1980, p. 267, Sion, Banque 1984, p. 18, Wymeersch, TPR 1986, p. 484, Pabbruwe, WPNR 1979, p. 181, Dolan, § 3.07[3], *Harbottle (Mercantile) Ltd. v. Nat. Westminster Bank Ltd.*, [1978] Q.B., p. 155, 156, *Esal (Commodities) Ltd., Reltor Ltd. v. Oriental Credit Ltd.*, [1985] 2 Lloyd's Rep. 546, *Paris, November 24 1981*, D. 1982 J. p. 296, *OLG Stuttgart, 25 January 1979*, RIW 1980, p. 729. See also *CA The Hague, 13 June 1980*, NJ 1982, 267. See further Chapter 15, No. 15-2.

[3] See for this aspect Dolan, § 3.07[3], Bataille, Arizona L.R. 1974, p. 828, Weisz and Blackman, University Illinois L.R. 1982, p. 355.

[4] Cf. Chapter 5, No. 5-2.

bank, if the bank has ascertained compliance with the terms and conditions and thereupon has proceeded to payment. This is what the involvement of the bank basically amounts to. The issuance of a guarantee may also give rise to certain risks which the account party presumably did not intend to accept, for example a fraudulent call on the guarantee or enforced payment despite non-compliance, a risk which is especially liable to occur in indirect guarantees. Such risks are inherent in guarantees and must be allocated to the account party, for it is the account party who selected the beneficiary and the guarantee format, not the bank which is merely expected to act as an intermediary.

7.2 THE BANK'S INTEREST IN INDEPENDENCE

7-2 In the context of the multi-party guarantee the meaning and legal basis of the principle of independence varies according to the selected point of issue.

The notion of independence may be used to describe the legal separation between the relationship of account party and bank – the mandate – on the one hand, and the relationship between bank and beneficiary – the guarantee – on the other hand. This aspect will be examined in Chapter 9, No. 9-5. The notion is, however, usually used to denote the independence of the contract of guarantee in relation to the underlying relationship. In this regard, independence signifies that the rights and obligations between issuing bank and beneficiary are solely governed by the terms and conditions of the guarantee and that the bank cannot invoke defences emanating from the principal contract. But here again, the assessment varies depending on whether the notion is considered from the point of view of the parties to the principal contract or from the point of view of the bank.

To the parties to the underlying relationship, independence on its own does not accord any particular advantage or disadvantage to either of them. Independence assumes significance only in combination with the agreed type of conditions of payment, for example payment on first demand without any evidence of default. It is this combination which brings about a major shift of risks, the beneficiary/creditor acquiring a very strong position at the expense of the principal debtor/account party.

For the bank, independence signifies that its role is confined to checking compliance with the terms and conditions of the guarantee only, which are ordinarily framed in a documentary fashion, see No. 7-3. The bank is merely supposed to compare the documents. It does not have to immerse itself in an appraisal of the precise rights and liabilities of the account party and beneficiary on the basis of the principal contract. This would be an onerous and precarious operation for which a bank is neither equipped nor paid. Independence as such is thus vital and a near necessity for the bank.

In relation to the account party, independence signifies that the right to reimbursement is not affected by defences which the account party/principal debtor may have against the beneficiary/creditor on the basis of the underlying relationship. This aspect of independence follows from the instruction of the account party to the bank to issue an independent guarantee. When the bank effects payment to the beneficiary exclusively on the basis of the terms and conditions of the guarantee, it does no more or less than carry out the instructions. If, thereafter, defences of the account party/principal debtor against the beneficiary/creditor were to affect the bank's right of recourse, it would result in the bank bearing the risks emanating from the independent nature of the guarantee, instead of the account party. This cannot be intended. In other words, by requesting the bank to furnish an independent guarantee and by the bank's acceptance of that request, the account party and the bank indicate that defences from the principal contract are extraneous to the obligation and the right of reimbursement. Accordingly, this notion of independence is necessarily implied as a matter of logic and need not be stipulated.

The reverse happens when the principal debtor instructs the bank, and when the bank accepts such instruction, to issue a traditional, accessory suretyship. In this situation the principal debtor's defences against the creditor are not extraneous elements, since these are inherent in the instruction. These defences do affect the position of the bank. If the bank wishes to avoid these consequences, it must stipulate expressly that as regards its customer it is entitled to reimbursement regardless of such defences.

The frequently used phrase 'the bank cannot invoke defences derived from the principal contract' is correct, but could be misleading inasmuch as it suggests something to the detriment of the bank. In actual fact, the disadvantage relates to the account party, not to the bank, in view of his obligation to reimburse the bank irrespective of those defences. Accordingly, the bank will usually have no inclination to attempt to invoke such defences. This may, however, be quite different when the bank anticipates problems with respect to repayment, for example in view of the (imminent) insolvency of the account party.[5]

---

[5] As occurred in at least fifty reported cases, see, for example, the trilogy of *Rb. Haarlem, 9 January 1987*, KG 1987, 85, *January 22 1987*, KG 1987, 86 and *6 February 1987*, KG 1987, 104, *CA The Hague, 20 April 1993*, NJ 1995, 542, Turkiye *Is Bankasi v. Bank of China*, [1996] 2 Lloyd's Rep. 611, *Balfour Beatty Civil Engineering v. Technical & General Guarantee*, [1999] 68 Con.L.R. 180, *Csarnikow-Rionda v. Standard Bank London*, [1999] 2 Lloyd's Rep. 187, *BGH, March 12 1984 (11 ZR 10/83)*, RIW 1985, p. 78, *Paris, 8 December 1977*, D. 1979 J. p. 259, *Trib. com. La Roche-sur-Yon, September 14 1981*, D. 1982 I.R. p. 199, *Cass., 20 December 1982*, D. 1983 J. p. 365, *Trib. com. Nantes, 22 September 1983*, D. 1984 I.R. p. 202, *Cass., 8 December 1987*, D 1988 Somm. p. 240, *Paris, 18 December 1991*, D. 1993 Somm. p. 106, *Cass., 30 January 2001*, D. Affaires 2001, p. 1024, *Trib. com. Brussels, March 11 1981*, BRH 1981, p. 361, *Trib. com. Brussels, 16 May 1991*, JT 1991, p. 711, Trib. com. Brussels, 10 January 1992, RDC 1993, p. 1052, *Trib. com. Namur, 12 September 1994*, RDC 1995, p. 68, *Trib. com. Charleroi, 23 April 1997*, JLMB 1998, p. 1073, *Trib. com. Brussels, 21 November 1997*, RDC 1998, p. 850, Trib. com. *Brussels, 11 February 1999*, RDC 2000, p. 725, *CA Brussels, 2 March 2001*, TBH 2002, p. 484, Chase *Manhattan Bank v. Equibank*, 394 F. Supp. 352 (1977), 21 UCCRS 247 (1977), *Wahda Bank v. Arab Bank*, [1993] 2 Bank L.J. 233. See also Chapter 12.3.3, No. 12-27 and Chapter 13.2.10, No. 13-30.

7.3 THE BANK'S INTEREST IN THE TERMS AND CONDITIONS OF THE GUARANTEE; DOCUMENTS

7-3 Since the bank enters into the contract of guarantee for the risk and account of the customer, the bank's own interest in the terms and conditions of the guarantee as such is, in general, small. The determination as to which provisions will or will not be included, the type of conditions of payment, the choice as regards a direct or indirect guarantee, the qualifications of the rights of the beneficiary, the maximum amount, etc., are matters which primarily concern the parties to the main contract. The bank will ordinarily not intervene in these affairs. It is of course not suggested that banks are totally indifferent to the vast risks to which their client may be about to expose himself. The happy combination of sound self-interest and genuine loyalty towards its client may well prompt the bank to endeavour to avert disaster, which is often only apparent to those standing at some distance. The fact is, however, that the client has already often committed himself extensively, leaving little room for even minor rescue operations.

For the bank it is of vital importance that the provisions of the guarantee have been drafted in such a way that the bank will be able to determine easily and readily when it is supposed and when it is not supposed to effect payment to the beneficiary. Apart from specifying the expiry date and the maximum amount, this is accomplished by making the payment obligations and the limitations thereof dependent on the submission of prescribed documents, and the bank will ordinarily ensure that this is the case. The guarantee should indicate which of the parties, the beneficiary or the account party, is to tender the relevant document(s) and the identity of the person who is to draw up the document, while the contents ought to be set forth as clearly and concisely as possible. The importance of drafting the conditions of payment in a documentary fashion is also restated throughout the URDG, see, for example, Arts. 2(b), 8, 9, 10, 19, 20 and 22, and in Rule 1.06(d) and Rule 4.11 ISP98.

Documents do not only play a part where the payment mechanism prescribes the submission of third-party documents evidencing default or an arbitral or court decision, but occasionally also in first demand guarantees. Apart from a statement of default, if required, a first demand guarantee may be subject to conditions precedent, a reduction or an increase of the maximum amount or an expiry framed in a documentary form.

Although the risk of payment as a result of ambiguous provisions in the guarantee lies primarily with the account party,[6] it is of course in the bank's interest to prevent disputes with its customer concerning the correctness of the payment. The vagueness of the provisions may therefore be a cause for the bank to refuse to accept the text as submitted or to insist on amendments. Another reason for objection could be that the

---

6   See Chapter 10.8, Nos. 10-24/26.

bank fears that the examination with respect to compliance with the terms and conditions is likely to be too exacting or cumbersome, for example if over-elaborate documentation is to be presented. Thus, Art. 3 URDG warns against conditions with excessive details.

7.4 FACTORS INFLUENCING (NON-)ACCEPTANCE OF THE REQUEST

7-4 When considering its customer's application for the issuance of a guarantee the terms and conditions as such are, as noted in No. 7-3, of minor importance. Unfortunate experiences in the past with first demand guarantees extended to countries rated more than usually risk-prone may, however, call for particular caution. Apart from these special situations, the financial position of the account party in particular, but also his ability to complete the main contract successfully, are considered the primary objects for review.

The bank will ascertain whether its customer will have sufficient liquid means at his disposal to warrant confidence in his capability to effect prompt repayment in due course. Factors to be taken into account include the maximum amount of exposure under the guarantee, the duration of the guarantee, other financial commitments and the financial and earning potential of the customer in general.

Access to credit facilities is another major factor for consideration. Banks ordinarily regard the issuance of a guarantee as a credit facility which increases the customer's contingent liabilities *(obligo)*. They, therefore, tend to put considerable weight on the volume of disposable funds within the existing credit line. On the other hand, credit facilities cannot be static. Procurement of the main contract, for which the issuance of a guarantee is a precondition, enhances the financial and earning potential, which would justify an increase of the credit facilities. In contrast, a refusal, which would result in the customer foregoing the contract, may well impair his financial position. It is also debatable whether it is sound practice to equate the issuance of a guarantee with an ordinary credit facility increasing the customer's liabilities by the maximum amount of the guarantee. In fact, the issuance of a guarantee gives rise to a contingent liability only, and actual payment is the real exception. The more rational approach would be to create a special credit facility for the issue of guarantees, administered in a separate account. This is clearly preferable when the customer's business requires the issuance of guarantees or standby letters of credit on a regular basis. Under these facilities the bank will issue guarantees up to the maximum amount of the facility without debiting the customer's current account or other credit lines.

The assessment of the customers's capability to complete the main contract is ordinarily confined to the general reputation of the customer, the type, complexity and magnitude of the contract and the country where the contract is to be performed. Naturally, such an appraisal can and will only be carried out in a rather superficial manner. When the contract involves a large-scale construction project, a more careful assessment will be called for, but it inevitably remains inadequate and haphazard. Successful completion not only depends on the customer's own capability, but also on other risk factors which are difficult to gauge, such as participation in the project by sub-contractors and/or the beneficiary himself, local conditions and the stability in the country concerned. In any event, whenever the bank has reasons to suspect that its customer is likely to encounter serious difficulties in completing the project, it will adopt a rather reserved attitude.

Where the prospect of prompt reimbursement and proper completion by the customer is unsatisfactory, the availability of (additional) collateral security will usually be insufficient to persuade the bank to decide in favour of issuing the guarantee. The furnishing of collateral is rather a further, but essential, requirement.

The procurement of security calls for closer attention than is the case with documentary credits. A guarantee is not 'self-executing', as the utilisation of the guarantee by the beneficiary does not generate the means which enable the account party to repay the bank. Secondly, the documents to be tendered under a guarantee or standby letter of credit have no intrinsic value from which the bank could recoup its payments, as is the case with documentary credits, on the strength of its security interest. Finally, the financial exposure of the bank tends to be substantially larger than with documentary credits.

Under its general terms and conditions, the bank will usually be entitled to recoup payments from collateral already granted under the existing credit line. The existing collateral may, however, be insufficient also to cover additional risks and the bank may then insist on fresh security, for example counter-guarantees by affiliated companies or other financial institutions. A type of security which is particularly suitable consists of the assignment or pledge of the future proceeds of the main contract accompanied by measures assuring actual payment into the customer's account with the bank. In this way full use is made of the earning power of the customer. As a further safety measure the customer's accounts or general credit facility may be blocked up to the maximum amount of exposure, to be released only for approved expenditures. However, requiring the account party to deposit cash collateral up to the maximum amount of the guarantee is, barring exceptional circumstances, objectionable from his point of view, since this would defeat one of the objects of furnishing first demand guarantees, namely to avoid the disadvantages of placing cash collateral with the beneficiary.[7]

A further factor to be considered is the availability of export credit insurance under the various national schemes securing the continued flow of payments to the applicant in the event of non-payment of the amounts due by the beneficiary/contracting partner in the principal contract. If available, the future proceeds of the insurance could be assigned, thus providing a source of collateral security for reimbursement to the bank. The risk of non-reimbursement is virtually eliminated if the export credit insurance company is prepared to issue a counter-guarantee in favour of the bank. This is also

---

[7] See Chapter 4.2, No. 4-6.

advantageous to the customer, because his credit facilities with the bank will then not be debited with the amount for which the bank guarantee has been issued. Export credit insurance companies, such as Gerling NCM, are often willing to furnish these counter-guarantees if the exporter/customer has also obtained cover against the risk of 'unfair calling' of the bank guarantee by the beneficiary. On the other hand, a refusal to extend export credit insurance might figure as a warning signal. It would render the earning power of the customer more hazardous and it may also indicate that the country of performance of the principal contract is rated as exceptionally risk-prone.

Banks generally proclaim to prefer issuing first demand guarantees free from any further restrictive clauses due to the simplicity of their execution. Indeed, such guarantees are more straightforward and hence easier to deal with than other types. Yet simplicity cannot be the sole factor. Whether and to what extent banks are and will be prepared to accept requests for first demand guarantees containing restrictive clauses drafted in a documentary fashion, or guarantees requiring third-party documents, very much depends on the prevailing conditions in the country of the bank, be it the country of the account party or the country of the beneficiary in the case of an indirect guarantee. If banks operate under a liberal system, free of government constraints and in competition with each other, they cannot afford to turn down the business of issuing such guarantees in the face of existing and perhaps growing demands from the market.

CHAPTER 8
DRAFTING AND CLAUSES

8.1 INTERESTS OF THE PARTIES; DOCUMENTARY NATURE

8-1 It is not only the guarantee format, i.e. a direct or indirect guarantee, and the type of conditions of payment, for example a guarantee payable on first demand without any evidence of default or a guarantee requiring the submission of third-party documents evidencing default, but also the determination of other clauses which are primarily of concern to the parties to the underlying relationship. This can be explained by the fact that the guarantee is a product of the underlying relationship,[1] and the fact that the bank issues the guarantee for the risk and account of its customer.

Nonetheless, the various clauses which the parties to the underlying relationship may have agreed upon must be acceptable to the bank too. On the whole the bank's main interest is to ensure that the clauses are framed in such a way that they clearly define the content and extent of its obligations towards the beneficiary.[2] With respect to most clauses this could be achieved by stating that they become operative on presentation of prescribed documents. As regards the maximum amount and duration of the guarantee the bank's principal concern is that the guarantee should contain specific and clear-cut provisions, but it is less concerned about what the maximum amount or duration is to be, provided it has obtained sufficient security for reimbursement. It is only with respect to set-off, jurisdiction and applicable law that the bank has a direct interest of its own.

8.2 DRAFTING OF THE TEXT, PATTERNS AND DEVELOPMENT

Drafting

8-2 It is vital for all parties concerned that the text of the guarantee provides absolute clarity as regards the nature of the security, namely an independent guarantee as distinct from an accessory suretyship. Texts submitted by their clients are especially scrutinised by banks in this respect. Over the course of time banks have gained experience in drafting texts which do provide the required clarity. They therefore prefer to

---

[1] See Chapter 6.1 and Chapter 6.2, Nos. 6-5/7.
[2] See further Chapter 7, No. 7-3.

employ their own standard models.[3] Nonetheless, several standard models and individual texts have been found lacking in precision. At any rate, litigation which turns on the construction of the type of security[4] demonstrates that too often insufficient care has been taken in properly drafting the text of the guarantee.[5]

In attaining the required clarity several aspects may be considered. The term 'guarantee' itself is apt to cause confusion.[6] When used in a common law scenario the term usually refers to an accessory guarantee or has a neutral meaning. In the latter case, whether the term denotes an independent guarantee or an accessory suretyship is only apparent by reference to the context and other clauses and phrases. In Continental practice too – especially in the Netherlands – the terms *'garantie'* (in French, Dutch and Belgian) and *'Garantie'* (in German) do not always signify independence, particularly when in translation the English term 'guarantee' is used. Additional phrases such as 'unconditional', 'irrevocable', 'abstract' or 'commitment to pay as our own debt' are inappropriate or insufficient, if they purport to express independence.[7] Not surprisingly, Rule 1.10(a) ISP98 discourages the use of these and other obscure terms.[8] The best and most simple means of achieving clarity is expressly to employ the term 'independent guarantee' in the heading of the document and/or in the text itself. It should also be noted that it is not necessary for the term 'guarantee' to figure in the text. Particularly where the heading of the document contains the designation 'tender' or 'performance guarantee', as the case may be, it is quite sufficient if the text reads 'With reference to ... (description of the underlying relationship) we undertake to pay ... (followed by the type of conditions of payment, for example on first demand or upon presentation of certain documents)'.

Obviously, the terms 'surety', *'borgtocht'*, *'Bürgschaft'*, *'cautionnement'* or '(performance) bond' should not be used. Astonishingly, these terms can still be found in instruments which purport to be independent guarantees. Certain specific clauses, terms

---

[3] Several banks allow their branch offices to employ standard texts only. Divergent texts require the approval of the head office.

[4] See Chapter 12.3.

[5] Unless account party and bank have purposely sought to devise an ambiguous text.

[6] See also Chapter 1, No. 1-2.

[7] Even in the case of a first demand guarantee is the bank's obligation to pay *conditional* upon the beneficiary making a demand for payment, accompanied by a statement of default if required, on or before the expiry date. A surety's obligation in the case of an accessory guarantee (suretyship) is also irrevocable in the sense that, after acceptance, it cannot unilaterally revoke its undertaking. In Germany, France and Belgium, the independent (first demand) guarantee is not considered to be an *abstract* undertaking (such as a bill of exchange), but a *causal* undertaking, namely to provide security.

[8] See also Chapter 12.3, No. 12-21.

Drafting and Clauses

and phrases derived from language employed with regard to suretyship should also be avoided. These include references to statutory provisions concerning suretyship and especially the common exclusions of certain rights and defences which the law accords to the surety. Phrases such as 'We hereby guarantee proper performance of ... (the principal contract)' or 'payment will be made in the event of failure of ... (the principal debtor) to execute ... (the principal contract)' are also still quite common. They are, however, risky since they have a strong suretyship connotation. Such phrases are also quite unnecessary, as the purpose of the guarantee will already be evident from the heading of the document reading 'payment', 'tender' or 'performance guarantee', as the case may be, from the reference to the underlying relationship in the preamble and the statement of default, if stipulated. Should one be minded to retain such phrases it is strongly recommended that they are put in the recitals (preamble) of the guarantee, but not in the operative clauses, or that they are immediately followed by phrases such as 'as determined by you .. (the beneficiary)' in the case of a first demand guarantee or 'as evidenced by ... (description of third-party documents)' in the case of a guarantee payable upon submission of third-party documents.

In conclusion, short and concise texts ordinarily provide far greater clarity as regards the independent nature of the security than lengthy and elaborate texts.

Patterns and development

8-3 At one time many texts employed in the Gulf area were drafted by American attorneys hired by local agencies. They adopted the traditional patterns of American performance bonds,[9] a hybrid of the accessory suretyship and the independent guarantee, to which were added clauses intended to assure prompt payment without proof of default. This approach caused the texts to be exceptionally lengthy, intricate and difficult to comprehend. Nowadays, standard texts employed in the Middle East are in general shorter than those employed in Western Europe. In addition to the caption, reference to the underlying relationship, amount and expiry date, a typical text would read: 'We undertake to pay you on first demand notwithstanding any contest by the supplier (accompanied by your statement regarding the supplier's default)'.

A similar development can be discerned in England. By virtue of the common law tradition, English law contracts in general are significantly more comprehensive, specific and detailed than texts drafted on the Continent. In the early phase of their development, texts closely adhered to the traditional patterns of the accessory guarantee, supplemented by provisions for prompt payment. Now English law guarantees, at least those prepared for use in international trade, are very much shorter than they used to be. They still tend to differ from texts employed elsewhere inasmuch as very often the only clue to the independent nature of the security consists of a provision that the beneficiary's statement in respect of the default of the principal debtor will be accepted

---

9 See also Chapter 1, No. 1-2.

as conclusive evidence for the purpose of the guarantee. The adjective 'primary' can also be found to express independence in contradistinction with the term 'secondary' which has suretyship connotations.

On the Continent, especially in Belgium and France, texts also used to be interspersed with terms and phrases derived from the language of traditional suretyship. The use of the term *'cautionnement'* (traditional suretyship) or suretyship language was not uncommon. This has now disappeared or is gradually doing so in relation to guarantees issued by banks for crossborder transactions. However, guarantees issued by non-financial institutions in domestic cases continue to suffer from obscure language which is borne out by the voluminous amount of litigation involving the proper construction of the nature of the security. In Spain, Italy and Latin America many texts continue to be fashioned after traditional suretyship models. As far as the United States is concerned, any risk of confusing texts has been avoided by the use of the standby letter of credit.

8.3 REFERENCE TO THE UNDERLYING RELATIONSHIP; CONSIDERATION

Reference to the underlying relationship

8-4 The text of the guarantee invariably contains a reference to the underlying relationship, usually at the beginning or in a recital (preamble).[10] Together with the heading of the document ('tender' or 'performance guarantee', as the case may be) this reference serves to identify the purpose and the risk against which the guarantee provides security. More specifically, the reference is meant to indicate in respect of which relationship the guarantee can be called.

The description of the underlying relationship is short. It is usually confined to the names of the parties, which will be the account party and beneficiary, the date of conclusion of the contract or the submission of the tender, the reference number of the contract or tender and sometimes a short description of the object, for example the supply of goods. References to the principal contract do not turn an independent guarantee into an accessory guarantee.

Guarantees may cover more than one transaction and such guarantees are sometimes called block guarantees. This technique ordinarily reduces the aggregate amount of charges owed to the bank, but they entail grave risks for the principal debtor/account party. Block guarantees put the beneficiary in a position to claim the full amount of the guarantee even if in fact all but one of the contracts have been executed.

---

[10] Mainly in the past, Libyan beneficiaries and Libyan banks have occasionally attempted to extract, or issue, guarantees without a clear reference to the principal contract. Instructing banks should be alert in this respect.

Drafting and Clauses

Consideration

8-5 English law requires consideration for a contract to be enforceable, unless executed as a deed. Consideration represents the idea of reciprocity, being one of the justifications for the binding force of promises and contractual obligations under English law. Texts of guarantees issued by U.K. banks therefore begin with phrases such as 'In consideration of your (beneficiary) entering into a contract ... (reference to the main contract) we undertake ... '. This technique is occasionally also used in guarantees issued by banks outside the United Kingdom and other common law countries.[11] In counter-guarantees the phrase ' In consideration of your (second issuing bank) issuing the above guarantee we (first instructing bank) undertake ... ' can be found regularly.

8.4 BENEFICIARY. CREDITOR'S BANK AS BENEFICIARY

8-6 The guarantee ordinarily designates the creditor/contracting party of the account party as the beneficiary. This might, however, be different, for example, in the case of payment guarantees relating to lease contracts which are administered by an administration firm or in the case of judicial guarantees,[12] where the creditor's attorney might be named as the one entitled to request payment. In connection with the conveyance of real estate, the guarantee may designate the notary public, instead of the creditor/seller, as the beneficiary in order to ensure proper use of the guarantee to protect the legitimate interests of the account party/buyer.

Where a bank is financing the creditor's trade transactions, it is possible that the bank insists that the guarantee designates the bank as the one who is entitled to call the guarantee, either as the sole benefeciary or in addition to the creditor. This structure is extremely dangerous for the account party since the bank/beneficiary is likely to consider the guarantee as security for the repayment of the credit facilities by the creditor rather than as security for the proper performance by the account party of the underlying contract.[13] Indeed, depending on the way the guarantee has been drafted, the bank/beneficiary might be entitled to demand payment without any reference or relation to the underlying transaction between the account party and the creditor. The practical result of this structure may then be that the issuing bank, for the risk and account of the account party, in fact guarantees repayment of the credit facilities to the bank/beneficiary instead of proper performance by the account party, and that even clear evidence of proper performance by the latter does not prevent the bank/beneficiary from calling the guarantee.

---

[11] Section 5-105 of the Uniform Commercial Code (UCC), which covers both documentary credits and standby letters of credit, expressly dispenses with the requirement of consideration.

[12] See Chapter 3.9.

[13] *BGH, 25 September 1996*, WM 1997, p. 13, provides an example of such increased risk.

8.5 CONDITIONS PRECEDENT

Introduction

8-7 Conditions precedent to the guarantee serve the interests of the account party/ principal debtor. They guard against the risk that the guarantee may become operative, at a time which would otherwise be from the date of issuance, and that the guarantee could therefore be called prior to the fulfilment of certain essential preconditions relating to the underlying relationship.

Performance guarantees

8-8 It is not exceptional for a performance guarantee to have been issued before a definite and final contract has been concluded. This is certainly not unusual when a definite contract has been concluded which itself is subject to conditions precedent. The reason for this is usually that the importer/beneficiary wants to be satisfied that he is dealing with a serious and financially reliable partner. The exporter/account party could also offer to make the guarantee available at this stage, in the hope that this will have a favourable effect on the negotiations.

In these situations it is important for the account party that the guarantee should contain a clause such as 'This guarantee does not become operative unless and until the ... contract has been concluded' or 'unless and until the conditions precedent in the ... contract have been fulfilled'.

Banks may be hesitant to accept such conditions precedent, since it could be difficult for the bank to ascertain whether the conditions precedent have been fulfilled. That may give rise to disagreements with the beneficiary and account party. The most satisfactory solution is to have the fulfilment of the condition precedent evidenced by the submission of certain documents. If the condition precedent is the final execution (= signing) of the underlying contract, that can be shown by either party by presenting a copy of the signed document to the bank. Should the condition precedent in the guarantee relate to the fulfilment of certain conditions precedent in the underlying contract, the most common technique is a statement to this effect from the account party.[14] As far as the beneficiary is concerned, there is indeed the risk that the account party will refuse to release the statement, even though the conditions precedent in the underlying contract have in fact been fulfilled, but in general this risk will be small. Such a refusal

---

[14] Some guarantees have a two-tier system, for example 'This guarantee will become operative upon issue of our (the bank's) amendment making it effective, which will be issued upon receipt by us of a written confirmation from ... (the account party) that ...'.

Drafting and Clauses

would deprive the account party of the benefits of the principal contract, since that contract will not become operative either.[15]

Where under the terms of the principal contract the importer/beneficiary is obligated to make an advance payment or to have a documentary credit or standby letter of credit (payment guarantee) issued, it is advisable for the exporter/account party to make the execution of that obligation a condition precedent to the performance guarantee becoming operative.[16] The ascertainment by the bank that these conditions have been fulfilled does not usually present any particular problems. This is especially the case if the advance payment from the importer is channelled through the same bank, which is sometimes expressly stipulated in the relevant condition precedent,[17] or if the documentary credit or standby letter of credit is to be advised or confirmed by the same bank. In other cases the guarantee should state that the relevant condition precedent is fulfilled if and when the beneficiary presents a copy of the documentary credit or standby letter of credit.

Standby letters of credit (payment guarantees)

8-9 Standby letters of credit or payment guarantees in favour of the exporter may contain conditions precedent similar to those in performance guarantees, such as conditions relating to the final conclusion of the principal contract and the issuance of a performance guarantee in favour of the importer.

Repayment, retention and maintenance guarantees

8-10 Repayment, retention and maintenance guarantees regularly stipulate that they only come into force upon actual receipt of the advance payment, the retention moneys or the last instalment. Sometimes they expressly provide that transfer has to be effected by payment into the accounts of the exporter/account party with the bank/guarantor. This so-called 'by us' (the bank) clause serves the interests of the bank, since such payment increases the credit balance in the account party's current account with the bank. This will then operate as a kind of added collateral security for immediate reimbursement of the bank.

---

[15] See Chapter 6.2, No. 6-8. There is no danger of circuity. Either the statement is released, in which event both guarantee and principal contract become operative, or the statement is not released, in which case neither enters into force.

[16] The dangers of the omission of such a precaution is demonstrated in such cases as *Howe Richardson Scale Co. v. Polimex-Cekop*, [1978] 1 Lloyd's Rep. 161, *Edward Owen Engineering Ltd. v. Barclays Bank Int. Ltd.*, [1978] Q.B. 159 and *KMW International v. Chase Manhattan Bank*, 606 F. 2d 10 (1979).

[17] Cf. No. 8-10.

Explicit inclusion of these conditions precedent seems an obvious and legitimate precaution, but not all repayment, retention and maintenance guarantees do in fact contain them. Their omission is liable to engender unnecessary disputes when the guarantee is called while no transfer has been made, not only between bank and beneficiary but also between bank and account party.[18]

8.6 PERIOD OF VALIDITY

Introduction

8-11 Guarantees should contain provisions regarding the period of validity. The specification is of great importance to all parties concerned. For the bank it marks the period during which it has a contingent liability for which it has to reserve funds. For the beneficiary it marks the period during which he can take advantage of the benefits of the guarantee. For the account party it marks the period during which he is exposed to a financial risk, has to pay bank charges and during which part of his credit facilities, collateral and other resources may be tied up as security for reimbursement to the bank.

The most important provision is the one dealing with the expiry date following which the guarantee can no longer be called and the rights and obligations under the guarantee and with it the attendant liabilities of the bank and account party terminate. It goes without saying that account parties look forward to the expiry date with great anxiety, especially when a first demand guarantee, which can be called so easily, is at stake. While being so crucial for the account party, it must be emphasised from the outset that expiry dates will often not bring the hoped for relief. In many instances the practical significance of an expiry date proves to be severely reduced by a practice known as 'pay or extend'. These aspects will not be examined here, but in Chapter 12.4. Clauses and practices concerning the period of validity of counter-guarantees will be discussed in Chapter 11.3.3, No. 11-27. Moreover, the guarantee may also contain an extension clause, see No. 8-13.

Expiry date – calendar date, expiry event, or a combination

8-12 The inclusion of an expiry date in the guarantee is the rule, the absence thereof being a real exception. There are three basic methods for formulating the expiry date, which can also be found in Art. 22 URDG and Art. 12 UNCITRAL Convention.[19]

---

[18] See Chapter 13.2.6, No. 13-20, and Chapter 14.5.16.

[19] ISP98 does not have a specific provision in this respect, but it clearly allows for all three methods provided that, in the event of an expiry event, it is in a documentary form, see also ISP98 Commentary on Rule 9.01.

Drafting and Clauses

First, the most common technique is the mention of a calendar date. This provides the greatest clarity and certainty for all parties concerned. The expiry date will be attuned to the contractually fixed or projected period for performance of the principal contract or tender period plus an additional period of a number of months, which may vary from three to twelve months depending on the nature of the underlying relationship. Guarantees sometimes state that they are valid 'for X months after issuance'. This variant affords less certainty than does the mention of a calendar date. It could result in unnecessary disagreements as to the precise date of commencement and termination.

Secondly, the expiry of the guarantee can also be expressed in terms of a certain event which is linked to the underlying relationship. For instance, a tender guarantee could state that it is valid until final award of the contract by the beneficiary/employer plus X months. A warranty, maintenance or retention guarantee could refer to the warranty or maintenance period of the principal contract (plus X months). Linkage to completion of the principal contract plus X months can regularly be found in performance guarantees where the performance of the contract will take a considerable length of time and where the final date of completion is difficult to project, as is the case in major construction projects. Linkage to the principal contract also occurs frequently in respect of long-term leases. On account of the absence of a fixed calendar date, this second method is apt to give rise to disagreements between all parties concerned as to whether or not the underlying relationship – and with it the guarantee – has terminated. The obvious solution to these difficulties is to turn the expiry event into a documentary event. Thus, a performance guarantee may provide, for example, that 'it ceases to be in force one month after completion as evidenced by the beneficiary's protocol of (provisional) acceptance', or 'it expires one month after completion as evidenced by a written statement from ... (for example an independent surveyor) to the effect that the equipment has been delivered and installed in accordance with the contract'. Since the bank may not be aware of the release of such documents, it is advisable that the guarantee or counter-guarantee from the account party states that the expiry event clause only becomes operative as far as the bank is concerned if and when the relevant documents have been presented to the bank. It will ordinarily be the account party who submits this kind of document.

A third method, which remedies the possible drawbacks of the two previous ones, consists of a combination of the two. Thus, a performance guarantee may provide that 'it terminates X months after completion of the main contract as evidenced by ..., but not later than, for example, 10 January 1996, whichever is the earlier', *cf.* Art. 22 URDG.

Most guarantees expressly state that calls must be made on or before expiry and that they become null and void or cease to have any effect upon expiry, pursuant to the terms of the guarantee. Such clauses are intended to clearly dispel any notion that the beneficiary could lodge a valid claim under the guarantee after the expiry date if the default of the principal debtor has occurred within the validity period, as may be the case with a traditional suretyship.

Guarantees regularly expressly state that the request for payment must have been 'received by us (the bank)' on or before expiry. The 'received by us' phrase avoids the problem of whether the date of despatch or the date of receipt of the call is to apply as a yardstick, since this question is answered differently by the laws of various countries. It is also advisable that the guarantee states the hour of the day on the expiry date on or before which the demand must have been received. A mere reference to 'banking hours' is inappropriate as it will often be unclear for the beneficiary what these are in the bank's country.[20]

Some guarantees distinguish between, or at least refer to, two dates: the expiry date and the last date for claim, which is, for example, two weeks or three months later.[21] Whatever the underlying motives for such a dual system may be,[22] the second date is the effective date.

Extension clause

8-13 Tender and performance guarantees sometimes accord the beneficiary a contractual right to have the period of validity extended upon his request. These clauses might be accompanied by phrases such as 'should (in your judgment) the principal contract (or tender proceedings) not (yet) have been completed'.

Extension clauses could be useful in situations where the date of adjudicating the tenders or the date of final completion is difficult to project or as an acceptable compromise between the beneficiary's preference for an exceptionally lengthy or unlimited period of validity and the account party's preference for a fixed, short period. Obviously, extension clauses effectively accommodate the interests of the beneficiary. Compared with a guarantee without an expiry date this technique has, however, two advantages for the account party and that bank. First, it forces the beneficiary to make his position clear before the expiry date so that they will know whether or not they have to reckon with possible, future claims. Secondly, if the beneficiary, inadvertently or for some other reason, fails to request a renewal within the current period of validity, the guarantee expires and can no longer be called.

Extension clauses are clearly perilous for the account party, since they entitle the beneficiary to have the guarantee prolonged as many times as it pleases him and for a virtually infinite length of time.[23] It must be borne in mind, however, that in respect of

---

[20] See Chapter 13.2.2, No. 12-22, for the ensuing problems if the expiry provision lacks the specifications mentioned in this paragraph.

[21] This can be found in guarantees issued in, for example, Greece, Indonesia and Bangladesh.

[22] There are some indications that the system originates from the local law on suretyship.

[23] In tender guarantees there are also the special risks of increases in costs and of problems concerning the planning of projected works.

first demand guarantees, the lack of such a clause means the account party is exposed to much the same risk in view of the common practice of 'pay or extend' demands.

In the Middle East, extension clauses are sometimes accompanied by a further clause to the effect that, should the validity period not be prolonged for whatever reason, the bank shall proceed to payment or put the amount at the disposal of the beneficiary.

Guarantees sometimes state that 'they shall automatically be extended for (successive) periods of X months', omitting the phrase 'upon your request'. Formulated this way the clause might possibly be construed as dispensing with the requirement of an explicit request for extension within the validity period, which would in effect convert the guarantee into one for an indefinite length of time. If this is indeed what the parties have intended, it would be desirable to add a phrase to this effect, for instance 'until discharge'. Should this not be the intention of parties, then the phrase 'upon your request' had better be inserted explicitly.

Commencement date

8-14 In the absence of contrary provisions, the period of validity of the guarantee commences upon its issuance. In respect of repayment, performance and payment guarantees this would mean that the beneficiary is in a position to call the guarantee immediately, although according to the terms of the principal contract performance was not yet due. In order to avoid this risk, the guarantee may state that, for example, the guarantee cannot be called prior to X date. Such clauses are also appropriate in guarantees payable upon the beneficiary's demand unless the account party submits documents evidencing, for instance, shipment or completion before a certain date.

Where, in addition to a performance guarantee, maintenance and/or retention guarantees are issued, the insertion of a commencement clause in the latter could be called for in order to avoid them running simultaneously. For example, a maintenance guarantee may stipulate that it enters into force upon release of the performance guarantee.

Return of the guarantee document

8-15 Guarantees often contain provisions dealing with the return of the guarantee document upon its expiry. They can be classified into four main groups:
- guarantees which obligate the beneficiary to return the document upon expiry,
- idem, but with the additional clause that the guarantee becomes null and void upon expiry whether or not the guarantee document is returned,
- guarantees which state that they become null and void upon expiry whether or not the document is returned,
- guarantees which merely state '*please* return the guarantee document upon expiry'.

It is an established rule of law, which is also endorsed in Art. 22 URDG, Rule 9.05 ISP98 and Art. 11(2) UNCITRAL Convention, that the guarantee ceases to have any effect upon the expiry date or expiry event as stated in the guarantee, irrespective of the return of the guarantee document.[24] However, the return of the document is deemed useful for administrative purposes ('closing the file') and in order to clear the balance sheet of contingent liabilities. This could explain the presence of such clauses. Also, the return of the document is generally viewed as the expression of the will of the beneficiary that he renounces his rights under the guarantee and this is no doubt the predominant motive for its insertion. However, it is self-evident that a beneficiary who takes the view that his rights are not terminated or simply retains the document as a means of putting sustained pressure on his contracting partner and who envisages the possibility of a call at some future date is not going to return the guarantee document. However incorrect his view may be and whatever legal or contractual obligations as regards the return may exist, there are no practicable means of making the beneficiary release the document. Such clauses are therefore hardly effective. If inserted, it is advisable to at least put beyond doubt that the non-return of the document is of no significance whatsoever as far as the rights of the beneficiary are concerned. Otherwise such clauses may do more harm than good, as they may convey the suggestion that the non-return in some way or other strengthens the legal position of the beneficiary after expiry.

Guarantees payable upon a court or arbitral decision; absence of expiry date; continuing guarantee

8-16 While on the whole guarantees without an expiry date, which consequently run for an indefinite period of time, are exceptional, there are certain specific situations where the absence of an expiry date is not uncommon or even regular practice.
– Guarantees which only become payable upon submission of a court or arbitral decision are often issued without mention of an expiry date. The preferred technique is, however, that such guarantees provide that the initial call must be made on or before a certain date (e.g. 6 months after the projected date for completion of the underlying contract) or, in the event of a judicial guarantee,[25] that the proceedings must have been initiated on or before a certain date, but that payment will only be made after submission of the decision, which may occur after the initial expiry date. This technique has the advantage that the bank and the account party will know on or before a specified date whether or not they have to reckon with a possible, future claim, while the beneficiary's rights under the guarantee are not impaired by the length of the proceedings. In addition, these guarantees may provide that the definite demand for payment

---

[24] See also Chapter 12.4, No. 12-57.
[25] See Chapter 3.9.

Drafting and Clauses 103

must be made within a certain period after the date of the judicial or arbitral decision.[26]

– Payment guarantees in favour of tax and subsidising authorities, as well as payment guarantees in favour of banks which extend continuing credit facilities to the account party, are regularly issued for an indefinite period of time. In that event, they often contain a clause permitting the bank to cancel the guarantee upon a certain period of notice. Should the account party be unable to arrange for a fresh guarantee, the creditors/beneficiaries will then discontinue the facilities previously granted.

Guarantees which do not contain expiry provisions only cease to have effect upon return of the guarantee document or upon a statement of release.

Apart from the two specific situations mentioned above, first demand guarantees for an indefinite period of time are comparatively rare nowadays, especially in the private sector. While at one time such guarantees were not uncommon, the recognition of the possibilities of 'extend or pay' requests and contractual extension clauses which adequately protect the interests of the beneficiary, has led to their gradual disappearance.

Generally speaking, not only account parties but also banks strongly object to or are not even allowed to issue guarantees without an expiry date, especially if payable upon demand. They pose grave difficulties with respect to balance sheet requirements. For the account party there is the continuing risk of a call. Perhaps worse could be continual threats by the beneficiary to call the guarantee in order to force the account party to yield to all kinds of demands, whether or not related to the principal contract, long after completion. An eternal and pervasive problem is that of sheer uncertainty. Unlike situations of 'extend or pay' demands or guarantees containing extension clauses, there is no incentive for the beneficiary to make his position clear. He can decide simply not to respond to queries from the bank or account party, as indeed happens very often, without forfeiting his power to call the guarantee if and when he chooses. This continuing uncertainty explains why banks are reluctant, even after a considerable lapse of time, to unblock the credit facilities and collateral of the account party, which is most detrimental to his business operations.

In respect of contracts with government agencies, guarantees without an expiry date and which remain in force until discharge are not unusual, both in Europe and especially in the Middle East, as well as in the Indian subcontinent.[27] It must be noted,

---

[26] See also Chapter 4.4, No. 4-15.

[27] Especially in Bangladesh, India, Marocco, Pakistan, Sri Lanka, Turkey (in respect of government agencies that are subject to Act No. 2886, September 9, 1983), Thailand, Tunisia, Bahrain and occasionally in other countries in the Middle East. These guarantees are nearly always issued by a local bank, thus in the form of an indirect guarantee. As the guarantee contains no expiry date, the counter-guarantee in favour of the local issuing bank provides that it remains in force until discharge or until the return of the (counter-)guarantee docu-

however, that guarantees for an indefinite period of time in favour of Western European authorities are found to give rise to fewer problems than do (indirect) guarantees with an expiry date issued in some other regions. This can be explained by the regular practice of 'extend or pay' demands, and by the fact that these guarantees may contain extension clauses. Also, the return of the guarantee document or a statement of release by Western European government beneficiaries upon completion of the contract rarely poses serious problems, in contrast with some countries outside Western Europe.[28] With respect to these countries, Western European exporters and banks are very wary of issuing guarantees without an expiry date or refuse as a firm principle to do so. This stance is, however, usually of little avail, as the guarantees are usually issued indirectly by a local bank. The counter-guarantee, whether or not it contains an expiry date, will then stipulate that it remains in force until the return of the guarantee document or a statement of release.

Art. 12(c) of the UNCITRAL Convention provides that, if the guarantee or standby does not contain a provision for an expiry date or expiry event, it expires 6 years after its issuance.

8.7 AMOUNT, CURRENCY

8-17 Apart from some rare exceptions in respect of payment guarantees in favour of tax and subsidising authorities and banks which extend credit facilities, all guarantees state the maximum amount of the guarantee as well as the currency.

In no circumstances could the beneficiary claim under the guarantee in excess of the maximum amount, even if he could demonstrate that his right to payment or damages and/or interest as measured by the underlying relationship would involve a higher amount.[29] Syrian as well as some Turkish repayment guarantees, however, provide expressly for payment of interest as from the date of the advance payment, tellingly referred to as a loan, on top of the maximum amount. Payment guarantees in favour of a bank which extends credit facilities to the account party may also provide that the

---

ment. Turkish banks issuing those guarantees do sometimes accept counter-guarantees with an expiry date, provided that they permit extension upon simple demand. Guarantees in favour of government agencies in Jordan and Lebanon may contain an expiry date, but with a clause providing for automatic extension upon expiry until discharge. If the latter clause has not been added, these beneficiaries adopt a practice of calling the guarantee immediately upon issue with the request to block the amount until discharge. A variant of such guarantees in favour of government agencies contains an expiry date but also explicitly states that the expiry date merely represents the expected date of completion of the secured transaction.

[28] See also Chapter 12.4.6, No. 12-58 *et seq.*

[29] This has nothing to do with the principle of independence. The rule equally applies to the contract of suretyship.

Drafting and Clauses

maximum amount is to be increased with interest and costs which are due and payable in accordance with the terms of the credit facility.

The maximum amount does not include interest in case of late payment by the bank. Payment is to be effected free of bank charges, stamp duties or any other levies. These are for the account of the bank, or the account party, as the case may be.

The currency of the guarantee does not have to be the same as that of the principal contract. If the amount is expressed in the local currency of the beneficiary's country, the guarantee may permit the beneficiary to claim the equivalent value in another currency.

8.8 REDUCTION AND INCREASE OF THE MAXIMUM AMOUNT

8-18 The guarantee may contain a reduction clause, *cf.* Art. 8 URDG, which envisages the reduction of the maximum amount upon progressive performance of the principal contract, thereby decreasing the contingent liability of bank and account party.

Such clauses are common in repayment (advance payment) guarantees securing proper application of the advance payment by the beneficiary. They nearly always envisage eventual reduction to zero once the account party/exporter has carried out works up to the value of the advance payment, except if the guarantee also operates as a performance guarantee. The guarantee ordinarily specifies the method of implementation, which should take a documentary form. In respect of contracts for the supply of goods this consists of the designation of certain documents to be presented by the exporter. They are often the documents which the exporter has to present in his capacity as beneficiary of a documentary credit. In respect of construction contracts and contracts for the installation of equipment, a reduction may take place upon presentation of the shipping documents or third-party documents attesting to the arrival of the goods or completion of the initial stages of the project.

A reduction of the maximum amount to zero in accordance with the reduction clause does not by itself bring about the expiry of the guarantee. The reduction and the validity period of the guarantee are two different aspects and should not be confused. The terms of the guarantee may, however, link them together. Thus, many repayment guarantees provide that the guarantee expires as soon as the maximum amount of the guarantee has been reduced to zero pursuant to the reduction clause. Such linking mechanisms do, however, require careful drafting.[30]

On the whole, reduction clauses are not very common in performance guarantees.[31] Especially where the maximum amount as a percentage of the contract value is sub-

---

[30] See *Trib. com. Brussels January 10 1992*, RDC 1993 p. 1052 for the consequences of an ill-drafted mechanism.

[31] The recommended forms for repayment (advance payment) guarantees and performance guarantees in the FIDIC Conditions of Contract contain reduction clauses.

stantial, there is no reason why the appropriateness of a reduction should not be seriously considered. In respect of construction contracts, a reduction could take place, for instance, upon the issuance of the taking-over certificate and then upon the performance certificate, leaving a reduced percentage for the maintenance period if that period is also covered by the performance guarantee.

In respect of construction contracts it may also happen that, in the initial phase, the maximum amount of the performance guarantee is relatively low. It will then provide that the maximum amount increases by the amount(s) equal to (a certain percentage of) the sum(s) paid by the beneficiary/employer as the performance of the project progresses. In this way the employer is assured of repayment if defects become apparent at a later stage.

8.9 AMENDMENTS TO THE SECURED CONTRACT

8-19 Guarantees occasionally state explicitly that amendments, alterations and modifications of the secured contract do not exonerate the bank from its obligations under the guarantee.

Such clauses are not really necessary, since this is taken to be a term implied by law.[32] The explanation is that the guarantee is independent of the underlying contract, but also the fact that such alterations do not materially affect the position of the bank. An exception to this term implied by law might possibly be justified where the nature of the underlying contract has been fundamentally altered, resulting in a substantial increase in risk for the bank.

8.10 GRACE PERIOD

8-20 The guarantee may provide for a mechanism which allows for a certain grace period between a formal notice of default by the beneficiary to the account party and payment under the guarantee. As such a grace period is especially relevant for first demand guarantees, it has been examined in Chapter 4.2, No. 4-3.

8.11 TIME OF PAYMENT; INTEREST

8-21 The guarantees may contain a provision to the effect that payment is to be effected within a certain period of time, ranging from three to ten days, after the request

---

[32] *Paris, October 1 1986*, D. 1987 Somm. p.171. Cf. Pabbruwe, rede p. 6, de Vroede /Flamee, TPR 1982, p. 372. It is conceivable that these clauses originate from the general law of accessory guarantees (suretyship) in common law countries where alterations in the principal contract in the absence of approval do exonerate the guarantor (surety).

for payment. This period only commences after the bank has established compliance with the terms and conditions of the guarantee.

If present, such clauses are usually inserted at the beneficiary's request. They can be useful in order to fix the date as from which the bank owes interest in case of late payment and if inserted they should also state the rate of interest or refer to, for example, the statutory interest or Libor/Euribor. Another motive for provisions concerning the time of payment and interest is to discourage attempts by the account party to delay payment by judicial proceedings. A contractual interest clause is particularly important if the account party has obtained a conservatory attachment order (or freezing order) under the bank, which prevents the bank from paying until the order is lifted. Practice shows that this often takes some time. While under the law governing the guarantee the bank may not be liable for statutory interest as long as the order is in force, it does owe the contractually agreed interest as from the agreed date.

A provision for the period for payment could also be inserted at the account party's request if it is intended to serve as a kind of grace period mechanism.[33] In that event the guarantee may provide that payment will not be made until, say, fourteen or thirty days after the demand has lapsed.

8.12 ASSIGNMENT; PLEDGE; TRANSFER

8-22 As a general rule the beneficiary can assign his rights pursuant to the guarantee to a third party, with or without a specific stipulation to this effect. This rule is also endorsed in Art. 4 URDG, Rule 6.06 ISP98 and Art. 10 UNCITRAL Convention. It is expressly noted that assignment of the rights of the guarantee means assignment of the proceeds only,[34] and that the assignee cannot call the guarantee without the cooperation of the beneficiary.[35] This only differs if the guarantee contains explicit provisions to the contrary. Such a stipulation would be extremely dangerous for the account party, since it virtually turns the guarantee into a negotiable instrument and the risk of a call, including a fraudulent call, will increase significantly.

The beneficiary's right to the proceeds of the guarantee upon a valid call is ordinarily also capable of being pledged, but this depends on the law which governs the guarantee. A pledge or a security assignment of this right in favour of the beneficiary's bank often occurs as part of the security provided in connection with the granting of credit facilities.[36] The observations made above also apply to pledges.

---

[33] See Chapter 4.2, No. 4-3.
[34] See further Chapter 12.5.
[35] See Chapter 12.5.3.
[36] See also Chapter 12.5.7.

Unless otherwise stated in the guarantee, the beneficiary is not entitled to transfer the guarantee, in the sense that the transferee is able to call the guarantee in its own right, independent from and without the cooperation of the beneficiary/transferor or in the sense that the transferee is entitled to request the issue of a second guarantee in his favour, see also Art. 4(a) URDG, Rule 6.02(a) ISP98 and Art. 9 UNCITRAL Convention.[37, 38] Accordingly, if the beneficiary wishes to obtain the right to have the guarantee transferred, he must negotiate for such a clause and, if agreed to, it is advisable that the clause sets forth the modalities and restrictions of the transfer. A transfer of the guarantee entails grave risks for the account party and he should, therefore, only agree to it in very specific circumstances.[39]

8.13 SET-OFF

8-23 As yet there exists no clear and established law on the permissibility of set-off by the bank with counterclaims against the beneficiary. Nonetheless, as regards counterclaims unrelated to the principal contract there are more decisions allowing set-off, at least in certain circumstances, than decisions which go decidedly the other way. Art. 18 UNCITRAL Convention permits set-off with the bank's counterclaims, except those claims which have been assigned by the account party, while case law and legal doctrine is divided on the subject.[40] Inclusion of an explicit provision may therefore be considered. In principle, such a provision may either exclude or allow set-off by the bank, but it is likely that any suggestion of a provision permitting set-off will be rejected by the beneficiary.

8.14 NON-RECOURSE OR SUBORDINATION CLAUSE

8-24 If the maximum amount of the guarantee is not sufficient to secure the entire claim of the beneficiary against the principal debtor/account party or if the beneficiary has other claims which are not secured, it is important to include a non-recourse or subordination clause. The effect of such clauses is that the guarantor cannot take any recourse against the account party unless and until all claims of the beneficiary against the principal debtor have been paid in full. This improves the beneficiary's chances of

---

[37] Idem: Art. 333 Commercial Code of Bahrain, Art. 289 Commercial Code of Iraq, Art. 1502 Civil Code of Yemen, Art. 384 Commercial Code of Kuwait.

[38] See also Chapter 12.6.

[39] See Chapter 12.6.

[40] See Chapter 13.2.12.

Drafting and Clauses 109

full recovery. In practice, such a clause is only feasible if the guarantee is issued by a parent company, as financial institutions will usually refuse such a clause.

8.15 JURISDICTION, APPLICABLE LAW

8-25 In respect of guarantees in favour of foreign beneficiaries, most banks routinely include a provision stipulating exclusive jurisdiction in their country and the application of their domestic law. Beneficiaries who feel uneasy with such provisions are likely to insist on guarantees issued by a bank in their country. At any rate, provisions to the contrary are rare.[41]

Indirect guarantees issued by a bank in the beneficiary's country often contain the same provisions too. This is hardly necessary, since both parties are located in the same country. The motive is possibly to draw the attention of the instructing bank and account party to the fact that the primary guarantee will be governed by local law and practice.

---

[41] The Saudi Arabian Monetary Agency (SAMA) permits a number of foreign banks to issue guarantees directly in favour of Saudi Arabian beneficiaries, provided that they use the SAMA models. In these cases the guarantees expressly state that they are governed by Saudi Arabian law.

CHAPTER 9
RELATIONSHIP BETWEEN ACCOUNT PARTY – FIRST INSTRUCTING BANK – SECOND ISSUING BANK. INTRODUCTION AND STRUCTURE

DIRECT GUARANTEE

9-1 The relationship between account party and bank is a contractual one comprising three major aspects. First, there is the instruction of the account party to the bank to issue a guarantee in favour of the beneficiary, with terms and conditions as specified in the instruction. Secondly, if the bank accepts the instruction, it is under a duty to issue the guarantee and to effect payment pursuant to the terms and conditions of the guarantee. Finally, the bank, having paid in the manner just indicated, is entitled to reimbursement by the account party.

Although the bank issues the guarantee upon the request of its customer, it assumes an obligation of its own towards the beneficiary. The bank does not act as the customer's agent and the customer is not privy to the guarantee. However, the bank issues the guarantee at the risk and for the account of the customer. This constitutes the basis for the duty of reimbursement by the bank's customer.

DIRECT GUARANTEE AND ADVISING BANK

9-2 The interposition of an advising bank does not alter the structure of the direct guarantee, nor the relationship between account party and bank. There is no privity of contract between account party and advising bank. However, the advising bank acts as the agent of the bank in the sense that it performs certain duties which are incumbent on the bank/guarantor as issuing bank.[1] Accordingly, delay in the notification of the issuance of the guarantee or errors in the transmission of the text of the guarantee will in principle be attributed to the bank and may render that bank liable to the account party. If the account party has instructed the bank to utilise the services of an advising bank, liability of this nature may have, however, been limited or excluded, as is the case in Art. 14(a) URDG subject to the good faith and reasonable care clause of Art. 15 URDG.

---

1   *Equitable Trust Co. of New York v. Dawson Partners Ltd.*, [1927] 27 Lloyd's Rep., 49; Canaris, No. 1116, Zahn/Ehrlich/Neumann, No. 9/95, 9/99.

In the relationship with the beneficiary the advising bank's function is to check the authenticity of the advised message, *cf.* Rule 2.05(a) ISP98. There is, however, no contractual relationship between the advising bank and the beneficiary.

INDIRECT GUARANTEE

9-3 In the case of indirect guarantees the account party requests the first bank (instructing bank) to instruct the second bank (issuing bank) to issue the (primary) guarantee in favour of the beneficiary upon terms and conditions specified by the account party and forwarded by the instructing bank. It is thus only the second bank that assumes the obligations of a guarantor and it does not act as the agent of the first instructing bank.[2]

The indirect guarantee gives rise to two distinct contracts of mandate, one between the account party and instructing bank, the other between the instructing bank and issuing bank. The latter is of the same nature as the former.[3] As is the case in a direct guarantee, the second issuing bank undertakes the obligations towards the beneficiary in its own name, but does so for the account of the first instructing bank. The duty of reimbursement may be contained and qualified in what is called a counter-guarantee.[4] In its turn the account party is bound to repay the first instructing bank the amount paid by the latter on the basis of its relationship with the second issuing bank.

No contractual relationship exists between the instructing bank and the beneficiary, nor is there privity of contract between the account party and the issuing bank.[5] The instructing bank has a duty to the account party to select the foreign issuing bank with due care,[6] but it may have excluded or limited its liability for errors or negligence by the issuing bank, as is the case in Art. 14(a) URDG but subject to the general duty of care pursuant to Art. 15 URDG. The issuing bank may, however, also owe a general duty of care towards the account party, breach of which constitutes the tort of negligence.[7]

---

[2] Cf. von Westphalen, pp. 225, 229, Canaris, No. 1116, Zahn/Ehrlich/Neumann, No. 9/97, 9/99.

[3] See further Chapter 11.1.1/2.

[4] See Chapter 11.2.

[5] *LG Stuttgart, 8 August 1980*, WM 1981, p. 633, *United Trading Corporation SA v. Allied Arab Ltd.*, [1985] 2 Lloyd's Rep. 554, *Paris, 26 July 1985*, D. 1986 I.R. p. 157 and note Vasseur, *Paris, 14 March 1988*, D. 1989 Somm. p. 152. Von Westphalen, pp. 225, 229, 343, Zahn/Ehrlich/Neumann, No. 9/99, Canaris, No. 1119a, Schlegelberger/Hefermehl, No. 291, Dohm, No. 260, Bark, ZIP 1982, p. 408, Prüm, p. 140.

[6] Zahn/Ehrlich/Neumann, No. 9/99, Canaris, No. 1116.

[7] Cf. *United Trading v. Allied Arab Bank*, [1985] 2 Lloyd's Rep. 554, 560, Canaris, No. 1119a, Mülbert, p. 142. In *Paris, 26 February 1985*, D. 1985 I.R. p. 244, the second issuing bank was ordered to pay damages to the account party on the grounds that it had failed to transfer

THE AMERICAN STANDBY LETTER OF CREDIT AS COUNTER-GUARANTEE

9-4 It has been pointed out in Chapter 2.3, No. 2-7, that indirect guarantees issued on behalf of American companies are sometimes structured differently in that the request to the foreign bank for the issuance of the guarantee originates directly from the American exporter. Consequently, there exists a direct contractual tie between account party and foreign issuing bank and it is under a duty to reimburse the issuing bank directly. The foreign bank will, however, only be prepared to issue the guarantee on condition that an American bank gives assurances as to reimbursement. This is accomplished by the issuance of a standby letter of credit (= counter-guarantee). The relationship between the American (first) bank and the foreign bank is, therefore, founded solely on the standby letter delivered by the American bank at the request of the exporter, there being no mandate relationship. The standby letter typically provides for repayment on demand in the event that the foreign bank has effected payment to the beneficiary under its primary guarantee. Accordingly, these standby letters of credit are not designed to secure the foreign issuing bank's right to reimbursement from the American exporter, but they confer a right of direct recourse against the American bank. Thus, while the structure is different in form, this technique functions in substance in the same way as the indirect guarantee supported by a counter-guarantee from the instructing bank.

This technique is, however, not confined to American practice. It may occur anywhere anytime a bank is approached by someone with whom it does not have a standing relationship or on whose creditworthiness it does not wish to rely.[8] Outside the U.S.A. the counter-security is then ordinarily referred to as a counter-guarantee, rather than a standby letter of credit.[9]

---

the advance payments, remitted by the beneficiary, to the accounts of the account party. Instead, it had transferred the down payments to the main contractor, which had gone bankrupt. In *Paris, 3 April 2002*, D.Affaires 2002, p. 1750, the second issuing bank was ordered to pay damages to the account party because it had paid under the primary guarantee while it was aware of the beneficiary's fraud. However, in *GKN Contractors v. Lloyds Bank*, [1985] 30 BLR 48, and especially in *Csarnikow-Rionda v. Standard Bank london*, [1999] 2 Lloyd's Rep. 187, it was doubted whether the account party has a cause of action against the issuing bank in the case of an indirect guarantee.

[8] A good example involving two tiers of counter-security is provided in *BGH, 24 November 1983*, WM 1984, p. 44.

[9] In banking practice the term 'standby letter of credit' meaning counter-guarantee is not only used in connection with guarantees, but also in connection with other credit facilities.

RELATIONSHIP BETWEEN ACCOUNT PARTY – FIRST INSTRUCTING BANK – SECOND ISSUING BANK AND THE GUARANTEE. INDEPENDENCE FROM MANDATE

9-5 Although the bank issues the guarantee for the purpose of implementing the instructions of the account party, or, as is the case in indirect guarantees, those of the first instructing bank, that motive does not affect the bank's relationship with the beneficiary. The guarantee between issuing bank and beneficiary is independent of the mandate relationship with the account party or first instructing bank.[10] As a result, circumstances such as avoidance, repudiation or rescission of the mandate, liquidation or insolvency of the account party or prior notice of refusal to repay the bank, currency exchange restrictions, etc. have no bearing on the obligations of the issuing bank pursuant to the terms of the guarantee. This principle of independence equally applies in respect of the two contracts of mandate in the case of indirect guarantees. From the above it will be apparent that the notion of independence as discussed here has a different meaning to the notion of independence of the guarantee in relation to the the underlying relationship between account party/principal debtor and beneficiary/creditor.

---

[10] *Paris, 22 September 1987*, D 1988 Somm. p. 248 (with respect to a counter-guarantee), *Trib. com. La Roche-sur-Yon, 14 September 1981*, D. 1982 I.R., p. 199. Mijnssen, p. 41, von Westphalen, p. 179, Canaris, No. 1136, Vasseur, No. 21, Gavalda/Stoufflet, RTDC 1980, p. 12, Wymeersch, TPR 1986, pp. 489, 491.

CHAPTER 10
RELATIONSHIP ACCOUNT PARTY – BANK. DIRECT GUARANTEE

10.1 INTRODUCTION

10-1 In general the relationship between the account party and his bank is governed by the same rules whether the guarantee is issued directly by this bank or indirectly by a second bank in the beneficiary's country. The fact that the guarantee is issued by a foreign second bank does, however, have certain consequences, particularly for the account party. These consequences will be examined in Chapter 11.

Chapter 10 contains an exposition of the rules of law as they exist, or are deemed to exist, in the absence of specific contractual provisions. Naturally, if the parties do not wish to adhere to the rules of general law, they can be modified, altered or excluded by specific and explicit stipulations. The relationship may also be subject to the general and/or specific standard terms and conditions of the bank, which are ordinarily contained in a counter-guarantee granted by the account party.[1]

The account party and bank are ordinarily located in the same country and accordingly their relationship is purely domestic. The need for transnational adjustment of legal rules will therefore be less pressing. Divergencies in legal systems and principles or in particular branches of law can to a large extent be accounted for on historical grounds. If, however, one recognises that the relationship between account party and bank forms an integral part of a wider guarantee transaction, which is a relatively recent phenomenon and evolved from international trade independent of national law, there appears to be no reason why these rules should not be substantially alike or why they should not develop along common patterns. Indeed, case law in the various jurisdictions shows that the rules pertaining to the account party – bank relationship are marked by a significant degree of uniformity.

---

[1] See further Chapter 10.3.

10.2 LEGAL NATURE

Mandate

10-2 In the Netherlands[2] and the Germanic legal family[3] the relationship between the account party and bank has been labelled as one of mandate (*lastgeving, Geschäftsbesorgungsvertrag gerichtet auf Werkleistung*, and *Mandat*). English law also classifies the relationship as a mandate.[4] Some Belgian authors have rejected the subsumption under mandate and the rendering of services, albeit for technical reasons.[5] Instead, the relationship has occasionally been dubbed a 'contract to extend credit', which is not particularly helpful. It is neither regulated by statute, nor does it have a fixed meaning with distinct legal consequences. In France the relationship has been classified either as one of mandate[6] or as a contract 'to extend credit' or 'to render a service'.[7]

Because of the general nature of the statutory provisions of mandate and the fact that a mandate may relate to a wide range of very dissimilar contracts, it is doubtful whether safe and clear guidance can be gleaned from this subsumption in relation to specific issues which may arise in the context of independent guarantees. In any event, one should be cautious when considering applying particular rules of mandate which have been developed in other contexts. Perhaps it would be more expedient to recognise that the relationship between account party and bank in the context of a wider guarantee transaction is governed by its own, distinct rules. To accord it any other

---

[2] Mijnssen, p. 31, Bannier, in Hague-Zagreb Essays 6, p. 72-73, Grootenhuis, AA 1986, p. 414, Bertrams, in International Contracts, p. 135.

[3] *OLG Frankfurt a/M, 27 April 1987*, WM 1988, p. 1480, *OLG Köln, 15 March 1991*, RIW 1992, p. 145, Von Westphalen, p. 335, Zahn/Ehrlich/Neumann, 9/73, Canaris, No. 1106 et seq., Schlegelberger/Hefermehl, No. 282, Mülbert, p. 95, Dohm, No. 120, Kleiner, No. 19.01, von Mettenheim, RIW 1981, p. 585.

[4] Goode, p. 18.

[5] Van Lier, JT 1980, No. 4.2., p. 355, Velu, Tours, p. 236, Wymeersch, TPR 1986, p. 480-483. The assumption is that a mandate is confined to the mandatory performing legal acts in the name of the mandator, while the bank concludes the contract of guarantee in its own name, and that the rendering of services relates to tangible services. The correctness of these objections has been questioned by Poullet, who favours a classification as mandate, DPCI 1979, p. 390 note 11, Tours, p. 22, thesis, Nos. 344, 345.

[6] *Trib. com. Paris, 8 July 1983*, D. 1984 I.R. p. 92, Villerey, Tours, p. 270, Poullet, cited in the previous note.

[7] Mattout, No. 215, Prüm, p. 12-14, Stoufflet, Garantie Bancaire Internationale, No. 27, Gavalda/Stoufflet, RTDC 1980, p. 21, Vasseur, Nos. 52, 53, D. 1986 I.R. p. 166.

Relationship Account Party – Bank

name might well be both meaningless and perilous.[8] It is noted that in the Netherlands, France and Belgium, no practical significance or consequences are attached to the various subsumptions of the relationship between account party and bank under the above-mentioned statutory categories, but the German attitude in this respect appears to be different.

Account party – bank and documentary credit

10-3 There is yet another reason why comparisons and subsumptions under traditional categories could perhaps be dispensed with. A great deal of the law neatly tailored to the relationship between customer and bank is already available, namely the law developed in the context of documentary credit. Both the nature and structure of the documentary credit as a multi-party relationship and the nature and structure of the relationship between account party and bank are the same as those in guarantees. Of course, this likeness should not lead to a mechanical transposition of each and every rule of documentary credits. There will be occasions when the relationship between customer and bank in the context of an independent guarantee requires its own solutions. Apart from this, many of the issues and problems differ.

Main features: instructions, duty of examination, reimbursement, duty of care

10-4 A characteristic feature of the relationship between customer and bank is that the bank enters into the contract of guarantee for the risk and account of the customer. It necessarily follows that the bank is entitled to reimbursement upon payment to the beneficiary, or, in the case of an indirect guarantee, upon payment to the foreign issuing bank.[9]

The right to repayment exists, however, on the assumption that the bank has properly carried out the instructions of the account party. The bank must have issued the guarantee in a manner and with terms and conditions as instructed (or at least agreed to) by the customer and it must have examined whether those terms and conditions of payment have been fulfilled.[10] Failure to discharge these obligations bars, in general,

---

[8] Cf. De Vroede/Flamee, TPR 1982, p. 374, 375.

[9] In this context German and Austrian writers refer to Sec. 670 BGB and Sec. 402(1) OR. These provisions relate, however, to incidental costs which the mandatory may or may not incur and which he deems justified and expedient for a correct execution of the instructions. Payment under a guarantee cannot be viewed as an incidental cost. It is a major, preconsidered object of the instructions. When the bank effects payment, it is not because the bank believes this to be appropriate, but because it is under a legal obligation to do so.

[10] See further Chapters 10.7 and 10.8.

the claim for reimbursement.[11] The same principles apply in the event of an indirect guarantee. This situation is, however, compounded by the fact that the instructing bank's duty to reimburse the foreign issuing bank is ordinarily determined by its counter-guarantee in favour of the issuing bank, which also impacts on the duty of reimbursement by the account party to its bank.[12]

In addition to the bank's principal obligations to adhere to the instructions of the account party when issuing the guarantee and to ascertain compliance with the terms and conditions of the guarantee, the bank owes a general duty of care. Depending on the particular circumstances of the situation and the legitimate interests of the account party this duty may oblige the bank to act or not to act in a particular way. The scope of this duty can never, however, be such that discharge thereof would result in the bank breaching its obligations to the beneficiary.

Although the account party has the power to withdraw the mandate, revocation does not prejudice the bank's right of repayment once the guarantee has been issued.[13] This is the consequence of the customer's own instruction to the bank to assume an irrevocable undertaking to the beneficiary in its own name, but for the risk and account of the account party.

10.3 COUNTER-GUARANTEE

Counter-guarantee by the account party

10-5 The bank usually requires the account party to issue a counter-guarantee in favour of the bank. Its purpose is, on the one hand, to explicitly confirm in writing the rights

---

[11] See, for example, *OLG Hamburg, 4 November 1977*, RIW 1978, p. 615, *Paris, 26 February 1985*, D. 1985 I.R. p. 244 (foreign issuing bank liable to account party, see Chapter 9, No. 9-3), *Cass., 26 January 1993*, D. 1995 Somm. p. 13 (the Cour du Cassation rejected the allegation of the bank, which had honoured a demand for payment made after the expiry date, that the account party had not objected to the payment and had agreed to an extension of his counter-guarantee in favour of the bank). See also the case law cited throughout Chapter 13; Von Westphalen, p. 174, Dohm, Nos. 120, 144, 153, 189-216, Mijnssen, p. 31, 43, Gavalda/Stoufflet, RTDC 1980, p. 21, Wymeersch, TPR 1986, p. 479.

[12] See Chapter 11.2.2.

[13] Mijnssen, p. 34. Sec. 671(1) BGB granting the mandator a right to revoke the mandate does not apply to *Geschäftsbesorgung*. On the other hand Canaris, No. 1113, and Schlegelberger/Hefermehl, No. 290, are of the opinion that the bank is entitled ex Sec. 775 BGB to repudiate the mandate in the case of imminent insolvency of the account party. See also von Westphalen, p. 370. One may query what purpose such repudiation may serve once the guarantee has been issued.

and obligations as they exist on the basis of the general rules of mandate and, on the other hand, to qualify those rules, for example by modification, enlargement, derogation, exclusion and by inserting provisions which are specifically attuned to the customer-bank relationship in the context of independent guarantees. The key provisions relate to the instructions by the account party, the manner in which they will be carried out by the bank, reimbursement to the bank and the provision of security by the account party, bank charges and reimbursement of costs, and certain exclusions of liability on the part of the bank. If the account party's business regularly requires the issue of guarantees, it will be expedient to conclude a master counter-guarantee which applies to each specific instance.

Counter-guarantees are nearly always based on the bank's standard terms and conditions and they tend to strengthen the position of the bank at the expense of the account party. However, under national statutory law certain standard terms and conditions are (in certain circumstances) prohibited or cannot be relied upon, while others are subject to judicial review on the basis of good faith and reasonableness in the light of the circumstances of the case. Pursuant to national law they may also be construed restrictively and against the bank.

As has been observed in Chapter 10.2, no. 10-4 and especially in Chapter 7, no. 7-2, the account party's obligation to reimburse the bank regardless of disputes or defences which he may have against the beneficiary and regardless of actual default, is the immediate and automatic consequence of his instruction to the bank to issue an independent guarantee, followed by payment by the bank after verification of compliance with the conditions of payment. Although it does not add anything to the already existing duty of repayment, it is useful to restate explicitly the extent of this obligation in the counter-guarantee. This is especially true in the event of a first demand guarantee, because such an explicit clause is designed to bring home clearly to the account party that the bank is not concerned with the propriety of the beneficiary's demand for payment and the risks to which he is exposed.[14]

The account party's obligation to reimburse the bank is usually stated in broad terms, for example 'the customer undertakes to indemnify the bank for all consequences which may arise as a result of the issue of the guarantee'.[15] Sometimes the duty of reimburse-

---

[14] Cf. *Brussels, 18 December 1981,* Rev. Banque 1982, p. 99.

[15] The effect of such a clause is well illustrated in *Gulf Bank v. Mitsubishi Heavy Industries,* [1994] 2 Lloyd's Rep. 145. The bank had issued a repayment guarantee in favour of the Kuwaiti Ministry in connection with a contract for the construction of plant and equipment by the account party. Following the Iraqi invasion in 1990, the government of Kuwait declared all public work contracts with the government void and terminated. The account party then alleged that the guarantee was also void and terminated and that his counter-guarantee, therefore, also ceased to be in full force and effect. This was, of course, challenged by the bank which sought a declaration that the counter-guarantee continued to be valid. This

ment is formulated in a rather sweeping fashion, for example, 'the customer hereby undertakes to repay the amount which the bank *in its sole discretion considered* owing to the beneficiary'. It is submitted that such phrases should not be understood as conferring a right to full repayment to the bank where it has breached its obligation to adhere to the instructions and to carefully ascertain compliance with the conditions of payment. A construction to the contrary would be wholly incompatible with these fundamental principles governing their relationship and these standard clauses cannot be assumed to have the effect of obliterating these principles.

Counter-guarantees sometimes state that the account party must repay the bank 'upon first demand'. This phrase does not, however, absolve the bank from its duty of examination for compliance with the conditions of payment.[16] Moreover, it has never been suggested that the phrase 'payment upon first demand' in the account party-bank relationship means that, if there is a genuine dispute regarding the bank's discharge of its duty of examination, the account party has agreed to first reimburse the bank and that he may thereafter try to recover the amount paid if he establishes that the bank was in breach of this duty.[17, 18]

There may, however, be situations where it would stand to reason that the obligation of repayment pursuant to the counter-guarantee is defined in broader terms than in the guarantee itself. This could be the case where the bank is prepared to issue a guarantee containing conditions of payment, compliance with which is difficult to ascertain, such as non-documentary conditions. While, as will be observed in Chapter 10.8, no. 10-26,

---

application was granted on the grounds that the terms of the counter-guarantee were sufficiently broad to cover a situation whereby the beneficiary makes a demand for payment in accordance with the terms of the guarantee, even if that guarantee might be unenforceable. It is noted that the counter-guarantee also stated that the account party's obligation was not affected by any total or partial invalidity of the guarantee. It is submitted that the account party should also have to indemnify the bank in the absence of such a clause, since because of the principle of independence one cannot expect the bank to investigate whether under the applicable law the nullity of the underlying contract also renders the guarantee unenforceable.

[16] *BGH, 19 September 1985*, NJW 1986, p. 310, *OLG Hamburg, 4 November 1977*, RIW 1978, p 615, *LG Stuttgart, 8 August 1980*, WM 1981, p. 633, von Westphalen, pp. 212-214, 364, Mülbert, p. 95 Zahn/Ehrlich/Neumann, 9/83-84, Canaris, No. 1108.

[17] However, this 'pay first, argue later' effect may still occur as a result of the fact that the bank is usually in a position to debit the accounts of the customer immediately. The latter may then seek to have the balance on his account restored through interlocutory proceedings until the dispute has been resolved.

[18] See Chapter 11.2.2, and especially No. 11-13, for counter-guarantees payable 'upon first demand' issued by the instructing bank in favour of the foreign issuing bank in the case of an indirect guarantee.

the bank already enjoys protection against the inherent risks thereof by force of law, it would be understandable if this safeguard were made explicit and perhaps enlarged by excluding liability altogether. It would appear, however, that such a stipulation does not entitle the bank to ignore completely such a condition of payment, but only expands the extent of the discretionary powers of the bank in its relationship with the customer.

Another clause which sometimes appears in counter-guarantees states that the account party renounces the right to contest the propriety of payments made by the bank. This clause does not, however, prevent the account party from commencing proceedings aimed at the procurement of stop-payment orders against the bank in appropriate cases, such as fraud or non-compliance with the terms and conditions of the guarantee.[19]

Along with the counter-guarantee, the bank may remit to the customer for his final accord the text of the guarantee, or, in the case of an indirect guarantee, the text of the instructions to the second issuing bank which usually also comprises the counter-guarantee in favour of that bank. However, due to time pressure this often takes place only after the issuance of the guarantee or the forwarding of the instructions to the foreign bank.

The implications of counter-guarantees by the account party on the basis of standard terms and conditions will not be examined in this study, as they vary from country to country and in most countries from bank to bank.

Instructions and counter-guarantee by a party other than the principal debtor; affiliated company

10-6 It may happen that the instructions for the issue of a guarantee and the counter-guarantee in favour of the bank do not originate from the principal debtor in the underlying transaction, but, for example, from its parent or affiliated company only, acting upon the request of the principal debtor.[20] Because of the absence of a contractual relationship it is obvious that the bank has no contractual right of recourse against the principal debtor. It is not certain, however, whether the bank might not have a right of recourse on the basis of (statutory) general law. Since this structure is often selected at the bank's insistence or, if not, because the bank has at least knowingly agreed to the absence of a counter-guarantee from the principal debtor, it could be argued that the bank must be presumed to have waived a right of recourse against the principal debtor

---

[19] The clause features among the standard provisions in French counter-guarantees. The proposition is affirmed by implication in the consistent trend of French case law dealing with such clauses. See in particular *Paris, 14 December 1987*, D. 1988 Somm. p. 248.

[20] See Chapter 2.3, No. 2-9 diagram 7.

which it might otherwise have had pursuant to (statutory) general law.[21] If this general presumption is correct, but the bank wishes otherwise, it should insist on the principal debtor co-signing the counter-guarantee.

10.4 SECURITY FOR REIMBURSEMENT

Security

10-7 Unless so stipulated, the bank is not entitled to advance payment from the account party by way of security.[22] From the latter's point of view, advance payment or cash collateral for the entire amount would defeat one of the objects of a guarantee, i.e. to dispense with the need for a cash deposit with the beneficiary. The bank cannot demand security unless this is stipulated. The general terms and conditions of the bank or the counter-guarantee usually contain provisions to this effect. The fact that the bank's right to reimbursement is only a contingent one, namely conditional upon a valid call on the guarantee and subsequent payment, is immaterial.[23]

In the case of a general facility for the issuance of guarantees, the credit balance on that facility will be debited by the maximum amount of the guarantee, but such debiting should not be regarded as actual payment by the account party or as the provision of security.

Release and prolongation

10-8 The issue concerning the point in time when the bank is to release the security is very much tied up with the validity period of the guarantee and counter-guarantee in the case of indirect guarantees. As a general rule, the security is to be released if no demand for payment has been made on or before the expiry date of the guarantee or counter-guarantee. This matter is discussed in Chapter 12.4.7 in more detail. In addition, the security should be released if for any other reason the guarantee or counter-guarantee can no longer be validly called.[24]

---

[21] See for subrogation Chapter 10.11.
[22] Cf. Von Westphalen, p. 368, Schlegelberger/Hefermehl, No. 290, Canaris, No. 1113.
[23] Cf. Von Westphalen, p 369.
[24] See. e.g., *Shanning and Others v. Rasheed Bank*, [2001] All ER (D) 321 (Jun), see further Chapter 13.4, No. 13-42.

10.5 COMMISSION

10-9 The account party owes the bank commission in return for its services and credit risk and for reserving or capitalising liquid assets in the event of payment. The commission amounts to a certain percentage of the maximum amount of the guarantee and is owing from the time of issuance of the guarantee, irrespective of any possible conditions precedent.[25] The obligation to pay bank charges ordinarily terminates upon the expiry date of the guarantee, which is the initial date mentioned in the guarantee, or a later date pursuant to 'pay or extend' requests. In the case of an indirect guarantee, specific provisions in the counter-guarantee in favour of a foreign issuing bank may, however, cause certain difficulties. These aspects are also examined in Chapter 12.4.7.

10.6 INCIDENTAL EXPENSES, LITIGATION AND COSTS

Incidental expenses

10-10 In the course of carrying out the contract of guarantee the bank may incur incidental expenses on several accounts. The ultimate allocation of these costs between bank and customer is examined in this subchapter.

Pursuant to their general terms and conditions or the counter-guarantee, banks are ordinarily entitled to charge the customer for incidental costs such as telephone, postal, telex, telefax and similar expenses.[26] This is, however, never done to the full extent. Banks will either charge a certain amount for such incidental costs on the basis of a flat rate or charge for telex and telefax costs only when they involve considerable amounts or they may employ a combination of these two possibilities.

If the (counter-) guarantee provides for payment in foreign currency, the bank is entitled to make the usual charges. Should there be any state regulations imposing levies on currency transfers abroad or stamp duties, these costs can be passed on too.

Litigation and costs. Risks

10-11 Parties to the guarantee may take different views regarding the right of payment under the guarantee and litigation cannot always be avoided. In that event, the question of whether the bank or the customer is the proper party to pursue the litigation arises. Should the bank be the proper party or be implicated in the proceedings, the further

---

[25] Cf. Von Westphalen, p. 374, Zahn/Ehrlich/Neumann, 9/88.

[26] Von Westphalen, p. 386, Zahn/Ehrlich/Neumann, 9/91, Dohm, No. 153 and Gavalda/Stoufflet, RTDC 1980, p. 21, invoke the statutory provisions of mandate.

question arises as to whether the bank or the customer is ultimately to bear the costs of litigation, which often involves considerable amounts of money. It is submitted that both questions should be resolved on the basis of the proper allocation of the risk in respect of litigation and the interests which are advanced by pursuing legal proceedings. It is therefore necessary to examine the particular object of litigation.

If the bank considers that the terms and conditions of the guarantee or, in the case of an indirect guarantee, the terms of the counter-guarantee, have not been complied with and accordingly refuses to pay, while the beneficiary or foreign issuing bank takes a contrary view, the costs of the ensuing litigation remain with the bank. Examination with respect to compliance is a principal task and responsibility of the bank and the refusal to pay in the event of non-compliance figures among its key duties. Litigation concerning compliance should therefore, as a general rule, be regarded as a risk incidental to the bank's own responsibilities. By contesting the position taken by the beneficiary or issuing bank the (instructing) bank is also seeking to protect its own interests. For, if the bank were to concede too readily to the demands for payment and if upon a challenge by the customer the terms and conditions are indeed found not to have been met, the bank will have forfeited its right to repayment. The counter-guarantee may, however, allow the bank to pass these costs on to the customer, the argument being that such costs are incurred as a result of the customer's instruction to issue a guarantee for the customer's risk and account and that such extraordinary costs have not been taken account of in the general rate for commission.

A different situation arises where the bank resists the demand for payment because of non-compliance with the terms of the (counter-) guarantee, but where the beneficiary or issuing bank is able to procure payment by seizing the assets of the bank in a jurisdiction where this proves to be possible, whether or not on the basis of a foreign court decree. Here, the bank has discharged its duties. The incidence of forced payment in these circumstances is a risk which is allocated to the customer and he is under a duty to indemnify the bank.[27] If legal proceedings aimed at preventing forced payment or at retrieving payment already procured are contemplated, the bank appears to be the proper party to conduct the litigation. The costs of litigation must, however, be borne by the customer, because the proceedings serve his interests only. Since he has to account for the costs, the decision whether or not to commence proceedings lies with the customer.

A third situation which may give rise to litigation occurs when, in the case of an indirect guarantee, the account party's (instructing) bank is obliged to repay the foreign issuing bank on the strength of its counter-guarantee, while the account party is of the opinion that the issuing bank has failed to discharge its duty of examination. Banks which utilise the services of another bank, i.e. the foreign issuing bank, for the purpose

---

[27] See Chapter 10.10.

of giving effect to the account party's instructions do so for the account and at the risk of that account party, cf. art. 14(a) URDG. Accordingly, if the instructing bank conducts the litigation in order to recover the amounts paid, it is entitled to reimbursement of the costs thereof.

A fourth area of litigation concerns the issue of (allegedly) fraudulent demands for payment. The bank may become implicated in fraud proceedings in two ways. In concert with the account party, the (instructing) bank may refuse payment and then be sued by the beneficiary or foreign issuing bank. Secondly, the customer may attempt to prevent payment by initiating proceedings, which are often directed against the bank, either as sole defendant or as co-defendant. The incidence of fraud falls in principle outside the ambit of the responsibilities of the bank. Fraud and its consequences are a typical risk allocated to the customer, since he is responsible for the selection of the beneficiary and the guarantee format. Preventing payment in the event of (alleged) fraud is therefore a matter of concern to the customer and he, not the bank, is the proper party to litigate the issue. Accordingly, in fraud cases attention should first be directed to measures to be taken by the customer which reduce the involvement of the bank as much as possible, thereby minimising the bank's expenditures at the same time. These measures will be examined elsewhere.[28] It suffices to say here that the costs of litigation concerning allegations of fraud which the bank may nevertheless incur are for the account of the customer. For this reason the bank should not decide of its own accord to proceed to litigation.

In general, banks are reluctant to commence legal proceedings against foreign correspondent banks for fear of damaging their international standing and of straining their business relationship. The argument is a valid one, but it is not always conclusive. There is no reason why the bank's interest should necessarily prevail over the interests of its customer, particularly in the event of non-compliance or improper conduct by the foreign bank. At any rate, there is nothing unusual about litigation between banks, as numerous guarantee, and especially documentary credit, cases show.

As a result of certain conduct by the account party, the bank may suffer a loss in yet another way, which is illustrated in two French cases. In the first case, the bank was persuaded by its customer to resist the demand for payment, although the terms and conditions had been complied with. Upon a suit brought by the beneficiary, the bank was ordered to pay damages in the amount of €15,000 in addition to the principal sum and interest, on the grounds that the reasons advanced for the refusal were devoid of any substance and plainly dilatory.[29] In the second case, the account party secured a conservatory attachment (freezing) order which prevented the bank from effecting pay-

---

[28] See Chapter 15, No. 15-4, and Chapter 16.

[29] *Paris, 29 January 1981*, D. 1981 J. p. 336, upheld by *Cass., 20 December 1982*, D. 1983, J. p. 365.

ment. After the lifting of the order, the bank did indeed proceed to payment, but meanwhile a delay of ten months had occurred. The court declared both bank and account party jointly and severally liable for damages.[30] In both cases the loss to the bank had been occasioned by the customer's conduct in furtherance of its own interests. It would therefore appear correct if in these and similar cases the customer were to be accountable for these losses.

It may, however, also happen that the bank attempts to resist or to delay payment on its own initiative and for its own purposes, for example if it fears that the account party will default on its obligation to effect prompt repayment because of insolvency. In these situations the costs of litigation and other possible losses cannot be passed on to the customer.

10.7 INSTRUCTIONS BY THE ACCOUNT PARTY. ADHERENCE TO THE INSTRUCTIONS. REVIEW AND ACCEPTANCE BY THE BANK

The principle of strict compliance, direct guarantees

10-12 As with documentary credits, it is an essential feature of their relationship that the bank must strictly adhere to the instructions of the account party as regards the type and contents of the guarantee.[31] The ambit of the principle of strict adherence is confined, however, to instructions in so far as they contain clear and specific particulars. Where the instructions of the account party are couched in general or perhaps vague terms, other principles apply, see no. 10-15. Obviously, the principle does not apply if the bank declines to accept the instructions.

The rule of strict adherence derives on the one hand from the fact that the determination of the terms and conditions of the guarantee is mainly the concern of account party and beneficiary and on the other hand from the fact that the bank issues the guarantee for the risk and account of its client. Accordingly, if the account party specifies the conditions of payment, e.g. payment upon first demand accompanied by a particular statement of default by the beneficiary or payment upon submission of certain documents drawn up by a particular agency, or if he specifies a number of protective clauses, e.g. the issuance of a documentary credit in his favour as a condition precedent or a reduction clause, or indicates a specific expiry date, maximum amount and

---

[30] *Trib. com. Paris, 15 February 1984*, D. 1984 I.R. p. 205, reversed by *Paris, 26 July 1985*, D. 1986 I.R. p. 157 in respect of the award against the bank. For cases, see Chapter 13.2.10, No. 13-30.

[31] *OLG Stuttgart, 25 January 1979*, RIW 1980, p. 729; Mijnssen, p. 31, Zahn/Ehrlich/Neumann, 9/76, Canaris, No. 1107, von Westphalen, p. 336, and Dohm, No. 127. See also *BGH, 10 February 2000*, WM 2000, p. 715, examined in No. 10-17.

currency, the bank should draft the guarantee precisely according to these instructions. No deviation from such instructions can be admitted on the pretext that they are insignificant, immaterial or unusual.

The bank will often find itself in the situation where it honestly believes that altering, adding or leaving out some of the prescribed terms would serve the interests of the account party. The bank may be aware of the fact that the terms indicated by the account party are unusual in international trade or likely to be rejected by the beneficiary. It may be convinced that certain terms do not serve any useful purpose or are even detrimental. Nonetheless, the bank will not be excused for substituting its own judgment for that of its customer without the latter's approval.[32] What is and what is not in his interest is to be adjudged by the account party only, primarily as a matter of principle but also as a matter of practical expedience, since in any given case the bank's judgment may prove erroneous.

If the instructions call for a direct guarantee, the bank must issue the guarantee itself.[33] In no circumstances is the bank permitted to seek the intermediation of a second bank in the beneficiary's country requesting that bank to issue the guarantee. As regards this particular instruction, any relaxation of the principle of strict adherence is totally out of the question, because the issuance of an indirect guarantee increases the risk to the customer considerably. Regulations in several countries prescribe that government beneficiaries established in those countries accept only (indirect) guarantees issued by their local banks. A knowledgeable bank will be aware of these regulations, but once again, it should resist the temptation to attempt to further the presumed interests of its client on its own initiative. In such situations, the only proper procedure for the bank is to consult its client and to obtain his approval.

The principle of strict adherence applies with equal force when the beneficiary refuses to accept the guarantee as presented to him. The beneficiary may have plausible reasons or he may even be entirely within his rights to reject the proposed text, for example because the terms and conditions do not accord with the terms agreed with the account party. Nonetheless, the bank continues to be bound by the instructions and whatever the account party and beneficiary may have agreed upon between themselves, or whatever position the beneficiary may take, is of no concern to the bank. Accordingly, the bank may not agree to modifications, whether or not the beneficiary is persistent or presents those changes as non-negotiable, without first obtaining the consent of the

---

[32] Von Westphalen, Zahn/Ehrlich/Neumann, Canaris and Dohm, cited in the previous footnote, reject the applicability of Sec. 665 BGB, c.q. Sec. 397 OR. These statutory provisions allow the mandatory to depart from the instructions if this should be in the interest of the mandator.

[33] Canaris, No. 1115. See also Zahn/Ehrlich/Neumann, 9/76, and von Westphalen, p. 345. See No. 10-15 for the question of whether the bank is allowed to arrange an indirect guarantee in the absence of explicit instructions.

account party. It is true that the contents of the guarantee are often dictated by the beneficiary on a 'take it or leave it' basis, but any decision in this respect must emanate from the account party, not from the bank. Should the account party choose to be equally adamant, the bank cannot but conclude that it is impossible to furnish a guarantee upon terms acceptable to both account party and beneficiary. The bank will then have to decline the request of the account party.

The principle of strict adherence could well be branded as rigid and harsh, especially if the bank believed honestly and with good reason that the modifications served the interests of the account party. However, one should also appreciate that its firmness adds to clarity and certainty, which promotes the interests of the bank as well. It knows exactly how it ought to act and it is forcefully discouraged from entering the perilous area of substituting its own judgment, which may well turn out to be mistaken. Moreover, any chance of falling victim to the strictness of the principle could so easily be avoided by consulting its customer. Finally, the deterrent force of the rule also helps to prevent disputes from arising in the first place, which is a not unimportant function of the law.

If, for reasons described above, the bank must revert to its customer, it is not liable for any delay in the issuance of the guarantee as a result thereof.

Once the contract of guarantee has been concluded, any instructions by the account party to have the terms of the guarantee amended can be ignored. Such amendments require the consent of both bank and beneficiary.[34]

Should the bank have issued a guarantee on terms which are more favourable to the beneficiary than those which have been agreed upon between the account party and beneficiary or than those which have been specified by the account party to the bank, then the bank is, as a general rule, bound to these more favourable terms in its relationship with the beneficiary.[35]

Indirect guarantees

10-13 If the account party instructs his bank to arrange for an indirect guarantee, specifying the terms and conditions, the bank is under a duty to request the foreign bank to issue the guarantee in accordance with those terms and conditions.[36] It is submitted that as between account party and first instructing bank the principle of strict adher-

---

[34] Cf. Article 9(d) UCP, Rule 2.06 ISP98.

[35] *BGH, 10 February 2000*, WM 2000, p. 715, see further No. 10-17.

[36] *LG Frankfurt, 11 December 1979*, NJW 1981, p. 56, *Trib. com. Versailles, 17 September 1981*, D 1982 I.R. p. 496 (errors in the transmission of the terms of the guarantee are to be accounted for by the bank, not by the customer), von Westphalen, pp. 226-228, 344, Coing, ZHR 1983, p. 137, Vasseur, No. 55.

ence applies no less than in the case of direct guarantees. According to this view, the instructions from the first instructing bank to the second issuing bank should not be at variance with clear and specific instructions from the account party to the first bank. Nor is the first bank allowed to agree of its own accord to modifications demanded by the second issuing bank. Some authors allow for a relaxation of the principle in the case of indirect guarantees.[37]

It may well be that the bank knows from experience that it is pointless to prescribe the terms and conditions in explicit detail or to include or omit certain terms. This does not, however, justify the bank making decisions on behalf and for the account of its customer. Again, the bank is to refer the matter to the customer and obtain his approval, but any delay as a result thereof is for the customer's account.

The issue of instructions and other pertinent aspects in the case of indirect guarantees are examined in further detail in Chapter 11.1.4.

Review by the bank. Duty of bank and account party in general

10-14 It does not follow from the rule of strict adherence that the bank is supposed to adopt a passive role, carrying out the instructions uncritically and without review.[38] As has been observed in no. 10-12, the scope of the principle is limited to situations where the instructions are clear and specific, whereas in practice the instructions are often marked by vagueness and imprecision.

There are two factors that would appear to require the bank to play a more active role than is the case with documentary credits. First, stipulations for the issuance of an independent guarantee in the secured contract are not such a matter of daily routine as with documentary credits. Consequently, the bank's customer may have less experience in adequately formulating instructions for an appropriate guarantee format. Secondly, the terms and conditions of guarantees as well as the texts themselves have not attained, and probably never will attain, the same degree of uniformity and standardisation as is the case with documentary credits. Applications for documentary credits are usually made by the account party completing a standard form which contains a comprehensive list of the usual types of documents and conditions of payment. Although most banks employ standard application forms for independent guarantees, the problem is that the parties to the underlying transaction have often agreed on terms and conditions that may be difficult to fit into the bank's standard formats or have only reached agreement in broad terms. As a result, the precise determination of the terms and the actual drafting of the guarantee may call for closer attention and care in each individual case. In both respects, the bank could and to some extent should be of assistance.

---

[37] Dohm, Nos. 128, 263-264, Zahn/Ehrlich/Neumann, 9/97, von Westphalen, p. 228, 344.

The scope of the bank's responsibility at the application stage can only be circumscribed in cautious and general terms. It would appear that the individual bank has to employ a standard of care which is determined by what may reasonably be expected of the experienced and prudent bank engaged in the business of issuing guarantees. Among the major elements determining responsibility are the relative ease with which the bank can avoid misunderstandings and errors by the account party and the importance for the account party of preventing these incidents.

Obviously, the account party is initially responsible for his instructions. In particular, his instructions should be clear, precise and complete and avoid ambiguous language, cf. art. 3 URDG and Rule 1.10 ISP98. This means that the consequences of instructions not attaining the required degree of precision could be attributed to the account party. In this respect, one could speak of concurrent responsibility. It would, of course, be impossible to say in general when instructions are inexact and where the respective responsibility of account party and bank begins and ends. Possibly the only formula that could tentatively be proffered is that, on the one hand, carelessness by the account party does not necessarily exculpate the bank and that, on the other hand, if the bank has discharged its duty of care, the residual risk of misunderstandings and errors lies with the account party.

Apart from the bank's limited joint responsibility for the drafting of the text and the conditions of payment of the guarantee, the bank is also serving its own interests by reviewing the application of its customer carefully. Such a review helps to avoid misunderstandings and imprecision in the formulation of the conditions of payment, which may otherwise be a source of future disagreement and strained relations.[39]

Imprecise and incomplete instructions

10-15 The account party's application as a whole, or certain elements of it, may be couched in such vague and general terms that it offers hardly any guidance to the bank. The reason for this could well be that the account party and beneficiary, having agreed upon the furnishing of a guarantee or upon something which they call a 'guarantee', have failed to express themselves sufficiently clearly as regards the meaning of that term, the precise contents of the guarantee and the payment mechanism. In such circumstances the bank should communicate with its customer in order to obtain clarification instead of drafting a guarantee on terms which it deems appropriate or on terms which it believes to be customary. Upon enquiry it may well turn out that the parties to the underlying transaction have in fact agreed on a traditional accessory guarantee, instead of a first demand guarantee.

---

[38] Cf. Zahn/Ehrlich/Neumann, 9/80-82, von Westphalen, pp. 336-339.

[39] See also Chapter 7, No. 7-3, and No. 10-26.

Relationship Account Party – Bank 131

The bank has some responsibility to draw the customer's attention to terms which lack unequivocal meaning or to conditions which do not clearly define the circumstances in which the bank is or is not to pay, and to suggest improvements.[40] This duty is, however, confined to situations where the inadequacies must be taken to be plain to the ordinary banker and where the instructions are inherently ambiguous, which must be apparent at the time of application. Where the instructions contain conditions of payment which have not been framed in a documentary fashion, the bank will have an interest of its own in converting those into documentary conditions.

The instructions may have to be considered to be incomplete. If the name of the beneficiary or the type of conditions of payment have not been indicated, the bank will be unable to issue a guarantee and hence be compelled to make enquiry to the account party. Greater difficulties are posed by applications which do not specify the underlying transaction, the maximum amount or an expiry date or expiry event. Since these elements are vital to the account party, it is submitted that the bank cannot remain inactive, but should consult the account party. Art. 3 URDG states that all guarantees should stipulate the account party (principal), beneficiary, reference to the underlying transaction, the maximum amount, the expiry date, the payment mechanism and a provision for the reduction of the guarantee amount (if any). Accordingly, both the account party and the bank are expected to run off a limited checklist. Rule 1.10 ISP98 contains a list of redundant or otherwise undesirable terms.

How is the bank to act if the type of guarantee, i.e. a direct or indirect guarantee, has not been indicated? It has been suggested that the bank is entitled to arrange for an indirect guarantee without further consultation, if that were the only possible way of carrying out the instruction. This is taken to be the case where the issuance of an (indirect) guarantee by a local bank in the country of the beneficiary is a mandatory requirement in that country, where an indirect guarantee has been agreed upon by the account party and beneficiary or where there is a custom to that effect.[41] Should the bank indeed follow this course, it would only expose itself to risks which could have so easily been avoided. How can the bank be sure in its knowledge? Apart from these practicalities, it could be objected to on the grounds that in the preparatory stage the bank has a contractual relationship, with the ensuing duties, with its account party only. It should not be influenced by whatever the account party and beneficiary are believed to have agreed upon or by whatever foreign laws, practices or custom may, supposedly, require. Moreover, it is a matter of principle that the bank should not make such important decisions on behalf of its customer who, if the question were put to him, would be quite capable of making that decision for himself.

---

40 Cf. Von Westphalen, p. 337, Zahn/Ehrlich/Neumann, 9/80, Stoufflet, Garantie Bancaire Internationale, No. 28.

41 Bark, ZIP 1982, p. 414, 415, Zahn/Ehrlich/Neumann, 9/76, von Westphalen, p. 346. Canaris' approach, No. 1115, is similar to the view of this study.

Banks are sometimes requested to issue a guarantee in accordance with the terms as provided for in the underlying contract. Such requests should be handled with great caution, as the bank in the case of *Trib. com. Versailles, 17 September 1981* had to find out.[42] Such a request was made by a French exporter to his regional branch office, which transmitted the request to the central department of the bank which, in its turn, requested a Dutch bank in the beneficiary's country to issue a first demand guarantee covering repayment of the advance payment. The underlying contract stated that the guarantee was to cease to have any effect once the exporter had carried out work in excess of the advance payment. Somewhere along the line, this clause was mislaid and did not reach the Dutch bank. The Dutch bank proceeded to pay upon the demand of the beneficiary, while the restrictive condition had been fulfilled. The court held that the French bank had failed to carry out the instructions and that accordingly the exporter was excused from reimbursing the bank.[43]

The problem with instructions of this kind is that they cannot be considered ambiguous or incomplete but they are certainly apt to give rise to errors. Banks are well-advised to insist that the applicant himself should specify all terms and conditions in a straightforward manner without blanket references to other documents. If the bank does not object to instructions of this kind, it may be deemed to have accepted the attendant risks. This might have been the rationale underlying the court's decision.

Speediness as regards the dispatch of the guarantee could be of importance to the account party in view of the stipulated time of issuance in the underlying contract, but if that should entail summary and deficient instructions, e.g. by telephone, or if the account party urges the bank just to go ahead, as often happens, he will be estopped from asserting that the bank has neglected its responsibilities as outlined above. Moreover, as long as the bank puts a reasonable interpretation on imprecise instructions when transposing these into the guarantee or if the bank fails to detect ambiguities in the conditions of payment in situations other than those described above, the risk thereof remains with the account party.

It is a sensible practice for banks to forward the text of the guarantee to the account party prior to its issuance. This will avoid disagreement between account party and bank regarding the contents of the guarantee, which would otherwise only become apparent at the time of a call by the beneficiary.[44] However, pressure of time does not always allow for this practice.

---

[42] D. 1982, I.R. p. 496.

[43] According to art. 12 URDG the bank is exempt from liability for mutilation or other errors arising in the transmission of any telecommunication, but subject to art. 15.

[44] Cf. *Cass. 22 May 1991*, D. 1992 Somm. p. 233, and *Nimes, 27 September 1989*, D. 1990 Somm. p. 200. In both cases the claim by the account party, who had given oral instructions, against the bank for not properly carrying out the instructions was rejected.

Advice to the account party

10-16 Banks regularly draw the customer's attention to the differences between the traditional accessory guarantee and the independent (first demand) guarantee and the attendant risks, as well as to the increased perils surrounding indirect guarantees in relation to certain countries. However, a general legal obligation on the bank to advise and warn its client cannot be said to exist.[45] Nor does the bank owe a general duty to advise its customer how to mitigate the risks, for example by adding protective clauses. A customer who engages in international trade can in general be expected to be aware of these risks or to seek legal advice. Moreover, the account party can at least be expected to read the text of the guarantee carefully when it has been forwarded by either the beneficiary or the bank, as well as the text of his counter-guarantee in favour of the bank.[46] Another reason for denying such a general duty is the impossibility of defining the extent of it, which then leaves the bank uncertain as to how it is supposed to act. Moreover, advice will often be of little consequence, since the terms and conditions may already have been fixed by the beneficiary, while the account party, rightly or wrongly, has decided that acceptance is unavoidable in order to win the contract.

A certain duty to advise its customer may, however, exist in special situations, for instance where the bank is aware of the inexperience of the account party[47], where the bank has actual knowledge of a particular piece of information which it knows to be vital to its customer, or where the bank insists that significant alterations be made to the terms or the type of guarantee.[48] An area of particular attention could be the validity period or absence of an effective expiry date in the (counter-) guarantee, which is of

---

[45] *Paris, 9 July 1986*, upheld by *Cass., 10 January 1989*, D. 1989 Somm. p. 153, *Cass., 26 January 1993*, D. 1995 Somm. p. 14, *Cass., 3 May 2000*, Droit&Patrimoine, November 2000, p. 98 (no duty to advise where the account party was a company which was familiar with international trade practices); Staudinger/Horn, No. 326, Von Westphalen, pp. 337, 339, Zahn/Ehrlich/Neumann, 9/81, Dohm, No. 129, Bark, ZIP 1982, p. 415. Contra von Mettenheim, RIW 1981, p. 585 and Nada Nassar Chaoul, Proche-Orient ètudes juridiques 1984/1985, p. 158. See also Beckers, IFLR October 1982, p. 33. In *Brussels, 18 December 1981*, Rev. Banque 1982, pp. 99, 121, it was held that failure to point out the risks and implications did not constitute breach of duty of care, where the bank had mentioned that payment was to be made on first demand without recourse to the statutory provisions of suretyship, while the text of the guarantee was clear.

[46] *Cass., 22 May 1991*, D. 1992 Som. p. 233, *Nimes, 27 September 1989*, D. 1990 Somm. p. 200. In both cases the text of the guarantee clearly stated that the bank would pay on the beneficiary's first demand regardless of disputes.

[47] Cf. *Cass., 18 December 1990*, D. 1991 Somm. p. 193, Vasseur D. 1995 Somm. p. 15, Staudinger/Horn, No. 326. See also Chapter 12.2, No. 12-5, in relation to the bank's duty to advise private individuals who issue a guarantee in favour of the bank.

[48] See, e.g., *BGH, 10 February 2000*, WM 2000, p. 715, see No. 10-17.

such importance to the account party. Other examples might be the regular practice of 'extend or pay' demands and the peculiarities of foreign laws and practices in the case of indirect guarantees.[49]

Acceptance and refusal by the bank

10-17 As a general rule the bank can freely decide whether to accept or to reject the application, cf. art. 7(b) URDG. It may also insist on more specific instructions or on adaptation of the text and terms or the format of the guarantee.[50] *BGH, 10 February 2000*, provides an interesting example of how the bank may have to act in such circumstances as regards the applicant, and in particular if the changes required by the bank result in a significant increase in the risks for the applicant.[51]

If the bank declines the application or if it insists on amendments, it should inform the applicant of its position forthwith so that the applicant does not unnecessarily lose time in considering alternatives, cf. art. 7(a) URDG in fine.

There could be special circumstances where, upon balancing the respective interests, a refusal to issue a guarantee may be considered unreasonable.[52] A typical and recurring case is where a tender guarantee has previously been issued and where the contract has been awarded to the account party. In such circumstances, banks tend to feel bound, and rightly so, to agree to the issuance of a performance guarantee as a natural sequel. Banks, therefore, consider applications for tender guarantees in conjunction with possible future requests for performance guarantees. Should the bank

---

[49] See also Chapter 11.1.4., No. 11-6.

[50] See also Chapter 7, No. 7-3.

[51] WM 2000, p. 715. In this case the applicant instructed the bank to issue a traditional suretyship in accordance with a specimen as had been agreed with the beneficiary. The bank declined to issue such suretyship and instead forwarded a text containing a guarantee payable on first demand to the account party who did not object. The German Supreme Court held that the bank should not only have obtained the approval of the account party but also clearly informed the account party of the significant increase of risk as a result of the issuance of a first demand guarantee in stead of a traditional suretyship. As the bank had failed to do so, the account party was entitled to raise defences against the bank's claim for reimbursement as if it had issued a traditional suretyship. The court also ruled that the bank in its relationship with the beneficiary was bound to the terms of the guarantee payable on first demand.

[52] See, for example, *Trib. com. Brussels, 30 October 1984*, RDC 1985, p. 572, where the court ordered the bank to extend the period of validity because of ongoing consultations between customer and beneficiary to resolve their differences of opinion. The court took into account the great potential damage to the interests of the customer (the likelihood of a call on the guarantee if no extension were to be granted) and the absence of significant harm to the bank.

have delivered a letter of commitment to the beneficiary of the tender guarantee or a letter of commitment in lieu of a tender guarantee, the issuance of a performance guarantee is, in those circumstances, also an obligation owed by the bank to the beneficiary.

If the bank accepts the instructions, it should proceed to issue the guarantee without undue delay. The need for further consultation with the beneficiary and account party regarding the text or other circumstances may cause a delay for which it cannot be held responsible.[53]

10.8 DUTY OF EXAMINATION WITH RESPECT TO COMPLIANCE WITH THE TERMS AND CONDITIONS OF THE GUARANTEE

Introduction. Relationship bank-beneficiary and bank-account party

10-18 Examination with respect to compliance with the terms and conditions of payment is an issue which relates both to the relationship between the bank and the beneficiary and to the relationship between the bank and the account party. As far as the first-mentioned relationship is concerned, the beneficiary is only entitled to payment if the conditions have been fulfilled and, conversely, the bank is entitled to refuse payment if it finds that the conditions are not met, cf. art. 19 URDG, Rule 2.01 ISP98 and art. 15 Uncitral Convention. In its relationship with the account party the bank owes a duty to ascertain compliance and to refuse payment if the conditions have not been complied with, cf art. 9 URDG and art. 16(1) Uncitral Convention. Breach of this duty debars the bank from claiming reimbursement.

Most of the conditions of payment ordinarily relate to the tender of specific documents and hence the examination predominantly consists in verifying whether the documents presented conform to the documents prescribed in the guarantee. With documentary credits, the bank performs a similar task. The principles applying to documentary credits are therefore also valid for guarantees.[54] The fact that the documents to be tendered under a guarantee are usually fewer in number and of quite a different nature does not alter this, but rather gives rise to special problems and considerations.

---

53   Cf. *Trib. com. Toulouse, 26 September 1990*, D. 1992 Somm. p. 238.

54   *Trib. com. Brussels, 21 November 1979*, JCB 1980, p. 140 (reversed by *Brussels, 25 February 1982*, JCB 1982, p. 349, on other grounds), *Trib. com. Brussels, 27 July 1984*, RDC 1985, p. 567, *Howe Richardson Scale Co. Ltd. v. Polimex-Cekop*, [1978] 1 Lloyd's Rep. 161, *Potton Homes Ltd. v. Coleman Contractors (Overseas) Ltd.*, [1984] 28 Build. L.R. 19. See also *OLG Hamburg, 7 July 1977*, WM 1978, p. 260. The application of the same principles by English courts is only natural, as (independent) guarantees and documentary credits are generally treated in the same way, as of course are standby letters of credit.

The basic principles concerning ascertaining compliance are applied identically to the relationship of the bank with the account party and with the beneficiary. This congruence ensures that the bank's obligation to pay tallies with the bank's right of reimbursement by the account party. Compliance will be discussed in further detail in Chapter 13 in relation to the specific terms and conditions.

Compliance with all positive conditions, fulfilment of negative conditions

10-19 The terms qualifying the banks's obligation to pay may relate to both positive and negative conditions. The fulfilment of positive conditions turns the contingent obligation to pay into an enforceable obligation. The fulfilment of negative conditions restricts, suspends or terminates the payment obligation.

A guarantee always contains positive conditions of payment. It is for the beneficiary to show that all these conditions have been met. As far as documentary conditions are concerned, this is and can only be done by tendering the prescribed documents, while the bank must verify that all these conditions have indeed been complied with, cf. art. 19 URDG and art. 16 Uncitral Convention. The bank will always have to ascertain whether the demand for payment has been made in the correct form and by the proper person and whether the beneficiary has submitted the statement of default, if so required according to the conditions of payment. In proper first demand guarantees these will be the only conditions for payment. If, according to the guarantee, the beneficiary is to substantiate the principal debtor's default by means of documentary evidence from third parties, the bank must examine whether all, and the correct, documents, particularly as regards the content and the persons or agencies who have issued those documents, have been submitted.

The bank's undertaking may also be subject to conditions of yet another type, for example an advance payment by the beneficiary, the issuance of a documentary credit in favour of the account party, the coming into force of the underlying contract or even the discharge of all or certain obligations of the underlying contract by the beneficiary. In that event, the guarantee will ordinarily, or hopefully, specify the documents by which the occurrence of these events can and must be evidenced. In addition to verifying compliance with the above-mentioned conditions, the bank must always see to it that the request for payment has been made on or before the expiry date.

Guarantees may contain provisions which restrict or remove the liability of the bank, for example clauses which reduce the maximum amount payable upon part and/or successive performance of the secured contract by the account party, clauses which terminate the obligation of the bank upon complete performance of the main contract or clauses which suspend the obligation in the event of *force majeure* relating to the main contract or in the event of pending arbitration. The fulfilment of these negative conditions has to be shown by the account party. Again, the guarantee will ordinarily, or hopefully, designate the pertinent documents, for example shipping documents with respect to a reduction clause or a certificate of completion by a named surveyor or engineer. If such negative conditions have been fulfilled, the bank should not pay.[55] If they have not, the bank cannot refuse payment on account of these conditions.[56]

While the bank must base its decision whether or not to pay upon due consideration of all the positive and negative conditions, it is not concerned with circumstances which the guarantee does not designate as conditions defining its liability. Phrases such as 'payment ... in case of failure of the account party to execute the contract' (*Effektivklauseln*) may cast doubt as to the nature of the security furnished, but if, upon final analysis, the contract is to be construed as an independent guarantee as opposed to an accessory suretyship, proof of default is not a condition of payment.[57]

Formal compliance

10-20 It is part of the essence of the independent nature of the guarantee and a prerequisite for the proper functioning of the bank that examination of compliance with the (documentary) conditions means examination of *formal* compliance. This fundamental priciple is also clearly expressed in art. 9 URDG, Rule 4.01(b) ISP98 and art. 16(1) Uncitral Convention.

If the beneficiary is to submit a unilateral statement of default, the bank will merely verify whether that statement on the face of it corresponds with the statement prescribed in the guarantee. The same applies with respect to other kinds of documents. As regards the beneficiary, the bank is not entitled to investigate the veracity or correctness of the statements contained in the documents or to verify or require proof of the principal debtor's default in any other way than as stipulated in the guarantee. The bank also owes no duty to its customer in this regard. Nor is the bank concerned with disputes regarding the rights and liabilities of the beneficiary and account party as they may exist on the basis of the underlying contract.[58] The reverse is also true. If the

---

[55] See, for example, *BGH, 12 March 1984 (llZR 198/82)*, NJW 1984, p. 2030, *OLG Hamburg, 4 November 1977*, RIW 1978, p. 615, *Paris, 2 June 1982*, D. 1983 J. p. 437 (no call to be made prior to a certain date, before which the account party could submit the documents).

[56] See, for example, *Paris, 1 February 1984*, D. 1984 J. p. 265.

[57] See Chapter 4.2, No. 4-8, No. 10-26, and Chapter 13, No. 13-13.

[58] See, for example, *BGH, 24 November 1983*, WM 1984, p. 44, *BGH, 12 March 1984 (ll ZR 198/82*, NJW 1984, p. 2030, *BGH, 31 January 1985*, WM 1985, p. 511, *OLG Hamburg, 4 November 1977*, RIW 1978, p. 615, *OLG Schleswig, 6 December 1983*, WM 1984, p. 651, *OLG Hamburg, 10 October 1985*, NJW 1986, p. 1691, *Kammergericht, 20 November 1986*, NJW 1987, p. 1774, *OLG Karlsruhe, 21 July 1992*, RIW 1992, p. 843 *Brussels, 25 February 1982*, JCB 1982, p. 349, *Brussels, 4 January 1989*, TBH 1990, p. 1073 *CA Amsterdam, 30 March 1972*, NJ 1973, 188, *CA The Hague, 13 June 1980*, in HR, 12 March 1982, NJ 1982, 267, *Howe Richardson v. Polimex-Cekop*, [1978] 1 Lloyd's Rep. 161, *Edward Owen v. Barclays Bank*, per Lord Denning MR, [1978] 1 All ER 976, 983, *Harbottle (Mercantile) v.*

conditions for payment of the guarantee have not been complied with, the beneficiary cannot claim payment under the guarantee by alleging that he is entitled to payment on the basis of the underlying contract.[59]

If the beneficiary is to submit more than one document, the bank must also ascertain whether these documents are consistent with one another, see no. 10-23.

Strict compliance

10-21 As with documentary credits, compliance also means that the conditions of the guarantee must have been *strictly* complied with. It is perhaps surprising that this major principle is not stated in the URDG,[60] ISP98[61] or Uncitral Convention,[62] but has been developed in case law and legal writing.[63]

Nat. Westminster Bank, [1977] 2 All ER 862, 870, *Siporex Trade SA v. Banque Indosuez*, [1986] 2 Lloyd's Rep. 146, *Turkiye Is Bankasi v. Bank of China*, [1996] 2 Lloyd's Rep. 250. However, in *CA Amsterdam, 3 September 1998*, JOR 1999, 128, the Court of Appeal took the view that the bank, in the course of its formal examination, could have concluded that the beneficiary had called the guarantee for a purpose which was not covered by the guarantee. In fact, the case turned on the beneficiary's fraud and the bank could not possibly have discovered such fraud, see the critical comment by Bertrams, WPNR 1999, pp. 706-711. See Chapter 14.5.5, No. 14-27, for the facts of this case.

[59] *Trib. com. Brussels, 15 March 1984/27 July 1984*, RDC 1984, p. 567. In *Brussels, 26 June 1992*, RDC 1994, p. 51, the Court of Appeal determined that the terms of the reduction clause had been fulfilled and rejected the beneficiary's argument that he did in fact have a claim against the account party. See also *Ghent, 25 February 1988*, TBH 1989, p. 40. The repayment guarantee in favour of the buyer was payable on demand but also provided that no payment was to be made if the account party/seller submitted a statement that the non-performance of the contract had been caused by one of the reasons stated in Article 9 of the underlying contract. The account party did submit the statement and the bank refused payment. The Court of Appeal dismissed the claim by the beneficiary ruling that the decision of the bank was correct.

[60] According to Affaki, No. 114 on p. 85, the principle of strict compliance is inherent to the URDG and was, as such, implicitly relied on by the ICC Banking Commission in an opinion of 6 June 2000, 470/TA.361.

[61] The ISP98 Commentary at Rule 4.01 notes that this Rule avoids the term 'strict compliance' because it is a crude and abstract formulation of the standard of examination.

[62] Numerous statements in the Uncitral documents put beyond doubt, however, that compliance means strict compliance, see for example doc. A/CN.9/316, p. 27, A/CN.9/330, p. 18, A/CN.9/330, p. 18, A/CN.9/WG.ll/WP.63, p. 5, and A/CN.9/WG.ll/WP.68, p. 15.

[63] See, for example, *BGH, 12 March 1984*, NJW 1984, p. 2030, *OLG Hamburg, 7 July 1977*, WM 1978, p. 260, *OLG Stuttgart, 25 January 1979*, RIW 1980, p 729, *OLG Karlsruhe, 21 July 1992*, RIW 1992, p. 843, *Cass. 5 February 1985*, D.1985 J. p. 269, *Cass. 24 March*

The purpose of the strict compliance rule is twofold. It protects the account party as, by specifying the conditions of payment, he intimates under what circumstances he is or is not prepared to accept the risk of payment, although no payment might have been due on the basis of the underlying contract. It is the bank's duty towards the account party to ensure that the conditions of payment have been strictly observed and failure in this respect renders the bank liable to the account party. At the same time and more importantly, the rule of strict compliance serves the interests of the bank, since it has the distinct advantage of clarifying and facilitating its position. In fact, the principle of strict compliance has evolved in banking practice and has subsequently been endorsed in case law and legal writing. When the terms and conditions have not been strictly complied with, for example if the documents submitted are at variance with the prescribed documents, or if the required statement of default has not been presented or if the demand for payment has been made shortly after the expiry date, the bank knows that payment is to be refused and there is no need to apply its judgment as to whether the interests of its customer would or would not be impaired or whether the discrepancies are material. The requirement of strict compliance also avoids the risk to the bank of becoming involved in differences of opinion between the parties to the underlying contract. Thus, the rule of strict compliance greatly facilitates the performance of the duties of the bank, which also helps to reduce the costs of its services.[64] On the other hand, the doctrine of strict compliance should not be allowed to produce results which are manifestly unreasonable or absurd.[65]

The ambit of the principle of strict compliance is limited. The principle postulates precision in respect of the terms and conditions of the guarantee and exactitude in the description of the nature and content of the prescribed documents. In documentary credits, the particulars of the various documents could be and are usually specified with precision. By their nature the circumscription of the particulars of the documents in guarantees cannot all and always have the same degree of exactitude. Precision can be, and usually is, achieved with respect to the identity of the person entitled to make the demand for payment, the statement of default by the beneficiary, if required, the expiry date or the expiry event if framed in a documentary fashion, the documents to be presented in connection with a reduction clause, the identity of the persons issuing third-party certificates and other purely factual matters such as dates and references to

---

1992, D. 1993 Somm. p. 99, *HR, 9 June 1995*, NJ 1995, 639, *CA Amsterdam, 27 February 1992*, NJ 1992, 735, *Trib. com. Brussels, 27 July 1984*, RDC 1984, p. 567, *Brussels, 4 January 1989*, TBH 1990, p. 1073, *Trib. com. Brussels, 15 December 1992*, RDC 1993, p. 1055, *Brussels, 26 June 1992*, RDC 1994, p. 51, *Trib. com. Brussels, 5 February 1996*, RW 1996/1997, p. 1263, OG *Austria, 24 March 1988*, JIBL 1988 N-154. See also von Westphalen, p. 165, Canaris, No. 1107, 1109, Dohm, No. 203, Nielsen, p. 82, and ZHR 1983, p. 150.

64   See for this aspect especially Dolan, § 6.02/3.
65   See also Chapter 13, Nos. 13-12 and 13-13.

the principal contract. However, when it comes to the substance of third-party documents and especially non-documentary and unascertainable conditions, matters tend to be different. These are areas where the doctrine of strict compliance cannot be employed and where the duty of examination by the bank is rather governed by the principle of reasonable care and discretion, see nos. 10-25 and 10-26.

The application of the rule of strict compliance in relation to specific conditions of payment is also examined in Chapter 13.

Relaxation of the principle of strict compliance? Substantial compliance

10-22 While the justifications for the principle of strict compliance are without any doubt sensible, solid and cogent, there could be situations where the justice of a rigid adherence to the doctrine could be called into question. The following cases serve as an example of the difficulties which the doctrine occasionally may produce.

In *OLG Hamburg, 7 July 1977*, the guarantee provided for payment upon submission of a London arbitral award.[66] The account party preferred to have the dispute with the beneficiary concerning the secured contract settled by the London courts. Judgment was given against the account party and the beneficiary submitted the court decision to the bank, which refused to pay. The Court of Appeal rightly observed that examination by the bank is subject to the principle of strict compliance in order to guard the interests of the account party, but it also ruled that in this case the legitimate interests would not be served by adherence to this rule.

Paris, 17 September 1991, provides a similar example of a court mitigating the rigidity of the rule of strict compliance. The case involved an indirect guarantee backed up by a counter-guarantee, both providing for payment upon submission of an arbitral award. The pertinent clause in the main contract stated that arbitration proceedings could only be initiated upon completion of the project. The difficulty in this case was caused by the fact that the account party, a construction firm, had abandoned the project leaving it uncompleted, with the result that the settlement through arbitration was frustrated. The Paris Court of Appeal ruled that the instructing bank could not escape liability under the counter-guarantee if the second issuing bank succeeded in procuring an alternative judgment which could be regarded as a substitute for the arbitral award as originally contemplated.[67] Because of a flaw in its argumentation this decision was, however, quashed by *Cass., 7 February 1995*.[68]

---

[66] WM 1978, p. 260. The decision has been criticised by Zahn/Ehrlich/Neumann, No. 9/117, Canaris, No. 1133b, Dohm, No. 208.

[67] *Paris, 17 September 1991*, D. 1992 Somm. p. 240.

[68] RJDA 1995/6, No. 754, p. 600.

Payment under the guarantee in *Paris, 10 November 1988,* was made subject to an extraordinary condition, namely submission of both an arbitral award from a Mauretanian expert and a 'concomitant' arbitral award from the Paris International Chamber of Commerce. Since, understandably, the beneficiary was unable to meet this condition of payment, the bank refused to pay and the beneficiary instituted main proceedings before the competent court in Mauretania. This court ruled that the condition for payment was incapable of fulfilment and had to be ignored, and also held the account party liable for breach of contract. The Mauretanian judgment was presented to the bank, which then proceeded to pay. This payment was subsequently challenged by the account party on the grounds that the bank had honoured a non-conforming demand. This complaint was rejected by the Paris court with the observation that the beneficiary had sufficiently shown its right to payment under the guarantee and that the bank was therefore entitled to effect payment.[69]

A recent and very important decision is that of the Dutch Supreme Court, *HR 26 March 2004*, which explicitly recognised the possibility of an exception to the rule of strict compliance and, more importantly, did in fact apply the exception. One of the conditions of payment was a report by a specified independent surveyor (X) to the effect that the account party/shipbuilder had defaulted under the secured contract for the building of a ship. The shipbuilder ran into financial and technical difficulties and ceased building the ship. The beneficiary then asked surveyor X to issue the required report which it declined to do because of a conflict of interests unless the shipbuilder would waive any objections. The shipbuilder refused to cooperate, however, and also refused to have the survey carried out by another independent surveyor (Y). The beneficiary, nonetheless, requested surveyor Y to issue the report, which it did, and the beneficiary presented this report to the bank which refused to pay because the report had not been drawn up by the surveyor X as mentioned in the guarantee. The beneficiary then sued the bank for payment while the shipbuilder had meanwhile been declared bankrupt. While recognising that the bank was entitled to *initially* refuse payment, the Dutch Supreme Court ordered the bank to pay because the non-compliance with the above-mentioned condition of payment had been frustrated by the account party/shipbuilder. In this context the Supreme Court referred to fraud on the part of the account party. It also ruled that, upon payment, the bank did not forfeit its right to take recourse against the account party. The fact that such recourse might be futile in the light of the account party's insolvency was a risk to be borne by the bank.

The decision of *Paris, 17 December 1992,* went the other way.[71] The case involved a repayment guarantee which was stated to take effect upon an advance payment to the

---

[69] D. 1990 Somm. p. 201.

[70] JOR 2004, 153.

[71] D. 1993 Somm. p. 98, affirmed by *Cass., 21 February 1995*, RJDA 1995/7, No. 883, p. 709.

account party by the beneficiary. Upon the initiative of and with the consent of the account party the advance payment had in fact not been made by the beneficiary, but was substituted by a loan to the account party from the beneficiary's bank, which in its turn obtained an accessory guarantee (suretyship) from the beneficiary of the repayment guarantee. When the account party failed to carry out the secured contract and to repay the loan to the bank and the bank had been indemnified by the beneficiary, the latter called the repayment guarantee in order to retrieve the advance payment. His claim for payment against the bank/guarantor was rejected by the Court of Appeal on the grounds that the condition precedent as set forth in the text of the guarantee, namely the advance payment to be made by the beneficiary, had not been fulfilled. Whereas the court of first instance was prepared to make an exception to the principle of strict compliance since the account party had in fact received the advance payment in accordance with the amended arrangements between the account party and the beneficiary, the Court of Appeal chose to enforce this principle strictly.

As has been mentioned in no. 10-21, the doctrine of strict compliance also serves the banks' own interests. Thus, it is submitted that in the above-mentioned cases the bank was quite entitled not to proceed to payment voluntarily. If, however, judgment were ultimately given in favour of the bank and against the beneficiary, the only practical effect would have been that the account party would have received an undeserved windfall as he would escape having to pay the sum which he so plainly owed to the beneficiary. This seems all the more unreasonable since in the *OLG Hamburg* case it was the account party who preferred and agreed to have the dispute adjudged by the London courts instead of by arbitration as originally envisaged, while in the 2004 *Dutch Supreme Court* case it was the account party which frustrated strict compliance. In the 1992 *Paris* case the account party had in fact received the advance payment and in a manner subsequently agreed to. It is noted that in none of the cases mentioned in no. 10-22 was any specific justified interest of the bank impaired, while, obviously, if eventually the bank is ordered to pay, it is entitled to reimbursement by the account party, as was expressly observed by the Dutch Supreme Court.

Albeit with considerable hesitation, this study is inclined to accept substantial as opposed to strict compliance in very special circumstances such as those in the above-mentioned cases, but this should indeed be confined to clearly exceptional situations and provided that no specific justified interests of the bank are harmed. The general interest of the bank in upholding the rule could be safeguarded by permitting the bank to refuse payment initially when the conditions of the guarantee have not been strictly fulfilled and by leaving it to the beneficiary to obtain a final decision in respect of compliance by the courts. In the case of *CA The Hague, 20 April 1993*, it was the bank which frustrated strict compliance. The repayment guarantee provided that claims had to be made, each time, within three months of the due date of the invoice. However, the bank contested the existence of the guarantee which resulted in protracted proceedings. When eventually the court in these proceedings had confirmed the valid existence of the guarantee, the beneficiary also called the guarantee for due dates in previous years, after the three months time limit, and the bank refused to pay. The Court of

Appeal emphasised the principle of strict compliance, but observed that application of this principle in this case would work as a trap, and judgment was given against the bank.[72]

The justification for a relaxation of the principle of strict compliance in favour of substantial compliance in appropriate cases could also be based on several significant differences which exist in this respect between bank guarantees and documentary credits. In the case of documentary credits, a request for payment is the rule and given their immense numbers any departure from the principle of strict compliance would prejudice the general interests of banks in an unacceptable manner. It would also invite litigation to an extent that would jeopardise the utility of a documentary credit as a smooth and easy payment instrument. In contrast, an actual call on a bank guarantee only occurs rarely, so that an exception to the rule in appropriate cases would have less far-reaching consequences. Secondly, the documents tendered under a documentary credit are often passed on to third parties or are used in back-to-back transactions which implies that the account party/buyer and occasionally the bank have a specific interest in strictly conforming documents. The same does not apply to documents presented under a bank guarantee. Finally, unlike in the case of documentary credits the documents which have to be submitted under a bank guarantee have no intrinsic value. It is noted that Staughton L.J. in *I.E. Contractors Ltd v. LLoyds Bank Plc. and Rafidain Bank* expressly observed that there is less need for the doctrine of strict compliance to apply to first demand guarantees than is the case in respect of documentary credits and he referred to several of the differences mentioned above.[73]

Inconsistencies

10-23 The bank must also verify that the beneficiary's demand for payment and other documents and statements, if required, are consistent with one and another and if this is found not to be the case the bank should refuse payment on the grounds of non-compliance, cf. art. 9 URDG in fine.[74] An example of this is where the beneficiary's demand for payment refers to breach of contract in respect of contract XYZ and a third-party document to contract ABC. Inconsistency does not necessarily have to relate to the submitted documents themselves. By implication, it can also be said to exist when the beneficiary's demand for payment or statement of default refers to contract

---

[72] NJ 1995, 542. It is noted that the account party had been declared insolvent which might explain the bank's attitude.

[73] (1990) 2 Lloyd's Rep. 496. See also *Siporex Trade v. Banque Indosuez*, (1986) 2 Lloyd's Rep. 146.

[74] According to Rule 4.03 ISP98 the bank is only required to examine documents for inconsistency if this is expressly provided in the standby.

XYZ, while the guarantee is expressed to secure performance of contract ABC.[75] This variant of inconsistency can be illustrated by the case of *CA Brussels, 4 January 1989*. According to its text, the indirect guarantee related to a contract between the account party and the beneficiary for the supply of 800 tons of milk powder, whereas this contract in fact provided for the delivery of 500 tons. When calling the guarantee the beneficiary presented a statement to the effect that the account party had failed to carry out its obligations in respect of the supply of 500 tons of milk powder and claimed the full amount of $ 66,400, which was honoured by the issuing bank. The Court of Appeal ruled that the issuing bank had not properly discharged its duty of examination, since a cursory reading of the text of the guarantee and the statement of default should have caused the average prudent bank to pay only part of the maximum amount, namely $ 41,500.[76] In accordance with the general principles for examination, the bank's duty to detect inconsistencies is confined to an examination of the face of the documents.

Reasonable care, discretion

10-24 The examination by the bank of compliance with the terms and conditions of the guarantee must be carried out with reasonable care, cf. art. 9 URDG and art. 14 Uncitral Convention. This standard describes the limit of the bank's duty of examination owed to the account party.[77] It should, however, be noted that this limitation of the bank's responsibility finds no application where the bank's duty is governed by the rule of strict compliance. The aforementioned articles should be read in conjunction with art. 11 URDG which excludes liability for forgeries which are not apparent from the face of the document and for the lack of sufficiency, accuracy and genuineness of the documents, etc. The standard of reasonable care, often in conjunction with the bank's discretionary powers, also affords protection against the risk of misinterpreting voluminous and intricate documents tendered by the beneficiary and against the difficulties

---

[75] Cf. Goode, p. 66.

[76] TBH 1990, p. 1073. The Court of Appeal also observed that if the beneficiary had stated that its loss in respect of the non-delivery of 500 tons ran to the full amount of $ 66,400, it would have been a conforming demand and that in that event the issuing bank would have been correct in paying the entire amount. The court was, however, of the opinion that this was not the case as the statement merely referred to a supply of 500 tons. Although it is true that this particular statement of default ought to have caused the issuing bank to make enquiries of the beneficiary, it would seem that the court overstretched the required standard of care if it expected the bank to discern this subtle distinction, also bearing in mind that the demand for payment did in fact relate to the secured contract and that the statement of default would have been in compliance with the prescribed statement if it had merely referred to the account party's default, without mention of the number of tons.

[77] Cf. Goode, p. 65. See *CA Brussels, 4 January 1989*, TBH 1990, p. 1073, discussed in the previous footnote.

which the bank may encounter in respect of third-party documents and non-documentary or unascertainable conditions of payment in particular, see nos. 10-25 and 10-26.

Reasonable care, discretion. Third-party documents

10-25 For a number of reasons the examination of third-party documents, if required under the terms of the guarantee, tends to be more problematic in guarantees than in documentary credits. Only to a limited extent do the documents relate to purely factual data, while the description of the contents of the documents in the guarantee is often couched in general terms. The basic problem stems, however, from the nature of the documents that are submitted to the bank. Third parties requested by the beneficiary to draw up certain documents, will ordinarily not be familiar with the purpose for which they will be used. If so, it will not always be a factor that can be taken into consideration. They are unable to use standard forms or to follow standard patterns. As a result, the documents may display great variety as regards structure, formulation, conciseness, clarity, etc., which compounds the bank's task of determining whether the submitted document satisfies the requirements of the prescribed document.

Third-party certificates of non-completion of the secured contract by the account party are particularly apt to cause problems. It is quite common that a guarantee which prescribes a third-party document, merely states that it is payable 'upon submission of a certificate drawn up by X'.[78] Does the presentation of a certificate which makes no mention of defects satisfy this condition of payment? With a view to the clear purpose of such a condition, the answer must be in the negative. As far as documentary credits are concerned it is trite law that documents which are, for example, worthless or not in good merchantable order or invite litigation must be rejected as a bad tender. A guarantee may require a certificate of non-completion setting forth the text of the certificate. Is the bank to reject a certificate which unequivocally confirms non-performance, but uses different language with a view to the principle of strict compliance? How should a bank decide when the certificate states 'that the contract has been properly executed, except with respect to ...' ? When a certificate of default is required, the bank may be confronted with a certificate which attests to non-performance of the contract or the defectiveness of the goods without mention of the phrase 'default' or it may indeed refer to default of the account party adding that the non-completion has been caused, to some extent, to a large extent or wholly by *force majeure* or by the non-performance by the beneficiary of his obligations.[79]

---

[78] See, for example, *Brussels, 25 February 1982*, JCB 1982, p. 349, *ICC Arbitration, No. 5639 (1987)*, D. 1988 Somm. p. 242.

[79] On the Continent the term 'non-performance' has in law a neutral meaning, while the term 'default' denotes non-performance for which one is accountable rendering the defaulter liable. Even in legal practice, however, the terms are often used indiscriminately. Third parties,

In these and similar situations the decision as to whether the document is or is not in order is a very difficult one and whichever way the bank decides, that decision could subsequently be found to be an error of judgment. It would, however, be no use to overturn the bank's decision on the basis that experts with the benefit of ample time, hindsight and specialised knowledge would have decided differently. The dilemma facing the bank is also recognised in documentary credits and has been resolved by according the bank a certain degree of discretion. In the case of guarantees, there is an even greater need for discretionary powers in situations such as described above in view of the absence of guidelines as given in Part D of the UCP.[80] If the situation is such as to entitle the bank to exercise its discretion and provided it puts a reasonable interpretation on the document presented in the light of the document prescribed, both account party and beneficiary are in principle bound by the decision and the room for judicial review will be limited. One has to bear in mind that the dilemma of the bank stems from the nature of the documents and the conditions for payment which are principally the making and responsibility of the account party and beneficiary. When exercising its discretionary powers the bank must act honestly and in good faith. It should be careful to retain a neutral position and not give priority to the interests of its customer. If the certificate is ambiguous it may also be appropriate for the bank, before reaching a final decision, to make further enquiries of the person who issued the certificate.

A practical consequence of the discretionary powers is that there could be situations in which the bank in its relationship with the beneficiary would be justified in rejecting a particular document, while, if it were to decide that the document was in order, it would be entitled to reimbursement from the account party.[81]

---

such as engineers and surveyors, are most certainly unfamiliar with the distinction and in any event they will not be capable of ascertaining default in the strict legal sense. It is therefore submitted that a certificate will not be refused on the sole ground that it does not refer to or establish default.

[80] At present a great number of the articles of Part D clarify the meaning of certain terms and phrases and indicate which documents will be accepted or rejected failing specific or contrary stipulations in the credit. As a result the room for discretion has been narrowed down severely. See also von Westphalen, p. 166.

[81] In *Brussels, 25 February 1982*, JCB 1982, p. 349, the Court of Appeal dismissed the account party's defence that the bank should not have paid against a report which, although confirming the defectiveness of the goods, stated that it was not the final report. One could only speculate about what the situation would have been if the bank had rejected the document and then been sued by the beneficiary.

Reasonable care, discretion. Non-documentary conditions of payment. *Effektivklauseln*

10-26 *Non-documentary conditions of payment.* Guarantees may contain conditions of payment which are framed in factual instead of documentary terms. In those situations, the guarantee does not prescribe as a condition of payment the tender of documents testifying the occurrence or non-occurrence of a certain event. Instead, the obligation to pay is made subject to the occurrence itself, without specification of the means of documentary evidence. The difficulty with non-documentary conditions is that they compel the bank to deal in realities, instead of documents and that they thereby render the bank's task unduly cumbersome. For beneficiary and account party they are apt to create uncertainty and a fair chance of disappointed expectations. It is therefore in the interest of all parties to ensure that non-documentary conditions are avoided or, if possible, are converted into documentary conditions. However regrettable, it remains a fact that independent guarantees occasionally still contain non-documentary conditions for payment. As far as documentary credits are concerned, art. 13(c) UCP provides that banks will deem such conditions as not stated and will disregard them.[82] The URDG for independent guarantees do not contain an explicit provision, but it has been suggested that a rule such as art. 13(c) UCP can be inferred from a combined reading of arts. 9 and 10 URDG.[83] It is submitted that a rule such as art. 13(a) UCP or any alternative to the effect that a non-documentary condition is deemed fulfilled if the beneficiary merely unilaterally certifies that the event has occurred, should not apply as a general rule to guarantees because it is too sweeping and because it would frustrate the intention and expectations of the parties to the underlying transaction. Any argument that examination in respect of non-documentary conditions is unduly cumbersome for the bank is negated by the fact that it is the bank itself which has agreed to the inclusion of such a condition. The protection, to which the bank is entitled and which is quite sufficient, lies in the limitation of its liability if it exercises reasonable care and in its discretionary power. Alternative protection is provided in the ISP98. While Rule 4.11(a) ISP98 states that non-documentary conditions must be disregarded, subparagraph (b) defines such conditions as those the fulfillment of which cannot be determined by the bank from the bank's own records or within the bank's normal operations. In any event, it should be emphasised that the presence of a non-documentary condition of payment does not turn an independent guarantee into an accessory guarantee (suretyship), unless the relevant condition is fundamental to the undertaking.

Nonetheless, there is no easy or general answer to the question of how banks and courts should deal with non-documentary conditions. If the guarantee requires as a condition of payment an advance payment or the issuance of a documentary credit or

---

[82] See for a critical comment Dolan, IBLJ 1994, pp. 149, 159, and 13 B.F.L.R., p. 7.
[83] Affaki, No. 114, p. 86.

payment guarantee in favour of the account party, or the award of the contract to the account party in the case of a tender guarantee, the absence of specification of (the documentary) evidence will ordinarily not give rise to great difficulties. The beneficiary will ordinarily be able to produce the relevant documents and thereby establish the fulfillment of such conditions of payment to the satisfaction of the bank. Conversely, if in the abovementioned examples the advance payment had to be made into an account with the issuing bank or if the issuing bank is also the bank which issued the documentary credit, the bank is in a very good position to ascertain compliance with these conditions from its own records, cf. Rule 4.11(b) ISP98. This may well be different if, for example, the guarantee states that 'it only takes effect if the conditions precedent of the principal contract have been fulfilled' or 'on condition always that the buyer (i.e. beneficiary) has fulfilled all his obligations under the said contract unless he has been prevented from so doing by an act or default of the seller (i.e. account party)'. Such clauses do not provide any yardstick against which compliance can be measured. It would appear that full and conclusive proof by the beneficiary of the event is not required, while, on the other hand, a mere unilateral statement by the beneficiary appears insufficient. All one can say is that the beneficiary must present *some* proof and that it is inevitably at the discretion of the bank to decide whether that proof is satisfactory, provided that it exercises reasonable care. A reasonable decision also binds the account party.

The guarantee may also stipulate that the bank's liability is limited or terminates upon a certain event without specifying the means by which the bank could ascertain fulfilment of these negative conditions, for example the expiry of the guarantee 'X months after delivery/final completion of the principal contract', or a clause suspending the obligation to pay in the event of *force majeure* in the execution of the main contract or pending arbitration, or a clause reducing the maximum amount 'in accordance with the progressive completion of the contract'. Just as the beneficiary must make his case, so must the account party and he will accordingly have to adduce some evidence to the bank.[84] The bank cannot be expected to ascertain the occurrence of the event and is, in any event, rarely capable of doing so. As regards the standard of proof and the discretionary powers of the bank, similar principles to those mentioned above apply.

Effektivklauseln. The view argued in this study is that if a 'guarantee' containing phrases such as payment upon first demand '*in the event of breach of contract*' or '*in the event that the contracting party has failed to comply with its obligations*' (*Effektivklauseln*) is, in the final analysis, construed as an independent guarantee, such phrases

---

[84] See with respect to reduction clauses Chapter 13.2.6., No. 21. Circular letters of several Libyan banks state that, as far as the counter-guarantee is concerned, reduction clauses only become effective after receipt in writing of the beneficiary's agreement to this effect.

do not constitute a condition for payment.[85] Accordingly, the beneficiary need not adduce evidence of default by the account party, and the bank is not required to investigate the matter and/or to demand evidence of default or loss from the beneficiary.[86] German doctrine recognises the contradictory nature of guarantees which are stated to be payable on first demand, but also contain these so-called *Effektivklauseln*. One considers, however, these 'guarantees' to be an independent guarantee payable on first demand or, as the case may be, a suretyship payable on first demand,[87] but yet requiring substantive proof of breach of contract or the beneficiary's loss as described in the *Effektivklausel*, while (other) defences stemming from the underlying relationship are to be discarded. In this approach, the phrases are construed as conditions of payment and, as the kind of proof of default has not been specified, they amount to non-documentary conditions. This view has led to the state of uncertainty that could be expected. These German authors disagree as regards the kind of evidence required, ranging from a mere formal statement of default to some or even full proof of the beneficiary's loss or the principal debtor's default.[88] Consequently, not only will the bank be surprised to learn that the guarantee is supposed to contain conditions of payment which are by no means apparent, but they are also kept in the dark as to the nature of the evidence they are expected to demand. German case law rejects, however, the view that the beneficiary has to produce some kind of evidence of default and that the bank has to inquire into this matter: in the case of such *Effektivklauseln* a submission by the beneficiary of a mere formal statement of default is sufficient.[89]

Limitations of liability, notification to account party

10-27 As has been observed in no. 10-19, it is not the bank's duty to investigate whether the terms for limitation or termination of liability have been fulfilled, if that is not

---

[85] References to 'breach of contract' or 'default by the account party' often appear in the recitals of the guarantee. These references merely serve to identify the purpose of the guarantee and they do not constitute a condition of payment as they do not form part of the operative clauses.

[86] Cf. *Cass.*, *5 February 1985*, D 1985 J p. 269, *Paris, 29 January 1981*, D. 1981 J. p. 336, *LG Braunschweig, 22 May 1980*, RIW 1981, p. 789, *OLG München, 6 May 1987*, WM 1988, p. 1554. See also Chapter 12.3.4, No. 12-21, and Chapter 13.2.3, No. 13-13.

[87] See Chapter 4.5 for the German type of suretyship payable on first demand.

[88] See especially Schmidt, WM 1999, p. 308-313 (with further references to legal writing), von Westphalen, p. 98-102, Zahn/Ehrlich/Neumann, 9/26, Canaris, No. 1131, Schlegelberger/Hefermehl, No. 297, p. 589, Kleiner, Nos. 21.02/3, 21.26, Dohm, Nos. 85, 200, Horn, Nos. 517-519, Staudinger/Horn, No. 236, Lienesch, p. 128.

[89] *LG Braunschweig, 22 May 1980*, RIW 1981, p. 789, *OLG München, 6 May 1987*, WM 1988, p. 1554, *BGH, 17 October 1996*, WM 1996, p. 2228, and *OLG München, 23 July 1997*, WM 1998, p. 342. See further Chapter 13.2.3, No. 13-13.

readily ascertainable. The account party will have to adduce the evidence. This allocation necessarily implies that the bank should immediately inform its customer of the demand for payment to enable him to produce evidence. If the guarantee does not fix the period of time,[90] the account party should be allowed a reasonable, but short, period. After all, the account party will often be in a position to procure evidence well before the demand for payment has been made, while, on the other hand, the beneficiary has a legitimate interest in obtaining quick payment, once he has complied with the conditions. Accordingly, account parties are well advised to forward the relevant documents immediately rather than to await an actual call on the guarantee.

10.9 BANK'S DUTY OF NOTIFICATION OF THE DEMAND FOR PAYMENT

Significance of notification

10-28 It is accepted, at least as a matter of principle, that the account party has the opportunity to obtain a preliminary stop-payment order, if he is able to establish fraud on the part of the beneficiary.[91] Should, however, payment by the bank already have been effected, his obligation to reimburse the bank will only lapse, if, in addition, he can prove that the bank was aware of the beneficiary's fraud at the time of payment.[92] The chances that the account party will be able to discharge this burden of proof is very small. Consequently, once payment has been effected, the (alleged) fraud has materialised and the harm to the account party has been inflicted. It is therefore of major importance to the account party that he becomes immediately aware of the demand for payment so that, by seeking interlocutory relief, he can attempt to prevent the imminent damage.

Opinions differ, the law at present, notice injunctions

10-29 Among legal writers on the Continent the question of a legal duty to notify the customer prior to payment has been much debated, but a unanimous view has not emerged. A vast majority favours such a duty,[93] while a small, but forceful minority

---

[90] See, for example, *Paris, 2 June 1982*, D. 1983 J p. 437 , in this respect upheld by *Cass., 5 February 1985*, D. 1985 J. p. 269 ('prior to 7 April 1983'), *Trib. com. Brussels, 15 November 1984*, RDC 1985, p. 569 ('within six months').

[91] See Chapter 16.

[92] See Chapter 15.

[93] Mijnssen, p. 36, Boll, p. 118, van Delden, HH p. 744, Bertrams, WPNR 1987, p. 516-518, von Westphalen, p. 194-196, 353-358, Staudinger/Horn, No. 33, 332, Lienesch, p. 127, 200-202, Nielsen, WM 1999, p. 2057,2058, Schlegelberger/Hefermehl, No. 286, Canaris, No.

opposes the proposition.⁹⁴ The issue has not been settled conclusively by case law, at least not in each of the several jurisdictions concerned.⁹⁵

In the United Kingdom, a general duty of notification has been rejected in *Esal (Commodities) Ltd., Reltor Ltd. v. Oriental Credit, Wells Fargo*. The fact that banks commonly give prior notice was found insufficient to conclude that a legal obligation to do so exists.⁹⁶

During the Iranian revolution of 1979-1980 American case law came up with a kind of in-between solution. In *Stromberg Carlson Corp. v. Bank Melli Iran*, the court was not prepared to accept the existence of a general duty, but in view of the particular circumstances of the case ('the fluid and precarious circumstances now prevailing in Iran') it did grant a so-called 'notice injunction' requiring the bank to inform the account party of the demand for payment and to allow a period of ten days before honouring the demand.⁹⁷ This restraint of payment for a short time was intended to enable the

---

1110, Kleiner, No. 21.15, Pleyer, WM 2/1973, p. 12, Schütze, RIW 1981, p. 85, von Mettenheim, RIW 1981, p. 585, Coing, ZHR 1983, p. 136, Bark, ZIP 1982, p. 415 (with qualifications), Dohm, No. 137-141, Schinnerer, O. Bank-Archiv 1982, p. 208, Simont, Tours, p. 486, Poullet, thesis, No. 342-345, De Ly, TBH 1986, p. 177, T'Kint, No. 847, RPDB, No. 124, Rives-Lange, Banque 1988, p. 236, Mattout, No. 227, Stoufflet, Garantie Bancaire Internationale, No. 43, Prüm, No. 485.

94 Zahn/Ehrlich/Neumann, 9/86, Schinnerer/Avancini, p. 319, Moschner, O. Bank-Archiv, 1987, p. 160, Vasseur, No. 102 , D. 1986 I.R. p. 160, 166 and D. 1988 Somm. p. 247. See also Pabbruwe, p. 25.

95 The existence of a general duty of prior notification has been affirmed in *Geneva, 14 March 1985*, D. 1986 I.R. p. 164. In *LG Stuttgart, 8 August 1980*, WM 1981, p 633, and in *OLG München, 6 May 1987*, WM 1988, p. 1554, the courts observed cursorily and as an obiter dictum that the bank was to notify the customer of its intention to pay, while the bank had in fact done so. *Trib. com. Melun, 29 April 1985*, D. 1986 I.R. p. 159, ordered the instructing bank to give prior notice of a fresh demand for payment by the issuing bank in cases involving indirect guarantees. In *Kammergericht, 20 November 1986*, NJW 1987, p. 1774 (first demand suretyship), the court held that the question did not have to be decided, since the omission of prior notification had not been deemed prejudicial to the interests of the account party. *BGH, 19 September 1985*, NJW 1986, p. 310, could only be an indirect authority, since the security furnished by the bank was a traditional suretyship. It was held that the former Sec. 13 of the general terms and conditions of German banks, which, in their relationship with the account party, entitles a bank to effect payment upon first demand, did not negate the bank's duty to notify the account party. The German Supreme Court found that there was clear evidence that the beneficiary/creditor had no right of payment against the account party/principal debtor and the claim for reimbursement was therefore dismissed.

96 [1985] 2 Lloyd's Rep. 546 (QB). The court allowed for an exception 'where there is a course of dealing giving rise to some implied agreement'.

97 467 F. Supp. 530, 532 (S.D.N.Y. 1979).

account party to adduce further evidence of fraud and then to take legal action aimed at a more indefinite injunction. Notice injunctions were subsequently during that period granted in several instances,[98] but they were refused on at least two occasions on the grounds that they were premature, as the account party had failed to demonstrate the likelihood of an imminent call on the guarantee and a threat of imminent harm.[99]

A legal duty of prior notification must surely be taken to exist at present in two specific instances. First, the situation where the bank's obligation is qualified by restrictive conditions, the fulfilment of which has to be shown by the account party, see no. 10-27. Secondly, where the beneficiary invites the bank 'to pay or to extend' the validity period of the guarantee. Clearly, this choice should be made by the customer, not by the bank. It is only when no timely response is forthcoming that the bank may serve its customer's interests by extending the period of validity.[100]

Arguments pro and contra a duty of notification

10-30 Opponents of a legal duty of notification argue that the bank's obligation is independent of the main contract, that no such duty exists in respect of documentary credits and that the bank has a legitimate interest in staying clear of disputes between account party and beneficiary. These arguments do not appear to be conclusive. Independence has no bearing on the issue whatsoever, while there are sound arguments for the absence of such a duty in documentary credits, which cannot be advanced with respect to guarantees.[101] It is true that the bank, if it proceeds to payment forthwith,

---

[98] See, for example, *Harris Int'l. Telecommunications Inc. v. Chase Manhattan Bank, Bank Melli Iran*, No. 79 Civ. 802 (S.D.N.Y. 23 February 1979), *PanAm World Airways Inc. v. Bank Melli Iran, Citybank N.A.*, 30 March 1979, Int.'l Trade Rep. U.S. Export Weekly (BNA) O-1, *KMW Int.'l. v. Chase Manhattan Bank N.A.*, 606 F.2d. 10 (2d. Cir. 1979). See for a complete list of notice injunctions granted in the period 1979-1980 Getz, Harv. Int. L.R. 1980, p. 216 note 135 and the Appendix pp. 248-252, and Zimmett, Law & Policy Int. Business 1984, pp. 937, 940. The waiting period ranged from three to twenty days.

[99] *Harris Corp. v. Bank Melli Iran*, No. 79 Civ. 560 (N.D. Ill., 22 March 1979), *Stromberg Carlson Corp. v. Continental Illinois Nat. Bank & Trust Co. of Chicago*, No. 79 Civ. 810 (N.D. Ill., 22 March 1979). In the latter case the bank had in fact promised to give prior notice and to observe a waiting period of three days.

[100] See further Chapter 12.4.3. No. 12-43.

[101] First, the utilisation of the letter of credit and payment is the ordinary course of events expected by all parties concerned. Secondly, the opportunities for fraud are smaller on account of the third-party documentation, although there exists a possibility of forged documents. Thirdly, having regard to the immense number of documentary credits such a duty would impose an undue burden on the bank.

will indeed avoid trouble with the beneficiary, but at the same it may well cause strained relations with its customer and result in litigation which could have been prevented.[102]

The argument in favour of a legal duty of notification is the fact that, while the interest of the account party in prior notice is clear and substantial, the factual and legitimate interests of the bank do not militate against such a duty. Banks do in fact frequently give prior notice, which does not particularly suggest a conflicting interest. Giving notice even has the advantage for the bank that it can never be accused of having effected payment in circumstances where fraud by the beneficiary should have been obvious to the bank. After notification it is for the account party to decide either to desist from seeking a restraining order, in which case fraud could never have been obvious to the bank, or to commence proceedings, in which case the court will pronounce judgment on the alleged fraud. Accordingly, the bank is freed from the burden and responsibility of having to make such a risky decision on its own and it can also preserve a neutral position.

From the beneficiary's viewpoint a duty of prior notification might be perceived as a form of the bank's siding with the account party and as a measure which frustrates his right to immediate payment, precisely because notice enables the account party to apply for restraining orders. On the other hand, the bank owes no duty to refrain from notification unless this has been explicitly stipulated.[103]

On balance, this study is not inclined to impose a general legal duty of prior notification on the bank, the main reason being that such a legal duty would be difficult to reconcile with the neutrality which is expected of the bank. It should also be pointed out that a call on the guarantee will rarely come as a total surprise to the account party and it appears more appropriate, as a matter of legal norms, to leave it to the account party to contact the bank on its own initiative in the case of an imminent call. Moreover, the account party could have stipulated a clause to the effect that the beneficiary is to submit to the bank, as one of the required documents, a copy of a prior notice of default to the account party so that he will always be aware of an imminent call.[104]

In the case of indirect guarantees there are compelling reasons to reject a general legal duty of notification on the foreign issuing bank. Whereas the first instructing bank might perhaps be naturally account party-oriented, the foreign issuing bank, which does not stand in a contractual relationship with the account party, might naturally be beneficiary-oriented. Both account party and beneficiary will expect nothing else. Against this background, imposing a legal duty of notification on the foreign issuing

---

[102] Striking examples are *BGH, 19 September 1985*, NJW 1986, p. 310 and *Kammergericht, 20 November 1986*, NJW 1987, p. 1774.

[103] Should the guarantee contain phrases such as 'without further question or reference to the account party' these should be understood as merely emphasising the independent nature of the guarantee and/or as excluding the need for approval of payment by the account party.

[104] See Chapter 4, No. 4-3.

bank just for the account party's sake should be rejected, the more so as it would inevitably put a strain on the foreign bank's position towards the beneficiary, perhaps not in a strictly legal sense, but certainly as a matter of fact.[105]

The question of whether the bank should defer payment, if the account party commences interlocutory proceedings for restraining orders, and await the court's judgment is examined in Chapter 16.5, no. 16-24.

Art. 17 and 21 URDG, Rule 3.10 ISP98: notification and transmission of documents

10-31 Art. 17 URDG requires the bank to inform the account party of the demand for payment 'without delay', which suggests a slightly lower degree of promptness than the phrase 'immediately'. This duty also applies to the foreign issuing bank in the case of an indirect guarantee in that this bank should inform the first instructing bank, which in its turn must inform the account party. It is expressly noted that art. 17 does not require the bank to notify the account party before paying. Accordingly, the bank acts within the scope of art. 17 if it receives a conforming demand for payment and pays it the next day whilst at the same time notifying the account party that it has received and honoured a demand for payment.[106] Art. 21 URDG prescribes that the issuing bank shall also transmit the beneficiary's demand for payment and other documents as they may be required to be submitted in accordance with the conditions of payment.[107] Rule 3.10 ISP98 explicitly negates a duty of the bank to notify the account party of a demand for payment and the ISP98 do not contain provisions in respect of the transmission of documents to the account party.

10.10 RECOURSE OF THE BANK AGAINST THE ACCOUNT PARTY. SPECIAL RISKS

10-32 As discussed in Chapter 10.8, the bank owes a duty to the account party to refuse payment if the terms and conditions of the guarantee have not been complied with. That same duty applies to the foreign issuing bank in the case of indirect guarantees. It has been argued that, if it is established that the foreign issuing bank has breached that

---

[105] In favour of such a duty: Poullet, thesis, No. 345, Prüm, No. 485, and Horn and Wymeersch, p. 485. See also von Westphalen, p. 355. Contra: Pabbruwe, p. 26.

[106] Cf. Goode, p. 86, 87, Affaki, No. 114(1). Interestingly, art. 35(2) of the Uniform Act on Securities of the OHADA countries, which generally follows the URDG patterns, does explicitly provide for notification before payment.

[107] While at some stage the Draft Uncitral Convention had a draft provision (art. 15) along the lines of art. 17 URDG, it has been deleted in a subsequent revision of the text.

obligation, the first instructing bank is to refrain from reimbursing the issuing bank.[108] It is also possible that the (instructing) bank has been prohibited to pay by virtue of a court order. It may happen, however, that although the (instructing) bank has resisted claims for payment for reasons stated above, the beneficiary and/or foreign issuing bank have been able to obtain judgment against the (instructing) bank in some jurisdiction and/or to seize its assets. It is noted that issuing banks are often in a position to procure payment by debiting the instructing bank's current account with the issuing bank. As guarantees are issued for the risk and account of the customer and as the bank has discharged its obligations, a loss of this nature is a typical risk that is to be allocated to the account party. The bank is, therefore, ordinarily entitled to be indemnified by the customer.[109]

An example of a possibly atypical risk is provided in *Paris, 27 June 1988*. A French bank had issued a direct guarantee in favour of an Iranian company and the guarantee was called in 1980 by an Iranian bank which had apparently taken charge of the beneficiary's business while the beneficiary itself had been liquidated. The French bank refused payment because the claim was evidently fraudulent. In 1984 another Iranian bank which had subsequently taken charge of the beneficiary's business managed to procure payment by debiting the accounts of the French bank, which were held with a German bank. The Court of Appeal ruled that the account party did not need to indem-

---

[108] Chapter 11.2.2, Nos. 11-13 and 11-20.

[109] *Esal (Commodities), Reltor v. Oriental Credit, Wells Fargo*, [1985] 2 Lloyd's Rep. 546 (instructing bank ordered to reimburse the issuing bank, customer ordered to reimburse the instructing bank), *LG Düsseldorf, 9 August 1984*, RIW 1985, p. 77 (fraud by the beneficiary as well as fraud by the second issuing bank, if it were to proceed to payment, had been established; the instructing bank was not to proceed to payment on the counter-guarantee *voluntarily*, but it was held to be entitled to debit the accounts of the customer in the two situations mentioned in the text; at the court hearing the instructing bank stated that it would not voluntarily proceed to payment and an injunction to this effect was therefore considered unnecessary), *LG Köln, 11 December 1981*, WM 1982, p. 438 (one of the reasons for not granting a stop-payment injunction against the first instructing bank was the fact that the second issuing bank could easily debit the accounts of the first bank). *Rockwell Systems Int. v. Citibank*, 719 F2d. 583 (2d. Civ. 1983) and *Collins Systems Int. v. Citibank*, 82 Civ. 613 (V.L.B.) (S.D.N.Y. 1982) (indirect guarantee; stop-payment injunction against instructing bank granted; account party ordered to indemnify the bank against possible losses arising from the injunction). See also *OLG Hamburg, 4 November 1977*, RIW 1978, p. 615 (order to release the collateral security in view of the absence of likelihood of enforced payment), von Westphalen, p. 387, Zahn/Eberding /Ehrlich, 9/91, Nielsen, ZHR, 1983, p. 157. Contra Dohm, No. 158 (referring to Sec. 402(2) OR), von Mettenheim, RIW 1981, p. 587. See also *Cass., 18 March 1986*, D. 1986 I.R. p. 166 (the beneficiary had obtained an arbitral award against the Egyptian, issuing bank. The claim of this bank for reimbursement by the French instructing bank was dismissed on the grounds that the call on the counter-guarantee had been made after its expiry date).

nify the French bank since he was not answerable for the manoeuvres of the Iranian bank, with which he had no relationship at all.[110]

10.11 SUBROGATION

10-33 Could the guarantor who has effected payment to the beneficiary pursuant to the terms of the guarantee, claim reimbursement from the principal debtor on the basis of subrogation, as could a surety in the case of an accessory guarantee? If so, other forms of security, such as a charge, which the principal debtor may have furnished to the beneficiary/creditor, would also pass to the guarantor.

The issue is ordinarily not of great practical relevance. A right to reimbursement flows directly from the the principal debtor's request to issue the guarantee for his account. The duty to repay the bank is often also contained in a counter-guarantee by the principal debtor, while banks usually make sure that the account party furnishes sufficient security for reimbursement. Subrogation is, however, important if the security proves to be insufficient while the principal debtor or a third party has furnished additional security to the beneficiary/creditor. Subrogation may also be important if the instructions for the issuance of the guarantee and the counter-guarantee do not originate from the principal debtor, but, for example, from a group company and if that group company is insolvent.[111] A third situation is the case where it is not the paying bank, but the bank's counter-guarantor who invokes subrogation.

In legal writing the controversy concerning subrogation reveals some misconceptions regarding the nature of independent guarantees. Certain commentators in, mainly, early legal writing reject subrogation, whether founded on the general statutory provisions concerning subrogation or founded on an analogous application of the pertinent provisions of suretyship. The persistent argument is that the guarantee, unlike suretyship, is independent of the underlying relationship and that the guarantor pays his own debt, not the debt of the principal debtor.[112] This view was followed in *CA Amsterdam, 10*

---

[110] D. 1989 Somm. p. 151. Vasseur, in his annotation, questions the correctness of the decision. It must, however, be noted that the loss incurred by the French bank did not solely arise as a consequence of the account party's request to issue a guarantee, but also from the fact that the bank maintained mutual accounts with the Iranian bank, which was not involved in the issuance of the guarantee and with which, as was observed by the court, the account party had no relationship at all. The Court of Appeal's judgment has been affirmed by *Cass. 6 February 1990*, D. 1990 Somm. p. 213.

[111] See further No. 10-6.

[112] Pabbruwe, WPNR, 1979, p. 183, Poullet, DPCI 1979, p. 435, de Vroede and Flamee, TPR 1982, p. 374, Herbots, RW 1983-1984, p. 1191, Wymeersch, TPR 1986, p. 480, RPDB, No. 174, Gavalda and Stoufflet, RTDC 1980, p. 21, Kleiner, No. 24.07, Dohm, No. 159, Lienesch, p. 206, Staudinger/Horn, No. 228 (with further references to general German writing).

August 2000,[113] and *Trib. com. Ghent, 12 February 1999*.[114] The aforementioned contradistinction is, however, false and reflects a superseded perception of the notion of independence. Just as the surety does, the independent guarantor satisfies both his own debt and the debt of the account party. Independence has no bearing on the issue of subrogation.[115] A significant number of German writers, therefore, correctly advocates the analogous application of the suretyship provisions relating to subrogation.[116] This is also the view under English law.[117] In France, legal writing derives the bank's right to invoke subrogation from two decisions by the French Cour de Cassation.[118] The 1995 revised Section 5-117(a) of the U.S. U.C.C. explicitly states that the paying bank is subrogated to the rights of the beneficiary as if the issuer were a secondary obligor (= surety, or accessory guarantor).[119] Art. 336 of the Law of Commerce of Bahrain, art. 292 of the Iraqi Commercial Code, art. 386 of the Commercial Code of Kuwait and art. 1503 of the Civil Code of Yemen also provide for subrogation in favour of the paying bank.

---

[113] JOR 2000, 205, with critical comments by Bertrams.

[114] TBH 1999, p. 727. In the case at hand the court, however, made an exception by allowing subrogation in favour of the counter-guarantor of the paying bank, who was a private individual. T'Kint, No. 33, is, however, in favour of subrogation. In a similar situation *OG Austria, 9 December 1987*, JIBL 1988 N-154, also allowed subrogation.

[115] Cf. Chapter 12.1, No. 12-6.

[116] See especially Castellvi, WM 1995, p. 868-872. Idem: Von Westphalen, p. 390, Zahn/Ehrlich/Neumann, 9/13, Canaris, No. 1112, Schlegelberger/Hefermehl, No. 288, Liesecke, WM 1986, p. 28, Pleyer, WM 1973 SBeil. Nr. 2, p. 21 and Tours, p. 194, 195, von Caemmerer, FS Riese, p. 306, Schinnerer/Avancini. p. 294.

[117] See Alan Ward and Gerry McCormack, A New Application for the Doctrine of Subrogation, [1999] JIBL, p. 39-44, citing several English decisions.

[118] *Cass., 23 February 1988*, D. 1988 I.R., p. 69, and *Cass., 9 May 1990*, RTD civ. 1990, p. 662. In these cases, which did not involve independent guarantees, the Cour de Cassation ruled that a party which pays his own debt, is nonetheless entitled to subrogation as regards the principal debtor if the latter is also discharged on account of that payment as against the creditor. See further Simler/Delebecque, Droit civil, Les suretés, La publicité foncière (2e. ed), No. 239.

[119] Interestingly, the clearer text of the 1995 revised version was felt necessary in order to dismantle a variety of technical impediments against subrogation that were previously raised in some court decisions and legal commentary. The 1995 text was designed, as the Official Comment 1 observes, to explicitly remove any suggestion that the independence principle is an obstacle to subrogation. See also McLaughlin, [2002] 119 BLJ, p. 538-540, Dolan, § 7.05[2].

CHAPTER 11
RELATIONSHIP ACCOUNT PARTY – FIRST INSTRUCTING BANK – SECOND ISSUING BANK. INDIRECT GUARANTEE. COUNTER-GUARANTEE

11.1 ACCOUNT PARTY – FIRST INSTRUCTING BANK – SECOND ISSUING BANK. GENERAL

11.1.1 Introduction. Structure and terminology

11-1 In the case of indirect guarantees the guarantee is issued by – and only by – the second foreign bank (=the issuing bank), ordinarily located in the beneficiary's country, upon the request of the first bank (= the instructing bank), which in turn acts upon the request of the account party.[1] After payment, the issuing bank looks to the instructing bank for reimbursement and the latter is entitled to repayment from the account party of the amount it had to pay to the issuing bank. The guarantee issued by the issuing bank is usually referred to as the 'primary' guarantee in order to clearly distinguish this undertaking from the instructing bank's express undertaking to reimburse the issuing bank which is called the counter-guarantee.

The counter-guarantee is issued by the instructing bank in its own name but for the risk and account of the account party. It often provides for payment to the issuing bank on terms which are broader than those of the primary guarantee. One should, therefore, bear in mind that in the case of indirect guarantees the risks to which the account party is exposed are not only determined by the terms and conditions of the primary guarantee but also by those of the counter-guarantee. This reveals, once again, that the various relationships which together make up the modern guarantee framework, are distinct and independent of each other in most respects and at the same time interdependent in other respects.

11.1.2 First instructing bank – second issuing bank. Legal nature. Mandate

11-2 In the relationship between first instructing and second issuing bank we find the same factual elements as in the relationship between account party and bank in direct guarantees: a request to issue a guarantee under certain terms and conditions, accept-

---

[1] See also Chapter 9, No. 9-3.

ance thereof, execution and reimbursement. The two relationships must therefore be regarded as the same in law too, at least in principle. This is certainly reflected in German case law and doctrine, where both relationships are labelled as *Geschäftsbesorgungsvertrag*, Sec. 675 BGB (mandate).[2] The same rules of law apply.

11.1.3 Various aspects

11-3 Various aspects of the inter-bank relationship are to be dealt with in the same way and for the same reasons as those between account party and bank in direct guarantees, see Chapter 10.

The right of reimbursement by the instructing bank is based on the proper discharge of obligations by the second issuing bank, the principal duties being the issuance of the guarantee in accordance with the instructions, and the examination with regard to compliance with the terms and conditions of the primary guarantee. It is noted, however, that the precise conditions of reimbursement are also affected by the terms of the counter-guarantee in favour of the issuing bank, see Chapter 11.2.2 and 11.4. The right to reimbursement need not be stipulated expressly as this right is implicit in the instructions. Nor is the right to reimbursement in any way affected by whatever may or may not occur between account party and first instructing bank or by whatever defences the account party may have against the beneficiary deriving from the underlying relationship, since the second issuing bank has been instructed to issue an independent guarantee. Accordingly the exclusion of those defences need not be stipulated expressly either.

The issue of furnishing security may also arise in the inter-bank relationship. If the instructing bank does not maintain a current account or have a standing relationship with the issuing bank, if the instructing bank is unknown or if the issuing bank has any doubts concerning the reliability of the instructing bank, the issuing bank may require security. This security will ordinarily be obtained from another, higher rated bank acting at the request of the instructing bank and can be accomplished in two ways. The other bank could provide a counter-guarantee to be called in the event that the instructing bank fails to promptly meet its obligations towards the second issuing bank, or the other bank could be interposed between the instructing and the issuing bank. The latter structure will be preferred by the issuing bank, as it then can deal directly with the other bank. That bank will in turn be reimbursed by the instructing bank. Certain Libyan banks pursue a policy of requiring a deposit of up to twenty-five per cent from the instructing bank, while some Egyptian banks ask for a power of attorney authorising the bank to draw on the instructing bank's accounts with a third bank.

---

[2] *OLG Saarbrücken, 23 January 1981*, RIW 1981, p. 338, *LG Dortmund, 9 July 1980*, WM 1981, p. 280, von Westphalen, pp. 225, 226, 229, 343, Zahn/Ehrlich/Neumann, 9/101, Canaris, no 1117, Schlegelberger/Hefermehl, no 291, Mülbert, p. 81, Nielsen, ZIP 1982, p. 257 and ZHR 1983, pp. 157, 158, Coing, ZHR 1983, p. 126, Kleiner, p. 139, Dohm, No. 269.

The second issuing bank is also entitled to a commission fee and reimbursement of incidental expenses as discussed in Chapters 10.5 and 10.6.

11.1.4 Instructions for the issuance of the primary guarantee. Advice

Instructions and adherence; imprecise instructions

11-4 In many instances the first instructing bank will advise its customer that it is futile or that it may cause uneasiness to instruct the foreign bank to issue a guarantee with certain terms and conditions, or the omission thereof, and/or on the basis of a text which purports to be fixed in minute detail. The reason for this is that issuing banks in foreign countries prefer to employ, or insist on employing, their own texts because they are familiar with the format and terminology. The issuing bank may also be bound under local mandatory law to agree only to issue guarantees which conform to state regulations. Foreign banks regularly disseminate circular letters to correspondent banks indicating the data which should (or should not) be included in the instructions, and containing a specimen of the various standard texts. In such circumstances, the customer and the instructing bank may confine themselves to stating the main items, such as the name of the beneficiary, circumscription of the secured contract, type of conditions of payment and other clauses, maximum amount and currency, and the expiry date, and to request the foreign bank to issue the guarantee 'as per your usual specimen X' or 'as per your usual specimen X as contained in your circular letter of …'. The latter phrase is to be preferred, since the standard texts are occasionally revised.

The principle of strict adherence to the instructions of the mandator, i.e. those of the first instructing bank, also applies to the second issuing bank.[3] It applies with equal force and regardless of whether the instructions are confined to the principal items, whether the text of the guarantee purports to be definite or whether the text is presented as a draft. Several authors allow for some deviation, if this is required by special usage or by local law.[4] This appears to be the wrong approach. Clearly, the second issuing bank is quite at liberty to decline to issue a guarantee as instructed for whatever reason and/or to insist on alterations or adaptations, but it is for the first instructing bank and account party to decide. The second issuing bank should, therefore, liaise with the instructing bank. To the extent that no consent for alterations has been obtained, the only relevant question is whether the variations are in any way material, having regard

---

[3] *LG Dortmund, 9 July 1980*, WM 1981, p. 280, von Westphalen, pp. 226-228, 344, Zahn/Ehrlich/Neumann, 9/97, Bark, ZIP 1982, p. 408, Dohm, Nos. 263, 264.

[4] See the authors mentioned in the previous footnote. Von Westphalen and Zahn/Ehrlich/Neumann do, however, recommend further consultation.

to the nature of the instructions, the reasonableness of the bank's understanding of the instructions in the light of local practices and the pressure of time. Whether the foreign bank is prepared to issue guarantees with terms and texts which deviate from their standard specimen depends on local conditions.[5]

In case of unclear instructions it would be commendable for the issuing bank to contact the instructing bank for clarification. The difficulty is, however, that the issuing bank may not fully appreciate that the instructions are, from an objective point of view, unclear due to different local perceptions and practice. Pressure of time may also be a factor. In two recent decisions, *LG Hamburg, 15 March 1999*, and *CA Liege, 8 June 1999*, the court ruled that the reasonable understanding of the issuing bank of the instructions prevails.[6]

In most instances it will be the second issuing bank which is entrusted with the drafting of the final text of the guarantee, which may be rendered in local language. It would be commendable if the issuing bank were to forward a (translated) copy of the text prior to its issuance in order to reduce the possibility of misunderstandings or deviations, thereby preventing subsequent disagreement. However, it appears that pressure of time and lack of facilities do not always allow for such precautions and that copies are only forwarded, if at all, after issuance of the guarantee.

Errors in the transmission of the instructions. Issuing bank's failure to carry out the instructions. Arts. 12, 14 and 15 URDG

11-5 It may happen that the instructions for the issuance of the guarantee, as received by the foreign issuing bank, contain errors due to a mistake on the part of the first instructing bank's staff or technical defects in its equipment with the result that, for example, a reduction clause has been omitted or the maximum amount or the expiry

---

[5] See Chapter 7, No. 7-4.

[6] In *LG Hamburg, 15 March 1999*, WM 1999, p. 1713, the instructing bank requested the foreign bank to issue a guarantee without specifying the nature of the guarantee or the conditions of payment and giving only the key elements, such as the name of the beneficiary and account party, the secured contract, amount and expiry date. The foreign bank issued a first demand guarantee and debited the account of the instructing bank after a call on the primary guarantee. The instructing bank, then, claimed repayment arguing that it had requested the foreign bank to issue a traditional suretyship. This claim was rejected. The court ruled that the issuing bank could reasonably have interpreted the request as an instruction to issue a first demand guarantee, *inter alia*, because the counter-guarantee was also payable on first demand and the expiry date thereof was linked to that of the primary guarantee. In a similar case *CA Liege, 8 June 1999*, RDC 2000, p. 731, ruled that, with a view to international practice and the customs developed in this matter, the issuing bank could reasonably have interpreted the instructions as an instruction to issue a first demand guarantee.

date has been misstated. Since the correct transmission of the instructions to the foreign bank is a key duty of the first bank, it is liable to its customer for any loss which is caused by such errors, except in the case of extraordinary supervening events beyond its control. This rule has been affirmed in *Trib. com. Versailles, 17 September 1981*.[7] If the URDG apply, the bank is, however, relieved of liability for technical defects in the transmission of the instructions by virtue of art. 12 URDG,[8] subject to the overriding duty to act in good faith and with reasonable care (art. 15 URDG).

If the second foreign bank refuses to issue the guarantee without informing the instructing bank (in time), or if it delays the issuance or if it issues a guarantee with terms and conditions which deviate from the instructions, it may incur liability towards the instructing bank. The difficulty is, however, that the loss as a result of such acts and omissions is ordinarily suffered by the account party and not by the instructing bank. Since there is no contractual relationship between the second foreign bank and the account party, the latter has no claim for damages in contract but only in tort.[9] In general, the instructing bank is not responsible for the acts or omissions by the foreign issuing bank. This is also stated in art. 14a/b URDG subject to art. 15 URDG. Its duty towards the account party is mainly confined to the exercise of reasonable care in the selection of a competent and properly functioning intermediary.[10] The instructing bank is also expected to contact the foreign bank if no response is forthcoming or in case of any indication that the foreign bank has not correctly carried out the instructions.

Advice with respect to local practices

11-6 As noted in Chapter 10.7, no. 11-6, the bank does not owe a general duty to advise its customer of the risks of first demand guarantees. However, the peculiarities of local practices and the patterns of behaviour in some countries may give rise to some responsibility in the case of indirect guarantees, especially towards those customers who have had no previous dealings with those countries.[11]

---

[7] D. 1982, I.R. p. 496, see Chapter 10.7, No. 10-15.

[8] This article contains a disclaimer for a range of events, such as delay in the transmission and errors in translations.

[9] See also the remarks in Chapter 9, No. 9-2, in respect of the remedies against the advising bank, which apply *mutatis mutandis* in relation to the second issuing bank.

[10] Cf. Goode, p. 79, von Westphalen, p. 229, Canaris, No. 1116.

[11] Cf. Zahn/Ehrlich/Neumann, 9/94.

11.1.5 Second issuing bank's duty of examination with respect to compliance

11-7 The duty of the second issuing bank to ascertain with reasonable care compliance with all terms and conditions of the primary guarantee features among its key obligations. This duty has the same content and operates in the same way as it does with regard to the bank in the case of direct guarantees.[12] This is also borne out by art. 9 URDG and art. 16 Uncitral Convention, which do not distinguish between direct and indirect guarantees. Failure to discharge its duty of examination bars the second issuing bank's claim for reimbursement founded on the mandate. The practical value of this rule, particularly from the viewpoint of the account party, is, however, greatly affected by the terms of the counter-guarantee, see Chapter 11.2.2.

11.2 THE COUNTER-GUARANTEE

11.2.1 General

11-8 The relationship between the instructing and issuing bank in the case of guarantees is different from that between the instructing and confirming bank in the case of letters of credit. In the former there is usually a counter-guarantee which formalises the legal relationship and in particular the conditions for reimbursment by the instructing bank to the issuing bank, which is absent in letters of credit. That gap is filled by the general provisions of the UCP.

The request from the instructing bank to the foreign issuing bank nearly always comprises two elements: the request to issue a guarantee in accordance with the specified text or particulars and some kind of express undertaking for reimbursement. These undertakings are commonly referred to as counter-guarantees. In American terminology, however, they are called standby letters of credit, which causes confusion, since the primary guarantee issued by the foreign bank in favour of the beneficiary/creditor is also called a standby letter of credit. In Germany the counter-guarantee is sometimes dubbed an indirect guarantee causing the same confusion, while in English law the term indemnity may be found.

The instructing bank issues the counter-guarantee in its own name, but for the risk and account of the account party. Accordingly, if the instructing bank is bound to pay the issuing bank in accordance with the terms of the counter-guarantee, it is entitled to reimbursement by the account party.

Counter-guarantees are rarely embodied in separate documents. This will only occur if the undertaking for reimbursement has, probably by oversight, not been included in the request or if the initial undertaking is not satisfactory to the foreign bank.

---

[12] See Chapter 10.8. for direct guarantees.

Counter-guarantees may take different forms. Counter-guarantees between Western European banks often consist of no more than the phrase 'please issue *for our account*' or 'under our full responsibility' or they may state 'we shall unconditionally repay the amounts which you have paid pursuant to the above-mentioned guarantee'. They may or they may not contain phrases such as 'payment upon first demand regardless of disputes between principal and beneficiary'. Outside Western Europe, foreign issuing banks often, but not always, prescribe a general formula for the counter-guarantee, which ordinarily contains the phrase '(re)payment upon first demand'. For example, 'we undertake to pay to you on your first demand despite any contestation by our principals any sum or sums that you may pay in accordance with the terms of your guarantee', or 'we undertake to hold you fully indemnified and harmless from any claim, loss or expenses which may arise as a result of your issue of the guarantee, or 'we undertake to pay to you without demur or protest in case the guarantee is invoked by the beneficiary and your notice of invocation is acceptable to us by simple tested telex', or 'in the event of execution by the beneficiary, reimbursement will be made on your first demand, irrespective of any contestation from whatever party and our counter-guarantee to cover you will be subject to the same terms and conditions of the letter of guarantee issued', or 'we hereby agree to reimburse you upon your first written or tested telex demand stating that you have paid the amount claimed under and in accordance with the terms of the guarantee', or 'we hereby undertake to reimburse you without delay and at your first simple cable/telex demand any amount you may be called upon to pay under said guarantee, DESPITE ANY CONTESTATION BETWEEN (X) AND (XX) and without it being necessary for you to produce or adduce any proof or any judicial or administrative proceedings whatsoever in support of your claim', or ' we hereby absolutely, irrevocably and unconditionally guarantee, under our counter-guarantee no. ... , to pay to you on your first demand by letter, telex or cable any amount up to ... as and when required to be paid by you to the above-mentioned beneficiary plus your charges and expenses as determined by you and to indemnify you against any loss or damage whatsoever resulting from issuing your guarantee, notwithstanding any objection and defiance by a third party arising from said obligation', or 'Any/and all claims will be paid on first demand despite any contestation between the Principal and Beneficiary or any third party'.[13]

In addition to the aforementioned hard core provisions, banks in the Middle East and North Africa regularly insist that other clauses be included in the counter-guarantee, and they sometimes prescribe a comprehensive text with detailed provisions. As they are standard texts it is very difficult to negotiate for changes or modifications.

---

13 These samples have been taken from circular letters from banks in the Middle East, the Indian subcontinent and Latin America. Similar texts can be found in the North African region.

Another reason for this is that in some countries banks are bound to issue guarantees and to insist on counter-guarantees which conform to local practices and regulations. This is particularly the case if the beneficiary of the primary guarantee is a state agency. Nonetheless, the texts disseminated by the various banks in any particular country often display some differences which it is worthwhile paying attention to. Sometimes the circular letters, instead of specifying the precise text, only state the particulars that have to be included. This permits the instructing bank at least to attempt to draft the counter-guarantee in a fashion which is more satisfactory to it and the account party. Finally, foreign banks do occasionally, by omitting to raise objections, accept texts which deviate from their standard texts. Accordingly, it could be more profitable just to forward a modified text rather than to attempt to negotiate for modifications.

Sometimes instructing banks merely state that they agree to the counter-guarantee 'as per your usual specimen (as contained in your circular letter of …)'.

11.2.2 Legal nature and effect of counter-guarantees

Introduction. The issue of independence between the primary guarantee and counter-guarantee

11-9 In view of the fact that the majority of guarantees in support of international transactions are furnished in an indirect manner, and as most instructions to the second issuing bank include some kind of counter-guarantee, an appraisal of the legal nature and effect of counter-guarantees is of considerable importance.

The paramount question regarding counter-guarantees relates to its (in)dependent nature: is the right of the second issuing bank to repayment by the first instructing bank to be defined solely by reference to the terms of the counter-guarantee (independent) or also and in addition by reference to fulfilment of the terms of the primary guarantee and/or proper performance by the second issuing bank of its duties deriving from the mandate, notably the duty to adhere to the instructions and the duty of examination in respect of the fulfilment of the terms of payment in the primary guarantee and, if so, in what manner and to what extent? The fundamental purport of this question can be illustrated by the following example. Suppose that, upon the instructions of the first bank, the second bank has issued a guarantee which is payable on demand provided that (i) the beneficiary submits a statement of default; (ii) the expiry date is 1 May 2004; (iii) the maximum amount of € 2 million will be reduced by 50% upon presentation of certain documents by the account party. The counter-guarantee in favour of the issuing bank provides for payment on first demand without further qualifications. Let us further suppose that the issuing bank has honoured the beneficiary's demand for payment for the full amount of € 2 million, although (i) he did not submit the required statement of default, (ii) he lodged the demand for payment after the expiry date of 1 May 2004, and (iii) the account party had presented the prescribed documents regarding the reduction clause to the issuing bank in time. The question then is whether or not the issuing bank is entitled to reimbursement (for the full amount) on the grounds that the counter-guarantee provides for repayment on first demand without further qualifications.

For over a decade French case law and German doctrine have expressed the view that a counter-guarantee is an independent undertaking (or in the French terminology an 'autonomous' undertaking) and that it functions in the same way as an ordinary independent guarantee. The view that the counter-guarantee is an independent undertaking in the same way as an ordinary independent guarantee, has also been expressed in art. 2(c) URDG and art. 6(c) Uncitral Convention and this fact might possibly justify the proposition that it reflects the current view. This perception of the counter-guarantee would suggest that the payment obligation of the instructing bank, which furnishes a counter-guarantee in favour of the issuing bank, is, in principle, solely defined by the terms of the counter-guarantee, and that, in the above-mentioned example, the second issuing bank would indeed, in principle, be entitled to repayment of the full amount. Whether this is indeed the case is the subject of the analysis in nos. 11-10/20.

If it can be said with some confidence that the principle stated above reflects the current view, the difficulty remains that several important aspects have not yet been resolved or continue to be controversial. For example, there exists neither clarity as regards the precise legal qualification of the counter-guarantee nor certainty concerning the precise meaning and limits of its independent nature. First of all, the typical notion of independence as it applies to the relationship between the guarantee and the underlying contract, cannot possibly be transposed to the relationship between counter-guarantee and primary guarantee.[14] Moreover and more significantly, there is reason to doubt that the failure by the issuing bank to verify compliance with the terms and conditions of the primary guarantee is indeed totally irrelevant because of the independent nature of the counter-guarantee. It should be emphasised from the outset that there is not any court decision, not even in French case law, to the effect that the issuing bank is entitled to reimbursement on the strength of a first demand counter-guarantee where there is clear evidence that it has failed to discharge its duty of examination regarding the fulfilment of the conditions in the primary guarantee. On the other hand, there is a significant number of cases where the court did indeed take this aspect into account when considering the issuing bank's claim for reimbursement.

Chapter 11.2.2 aims to give insight into the meaning, effect and limits of the independent nature of counter-guarantees. No. 11-10 describes the view that the counter-guarantee is independent of the primary guarantee, no. 11-11 relates to the German view that the counter-guarantee is independent of the mandate and no. 11-12 deals with the established principle that the counter-guarantee is independent of the underlying relationship. No. 11-13 contains a summary and an exposition of the view of this

---

14 See further No. 11-13 (Counter-guarantee as indemnity).

study, while case law is examined in nos. 11-14/19, with a summary in no. 11-20. Chapter 11.2.2 focuses on counter-guarantees which are payable on demand, as they ordinarily are, because the implications of the principle of independence are greatest in this type. It does not deal with the issue of fraud by the beneficiary, since the central theme of this subchapter (11.2.2) concerns the possible impact of the non-performance by the issuing bank of its duty of examination. Fraud by the beneficiary and the possible issuing bank's knowledge thereof is a quite different topic which requires separate discussion.[15] It is only referred to whenever this proved to be unavoidable with a view to legal writing and case law.

This study argues that the principle of independence between the counter-guarantee and the primary guarantee does not mean that the issuing bank is entitled to reimbursement from the instructing bank, if it is established that the issuing bank has failed to perform its duty of verifying compliance with the terms of the primary guarantee, see no. 11-13 (limits of independence. the exception) and no. 11-20.

The view that the counter-guarantee is independent of the primary guarantee and operates as an ordinary independent guarantee

11-10 On several occasions, the French Cour de Cassation has explicitly stated that a counter-guarantee is an autonomous undertaking which is independent of the primary guarantee and which operates in the same way as an ordinary independent (primary) guarantee, see *Cass. 27 November 1984*,[16] *Cass. 5 February 1985*,[17] *Cass. 20 November 1985*,[18] *Cass. 18 March 1986*,[19] *Cass. 29 April 1986*,[20] *Cass. 14 December 1987*,[21] *Cass. 27 February 1990*,[22] *Cass. 29 March 1994*,[23] and *Cass. 26 November 1996*.[24] On the basis of this principle the French Cour de Cassation has affirmed that the conditions for payment under the counter-guarantee do not have to coincide with those of the primary guarantee. For example, the expiry dates could be different, the primary

---

[15] See Chapters 14, 15 and 16.
[16] D. 1985 J. p. 269.
[17] D. 1985 J. p. 269.
[18] D. 1986 J. p. 213.
[19] D. 1986 I.R. p. 166.
[20] D. 1987 J. p. 17.
[21] D. 1988 Somm. p. 248.
[22] D. 1990 Somm. p. 213/D. 1991 Somm. p. 197.
[23] D. 1995 Somm. p. 20. See also the case law cited in Nos. 11-16/17.
[24] RJDA 1997/3, No. 397, p. 252.

guarantee may contain a reduction clause which does not appear in the counter-guarantee, or the primary guarantee might require the beneficiary to submit a statement of default, whereas the counter-guarantee may not refer to such a condition. Moreover, the beneficiary's fraud in respect of the primary guarantee does not as such render the issuing bank's call on the counter-guarantee fraudulent too. These affirmations are unquestionably correct and are in fact trite law. However, certain statements in the aforementioned case law also appear to indicate that the payment obligations of the instructing bank are solely defined by the terms of the counter-guarantee and that fulfilment of the terms in the primary guarantee, c.q. proper examination by the issuing bank is irrelevant. It is noted, however, that in these and many other decisions, in which reference has been made to the rule of independence, the conditions for payment in the primary guarantee were in fact fulfilled, c.q. the issuing bank was not in breach of its duty regarding examination, see no. 11-15. Moreover, there is also case law in which the court did consider whether the terms of the primary guarantee had been complied with, see no. 11-16 and no. 11-17.

Case law in other countries does not contain clear and conclusive statements regarding the legal nature of counter-guarantees or their independence of the primary guarantee.[25]

As far as legal writing is concerned, several authors, and notably the French professor Vasseur, have also expressed the view that a counter-guarantee is independent of the primary guarantee with the implications as mentioned in respect of the above-stated case law.[26] Interestingly, the French professor Mattout vigorously challenges the idea that the counter-guarantee is independent of the primary guarantee and argues that a counter-guarantee can only be called in relation to a call on the primary guarantee, unless otherwise stipulated.[27] Mattout suggests that the notion of independence has been introduced in order to explain why a fraudulent call on the primary guarantee by the beneficiary does not necessarily also render a call on the counter-guarantee fraudulent. He correctly points out that that one does not need to invoke this notion of

---

[25] But see the ambiguous observations in *CA Amsterdam, 4 February 1993*, KG 1993, 113, and *Trib. com. Brussels, 26 May 1988*, JT 1988, p. 460. In *Wahda Bank v. Arab Bank*, Lloyd's Rep. 470, 473, Staughton LJ observed that 'counter-guarantees are in one sense autonomous contracts,.. but they are intimately connected with the (primary) guarantees.'

[26] Vasseur, annotations to the above-cited case law and RDAI 1990, pp. 367-369, RDAI 1992, p. 279. It is quite likely that Vasseur's annotations have strongly influenced both French case law and other authors: France: Prüm, p. Nos. 292-301, Maotti, Journal des Notaires et des Avocats 1989, pp. 672-674, Rives-Lange, Banque 1986, p. 712, Banque 1987, p. 14; Belgium: Simont and Bruyneel, Rev. Banque 1989, p. 529, De Ly, Rev. Banque 1990, p. 167, 171, Martin and Delierneux, RDC 1993, p. 308; The Netherlands: Pabbruwe, p. 18/9.

[27] Mattout, No. 224.

independence in order to explain this rule and that the true explanation is, in fact, far more direct and simple.[28]

The independence approach has now found support in the URDG. Art. 2(c) unequivocally states that 'Counter-Guarantees are by their nature separate transactions from the Guarantees to which they relate ... and Instructing Parties are in no way concerned with or bound by such Guarantees...despite the inclusion of a reference to them in the Counter-Guarantee'. Under the URDG regime, counter-guarantees are considered to operate as ordinary guarantees and most provisions also apply to counter-guarantees, although this has not been stated explicitly due to the fact that the provisions regarding counter-guarantees were added at a later stage.[29] Art. 20(b) URDG brings about a certain link between the counter-guarantee and the primary guarantee. According to this provision the issuing bank, when requesting payment under the counter-guarantee, must state that it has received a demand for payment under the primary guarantee in accordance with its terms and art. 20(a). Contrary to the views of some authors,[30] this provision does not detract from the URDG's rule that counter-guarantees are independent of the primary guarantee but is much rather an expression of this rule. For, the issuing bank does not have to prove that the primary guarantee was called in accordance with its terms, but merely has to submit a statement to this effect. It is thus a documentary condition of payment, which is similar to a provision in a guarantee requiring the beneficiary (merely) to state that the account party is in default.

Under the regime of the Uncitral Convention, the counter-guarantee is also regarded as an ordinary independent guarantee. This is apparent from art. 6(a) which defines a guarantee as including a counter-guarantee. By means of such a definition all provisions in respect of the guarantee also apply to the counter-guarantee and the latter's independence of the primary guarantee follows implicitly from art. 3, which gives a definition of an independent guarantee. Nonetheless, art. 6 (c) Uncitral Convention produces a similar link between the counter-guarantee and primary guarantee, as does art. 20(b) URDG, by providing that a demand for payment under the counter-guarantee must indicate that the primary guarantee has been called.

---

[28] See Chapter 16.4.2, No. 16-13.

[29] Goode, p. 26, and Lloyd's Mar. & Com. L.Q. 1992, p. 197, Vasseur RDAI 1992, pp. 281-284, Martin and Delierneux, RDC 1993, p. 308.

[30] Vasseur, RDAI 1992, pp. 279, 284, Martin and Delierneux, RCD 1993, p. 309.

The view that the counter-guarantee is independent of the mandate and operates as an ordinary independent guarantee. Germany

11-11 The legal nature of the counter-guarantee has been the subject of extensive analysis by German authors. A unanimous view has emerged.[31] Where a counter-guarantee has been issued, the legal relationship between the first instructing bank and the second issuing bank is split into two, one based on mandate, i.e. the first bank's instructions to the second bank to issue a guarantee for the first bank's account, governed by the relevant statutory provisions,[32] the other embodied in the counter-guarantee. Both relationships create different rights and obligations and they are considered distinct from and independent of each other. The view that the counter-guarantee merely particularises and qualifies the relationship as defined by the mandate has been rejected.[33] There being two distinct relationships, the issuing bank is entitled to claim reimbursement both on account of the mandate and on account of the counter-guarantee. They are also governed by different laws: the mandate by the law of the issuing bank's country, the counter-guarantee by the law of the instructing bank's country.

The purpose of the counter-guarantee is thought to be to strengthen the position of the issuing bank by affording protection beyond that accorded by the statutory provisions of mandate. In particular, it provides protection against any defences arising under the relationship between account party and instructing bank and against defences derived from the underlying relationship between account party and beneficiary. It is argued that the counter-guarantee establishes the required independence.

The counter-guarantee is perceived as an ordinary guarantee and is payable in accordance with its own terms. The only difference between the two is that the (primary) guarantee secures the claim of the beneficiary/creditor against a third party, i.e. the account party/principal debtor, on account of breach of contract, while the counter-guarantee secures the issuing bank's right of reimbursement by the instructing bank. The counter-guarantee, being an ordinary independent guarantee, entitles the issuing bank to payment once the terms and conditions of payment as specified in the counter-

---

[31] Mülbert, pp. 9, 21-22, 28-29 and in particular pp. 81-88, von Westphalen, pp. 234-243, 350-352, and WM 1981, p. 301, Nielsen, pp. 95-100, ZIP 1982, pp. 257-258 and ZHR 1983, pp. 157-158, Lienesch, pp. 210-212, Zahn/Ehrlich/Neumann, 9/, 9/101-107, 9/120, Canaris, No. 1118, Schlegelberger/Hefermehl, No. 291, Dohm, Nos. 105-108, No. 270, Nos. 274-282 and DPCI 1980, pp. 267, 269, Kleiner, 20.07-20.10, Pleyer, WM 2/1973, p. 15 and Tours, p. 188, Bark, ZIP 1982, pp. 409-412, Schütze, WM 1982, pp. 1398-1399.

[32] See Chapter 11.1.2, No. 11-2.

[33] But see Nielsen, p. 96/97, who describes the counter-guarantee as a formalisation of the obligation of reimbursement stemming from the mandate, whereby the position of the foreign issuing bank is reinforced. See also Zahn/Ehrlich/Neumann, 9/105.

guarantee are fulfilled.³⁴ If the counter-guarantee contains the phrase 'payment upon first demand', as is often the case, the issuing bank is indeed entitled to immediate payment once the request is made. This effect is expressly stated to be the consequence of the clause 'payment upon first demand'.

It is perhaps surprising that German doctrine has paid comparatively little attention to the question of whether or not the counter-guarantee is independent of the primary guarantee. However, certain German authors do take the view that payment under the counter-guarantee does not depend on fulfilment of the terms of payment in the primary guarantee, c.q. performance by the issuing bank of its duties under the mandate,³⁵ but acknowledge that this independence is subject to certain limits.³⁶ This view is also expressed in *BGH, 10 October 2000*.³⁷

The counter-guarantee is independent of the underlying relationship

11-12 It is trite law that the counter-guarantee is independent of the underlying relationship between the account party and the beneficiary of the primary guarantee. This is explained by the simple fact that the issuing bank has been instructed to furnish a guarantee which is independent of that relationship. Accordingly, the foreign issuing bank – like the issuing bank in the case of a direct guarantee – is not concerned with the relationship between the parties to the underlying relationship and the instructing bank can therefore never raise defences which are derived from that relationship. These clear rules are not specific to the counter-guarantee but equally apply to the mandate relationship between instructing and issuing bank. In short, it is not the counter-guarantee 'payable on first demand' itself but the instructions to the issuing bank to issue an independent guarantee which render the counter-guarantee independent of the underlying relationship. The phrase 'payable on first demand' merely affirms this principle.

The view of this study. The counter-guarantee is an independent indemnity and operates as an ordinary independent guarantee, subject to certain limitations. Summary

11-13 – *Counter-guarantee as an indemnity*. A guarantee is ordinarily perceived as a contract which provides security to the beneficiary with regard to default by a third party in respect of a contractual obligation owed to the beneficiary. The counter-guar-

---

34 Canaris, von Westphalen, Mülbert, cited above.
35 Canaris, von Westphalen, Mülbert, cited above.
36 See No. 11-13 (Limits of independence. The exception).
37 WM 2000, p. 2334.

antee does not, however, guarantee a third party's obligation to the issuing bank but relates to reimbursement to the issuing bank in view of payment by that bank under the primary guarantee. Moreover, the instructing bank is already bound to reimburse the issuing bank on account of the mandate as it has instructed that bank to issue the primary guarantee for the account and risk of the instructing bank. It seems somewhat odd for the instructing bank to guarantee its own, already existing, obligation. Juridically, the counter-guarantee is, therefore, not quite the same as an ordinary (primary) guarantee,[38] and it seems more appropriate to regard the counter-guarantee as an indemnity provided by the instructing bank in favour of the issuing bank.

– *Relationship with mandate.* Since the counter-guarantee relates to the indemnification of the issuing bank in connection with the first bank's instructions to issue a guarantee, primary attention should be directed towards the relationship between the mandate and counter-guarantee. A careful reading and analysis of the actual instructions by the first bank to the foreign second bank show that they contain two elements, apart from the references to the text and particulars relating to the primary guarantee. First, there is the request to issue the primary guarantee for the account and risk of the instructing bank, usually accompanied by a general undertaking to indemnify the issuing bank for the consequences of its issuing the guarantee ('Please issue *under our full responsibility*'). This element reflects and reaffirms the mandate relationship as it exists by law and the duty to reimburse the issuing bank directly follows from the instructions. Secondly, there are provisions which particularise the aforementioned right of reimbursement and these specific provisions are commonly known as the counter-guarantee. Both elements are contained in the same document, namely the instructions to the issuing bank, and virtually merge into one another. This being so, it is difficult to assume that one document (the instructions) which relates to one transaction is intended to create two separate contracts, namely a mandate and a counter-guarantee, which are independent of one another, as does German doctrine. The correct view appears to be that the counter-guarantee qualifies and elaborates on the rights and obligations of instructing and issuing bank as they exist under the general rules of law relating to mandate by substituting the counter-guarantee provisions for those general rules.[39]

– *Independence.* The counter-guarantee is drafted in such a manner that it provides for payment in accordance with its own terms and conditions and is, therefore, payable once its conditions of payment have been fulfilled and within the scope of the other terms, such as those relating to the maximum amount and period of validity. It is only in this sense that the counter-guarantee can be said to operate as an ordinary independent (or autonomous) guarantee. The counter-guarantee is unquestionably independent

---

[38] Cf. Zahn/Ehrlich/Neumann, 9/66, Mülbert, pp. 86, 87, Dohm, No. 278, Prüm, p. 147.
[39] Cf. Nielsen, p. 96/97.

of the underlying relationship between the account party and beneficiary since the issuing bank has been requested to issue an independent guarantee.

– *Purpose. Pay first, argue later.* The purpose of the counter-guarantee is to strenghten and improve the position of the issuing bank compared with its position under the rules of the general law of mandate. Under these general rules, if the issuing bank claims reimbursement and the instructing bank challenges this claim, for example because the issuing bank has (allegedly) failed to carry out the instructions or to check fulfilment of the conditions of payment in the primary guarantee, a court will not give judgment in favour of the issuing bank until this issue has been resolved in his favour. Moreover, it might well be that the burden of proof in this respect lies with the issuing bank. Its position is essentially no different from that of any contracting party who alleges that the other party owes him money and whose difficulties of enforcing his claim have been described in Chapter 6.1. Just as that contracting party seeks to avoid these risks by stipulating a first demand guarantee, so does the issuing bank by insisting on a counter-guarantee which is payable on first demand. Such a counter-guarantee performs the same function as an ordinary first demand guarantee in that it brings about the same reversal of risks and affords the issuing bank the same advantages, namely that it is entitled to payment forthwith without having to prove that it has carried out the instructions and verified compliance with the conditions of payment of the primary guarantee.[40] These aspects are not an issue as far as the counter-guarantee is concerned, just as actual default of the account party is not relevant under the ordinary (primary) guarantee. Therefore, if the terms and conditions of the counter-guarantee have been fulfilled, the issuing bank must pay forthwith, even though it or the account party might be of the opinion that the issuing bank has not properly performed its duties. After payment, the issuing bank, or rather the account party, may seek to recover the amount paid under the counter-guarantee from the issuing bank but this might prove to be very difficult ('pay first, argue later').[41]

A counter-guarantee usually contains other provisions in addition to the 'payment on first demand' clause. These provisions are examined in Chapter 11.4.

– *Independence of the primary guarantee.* As explained above, proper examination by the issuing bank regarding compliance with the terms and conditions of the primary guarantee, c.q. non-compliance with those terms is not an issue as far as a first demand counter-guarantee is concerned, and the issuing bank must proceed to payment forthwith once the conditions of the counter-guarantee have been met. In this sense it can indeed be said that a counter-guarantee is independent of the primary guarantee.

---

[40] Cf. Nielsen, p. 96, who rightly refers to the liquidity function of counter-guarantees.
[41] See also Chapter 6.2.

– Limits of independence. The exception. The principle of independence of the counter-guarantee in relation to the primary guarantee is not absolute but is subject to certain limits which are similar to those in respect of the ordinary independent guarantee. In the case of the ordinary independent guarantee, the bank is entitled to refuse payment despite the principle of independence if there is clear evidence that the beneficiary's demand for payment is fraudulent, for example clear evidence that the account party has completely performed the contract. A similar exception to the principle of independence applies to counter-guarantees: despite the principle of independence the instructing bank as counter-guarantor is entitled to refuse payment if there is clear evidence that the issuing bank has not performed its obligations in respect of adherence to the instructions or examination of compliance with the terms and conditions of the primary guarantee.[42] In general, it is for the account party, not for the instructing bank, to adduce the evidence.[43] Mere allegations or insufficiently persuasive evidence of breach of contract by the issuing bank or evidence which cannot be produced forthwith will not suffice. In these situations the instructing bank must proceed to payment in accordance with the principle 'pay first, argue later'. If indeed established, such a breach of contract by the issuing bank does not, however, ordinarily amount to fraud and it seems, therefore, inappropriate to use that term in this context.[44]

It is noted that the non-fulfilment of the terms and conditions of the primary guarantee does not automatically warrant the conclusion that the issuing bank has breached its duty of examination. This is especially true for conditions the (non-)fulfilment of which is difficult to ascertain, such as, for example, expiry events or reduction clauses which have not been drafted in a documentary fashion. It could, therefore, happen that in actual fact the expiry event has occurred or the conditions for the reduction clause have been fulfilled, and that the issuing bank, nonetheless, pays the full amount of the guarantee because it has not been provided with the evidence of these occurrences. In situations like these the issuing bank is not at fault[45] and is, therefore, entitled to repayment in accordance with the terms of the counter-guarantee.

---

[42] Cf. von Westphalen, p. 241/242, p. 250, and the Uncitral Secretariat's second draft for the Draft Uncitral Convention ad art. 19(2)(e) variant Y, doc. A/CN.9/WG.ll/WP.76/Add.1 of 29 October 1992: 'a demand for payment is improper if: (…) In the case of a counter-guaranty letter, the beneficiary (issuing bank, R.B.) has not received a demand for payment under the guaranty letter issued by it, or the beneficiary has paid upon such a demand although it was obliged [under the law applicable to its guaranty letter] to reject the demand [as lacking *conformity* (italics added, R.B.) or as being improper]'.

[43] See Chapter 11.3.

[44] Unfortunately, the case law discussed in Nos. 11-16/19 usually employs the term 'fraud' both in situations where the issuing bank is aware of the beneficiary's fraud and in situations where the issuing bank has not properly discharged its duty of examination.

[45] See Chapter 10.8, No. 10-26.

– *Summary.* In accordance with French case law, German doctrine and several authors from other jurisdictions, the URDG and the Uncitral Convention, this study takes the view that a counter-guarantee is an independent (or autonomous) undertaking (or indemnity) which operates in the same way as the ordinary independent guarantee. The instructing bank as counter-guarantor must, therefore, pay if the terms and conditions of payment as stated in the counter-guarantee have been fulfilled. Proper examination by the issuing bank in respect of compliance with the terms of the primary guarantee, c.q. non-fulfilment of those terms is, in principle, not an issue in this respect if the counter-guarantee provides for payment on first demand. The principle of independence is, however, subject to an exception which is similar to that in the ordinary guarantee: the instructing bank is entitled to refuse payment if there is clear evidence that the issuing bank did not carry out the instructions or did not properly verify compliance with the terms of the primary guarantee. These aspects are, therefore, not without relevance.

The independent nature of counter-guarantees and its limits in case law. Introduction

11-14 In no. 11-13 it has been argued that a counter-guarantee is an independent undertaking, but subject to an exception, and that in this context proper examination by the issuing bank in respect of compliance with the terms of the primary guarantee, c.q. (non-)fulfilment of those terms are not without relevance. In nos. 11-15/19 we will examine whether this proposition regarding the exception to the principle of independence finds support in case law. We will therefore focus on the question of whether and to what extent courts have indeed paid attention to proper examination by the issuing bank, c.q. fulfilment of the terms of the primary guarantee and especially whether a claim for repayment under the counter-guarantee is indeed rejected if it is established that the terms of the primary guarantee have not been fulfilled, c.q. that the issuing bank has breached its duty of examination. The case law examined in nos. 11-16/19 indicates that courts do indeed consider these aspects. Nos. 11-15/17 involve cases which have been decided on the basis of the principle of independence, whereas the cases discussed in nos. 11-18/19 do not refer to this principle.

Cases decided on the basis of independence. Fulfilment of the terms of the primary guarantee not considered. No evidence of fault by the issuing bank

11-15 There are several French decisions, notably some of the Cour de Cassation, in which it has been clearly stated that the counter-guarantee is independent of the primary guarantee and in which no attention has been paid to the question whether or not the issuing bank had properly examined compliance with the terms of the primary guarantee, c.q. whether or not those terms were fulfilled. These decisions do not, however, disprove this study's proposition regarding the exception to the principle of independence since in actual fact there was no evidence of fault on the part of the issuing bank.

These cases decided on the basis of independence of counter-guarantee and guarantee can be grouped into four categories.

- In the case of *Paris, 2 June 1982* the performance guarantee stated that it was 'payable upon first demand in the event that the principal debtor had failed to execute his obligations'.[46] In the case of *Paris, 24 January 1984* the guarantee stated that it was 'payable upon demand provided that the call related to the principal contract'.[47] In both cases the Court of Appeal enjoined the instructing bank from proceeding to repayment of the issuing bank, because that bank should have obtained some corroboration from the beneficiary in respect of default of the principal debtor, and, in the second decision, corroboration that the call did indeed relate to the principal contract. Both rulings were rightly quashed by *Cass., 5 February 1985*,[48] and *Cass., 20 November 1985*.[49] The decisions of the Cour de Cassation were founded on the independence of counter-guarantee and guarantee. The reports of these cases show, however, that the issuing bank had not in fact breached its duty of examination, since the procurement of corroboration or statements from the beneficiary was not stated to be a condition of payment under the primary guarantee.[50] The same observation applies to the decision of *Paris, 14 March 1988*, affirmed by *Cass., 27 February 1990*,[51] which ruled, on the grounds of independence, that the instructing bank could not invoke a reduction clause which formed part of the primary guarantee, but which was not inserted in the counter-guarantee. However, the report of the decision does not state whether the issuing bank was presented with data which would have rendered the reduction clause operative. Moreover, the Court of Appeal recognised that the instructing bank could have refused reimbursement in the event of fraud, which probably means evidence that the issuing bank knew that

---

[46] D. 1983 J. p. 437.

[47] D. 1984 I.R. p. 203.

[48] D. 1985 J. p. 269.

[49] D. 1986 J. p. 213. Upon referral *Amiens, 6 June 1988*, D. 1989 Somm. p. 151, finally ruled that the instructing bank had to reimburse the second issuing bank and that the account party had to reimburse the instructing bank.

[50] See also Chapter 10.8, No. 10-26 and Chapter 13.2.3, No. 13-12.

[51] D. 1991 Somm. p. 197.

[52] D. 1989 Somm. p. 152. See Chapter 13.2.6, No. 13-21, for the bank's responsibilities in connection with reduction clauses. *Amiens, 6 June 1988*, D. 1989 Somm. p. 151, also observed that fraud allows for an exception to the principle of independence between counter-guarantee and guarantee.

the reduction clause had become operative.[52] Thus, the issuing bank's duty of examination in this respect was apparently viewed as a relevant factor.

– *Paris, 26 April 1983*, held that the fact that the beneficiary of the primary guarantee had not made a call on the guarantee, let alone a call within the stated validity period, did not preclude the issuing bank from rightly calling the counter-guarantee.[53] This decision was affirmed by *Cass., 27 November 1984*, on the grounds that counter-guarantee and guarantee are independent and that the counter-guarantee did not state as a condition of repayment that the beneficiary of the primary guarantee must have made a (timely) written demand for payment.[54] Another explanation for this decision is that the issuing Syrian bank had explicitly advised the French bank that expiry dates are not enforceable in Syria and that the counter-guarantee, therefore, remained in force until discharge and especially that the primary guarantee clearly stated that it became automatically payable upon the expiry date.[55] Accordingly, the terms of the primary guarantee had been fulfilled and the Syrian bank had not breached its duty of examination.

– In *Cass., 12 December 1984*,[56] *Paris, 14 December 1987*,[57] *Paris, 23 November 1990*,[58] and *Aix-en-Provence, 19 January 1995*,[59] the independence of counter-guarantee and primary guarantee was invoked as the rationale for the decision that in respect of fraud cases a stop-payment order against the instructing bank can only be granted if fraud on the part of the beneficiary has been established and if in addition some kind of knowledge on the part of the issuing bank regarding the beneficiary's fraud has been shown.[60] In none of these cases was there any evidence of such knowledge on the part of the issuing bank and it was, therefore, not at fault when it proceeded to payment.

---

[53] D. 1983 I.R. p. 485.

[54] D. 1985 J. p. 269.

[55] Stoufflet, too, JCP 1985 ll no 20436 (14), refers to this particular stipulation as the rationale of the decision.

[56] D. 1985 J. p. 269.

[57] D. 1988 Somm. p.248.

[58] D. 1991 Somm. p. 199

[59] Banque et Droit 1995, No. 43, p. 30.

[60] See also *Cass., 29 March 1994*, D. 1995 Somm. p. 20. These decisions are in line with the unanimous view of legal writing in France and elsewhere and with established case law in France and elsewhere, see Chapter 16.4.2. Apart from these decisions it has not been found appropriate or expedient to refer to the principle of independence as the rationale for the requirement that the issuing bank's knowledge of the beneficiary's fraud is also to be demonstrated. See also Mattout, No. 224.

– A fourth group of decisions concerns the validity period of primary guarantee and counter-guarantee. They merely acknowledge the fact that the expiry date of the counter-guarantee does not have to be the same as that of the primary guarantee and that the counter-guarantee has to be called within its own validity period.[61] In none of these cases was there any evidence of fault by the issuing bank in respect of honouring a claim on the primary guarantee lodged after its expiry date.

Cases decided on the basis of independence. Fulfilment of the terms of the primary guarantee considered. No evidence of fault by the issuing bank.

11-16 In two French cases the court clearly stated that a counter-guarantee is independent of the primary guarantee and that it is governed by its own terms and conditions. In *Paris, 8 November 1988*, the court went on, however, to consider whether the terms of the primary guarantee were fulfilled, namely whether or not the primary guarantee had been called by the right person and whether or not it had expired prior to the call.[62] Thus, the independent nature of the counter-guarantee in relation to the primary guarantee does not imply that the (non-)fulfilment of the terms of the primary guarantee, c.q. proper examination by the issuing bank, is irrelevant. The court found, however, that the terms of the primary guarantee had indeed been complied with, c.q. that there was no evidence of fault by the issuing bank in respect of its duty of examination. On these grounds, applications by the account party for an injunction against the instructing and issuing bank were rejected. In *BGH, 10 October 2000*, the German Supreme Court ruled that a counter-guarantee is payable in accordance with its own terms, but also observed that the terms of the primary guarantee had been fulfilled.[63] In *CA Amsterdam, 4 February 1993*, the court also observed that, despite its independent nature, a call on the counter-guarantee should be rejected if the issuing bank had proceeded to payment on grounds which were evidently inappropriate. This was not the case.[64]

---

[61] *Cass., 11 November 1984*, D. 1985 J. p. 269, *Cass., 29 April 1986*, D. 1987 J. p. 17, *Cass., 18 March 1986*, D. 1986 I.R. p. 166, and *Paris, 27 November 1990*, D. 1991 Somm. p. 200, see also Chapter 13.3, No. 13-39.
[62] D. 1990 Somm. p. 206.
[63] WM 2000, p. 2334.
[64] KG 1993, 113.

Cases decided on the basis of independence. Terms of the primary guarantee not fulfilled. Claim under the counter-guarantee rejected.

11-17 The following two decisions clearly show that recognition of the independent nature of the counter-guarantee in relation to the primary guarantee does not imply that the (non-)fulfilment of the terms of the primary guarantee is without significance and that claims under the counter-guarantee should indeed be rejected, c.q. that applications for restraining orders should be granted if it is established that these terms have not been complied with.

The Court of Appeal in *Versailles, 29 March 1985* granted a stop-payment order against the instructing bank, observing that, while the counter-guarantee is independent of the primary guarantee, it does not follow that a counter-guarantee payable upon first demand can be called where the primary guarantee itself had not been called.[65] In other words, the issuing bank has no right to payment under the counter-guarantee, although stated to be payable on demand without any other condition of payment, where the terms of the primary guarantee have not been met.

In the case of *Trib. com. Brussels, 26 May 1988*, the primary guarantee stipulated that the demand for payment had to be made by registered mail and that the beneficiary had to state the reasons for his call. The counter-guarantee was payable on first demand and did not refer to the above-mentioned clauses of the primary guarantee. While reaffirming the principle of independence, the court did grant restraining orders against the instructing and issuing bank, one of the reasons being that the terms of the primary guarantee had not been fulfilled.[66]

A most remarkable decision is that of *Paris, 25 February 1988*, which involved a call on the primary guarantee after its expiry date.[67] The Court of Appeal rejected the claim for payment under the counter-guarantee on the grounds that the terms of the primary guarantee must also be deemed incorporated into the counter-guarantee, with the result that the demand for payment under the counter-guarantee was also too late. The Cour de Cassation affirmed the decision and observed that the Court of Appeal had not misjudged the principle of independence, which seems quite inconsistent with its previous case law.[68] If the issuing bank's claim under the counter-guarantee were to be rejected, it should not have been on the grounds that it had expired but because the issuing bank had incorrectly honoured a call on the primary guarantee which was made after its expiry date.

---

[65] D. 1986 I.R. p. 156. See also Chapter 13.3, No. 13-40 for other case law and sources.

[66] JT 1988, p. 460. The second ground was the issuing bank's awareness of the beneficiary's fraud.

[67] D. 1989 Somm. p. 150.

[68] D. 1991 Somm. p. 195. The decision has been rightly criticised by Vaseur.

Other cases. Fulfilment of the terms of the primary guarantee considered. No evidence of fault by the issuing bank.

11-18 There are several other cases where, in relation to a call on the counter-guarantee, the court considered whether the terms of the primary guarantee were fulfilled, c.q. whether the issuing bank had discharged its duty of examination. A good example of this approach is *CA The Hague, 3 June 1993*, where the Court of Appeal observed that the instructing bank must pay under the counter-guarantee in accordance with its terms unless it is established that the issuing bank had honoured an invalid call on the primary guarantee.[69] In this context it considered whether the call on the primary guarantee was made within the period of validity and in accordance with the prescribed wording. The Court of Appeal found that the account party had failed to establish that these terms had not been complied with, c.q. that the issuing bank had acted improperly by honouring the demand for payment and rejected the application for a stop-payment injunction. In connection with a call on the counter-guarantee the Court of Appeal in *I.E. Contractors v. Lloyds Bank* also examined whether the primary guarantee had been called in the correct manner. This was found to be the case.[70] A similar approach with the same final result can be found in many other cases too.[71]

---

[69] KG 1993, 301.

[70] [1990] 2 Lloyd's Rep., p. 496, 501.

[71] In *Paris, 13 December 1984*, D. 1985 I.R. p. 239, affirmed by *Cass., 10 March 1987*, D. 1987 Somm. p. 172, and *Brussels, 25 February 1982*, JCB 1982, p. 349, applications for injunctions restraining the instructing bank from paying under the counter-guarantee were dismissed on the grounds that the issuing bank had correctly, or at least not incorrectly, proceeded to payment to the beneficiary of the primary guarantee. In *Esal, Reltor v. Oriental, Wells Fargo*, [1985] 2 Lloyd's Rep. 546, the court took the view that the terms of the primary guarantee had not been complied with, but ordered the instructing bank to reimburse the issuing bank because that bank was not at fault as it had been forced to pay by an order of an Egyptian court. *CA Amsterdam, 5 February 1993*, KG 1993, 113, involving an indirect guarantee. The Court of Appeal dismissed the application for an injunction restraining the instructing bank from reimbursing the issuing bank, on the grounds that the account party had by no means proven the event which would terminate the primary guarantee, and that the issuing bank's decision that the primary guarantee was still in force was not incorrect. See also *LG Dortmund, 9 July 1980*, WM 1981, p. 280. The issuing bank had been instructed to issue a first demand guarantee in favour of the Imperial-Iranian Government Ports and Shipping Organisation, which was the contracting partner of the account party. In fact the guarantee had been issued in favour of the Imperial-Iranian Marine, which was not a contracting partner. It was not clear who had called the guarantee. These facts were mentioned as one of the reasons for granting a stop-payment order against the instructing bank.

Other cases. Terms of the primary guarantee not fulfilled. Claim under the counter-guarantee rejected.

11-19 In addition to the case law mentioned in no. 11-18 there are also other cases where the court admitted evidence concerning the non-fulfilment of the terms of the primary guarantee, c.q. breach by the issuing bank of its duty of examination in respect of compliance. In none of these cases was reference made to the principle that the counter-guarantee is independent of the primary guarantee. No. 11-19 deals with cases where the court was satisfied with the evidence and dismissed the issuing bank's claim for payment under the counter-guarantee, c.q. granted an injunction restraining the instructing bank from paying under the counter-guarantee or ordered the issuing bank to repay the amount received under the counter-guarantee.

In *Paris, 22 January 1991*, the Court of Appeal gave judgment in favour of the account party and instructing bank who applied for a judicial declaration that no payment was due under the counter-guarantee for the reason that the primary guarantee had been called after its expiry date.[72] *Trib. com. Paris, 7 February 1989*, granted an injunction against the instructing bank enjoining it from paying the full amount of the counter-guarantee upon evidence by the account party that the terms of the reduction clause in the primary guarantee had been fulfilled.[73] A similar injunction was granted in *Brussels, 4 January 1989*, on the grounds that the issuing bank had failed to properly examine compliance with the terms of the primary guarantee.[74] In *Trib. com. Paris, 1 August 1984* the primary guarantee explicitly required the submission by the beneficiary of a statement of default. The second, issuing bank had failed to procure this statement or, at any rate could not produce the statement when calling the counter-guarantee. This was one of the grounds upon which the court granted a stop-payment order against the first instructing bank.[75] In *Paris, 3 April 2002*, the Court of Appeal

---

[72] D. 1991 Somm. p. 200. As a matter of fact, the issuing bank had refused to pay on the primary guarantee for the same reason, but called the counter-guarantee nonetheless. See also *Paris, 2 June 1982*, D. 1983 J. p. 437, involving a repayment guarantee which stipulated that it could not be called prior to 7 April 1983. The Court of Appeal allowed the account party's application for a stop-payment injunction and ordered the sequestration of the funds of the counter-guarantee on the grounds that the primary guarantee and the counter-guarantee were called prior to that date. This decision was affirmed in *Cass., 5 February 1985*, D. 1985 J. p. 269.

[73] D. 1990 Somm. p. 207.

[74] TBH 1990, p. 1073. It is, however, questionable whether the issuing bank was indeed at fault, see Chapter 10.8, No. 10-23.

[75] D. 1986 I.R. p. 159. The other reason was clear evidence that the beneficiary had called the guarantee in relation to another project which was not covered by the guarantee. See, however, for this aspect Chapter 10.8 No. 10-26 last paragraph, and Chapter 13.2.2.

had construed the primary guarantee as an accessory suretyship and the counter-guarantee as an independent undertaking payable on first demand without reference to the underlying transaction.[76] Following a call on the primary undertaking, the issuing bank requested payment under the counter-guarantee in 1987 and in the period 1993-1994 whereupon the instructing bank effected payment in 1994 and the account party reimbursed the instructing bank. Meanwhile in 1991 the account party had notified the issuing bank of an arbitral judgment in proceedings between the account party and beneficiary to the effect that the beneficiary had no claim against the account party and that it had no right to call the guarantee. This being so, the Court of Appeal ruled that the issuing bank should not have paid under the primary undertaking and, consequently, that it was not entitled to payment under the counter-guarantee, ordering the issuing bank to repay the amount received to the account party as the party which suffered the loss.

The limits and exception to the independence of counter-guarantees in relation to the primary guarantee. Conclusions in respect of case law.

11-20 The case law examined in nos. 11-18/19 show that the non-fulfilment of the terms of the primary guarantee, c.q. breach by the issuing bank of its duty of examination in respect of compliance, is not irrelevant as far as the counter-guarantee is concerned. The same is true for the decisions discussed in nos. 11-16/17, which is even more significant because they were expressly founded on the principle that the counter-guarantee is independent of the primary guarantee. In the cases examined in no. 11-15, no attention was paid to the aforementioned issues, but the reports of these cases reveal that the terms of the primary guarantee were in fact fulfilled, c.q. that the issuing bank had not acted improperly. As a matter of fact, there is not one single instance of a court giving judgment in favour of the issuing bank in the face of evidence that the terms of the primary guarantee had not been complied with or that the issuing bank was in breach of its duty of examination. In conclusion, case law lends clear support to this study's view, as expounded in no. 11- 13, that a counter-guarantee is an autonomous undertaking pursuant to which the instructing bank must pay if the terms of the counter-guarantee are fulfilled and, if payable on first demand, without reference to the terms of the primary guarantee but subject to an exception. This exception occurs where there is evidence that the terms of the primary guarantee have not been complied with, c.q. that the issuing bank did not properly discharge its duty of examination. No. 11-17 and no. 11-19 contain examples of cases where this exception was indeed applied.

---

[76] D.Affaires 2002 p. 1750.

11.3 THE INSTRUCTING BANK OWES NO GENERAL DUTY TO THE ACCOUNT PARTY TO INVESTIGATE FULFILMENT OF THE TERMS OF THE PRIMARY GUARANTEE

Introduction

11-21 Since a counter-guarantee is independent of the primary guarantee, the issuing bank, when demanding payment under the counter-guarantee, need not show that it has discharged its duty of examination regarding compliance with the terms of the primary guarantee. For the same reason, the instructing bank is not concerned with this aspect either. The principle of independence is, however, subject to an exception, namely where there is evidence that the terms of the primary guarantee have not been fulfilled, see no. 11-20. Against this background, the question arises as to whether the instructing bank owes some kind of duty to the account party to investigate whether the terms of the primary guarantee have been complied with or to assist the account party in some other way. This is important from the account party's point of view, because he has no contractual relationship with the issuing bank and because the reality is such that it is virtually impossible for him to establish contact with the foreign issuing bank.

No general duty

11-22 German legal writing takes the view that examination of compliance with the terms and conditions of the primary guarantee is the sole concern of the foreign issuing bank, that the instructing bank is bound by the issuing bank's decision in this respect ('Tatbestandswirkung'), and that the instructing bank does not owe a duty to the account party to verify proper examination by the issuing bank or fulfilment of the terms of the primary guarantee.[77] Generally speaking, case law has also rejected a general duty on the part of the instructing bank to investigate whether the terms of the primary guarantee have been complied with.[78] This study agrees with this view. One argument is that the instructing bank has furnished a counter-guarantee which is independent of the primary guarantee, with the result that it is not concerned with the fulfilment of the

---

[77] Von Westphalen, p. 232, 233, 240-245, 350-352, Zahn/Ehrlich/Neumann, 9/120, Nielsen, ZIP 1982, p. 259, Bark, ZIP 1982, p. 441, Dohm, no 280.

[78] *CA Amsterdam, 4 February 1993*, KG 1993, 113, *CA The Hague, 8 June 1993*, KG 1993, 301, *Paris, 14 March 1988*, D. 1989 Somm. p. 152, affirmed by *Cass., 27 February 1990*, D. 1991 Somm. p. 197, and *Amiens, 6 June 1988*, D. 1989 Somm. p. 151. See, however, Staughton L.J. in *I.E. Contractos v. Lloyds Bank*, [1990] 2 Lloyd's Rep. pp. 496, 502 r.c, who observed that the instructing bank is in a position to determine whether the issuing bank was obliged to pay under the primary guarantee by asking to see the beneficiary's demand for payment.

terms of the primary guarantee and that it must pay in accordance with the terms of the counter-guarantee. In principle, the instructing bank's duty to the account party is confined to an examination of the terms of the counter-guarantee. A second reason is that the instructing bank utilises the services of the foreign issuing bank at the risk of the account party, cf. art. 14(a) URDG. The issuing bank's failure to verify compliance with the terms of the primary guarantee is, therefore, a risk which is borne by the account party. From this it also follows that, with a view to a possible exception to the principle of independence, it is for the account party and not for the instructing bank to present evidence of such a breach of contract by the issuing bank.

Banking practice

11-23 Current banking practice in connection with enquiries as to the fulfilment of the terms of the primary guarantee shows a haphazard pattern if the counter-guarantee does not contain any particulars in this respect.[79] When claiming reimbursement, foreign issuing banks do not normally forward a copy of the beneficiary's request nor a copy of the statement of default should that be required under the terms of the primary guarantee. Instructing banks neither ask for these documents on their own initiative nor enquire whether the primary guarantee has been called within its period of validity. In the case of guarantees prescribing the submission of third-party documents, foreign banks occasionally forward these documents but in most cases they do not, while instructing banks do not, as a matter of standard practice, ask for them. As far as instructing banks are concerned, their pattern of action is to a large extent determined by practical considerations. While they basically adopt a passive stance, they do respond to signals from their customers who query compliance with the terms of the primary guarantee by the beneficiary. Whether and to what extent banks will then proceed to some kind of enquiry depends on a variety of factors such as the seriousness and the weight of the queries, the status of the particular client, the kind of response by the foreign issuing bank, its general reputation and the importance of or comparative indifference to preserving a smooth and untroubled relationship with the foreign bank. There exists no standard procedure for dealing with queries from the account party and one proceeds from case to case taking into account all the facts of the case at hand. Nonetheless, two kinds of general pattern of behaviour have evolved. First, the account party's bank will not ignore serious queries, but take up the matter with the foreign issuing bank and it may also ask for a copy of the beneficiary's demand for payment and of other documents which he was required to submit.[80] Secondly, if the foreign bank does not respond

---

[79] The representations are based on recurrent in-depth interviews with Dutch banks and experience with banks for many years.

[80] Cf. Staughton L.J.'s statement in *I.E. Contractors v. Lloyds Bank*, see note 78.

at all, or in a totally unsatisfactory manner, instructing banks will, as a general rule, not proceed to reimbursement but wait and see or make further enquiries. During this phase, instructing banks carefully avoid both clear statements to the issuing bank that they will refuse to pay and statements to the account party that they will refrain from paying. The crucial stage arrives when the foreign bank finally and persistently confirms that the terms of the guarantee have indeed been complied with without, however, producing the documents relating to the primary guarantee from which the instructing bank could verify compliance. It appears that this is not an uncommon situation. At this stage instructing banks tend not to insist any longer and proceed to reimbursement. Banks point out that ultimately the overriding consideration is that inter-bank dealings are based on mutual trust and reliance and that they, therefore, eventually ought to take the foreign bank at its word. However, this does not appear to be the kind of practice to which all banks in all circumstances will adhere without reserve. Several banks have expressed doubts as to whether such reliance is warranted in each and every case and these banks are not prepared to say that they would always and definitely pay in the end, without first having been able to verify compliance for themselves. Most banks also indicate that they would probably be inclined to distinguish between first demand primary guarantees on the one hand and primary guarantees prescribing the submission of third-party documents on the other hand. In the latter case they would be more adamant in their efforts to obtain the documents for the purpose of verification.

In those situations where the foreign issuing bank does forward the documents, instructing banks will, as a general rule, look at those documents and confer with the foreign bank when the documents give rise to queries. Ultimately instructing banks tend to abide by the judgment of the foreign bank, except where they feel quite certain that the terms of the primary guarantee have not been complied with. With respect to this restriction common banking practices cannot, however, be said to exist.

Limited duty to assist the account party

11-24 The survey of bankers' attitudes in no. 11-23 shows that the imposition on the instructing bank of a limited duty to assist the account party where there are serious doubts as to the fulfilment of the terms of the primary guarantee tallies with current banking practices. Thus, in the circumstances described in no. 11-23, the instructing bank ought to make some kind of enquiries to the foreign issuing bank. There are several arguments which justify the imposition of such a limited duty. The first reason is that the instructing bank's exclusion of liability for acts by the issuing bank is subject to its duty to the account party to act in good faith and with reasonable care, cf. art. 14(a) j. art. 15 URDG. Secondly, the account party may expect some degree of assistance from the instructing bank beyond the passing on of the instructions to the issuing bank and the examination regarding the terms of the counter-guarantee in return for its charges. A third argument relates to the credibility of indirect guarantees. While it appears justified to proceed on the general assumption that issuing banks correctly fulfil their duty of examination in respect of the primary guarantee, it appears equally justified to question whether all banks all over the world in all circumstances meet the required standards. It seems that if there are serious doubts in this respect one should no longer stick to this general assumption. In these circumstances enquiries by the instructing bank to the issuing bank could only be described as appropriate and will also enhance the credibility, and hence the utility of indirect guarantees supported by a counter-guarantee as a useful commercial instrument.

After having made appropriate enquiries to the issuing bank, the instructing bank is, however, entitled and obliged to proceed to payment if the foreign issuing bank unambiguously states that the terms of the primary guarantee have been fulfilled, unless there is clear evidence to the contrary. This could be the case, for example, if the instructing bank is in possession of the documents which the beneficiary submitted under the primary guarantee and which are evidently not in conformity with the required documents, or if it has itself forwarded the correct documents from the account party to the issuing bank which should have triggered an expiry event or a reduction clause in the primary guarantee.

If the counter-guarantee prescribes a statement from the issuing bank and the transmission of documents. Art. 20(b) and 21 URDG

11-25 Counter-guarantees sometimes require as a condition of payment that the issuing bank submit a statement to the effect that the primary guarantee has been called in accordance with its terms and that the issuing bank transmits the related documents. The purpose of such clauses is to provide the account party with a fair degree of protection with a view to ensuring compliance with the terms of the primary guarantee and to clarify the position of the instructing bank, for, pursuant to these clauses in the counter-guarantee, the instructing bank is entitled to request and the issuing bank must present the above-mentioned statement and the related documents. This latter aspect is crucial. Since the conditions for payment of the primary guarantee are ordinarily framed in a documentary fashion, the instructing bank is usually in a position easily to check whether, for example, the beneficiary has made a demand for payment, whether the demand has been lodged prior to the expiry date, whether the demand was accompanied by the beneficiary's statement of default, if required, or whether a prescribed third-party document has been submitted. If it is beyond reasonable doubt that the documents do not meet the requirements as set forth in the primary guarantee, the issuing bank's statement that the primary guarantee has been called in accordance with its terms must be considered as proven to be untruthful (or fraudulent). The consequence of this is that in this respect the terms of the counter-guarantee have not been met, which entitles the instructing bank to refuse payment. In situations like these, there is no need to resort to the exception to the principle of independence.

It is expressly noted that because of the principle of independence verification by the instructing bank should not amount to a complete re-examination of compliance with the terms of the primary guarantee. It is confined to the documents which have been and must be transmitted and only to the extent that the documentary fulfilment of the conditions of payment is governed by the principle of strict compliance.[81]

Where the foreign issuing bank is entitled to exercise its discretionary powers or where its duty is confined to applying reasonable care,[82] its judgment is binding, unless it is manifestly unreasonable.

If the URDG apply, the issuing bank must, when requesting payment from the instructing bank, also confirm that it has received a demand for payment under the primary guarantee in accordance with its terms, see art 20(b) URDG.[83] While art. 21 URDG obliges the issuing bank to transmit the beneficiary's demand under the primary guarantee and the related documents without delay to the instructing bank, such a duty is not expressed as a condition of payment. Neither ISP98 nor the Uncitral Convention contain specific provisions in respect of the conditions of payment under the counter-guarantee.

11.4 CLAUSES IN THE COUNTER-GUARANTEE

Clauses relating to payment

11-26 The instructions from the instructing bank to the issuing bank always contain statements to the effect that the request for the issuance of the guarantee is made for the account of the instructing bank or under its full responsibility, or, more elaborately, that it will fully indemnify the issuing bank for all consequences of its issuing the guarantee. Such general undertakings for reimbursement are often repeated in the counter-guarantee, followed by more specific clauses.

- Counter-guarantees often provide that payment will be made upon the issuing bank's first demand, to which may be added phrases like 'without any contestation by the principal' or 'regardless of disputes between the principal and beneficiary'.[84]
- In addition, the aforementioned clauses often refer to the primary guarantee, for example 'we (re)pay you (on your first demand) the amounts which you may have to pay in accordance with the terms of your guarantee' or 'we undertake to pay to you (on your first demand) the amounts which you may be obliged to pay under your guarantee' or 'in the event of execution of the guarantee by the

---

[81] See Chapter 10.8 No. 10-21.
[82] See Chapter 10.8, Nos. 10-24/26.
[83] Art. 34(2) of the OHADA's Uniform Act on Securities contains the same provision.
[84] See Chapter 11.2.2, No. 11-13 for the effect of the 'first demand' clause.

beneficiary, payment will be made upon your first demand'. These clauses do not detract from the principle that the counter-guarantee is independent of the primary guarantee and evidence by the issuing bank that, for example, it has paid in accordance with the terms of the primary guarantee is not a condition of payment as far as the counter-guarantee is concerned. They merely provide the consideration for payment under the counter-guarantee and explain the underlying reason for it in a manner which is similar to the references in the (primary) guarantee to the underlying contract and default by the account party.

- Counter-guarantees sometimes stipulate as a condition of payment that the issuing bank certifies that the demand for payment under the primary guarantee was made in accordance with its terms. Again, this clause does not negate the principle of independence, since it merely obliges the issuing bank to submit a formal statement without having to prove the correctness of its content. This is comparable to a unilateral statement of default in relation to the underlying transaction which the beneficiary of the (primary) guarantee may be required to submit. The aforementioned clause also applies if the counter-guarantee has been made subject to the URDG, see no. 11-25.

- The counter-guarantee may also require the issuing bank to transmit the beneficiary's demand for payment under the primary guarantee and the related documents. Such a clause is important for the account party and instructing bank since it enables them to verify whether the terms of the primary guarantee have indeed been fulfilled and, in appropriate cases, to prove that the issuing bank has breached its duty of examination.[85]

- Counter-guarantees sometimes contain provisions which link the counter-guarantee more closely to the primary guarantee, for example when the counter-guarantee does not contain a 'payment on first demand' clause but provides that payment is only due if the conditions of payment in the primary guarantee have been fulfilled. This technique serves the interests of the instructing bank and the account party in particular since the issuing bank cannot rely on the above-mentioned advantages of a first demand counter-guarantee.

- Repayment guarantees often contain specific clauses with respect to the reduction of the maximum amount.[86] In that event, the counter-guarantee is likely to contain a similar clause for reduction.

- If the issuing bank is prepared to issue a traditional accessory guarantee, it may require a counter-guarantee which entitles it to payment without proof of default by the account party.

---

[85] See Chapter 11.2, No. 11-13 under 'limits of independence. the exception', and No. 11-20, and Chapter 11.3, No. 11-25.

[86] See Chapter 8.8.

Duration, expiry date

11-27 Counter-guarantees usually provide for a period of time within which the issuing bank must submit its claim for repayment. Its duration is attuned to that of the primary guarantee. If the primary guarantee contains a fixed expiry date, the duration of the counter-guarantee will be fixed according to that date plus an additional, short period of time, which usually ranges from three to thirty days. The purpose of this additional period, sometimes erroneously referred to as a grace period, is to allow the issuing bank some time for administration and mailing of its request for payment under the counter-guarantee. The additional period is not meant to allow the beneficiary a grace period for claiming under the primary guarantee after its expiry date.

Since every first demand guarantee is subject to a possible request from the beneficiary 'to pay or extend' or 'to hold for value', the counter-guarantee often stipulates expressly that, should the period of validity of the primary guarantee be extended, the counter-guarantee will also be extended automatically for the same length of time. By no means do all counter-guarantees contain an explicit provision to this effect and the absence thereof may create grave difficulties. It is submitted, however, that extension of the counter-guarantee following similar requests from the beneficiary is an implied term of the counter-guarantee.[87]

If the primary guarantee is extendable at the request of the beneficiary, the counter-guarantee will contain matching clauses. It may provide, for example, that, in the event of extension of the primary guarantee, the counter-guarantee becomes payable on its expiry date unless it is extended, that it is automatically extended or that it is extended on the request of the issuing bank. Issuing banks in certain jurisdictions sometimes require a counter-guarantee which remains in force until discharge even though the primary guarantee contains an expiry date which is enforceable under local law. Instructing banks and account parties should object to this practice.

Where the primary guarantee does not contain an expiry date, but an expiry event, for example submission by the account party of the certificate of acceptance, the counter-guarantee will refer to the same event, with an added period for administration and mailing. It is advisable that the counter-guarantee stipulates that the additional period does not commence until the account party has notified the issuing bank of the event in the appropriate manner.

If the primary guarantee does not contain an expiry date or expiry event, the counter-guarantee is not likely to have an expiry date either but will stipulate that it remains in force until discharge.

---

[87] See further Chapter 12.4.3, No. 12-44, and Chapter 13.3, No. 13-39.

Amount and currency, transfer

11-28 Counter-guarantees invariably specify the maximum amount, which corresponds with the maximum amount of the primary guarantee. Within this maximum amount the issuing bank is, of course, only entitled to reimbursement of the amount actually claimed by the beneficiary of the primary guarantee.

The amount of the primary guarantee is often expressed in local currency. The issuing bank may, however, prefer to be reimbursed in another currency, especially that of a Western industrialised country. If so, the counter-guarantee should also specify the basis of the conversion, for example the official rate of exchange in the issuing bank's country, as well as the date for the determination of the rate of exchange, for example the date of payment by the issuing bank or the date of payment by the instructing bank under the counter-guarantee.

Unless otherwise provided, the maximum amount does not include incidental costs, bank charges, taxes and other levies. Counter-guarantees sometimes provide expressly for payment of interest, commonly calculated at LIBOR (London Interbank Offered Rate) and the date as from which interest is due, which is usually the date of the request for payment.

Some foreign banks require an express statement from the instructing bank that overseas transfers are not subject to exchange control regulations or, as the case may be, that the required approvals have been obtained.

Choice of law, jurisdiction

11-29 The counter-guarantee may contain a choice of law and jurisdiction clause for the settlement of disputes which may arise between instructing and issuing bank. If so, these clauses invariably provide for the law of and jurisdiction in the issuing bank's country.

Garnishment ('Kuwaiti') clauses

11-30 Counter-guarantees in favour of some banks in Kuwait, Egypt, Sudan, Yemen and Libya contain clauses providing for reimbursement irrespective of stop-payment and conservatory attachment (freezing) orders initiated by the account party or, sometimes, even by third parties.[88] These clauses are known as 'garnishment' or 'Kuwaiti'

---

[88] See, for example, the specimen in a counter-guarantee in favour of a Kuwaiti bank: 'In the event any legal injunction or any other legal action or enforcement, or any order of any Governmental, semi-Governmental or Public authority is issued restraining or precluding our (instructing, R.B.) Bank from payment to you as counter-Guarantors, then this Letter will be immediately and automatically converted into a direct obligation on our Bank

clauses. In the past, this practice was far more widespread and extended to virtually all banks in the countries mentioned.

Opinions regarding the validity, enforceability and legal effects of such garnishment clauses differ. One author appears to uphold their validity,[89] others reject their validity as contravening public policy,[90] whereas yet others suggest that a distinction is to be made between the inter-bank relationship and the relationship between account party and instructing bank.[91] Indeed, as far as the inter-bank relationship is concerned, clauses providing for reimbursement despite stop-payment orders do not violate public policy. Judicial relief, if granted at all, is not aimed at protecting the interests of the instructing bank, but the interests of the account party. Banks could well agree to such clauses and effect reimbursement accordingly but they cannot, in principle, subsequently turn to their customer in the face of judicial relief extended to them. The acceptance of such clauses by the instructing bank is thus viewed as constituting a separate undertaking, solely confined to the inter-bank relationship and distinct from the relationship between instructing bank and customer, as is indeed reflected in the wording of counter-guarantees containing such garnishment clauses.

Western European banks are gravely concerned about these requirements and they are most reluctant to agree to their inclusion for fear of contravening public policy and, as far as the United Kingdom is concerned, for fear of contempt of court. The clauses have been the subject of continual consultation among banks on a national level as well as within the Fédération Banquaire. Dutch, German and British banks have stated that, as a general policy, they refuse to accept these clauses. Current practice shows that if the instructing bank clearly expresses objections, most of the foreign banks concerned will agree to the deletion of a garnishment clause.[92]

---

towards you as if our Bank, for all intents and purposes, is a primary obligor towards you for a Cash indebtedness of the amount above stated.'

[89] Vasseur, Tours, p. 352, Nos. 22-23 and note to *Trib. com. Paris, 15 February 1984*, D. 1984 I.R. p. 205. It is noted, however, that the court did not pronounce on this issue.

[90] Dohm, DPCI 1980, p. 271, von Mettenheim, RIW 1981, p. 585, Stoufflet, Garantie Bancaire Internationale, No. 48.

[91] Simont, Tours, pp. 490, 491 and Rev. Banque 1983, p. 585, Poullet, thesis, Nos. 369, 370.

[92] The Central Bank of Libya recently advised Libyan banks not to insist on garnishment clauses.

11.5 INSTRUCTING BANK'S DUTY TO INFORM THE ACCOUNT PARTY OF THE CONTENT OF THE COUNTER-GUARANTEE

11-31 The issuance of an indirect guarantee gives rise to additional risks for the account party. He is exposed not only to the risks related to the primary guarantee, but also to those which ensue from the counter-guarantee, which the instructing bank has issued for his account. The reason why a counter-guarantee adds to the risks flowing from the primary guarantee is that the counter-guarantee is independent of the primary guarantee and that the payment obligation under the counter-guarantee might be stated in broader terms. Thus, if the counter-guarantee provides for payment upon the issuing bank's first demand, the instructing bank, and in turn the account party, must pay without the issuing bank having to prove that the terms of the primary guarantee have been fulfilled. Accordingly, the account party must reimburse his bank even though actual compliance with the terms of the primary guarantee is uncertain or even disputed. Other additional risk factors could be that, for example, the primary guarantee contains an expiry date while the counter-guarantee remains in force until discharge, or that the counter-guarantee contains no matching reduction clause.

The terms of the primary guarantee should be known to the account party, since, ordinarily, he passed those on to his bank for transmission to the issuing bank but he might not be aware of the fact that his bank has issued a counter-guarantee or of the terms thereof. Since the counter-guarantee has been issued for the risk and account of the account party, the instructing bank should inform him of this. This is normally done by sending a copy of the instructions to the issuing bank which contains the counter-guarantee, or a copy of the final text if and when it has been amended pursuant to objections of the issuing bank. Because of practical reasons and/or pressure of time, it is often impossible to forward a copy to the account party prior to the transmission of the counter-guarantee to the issuing bank. Failure to advise its client promptly of the issuance of a counter-guarantee does not necessarily bar the instructing bank's claim for reimbursement because the account party owes a paramount duty to indemnify his bank for the consequences of its instructing the foreign bank, because the terms of the counter-guarantee are often non-negotiable and because the account party is often aware of the practice of issuing counter-guarantees from previous transactions.[93]

---

[93] Cf. *Trib. com. Toulouse, 26 September 1990*, D. 1993 Somm. p. 97.

CHAPTER 12
OTHER ASPECTS OF THE BANK GUARANTEE

12.1 THE PRINCIPLE OF INDEPENDENCE RE-EXAMINED

12.1.1 Recapitulation

Introduction

12-1 The chief characteristic feature of the modern multi-party guarantee is the principle of independence. Insight into this phenomenon will be enhanced if one bears in mind that the meaning of independence as well as the underlying explanation vary according to the selected point of reference. This has been examined elsewhere but will be briefly recapitulated. Proper understanding of the various notions of independence avoids attributing all kinds of unwarranted legal effects to this principle. It also avoids invoking the principle too readily as the rationale for resolving all sorts of issues and specific rules of law where it has in fact no bearing on the matter at all. Independence explains a lot but not everything.

Between bank and beneficiary

12-2 The notion of independence in respect of the relationship between bank and beneficiary comprises two aspects. First, that relationship is not affected by the mandate relationship between bank and account party.[1] Secondly – and what is more important – the payment obligations of the bank and the beneficiary's right to payment are to be determined by reference to the terms and conditions as stated in the guarantee and not by reference to the underlying relationship.[2] Accordingly, the bank must pay and only pay if the terms of the guarantee have been met and it cannot raise defences which emanate from the underlying relationship in the way a surety (accessory guarantor) can. More specifically, the determination of default by the principal debtor as measured by the underlying relationship and differences of opinion in this respect are not an issue in the relationship between bank and beneficiary. In order to be entitled to payment by way of compensation, the beneficiary merely has to satisfy the terms of the guarantee and need not show default in any other way.

---

[1] See Chapter 9, No. 9-5.
[2] See Chapter 2.1, and Chapter 7, No. 7-2.

Between account party and bank, indirect guarantee and counter-guarantee

12-3 As far as direct guarantees are concerned, independence in this context means that the obligation and right to reimbursement are not affected by the rights and obligations, or defences against compensation as measured by and originating from the underlying contract. The bank cannot be implicated in disputes which may divide parties to the underlying relationship. In this respect the bank has an interest of its own in the principle of independence. The same applies to the inter-bank relationship in the case of indirect guarantees.[3] Moreover, the counter-guarantee furnished by the instructing bank in favour of the issuing bank is independent of the primary guarantee which is furnished by the issuing bank. This means that the counter-guarantee is payable in accordance with its own terms.[4]

Between parties to the underlying relationship

12-4 The notion of independence can also be related to the parties to the underlying relationship. It finds expression in their agreement to 'pay first, argue later', i.e. their agreement that payment by way of compensation is to be effected (first) once the agreed conditions of the guarantee have been complied with, for instance a simple demand for payment with or without a statement of default or the presentation of third-party documents evidencing default, in derogation of the ordinary determination of default, which would have to be pursued but for this special agreement.[5] At the heart of the matter, it is this notion of independence that best explains the principle of independence as it exists as an inherent part of the other relationships mentioned above.

12.1.2 Independence and functional interdependence

Synthesis instead of antithesis

12-5 Emphasising the independent nature of the guarantee as a contract between bank and beneficiary in respect of the secured contract and mandate is only possible by virtue of their functional interdependence. One would not speak in terms of independence if these relationships were totally unrelated. But they are not and the existing interdependence accords sense and meaning to the principle of independence. The various segments are functionally and commercially correlated in some aspects and at the same time independent of each other in other respects and this is so because

---

[3] Chapter 7, No. 7-2.
[4] See Chapter 11.2.2.
[5] Chapter 6.1.

the parties to the underlying relationship themselves agreed to an independent guarantee.[6]

A sustained awareness of the functional interdependence of the various relationships is essential for understanding the mechanics of the modern guarantee. It explains why most of the disputes revolve not around one single relationship on its own but in relation to one of the other segments. It explains several basic rules of law and factual matters, such as the rule that the determination of the terms and conditions of the guarantee is not just a matter to be decided upon by the parties to the guarantee (bank and beneficiary), the rule that the principal debtor is to reimburse the bank for payments to the beneficiary but only if the bank has duly ascertained compliance with the terms of the guarantee, the rule that in matters concerning the proper construction of the guarantee reference could be had to the underlying relationship, the rule that petitions by the principal debtor for conservatory attachment and freezing injunctions are ordinarily dismissed or lifted and the rule that the issue of fraudulent calls on the guarantee is essentially a matter which pertains to the parties to the underlying relationship and which only marginally affects the position of the bank, if at all.

Most of these rules are too obvious and too plain for words, and that is so by virtue of the interdependence of the various segments. These and other rules of law also seem to endorse the view that the guarantee as a contract between bank and beneficiary is essentially a vehicle assuring the realisation of the contemplated reallocation of risks between principal debtor and creditor.[7]

Antithesis instead of synthesis

12-6 Obdurate and undue emphasis on the principle of independence, which may stem from a mistaken perception of the principle in disregard of the equally valid principle of interdependence, has led to observations and views which could be considered as unhelpful and confusing,

- Some authors of the Germanic legal tradition state that, as a result of its independence and in contrast to accessory suretyship, the independent guarantee assures a certain 'result' (*Erfolg, Leistung, Zustand, or Umstand*), as described in the underlying relationship, but regardless of whether such a result is owed.[8]

---

6   Cf. Mattout, No. 214.

7   See Chapter 6.1, No. 6-2.

8   Kleiner, pp. 33, 34, Roesle, p. 24 et seq., p. 36 et seq., Dohm, Nos. 71, 78, 94, Mülbert, pp. 39, 41, 83, Schinnerer/Avancini, pp. 287, 291, 293, 313, Bärmann, Recht der Kredietsicherheit in europäischen Ländern, Band ll, Teil 1 (1976), No. 186, Käser, RabelsZ. 1971, pp. 608, 609, Guggenheim, FS Schnitzer, pp. 172, 174, Bernstein, FS Imre Zajtay, pp. 22, 23, Mühl, FS Imre Zajtay, pp. 400, 406.

Accordingly, payments pursuant to the guarantee are not related, it is said, to the beneficiary/creditor's rights against the account party/principal debtor. These observations fit the German *Garantievertrag* (autonomous guarantee) as described in Chapter 3.11 but they are misleading in the context of a multi-party guarantee. Independence merely means that, if the terms of the guarantee are met, the beneficiary has a right to payment of compensation without the need to produce (further) evidence of default and that the bank cannot invoke defences from the underlying relationship. This follows from the agreement to this effect by the parties to the underlying relationship, the execution of which has been transferred to the bank. Thus, the beneficiary only receives what is owed to him when it is owed to him by the bank and account party by virtue of their agreement.[9] There is no magic in the principle of independence.

– Especially in the early period of the development of the notion of independent guarantees one occasionally encounters the view that the guarantor solely pays his own debt, not the debt of the principal debtor, as the surety does.[10] Such thoughts reflect a misunderstanding of the principle of independence as well as the principle of co-extensiveness in the case of suretyship. Both the independent guarantor and the surety pay their own debt, the one pursuant to the contract of guarantee, the other pursuant to the contract of suretyship. In both situations, that payment also constitutes payment on behalf of the principal debtor to the

---

[9] Cf. *Trib. Brussels, 3 September 1993*, RDC 1994, p. 1126: 'The principle of independence stems from the will of the parties (account party and beneficiary) of the underlying relationship and that of the account party and bank'; Bouloy, JCP 1981 ll No. 19702 last paragraph: 'if extraordinary, independence is nothing but the proclamation of the paramountcy of the principal contract: it is the principal contract which brings about independence'. *Geneva, 12 September 1985*, D. 1986 I.R. p. 165: 'In respect of a guarantee the true parties are the parties to the underlying contract. The bank is merely an intermediary mandatory charged with the execution of one of the modalities of the principal contract'. *ICC Arbitration, No. 5721/1990*, J.D.I. 1990, p. 1020: 'The independent nature of the guarantee does not mean that it does not originate from the underlying contract and that it is not closely related to that contract'.

[10] See, for example, *Trib gr. inst. Paris, 13 May 1980*, D. 1980 J. p. 488, *Trib. com. Brussels, 6 April 1982*, Rev. Banque 1982, p. 683, *Trib. com. Brussels, 28 April 1982*, RDC 1984, p. 57, *Trib. com. Brussels, 15 November 1984*, RDC 1985, p. 569. See for a recent example: *CA Amsterdam, 10 August 2000*, JOR 2000, 205. Legal writing: Schinnerer/Avancini, pp. 297, 283, Moschner, O Bank-Archiv 1983, p. 130, Poullet, DPCI 1979, pp. 398, 435 and Tours, p. 154, van Lier, JT 1980, p. 355, de Vroede and Flamee, TPR 1982, p. 374, De Smedt, IFLR December 1983, p. 19, Herbots, RW 1983-1984, p. 1191, Wymeersch, TPR 1986, p. 480 and Hague-Zagreb Essays 6, p. 92, Eisemann, Rev. Arbitrage 1972, p. 383, Vasseur, e.g., No. 23, D. 1983 J. pp. 367 and 444, D. 1983 I.R. p. 304, D. 1986 I.R. p. 166, Tours, pp. 326, 331, Croiset van Uchelen, WPNR 1989, p. 271.

creditor.[11] The contrary view raises non-existent problems, for it then becomes exceedingly difficult to explain why the principal debtor should have to reimburse the guarantor and why the creditor cannot once more revert to the principal debtor for payment of amounts which he has already received under the guarantee. It would also be difficult to explain why it is the parties to the underlying relationship who determine the terms and conditions of the guarantee.[12]

– The independent nature of the guarantee has spawned extensive debates in France and Belgium as to whether the independent guarantee has a *causa*, being one of the requirements for a valid and enforceable contract and, if it has, what the *causa* should be. One is inclined to suspect that the difficulties stem from an ill-conceived and inflated notion of independence. It is worth noting that the issue has incited little or no fuss in respect of the contract of suretyship and that all propositions for the identification of the *causa* of the independent guarantee could equally be applied to suretyship and vice versa. In any event, at present it is fully accepted that the independent guarantee has a *causa*. The prevailing view is that the *causa* consists in the bank's wish to be instrumental in the realisation of the underlying relationship, but that the obligation of the bank is detached from that *causa*, and/or in the will of the parties to the underlying relationship to provide security in a manner which is independent of the underlying relationship.[13]

The phenomenon '*causa*' has not been an issue in Germany, nor in the Netherlands. At any rate, the principle of independence has, rightly, never been regarded as a possible source of difficulty in this respect. According to the prevailing view in the Netherlands

---

[11] *Baytur S.A. v. Moona Silk Mills, 20 December 1984*, JBL 1985, p. 324 (Mustill J.: 'Payment under a guarantee is not an extrinsic benefit and should be taken into account when assessing damages under the main contract'). Cf. Picod, D.-RDA 2000 J., pp. 112, 114, Mijnssen, p. 34. See also Mülbert, p. 36 note 31.

[12] See Chapter 8.1.

[13] *Riom, 14 May 1980*, D. 1981 J. p. 336, *Trib. gr. inst. Montlucon, 9 January 1981*, D. 1981 J. p. 336, *Trib. com. Paris, 24 March 1981*, D. 1981 J. p. 482, *Brussels, 18 December 1981*, Rev. Banque 1982 p. 99, *Trib. Brussels, 3 September 1993*, RDC 1994, p. 1126, *Trib. com. Brussels, 21 November 1997*, RDC 1998, p. 850. *Paris, 27 November 1990*, D. 1991 Somm. p. 200, held that the *causa* is situated in the instructions from the account party. In two decisions of 20 December 1982, D. 1983 J. p. 365 the Cour de Cassation affirmed the causal nature of the independent guarantee, without taking a position as to what constitutes the *causa*. Legal writing on the subject is prolific. Summaries can be found in Mattout, No. 202, Prüm, pp. 55-69, Cabrillac/Mouly, Nos. 426-427, Stoufflet, Garantie Bancaire Internationale, Nos. 38-39, Vasseur, Nos. 39-49, Wymeersch, TPR 1986, pp. 489-494, De Ly, TBH 1986, pp. 182-184, RPDB, Nos. 27-34, T'Kint, No. 826.

and the unanimous view in Germany, the *causa* of the independent guarantee is the furnishing of security to the beneficiary with a view to proper performance of the underlying relationship. Particularly in this context, it is widely acknowledged that independence does not mean that guarantee and underlying contract are unrelated to each other.[14]

12.1.3 Independence as an abstract concept and as a matter of construction. Relativeness and evolution

12-7 On the Continent, case law and especially legal writing neatly distinguish between the concepts of accessory suretyship and the independent guarantee and it is, indeed, expedient to do so. However, they are abstract concepts. The existence of and the distinction between the two concepts as such afford no aid when one has to answer the question of whether a particular contract under review is to be understood as one or the other. Businessmen, bankers and practising lawyers are not minded to think in such abstract concepts. They are interested in whether payment is to be made upon full proof of default, upon third-party documents or upon demand without evidence of default, and, if all is well, the terms and conditions will be drafted accordingly. Whether the law classifies the contract as either an accessory suretyship or an independent guarantee is of less importance to them. This explains why those engaged in legal practice – but probably less so in Germany – often employ both terms indiscriminately. Also the texts of the security instruments, at least at one time, reveal that one was not conscious of there being two different concepts of security. It is worth noting that long before the influx of first demand guarantees from the Middle East area, beneficiaries in the public sector on the Continent began to require exactly the same type of security – a suretyship payable upon first demand.[15] Why the term 'suretyship'? No doubt because that was the familiar and common term. The awareness that two different concepts exist, namely the accessory suretyship and the independent guarantee, only grew over time.

American law and practice employ two terms covering two distinct concepts, the guarantee (or guaranty) being the accessory type of security and the standby letter of credit being the independent type of security. The American performance bond is a hybrid form. The extent of co-extensiveness or independence and the rights and obligations of parties can only be derived from the particular terms and conditions of the bond but it always requires some kind of proof of default.

---

[14] See, for example, Mijnssen, pp. 40, 38, Pabbruwe, rede p. 5 and Tours p. 197, Bannier, in Hague-Zagreb Essays 6, p. 69, Schoordijk, RMThemis 1985, p. 388, von Westphalen, p. 58, Canaris, No. 1125, Mülbert, pp. 33, 59, Dohm, Nos. 100, 102, Kleiner, Nos. 18.01-18.05, Bouloy, JCP 1981 ll, No. 19702, Stoufflet, JCP 1985 ll No. 20436.

[15] See Chapter 4.5, No. 4-17.

English law and practice do not principally distinguish between the two concepts. The focal point is the terms and conditions of the instrument. They will indicate whether the guarantee is payable on proof of default (accessory guarantee) or upon fulfilment of the terms of the guarantee, such as a demand for payment accompanied by the beneficiary's unilateral statement of default (independent guarantee) and that will answer most questions. Co-extensiveness and independence are mainly a finding resulting from the construction of the particular security instrument being considered.

A clear conceptual distinction is lacking in many other regions too, whether or not the law has been shaped in the Common Law tradition. For instance, the Arab language has only one term which refers to both the accessory and the independent guarantee. Present legislation in Kuwait, Iraq, Bahrain and Yemen merely states that a guarantor may invoke defences derived from the underlying transaction (accessory guarantee), but that a bank guarantor cannot do so (independent guarantee). Originally, many texts of security instruments employed in the Arabian Gulf followed the pattern of the American performance bond but, nonetheless, provided for payment upon demand.[16] The lingering uncertainty as regards the enforceability of expiry dates in some countries is probably also a consequence of not distinguishing between the two types of security.[17]

12.2 FORMATION

Unilateral engagement or consensual contract. Formation

12-8 Two schools of thought exist regarding the nature of the bank's obligation and the time and manner of its coming into force. The same issue has been raised in respect of documentary credits.

According to one view, the bank's obligation is considered to be a unilateral engagement and the binding force of this engagement merely depends on and arises from the bank's unilateral declaration to commit itself to the beneficiary. This declaration is contained in the advice stating the terms and conditions of the guarantee. Accordingly, the binding force of the bank's obligation attaches and the terms and conditions are fixed as from the time of the issuance of the guarantee document. Acceptance by the beneficiary is not required.

The second school of thought views the bank's obligation as one stemming from a consensual contract which comes into being upon offer and acceptance. Accordingly, the issuance of the guarantee merely amounts to an offer which must be accepted by the beneficiary. It is common ground that the offer can be and usually is accepted tacitly. A call on the guarantee certainly evidences that the offer has been accepted.

---

[16] See also Chapter 8, No. 8-3.
[17] See further Chapter 12.4.5.

The view that the obligation of the bank is a unilateral engagement with the legal effects mentioned above has been expressed in *Brussels, 15 October 1987*.[18] Belgian legal writing is divided.[19] German doctrine unanimously adopts the contractual view whereby the contract of guarantee comes into being upon the bank's offer and the (tacit) acceptance thereof by the beneficiary.[20] German case law has taken the same position.[21] French case law also adheres to the contractual approach,[22] as does Dutch law.[23] While English law is more concerned with the issue of (ir)revocability of the bank's undertaking, it would appear that, at least in respect of documentary credits, the obligation of the bank is viewed as a contractual one resulting from the offer and its acceptance.[24]

Art. 6 URDG, Rule 1.06(e) and 2.03 ISP98 and art. 7(1/3) Uncitral Convention provide that the guarantee (or standby letter of credit) enters into effect as from its issuance. These provisions seem to suggest that the guarantee (or standby) is viewed as an unilateral undertaking, but it is doubtful whether it was intended to take a particular stand in this matter. It probably means no more than that, upon issuance, the bank is bound by the terms of the guarantee and that the beneficiary is entitled to call the

---

[18] Rev. Banque 2/1988, p. 29.

[19] Unilateral engagement: Velu, Tours, pp. 218, 223, 227-228, Simont, Rev. Banque 1983, p. 588 (who, oddly, views the counter-guarantee as a consensual contract), van Lier, JT 1980, p. 346, van Ommeslaghe, JT 1982, p. 148, Herbots, RW 1983-1984, p. 1185, Devos, Rev. Banque 2/1988, p. 32. Consensual contract: Poullet, thesis No. 243, 247, de Vroede and Flamee, TPR 1982, p. 376, T'Kint, Nos. 828-829, W. Derijcke, TBH 2002, p. 492, footnote 10. According to the last mentioned author *CA Brussels, 2 March 2001*, TBH 2002, p. 484, views the independent guarantee as a consensual contract. See in general RPDB, Nos. 54-59.

[20] See, for example, von Westphalen, p. 110, Lienesch, p. 71, Canaris, No. 1121, Zahn/Ehrlich/Neumann, 9/109, Kleiner, No. 16.01, Dohm, No. 165, Schinnerer/Avancini, p. 302.

[21] *BGH, 3 May 1984*, WM 1984, p. 768, *BGH, 19 September 1985*, NJW 1986, p. 310, *OLG Schleswig, 6 December 1983*, WM 1984, p. 651, *OLG München, 6 May 1987*, WM 1988, p. 1554,*BGH, 6 May 1997*, WM 1997, p. 1242, *BGH, 10 February 2000*, WM 2000, p. 715.

[22] *Cass., 2 February 1988*, D. 1988 Somm. p. 239, *Trib. com. Paris, 26 May 1989*, D. 1990 Somm. p. 206, Prüm, p. 112, Gavalda and Stoufflet, RTDC 1980, p. 6, Villery, Tours, pp. 269, 270, Vasseur, Tours, p. 322, and RDAI 1992, p. 266, Stoufflet, Garantie Bancaire Internationale, No. 35. But see *Rouen, 19 February 1992*, D. 1993 Somm. p. 108, mentioned in No. 15.

[23] Mijnssen, p. 40, Boll, preadvies, p. 102, Bannier, in Hague-Zagreb Essays No. 6, pp. 77, 79, Pabbruwe, p. 6.

[24] Schmitthoff, Export Trade, p. 423, 424, Gutteridge/Megrah, Chapter Four, especially pp. 31-32 and case law cited, Ellinger, in Chitty on Contracts vol. 2, No. 2668, Harfield, pp. 52, 55. See further Todd, Sellers and Documentary Credits, JBL 1983, pp. 468-481. See for guarantees Goode, p. 28.

guarantee, regardless of whether the bank's liability is founded on its unilateral undertaking or on contract.[25]

In most cases it will not matter whether the law adopts one or the other approach.[26] This study prefers the consensual approach, but primarily because it accords with the generally accepted principles of the law of obligations in the countries concerned, while no reasons compel a departure from those principles with respect to independent guarantees and documentary credits. The contract of guarantee comes into being by virtue of an irrevocable offer from the bank, followed by the – usually tacit – acceptance by the beneficiary.[27] As the beneficiary is expecting the issuance of a guarantee and as a guarantee only confers advantages on him and no obligations, tacit acceptance can be deemed to exist when the beneficiary does not object to the terms and conditions within a reasonable, i.e. short, period of time after receiving the advice. As from this time, not only the bank, but also the beneficiary is contractually bound by the terms of the guarantee and he can no longer demand changes or amendments. The beneficiary should, therefore, check without undue delay whether the terms and conditions of the guarantee are satisfactory and correspond with those which have been agreed upon between him and the account party. He should also verify whether the various terms and conditions of payment are consistent with each other and capable of fulfilment.[28] If not, he should forthwith contact the bank and account party in order to have the terms amended. In the absence of a very specific relationship, there is no duty on the part of the bank to draw the beneficiary's attention to unusual conditions of payment or conditions which are impossible to fulfil.[29]

The reverse situation occurred in *BGH, 10 February 2000*, where the bank issued a guarantee on terms which were significantly more favourable for the beneficiary than had been agreed upon between him and the account party, and the beneficiary had

---

[25] In respect of the URDG Affaki, No. 66, notes that it is left to national law to decide whether a guarantee should be considered as a consensual contract or an unilateral act, but in either view the guarantor cannot revoke its undertaking.

[26] In relation to American law Wunnicke/Wunnicke/Turner, § 2.07 and § 1.05, seem to favour the contractual approach, but observe that the issue is, to a considerable degree, a semantic one. See also Dolan, § 5.01[1/2].

[27] See for tacit acceptance especially *BGH, 6 May 1997*, WM 1997, p. 1242, *BGH, 10 February 2000*, WM 2000, p. 715.

[28] In *Exxon Co. U.S.A. v. Banque de Paris et des Pays-Bas*, 828 F2d 1121 (5th Cir. 1987), see further Chapter 13.2.7, No. 13-23, and *Cass., 3 June 1986*, D. 1987 Somm. p. 174, see further Chapter 13.3, No. 13-39, the (counter-)guarantee contained (inconsistent) expiry provisions which could not possibly be complied with. See also Chapter 12.3.5, No. 12-37.

[29] See Dolan, § 6.08[1] for a discussion of some, apparently conflicting American cases.

tacitly accepted this guarantee. The German Supreme Court ruled that the bank was bound to these terms in its relationship with the beneficiary.[30]

It is noted that, pursuant to the above-mentioned view, the interval between the bank's liability arising from its irrevocable offer and its liability founded on the contract of guarantee is of short duration only.

Arguments

12-9 Those who advocate the unilateral engagement theory do so because of some alleged defects in the offer and acceptance theory. They point out that if the binding force of the bank's obligation depends on acceptance by the beneficiary, it would be possible for the bank to withdraw or to alter its offer before acceptance. The major flaw in the reasoning is the fact that it is founded on a questionable premise, namely the revocability of the bank's offer. While, in general, Continental case law and legal writing is divided on the question of whether and in what circumstances an offer should be considered (ir)revocable, it is accepted that an offer is irrevocable if so indicated, or if it was reasonable for the offeree to rely on the offer as irrevocable and has acted in reliance on the offer, or if the offer is irrevocable pursuant to usage.[31] Should neither of the two first-mentioned conditions be met, it is submitted that the irrevocability of the bank's offer follows from international usage. In any event, art. 5 URDG, Rule 1.06(e) and Rule 2.03 ISP98 and art. 7(4) Uncitral Convention state that the guarantee is irrevocable and takes effect upon issuance.

A further argument in favour of the unilateral engagement theory is that Common Law countries do not generally recognise the concept of the irrevocability of offers. If true, the rule is subject to numerous exceptions.[32] In any event, it does not apply to documentary credits and bank guarantees but it may explain why they usually provide that 'the bank herewith *irrevocably* undertakes to …'. A final argument that has been made is that banks feel bound as from the date of communication of their offer. That 'feeling' is correct. They are bound, namely by their offer, meaning that they cannot withdraw or alter it.

In conclusion, the alleged defects of the offer and acceptance theory prove to be erroneous. On the other hand, the unilateral engagement approach may give rise to some problems in matters of construction. In that approach, it becomes more difficult to explain that the precise contents of the rights and obligations are to be found by reference to the mutual intention and expectations of bank *and* beneficiary, and occa-

---

[30] WM 2000, p. 715. See for the facts of this case Chapter 10.7, No. 10-17.

[31] Art. 16 (2) and art. 9 of the 1980 Vienna Convention on Contracts for the International Sale of Goods (CISG), which may be deemed to reflect current views.

[32] See, for example, Treitel, *The Law of Contract*, 6th. ed., pp. 34, 35.

sionally by reference to the underlying relationship. There could be a second kind of problem. If the beneficiary were to suggest some amendments and if the bank were to agree, then the obligation of the bank pursuant to its original offer surely ceases to have effect. But how is this to be explained in the unilateral engagement theory? And what is the position prior to the bank's acceptance of the amendments?[33]

Rejection, counter-proposals

12-10 An outright, unequivocal rejection by the beneficiary terminates the binding force of the offer. The bank owes no duty to the beneficiary to submit a fresh offer on more favourable terms. Whether or not the non-conclusion of the contract of guarantee results in breach of contract by the principal debtor in his relationship with the beneficiary is quite a different matter.[34]

However, the beneficiary is not likely squarely to reject the offer. Instead, he will request some amendments, because, for example, the terms and conditions stated in the advice do not correspond with those agreed with the account party. Clearly, the bank will only be bound by these counter-proposals if it has accepted them, as was decided in *BGH, 3 May 1984*.[35] Contrary to the position of the beneficiary, silence or inactivity on the part of the bank cannot generally be deemed to amount to acceptance.

A more thorny question is whether the bank, if it does not agree to the counter-proposals, continues to be bound by its original offer, with the result that the beneficiary no longer has the power to bring about a valid contract by accepting the original offer. It is a general rule of law that a reply to an offer which contains material modifications is a rejection of the offer and constitutes a counter-offer.[36] Thus, in general, the law answers this question in the affirmative. It is submitted, however, that the general rule should not, at least not automatically, be applied to guarantees. Some support for this proposition can be derived from case law.

In *BGH, 3 May 1984*, the claim by the beneficiary for payment was rejected, one of the grounds being that no valid contract of guarantee had been concluded, since the bank had persistently rejected the counter-proposals. The question just posed does not seem to have been addressed directly in this case. However, the main reason for dismissing the claim was non-fulfilment of a condition precedent. That reasoning would have been superfluous if no contract or no obligation whatsoever had existed. It is, therefore, submitted that this decision affirms the rule that counter-proposals must

---

[33] Cf. Vasseur, RDAI 1992, p. 266.
[34] See Chapter 6.2. No. 6-8.
[35] WM 1984, p. 768.
[36] See, for example, art. 17 j. art. 19(1) CISG.

be accepted in order to be binding, while it leaves room for the proposition that the beneficiary continues to have the power to accept the original offer.

Brussels, 15 October 1987 did answer the question directly.[37] In this case the bank forwarded a guarantee providing for a very short period of validity and the beneficiary, thereupon, asked for a guarantee allowing for a longer period. The bank did not respond – at least it expressed no agreement. When the beneficiary called the guarantee within the period of validity stated in the original offer, the bank refused payment arguing that no valid contract had been concluded, since the beneficiary had rejected the offer, while the bank had not accepted the counter-offer. The court rightly dismissed this defence but did so by rejecting the offer and acceptance theory and endorsing the unilateral engagement approach.[38] It is submitted that the consensual offer and acceptance theory would have led to the same result, provided that the submission of counter-proposals is not viewed in law as a rejection of the original offer. This appreciation of the facts would ordinarily be the proper one, because, as stated above, an actual unequivocal and definite rejection will be rare.

The facts of both cases perhaps illustrate that it is often more productive to enquire what terms and conditions parties have agreed than it is to ponder whether a contract has or has not come about.

Requirements as to form

12-11 There are no statutory requirements as to the form of conclusion with regard to the contract of guarantee.[39] This should not come as a surprise, as the modern, independent guarantee is not regulated by statute. In respect of traditional suretyship, some national laws require as a means of protection that the contract be concluded in writing, either as a rule of general application or confined to those not acting in a professional capacity. It is submitted that by analogy such requirements, if relevant, also apply to independent guarantees.[40] It is, however, all but inconceivable that guarantees are not put into writing. Art. 7 (2) Uncitral Convention and art. 2(a/d) URDG

---

[37] Rev. Banque 2/1988, p. 29.

[38] See for a similar case with the same outcome *Amoco Oil, First Bank & Trust*, 759 SW2d 877 (Mo. Ct.App. 1988).

[39] Cf. Canaris, No. 1122, Zahn/Ehrlich/Neumann, No. 9/109, Dohm, No. 166.

[40] Contra Kleiner, No. 16.03, for the curious reason that the guarantee is independent and that the risks assumed are so much greater that a guarantor does not expect to be protected, and von Westphalen, p. 91.

require the guarantee to be in writing, which includes authenticated teletransmission or tested electronic data interchange.[41]

English law requires the presence of consideration for the guarantee to be enforceable.[42]

Transmission, authenticity, authority, operative instrument

12-12 The advice stating the terms and conditions of the guarantee is ordinarily transmitted by letter, telefax or telex, either directly or through an advising bank. In order to ensure authenticity, telex messages ordinarily contain test codes. In *Rb Arnhem, 27 October 1983*, the court held that, in accordance with prevailing practice concerning international communications between banks, banks should ascertain the authenticity of telex messages, especially if the message does not contain the test code. Inclusion of the test code is usual as well as required in such communications.[43]

Whether a particular officer within the bank does or does not have authority to issue a guarantee is a matter of agency. Courts are, however, reluctant, and rightly so, to accept a defence based on lack of authority of the particular officer. In *Paris, 29 June 1990*, the bank was ordered to pay despite the fact that the guarantee had been issued by an officer who lacked the authority to do so, because the beneficiary, a bank, had no reason to question the officer's authority and it had verified the authenticity of the telex message by means of the test code.[44] In *Versailles, 9 June 1994*, the court observed that the guarantee had been issued in accordance with international practice and regular procedures established between the two parties.[45]

The advice, in whatever manner communicated, is deemed to be the operative instrument, barring contrary provisions, and no further confirmation is required.

---

[41] See for a general discussion on matters relating to electronic applications of bank guarantees: S. Kröll, Rechtsfragen elektronischer Bankgarantien, WM 2001, pp. 1553-1360, and the same, Electronic Bank Guarantees and Stand-by Letters of Credit, in 'Legal Issues in Electronic Banking', pp. 288-306.

[42] See Chapter 8, No. 8-5.

[43] NJ 1986, 79. The claim for payment was dismissed upon expert evidence revealing that the telex message, which, on the face of it, had been sent by the bank, was a forgery, the clue being the absence of the test code. The court also held that the bank was not responsible for the failure of the advising bank to ascertain the authenticity of the telex message. In *Trib. com. Antwerp, 25 September 1987*, TBH 1989, p. 100, the advising bank was held liable to the 'beneficiary'/ creditor for this failure.

[44] D. 1993 Somm. p. 98.

[45] D. 1995 Somm. p. 15. The court also rejected the argument of the Turkish bank that the issue should be resolved in accordance with Turkish law.

Nonetheless, written confirmation of telex and telefax messages is not unusual. The advice may consist of one or more documents.[46]

Commencement, taking effect

12-13 As from the date of its issue the guarantee can be called pursuant to the stipulated terms. The terms may, however, postpone the power to call the guarantee, although stated to be payable on demand. For example, the guarantee could stipulate that it enters into effect at some later date, or that it cannot be called prior to a certain date or the guarantee may be subject to conditions precedent, such as an advance payment in respect of a repayment guarantee.[47] Barring such stipulations the guarantee takes immediate and full effect and can be called at once, cf. art. 6 URDG and art. 7(3) Uncitral Convention.

Amendments, irrevocability

12-14 Once the contract of guarantee has been concluded, its terms and conditions cannot be amended without the agreement of the issuing bank and beneficiary. An amendment enters into effect in the same way as a guarantee. *A fortiori* the bank cannot unilaterally cancel its obligations, since its undertaking is irrevocable.[48]

In respect of indirect guarantees, amendments made without the consent of the instructing bank or account party do not affect their rights and obligations towards the issuing bank. It is noted that the issuing bank might be entitled to agree to an extension of the period of validity without their consent pursuant to the terms of the counter-guarantee.

Guarantees issued by private individuals and non-financial institutions. Duty to advise guarantor

12-15 First demand guarantees issued by private individuals are ordinarily furnished by persons who occupy a major position, for example as managing director and/or major shareholder, in a small company which is to procure such a guarantee, usually in favour of a bank which extends credit facilities to that company. These persons may be unfamiliar with the far-reaching differences between accessory suretyship and a first

---

[46] In *BGH, 3 May 1984*, WM 1984, p. 768, it was held that the terms and conditions were those as stated in the formal instrument in conjunction with those of the covering letter.

[47] See Chapter 8.4.

[48] Unless stated otherwise, cf. art. 5 URDG and art. 7(4) Uncitral Convention. Revocable guarantees are unknown in practice.

Other Aspects of the Bank Guarantee 209

demand guarantee. Moreover, the financial strength of the company/account party is often weak, with the result that recourse by the individual guarantor against the company/account party often proves ineffectual. First demand guarantees, therefore, pose particular risks for those individuals and they are entitled to be informed thereof. This is exemplified in a number of French decisions where the first demand guarantee was held to be invalid because the beneficiary (a bank) had failed to explain the meaning and effect thereof and the differences with an accessory suretyship.[49]

A decision by the German Supreme Court, *BGH, 5 July 1990*, at one time caused grave concern among banks in relation to the validity of first demand guarantees issued by affiliated companies in favour of the bank in connection with credit facilities to a group company.[50] In this case the Supreme Court held that only financial institutions can issue a first demand suretyship or a first demand guarantee and that those furnished by a non-financial institution are invalid. The decision was met with severe criticism.[51] It is important, however, to note the context of the decision: the 'payment on first demand' clause was contained in non-negotiated general conditions of the bank/beneficiary, while the instrument was labelled as 'suretyship', and the security was given by a private individual. The particular facts of that case were considered in a subsequent decision of the German Supreme Court, *BGH, 23 January 1997*.[52] In this decision the German Supreme Court confined the invalidity of first demand guarantees to cases such as occurred in its 1990 decision, with particular reference to guarantees issued by private individuals, and recognised that non-financial entities, such as business enterprises and holding or affiliate companies, can also validly issue first demand guarantees. In *BGH, 2 April 1998*, the German Supreme Court possibly took the matter a step further. It stated that, with a view to the principle of freedom of contract, '*everyone*' – which term may include individuals – is allowed to issue a first demand guarantee provided that it is not just a term in standard documentation and that, if the

---

[49] *Paris, 27 June 1990*, D. 1991 Somm. p. 193, *Paris, 5 February 1992*, D. 1993 Somm. p. 107, *Paris, 16 April 1996*, JCP 1997 Éd. E I, No. 633. See also *Rouen, 19 February 1992*, D. 1993 Somm. p. 108, where, contrary to the prevailing view, the court opted for the unilateral engagement approach (see No. 13-8 supra), which was evidently inspired by the court's resolve to have the first demand guarantee declared invalid on technical grounds. In *Trib. civ. Antwerp, 16 January 1997*, RW 1998/1998, p. 679, the court did not refer to a duty of the beneficiary (a bank) to explain the risks of a guarantee, which was construed by the court as a first demand guarantee, issued by the managing directors of the principal debtor.

[50] WM 1990, p. 1410.

[51] Bydlinski, WM 1991, pp. 257-262, WM, 1992, pp. 1301, 1308, Heinsius, Festschrift f. Merz, pp. 177, 184, v. Stebut, EWiR 1990, p. 981, Tiedtke, EWiR, 1992, pp. 865-866.

[52] WM 1997, p. 656. The absolute character of the BGH 1990 decision had already been mitigated in *BHG, 12 March 1992*, WM 1992, p. 854.

guarantor is not familiar with the risks of such guarantee, the beneficiary has fully explained these risks to the guarantor.[53]

German Act on General Terms and Conditions. Invalidity of suretyship and guarantee payable on first demand

12-15a Art. 9 of the German Act on General Terms and Conditions provides that a clause in general terms and conditions which imposes a disproportionate detriment on the counterparty, is invalid. In relation to domestic construction contracts German courts have, on several occasions, held that a requirement for the contractor to furnish a suretyship (or guarantee) payable on first demand contained in the employer's general terms and conditions violates art. 9 of the German Act which renders the first demand suretyship (or guarantee) invalid and unenforceable.[54] The reasoning is that this type of security imposes an inordinate degree of risk on the contractor/account party. An exception is made when the furnishing of security has been the subject of genuine negotiations whereby the contractor has had a true opportunity to influence the final result of the contract terms.[55] In that case the carve-out of art. 1(2) of the German Act applies.

12.3 CONSTRUCTION

12.3.1 Independent guarantee or accessory suretyship. Introduction

12-16 A considerable body of case law deals with the issue of whether the security instrument labelled as 'guarantee' is to be construed as an independent guarantee or as an accessory suretyship (accessory guarantee).[56] Several circumstances may account for this phenomenon. Universally adopted standard texts for guarantees do not exist.

---

[53] WM 1998, p. 1062. In the present case the guarantor was not an individual, but a company which was affiliated to the account party and which was fully aware of the risks of first demand guarantees. See also *BGH, 12 March 1992*, WM 1992, p. 854. See further Chapter 12.3.3, No. 12-28.

[54] *BGH, 5 June 1997*, WM 1997, p. 1675, *BGH, 2 March 2000*, WM 2000, p. 1299, *BGH, 8 March 2001*, NJW 2001, p. 1857, *OLG Düsseldorff, 9 August 2001*, WM 2001, p. 2294, *BGH, 18 April 2002*, WM 2002, p. 1415.

[55] See especially *BGH, 18 April 2002*, WM 2002, p. 1415, and *BGH, 5 March 2002*, WM 2002, p. 743.

[56] Inverted commas ('guarantee') have been added in order to express that the term guarantee is used in a neutral sense.

While it is true that banks increasingly use their own standard texts, the clarity of which has been proven, deviations from them continue to occur, possibly in order to accommodate the specific requirements of account party and beneficiary. Carelessness in drafting is another, obvious reason. Case law clearly evidences that lengthy texts containing an abundance of terms, phrases, details and provisions are likely to cause ambiguity, while short and concise texts tend to be clear. Difficulties also arise when the drafters continue to use traditional suretyship texts and attempt to convert these instruments into an independent guarantee by just adding some terms and phrases, such as 'payment on first demand', 'payment as our own debt', 'irrevocable and unconditional undertaking'. In any event, it is surprising and also disturbing that even at present ambiguous texts are by no means a rare phenomenon. This is especially the case in relation to 'guarantees' issued by entities other than banks.

The practical significance of the issue of construction in nearly all cases revolves around the question of whether, and in what manner, the beneficiary has to adduce evidence of default by the principal debtor and whether the bank is permitted to raise defences derived from the principal contract. As shown by case law, the issue may arise in several situations: between bank and beneficiary, between account party and bank and/or beneficiary when the account party seeks a preliminary stop-payment injunction, often in conjunction with allegations of fraud, and between the account party and bank when the former challenges his duty to reimburse the bank after payment.

When the 'guarantee' has been made subject to the URDG, the independent nature of the guarantee is evident. Nor can standby letters of credit as issued by American banks give rise to difficulties as regards their independent nature, particularly when they are made subject to the ISP98.

12.3.2 Suggestions for some general guidelines

Introduction

12-17 If there is one kind of litigation where the specific facts and circumstances of the case play a preponderant role with minimum impact from rules of law, it is likely to be cases involving the construction of the contract. To the extent that certain rules of law concerning interpretation exist, they hardly venture beyond the commonplace and their practical use may be called into question. It is not surprising to find courts, dealing with the construction of the 'guarantee', just resolving the issue either way without reference to or mention of some general precepts which underly their decision.[57]

---

[57] In an obiter dictum *OG Austria, 7 Ob 653/85*, JIBL 1986 N-50, provides a rare example of a court setting out a sequence of general rules of construction: the will and intention of parties to be derived from the wording; construction to accord with fair practice; construction according to the *contra proferentem* rule. *Trib. com. Charleroi, 23 April 1997*, JLMB 1998,

The following suggestions for some general guidelines are, therefore, put forward with some diffidence. While insofar as possible they are put in a certain order of preference, there are no clear dividing lines between the various phases. Moreover, in some cases certain guidelines might be more or less relevant than in other cases or even be of no relevance at all. Construing contracts remains a matter of dealing with facts. At any rate, the general guidelines are specifically tailored to the interpretation of 'guarantees'.

When does the issue of construction arise?

12-18 The obvious answer to this question is when the text of the 'guarantee' suffers from ambiguity. It is a working rule that the issue of interpretation of the 'guarantee' should be addressed once the parties to the litigation entertain divergent views in this respect. Such divergence becomes apparent, for example, where the account party and/or bank argue that the beneficiary is to prove default, while the beneficiary takes the view that evidence of default is not a condition of payment. However, in *Esal (Commodities) Ltd., Reltor v Oriental Credit*, the court brushed this contention of the account party aside, ruling that to require such proof would defeat the entire object of the guarantee.[58] It is submitted that this response is inappropriate, since it ignores the issue.

When dealing with the issue of construction it is of little use to expound the differences between accessory suretyship and the independent (first demand) guarantee. These differences are well known. However, it becomes reprehensible when the decision is made either way just by reference to these abstract differences.[59]

Finding the intention of parties

12-19 The essence and/or purpose of construing the contract consists in finding the intention of parties,[60] that is the intention of the individual parties to the 'guarantee' at

---

p. 1998, p. 1073, provides another example of a court enumerating a series of precepts for interpretation. In neither decision is it clear whether these rules actually played a part in the decision, and if so, which, and in what manner.

[58] [1985] 2 Lloyd's Rep. 546. Similar *CA The Hague, 13 June 1980*, NJ 1982, 267.

[59] This appears to have happened in *Trib. com. Brussels, 28 April 1983*, RDC 1984, p. 57 (but reversed by *Brussels, 3 April 1987*, RGDC 1989, p. 475), *Trib. com. Antwerp, 5 July 1984*, TBH 1985, p. 571, *Trib. com. Brussels, 15 November 1984*, RDC 1985, p. 569, all decisions in favour of suretyship. See also No. 12-20.

[60] Thus explicitly with respect to 'guarantees' *OLG Hamburg, 18 December 1981*, WM 1983, p. 188, affirmed by *BGH, 14 October 1982*, WM 1982, p. 1324, *BGH, 19 September 1985*, NJW 1986, p. 310, *Trib. com. Nantes, 22 September 1983*, D 1984 IR p. 202, *Trib. com.*

hand. This conclusion is important, for it follows that the requirements and needs of international trade or international practice, usage, lex mercatoria, etc., could only be a secondary source for the construction of the 'guarantee'.

Who are the parties whose intentions have to be ascertained? It is submitted that it is not only the intention of the bank and beneficiary that counts, but also that of the parties to the underlying relationship. The legal basis for resorting to the underlying relationship is the fact that the 'guarantee' issued by the bank in favour of the beneficiary could be regarded as a vehicle ensuring the realisation of the agreements made by the parties to the underlying relationship and the fact that the bank issues the 'guarantee' for the risk and account of the account party.[61] Moreover, it often happens that the drafting of (parts of) the text and the various clauses in particular do not originate from the bank, but from the parties to the underlying transaction.[62]

If, however, the issue of interpretation arises between account party and bank after payment, then their intention has to be determined and no regard should be had to the underlying relationship, unless the bank was aware of the intention of the account party and beneficiary. This is not so much a matter of construing the 'guarantee', but rather a matter of construing the instructions from the account party.[63]

Full and entire text as primary source

12-20 The written contract is deemed to represent and record the final and definite agreement of parties. The text of the 'guarantee' is, therefore, the paramount source for ascertaining their intention. Thus, if a court after due consideration of the text is satisfied that the 'guarantee' is an independent guarantee or accessory suretyship, it need not look any further. More specifically, a 'guarantee' when so construed as a suretyship cannot be turned into an independent (first demand) guarantee under the pretext that that would better accord with international usage.

It is crucial to bear in mind that the object of construction is the full and entire text of the 'guarantee', not just one or a number of isolated phrases which form part of the text. The various single phrases are generally speaking crystal clear. What is ambiguous about the term 'suretyship' or the phrase 'we renounce the rights pursuant to article ... (statutory provisions conferring certain protective rights to the surety)', or 'we shall pay forthwith in the event of non-performance by ...'? What is unclear about the phrase

---

Charleroi, 23 April 1997, JLMB 1998, p. 1998, p. 1073, *OG Austria, 7 Ob 653/85*, JIBL 1986 N-50, Mijnssen, pp. 5,6.

[61] See Chapter 6.1, No. 6-2 and Chapter 8.1.

[62] See further No. 12-23.

[63] *Brussels, 17 November 1988*, RDC 1990, p. 91. See also Chapter 10.7, Nos. 10-12/13/15.

'we undertake to pay upon your first demand'? One need not resort to international usage to grasp that that phrase means that the bank is to pay on first demand. Case law bears out that ambiguity is caused by the fact that one or a number of phrases point to suretyship, while another or a series of terms hint at an independent guarantee. One should look, therefore, at all terms and phrases in conjunction with each other as one finds them.[64]

In contrast, a selective approach can be found in some Belgian and French decisions.[65] Because of one or certain terms which pointed to accessory suretyship the court in those cases decided in favour of that type of security. As the contract of suretyship, the court went on to observe, is incompatible with an independent (first demand) guarantee, the clauses hinting at that type had to be disregarded and ignored. Of course, had the court first focused on the latter clauses, such a selective approach would have led to the opposite result.

Drafting technique in historical perspective, weighing of terms and phrases. 'Effektivklauseln'

12-21 It has been observed elsewhere that independent guarantees have evolved from practice, that practice when drafting the 'guarantee' naturally followed existing patterns with which it was familiar, namely those of suretyship, and that practice only gradually began to recognise that it was creating a new and distinct type of security calling for new and distinct textual patterns. Moreover, the law in many countries does not recognise the existence of two, clearly distinct types of 'guarantee', but just one, being neutral. From this, just one generic pattern for texts of 'guarantees' ensued. Independence is then achieved by adding pertinent clauses and phrases.[66]

It is submitted that these circumstances should be viewed as important factors when construing the 'guarantee'. It follows that when the text contains phrases such as 'payment on (first) demand', 'payment without contestation' or 'payment without objections', etc., these phrases are to be accorded greater weight than one or even a number of phrases indicating suretyship. There is a second group of phrases which recur in

---

[64] Cf. *HR, 25 September 1998*, NJ 1998, 892, *Rb Amsterdam, 5 April 1984*, KG 1984, 122, *Siporex Trade v. Banque Indosuez*, [1986] 2 Lloyd's Rep. 146.

[65] *Trib. com. Brussels, 28 April 1983*, RDC 1984, p. 57 (but reversed by *Brussels, 3 April 1987*, RGDC 1989, p. 475), *Trib. com. Antwerp, 5 July 1984*, TBH 1985, p. 571, *Trib. com. Brussels, 15 November 1984*, RDC 1985, p. 569; *Cass., 9 December 1997*, Rev. Droit Bancaire 1998, p. 66, Bordeaux, *7 March 1991*, D. 1992 Somm. p. 235, *Paris, 7 January 1992*, D. 1993 Somm. p. 96. See also the French cases mentioned in No. 12-31. See for a critical comment Contamine-Raynaud, Revue Droit Bancaire 1997, p. 123, and 1998, p. 66.

[66] See Chapter 8.2, No. 8-3, and Chapter 12.1.3.

texts of 'guarantees'. For example, the undertaking is described as 'unconditional', 'irrevocable' or 'primary', or it is mentioned that payment will be made 'as our own debt' or 'forthwith'. These terms are not likely to be found in straightforward texts for traditional suretyship. This might be a reason to assume that such phrases have been added in an effort, clumsy though it may be, to express independence.

The heading of the document, for example 'suretyship' or 'guarantee', is never decisive. There are instruments which are labelled as 'suretyship' but which are, in fact, clearly independent (first demand) guarantees in view of other terms and phrases in the same document.[67] On the other hand, commercial practice often uses the term 'guarantee' indiscriminately and it may refer to an accessory guarantee (suretyship) or to an independent guarantee. The true nature will then become apparent from the other terms and phrases of the instrument.

Texts containing phrases such as '(payment will be made) in the event of failure of the account party to execute the contract' have repeatedly given rise to difficulties, since they have a clear suretyship connotation. German legal writing refers to these phrases as *Effektivklauseln*. In the cases cited in no. 12-34 the significance of these phrases was outweighed by phrases such as 'payment on first demand' and those mentioned above and in no. 12-22, and the 'guarantees' were construed as first demand guarantees requiring no evidence of default, except, sometimes, for a unilateral statement of default by the beneficiary.[68] Clearly, if parties envisage a first demand guarantee, such *Effektivklauseln* which merely describe the generic purpose of the 'guarantee', should not be put in the operative clauses, but in the preamble.[69] Their continued insertion in the operative clauses could be explained in the light of the historical developments in the drafting technique. The Dutch Court of Appeal in the case of *HR, 12 March 1982*, had to deal with a text drafted in a particularly awkward fashion. The 'payment guarantee' was payable 'on written demand without further question or reference to the buyers in case of failure of the buyers to execute the sales contract..., *copy of which is attached to this guarantee and forms an integral part of it* [italics added], in case of any default on the part of the buyers in the due performance...' This text went much further than the common '*Effektivklausel*'. The Dutch Court of Appeal ruled that the purport of bank guarantees in international trade such as the one under review is that the bank effects payment without delay upon the first demand of the beneficiary and without enquiry into the alleged default of the account party. While not arguing with the outcome, the observation appears somewhat perfunctory. The Court of Appeal correctly defined the most significant features of a first demand guarantee, i.e. the abstract

---

[67] See No. 12-34.

[68] See Chapter 13.2.3, No. 13-13 for specific reference to case law. See also Chapter 8.3, No. 8-4, and Chapter 10.8, No. 10-26.

[69] See also Chapter 8, No. 8-2.

notion of such a guarantee, but it did not give reasons why this particular 'guarantee' amounted to a first demand guarantee. The Supreme Court upheld the decision, but wisely noted that the Court of Appeal must evidently have had in mind the phrase 'on written demand without further question or reference' in particular.[70]

Specification of the means of proof; documentary proof; statements by beneficiary

12-22 Where the text of the 'guarantee' specifies the means by which non-performance or performance have to be proven, but where the text could otherwise be considered ambiguous, it is submitted that such specification constitutes an all but conclusive indication in favour of an independent guarantee. This is especially true when the 'guarantee' refers to documentary evidence. This comprises guarantees calling for the submission of third-party documents and guarantees stipulating presentation of an arbitral or judicial decision. For example, if the 'guarantee' states, *inter alia*, that payment is to be made 'on the basis of a survey report of appointed surveyors at the port of discharge', that would be decisive for a finding of an independent guarantee as opposed to an accessory suretyship.[71] The same applies if the 'guarantee' stipulates, *inter alia*, that payment is to be made 'on demand, unless the principal debtor produces the specified documents within six months'.[72]

---

[70] NJ 1982, 267. This decision should be contrasted with *HR, 23 September 1998*, NJ 1998, 892, mentioned in No. 12-31.

[71] The example is taken from the case of *Trib. com. Brussels, 21 November 1979*, JCB 1980, p. 140. The court held the 'guarantee' to be an accessory suretyship and dismissed the claim for payment. This decision was reversed by *Brussels, 25 February 1982*, JCB 1982, p. 349. Upon review of all terms and phrases and especially the phrase 'payment on demand' which also appeared in the text, the Court of Appeal ruled in favour of an independent guarantee, requiring no proof of default except for the stipulated certificate. In *Paris, 20 March 1992*, D. 1993 Somm. p. 96, the Court of Appeal ruled that an instrument, which was labelled as suretyship, but which was payable on first demand provided the beneficiary submitted a statement from the engineer or surveyor confirming the account party's default, was an independent guarantee payable upon presentation of the aforementioned documents. In *Trib. gr. inst. Paris, 26 January 1983*, D. 1983 I.R. p. 297, involving a 'guarantee' payable on submission by the beneficiary of certain third-party documents confirming non-performance, the court ruled that the instrument did not amount to a first demand guarantee – which seems quite plain – but to a suretyship. However, the court in fact treated the instrument as an independent guarantee and rejected the account party's claim against the bank, as the latter had proceeded to payment upon submission of the correct documents. See for other cases *Aix-en-Provence, 13 March 1980*, D. 1981 I.R. p. 505 and *ICC Arbitration No. 5639 (1987)*, D. 1988 Somm. p. 242.

[72] The example is taken from the case of *Trib. com. Brussels, 15 November 1984*, RDC 1985, p. 569. The court decided, however, in favour of suretyship and ruled that no payment was to

It is, further, submitted that where a 'guarantee' requires a unilateral statement from the beneficiary as regards non-performance of the contract or in respect of the amount owing to it, such a requirement should ordinarily also be regarded as a decisive indication of an independent (first demand) guarantee.[73] This would be particularly true when the clause states that such a statement will be accepted as conclusive evidence. Inclusion of such clauses is a common technique for English banks to express the independent (first demand) nature of the security, while the phrase 'payment on demand' is often left out. In fact, guarantees requiring the submission by the beneficiary of a unilateral statement of default is one of the most common types of independent (first demand) guarantees.

Reference to the underlying relationship

12-23 In order to establish the intention of the parties regard could be had to the underlying relationship.[74] This may include examination of the relevant clauses in the main contract and negotiations, communications and correspondence between the parties to the underlying contract. Thus, for example, in *Cass., 19 May 1992*,[75] and in *OLG Köln, 24 October 1997*,[76] the court held that the security was to be construed as an independent guarantee payable on first demand, and a suretyship payable on first demand in the second case since the underlying contract required the furnishing of this type of security. Case law provides several examples of this technique.[77]

---

be effected. It is worth noting that the principal debtor had not been able to produce the documents. The same decision in the same circumstances was made in *Paris, 9 July 1986*, D. 1988 Somm. p. 243.

[73] Cf. the cases of *Cass., 20 February 1985*, D. 1986 I.R. p.153, *Cass., 7 October 1997*, JCP 1998 Éd. E, p. 226 ('payment of amount which the beneficiary *stated* that it has paid'),*Siporex Trade SA v. Banque Indosuez*, [1986] 2 Lloyd's Rep. 146 ('Any claims hereunder must be supported by *your declaration to that effect…*'), *I.E. Contractors v. Lloyds Bank*, [1990] 2 Lloyd's Rep. 496 ('payable on a demand being made *stating that it was a claim for damages brought about by the account party*'), *Frans Maas (UK) Ltd v. Habib Bank AG Zurich*, 3 August 2000, unreported, but mentioned in Jack, No. 12.55 ('Your claims should be received by us in writing *stating therein that the Principals have failed to pay you under their contractual obligations*').

[74] See No. 12-19 for the justification of this technique.

[75] D. 1993 Somm. p. 104 (3rd decision).

[76] WM 1998, p. 1443.

[77] *CA Amsterdam, 4 June 1982*, reprinted by Bannier, in Hague-Zagreb Essays 6, p. 208, *OLG Hamburg, 18 December 1981*, WM 1983, p. 188, *Trib. com. Brussels, 11 March 1981*, BRH 1981, p. 361, *Brussels, 18 December 1981*, Rev. Banque 1982, p. 99, *Versailles, 13 June*

Obviously, the fact that the security document refers to the underlying contract does not in any way give rise to an argument in favour of an accessory suretyship.[78] Independent guarantees invariably contain such a reference.[79]

Reference to international usage

12-24 Case law[80] and legal writing[81] provide several examples of references to international usage, international practice, lex mercatoria and the needs or requirements of the beneficiary and international trade as an aid to the interpretation of the 'guarantee'. It has been suggested that with a view to these sources the presence of the phrase 'payment on (first) demand' amounts to a (almost) decisive indication of an independent (first demand) guarantee.

The significance of the aforementioned sources should not be overrated. While the needs and requirements of the beneficiary/creditor and/or international trade have engendered the independent guarantee, and especially the first demand guarantee, these factors cannot in themselves be considered as predominant aids for the construction of

---

1990, D. 1991 Somm. p. 191, *ICC Arbitration No. 3316 (1979)*, JDI 1980, p. 970. All decisions were in favour of an independent (first demand) guarantee. In *BGH, 19 September 1985*, NJW 1986, p. 310, the 'guarantee' was held to be a traditional suretyship, and in *Trib. com. Charleroi, 23 April 1997*, JLMB 1998, p. 1073, the security was construed as a suretyship payable on first demand. See also No. 12-37.

[78] See explicitly *Cass., 18 May 1999*, JCP 1999 Éd G ll 10 199, p. 2044, *Cass., 30 January 2001*, D.Affaires 2001, p. 1024, and *CA Liege, 8 June 1999*, RDC 2000, p. 731.

[79] See Chapter 8.3, No. 8-4.

[80] See, for example, *CA The Hague, 13 June 1980, and HR, 12 March 1982*, NJ 1982, 267, *BGH, 24 November 1983*, WM 1984, p. 44, *Trib. com. Brussels, 11 March 1981*, BRH 1981, p. 361, *Harbottle (Mercantile) v. Nat. West. Bank*, [1977] 2 All E.R. 862, *Esal (Commodities), Reltor v. Oriental Credit*, [1985] 2 Lloyd's Rep. 546, *Zürich, 9 May 1985*, D. 1987 Somm. p. 177, *OG Austria, 7Ob 653/85*, JIBL 1986 N-50. Also in *CA Liege, 8 June 1999*, RDC 2000, p. 731, international practice and the customs developed in this matter were viewed as a key factor for a construction in favour of a first demand guarantee. It should be noted, however, that in this case the issue of construction arose in relation to the instructions from the instructing bank to the issuing bank, and not in relation to the 'guarantee' itself, see further Chapter 11.1.4, No. 11-4.

[81] See, for example, Pabbruwe, rede p. 5, Boll, p. 95, von Westphalen, p. 79, and WM 1981, p. 295, Zahn/Ehrlich/Neumann, 9/12, 9/19, Schlegelberger/Hefermehl, No. 278, Dohm, Nos. 87, 88, Schinnerer/Avancini, p. 300, Nielsen, ZIP 1982, p. 255, von Marschall, in Dokumentenakkreditive und Bankgarantien, pp. 31, 35, Vasseur, No. 29, and D. 1984 I.R. pp. 201, 202, D. 1986 I.R. p. 154

a specific instrument.⁸² Since the process of construing the 'guarantee' is aimed at finding the intention of the individual parties to the particular 'guarantee' at issue, they could only be a secondary source for establishing the intention of parties or for determining whether the beneficiary's understanding of the 'guarantee' document as an independent guarantee is reasonable. The difficulty, however, is that there exists no international usage, practice or lex mercatoria to the effect that security is ordinarily provided in the form of an independent guarantee, and more specifically a first demand guarantee. Other types of security, including the traditional suretyship, continue to be utilised too. It could, however, be safely stated that the phrase 'payment on first demand' in an crossborder context is generally perceived as referring to an independent first demand guarantee, see nos. 12-21 and 12-34. While such a clause therefore constitutes a strong indication of a first demand guarantee, this does not mean that other clauses and phrases with suretyship connotations can be ignored.

To what terms have parties agreed

12-25 The ultimate objective of construction is to ascertain the terms and conditions to which parties have agreed. This is of importance in two respects.

Where the text of the 'guarantee' is ambiguous as regards its nature, but where the issue relates to the implications of some specific terms which are not ambiguous, it is unnecessary to address the question of whether the 'guarantee' is an independent or accessory one. Thus, in a case where the text of the 'guarantee' was most unclear *OLG Frankfurt a.M., 25 November 1977,* declined to pronounce on its nature because the claim for payment had to be dismissed in any event since a condition precedent had not been met.⁸³

Disputes concerning construction are not always just a matter of a straightforward choice between either an independent guarantee or an accessory suretyship. If the 'guar-

---

[82] The comparatively low rating is highlighted in *OLG Hamburg, 18 December 1981,* WM 1983, p. 188, affirmed by *BGH, 14 October 1982,* WM, 1982, p. 1324, and *ICC Arbitration No. 3316 (1979),* JDI 1980, p. 970. In this case the bank (!) argued that accessory suretyship, much rather than the independent guarantee, was the common type of security in international trade. Arbitrators ruled that even if that contention was correct, it would not be decisive for the particular 'guarantee' at hand. The significance of these sources has also been called into question by Stoufflet, JCP 1982, No. 19876 (1), and in the comments to the Belgian decision of *CA Liege, 8 June 1999,* RDC 2000, pp. 731, 735.

[83] WM 1978, p. 1188. It cannot come as surprise that especially in English cases texts which are confusing as regards the nature of the security have not occasioned a choice either way. See, for example, *Hyundai Heavy Industries v. Papadopoulos,* [1980] 2 All E.R. 29, *Bank of India v. Transcontinental Commodity Merchants Ltd.,* IBL March 1984, p. 119, *Offshore Enterprises Inc. v. Nordic Bank PLC,* IBL November 1984, p. 86.

antee' is found not to be a suretyship, one must be careful not to conclude that the guarantee must therefore be a first demand guarantee 'calling for immediate payment without question'.[84] A 'guarantee' which turns out to be a first demand guarantee may well be subject to, for instance, a condition precedent or reduction clause. And further, when the 'guarantee' has been construed as an independent guarantee, there could be uncertainty as to whether it is a first demand guarantee or an independent guarantee with a different payment mechanism. *Aix-en-Provence, 13 March 1980*[85] and *Brussels, 25 February 1982*[86] provide excellent examples. In both cases the Courts of Appeal rightly ruled that a clause calling for the presentation of third-party certificates prevailed over a 'payment on first demand' clause.

Resort to general (statutory) rules for construction; presumptions

12-26 Some national laws have general, statutory rules for construction.[87] Reference has been made to two rules in particular which apply in cases of doubt.

At least as far as France is concerned the impact of the rule that the contract ('guarantee') is to be interpreted in favour of the debtor, resulting in accessory suretyship, has been severely undermined by *Cass., 2 February 1988*.[88] In the face of a text which suffered from an inordinate degree of ambiguity, the Cour de Cassation tersely stated that no uncertainty existed and ruled in favour of an independent first demand guarantee. Two recent Belgian decisions referred to the rule as a technique of last resort and did not, in fact, apply it.[89] Only a few authors advocate this rule of construction,[90] while others confine the rule to domestic situations. In an international context, the presumption should rather be in favour of an independent guarantee if the 'guarantee' contains

---

[84] The danger of such rash conclusions is occasioned by *Cass., 2 February 1988*, D. 1988 Somm. p. 239, where the Cour de Cassation proffered a definition of the independent guarantee in contradistinction to accessory suretyship in terms as stated in the text.

[85] D. 1981 I.R. p. 505.

[86] JCB 1982, p. 349. See also *Paris, 20 March 1993*, D. 1993 Somm. p. 96, and *Trib. gr. inst. Paris, 26 January 1983*, D.1983 I.R. p. 297, see No. 12-22.

[87] Articles 1156-1164 of the French and Belgian Civil Code.

[88] D. 1988 Somm. p. 239. The Cour de Cassation quashed a decision of the Court of Appeal, which did apply the rule, with the consequences as stated in the text.

[89] *Trib. com. Charleroi, 23 April 1997*, JLMB 1998, p. 1073, and *Trib. com. Brussels, 11 February 1999*, RDC 2000, p. 725.

[90] Canaris, No. 1124, Käser, RabelsZ. 1971, pp. 608, 610, Bärmann, p. 88. See also Stoufflet, JCP 1982 ll, No. 19876(1).

a 'payment on first demand' clause.[91] The significance of such presumption would, however, be limited, since it could only be brought into play where the instrument is ambiguous and when, after applying the techniques examined above, the nature of the 'guarantee' is still considered to be unclear. Thus, if a 'guarantee' in an international context has been found to be accessory suretyship, it cannot upon second thoughts be turned into an independent guarantee. Nor could a first demand guarantee in a domestic case be converted into suretyship.

In two decisions, reference has been made to the rule that in case of uncertainty the 'guarantee' is to be interpreted *contra proferentem*: one in an affirmative manner,[92] the other in a negative manner by simply stating that there was no uncertainty.[93] A variant of this technique is the method according to which the 'guarantee', which is often a unilateral instrument from the 'guarantor' which is forwarded to the beneficiary for (tacit) acceptance, is to be given a meaning which the addressee (the beneficiary) could reasonably attribute to it.[94] Both methods have an inherent difficulty: it should not automatically be assumed that it is the 'guarantor' which has drafted the entire text of the instrument and all of its provisions. In most cases the format of the 'guarantee' and its provisions are the result of the agreement in this respect between the parties to the underlying relationship, followed by a review by the bank with a view to its own interests.[95] Sometimes the text of the 'guarantee' and its provisions have been dictated by the beneficiary.[96] Accordingly, when using these two methods, the question always is whether the bank, the account party and beneficiary or the beneficiary only or any combination thereof should be regarded as the one having formulated the terms of the 'guarantee'.

---

[91] *Versailles, 13 June 1990*, D. 1991 Somm. p. 191, *Paris, 1 March 1989*, D. 1990 Somm. p. 196, *Trib. Féd. Switzerland, 20 August 1991*, D. 1992 Somm. p. 233, *Trib. Féd. Switzerland, 25 July 1988*, D. 1990 Somm. p. 195, *Trib. Féd. Switzerland, 13 April 1993*, D. 1995 Somm. p. 12; Von Westphalen, p. 78, Zahn/Ehrlich/Neumann, 9/12, 9/19, Dohm, Nos. 87, 88, Schinnerer/Avancini, p. 300.

[92] *OG Austria, 7Ob 653/85*, JIBL 1986 N-50.

[93] *ICC Arbitration No. 3316 (1979)*, JDI 1980. p. 970.

[94] See, e.g., *BGH, 12 March 1992*, WM 1992, p. 854, *OLG Frankfurt, 18 March 1997*, RIW 1998, p. 477, *OLG München, 23 July 1997*, WM 1998, p. 342, *OLG Köln, 24 October 1997*, WM 1998, p. 1443. These decisions also apply to the construction of unclear terms in a guarantee or suretyship payable on first demand, see further No. 12-37.

[95] See Chapter 6.1 and Chapter 8.1.

[96] See, e.g., *BGH, 12 March 1992*, WM 1992, p. 854, *OLG Frankfurt a.M., 18 March 1997*, RIW 1998, p. 477.

12.3.3 Miscellaneous aspects

Special rules for banks?

12-27 It is well known that banks do not not wish to become enmeshed in disputes between the account party/principal debtor and beneficiary/creditor. They have an interest of their own in independence.[97] Must one, then, conclude that 'guarantees' issued by a bank are bound or at least presumed to be independent guarantees?[98] It would indeed be most tempting to subscribe to such an inference where it is the bank that refuses payment, arguing that it only acted as a traditional surety.[99] It is, however, doubtful whether security furnished by a bank should generally be construed as an independent guarantee and payable on demand, as the case may be. It finds no support in case law and has indeed explicitly been rejected in *BGH, 19 September 1985*, and *HR, 25 September 1998*.[100] Two interrelated aspects have to be borne in mind. First, it

---

[97] See Chapter 7, No. 7-2.

[98] Affirmative view taken by Zahn/Ehrlich/Neumann, 9/12, Dohm, No. 88, Poullet, Tours, p. 135, either as a sufficient reason in itself or in combination with the needs of the beneficiary and/or international trade.

[99] As has been the case in, for example, *Rb Amsterdam, 5 April 1984*, KG 1984, 122, *OLG Hamburg, 18 December 1981*, WM 1983, p. 188, *OLG München, 23 July 1997*, WM 1998, p. 342, *OLG Köln, 24 October 1997*, WM 1998, p. 1443, *Cass., 20 December 1982*, D. 1983 J. p. 365, *Cass., 8 December 1987*, D. 1988 Somm. p. 240, *Cass., 2 February 1988*, D. 1988 Somm. p.239, *Cass., 1 February 1994*, D. 1995 Somm. p. 11, *Cass., 30 January 2001*, D. Affaires 2001, p. 1024, Aix *en Provence, 13 March 1980*, D. 1981 I.R. p. 505, *Paris, 1 July 1986*, D. 1987 Somm. p. 177, *Paris, 1 March 1989*, D. 1990 Somm. p. 196, *Versailles, 13 June 1990*, D. 1990 Somm. p. 191, *Bordeaux, 7 March 1991*, D. 1992 Somm. p. 235, *Paris, 7 January 1992*, D. 1993 Somm. p. 96, *Paris, 20 March 1993*, D. 1993 Somm. p. 96, *Trib. com. Nantes, 22 September 1983*, D. 1984 I.R. p. 202, *Antwerp, 15 October 1985*, TBH 1986, p. 646, *Trib. com. Brussels, 11 March 1981*, BRH 1981 p. 361, *Trib. com. Brussels, 28 April 1983*, RDC 1984 p. 57, *Trib. com. Tournay, 27 May 1987*, Rev. Reg. Dr. 1987, p. 387, *Trib. com. Charleroi, 23 April 1997*, JLMB 1998, p. 1073, and *Trib. com. Brussels, 11 February 1999*, RDC 2000, p. 725, *Siporex Trade v. Banque Indosuez*, [1986] 2 Lloyd's Rep. 146, *Trib. Féd. Switzerland, 25 July 1988*, D. 1990 Somm. p. 195, *Trib. Féd. Switzerland, 13 April 1993*, D. 1995 Somm. p. 12, *ICC Arbitration No. 3316 (1979)*, JDI 1980, p. 970, and *ICC Arbitration No. 5639 (1987)*, D. 1988 Somm. p.242. Particularly when the account party is insolvent, banks seem not to object to being engaged as an accessory guarantor and thus to becoming involved in the underlying relationship.

[100] *BGH, 19 September 1985*, NJW 1986, p. 310, *HR, 25 September 1998*, NJ 1998, 892. See also *Cass., 10 May 1994*, D. 1995, Somm. p. 12. In *Siporex Trade v. Banque Indosuez*, [1986] 2 Lloyd's Rep. 146, the court made two interesting observations: 'A bank guarantor was not and should not be concerned in any way with the rights and wrongs of the underlying transaction. Although every bond had to be construed in accordance with its terms, there

Other Aspects of the Bank Guarantee

is inappropriate to focus solely on the position of the beneficiary and that of the bank in particular, since the 'guarantee' is to be viewed as a vehicle ensuring the realisation of the agreements made by the parties to the underlying relationship. They could well have agreed to a traditional suretyship. Moreover, the text of the 'guarantee' or certain parts thereof might not originate from the bank, but from the parties to the underlying transaction.[101] The second aspect is that, if these parties agreed to a tradional suretyship, the bank could protect itself against becoming involved in the underlying relationship by stipulating as against the account party only that it is exempt from the duty to ascertain default or by requiring a counter-guarantee from the account party which is payable on demand. This technique enables a bank to issue an accessory guarantee without the risks and difficulties that would otherwise ensue.[102] A general presumption that banks would only issue independent guarantees is, therefore, unwarranted.

Nonetheless, in the event of doubt, the special position of the bank could be a factor in favour of a construction as an independent (first demand) guarantee.[103]

Special rules for domestic cases and for 'guarantees' issued by private individuals or non-financial institutions?

12-28 It has been argued that in the event of uncertainty the 'guarantee' should be construed in favour of suretyship rather than as an independent guarantee as far as domestic cases are concerned.[104] The reasoning is that such construction better accords with the (presumed) intention and legitimate needs of parties because the need for independent security is less urgent. This argument is rather weak. While the need for independent (first demand) guarantees might perhaps be less compelling in domestic

---

could be no blind categorisation of its character or blind assumption of the obligations which it created.'

[101] See Chapter 6.1, Nos. 6-1/2 and Chapter 8.1.

[102] See also Chapter 7, No. 7-2, Chapter 10.3, and No. 12-37a.

[103] *Trib. Féd. Switzerland, 25 July 1988*, D. 1990 Somm. p. 195, *Trib. Féd. Switzerland, 13 April 1993*, D. 1995 Somm. p. 12. In *OLG Hamburg, 18 December 1981*, WM 1983, p. 188, affirmed by *BGH, 14 October 1982*, WM 19 1982, p. 1324, the Court of Appeal observed that the consistent use of the term guarantee as opposed to suretyship was especially relevant when employed by a bank, since banks are well aware of the different meaning. In *Paris, 11 February 1986*, affirmed by *Cass., 8 December 1987*, D. 1988 Somm. p. 240, the Court of Appeal ruled that as a professional, financial institution the bank could not possibly have misunderstood the independent nature of the security, and ordered the bank to pay damages for delaying payment, in addition to the amount of the guarantee.

[104] Von Westphalen, p. 45, WM 1981, p. 295, Dohm, Nos. 87, 88, Käser, RabelsZ. 1971, pp. 608, 610, Pabbruwe, rede p. 5.

cases, the advantages for the beneficiary are no less substantial. Accordingly, there are many sound reasons for beneficiaries to require an independent (first demand) guarantee in domestic cases too. On the other hand, it might be true that, depending on their status, parties in a domestic setting are not sufficiently familiar with the meaning of a 'payment on first demand' clause which is usually attributed to it in international trade.[105]

The proposition that in domestic cases, in case of ambiguity, a 'guarantee' should be construed as a traditional suretyship finds no support in case law.[106] In *Aix-en-Provence, 13 March 1980*,[107] *OLG Hamburg, 10 October 1985*,[108] and *Paris, 5 February 1992*[109] it was expressly observed that first demand guarantees and first demand suretyships are not confined to international trade. Indeed, first demand guarantees in a domestic setting are by no means exceptional and they are becoming as usual as in crossborder situations.[110]

A more valid distinction is that between a 'guarantee' issued by a bank, a parent company or by a company engaged in business activities and, on the other hand, a 'guarantee' issued by a private individual. It is quite arguable that in the case of ambiguity a private individual should have the benefit of the doubt. In any event, it appears that this aspect prompted *Paris, 21 February 1992*, to construe the instrument as an accessory suretyship, although it contained several clauses and phrases which pointed to a first demand guarantee.[111] A slightly different distinction is made in German case

---

[105] For example, in *Trib. com. Charleroi, 23 April 1997*, JLMB 1998, p. 1073,and *Trib. com. Brussels, 11 February 1999*, RDC 2000, p. 725, the courts regarded a 'payment on first demand' clause in an crossborder situation as a very strong indication of an independent first demand guarantee, but not necessarily so in a domestic case.

[106] See, for example, *CA Amsterdam, 4 June 1982*, reprinted by Bannier, in Hague-Zagreb Essays 6, p. 208, *Rb Utrecht, 22 January 1998*, JOR 2000, 40, *Cass., 20 December 1982*, D. 1983 J p. 365, *Cass., 8 December 1987*, D. 1988 Somm. p. 240, *Cass., 7 October 1997*, JCP 1998 Éd. E, p. 226, *Paris, 1 July 1986*, D.1987 Somm. p. 171, *Antwerp, 15 October 1985*, TBH 1986, p. 646, *Potton Homes Ltd. v. Coleman Contractors*, [1984] 28 Build. L.R. 19, *OG Austria, 18 December 1987*, IBL November 1988, p. 92, and the numerous German decisions in favour of a first demand suretyship which all involved domestic cases, see No. 12- 35. See also Boll, p. 95.

[107] D. 1981 I.R. p. 505.

[108] NJW 1986, p. 1691.

[109] D. 1993 Somm. p. 107.

[110] See also Chapter 5, No. 5-5.

[111] D. 1993 Somm. p. 108. See also *Trib. Féd. Switzerland, 13 April 1993*, D. 1995 Somm. p. 12 (general observation), *Cass., 8 June 1993*, D. 1995 Somm. p. 11. But see *Paris, 14 February 1991*, D. 1993 Somm. p. 109, which went the other way. The Court of Appeal carefully observed that the meaning and effect of the undertaking was perfectly clear to the guarantor. The two CA Paris cases involved security provided by private individuals who also held

law. In *BGH, 12 March 1992*[112] and in *BGH, 2 April 1998*, it was held that if the 'guarantee' was issued by a non-financial institution and if the 'guarantor' was not familiar with the risks of a first demand guarantee, the beneficiary should fully explain these risks to the 'guarantor'. If the beneficiary fails to do so, the 'guarantee' is to be construed as or converted into an ordinary accessory suretyship.[113] However, in *Trib. civ. Antwerp, 16 January 1997*, the court construed the security, issued by the managing directors of the principal debtor in favour of a bank, as in fact amounting to a first demand guarantee, without reference to a duty to advise the guarantors of the risks thereof.[114]

Procedural aspects

12-29 Disputes concerning the construction of the 'guarantee' as a traditional accessory suretyship or as an independent first demand guarantee sometimes arise in summary proceedings for payment initiated by the beneficiary against the guarantor or in applications for preliminary restraining orders filed by the account party. Such proceedings do not allow for lengthy hearings and time-consuming gathering of evidence. This presents some difficulties. Where the court is not satisfied that the arguments and evidence are such as to warrant making a decision either way, the court may contemplate referring the case to main proceedings with trial. However, it would be sound policy that, if this should result in deferring payment to the beneficiary, it should be done only when serious difficulties as regards construction render a decision virtually impossible.[115] Otherwise, guarantors or account parties will be tempted just to conjure up issues of construction in order to delay payment.

---

major positions in the business of the account party/principal debtor. French case law has not rejected the possibility of first demand guarantees issued by private individuals. The Court of Appeal in the cases resulting in the decisions of *Cass., 13 December 1994*, and *Cass., 23 February 1999*, explicitly affirmed this possibility and construed the security as first demand guarantees. These decisions were quashed on other grounds, see No. 12-31. See also Chapter 12.2, No. 12-15 for the duty to advise private individuals on the risks of first demand guarantees.

[112] WM 1992, p. 854.

[113] WM 1998, p. 1062. In the present case the guarantor, which was a construction company affiliated to the account party, was fully aware of these risks.

[114] RW 1998/1999, p. 679. See also No. 12-32.

[115] See *Paris, 10 April 1986*, D. 1988 Somm. p. 244, *Paris, 10 January 1986*, D. 1986 I.R. p. 154, *BGH, 23 January 1997*, WM 1997, p. 656, *BGH, 2 April 1998*, WM 1998, p. 1062. See also Chapter 13.2.12, No. 13-32, and Chapter 14.6.

12.3.4 Overview of case law

Introduction

12-30 The following groups of cases are presented for the sake of reference. They all involve cases where the construction of the 'guarantee' instrument was a contested issue. Uncertainty as regards the nature of the security in all cases stemmed from the mixture of terms and phrasing that had a plain or assumed suretyship connotation with terms and phrases pointing to an independent (first demand) guarantee.

'First demand' clause. Held: suretyship.

12-31 The mere presence of the phrase 'payment on first demand' does not necessarily compel a construction in favour of an independent first demand guarantee, if the instrument also contains clauses and phrases with a strong suretyship connotation.[116] Indeed, there are several examples of cases involving texts which, *inter alia*, contain the 'payment on first demand' clause and which have been construed as a traditional, accessory suretyship.[117] Such construction frequently occurs in domestic cases,[118] and/ or in cases where the 'payment on first demand' clause is the only indication of a first demand guarantee and/or where the 'guarantee' does not contain a documentary payment mechanism, and particularly in cases of a combination of the above. A typical example of a 'guarantee' instrument which lacks a documentary payment mechanism, is provided in the Dutch Supreme Court decision *HR, 25 September 1998*, in relation to a 'guarantee' with the following text:'The Guarantor undertakes to pay Owner on

---

[116] This is particularly true for English law instruments. The phrase 'payment on (first) demand' frequently occurs in security documents which unquestionably provide for a traditional accessory suretyship. In that context the phrase merely means that the payment obligation of the guarantor (surety) is triggered by the demand for payment by the beneficiary, whether or not a demand for payment on the principal debtor has been made, but the guarantor (surety) can raise defences derived from the principal contract.

[117] *Rb Amsterdam, 5 April 1984*, KG 1984, 122, *OLG Stuttgart, 8 September 1976*, WM 1977, p. 881, *Cass., 10 May 1994*, D. 1995 Somm. p. 12, *Paris, 7 January 1992*, D. 1993 Somm. p. 96, *Bordeaux, 7 March 1991*, D. 1992 Somm. p. 235, *Trib. com. Antwerp, 5 July 1984*, TBH 1985, p. 571, *Trib. com. Brussels, 15 November 1984*, RDC 1985 p. 569.

[118] For example, in *Trib. com. Charleroi, 23 April 1997*, JLMB 1998, p. 1073,and *Trib. com. Brussels, 11 February 1999*, RDC 2000, p. 725, the courts regarded a 'payment on first demand' clause in an crossborder situation as a very strong indication of an independent first demand guarantee, but not necessarily so in a domestic case. In both cases the court construed the security as a 'suretyship payable on first demand', see further Chapter 4.5, No. 4-19.

first demand made in writing by or on behalf of the Owner all that which the owner may or shall as a result of any provisions contained in the aforementioned Construction Contract claim from the Contractor (…), without any further notice of default or legal proceedings being required in the matter'.[119] The difficulty of this wording is that payment by the bank does not clearly depend on the submission of a document, such as a unilateral statement by the beneficiary that certain amounts are owing, but seems to be connected with events pertaining to the underlying contract.

A rather restrictive approach is apparent in a number of recent French decisions. Although the 'guarantees' were stated to be payable on first demand and also contained other clauses which clearly pointed to a first demand guarantee, such as 'payment without contestation' or 'payment without raising any defences (from the underlying contract)', these 'guarantees' were nonetheless construed as a traditional suretyship for the sole reason that the text also contained the phrase that the guarantor guaranteed payment of the amounts *which are due by the account party*. Accordingly, this sole phrase outweighed the entirety of all other indications in favour of a first demand guarantee. It should be noted that all these decisions involved domestic cases,[120] while in some of them the security was provided by private individuals,[121] although these facts were not mentioned as the reason of the decisions.

No 'first demand' clause. Held: first demand guarantee

12-32 The abstract notion of a first demand guarantee relates to an independent guarantee which is payable on demand without any proof of default whatsoever, apart from the presentation of a formal, unilateral statement by the beneficiary to this effect, if so required pursuant to the terms of the guarantee. In order to be a first demand guarantee it is not absolutely necessary that the text contains the phrase 'payment on first

---

[119] NJ 1998, 892. The issue in this case was whether the bank had to pay on the mere fact of termination of the underlying contract, or whether such a termination must have been made in accordance with the requirements specified in certain clauses in the underlying contract, which only allowed termination in the event of material breach by the account party. This decision should be contrasted with *HR, 12 March 1982*, NJ 1982, 267, which went the other way, see No. 12-34.

[120] *Cass., 13 March 1996*, JCP 1997 Éd. E l No. 633, p. 102, *Cass. 11 March 1997*, Bull. Civ. 1997 No. 67, p. 60, *Cass., 27 June 2000*, Revue Droit Bancaire et Financier 2000, p. 355, *Cass., 25 June 2002*, D.Affaires 2002, p. 3333. See for a critical comment Contamine-Raynaud, Revue Droit Bancaire 1997, p. 123, and 1998, p. 66.

[121] *Cass., 13 December 1994*, D. 1995 J. p. 209, *Cass., 12 January 1999*, Revue Droit Bancaire 1999, p. 76, *Cass., 23 February 1999*, JCP 1999 Éd. G. ll 10 189, p. 1940, *Cass., 14 June 2000*, Revue Droit Bancaire et Financier 2000, p. 355, *Paris, 6 July 2001*, D.Affaires 2001, p. 2820.

demand'. The notion of a first demand guarantee could be expressed by other means, such as the phrase 'payment on request', 'payment without objection', 'without contestation', 'without proof or justification', 'payment will be made upon the contractor's default as determined by you at your absolute discretion'.[122] A requirement of a unilateral statement of default to be submitted by the beneficiary is also a very strong indication of a first demand guarantee.[123] Whether, in the light of the entire text, these and other phrases do in fact convey the notion of a first demand guarantee remains, of course, a matter of construction.

Payment on 'first justified demand'

12-33 'Guarantees' which state, *inter alia*, that they are payable 'on first justified demand' have led to difficulties as regards the meaning of the phrase 'justified'. In *Cass., 19 May 1992*, the Cour de Cassation ruled that the instrument was to be construed as an independent guarantee which merely requires some motivation by the beneficiary for his demand for payment or his statement regarding the account party's default, without the need for adducing any further justifications or evidence of default.[124] Accordingly, this type of instrument is treated in the same way as an independent first demand guarantee requiring the presentation of the beneficiary's unilateral statement of default and the kind of request for payment as envisaged in art. 20(a) URDG.[125]

---

[122] See, for example, *OLG Hamburg, 18 December 1981*, WM 1983, p. 188, affirmed by *BGH, 14 October 1982*, WM 1982, p. 1324, *OLG Frankfurt a.M., 26 June 1984*, RIW 1985, p. 407, affirmed by *BGH, 22 April 1985*, RIW 1985, p. 650, *Cass., 20 February 1985*, D. 1986 I.R. p. 153, *Cass., 2 February 1988*, D. 1988 Somm. p. 239, *Paris, 6 May 1986*, D. 1987 Somm. p. 175, *Trib. civ. Antwerp, 16 January* 1997, RW 1998/1999, p. 679 (in this case the instrument followed the usual pattern of a suretyship and it did not contain a 'payment on first demand' or similar clauses. However, because of the exclusion of statutory defences pertaining to suretyship and a number of other clauses the court ruled that the security in fact amounted to an independent first demand guarantee), OG *Austria, 18 December 1987*, IBL November 1988, p. 92.

[123] See No. 12-22.

[124] D. 1993 Somm. p. 104 (3e. decision). Idem: *Cass., 3 November 1992*, D. 1993 Somm. p. 96, *Cass., 7 June 1994*, D. 1995 Somm. p. 20, *Paris, 9 January 1991*, D. 1991 Somm. p. 196, *Trib. com. Paris, 3 October 1989*, D. 1990 Somm. p. 202, *Paris, 24 November 1981*, D. 1982 J. p. 296, *Paris, 9 January 1978*, mentioned by Gavalda and Stoufflet, RTDC 1980, p. 13, *OLG Köln, 24 October 1997*, WM 1998, p. 1443. However, in *Trib. com. Paris, 24 March 1981*, D. 1981 J. p. 482, the instrument was construed as an accessory guarantee requiring full proof of the account party's default.

[125] See Chapter 4, Nos. 4-3/3a.

Other Aspects of the Bank Guarantee 229

Held: independent (first demand) guarantee

12-34 In the vast majority of crossborder cases involving business entities, 'guarantee' instruments containing phrases and clauses as mentioned in nos. 12-21/22 have been construed as an independent guarantee, most of them being first demand guarantees.[126] In most decisions the phrase 'payment on (first) demand' was considered an important indicator, sometimes in combination with the documentary nature of the payment

---

[126] See for example: The Netherlands: *CA The Hague, 13 June 1980*, upheld by *HR, 12 March 1982*, NJ 1982, 267, *CA Amsterdam, 4 June 1982*, reprinted by Bannier, in Hague-Zagreb Essays 6, p. 208. Germany: *LG Frankfurt a.M., 16 October 1962*, NJW 1963, p. 450, *LG Braunschweig, 22 May 1980*, RIW 1981, p. 789, *OLG Hamburg, 18 December 1981*, WM 1983, p. 188, affirmed by *BGH, 14 October 1982*, WM 1982, p. 1324, *OLG Frankfurt a.M., 26 June 1984*, RIW 1985, p. 407, affirmed by *BGH, 22 April 1985*, RIW 1985, p. 650. France: *Cass., 20 December 1982*, D. 1983 J. p. 365, *Cass., 20 February 1985*, D. 1986 I.R. p. 153, *Cass., 8 December 1987*, D. 1988 Somm. p. 240, *Cass., 2 February 1988*, D. 1988 Somm. p. 239, *Cass., 22 May 1991*, D. 1992 Somm. p. 233, *Cass., 3 November 1992*, D. 1993 Somm. p. 96, *Cass. 1 February 1994*, D. 1995 Somm. p. 11, *Cass., 7 October 1997*, JCP 1998 Éd. E, p. 226, *Cass., 30 January 2001*, D. Affaires 2001, p. 1024, *Paris, 2 June 1982*, D. 1983 J. p. 437 (first demand guarantee, but the bank should have obtained a statement of default; this last part of the judgment was quashed by *Cass., 5 February 1985*, D. 1985 J. p. 269), *Aix-en-Provence, 13 March 1980*, D. 1981 I.R. p. 505, *Paris, 14 October 1983*, D. 1984 I.R. p. 202, *Poitiers, 13 March 1985*, D. 1988 Somm. p. 241, *Paris, 6 May 1986*, D. 1987 Somm. p. 175, *Paris, 1 July 1986*, D. 1987 Somm. p. 171, *Versailles, 13 June 1990*, D. 1991 Somm. p. 191, *Toulouse, 9 January 1992*, D. 1992 Somm. p. 236, *Paris, 20 March 1993*, D. 1993 Somm. p. 96, *Paris, 18 December 1991*, D. 1993 Somm. p. 106, *Trib. com. Nantes, 22 September 1983*, D. 1984 I.R. p. 202, *Trib. com. Paris, 7 October 1988*, D. 1989 Somm. p. 145. Belgium: *Brussels, 18 December 1981*, Rev. Banque 1982, p. 99, *Brussels, 25 February 1982*, JCB 1982, p. 349, *Antwerp, 13 October 1982*, BRH 1982, p. 642, *Antwerp, 15 October 1985*, TBH 1986, p. 646, *Brussels, 3 April 1987*, RGDC 1989, p. 475, *Brussels, 26 June 1992*, RDC 1994, p. 51, *Trib. com. Brussels, 23 December 1980*, Rev. Banque 1981, p. 627, *Trib. com. Brussels, 11 March 1981*, BRH 1981, p. 361, *Trib. com. Brussels 30 January 1992*, RDC 1993, p. 1052. United Kingdom: *Potton Homes Ltd. v. Coleman Contractors*, [1984] 28 Build. L.R. 19, *Esal (Commodities) Ltd., Reltor v. Oriental Credit*, [1985] 2 Lloyd's Rep. 546, *Siporex Trade v. Banque Indosuez*, [1986] 2 Lloyd's Rep. 146, *I. E. Contractors v. Lloyds Bank*, [1990]2 Lloyd's Rep. 496, *Balfour Beatty Civil Engeneering v. Technical & General Guarantee*, [1999] 68 Con. LR 180. Switzerland: *Zürich, 9 May 1985*, D 1987 Somm. p. 177. Austria: *OG Austria, 7Ob 653/85*, JIBL 1986 N-50, *OG Austria, 18 December 1987*, IBL November 1988, p. 92. *ICC Arbitration No. 3316 (1979)*, JDI 1980 p. 970, *ICC Arbitration No. 5639 (1987)*, D 1988 Somm. p. 242. In *Brussels, 17 November 1988*, RDC 1990, p. 91, the 'guarantee' did not contain the phrase 'payment on first demand', nor a clause in which the bank renounced all defences under the principal contract. The account party's argument that the bank should not have paid without evidence of default was rejected because the account party had clearly instructed his bank to issue a first demand guarantee.

mechanism. It should be noted, however, that French case law attributes particular significance to (additional) phrases such as 'irrevocable and unconditionally', 'payment without deferment', 'payment without any contestation (or objection)' and 'payment without raising any defences (from the principal contract)' in order to construe a 'guarantee' as an independent first demand guarantee.[127] And further, courts in numerous decisions rightly ruled that the labelling of the contract as 'suretyship' does not command an interpretation in favour of suretyship and, in the light of other terms and phrases, found that the particular instrument was an independent guarantee.

The fact that in the vast majority of cases the 'guarantee' has been construed as an independent (first demand) guarantee cannot, however, give rise to any general 'blind assumption' to this effect. Each case has to be decided on its own merits.[128]

Held: first demand suretyship. Germany

12-35 Recognition of a first demand suretyship as a seperate species, to be distinguished from both the traditional suretyship and the first demand guarantee, is peculiar to Germany.[129] All cases involved domestic situations. The decision in favour of a

---

[127] See, *Cass., 2 February 1988*, D. 1988 Somm. p. 239, *Cass., 9 January 1990*, D. 1991 Somm. p. 191, *Cass., 3 November 1992*, D. 1993 Somm. p. 96, *Cass., 7 October 1997*, JCP 1998 Éd. E, p. 226; see also *Cass., 10 May 1994*, D. 1995 Somm. p. 12, and *Cass. 15 June 1999*, D.Affaires 2000, p. 112 (held: suretyship, despite the phrase 'payable on first demand', because the 'guarantee' did not contain the phrases mentioned in the text) and *Paris, 3 April 2002*, D.Affaires p. 1750 (held: suretyship, because the 'guarantee' did not contain the phrases mentioned in the text). The inclusion of these phrases does not, however, ensure an interpretation in favour of a first demand guarantee, see *Cass., 9 December 1997*, Rev. Droit Bancaire 1998, p. 66, *Cass., 25 June 2002*, D.Affaires 2002 p. 3333, and the French case law cited in No. 12-31.

[128] Cf. *Siporex Trade v. Banque Indosuez*, [1986] 2 Lloyd's Rep. 146.

[129] *BGH, 2 May 1979*, NJW 1979, p. 1500, *BGH, 24 November 1983*, WM 1984, p. 44 (domestic counter-security forming part of a chain of crossborder guarantees), *BGH, 31 January 1985*, WM 1985, p. 511, *BGH, 11 December 1986*, WM 1987, p. 367, *BGH, 26 February 1987*, NJW 1987, p. 2075, *BGH, 21 April 1988*, WM 1988, p. 934, *BGH, 9 March 1989*, NJW 1989, p. 1606, BGH, *2 April 1998*, WM 1998, p. 1062, *OLG Hamburg, 10 October 1985*, NJW 1986, p. 1691, *Kammergericht, 20 November 1986*, NJW 1987, p. 1774, *BGH, 13 July 1989*, WM 1989, p. 1496, *OLG München, 23 July 1997*, WM 1998, p. 342, *OLG Köln, 30 October 1997*, WM 1998, p. 1443. In *OLG Hamburg, 18 December 1981*, WM 1983, p. 188, affirmed by *BGH, 14 October 1982*, WM 1982, p. 1324, the instrument was construed as a first demand guarantee, although it contained terms and phrases with suretyship connotations. In *BGH, 23 February 1984*, WM 1984, p. 633, *BGH, 17 January 1989*, NJW 1989, p. 1480, and in *BGH, 23 January 1997*, WM 1997, p. 656, a decision either way was deemed unnecessary for the purposes of resolving the issue.

suretyship payable on first demand as opposed to a traditional suretyship is consistently based on specific clauses to this effect. The interpretation in favour of a first demand suretyship, rather than a first demand guarantee, turns consistently on the use of the term 'surety(ship)' (*Bürgschaft*) as opposed to 'guarantee' (*Garantie*). It has been pointed out that for all practical purposes the effect is the same.[130]

Held: suretyship

12-36 In the minority of crossborder cases the court decided in favour of a traditional suretyship in situations where the instrument contained phrases which pointed both to suretyship and to an independent (first demand) guarantee.[131]

12.3.5 Construction of terms and clauses in independent guarantees and counter-indemnities

Independent guarantees

12-37 Problems concerning proper construction could, of course, also arise in respect of certain terms and clauses in an independent guarantee which are unclear or ambiguous. It would seem that there exists no single criterion for proper construction, but several of the suggested guidelines discussed in Chapter 12.3.2 could also be useful in this context. Thus, when construing the terms of an independent guarantee, one should try to find the intention of the parties, while the legitimate expectations of the parties and the perceptions in international trade in general should also be taken into account. For reasons mentioned in nos. 12-19 and 12-23 one could also have regard to the terms of the underlying contract and to the negotiations and communications between the parties to the underlying transaction. In *BGH, 26 April 1994*, the German Supreme Court expressly observed that this method of construction is not inconsistent with the principle of independence; this principle merely prohibits a construction in a manner for which the text of the guarantee does not contain a reference or point of departure.[132]

---

[130] See Chapter 4.5, No. 4-18/19.

[131] See the decisions mentioned in No. 12-31, and in addition *BGH, 19 September 1985*, NJW 1986, p. 310, *Cass., 10 May 1994*, D. 1995 Somm. p. 12 (see No. 12-34), *Cass., 9 December 1977*, Rev. Droit Bancaire 1998, p. 66 (see No. 12-34),*Paris, 9 July 1986*, D. 1988 Somm. p. 243, *Paris, 3 April 2002*, D.Affaires p. 1750 (see No. 12-34). In *Trib. com. Lyon, 27 June 1989*, D. 1990 Somm. p. 206, the instrument was expressed to be 'an irrevocable and unconditional guarantee', but was construed as a suretyship because the text did not state that it was payable on first demand or that the bank could not raise any defences.

[132] WM 1994, p. 1063. The issue related to a clause stating that 50% of the invoices were covered by the standby letter of credit. Idem: *OLG Frankfurt a.M., 18 March 1997*, RIW

Other useful illustrations of this technique are provided in *Rb. Amsterdam, 5 September 1991*, where an unclear non-calendar expiry provision was interpreted by reference to the main contract,[133] in *Rb Utrecht, 22 January 1998*, in relation to the validity period and the purpose of the guarantee,[134] in *Rb Amsterdam, 28 June 2000*, in relation to a certain third-party document,[135] and in *BGH, 25 February 1999*, in relation to the question of whether the guarantee provided security for non-performance by the account party in connection with a construction contract only or whether it also covered non-payment of rentals by the account party.[136]

If the issue of interpretation arises between account party and bank after payment, no regard should be had to the underlying relationship since the bank is not a party thereto, unless the bank was aware of the particular meaning of the term at issue ascribed to it by the parties to the underlying relationship.[137]

The difficulties of the *contra proferentem* method and the method focusing on the perception of the addressee of the guarantee have been described in no. 12-26.[138] However, if it is possible to identify the drafter of the ambiguous term or condition, the *contra proferentem* method could serve as a means of construction.[139]

Because of its independent nature (or, in the case of the German 'suretyship payable on first demand', because of the temporary suspension of the accessory nature thereof)

1998, p. 477. It should be noted that in the cases cited in this paragraph, the dispute was mainly between the account party and beneficiary, the bank not having a predominant interest of its own in the outcome of the controversy. Dolan, § 2.09[3], § 4.08[1], advocates against a construction of ambiguous terms by reference to the underlying transaction, but this might be explained by the fact that he focuses on the position of the bank in relation to the bank's examination of compliance and commercial letters of credit where a demand for payment is the rule, not the exception. See also the next paragraph.

[133] KG 1991, 335.

[134] JOR 2000, 40.

[135] JOR 200, 249 (subject to appeal).

[136] WM 1999, p. 895. Another example is provided in *BGH, 24 September 1998*, WM 1998, p. 2363.

[137] *CA 's-Hertogenbosch, 17 September 2002*, JOR 2003, 19. In this case the bank had paid while the account party argued that it should not have paid because the guarantee had been terminated prior to the demand. The issue related to the construction of the termination clause. See also No. 12-19, last paragraph.

[138] See also Dolan, § 4.08[3].

[139] In respect of commercial credits, Dolan, § 4.08[3], notes that some American courts prefer to invoke a rule construing an ambigious term against the drafter thereof, while other courts construe it against the issuer of the credit.

and the need for certainty, guarantees may only be interpreted on the basis of the text of the guarantee, including other documents and contracts to which the operative clauses of the guarantee refer.[140] Courts should, therefore, be most reluctant to imply, by way of interpretation, additional terms and conditions which either restrict or broaden the beneficiary's rights, or to deviate from clear stipulated terms, unless the operative part of the guarantee contains an appropriate point of departure thereto.[141] Accordingly, *Trib. com. Turnhout, 30 October 1995*, refused to give a clear calendar expiry date any other meaning than its literal meaning,[142] and *Trib. com. Brussels, 5 February 1996*, adhered to a strict construction of a condition precedent in relation to an advance payment of DEM 140,220 (approx. euro 70,000).[143]

It may also happen that the guarantee contains conditions which are impossible for the beneficiary to fulfil. In two such cases, *Exxon. Co. U.S.A. v. Banque de Paris et des Pays-Bas*[144] and *Cass., 3 June 1986*,[145] the beneficiary could not possibly make a valid demand for payment on or before the expiry date. In both cases the court rejected the beneficiary's argument that the expiry provision was ambiguous and had to be con-

---

[140] Cf. *BGH, 26 April 1994*, WM 1994, p. 1063, *BGH, 14 December 1995*, WM 1996, p. 193, *BGH, 25 February 1999*, WM 1999, p. 895, *BGH, 26 April 2001*, WM 2001, p. 1208. Belgian case law and legal writing often state that one of the main features of independent guarantees is their 'literal' nature. This characteristic does not entail a precept for interpretation, but merely relates to the rule of strict compliance and the independent nature of this type of security, i.e. the rights and obligations of the guarantor and beneficiary are to be determined by reference to the terms and conditions stated in the guarantee, and not by reference to the secured contract, cf. T'Kint, No. 827, and *CA Brussels, 14 February 2000*, R.N.B. 2000, p. 403.

[141] See also *Cauxell v. Lloyds Bank*, *The Times*, 26 December 1995, mentioned in No. 12-37a.

[142] RW 1996/1997, p. 328. In this case the guarantee had been issued on 26 September 1991 and provided for an expiry date of 7 October 1991, while the secured contract lasted much longer. The court rejected the beneficiary's argument that this (clear) expiry date should be construed in accordance with the precept of reasonableness and fairness.

[143] RW 1996/1997, p. 1263. The repayment guarantee required, as a condition precedent, the advance payment of '30%, i.e. DEM 140,220' (approx. € 70,000). In fact, the beneficiary made an advance payment of DEM 123,000, being 30% of the purchase price, exclusive of VAT. The beneficiary's claim for payment of DEM 123,000 was rejected because the stated condition precedent had not been fulfilled. The court observed that the condition precedent was clear and not ambiguous and therefore, rejected the beneficiary's argument that the amount mentioned therein should be interpreted in the light of the underlying contract. See also Chapter 13.2.6, No. 13-20.

[144] 828 F2d 1121 (5th. Cir. 1987). See Chapter 13.2.7, No. 13-23, for the facts.

[145] D. 1987 Somm. p. 174. See Chapter 13.3, No. 13-39, for the facts. See also *Trib. com. Turnhout*, mentioned above.

strued against the issuer of the guarantee, and instead kept the beneficiary to a strict reading of the expiry provision.[146] The result was that a post-expiry demand for payment was held to be invalid.

Indemnity ('counter-guarantee') by instructing bank to issuing bank in the case of an indirect guarantee

12-37a In the case of indirect guarantees, the indemnity ('counter-guarantee') furnished by the instructing bank in favour of the issuing bank cannot possibly be a contract of suretyship. The explanation is simple. Such an indemnity does not assure payment to the issuing bank in the event of non-performance by a third party in relation to the issuing bank, but indemnifies that bank in its capacity as a debtor for payment consequential to its undertaking towards the beneficiary of the primary guarantee.[147] The only question that could arise is whether payment under the indemnity is in some or other way linked to default of the account party, especially proof of default. If the foreign issuing bank has been requested to issue an independent guarantee, it necessarily follows that the indemnity is also independent of the underlying relationship.[148] Where the issuing bank has been instructed to act as a surety, one must be alert to stipulations in the indemnity exempting the issuing bank from liability for ascertaining default by the principal debtor as measured by the secured contract. In this way the issuing bank is protected against the risk of becoming involved in (disputes regarding) the underlying contract. In appropriate circumstances, such exemption may be evident from a 'repayment on first demand' clause. Thus, for example, the indirect accessory suretyship in *Cass., 29 April 1986*, *Cass., 15 June 1999*, Paris, *18 November 1986*, and *Paris, 3 April 2002* was backed up by an instrument which was construed as an independent counter-guarantee payable on first demand without reference to the terms of the suretyship and without the need to adduce evidence concerning the principal debtor's default.[149]

---

[146] In the *Exxon* case the court based its decision both on the beneficiary's failure to check the conditions of payment upon issuance and on the strong policy in favour of firm expiry rules, see further Dolan, § 4.08[5].

[147] See Chapter 11.2, No. 11-13 (Counter-guarantee as an indemnity).

[148] *Trib com. Brussels, 23 December 1980*, Rev. Banque 1981, p. 627, *Trib. com. Brussels, 11 March 1981*, BRH 1981, p. 361, *Trib. com. Nantes, 22 September 1983*, D. 1984 I.R. P. 202. See further Chapter 11.2, No. 11-12. See also *CA Liège, 8 June 1999*, RDC 2000, p. 731, and *BGH, 24 November 1983*, WM 1984, p. 44 (held: suretyship payable on first demand, without regard to defences from the underlying relationship).

[149] *Cass., 29 April 1986*, D. 1987 J. p. 17, *Cass., 15 June 1999*, D.Affaires 2000 p. 112, *Paris, 18 November 1986*, D. 1988 Somm. p. 247, *Paris, 3 April 2002*, D.Affaires 2002 p. 1750 (see also Chapter 11, No. 11-19); see also *Trib. com. Lyon, 27 June 1989*, D. 1990 Somm. p.

As far as the construction of terms in a counter-guarantee in general is concerned, it was held in *Cauxell v. Lloyds Bank* that courts should be reluctant to imply certain terms in a counter-guarantee which are not mentioned therein, with a view to the need for certainty in commercial transactions between banks.[150]

12.4 PERIOD OF VALIDITY. LAW AND PRACTICE

12.4.1 Significance of expiry date. The risk of the 'perpetual' (counter-)guarantee

12-38 Most guarantees contain an expiry date, the absence thereof being the exception.[151] While the importance of an expiry date is considerable, especially in respect of first demand guarantees,[152] the practical significance is often severely eroded by virtue of extension clauses, 'extend or pay' and 'hold for value' requests from the beneficiary. It is rather the rule than the exception that factors such as those just mentioned cause the guarantee to remain in force far longer than the original expiry date. In the case of indirect guarantees the predicament of the first instructing bank and the account party is often aggravated by stipulations concerning the period of validity of the counter-guarantee and these clauses ultimately define the extent of the account party's risk exposure. Clauses stating that the counter-guarantee remains in force until discharge are particularly troublesome. Such clauses were not unreasonable in the period when expiry dates mentioned in the primary guarantee were not enforceable under local law or practice or where the enforceability was uncertain, as was the case in respect of some countries. Unfortunately, these clauses sometimes still appear although at present the enforceability of expiry dates is beyond any doubt.[153] Another reason for concern is that certain banks in certain jurisdictions are in the habit of routinely lodging an 'extend or pay' request irrespective of whether such a request has been made by the ultimate beneficiary of the primary guarantee.

In respect of contracts with government agencies, guarantees without an expiry date and which remain in force until discharge are not unusual, both in Europe but especially in the Middle East and the Indian subcontinent.[154] In that event, the counter-guarantee contains matching clauses.

---

206. But see *Cass., 28 January 1992*, D. 1992 Somm. p. 234, where the indemnity in favour of the issuing bank was construed as a suretyship.

[150] *The Times*, 26 December 1995.
[151] See Chapter 8.6, No. 8-16.
[152] See also Chapter 8.6, No. 8-11.
[153] See No. 12-49.
[154] See Chapter 8.6, No. 8-16.

The risk of perpetuity of the (counter-)guarantee as a result of the above-mentioned practices and clauses is generally perceived by (instructing) banks and especially account parties as one of the most perturbing aspects of demand guarantees. The effect of the continuing duration of the (counter-)guarantee is that the account party continues to owe charges to the bank, that the credit facilities remain blocked and that the security will not be released, even apart from the continual risk of an actual call for payment. This often has a paralysing impact on the account party's business activities and his ability to finance his operations, particularly if the nature of his business requires the issuance of large numbers of demand guarantees.

12.4.2 Extension clauses

12-39 An extension clause accords the beneficiary a contractual right to have the period of validity of the guarantee extended on demand. The reasons for exercising this right are generally the same as those underlying 'extend or pay' requests. As an additional safeguard, guarantees and especially counter-guarantees sometimes state explicitly that payment is to be made if the extension has not been granted or not granted in time.

12.4.3 'Extend or pay' requests

Practice and motives

12-40 By an 'extend or pay' request the beneficiary requests an extension of the period of validity of the guarantee or, if not granted, payment. An UNCITRAL survey showed that 95 per cent of the calls on first demand guarantees concern 'extend or pay' requests. It is a widespread and common practice. Nor is it unusual that such requests are lodged over and again, carrying the repeatedly extended expiry date far beyond the initial expiry date.

Several motives may underlie such requests. The objective could be to allow the beneficiary more time, while preserving his rights under the guarantee, for example, where the principal debtor has failed to complete the contract within the period originally contemplated, or where the parties to the underlying contract are in consultation in order to overcome difficulties concerning the completion of the contract or to resolve differences of opinion as regards the performance. Made in these circumstances, an 'extend or pay' request could well be described as benevolent and constructive. A second reason could be that the beneficiary has not yet taken a final decision or that he is still undecided regarding the amount to be claimed. Another objective could be just to gain time where there are diffuse decision-making patterns or bureaucratic impediments within the organisation of the beneficiary or where in such situations the beneficiary is just incapable of taking the decision that the guarantee is no longer needed. The request may, however, also be inspired by the improper motive of putting pressure on the account party to agree to what is effectively an extended warranty period or to works in excess of the contractually agreed works or to exact discounts on further contracts.[155]

Since the request must be made within the period of validity as it exists from time to time, it is advisable for the beneficiary to lodge his request well before the expiry date. Thus, for example, the Saudi Arabian Monetary Agency (SAMA) and the Commercial Bank of Syria recommend beneficiaries to request an extension, if necessary, of one month and at least fifteen days respectively, before expiry.[156]

The request for extension is ordinarily granted, since the bank and, especially, the account party naturally prefer prolongation to actual payment. It remains, however, a fact that the account party is virtually forced to agree to an extension. The situation is different in the case of guarantees which require the submission of third-party documents attesting to the account party's default. If the account party anticipates that the beneficiary will not be able to meet that particular condition of payment within the current period of validity, he will obviously not wish to have that period extended. The text hereafter focuses on first demand guarantees.

Legal position

12-41 When the beneficiary secures an extension by means of an 'extend or pay' request, he is effectively exercising a power inherent in first demand guarantees, not a right. As explained in no. 12-40, this does not in itself imply any improper conduct on the part of the beneficiary. Only the particular circumstances and motives may render the request oppressive. It should be noted that a beneficiary asking for prolongation pursuant to an extension clause might abuse his contractual right just as much.

When a beneficiary lodges an 'extend or pay' request, he is, in the first instance, seeking an extension, not payment, as is apparent from the wording of the request. Nonetheless, it would appear evident that, if no extension has been granted, such a

---

[155] Dohm, No. 142, Horn, IPRax 1981, p. 153, and Stumpf/Ullrich, RIW 1984, p. 843, argue that repeated 'pay or extend' requests are a (clear) indication of fraud. See also von Westphalen, pp. 209-211, 356. This presumption has rightly been rejected in *LG Köln, 11 December 1981*, WM 1982, p. 438, *OLG Frankfurt a.M., 3 March 1983*, WM 1983, p. 175, *Paris, 1 October 1986*, D. 1987 Somm. p. 171, *Trib. com. Brussels, 23 December 1980*, Rev. Banque 1981, p. 627. See also *LG Braunschweig, 22 May 1980*, RIW 1981, p. 789, *Rb Amsterdam, 7 April 1988*, KG 1988, 181. In several of these decisions the court opined that in the light of the evidence the requests in fact indicated that the contract had not been fully performed.

[156] Pursuant to a circular letter of SAMA, No. 2504/M/A 286, dated 9 June 1969, banks are to remind the beneficiary one month before the expiry date of the forthcoming expiry, thus enabling the beneficiary to decide whether to call the guarantee, or to have the validity period extended, or to allow the guarantee to lapse. It is uncertain whether this regulation also applies to banks outside Saudi Arabia.

request constitutes a proper demand for payment with the result that the bank is obliged to pay. This proposition has been confirmed in *BGH, 23 January 1996*,[157] *Paris, 9 January 1991*[158] and *CA The Hague, 8 June 1993*,[159] and is also laid down in art. 26 URDG and Rule 3.09 ISP98. Yet, in some other cases the 'extend or pay' request was not viewed as a proper demand for payment where no extension was granted.[160] The startling result of these decisions was that a formal demand for payment after the unamended expiry date was held to be too late and that the bank's obligation to pay had lapsed in the meantime. Surely, an 'extend or pay' request should result in either an extension or in payment, and not in a lapse of the period of validity.

BGH, 23 January 1996, ruled that a reply by the bank that it had contacted the account party and that it would revert to the matter, did not amount to an implied agreement to extend the validity period. It should be noted that in this case the bank did not inform the beneficiary of its decision not to extend the validity period until after the expiry date, with the consequences mentioned hereafter.[161] With a view to this particular fact of the case one may feel ill at ease with this decision. This study suggests that the absence of a timely response by the bank should be deemed to amount to an implied consent to the requested extension in order to discourage unfair delaying tactics.[162] Such a rule would correspond to the rule that, if the bank determines that a demand for payment does not comply with the terms of the guarantee, it must notify the benefeciary thereof without delay and that, if it fails to do so, it is precluded from claiming that the terms of the guarantee have not been complied with.[163]

The fact that, if extension has been refused, an 'extend or pay' request constitutes a proper demand for payment, does not necessarily mean, according to the sources mentioned hereafter, that the demand is also a valid demand. Art. 26 URDG states that an 'extend or pay' request should be made in accordance with the terms and conditions of

---

[157] WM 1996, p. 393.

[158] D. 1991 Somm. p. 196.

[159] KG 1993, 301. See also *Paris, 22 November 1985*, D. 1986 J. p. 213, von Westphalen, p. 208, Goode, p. 113, Kleiner, No. 21.13, RPDB, No. 132, Mattout, No. 225.

[160] *Esal (Commodities), Reltor v. Oriental Credit*, [1985] 2 Lloyd's Rep. 546, *Paris, 28 May 1985*, D. 1986 I.R. p. 155, *Paris, 2 April 1987*, D. 1988 Somm. p. 248, upheld by *Cass., 24 January 1989*, D. 1989 Somm. p. 159, *Paris, 23 June 1995*, JCP 1995, Éd. E ll, No. 735, with critical note by Affaki. These cases involved 'extend or pay' requests relating to the counter-guarantee.

[161] *BGH, 23 January 1996*, WM 1996, p. 393,

[162] According to Ben Slimane, DPCI 1986, p. 287, in the Middle East the bank's failure to respond in time is deemed to be a consent to extension. See also Chapter 13.2.7, No. 13-24

[163] See Chapter 13.2.11, No. 13-31.

the guarantee and the Rules. In conjunction with art. 20(a) of the Rules this implies that the beneficiary, when lodging the 'extend or pay' request, must also submit a statement to the effect that the account party is in default. *BGH, 23 January 1996*, also ruled that such a request only constitutes a valid demand for payment, in the event that an extension has not been granted, if all conditions of payment as stated in the guarantee, have been fulfilled prior to the non-extended expiry date.[164] The effect of Rule 3.09 ISP98 is the same. One may question the wisdom of this requirement if the result is that the beneficiary forfeits his right to payment when he submits these unilateral statements after the non-extended validity period.[165] It often happens that performance of the underlying transaction takes more time than initially contemplated because of, for example, *force majeure*, amendments of the underlying contract, additional works or because the period for performance of the underlying contract has been extended. In these situations, there need not be default on the part of the account party, while an extension of the period of validity is fully justified.[166] Even apart from these situations, requiring a statement of default or other statements might unnecessarily strain the relationship between the parties to the underlying relationship as the beneficiary merely envisages securing an extension, for example in order to allow the account party more time to complete the project. Nonetheless, beneficiaries are strongly advised to either lodge their 'extend or pay' request well in advance of the expiry date in order to be able to still present the required statements in time or to ensure that the request immediately complies with all conditions of payment.

Tender guarantees, 'extend or withdraw' requests

12-42 'Extend or pay' requests relating to tender guarantees can be lodged in order to allow the employer/beneficiary more time to evaluate the tenders. While such requests

---

[164] WM 1996, p. 393. In this case the beneficiary had to submit a statement confirming that his request for payment to the contracting party/account party had not been complied with within 10 working days of the request. The 'extend or pay' request did not contain this confirmation. When the beneficiary did present the statement after the non-extended expiry date, the validity period had meanwhile lapsed and the claim for payment was rejected. This case should be contrasted with *CA Liège, 24 September 1999*, RDC 2000, p. 734, in which the court ruled that the bank could not refuse payment because of certain irregularities in a fourth 'extend or pay' request as it had not objected to three previous requests which suffered from the same defects. See also Chapter 13.2.7, No. 13-24.

[165] Cf. Vasseur, RDAI 1992, p. 270. See further Chapter 13.2.7, No. 13-24.

[166] Nevertheless, it is sometimes possible for the beneficiary to submit a statement of default if the account party refuses an extension, since the latter is often obliged under the terms of the underlying contract to ensure that the guarantee remains in force for the duration of the contract.

may not be unreasonable, they pose additional disadvantages for the account party/ contractor in view of his planning of projected works and possible increases in cost levels. This could be a reason for refusing prolongation. The risk of an effective call for payment is likely to be smaller than in the case of other types of first demand guarantees. Tender guarantees cannot be called if the contract has not been awarded to the account party and the likelihood that a court will be satisfied with the evidence in this respect is usually substantial.[167]

An alternative is the 'extend or withdraw' request. Such requests better accommodate the mutual interests of both account party and employer, and are therefore recommended.[168]

Account party and bank. Who is to decide? Art. 26 URDG

12-43 Since the choice between extension and payment primarily affects the interests of the account party, it would appear evident that the choice is to be made by the account party, not by the bank, cf. art. 26 URDG.[169] It is only when no timely response from the account party is forthcoming that the bank could and perhaps should serve the interests of its client by extending the period of validity rather than by proceeding to payment, since the latter action would be irreversible and because the beneficiary is primarily seeking an extension instead of payment.[170] The counter-guarantee from the

---

[167] See Chapter 14.5.15.

[168] Pursuant to SAMA's 1991 Circular Saudi Arabian employers are entitled to an extension of the validity period of both tender and tender guarantee. If requested, the extension is considered granted unless the contractor withdraws his tender in which event the employer should immediately release the tender guarantee.

[169] *Paris, 12 October 1988*, D. 1990 Somm. p. 205; Ben Slimane, DPCI 1986, p. 287, and IFLR September 1986, p. 28. See also *OG Austria, 18 December 1987*, IBL November 1988, p. 92, von Westphalen, pp. 133, 207, 209, RPDB, No. 134. In *Trib. com. Brussels, 21 November 1997*, RDC 1998, p. 850, the court rejected the bank's claim for reimbursement as it had not obtained the account party's consent for the requested extension and had paid following a subsequent definite demand for payment. It should be noted that with respect to a previous 'extend or pay' request the account party had explicitly asked the bank to agree to an extension. The author of a critical comment on this decision observes that the bank should at least have a claim for unjust enrichment. Under Rule 3.09 ISP98 the bank may exercise its discretion to either seek the approval of the account party to the requested extension or to treat the request as a demand for payment.

[170] This proposition is not inconsistent with art. 26 URDG which states that, unless an extension is granted within a reasonable period of time, the bank is obliged to pay. This Rule merely ensures that the beneficiary secures either an extension or payment. But see Affaki, No. 129, and von Westphalen, p. 208, who take the view that, in this event, the bank should proceed to payment.

account party may contain specific clauses to this effect. In any event, the bank should under no circumstances proceed to payment without first consulting the account party.[171] Art. 26 URDG, therefore, states that the bank shall suspend payment of the demand for such time as is reasonable to permit the account party and beneficiary to reach agreement on the granting of such an extension.[172]

Is the bank entitled to refuse prolongation when the account party chooses, as he is likely to do, to have the period of validity extended? When answering this question one has to bear in mind that a refusal by the bank inevitably triggers payment by the bank while the beneficiary does not seek payment. Moreover, such payment will immediately be followed by the bank's demand for reimbursement. This puts the account party in a difficult position and may well imperil his ability to complete the project. It is, therefore, submitted that the bank is not permitted to withhold its consent in the absence of special circumstances.[173] That might, for instance, be the case where the financial and trading position of the customer is rapidly deteriorating and where no adequate collateral is available to ensure reimbursement at a future date. Art. 26 URDG states, however, in a general fashion that no extension shall be granted unless the bank also agrees to it, while the bank's position under Rule 3.09 ISP98 is much the same.

Indirect guarantee, extension of counter-guarantee

12-44 The rule that the account party and not the bank should take the decision in respect of the beneficiary's 'extend or pay' request also applies to indirect guarantees, cf. art. 26 URDG which applies to both direct and indirect guarantees. The procedure

---

[171] Cf. *Trib. com. Brussels, 30 October 1984*, RDC 1985, p. 572, *Paris, 12 October 1988*, D. 1990 Somm. p. 205 (in view of the particular circumstances of the case liability of the bank for not first referring to the account party was rejected, because the account party had not been prejudiced by this omission). In *Paris, 22 November 1985*, D. 1986 I.R. p. 155, the Court of Appeal also dismissed the account party's complaint that the bank had effected payment without first referring to him.

[172] SAMA's 1991 Circular provides that the beneficiary should first contact the account party and that the bank should be supplied with a copy of the 'extend or pay' request.

[173] See also von Westphalen, p. 209. In the case of *Trib. com. Brussels, 30 October 1984*, RDC 1985, p. 572, the customer and beneficiary were in consultation in respect of certain difficulties concerning the completion of the project. The beneficiary indicated that he would not call the guarantee if the period of validity were extended. The customer applied for an extension which the bank refused. The court, however, ordered the bank to grant the extension having regard to the great and imminent damage to the customer's interests and the absence of significant harm to the bank. The court also enjoined the bank to proceed to payment during the extension period. This order, if permissible at all, was quite unnecessary since according to the report of the case the customer did not even apply for this order.

then is that the issuing bank passes the beneficiary's 'extend or pay' request on to the instructing bank and the instructing bank informs the account party. At the same time the issuing bank will, of course, also lodge an 'extend or pay' request relating to the counter-guarantee.[174] These actions should result in either the extension of both the primary and counter-guarantee or in payment under both the primary and counter-guarantee.

It is to be expected that in the case of indirect guarantees the communication from the issuing bank to the instructing bank and then on to the account party and back again will take much longer than is the case in direct guarantees. Indeed, as is evident from numerous decisions, it often happens that no timely and clear response from the instructing bank and account party is forthcoming. On the other hand, the (issuing) bank's duty to pay is suspended for a reasonable period only and such inactivity leaves the issuing bank in an untenable predicament. It is submitted that in this kind of situation the issuing bank could and perhaps should for reasons mentioned in no. 12-43, best serve the interests of the account party by extending the validity period of the primary guarantee instead of proceeding to payment.

As a corollary to an extension of the primary guarantee, the counter-guarantee must be considered prolonged for the same period of time too, whether or not this is expressly provided for in the counter-guarantee and even though the instructing bank and account party have not explicitly given their consent to the extension of the counter-guarantee. In other words, the instructing bank and account party are estopped from asserting that they have not given their consent to the extension of the counter-guarantee. Accordingly, the general rule that silence does not amount to acceptance should find no application in this kind of situation. A contrary view would yield counter-productive results: issuing banks may then feel compelled to insist on counter-guarantees remaining in force until discharge, or to proceed to payment, which they are entitled to do but which would not be in the account party's interest. Issuing banks might even be tempted to precipitate actual calls for cash payment by the beneficiary and issuing banks could hardly be reproached for such manoeuvres.

Counter-guarantees may also contain explicit clauses in relation to 'extend or pay' requests by the beneficiary of the primary guarantee. Thus, the counter-guarantee may

---

[174] Art. 26 URDG states that the request should be a 'conforming' demand, see No. 12-41, last paragraph. In relation to the 'extend or pay' request regarding the counter-guarantee this requirement would mean that the issuing bank should state in accordance with art. 20(b) URDG that it has received a conforming demand for payment from the beneficiary relating to the primary guarantee. The issuing bank is, of course, unable to present such a statement and it is submitted that this particular requirement has no application to 'extend or pay' requests relating to the counter-guarantee. This is one of the many instances which reveal that counter-guarantees were included in the URDG at a later stage without proper reflection.

provide that it is automatically extended for the same period of time or that the issuing bank has a right to an extension if requested. Such clauses may also have the effect that the decision whether or not to agree to an extension is not made by the account party, but by the issuing bank.

Counter-guarantee, absence of 'extend or pay' request from the beneficiary

12-45 It is not an uncommon phenomenon that the second issuing bank asks for an extension of the counter-guarantee, while the beneficiary of the primary guarantee has not lodged an 'extend or pay' request with the issuing bank or where this remains unclear. Is the issuing bank entitled to ask for an extension, could the instructing bank and account party refuse and what are the consequences thereof? It is this situation which is truly problematical, both from a legal and from a practical point of view. Requests from the issuing bank for an extension of the counter-guarantee, while the beneficiary of the primary guarantee has not lodged an 'extend or pay' request, are often inspired by a desire to continue charging commission but also to ameliorate its position towards the instructing bank with a view to possible requests for payment or extension from the beneficiary after the expiry date of the primary guarantee. Naturally, the existence of the rule that the issuing bank should not honour such requests may not deter that bank from attempting to improve its position. Under these conditions the instructing bank would be justified in refusing an extension of the counter-guarantee. Should such a refusal trigger a demand from the issuing bank for payment, the instructing bank would be justified in refusing payment, if it can indeed be shown that the beneficiary has not made any demand for payment or that the demand was made after the expiry date of the primary guarantee.[175]

The practicalities of the matter may, however, sometimes call for a different response. Neither the instructing bank nor the account party will always know for certain that the beneficiary of the primary guarantee has not made any demand for extension or payment and the instructing bank does not owe a duty to the account party to investigate compliance with the terms of the primary guarantee. Under these circumstances the instructing bank is, in principle, obliged to honour a conforming demand under the counter-guarantee.[176] That bank and the account party may, therefore, deem it wise policy to agree to a possibly unjustified request for extension of the counter-guarantee rather than to refuse such request and run the risk of a call under the counter-guarantee. Obviously, after having consented to such a possibly unjustified request the account party should contact the beneficiary in order to learn the true position and to prevent future unjustified requests for an extension of the counter-guarantee.

---

[175] See Chapter 13.3, No. 13-40.
[176] See Chapter 11.2.2, No. 11-13 and Chapter 11.3, No. 11-22.

12.4.4 'Hold for value' requests

Practice and motives

12-46 Beneficiaries and second issuing banks sometimes lodge shortly before the expiry date a request with the (instructing) bank to 'Please block the amount of the (counter-)guarantee and do not consider the period of validity as expired'. These requests are known as 'hold for value' requests and they are a common phenomenon in the Gulf area.[177] Variants include 'extend or hold for value' or 'pay or hold for value' requests and these should be treated in the same way.

The general idea of such requests is to avoid making a cash call on the guarantee and counter-guarantee which might have to be refunded later and, at the same time, to avoid the lapse of the (counter-)guarantee. The underlying motives and circumstances may vary. The request could be made as a preliminary to a definite demand for payment, enabling the bank to collateralise the funds, or as a provisional call whilst the beneficiary is still calculating the precise amount. It is equally possible that, at the time, the beneficiary is not truly contemplating a demand for payment but that the contract has not been completed or that the account party and beneficiary are in consultation with each other. A demand for cash payment would then only adversely affect the chances of proper completion to the detriment of all concerned. Thus it depends on the particular circumstances whether the 'hold for value' request amounts to a precursor to a demand for payment at a future date or whether it is merely meant to secure extension.

Legal characterisation

12-47 The legal nature and significance of 'hold for value' requests are unclear. According to one view the request is to be deemed a demand for payment, although at a future date,[178] while according to another view the request 'is, for all practical purposes, not a demand for payment, but a request for extension..., but perhaps, conceptually,... a demand for payment but on an unspecified future date'.[179]

---

[177] See Kronfol, JBL 1984, pp. 13, 18, van Orden Gnichtel, BLJ 1983, pp. 357-359, Ben Slimane, DPCI 1986, p. 288, and IFLR September 1986, p. 28. The texts of counter-guarantees in favour of Saudi Arabian banks have recently been adapted to provide explicitly for these situations.

[178] Ben Slimane, DPCI 1986, p. 289, and IFLR September 1986 p. 28. See also *OG Austria, 18 December 1987*, IBL November 1988, p. 92.

[179] Van Orden Gnichtel, BLJ 1983, p. 358.

Other Aspects of the Bank Guarantee 245

The true difficulty appears to be that it is one thing to conceive mentally of a legal category of requests which are proper demands for payment to be effected at a future date, but it is quite a different matter to determine whether a particular request containing phrases like 'hold for value' should indeed be subsumed under this abstract, legal category of deferred payment requests.[180] As mentioned in no. 12-46, the objectives of the request may vary and are most likely to be diffuse. Moreover, the actual benefits of the request being granted become apparent only later on and are shaped by future, often uncertain, developments. These aspects render a general legal classification either impossible or futile. As far as the practical consequences are concerned it is submitted that, as a point of departure, 'hold for value' requests ought to be treated in much the same way as 'extend or pay' requests. For one thing is certain: the beneficiary does not seek payment at the time but wishes to avoid the lapse of the guarantee. It is, however, possible that the request should be construed as a proper demand for payment to be effected on an unspecified future date, for example if the request reads 'pay *and* hold for value'. The effect of such a request would then be that the bank's obligation to effect actual payment is deferred rather than that the validity period of the guarantee is extended.

Implications

12-48 The following observations are primarily meant for situations where 'hold for value' requests are not contractually provided for. Moreover, as 'hold for value' requests cover an amorphous range of individual instances, the particular circumstances of the case and the specific wording of the request are, as always, decisive.

If the request is lodged within the current period of validity, the beneficiary and/or issuing bank could make a valid call for cash payment after the current expiry date.[181] Of course, when a demand for cash payment is made, all conditions such as, for example, the submission of a statement of default if required, must be met. Should the request be construed as a proper demand for payment but on a future date, all conditions must of course be complied with at the time of the 'hold for value' request.[182]

---

[180] In the case of *OG Austria, 18 December 1987*, IBL November 1988, p. 92, the beneficiary lodged a request which could only be described as a 'pay, but not yet, or extend, but pay if no timely extension is granted' request. The Austrian Supreme Court referred to this request as an 'extend or pay' request. However, it also seemed to observe that, in contrast to precautionary calls resulting in extension, this particular request did not cause the guarantee to be extended; it created a deferred payment obligation, the demand for payment having been made and requiring no further act from the beneficiary.

[181] *OG Austria, 18 December 1987*, IBL November 1988, p. 92. See also No. 12-41.

[182] Cf. Ben Slimane, DPCI 1986, p. 289, and IFLR September 1986, p. 28.

A recurrent problem is that the beneficiary rarely indicates a particular period for which the freeze is requested. This, in effect, would result in an extension for an indefinite length of time. In their reply, banks, therefore, regularly state a fixed period, usually corresponding to the customary period of extension following 'extend or pay' requests. It is debatable whether the beneficiary is bound by this restriction, unless explicitly agreed to. The question is important, since if the beneficiary were bound, he would have to take action in some way or another within that period, otherwise the guarantee would lapse. This is different if the request is construed as a proper demand for payment but on an unspecified future date. At some point in time the beneficiary should then either request actual payment or release the amount.

As the 'hold for value' request does not entail a cash payment by the bank, it would appear that the bank cannot demand immediate reimbursement or debit the current account of its customer,[183] unless the request should be treated as a proper demand for payment on a future date.[184]

12.4.5 Enforceability of expiry dates

General trend towards enforceability

12-49 One of the most pivotal features of independent guarantees and standbys is the rule that expiry dates are enforceable: the beneficiary of a guarantee or counter-guarantee no longer has any right to payment if the demand for payment has not been made on or before the expiry date. This has always been a well established and undoubted rule in countries with a mature system of law in relation to independent guarantees and standbys and it is also the rule under the URDG, ISP98 and Uncitral Convention. Such a clear rule provides certainty and is of particular importance for the account party as he is liberated from the severe risks associated with first demand guarantees as from the expiry date. However, ever since the emergence of this type of security in the mid-1960s much has been said and written in both the banking community and legal writing about the fact (or, should one say, assumed fact) that in many countries and regions, notably the Middle-East and North Africa, expiry dates are (deemed to be) *un*enforceable, whilst in other countries the enforceability of expiry dates is (deemed to be) uncertain. As a result, counter-guarantees in favour of issuing banks in those countries invariably contained matching clauses to the effect that they remain in force (irrespective of the expiry date of the counter-guarantee) until discharge. This practice dramatically increases the risk for the account party as it is well known that it is often very difficult to obtain formal discharge from either the ultimate beneficiary of the

---

[183] See *Paris, 21 January 1987*, D. 1987 Somm. p. 176.

[184] Cf. Ben Slimane, DPCI 1986, pp. 289, 290.

primary guarantee or from the issuing bank, even a long time after the completion of the secured contract.

Based on documentation from local banks and/or local lawyers available at the time, the 2nd edition of this study in 1996 listed four countries in which expiry dates were deemed to be unenforceable: Jordan, Lebanon, Syria and Thailand, and six countries in which the enforceability of expiry dates was uncertain: Brazil, India, Malaysia, Pakistan, Sri Lanka and Sudan. However, more recent documentation shows a clear and general trend towards respecting the enforceability of expiry dates and this also pertains to the above-mentioned countries, with the possible exception of Syria (see no. 12-51).[185] Whether this has in fact always been the true position in respect of all countries concerned or whether this development represents a true change of law is a question which can probably never be answered with any degree of accuracy.[186]

Three factors may account for the (true or supposed) unenforceability of expiry dates or uncertainty in this respect which has prevailed, at least for some period of time, in certain jurisdictions. Probably the most important reason is that in countries with an immature system of law on this particular subject no or insufficient distinction is or has been made between the traditional accessory (or secondary) guarantee and the independent guarantee (see further no. 12-50). Another factor is that government agencies in a great number of countries often require guarantees without an expiry date or guarantees which provide that they remain in force until discharge.[187] Such requirements from government agencies may well have led to the general but (probably) erroneous supposition that in respect of guarantees which do contain an expiry date without further qualifications, such an expiry date is unenforceable. A third, rather prosaic reason could be that foreign issuing banks may have a great deal of self interest in the unenforceability of expiry dates or the uncertainty in this respect as it enables them, on the strength of matching clauses in the counter-guarantee in their favour, to continue to claim charges until discharge by the ultimate beneficiary. Such foreign banks would then have little interest in litigating the matter in local courts as long as they feel comfortable that they will be reimbursed by the instructing bank.

Finally, the international banking community has always and increasingly emphasised the utter importance of the enforceability of expiry dates and absolute clarity in

---

[185] The representations in Chapter 12.4.5. are, for the sake of reliability, exclusively derived from documentation of local banks, local bankers' associations and/or local lawyers. No representations are made in respect of countries on which no reliable documentation is available.

[186] It is also fair to note that there may well be a difference between what certain banks in some foreign countries represent as being local law and practices and what local law and practices having force of law actually amount to.

[187] See Chapter 8, No. 8-16.

this respect and this has no doubt greatly contributed to the general trend towards respecting expiry dates.

Assimilation to accessory guarantees. Statute of Limitation

12-50 In several countries there has been a lack of clear distinction between the independent guarantee and the traditional accessory guarantee, i.e. suretyship. This has had consequences for the significance of expiry dates in that the period during which a valid demand for payment could be lodged was not determined by the expiry date but by the statutory provisions on limitation of actions. Now, there is however a distinct tendency towards recognising the differences between the two types of security which has had an impact on the enforceability of expiry dates. In three countries this development is well documented.

According to a 1976 decision of the Turkish Supreme Court, guarantees containing an expiry date could be called thereafter provided that the beneficiary proved that the default had occurred prior to the expiry date. It was stated that this rule followed from Turkish legislation on limitation of actions. The effect of the decision was that first demand guarantees were virtually turned into traditional accessory guarantees: if a claim was lodged after the expiry date and if the account party or guarantor challenged the claim, alleging that there had been no breach of contract or that the default had occurred after the expiry date, Turkish banks would not proceed to payment voluntarily. This forced the beneficiary to initiate proceedings whereby he had to prove that the default had occurred within the period of validity, which implied proof of default itself. These complications caused beneficiaries to observe expiry dates. Nonetheless, the Turkish banking community expressed their embarrassment about the non-enforceability of expiry dates in independent guarantees to banks abroad and dissatisfaction to government bodies. The Supreme Court decision has now been superseded by an amendment to Sec. 110 of the Law of Obligations, no. 2486, dated 8 July 1981, to the effect that expiry dates are valid and enforceable provided that the guarantee states that it becomes null and void after the expiry date. This change in attitude has no doubt been brought about by the increasing familiarity with the modern type of independent first demand guarantees and growing awareness that enforceability of expiry dates is vital for international commerce.

Until 1993 it was common knowledge that expiry dates in Algeria were not effective, which was said to result from certain provisions of the Civil Code and in particular art. 657 relating to accessory guarantees. This was changed by regulation no. 93-02 of 3 January 1993 and the instruction no. 05/94 of 2 February 1994 of the Central Bank of Algeria. The effect of this reform in the law was that expiry dates in independent guarantees are now enforceable.

India figured among the countries in which the enforceability of expiry dates was uncertain due to the fact that the period within which a demand for payment could be lodged was believed to be governed by the legislative provisions on limitations of actions. This supposition had been reinforced, rightly or wrongly, by the Indian Contract (Amendment) Act of 1996 which provided that contractual provisions which shorten the time limits as provided in the legislative provisions on limitation of actions, are void. After some period of confusion, a circular letter of 22 July 1998 from the Indian Banks' Association, which was published on the strength of legal opinions from eminent Indian jurists, has clarified the true position: guarantees must be called on or prior to the expiry date in order to be valid and the fact that the expired guarantee document had not been returned by the beneficiary would not alter the legal position of the bank, even after the 1996 amendment to Section 28 of the Indian Contract Act. It was made clear that the 1996 amendment did not have the effect of conferring a right to the beneficiary which had not materialised, which is the case in the event that no demand for payment has been made on or before the contractual expiry date. Clearly, the insertion of an expiry date is not the same as a provision shortening the legislative periods for limitation of actions.

The growing awareness of the differences between independent and accessory guarantees and the correct understanding of the meaning of statutory provisions on limitation of actions in Turkey, Algeria and India have no doubt been a model for developments in other countries. For example, while countries such as Brazil, Malaysia, Pakistan, Sri Lanka and Sudan were , in addition to India, listed in the 2nd edition of this study in 1996 as jurisdictions in which the enforceability of expiry dates was uncertain due to the assimilation to accessory guarantees, is this no longer the case in these countries.

Enforceability of expiry date uncertain. Syria

12-51 Although, as mentioned in no. 12-49, there is a general and clear trend towards respecting the enforceability of expiry dates and although in respect of a vast number of countries the enforceability is, at present, beyond any doubt (see. no. 12-52/53), the possibility that this might still be different in some countries cannot be ruled out entirely.

One of those countries (if there are any others) is Syria. According to Resolution no. 4407 dated 21 March 1973 issued by the Board of Directors of the Commercial Bank of Syria, which is the only bank in Syria with the power to issue guarantees, expiry dates in respect of performance guarantees were not enforceable and such guarantees could not be cancelled until the beneficiary had returned the original guarantee document.[188] Although the official texts of performance guarantees had been changed pursuant to a Circular Letter of 19 January 1988, to the effect that the demand for payment has to be made on or before the expiry date and that automatically thereafter the bank's obligation ceases without the need for warning or any other procedure, and although the standard text of counter-guarantees in favour of the Commercial Bank of

---

[188] Expiry dates in tender guarantees have always been considered valid.

Syria had also been adapted in that Circular Letter,[189] uncertainty continued to prevail due to confusing and sometimes conflicting documentation from the Commercial Bank of Syria in the past. Clarity appears to have emerged from a Circular Letter of 30 July 1999 and 25 September 1999 from the Board of Directors of the Commercial Bank of Syria, stating that performance guarantees will be cancelled after their expiry date if there has been no request for payment within their validity period even though the original document has not been returned. If any doubt still exists in respect of the enforceability of expiry dates and particularly of those in counter-guarantees in favour of the Commercial Bank of Syria, it is because of some phrases in the official text thereof which may be open to diverging interpretations. In the relevant part, the official text provides for an undertaking by the instructing bank to the Commercial Bank of Syria 'to pay on simple demand within the validity period *of the letter of guarantee, regardless of the date when such demand reaches you*' (i.e. the Commercial Bank of Syria) [italics added]. According to some representatives of the Western banking community the phrase in italics shows that, at least in respect of the counter-guarantee, expiry dates are not enforceable. It is more likely, however, that the provision, read as a whole, either means that, if the term '*letter of guarantee*' relates to the primary guarantee issued by the Commercial Bank of Syria, it merely allows that bank a certain undefined mailing period for lodging a claim under the counter-guarantee provided that the primary guarantee has been called on or before its expiry date, or that, should the term '*letter of guarantee*' relate to the counter-guarantee, the date of despatch of the demand by the Commercial Bank of Syria (as opposed to the date of receipt by the instructing bank) determines its timeliness.[190]

Expiry date enforceable

12-52/53 Whatever may have been the position in the past, at present the enforceability of expiry dates of guarantees and counter-guarantees is beyond any doubt in a great number of countries. Apart from European countries, the United States, Canada, Japan

---

[189] The official standard texts of 1988 are still in force.

[190] Based on correspondence after 1999 between the Commercial Bank of Syria and ABN AMRO and ING Bank, the first alternative is most probably the correct one. In this context it should be noted that banks, when giving instructions to the Commercial Bank of Syria, usually do not spell out the terms of the counter-guarantee, but merely refer to the standard text as contained in the Circular Letter of 19 January 1988, thus also leaving out any specification of an expiry date of the counter-guarantee, or state that the primary guarantee must have been called within its stated validity period and that any claim under the counter-guarantee must have been received by the instructing bank '*soonest*' or '*shortly*' thereafter, whether or not with the addition '*without fixing any mailing period*'.

and Australia, this also holds true for countries such as Algeria,[191] Armenia, Bahrain (art. 335 Commercial Code), Bangladesh, Brazil,[192] Burma, Bolivia, Bulgaria, Costa Rica, Egypt, Ethiopia, Ghana, India,[193] Indonesia, Iran, Iraq (art. 291 Commercial Code), Jordan,[194] Kazakhstan, Kuwait (art. 386 Commercial Code), Lebanon,[195] Libya, Malaysia,[196] Morocco, Mexico, Nigeria, Oman, Pakistan,[197] Peru, Philippines, Qatar, Saudi Arabia, Sri Lanka,[198] Sudan,[199] Thailand,[200] Turkey,[201] United Arab Emirates, Yemen (art. 1500 Civil Code), the member states of the Uncitral Convention (at present: Belarus, Ecuador, El Salvador, Kuwait, Panama and Tunisia) and the 15 OHADA countries in West Africa (art. 34(3) and 38 Uniform Act on Securities).[202, 203] Guarantees issued in Bangladesh, Greece, India, Malaysia and Indonesia are sometimes subject to a dual system for the validity period: the expiry date and the last date for calling, the latter being the effective date. In the Far East and in several Latin American countries guarantees and counter-guarantees are regularly issued in the form of standby letters of credit and made subject to the UCP or ISP98 so that the enforceability of expiry dates has never been in doubt.

Since expiry dates in guarantees governed by the laws of the above-mentioned countries are valid and enforceable, there is no sound reason why counter-guarantees relating to these guarantees should have a clause to the effect that they remain in force until discharge. Nonetheless, a number of banks in some of those countries still circulate sample texts of counter-guarantees containing such a clause. Instructing banks should object to this and it is advisable that they select the local, issuing bank with care.

---

[191] See No. 12-50.

[192] See Nos. 12-49 and 12-50.

[193] See No. 12-50.

[194] See Nos. 12-49 and 12-50.

[195] See Nos. 12-49 and 12-50.

[196] See Nos. 12-49 and 12-50.

[197] See Nos. 12-49 and 12-50.

[198] See Nos. 12-49 and 12-50.

[199] See Nos. 12-49 and 12-50.

[200] See Nos. 12-49 and 12-50.

[201] See No. 12-50.

[202] See Chapter 2, No. 2-17 for the OHADA countries.

[203] This list is not exhaustive. In particular, it is not suggested that uncertainty exists in respect of countries not mentioned, although such possibility might not be ruled out entirely.

It should be borne in mind that the enforceability of expiry dates does not, of course, mean that guarantees and counter-guarantees necessarily terminate upon the original expiry date. 'Extend or pay' or 'hold for value' requests are regular practice, while guarantees and especially counter-guarantees often provide explicitly for prolongation on demand. The practical significance of enforceability is that requests for extension must be made within the then existing period of validity. It may, however, also happen that the counter-guarantee explicitly states that it is automatically extended when the primary guarantee is extended. Moreover, it is not uncommon that guarantees in favour of government agencies do not contain an expiry date or that they explicitly state that they remain in force until discharge.[204] In that event, the counter-guarantee will have matching clauses.

12.4.6 (Non-)Return of the guarantee document. (No) statement of discharge

Return of the guarantee document. Statement of discharge. Legal significance

12-54 International practice attributes great significance to the return of the guarantee document. It is ordinarily viewed as a declaration by the beneficiary that claims for compensation for breach of contract have not materialised and that he, therefore, relinquishes any rights under the guarantee, cf. art. 23 URDG.[205] A written statement of discharge from the beneficiary has, of course, the same effect, cf. art. 23 URDG, Rule 7.01 ISP98 and art. 11(1)(a) Uncitral Convention.

The return of the document or a statement of discharge is of special importance when the guarantee does not contain an expiry date. In that event, the retrieval of the document or a statement of discharge constitutes virtually the only means by which guarantor and account party can be certain that the guarantee will not be called.
The above observations equally apply to counter-guarantees.

Return by mistake. Avoidance of payment

12-55 In *OLG Hamburg, 10 October 1985*, the Court of Appeal held that if the guarantee document has been returned by mistake, the true will and intention of the beneficiary

---

[204] See also Chapter 8.6, No. 8-16.

[205] Rule 7.01 ISP98 provides that the beneficiary's consent to cancellation may be evidenced in writing (such as a statement of dicharge) or by an action such as the return of the original standby in a manner which implies that the beneficiary consents to cancellation. See further Von Westphalen, pp. 124-125, who takes a view which is more favourable to the beneficiary: there must be consent between beneficiary and bank as regards the termination of the guarantee, while the return of the instrument is an indication thereof. See also Canaris, No. 1161.

is decisive, provided that that true will was evident to the guarantor.[206] In the case at issue the court was satisfied that the beneficiary had acted by mistake when he returned not only the repayment guarantee but also the performance guarantee and that this mistake must have been plain to the guarantor and account party. This finding was based on evidence that the account party – a building firm – and guarantor had only asked for the return of the repayment guarantee, not for the performance guarantee, knowing that there were ongoing differences of opinion concerning the completion and that the contract had in fact not been completed.

The above case, involving a true and manifest error on the part of the beneficiary, could be described as an exceptional one. Beneficiaries, particularly in a crossborder business context, are very much aware of the significance of the return of the document. They are not in the habit of making mistakes. It would, therefore, take an unusual case where the beneficiary would be able to establish that the return of the document with the implications as described in no. 12-54 did not reflect his true will and intention. It would take an even more unusual case where it could be said that the guarantor and account party could not properly rely on the return of the document, precisely because, ordinarily, they need not reckon with the possibility of mistakes. Such an unusual case occurred in *HR, 15 January 1999*. The Dutch Supreme Court ruled that the return of the guarantee document did not, in this particular case, terminate the guarantee because payment by the account party to the beneficiary was subsequently avoided because of fraudulent preference and the bank knew that this was likely to happen. Moreover, this case involved a domestic, traditional suretyship while the beneficiary was a private individual.[207]

Non-return of the guarantee document. Reasons

12-56 Irrespective of its legal significance, several reasons and motives could account for the beneficiary's decision not to return the guarantee document. The most obvious reason is that the beneficiary is of the opinion that the contract has not yet been completed. In that situation he is likely to also ask for an extension. There could also be administrative reasons or bureaucratic conditions and slackness which account for the non-return of the document or the document may have been lost. The beneficiary may also refuse to release the document as a means of putting pressure on the account party, for example, to carry out works in excess of the agreed works or to exact discounts on further contracts or cash payments. Above all, one should appreciate that there is often little incentive for the beneficiary to return the document upon completion or expiry.

---

[206] NJW 1986, p. 1691.

[207] NJ 1999, 241. In order to avert the risk as a result of subsequent avoidance, both accessory and independent guarantees sometimes contain a reinstatement clause.

As far as counter-guarantees are concerned, the second issuing bank will ordinarily not release the counter-guarantee document or issue a statement of discharge, if it has not itself been discharged by the beneficiary of the primary guarantee. Another motive might be the desire to continue to charge commission.

Non-return of the guarantee document. Legal significance

12-57 The guarantee document is neither a commercial paper nor a negotiable instrument. The retention of the document in itself is, therefore, of no legal significance. Thus, if the guarantee or counter-guarantee has expired in accordance with its own terms, either on the original or on the amended expiry date, the physical possession of the document does not confer any rights upon the beneficiary and the (counter-)guarantee can no longer be validly called. This rule is clearly confirmed in art. 24 URDG, Rule 9.05 ISP98 and art. 11(2) Uncitral Convention.[208] Many guarantees contain specific provisions to this effect.[209]

Counter-guarantees in support of primary guarantees without an expiry date will stipulate that they remain in force until discharge. The legal consequence of not returning the counter-guarantee document or the refusal to give discharge is clearly that the counter-guarantee continues to have full force and effect.

No statement of discharge in respect of the counter-guarantee. Primary guarantee expired

12-58 Real problems are occasioned by counter-guarantees which state that they remain in force until discharge, while the primary guarantee has expired without discharge having been given. Does such a clause in the counter-guarantee permit the issuing bank to make a valid call on the counter-guarantee, although it has (allegedly) honoured a claim by the beneficiary made after the expiry date of the primary guarantee? One thing is certain: the instructing bank cannot refuse payment on the grounds that the call on the counter-guarantee has not been made within its period of validity. Apart from this, the clue to answering this question lies in the principle of independence between counter-guarantee and primary guarantee on the one hand, and the exception to this principle on the other hand. Because of the principle of independence, noncompliance with the terms of the primary guarantee, c.q. the lack of proper examination by the issuing bank in this respect is, in principle, not a relevant factor as far as the counter-guarantee is concerned. This principle is, however, subject to an exception,

---

[208] See also Schütze, WM 1982, p. 1399, Kleiner, No. 25.03. See further von Westphalen, p. 123. See for the Middle East: Mohamed Abdel Khalek Omar, Arab Law Quarterly, 1989, p. 111

[209] See Chapter 8.6, No. 8-15.

namely if there is clear evidence that the primary guarantee has been called after its expiry date.[210]

The practical attitude of banks is, depending on the position they are in, as might be expected. Regardless of whether it has honoured claims by the beneficiary made after the expiry date of the guarantee, the second issuing bank may feel that it is entitled to reimbursement from the instructing bank. As regards the issuing bank, the instructing bank would prefer to remain non-committal as long as possible. Its attitude is affected significantly by the firmness and status of the issuing bank and the kind of response from the account party. The instructing bank is likely to convey to the account party that the terms and conditions of the counter-guarantee have been fulfilled and that it must, therefore, reimburse the issuing bank and leave the initiative with the account party to make a reasonable case against the issuing bank. If he provides convincing indications that the primary guarantee has been called after its expiry date, the instructing bank is likely to cooperate, seek clarification from the issuing bank and act as it feels appropriate in the light of the issuing bank's response.[211]

Initiatives by the account party and instructing bank if the (counter-)guarantee document has not been returned or if no discharge has been given

12-59 When the account party is of the opinion that the secured transaction has been completed, he is likely to develop initiatives aimed at the retrieval of the (counter-)guarantee document or a statement of discharge. His bank will often join in these efforts, not only with a view to protecting the interests of its customer but also because it has an interest of its own to obtain discharge. This course of action is initiated especially where the guarantee contains no expiry date or where the counter-guarantee remains in force until discharge while the primary guarantee has expired.

Attempts to have the documents returned or to obtain a statement of discharge after the (alleged) completion of the principal contract and/or after the expiry date are often fraught with great difficulties.[212] In many cases the beneficiary and/or issuing bank, as the case may be, will not respond or will refuse to comply with the request and they

---

[210] See Chapter 11.2, No. 11-13.

[211] See further No. 12-59 and Chapter 11.3, No. 11-23.

[212] In the case of *Trib. com. Paris, 6 March 1987*, D. 1988 Somm. p. 249, all parties to the principal contract had signed a formal instrument in settlement of all outstanding accounts. Eighteen months later the Egyptian beneficiary had still failed to return the guarantee document or to issue a statement of discharge. The court ruled that the instructing bank was entitled to continue to charge commission to the account party, but the beneficiary was ordered to indemnify the account party for this loss. It appears that financial inducements might sometimes also induce the return of the document.

may or may not have good reasons for such a refusal. The failure to recover the documents or to obtain a statement of discharge does not necessarily mean that all efforts have been in vain. In their communications, the account party and instructing bank will also employ language which conveys in plain or guarded terms that they consider the guarantee and/or counter-guarantee to be terminated, regardless of whether this stance is legally correct. Depending on the particular circumstances of the case and the sway of the initiatives, these efforts may well cause the beneficiary to be more cautious and the second, issuing bank to display greater reserve in respect of honouring demands for payment by the beneficiary, particularly when made after the expiry date of the primary guarantee. Moreover, experience shows that communications to the effect that the (counter-)guarantee is considered to be cancelled, if repeated a number of times, are more often than not followed by an everlasting silence on the part of the beneficiary and/or issuing bank, without there ever being a demand for payment.

12.4.7 Release of security furnished by the account party, unblocking of the credit facility, release of the duty to pay commission. Discharge of the account party's liability

Introduction

12-60 One would expect that, as a matter of principle, the right of the bank to earmark, retain or request further collateral as security for repayment by the account party, the right to block the account party's credit facility as well as the right to claim charges lapses upon the expiry date of the (counter-)guarantee. The difficulty is, however, that some banks may take the position, rightly or wrongly,[213] that in certain countries expiry dates are not enforceable or that the legal position is unsettled. It is also possible that the (counter-)guarantee does not contain an effective expiry date. This raises the question of whether and in what circumstances the bank is entitled to hang on to the security to cover the risk of an effective call after the expiry date, if any, as long as this risk could conceivably materialise.[214] In one respect near certainty does exist: no valid call can be made once the guarantee document has been returned or once a statement of discharge from the beneficiary has been issued.[215] This reduces the issue to the question of whether and in what circumstances a case for release of the security, the unblocking of the credit line and the termination of the duty to pay a commission could

---

[213] See Chapter 12.4.5, Nos. 49-52/53.

[214] Should this risk indeed materialise, then the account party must reimburse the bank, see Chapter 10.10.

[215] See Chapter 12.4.6.

be made prior to or irrespective of the return of the guarantee document or a statement of discharge.

The issue is of great importance and the bank and account party are likely to have conflicting interests in this respect. For the bank it is of course important to retain the security and/or to block the credit facilities for an amount equal to the maximum amount of the guarantee as long as the beneficiary of the (counter-)guarantee can validly demand payment or procure payment in any other way, for example by seizing the bank's assets in a foreign jurisdiction. By contrast, once the (counter-)guarantee has expired or once the obligations under the underlying contract have been performed, the account party has a legitimate interest in the release of the security and/or the unblocking of his credit facility. A bank's refusal in this respect is likely to have an adverse impact on the account party's business since he may be faced with great difficulties in financing his current and future activities. This is particularly the case if the account party has to procure a large number of guarantees. As a matter of fact, many big companies consider the furnishing of security and/or the blocking of their credit lines a more disconcerting draw-back of demand guarantees than the risk of an actual call. As far as bank charges are concerned, a duty to continue to pay charges is obviously also most burdensome for the account party.

Direct guarantees

12-61 The text of no. 12-61 is based on the premise that expiry dates are enforceable under the applicable law. Direct guarantees are governed by the law of the country where the issuing bank has its place of business. If the guarantee does not contain an (effective) expiry date, the issue should be approached in the same way as discussed in no. 12-64.

In a case concerning a direct guarantee, *OLG Hamburg, 4 November 1977*, the bank was denied the right to transfer the balance of a current account to a blocked account after the expiry date, since there was no plausible likelihood that the beneficiary would be able to procure payment.[216] In order to arrive at that finding, the court considered it unlikely that an Egyptian court, in the beneficiary's country, would accept jurisdiction or, if so, that it would apply any other law than German law or that it would ignore the

---

[216] RIW 1978, p. 615. See also *Gur Corporation v. Trust Bank of Africa Ltd*, IBL July 1986, p. 24. Although the demand for payment by the beneficiary, the Department of Public Works of Ciskei, had been rejected by the bank, it refused to release the deposit of the account party in view of imminent litigation. The court ordered the release of the deposit, since the demand was not accompanied by the required certificate of a registered quantity surveyor and no valid demand had been made within the operative period of the guarantee. The counterclaim by the beneficiary against the bank in third-party proceedings could not be adjudicated for reasons of public policy.

expiry date for other reasons. Even if the Egyptian court were to give judgment against the German bank, such a judgment, the court observed, could neither be enforced in Germany nor in Egypt since the bank had no assets in that country. In addition, the court referred to the fact that there was no indication of any intention on the part of the beneficiary to call the guarantee. Interestingly, the court rejected the argument that the non-return of the guarantee document was evidence of such an intention.

In short, the security is to be released and the credit facility should be unblocked after the expiry date.[217] This might only be different if it is shown that, as the Court of Appeal put it, there is a real likelihood, as opposed to a theoretical possibility, of the beneficiary being able to exact payment, to be adjudged by the criteria laid down by the court. The duty to pay commission to the bank certainly terminates on the expiry date of the guarantee.[218]

Indirect guarantees

12-62 German authors take the view that, in the case of indirect guarantees, the instructing bank is entitled to continue to claim charges until the guarantee document has been returned or until the foreign bank has issued a statement of discharge.[219] Their main argument is that certain countries do not recognise the enforceability of expiry dates. That argument has, however, been superseded by more recent developments, see Chapter 12.4.5. The proposition is, therefore, too sweeping. It would appear that the guiding principles as laid down by *OLG Hamburg, 4 November 1977,* are also relevant for indirect guarantees. The actual outcome of these guidelines may, however, be different. The major difference between direct and indirect guarantees is that in the latter situation the liability of the instructing bank and that of the account party, and thereby the issue of release or prolongation of the security, is to be determined by having regard to the relevant provisions of the counter-guarantee, which is governed, on account of an implied or explicit clause to this effect, by the law of the foreign issuing bank's country.

---

[217] Cf. Affaki, p. 46.

[218] Cf. von Westphalen, p. 377, Zahn/Ehrlich/Neumann, 9/90. If the guarantee is governed by foreign law, they express the view as mentioned in No. 12-62 with respect to indirect guarantees.

[219] Canaris, No. 1159, Dohm, No. 151, Schütze, WM 1982, p. 1402, Zahn/Ehrlich/Neumann, 9/89-90, Von Westphalen, pp. 378, 380 (unless the account party proves that expiry dates are enforceable).

Indirect guarantees. Counter-guarantee contains expiry date

12-63 If the counter-guarantee contains an expiry date without the clause that it remains in force until discharge, the contingent liability of the instructing bank ceases on that date, whether this is the original expiry date or the current expiry date in the case of an extension. That is the law of the countries covered in this study, the law in the countries which have been mentioned by way of example in nos. 12-52/53, and the rule under the URGD, ISP98 and the Uncitral Convention. It is true that the foreign beneficiary will be able to sue the issuing bank and that the issuing bank will be able to sue the instructing bank in their home country and that the local court will apply local law. The crucial point, however, is that the absence of a clause in the counter-guarantee as referred to above constitutes an all but certain indication that expiry dates are enforceable under local law, even apart from the general trend in this respect.[220] Accordingly, in the event of a call after the expiry date of the primary guarantee, judgment in favour of the beneficiary is highly unlikely. Similarly, in the event of a call after the expiry date of the counter-guarantee, judgment in favour of the issuing bank is equally unlikely. The account party has, therefore, a strong case when applying for the release of the security and/or the unblocking of the credit lines, once the counter-guarantee has ceased to be valid according to its terms. Indeed, *Paris, 23 June 1995* ruled in favour of the release of security.[221] This may only be different in wholly exceptional circumstances where there is a real likelihood that the foreign issuing bank both intends to call the counter-guarantee after its expiry date and is in a position to exact actual payment, for example where it can debit the instructing bank's account. The duty to pay charges to the instructing bank should certainly terminate upon the expiry of the counter-guarantee, while, in that event, the bank should also refuse to pay charges to the foreign issuing bank.

Indirect guarantees. Counter-guarantee valid until discharge. Release of security, unblocking of the credit facility

12-64 A quite different situation arises where the counter-guarantee stipulates that it remains in force until discharge. This might possibly be an indication, but not necessarily,[222] that the expiry date in the primary guarantee is not enforceable under local law. A more likely reason is that the primary guarantee does not contain an expiry date. In both situations there is a continuing risk of a call on the primary guarantee and then on the counter-guarantee and the instructing bank has, therefore, a legitimate interest

---

[220] See Chapter 12.4.5, No. 12-49.

[221] JCP 1995 Éd. E ll, No. 735.

[222] See Chapter 12.4.5, No. 12-49 and Nos. 12-51/52/53.

in retaining the security and/or blocking the credit facility until discharge by the issuing bank. On the other hand, the account party has a legitimate interest in avoiding situations whereby the collateral could be retained for an indefinite length of time. At this point, the only issue that needs clarification is the likelihood that an actual call will be made. One must bear in mind that in many cases the (counter-)guarantee document has never been returned or that a statement of discharge has never been given, but neither has a call ever been made.[223] The observations in this respect by the *OLG Hamburg*, cited in no. 12-61, deserve close attention. Applied to a counter-guarantee without an (effective) expiry date, these observations would lead to the proposition that an application for the release of the security and/or the unblocking of the credit line before discharge by the issuing bank stands a fair chance of success if the account party establishes beyond reasonable doubt that a call on the primary guarantee and counter-guarantee is merely a theoretical possibility. Factors which should be taken into account include the absence of complaints by the beneficiary, reticence on the part of the beneficiary and issuing bank, evidence of completion by the account party of his obligations under the secured contract and passage of time.

Clarifying case law concerning the release of security and/or the unblocking of the credit facilities in the case of an indirect guarantee which remains in force until discharge, does not exist.[224]

Indirect guarantees. Counter-guarantee valid until discharge. Release of the duty to pay commission

12-65 It would appear that the bank's interest in retaining the security and/or in blocking the credit lines until discharge by the issuing bank is more powerful than its interest in the continuation of the right to commission. The requirements for a release from that duty should, therefore, be less stringent. Moreover, the interests of both parties can be accommodated by means of a release under reserve: the instructing bank's right to claim charges terminates if a call on the counter-guarantee is not likely to occur anymore, but it revives in the event that the issuing bank still validly calls the counter-guarantee. At present, banks regularly agree to such a release under reserve. It could even be argued that a refusal must be considered unreasonable, but this depends on the particular situation.[225] In *Trib. com. Paris, 6 March 1987*, the court, however, ruled that the

---

[223] See Chapter 12.4.6, No. 12-59.

[224] But see *Cass., 25 January 2000*, Banque & Droit 2000, p. 44, as an example of a case where the account party's claim against the instructing bank for the release of the security was dismissed.

[225] Cf. Canaris, No. 1159. See also von Westphalen, p. 384, Zahn/Ehrlich/Neumann, 9/90-91.

instructing bank was entitled to claim charges until a release by the issuing bank.[226]

The foregoing remarks do not apply to charges in respect of the counter-guarantee. If the counter-guarantee states that it remains in force until discharge, the account party continues to be obliged to reimburse his bank for the commission which that bank has to pay to the foreign issuing bank. The reason is that the instructing bank cannot be expected to resist the issuing bank's demand for payment of charges. An example of this rule is provided in *Trib. com. Toulouse, 26 September 1990*.[227]

In relation to counter-guarantees which remain in force until discharge, it has often been suggested that some banks in certain regions tend to delay or withhold discharge because of laxness or just for the sake of continuing to charge commission, even in situations in which a valid call on the primary guarantee can no longer be made or where the account party has fully performed his obligations without complaints by the beneficiary. This would be a most regrettable practice which would call for initiatives as described in no. 12-59. The effect of such efforts is often that, while the foreign bank may still withhold discharge, it does not claim charges any more either.

Discharge of account party's liability

12-66 In the case of a direct guarantee, the bank is usually prepared to discharge the account party from liability under his counter-guarantee after the expiry date of the guarantee. In the case of the account party's counter-guarantee in the context of an indirect guarantee, the instructing bank is often willing to do the same after the expiry date of the counter-guarantee if the foreign bank is considered to be reliable. If there are any doubts in this respect, the instructing bank will normally first seek to obtain a formal statement of discharge from the issuing bank while emphasising that the counter-guarantee has expired according to its terms. Should the issuing bank fail to respond and desist from claiming charges, then most banks are prepared to give discharge to the account party on a case by case basis or to give discharge under reserve of rights. Banks are ordinarily not prepared to issue a formal statement of discharge to the account party if the guarantee or counter-guarantee does not contain an (effective) expiry date, unless they themselves have been released from liability. In exceptional circumstances, for example where there is merely a theoretical possibility of a call on the primary guarantee or counter-guarantee, banks may be willing to give discharge under reserve of rights.

---

[226] D. 1988 Somm. p. 249, see No. 12-59.

[227] D. 1993 Somm. p. 97. This decision was particularly awkward for the account party, since the beneficiary of the indirect guarantee was obliged under the terms of the underlying transaction to return the primary guarantee upon completion of the contract. This aspect was, however, rightly disregarded by the court on account of the principle of independence.

12.5 ASSIGNMENT. PLEDGE

12.5.1 Meaning and significance of assignment

12-67 The terms assignment and transfer are often used indiscriminately. Assignment of the guarantee is here taken to mean assignment of the right to the proceeds of the guarantee as opposed to a transfer of the guarantee itself to a new beneficiary, which is examined in Chapter 12.6.

The practical significance of assignment lies in the fact that it is a means of furnishing security for credit facilities to the beneficiary. This explains why the rights of the guarantee are often assigned to a bank. Thus, an exporter (beneficiary of a payment guarantee) or an importer (beneficiary of a performance guarantee) may assign the rights pursuant to the guarantee to his bank with a view to obtaining credit.

12.5.2 Contractual assignment

12-68 It is beyond doubt that the right to the proceeds of a guarantee is capable of being assigned. This is effected by means of a contract between beneficiary/assignor and a third party/assignee in accordance with the formalities as prescribed by the law that governs the assignment. Under most laws assignment as such does not require the consent of the bank as the debtor, but it only takes effect against the bank upon giving notice. As from that moment the bank can no longer validly make payment to the beneficiary. Nor does assignment require consent from the contracting partner/account party.

Contractual assignment of the proceeds is permissible, with or without a clause to this effect in the guarantee.[228] This follows from the general rule of law that contractual rights are capable of being assigned. The fact that assignment does not adversely affect the position of the account party and bank might be found a more persuasive argument. The guarantee could, however, stipulate that the rights of the guarantee cannot be assigned.[229]

Assignment could be confined to the rights pursuant to the guarantee only or could extend to the rights under the secured contract as well.[230] Especially when assignment is a means of providing security, assignment of the rights under the secured contract as well will ordinarily be confined to situations whereby the beneficiary/creditor in the

---

[228] See explicitly *Trib. com. Paris, 22 February 1989*, D. 1990 Somm. p. 204, and implicitly the case law and legal writing referred to in this Chapter 12.5.

[229] See Chapter 8.12.

[230] But see Blomkwist, WPNR 1986, p. 555, and Pabbruwe, WPNR 1983, p. 429, who discern certain difficulties in the event of assignment of the guarantee only.

principal contract is entitled to payment of moneys, as is, for example, an exporter, lessor or employer who has made advance payments to a construction firm/account party.

Art. 4(2) URDG makes it clear that assignment of the proceeds is not prohibited by the Rules, but it does not deal in a positive manner with the question whether of assignment is allowed and the effect thereof. This is left to the applicable law.[231] ISP98 also defers to the applicable law in respect of the permissibility of assignment of the proceeds of the standby. If so permitted, Rule 6.06-6.10 then provides some specific rules which apply unless the applicable law requires otherwise. Art. 10 Uncitral Convention does permit assignment of the proceeds in a positive manner.

12.5.3 Effect of contractual assignment. Position of assignee

General

12-69 Contractual assignment raises one particular issue of real significance, both from the legal and from the practical point of view: is the assignee of a first demand guarantee entitled to payment by merely calling the guarantee all by himself and by submitting a statement of default, if required, which has been drawn up by him instead of by the beneficiary/assignor? Or must the claim be accompanied by a request for payment from the beneficiary/assignor as the expression of his opinion that the account party is in default, and by a statement of default, if required, which originates from the beneficiary/assignor?

As the notion of assignment is confined to assignment of the proceeds of the guarantee, the answer must be that the cooperation of the beneficiary/assignor in the manner described above is, without question, indispensable. The explanation is that the right to payment under the guarantee does not arise unless and until the conditions of payment have been satisfied. Without a demand for payment from the beneficiary and without his statement of default, if required, these conditions are not complied with and consequently the right to payment has not arisen.

In addition, there are other arguments of a more substantive nature for an answer in the affirmative. The identity of the person who exercises rights under the guarantee is not a matter of mere formalities. When agreeing to furnish a first demand guarantee, the account party is prepared to accept a grave risk, but it is to some extent a defined and calculable risk. He expects or at least believes that the particular contracting partner he is dealing with, will not call the guarantee for frivolous reasons or for improper motives. When the beneficiary knows that there has been no breach of contract, the requirement to submit a statement of default will force him to commit a lie to writing

---

[231] See Goode, p. 53.

and there are many good reasons why the beneficiary should proceed with restraint.[232] Moreover, if the guarantee has been called, there is often still occasion for the account party to try to sort out difficulties and differences of opinion. The account party would be deprived of all these protective elements if the assignee were entitled to collect the benefits of the guarantee without endorsement by his contracting partner/assignor. It would also fundamentally alter the nature of the contract of guarantee, since it would for all practical purposes turn the guarantee into a negotiable instrument, which it is not. The risk that the guarantee will in fact be called would increase substantially and, moreover, for reasons which may not be related to the underlying contract between the account party and the beneficiary. The assignee, who has extended credit or has paid moneys in consideration of the assignment, is not likely to display the same degree of restraint as could be expected from the beneficiary.[233] It is also futile to argue that fraudulent calls can be prevented by stop-payment injunctions. The difficulty and small chance of securing such court orders in time, especially in the case of indirect guarantees, are well known.

In the case of guarantees requiring evidence of default by means of third-party documents, the increase of the risk of improper calls will, of course, be smaller. This is, however, insufficient reason to dispense with the requirement of cooperation by the beneficiary, because he may have good reasons to refuse to support the assignee's request for payment.

In conclusion, the assignee acquires no status of his own under the guarantee and his right to payment entirely depends on that of the beneficiary.[234] Therefore, the assignee may be entitled to lodge the request for payment and to receive payment, but the demand itself as well as the statement of default, if required, must originate from the beneficiary/assignor.[235] The same should apply to 'extend or pay' requests.[236] This might

---

[232] See Chapter 6, No. 6-4.

[233] Cf. the case of *Cass., 12 January 1993*, D. 1995 J. p. 24. The claim by the assignee/bank for payment had been rejected because of established fraud. Moreover, it was quite telling that the amount of the guarantee did not correspond with the amount which the account party might owe to the beneficiary pursuant to the underlying contract, but with the amount of the loan granted by the bank/assignee to the beneficiary. See also Paris, *23 September 1988*, D. 1989 Somm. p. 156, in No. 12-71 which relates to the same case.

[234] The same applies under the URDG, see Affaki, Nos. 87-89, Rule 6.07(b) ISP98 and art. 10 Uncitral Convention.

[235] Cf. Mattout, No. 226, Bartman, NJB 1987, p. 1089, Boll, p. 103, Blaurock, IPrax 1985, p. 204, Zahn/Ehrlich/Neumann, 9/136, Canaris, No. 1130, von Westphalen, pp. 136-140, Dohm, No. 186, Nielsen, WM 1999, p. 2019, Lienesch, pp. 97-98. See also Prüm, p. 105, Pabbruwe, WPNR 1983, pp. 429-432, and RMThemis 1994, p. 149. See No. 12-70 for case law.

[236] But see *Rb Haarlem, 12 January 1993*, NJ 1995, 53, discussed in No. 12-70.

be different in very special circumstances only, such as for example in the case of collusion between beneficiary/assignor and account party,[237] and, perhaps, in the case of guarantees requiring the submission of an arbitral or judicial decision.[238]

Case law

12-70 The case of *BGH, 12 March 1984 (II ZR 198/82)* involved a payment guarantee in connection with the lease of a plot of industrial land in Iran.[239] The guarantee stated that it could be called by X or by the assignee, Y. The guarantee also stated that a request for payment from X should be accompanied by a statement of default, but it did not mention whether this statement should emanate from X or Y, or from both of them. However, certain other statements could be made by either of them. The lease contract stated that it had been concluded by X in his capacity as attorney for Y, being the owner of the land, but this was not mentioned in the guarantee. Upon construction of the terms of the guarantee it was held that Y in his capacity as assignee was entitled not only to claim payment without the cooperation of X, the designated beneficiary, but also to submit his own statement of default. The situation where the guarantee does not contain provisions to this effect was left for future consideration.

This question had already been addressed in the lower courts, namely *LG Frankfurt a.M., 30 November 1977*.[240] The court decided that, with regard to the legitimate interests of the account party, the required statement of default could only be issued by the beneficiary/assignor. A similar decision was reached in *CA Amsterdam, 22 February 1991*, where the Court of Appeal ruled that the guarantee could be called by the assignee, but that the actual request for payment must emanate from the beneficiary/assignor.[241]

In the case of *BGH, 26 February 1987*, both the principal contract and the 'guarantee' had been assigned to the bank.[242] The beneficiary had been declared insolvent and had ceased to exist. The 'guarantee' in question was construed as a suretyship payable on first demand, as opposed to an independent guarantee payable on demand. The German Supreme Court laid down the general rule that the assignee of a first demand suretyship is indeed entitled to submit his own statement of default. This would only

---

[237] See for another example the case of *BGH, 26 February 1987*, NJW 1987, p. 2075, discussed in No. 12-71.

[238] Cf. *Rb Utrecht, 10 September 1997*, JOR 1998, 34, mentioned in No. 12-72.

[239] NJW 1984, p. 2030.

[240] WM 1978, p. 442.

[241] NJ 1992, 141.

[242] NJW 1987, p. 2075.

be otherwise in the event of stipulations to the contrary or special circumstances. In this case, no such special circumstances were apparent, the more so since the beneficiary/assignor had ceased to exist. In giving this judgment the Supreme Court heavily relied on the fact that the 'guarantee' was an accessory suretyship on first demand, not an independent first demand guarantee. As far as independent guarantees are concerned it did refer to the decision of *LG Frankfurt a.M., 30 November 1977*, and legal writing, but it did not take a position itself. In *OLG Köln, 30 October 1997*, the Court of Appeal also ruled that, in the case of a first demand suretyship, the assignee is entitled to submit his own statement of default and observed that in relation to first demand guarantees uncertainty exists in this respect.[243] Considering the great similarity between a first demand guarantee and a first demand suretyship,[244] it would appear that the legitimate interests of the account party are prejudiced to exactly the same degree. The Court of Appeal in the above-mentioned 1987 *BGH* case ruled that the statement of default must originate from the beneficiary/assignor of the first demand suretyship, but that the special circumstances of the case called for an exception. With respect, the latter approach is to be preferred.[245]

Rb Amsterdam, 7 April 1988, provides an example of the correct execution of the assignment by the beneficiary to his bank, apart from an innocuous flaw.[246] The assignment had been notified to the issuing bank. The beneficiary/assignor requested by letter the assignee/bank to call the guarantee and the letter contained the correct statement of default, i.e. a statement which originated from him, the beneficiary, as required by the guarantee. The subsequent demand for payment lodged by the assignee contained the phrase that 'in *our* (i.e. the assignee's) judgment' the account party had committed a breach of contract. The account party's complaint that this formulation was incorrect was rightly rejected. The court observed that the assignee evidently claimed payment on behalf of the beneficiary and on the basis of the statement of default formulated by the latter.[247]

---

[243] WM 1998, p. 707. The case of *BGH, 24 November 1998*, WM 1999, p. 72, involved a first demand guarantee which explicitly permitted the beneficiary to assign the guarantee in which case the assignee was entitled to call the guarantee and to submit his own statement of default. Again, the German Supreme Court declined to take a position as regards guarantees without such an explicit provision.

[244] See Chapter 4.5, Nos. 4-18/19.

[245] Cf. the critical comments in respect of the *BGH* decision by von Westphalen, pp. 136, 137, Zahn/Ehrlich/Neumann, 9/136 (with further references).

[246] KG 1988, 181. This decision was reversed by *CA Amsterdam, 19 January 1989*, KG 1990, 74, on other grounds.

[247] See also *Rb Arnhem, 20 October 1986*, KG 1986, 482. The beneficiary of a payment guarantee had assigned his rights pursuant to the underlying contract and guarantee to his bank.

In *Rb Haarlem, 12 January 1993*, the court expressed the view that the general rule that the assignee cannot call the guarantee without the beneficiary's cooperation does not apply to 'extend or pay' requests on the grounds that the assignee's interest in preventing the lapse of the guarantee independently of the beneficiary should prevail over the account party's interest concerning the identity of the person who exercises rights under the guarantee.[248] This view should be rejected, unless unusual circumstances compel otherwise. An assignee is entitled to the proceeds of the guarantee if the conditions of payment have been fulfilled, but he is ordinarily not entitled and he has no authority to request an amendment to the terms of the guarantee. Moreover, such requests constitute a proper demand for payment if the request is refused, as indeed occurred in this case.

12.5.4 Strengthening the position of the assignee; special provisions; irrevocable power of attorney?

12-71 Banks sometimes complain that their interests as a security assignee are impaired by the requirement regarding the cooperation of the beneficiary. It is doubtful whether this complaint has substance. Why should a beneficiary who takes the view that the account party has defaulted on his obligations, refuse to cooperate? It is true that the proceeds will not flow to the beneficiary, but to the bank. Such payments do, however, reduce his debit balance with the bank/assignee. It is no different when the beneficiary has been declared insolvent and when a receiver has been appointed, although there is a possibility of the receiver attempting to extract some advantage in exchange for his cooperation. Should the beneficiary have ceased to exist, any reasons to fear have been removed by the judgment of the Court of Appeal leading to the decision of *BGH, 26 February 1987*.[249]

Whether or not compelling reasons exist for the bank/assignee to strengthen its position, the safest way would be a provision in the guarantee which entitles the bank/assignee to call the guarantee and to submit the statement of default, if required, without the cooperation of the beneficiary. Such a provision allows, in fact, a complete transfer of the guarantee and there are good reasons why the guarantor and the account party in particular would refuse such a provision.[250] The same is true if the guarantee

---

The beneficiary called the guarantee. The account party's complaint that the guarantee could only be called by the assignee, but not by the beneficiary, was rightly dismissed.

[248] NJ 1995, 53. See also Pabbruwe, WPNR 1995, pp. 605-606.

[249] See No. 12-70.

[250] See No. 12-69.

would designate the bank which finances the creditor's business as the beneficiary of the guarantee, instead of the creditor himself.[251]

It has been suggested that the bank/assignee could strengthen its position by obtaining a general irrevocable power of attorney from the beneficiary to demand payment and to draw up and submit the statement of default, if required, on behalf of the latter.[252] It would appear, however, that this device is ineffective, since exercising the power of attorney still does not lead to the conditions of payment of the guarantee being fulfilled. Moreover, the arguments against the bank/assignee's right to demand payment independently of the beneficiary, mentioned in no. 12-69, remain the same. The actual decision to call the guarantee must be taken by the beneficiary and could not be left to the discretion of the bank/assignee. This proposition is affirmed by *Paris, 23 September 1988*. Immediately upon the issue of a first demand guarantee, which could be called between 1st and 15th May 1988, the beneficiary assigned his rights and delivered a letter in which he demanded payment and which was postdated 1 May 1988, to his bank/assignee. This course of conduct was condemned by the Court of Appeal.[253] Something similar happened in *Brenntag International Chemicals v. Norddeutsche Landesbank GZ*.[254]

It remains, of course, possible for the beneficiary specifically to instruct the assignee to call the guarantee on his behalf (mandate) and to give a power of attorney to this effect.[255]

12.5.5 Assignment by operation of law

12-72 By operation of law contractual assignment of rights pursuant to a contract comprises assignment of rights ancillary to that contract. For example, if a seller has obtained security for payment of the contract price by means of a suretyship, assignment of the right to payment entails by force of law assignment of the rights pursuant to the suretyship without the need for specific agreement to this effect. Assignment by operation of law is confined to ancillary rights, such as suretyship. This raises the question

---

[251] See Chapter 8.4.

[252] Pabbruwe, WPNR 1983, p. 432.

[253] D. 1989 Somm. p. 156 (quashed by *Cass., 6 November 1990*, D. 1991 Somm. p. 201 on other grounds). See also *Cass., 12 January 1993*, D. 1995 J. p. 24, mentioned in No. 12-69, which relates to the same case. See also Boll, p. 103.

[254] 70 F. Supp. 2d 399 (SDNY 8 November 1999). In this case the beneficiary discounted the standby with a lender and supplied that party with an undated statement of default which he authorised the lender to date when making a demand for payment. Such behaviour was condemned by the court.

[255] See Chapter 13.2, No. 13-5.

of whether or not the independent guarantee must be considered included in this category of ancillary rights for the purpose of assignment by law. Several authors are of the opinion that an independent guarantee does not belong to this category. They emphasise that the guarantee, as opposed to suretyship, is a contract independent of the underlying relationship.[256] This view is probably the result of a misapprehension of the concept of independence.[257] Independent guarantees always relate to and secure an underlying relationship without which they cannot, as a matter of fact, come into being or exist. The practical consequences of a rule that the rights of the guarantee do not pass to the assignee of the secured claim by operation of law would be startling too. Does the original beneficiary continue to be entitled to call and receive payment pursuant to the guarantee, although he is no longer entitled to the secured claim thereby also foiling the interests of the assignee of the underlying claim? Or could the third party in his capacity as assignee of the principal contract pursue his rights as well? Or could neither claim payment? In short, there are cogent arguments in favour of the proposition that independent guarantees should, in general, be viewed as ancillary rights for the purpose of assignment by operation of law.[258] However, the substitution of the assignee of the underlying claim as the new beneficiary for the original beneficiary may entail grave risks for the account party, particularly in the case of a first demand guarantee, for reasons explained in Chapter 12.5.3, no. 12-69. Therefore, the recognition of independent guarantees, in general, as ancillary rights, does not necessarily command the conclusion that the assignee of the underlying claim as the new beneficiary can always exercise the rights under the guarantee in the same way as the original beneficiary could have done. A definite answer with general application is impossible and much depends on the particular facts of each individual case.

As could be expected, case law has not settled this issue in a straightforward manner. In *OLG Frankfurt a.M., 26 June 1984*, it was upon construction of the deed of assignment that the Court of Appeal arrived at the finding that the assignment of the rights pursuant to the underlying contract included the assignment of the payment guarantee.[259] But the Court of Appeal did observe that assignment of the rights from the underlying contract only would make little sense. In *BGH, 26 February 1987*,

---

[256] Von Westphalen, p. 134, Staudinger/Horn, No. 257 (but allowing for the possibility of an implied contractual assignment), Mühl, FS Imre Zaytay, p. 403, Schinnerer/Avancini, p. 294 note 75, p. 324, Moschner, O. Bank-Archiv 1983, p.140, Kleiner, No. 23.02, Dohm, No. 185, Pabbruwe, WPNR 1983, p. 430, RMThemis 1994, p. 149. See also Blomkwist, WPNR 1986, p. 555.

[257] See Chapter 12.1, No. 12-6.

[258] Idem Canaris, No. 1150, Rebman/Sacks, Münchener Kommentar BGB, Band 2, par. 398, No. 12, Mijnssen, p. 70.

[259] RIW 1985, p. 407, upheld by *BGH, 22 April 1985*, RIW 1985, p. 650.

assignment by operation of law was recognised. However, the contract of security had been construed as a first demand suretyship as opposed to a first demand guarantee, and this was emphasised when considering the statutory provisions concerning assignment by operation of law.[260] The applicability of those provisions to independent guarantees did not need to be considered. However, *OLG Düsseldorff, 9 August 2001*, unequivocally ruled that an assignment of a claim entails, by operation of law, the passing of both the rights under a (first demand) suretyship and the the rights under a (first demand) guarantee.[261] In the case of *Rb Utrecht, 10 September 1997*, a creditor assigned his claim for payment to his bank and the court ruled that the rights under the guarantee, which secured this claim, had passed to the bank by operation of law.[262] It should be noted, however, that the guarantee was payable upon submission of a court judgment so that the additional risk for the account party, discussed in no. 12-69, did not arise.

12.5.6 The effect of transfer of the secured contract; lease contracts

12-73 The concept of transfer of contract is somewhat ambiguous and is often used interchangeably with the concept of assignment, at least on an international level. Here, transfer of contract is taken to mean the entire substitution of the original party to the contract by a new party such that the latter assumes the position of the former and takes over all rights and obligations pursuant to the contract. For example, a construction firm X transfers its role as party to the construction contract to firm Y who will then carry out the project and receive the contract price, or a buyer transfers his position to a new buyer who will then be entitled to delivery of the merchandise on the same terms and be obliged to pay the purchase price. Transfer of contract requires, of course, the consent of the other contracting partner.

Does the transfer of the secured contract affect the guarantee and, if so, in what manner? If it is the account party who transfers his role as contracting partner, it affects neither the guarantee nor the position of the beneficiary.[263] This rule is founded not so much on the principle of independence, but on the fact that the guarantee assures proper execution of the secured contract, which remains unaltered. The only change is that statements of default or third-party documents will refer to the new contracting partner. The transferor should, of course, see to it that his position as account party *vis-à-vis*

---

[260] NJW 1987, p. 2075; idem *OLG Köln, 30 October 1997*, WM 1998, p. 707. See Chapter 4.5, Nos. 4-18/19, for the question of whether the difference between a first demand guarantee and a first demand suretyship is a matter of true substance.

[261] WM 2001, p. 2294.

[262] JOR 1998, 34.

[263] Cf. *Paris, 1 October 1986*, D. 1987 Somm. p. 171.

the bank is also transferred to the new contracting partner because otherwise he would continue to be liable to the bank by virtue of his counter-guarantee. The transfer of his liabilities under the counter-guarantee requires the consent of the bank.

A different situation arises if it is the beneficiary who transfers his role as party to the underlying transaction. The transferor and transferee obviously intend that upon the transfer the latter should be entitled to exercise the rights pursuant to the guarantee. This would result in an alteration of the terms of the guarantee which requires the consent of the account party and bank. Consent on the part of the account party must, however, be deemed to be included in his consent to the transfer of the secured contract. The bank must also agree to the change in the beneficiary's identity, but it is submitted that, in the absence of very special circumstances, the bank cannot object thereto since such a change does not affect the bank's credit risk on the account party. Once this consent has been obtained, the transferee will be the new beneficiary of the guarantee who will be able to exercise his rights without the cooperation of the transferor/original beneficiary. Moreover, cooperation by the latter would make no sense, since he is no longer involved in the underlying contract.[264]

The sale and transfer of rented real estate to a new owner often give rise to difficulties relating to payment guarantees in favour of the previous owner/lessor as the beneficiary of such guarantees. In the event of such a sale and transfer, the existing lease contracts with the lessees are transferred by operation of law to the new owner, who will then be the new lessor. This situation is very much akin to the contractual transfer of the underlying contract by the original beneficiary, as discussed in Chapter 12.5.5, and the consequences thereof, as far as any guarantees are concerned, should be the same too.[265] It is true that the transfer of the lease takes place irrespective of the consent of the lessee/account party, but his rights remain unaltered by virtue of law. In any event, if the guarantee were not to pass to the new lessor, the lessee would have to put up a fresh guarantee in favour of the new lessor anyway. Accordingly, the interests of the account party/lessee do not militate against the passing of the rights pursuant to the guarantee to the new lessor. Obviously, the bank should also be informed of the change in the beneficiary's identity, but, as stated above, it cannot usually object to it. Indeed, *CA Amsterdam, 21 April 1988*, rejected the bank's defence and admitted the new lessor's claim against the bank based on the existing guarantee.[266]

It is of course advisable to make proper arrangements between all parties concerned in order to avoid all kinds of practical difficulties which may attend the transfer of the guarantee. Also, many guarantees for lease rentals explicitly provide that a new lessor

---

[264] See also Chapter 12.6.

[265] Cf. Mijnssen, p. 74. Contra: Pabbruwe, WPNR 1983, p. 432, Blomkwist, WPNR 1986, p. 555.

[266] Unreported, docket number 466/87.

is entitled to call the guarantee in the same way as the original beneficiary/lessor provided that the bank has been advised of the change of identity of the beneficiary.

12.5.7 Pledge of the guarantee

12-74 If national law allows for the possibility of pledging receivables, such a possibility extends to the pledge by the beneficiary of the proceeds of a guarantee, for example to his bank as security for credit facilities. The effect is the same as in the case of assignment as discussed in Chapter 12.3, nos. 12-69/70. Accordingly, the pledgee is entitled to lodge the demand for payment and to receive payment, but the demand itself as well as the statement of default, if required, must originate from the beneficiary/pledgor, while an irrevocable power of attorney to call the guarantee and demand payment without the cooperation of the beneficiary/pledgor is ineffective.

12.6 TRANSFER

Transfer and documentary credits; back-to-back credits

12-75 Sellers/beneficiaries of a documentary credit may request the buyer and bank to make the credit transferable. Such requests are usually made where the seller is a middleman who, in his turn, procures the merchandise from his supplier. The purpose of a transferable credit is to enable the intermediate seller, the first beneficiary, to finance his purchase from the supplier by making the credit available to him, the transferee, also called the second beneficiary. The credit can be transferred only on the terms and conditions of the original credit, with a few exceptions such as the amount of the credit. This will be lower than the amount of the original credit, the difference being the profit for the first beneficiary/intermediate seller. The second beneficiary may tender his own invoice. In short, although the transfer entails the issuance of a new letter of credit to the transferee, who can claim payment in his own right, basically one and the same credit is used as a means of payment to both supplier and middleman concerning the same merchandise shipped on the same terms and conditions.[267]

The same result can be accomplished by the device of back-to-back credits. This device involves the issuance of an entirely new and separate credit, although the terms and conditions of the new credit are geared to the first. The beneficiary of the first credit then acts as the account party/buyer in the second credit which the bank is prepared to issue on the strength of the first credit.

---

[267] Transfer is regulated by art. 48 UCP.

Transfer and guarantees; back-to-back guarantees

12-76 According to Rule 6.02 ISP98, art 4(1) URDG and art. 9 Uncitral Convention, the beneficiary can transfer his right to demand payment to a second beneficiary if this is expressly stated in the guarantee or standby. Transfer in the sense of a substitution of a new beneficiary for the original beneficiary, who may then request payment in its own right, may be useful in the following situations.

- Transfer may occur where the contractual position of the original beneficiary in the underlying transaction has been transferred to the new beneficiary. The result is that the new beneficiary entirely occupies the position of the original beneficiary with respect to both the underlying transaction and the guarantee. This notion of transfer does not raise particular difficulties.[268] Such a transfer is also possible when a bank issues a standby letter of credit as a credit facility (a 'direct pay standby') for its own account whereby the beneficiary is entitled to transfer the right to draw under the facility to a third party. This often occurs in relation to inter-company credit facilities. It should be noted, however, that both types of transfer are different from the notion of transfer in the context of documentary credits, see no. 12-75.

- Secondly, the transfer relates to a chain of contracts without a transfer of the underlying transaction whereby the transferee is a second beneficiary who is entitled to call the guarantee without the issue of a second guarantee. This may occur where a seller furnishes a transferable performance guarantee in favour of an intermediate buyer who resells the merchandise to an end-buyer on exactly the same terms and conditions. Such a transfer then allows the end-buyer, in case of defects in the merchandise, to call the guarantee issued on behalf of the first seller. The justification for a transferable guarantee in this case is that non- or defective delivery in the second sale contract will be brought about by non- or defective delivery by the first seller.

- A transfer does not appear to be an appropriate mechanism for payment guarantees in the context of a chain of contracts whereby the buyer furnishes a payment guarantee in favour of the intermediate seller who then 'transfers' the guarantee to his supplier. If the buyer has paid the intermediate seller, it would be wrong or at least unacceptable for the buyer, to allow the supplier to call the guarantee, for example because the intermediate seller has failed to on-pay the supplier. In other words, non-payment by the intermediate seller to the supplier

---

[268] See Chapter 12.5.6. Rule 6.11 ISP98 also provides for a transfer in the event of an heir, personal representative, liquidator, trustee or successor company which by operation of law takes over the interests of the beneficiary.

is not necessarily brought about by non-payment by the buyer to the intermediate seller. A back-to-back payment guarantee provides, however, a suitable alternative for a transfer of a payment guarantee. In this technique, the bank is prepared to issue a second guarantee under which the beneficiary of the first guarantee, for example the intermediate seller, is the account party in the second guarantee in favour of the end-supplier and whereby the first guarantee provides the financial basis for the second guarantee.[269] This construction does not affect the position of the account party in the first guarantee because the two guarantees are independent of each other and the fact that the second guarantee has been called does not as such entitle the beneficiary of the first guarantee also to call the guarantee.[270]

– Transfer of the guarantee can be used to enable a bank which finances the beneficiary's business, to call the guarantee and to obtain payment without the cooperation of the beneficiary/transferor. A clause in the guarantee which permits transfer for this purpose is very dangerous for the guarantor and the account party in particular.[271]

Apart from some specific situations described above, guarantees should not be freely negotiable as this would in fact turn these security instruments into negotiable instruments which they are not, and invite dubious trading practices, see no. 12-77.

Fraudulent trading schemes

12-77 During the last decade various fraudulent schemes have been operated which involve so-called prime bank instruments, such as 'prime bank' standby letters of credit or bank guarantees. Those promoting these schemes claim that such 'prime bank instruments' are off-balance activities of banks, only available to a select group of special customers, and that they can be traded in the secondary market with risk-free high yield returns. In fact, they are forged instruments from reputable existing banks, instruments issued by non-existing banks or by banks of doubtful repute in doubtful jurisdictions. Genuine standby letters of credit and bank guarantees are on-balance activities and they are only payable in relation to default in a particular underlying transaction. This also explains why genuine instruments are ordinarily not freely negotiable or transferable. As a consequence, a secondary market in these instruments does

---

[269] See Chapter 2.3, No. 2-11.

[270] *Trib. com. Paris, 14 December 1990*, D. 1991 Somm. p. 201. See also *HR, 12 March 1982*, NJ 1982, 267, for another example of the back-to back technique.

[271] See Chapter 12.5.3, No. 12-69. See further Chapter 8.4, No. 8-6 for a similar device.

not and cannot exist.[272] Several government agencies, many banks as well as the ICC have repeatedly warned against these fraudulent schemes.[273]

---

[272] Cf. *LG Hamburg, 24 April 1995*, RIW 1996, p. 686, in a case against a broker who was involved in such fraudulent scheme.

[273] See in particular the Special Reports 'Prime Bank Instrument Frauds' 1994 and 1996, by the ICC Commercial Crime Bureau. See further Dolan, § 2.02[2], and Wunnicke/Wunnicke/Turner, § 2.07 [E/F] for a vivid description of various fraudulent practices and relevant case law.

CHAPTER 13
THE DEMAND FOR PAYMENT

13.1 GENERAL ASPECTS

Percentages and their significance for the account party

13-1 According to bankers' estimates, demands for actual payment are made in approximately three to five per cent, or even less, of all guarantees and standby letters of credit. In this respect guarantees and standbys differ markedly from documentary credits. This difference reflects the distinct character of the two instruments. The utilisation of the documentary credit, that is the exchange of the prescribed documents (representing the merchandise) for the amount stated in the credit (representing the purchase price), is what both seller and buyer contemplate. A request for payment and actual payment thus occur in the ordinary course of events. Guarantees are designed to assure protection if the secured contract has not been carried out according to plan, which is ordinarily the exception. They operate as safety devices.

The above-mentioned percentage is an overall figure. It would not be safe for the individual account party to derive any comfort from this figure or to assume that the perils of first demand guarantees are being grossly exaggerated. The rate for each single guarantee is determined by numerous factors, which are often difficult to assess in advance, such as the nature of the contract, the country of performance and the identity and nationality of the beneficiary. Moreover, it is not only the actual demand for payment as the ultimate materialisation of the risk which the account party has to reckon with, but also the continuing possibility that such a demand could be made at some time in the future. One should bear in mind that guarantees tend to be valid for a considerable length of time, while expiry dates are regularly extended by virtue of 'extend or pay' requests or are lacking, especially in the public sector. This adversely affects the position of the account party in terms of charges owed to the bank, retention of security for reimbursement, the blocking of credit facilities and its liquidity position. If the guarantee is extended repeatedly, the continuing uncertainty as regards a future call, along with the side-effects just mentioned, appear to be feared nearly as much as an actual call for payment itself. Another discomforting aspect is the power the beneficiary of a first demand guarantee has to compel the account party, under the threat of a call, to concede to all kinds of requirements by the beneficiary. Construction firms in particular complain that they are regularly forced to carry out works in excess of the agreed works under threat of a call. Such practices could also account for the low percentage of demands for payment.

Bank's examination with respect to compliance with the terms and conditions of the guarantee. Summary

13-2 When the beneficiary requests payment, he must satisfy the terms and conditions of the guarantee. In its relationship with the beneficiary, the bank is entitled to ascertain compliance and, in its relationship with the account party, the bank owes a duty to verify compliance and a duty to refuse payment if the terms and conditions have not been met. The general aspects of examination with respect to compliance have been discussed in detail in Chapter 10.8. The key features will be repeated here only briefly.

All terms and conditions have to be complied with. There must always be a demand for payment lodged in the prescribed manner and within the period of validity. Also first demand guarantees can be subject to other terms such as the the fulfilment of conditions precedent or advance payments. The guarantee may contain provisions which limit or negate the beneficiary's right to payment, for example reduction clauses or clauses terminating the guarantee upon completion of the secured contract. In this event, it is for the account party to show that these restrictive conditions have been met.

Undoubtedly the most outstanding feature of compliance and the ascertainment thereof relates to its *formal* nature. The beneficiary is entitled to payment once the conditions as stated in the guarantee have been met and he need not establish default of the account party in any other way than is prescribed by the guarantee. In its turn, the bank is not entitled in its relationship with the beneficiary and owes no duty as regards the account party to require proof of default. It is not concerned with the rights and liabilities as measured by the underlying relationship, or with disputes between account party and beneficiary. This aspect is founded on the independent nature of the guarantee.

A third aspect is the rule that the terms and conditions of the guarantee are to be *strictly* complied with. As far as the bank is concerned, there is the further aspect of a certain degree of discretion in appropriate circumstances and reasonable care in deciding whether or not the terms of the guarantee have been met. This is particularly relevant in relation to conditions of payment which, unfortunately, have not been drafted in a documentary manner.

Disputes regarding compliance and proper examination may occur in two sets of circumstances. It is possible that the bank is of the opinion that the conditions have not been fulfilled, triggering off litigation initiated by the beneficiary. It could also be that the account party takes that view and commences proceedings. This he may do after payment by the bank when the bank has reimbursed itself by debiting his accounts, or before payment in a preventive action, often in conjunction with allegations of fraud. In fact, the majority of litigation concerning compliance is initiated by the account party.

Specific aspects of compliance with the terms and conditions of the guarantee and the bank's duty of examination are examined throughout this Chapter.

Direct and indirect guarantees. Applicable law

13-3 In the absence of provisions to the contrary, guarantees are governed by the law of the country where the issuing bank or the issuing branch of the bank has its place of business. In the case of direct guarantees, this law ordinarily coincides with the law of the account party's place of business. In the case of indirect guarantees, it nearly always coincides with the law of the beneficiary's place of business. However, the issue of the applicable law is scarcely of practical significance. There are no indications whatsoever that the rules of law concerning compliance and examination vary from country to country. The issue of applicable law may, however, arise in respect of some ancillary matters, for example interest and damages as well as the requirement of a formal notice of default from the beneficiary in case of non- or late payment. Uniformity of law in these matters is not essential and can probably not be achieved anyway.

The demand for payment pursuant to a counter-guarantee in favour of the second issuing bank is examined in Chapter 13.3. Most of the aspects discussed in Chapter 13.2 are, however, equally relevant to counter-guarantees.

13.2 CALL ON THE GUARANTEE

13.2.1 The call

The guarantee must have been called

13-4 It is evident that the bank is neither to pay, nor to seek reimbursement, if the guarantee has not been called. The account party is entitled to ask the bank for a copy of the beneficiary's request for payment.

It may happen that the bank solicits a call on the guarantee with a view to serving its own interests, for example when the financial position of the account party is deteriorating,[1] or when a counter-guarantee is about to expire. In such a situation, the bank may deem it expedient to precipitate a call, enabling it to secure repayment or to liquidate the collateral at a time when this is still possible. Such practices are equally improper.

---

[1] Cf. the case of *Versailles, 29 March 1985*, D. 1986 I.R. p. 156, where the second, issuing bank called the counter-guarantee in view of the liquidation of the account party, while the primary guarantee itself had not been called. The Court of Appeal granted a stop-payment injunction against the instructing bank.

Who is entitled to call; identity of the person calling the guarantee; change of status; agency and power of attorney

13-5 The person entitled to call the guarantee is the one which the guarantee designates as the beneficiary and the bank should refuse payment if the guarantee is called by a person other than the beneficiary.[2] The beneficiary is ordinarily the creditor/contracting party of the account party but this might be different in specific circumstances.[3]

The bank is entitled to require proof from the person calling the guarantee in order to ascertain his identity and to ensure that the correct person is making the call. In this respect the bank owes a duty to the account party to apply reasonable care in accordance with prevailing bank practice and taking into account the particular circumstances of the call.[4] For example, a request to remit the amount of the guarantee to an account not held in the name of the beneficiary is clearly suspicious. The beneficiary is ordinarily a legal entity and it may be necessary for the bank to enquire into the authority of

---

[2] In *Paris, 8 November 1988*, D. 1990 Somm. p. 206, the guarantee was called by the Iranian Ministry of Petrol, while the guarantee designated as the beneficiary the Iranian Gaz Agency which hierarchically formed part of the former. The Court of Appeal ruled that this was acceptable, but the propriety of this ruling may be questioned. *Trib. com. Paris, 14 December 1990*, D. 1991 Somm. p. 201, ruled that an advising bank cannot call the guarantee in its own name. In *BGH, 24 November 1998*, WM 1999, p. 72, it was held that the absence of an original signature in the request for payment made by telefax, did not render the call invalid, but the absence of the name of the person making the demand, did render the call invalid.

[3] See Chapter 8.4. In *CA Amsterdam, January 1987*, KG 1988, 300, the attorney of the creditor/contracting partner had been named as beneficiary. The creditor made a demand for payment, which was refused by the bank, and commenced proceedings. The Court of Appeal held that, in the absence of particular circumstances requiring otherwise, a reasonable construction of the text of the guarantee led to the conclusion that the bank had assumed an obligation to pay the creditor or to pay the attorney nominated by the creditor. In the case of *Rb Arnhem, 20 October 1986*, KG 1986, 482, the guarantee named the assignee/bank of the creditor as the beneficiary. However, the guarantee did not state that the assignee/bank was the only person entitled to call but provided that payment was to be made upon a statement from the creditor.

[4] See for this duty in general *CA Amsterdam, 13 January 1983*, No. 65/81 KG, not reported, but referred to by Mijnssen, p. 46, and Boll, pp. 111, 128, and their observations. See further *LG Dortmund, 9 July 1980*, WM 1981, p. 280. The Iranian bank had issued the guarantee at variance with the instructions in favour of another agency, which was not the contracting partner. It was not clear who had called the guarantee. These facts were mentioned as one of the reasons for granting an injunction against the instructing bank restraining it from paying the issuing bank.

the officer lodging the request for payment.⁵ In the event of intermediation by an advising bank, this bank could check the officer's authority.⁶

A particular problem is caused by changes in the formal status or corporate identity of the beneficiary, for instance where the original beneficiary/legal entity has ceased to exist and is succeeded by a new legal entity. A prime example is furnished by the events following the Iranian revolution in 1978, when a new government and new government agencies were substituted for the previous government and agencies. These changes have given rise to litigation concerning both guarantees and counter-guarantees. In these cases, it was mostly the account party who sought to obtain restraining orders, arguing that the guarantee and/or counter-guarantee had been called by a person whom the guarantee did not mention as the beneficiary and that the demands for payment did not, therefore, comply with the conditions for payment. These arguments did not find favour with the courts.⁷ This infringement of the rule of strict compliance is indeed justified. It is true that a change in the formal status of the beneficiary, espe-

---

5   During the upheaval at the time of the Iranian revolution several U.S. exporters sought to obtain restraining orders, arguing the substantial likelihood of unauthorised persons making demands on the guarantee. In *Pan American World Airways v. Bank Melli*, No. 79 Civ. 1190 (S.D.N.Y. 3 April 1979) and in *Stromberg-Carlson v. Bank Melli*, 467 F. Supp. 530 (S.D.N.Y. 1979) this contention was accepted and was one of the reasons why the court granted a temporary notice injunction restraining the issuing Iranian bank from honouring any demands. In *Dynamics Corp. v. Citizens & Nat'l Bank*, 356 F. Supp. 991 (N.D. Ga. 1973) the performance guarantee specified that 'the President of India' sign the demand, but the court permitted a signature from a minister authorised to sign on behalf of the president. Although perhaps not strictly in accordance with the terms of the guarantee, the call is indeed consistent with that term, also taking into account the peculiar nature of the specification. See also von Westphalen, pp. 142-143, Dohm, No. 191.

6   Cf. *Paris, 1 March 1989*, D. 1990 Somm. p. 196.

7   See especially *American Bell v. Islamic Republic of Iran*, 474 F. Supp. 420, 424 (S.D.N.Y. 1979) where Judge Macmahon observed that 'to do otherwise would only elevate form over substance'. This ruling was primarily based on the international rules of state succession and the pertaining U.S. legislation. The decision, as well as the issue in general, has been commented upon by Gable, Law & Policy Int. Business, 1980, pp. 938-940, Driscoll, Virginia Journal of Int. Law, 1980, pp. 479-480, Reed, Columbia Journal Int. Law, 1981, pp. 306-307, 318-321, Weisz and Blackman, University Illinois L.R., 1982, pp. 365-368. Similar decisions were reached in *Paris, 2 June 1982*, D. 1983 J. p. 437, *Brussels, 18 December 1981*, Rev. Banque 1982, p. 99 (Syrian case), and *Trib com. Brussels, 6 April 1982*, Rev. Banque 1982, p. 683. See also *Rb Rotterdam, 9 June 1989*, KG 1989, 270, and *Rb Rotterdam, 20 November 1990*, KG 1990, 405, which related to a change in corporate identity as a result of the *Treuhandgesetz* concerning the former German Democratic Republic. See also *GKN Contractors v. Lloyds Bank*, [1985] 30 BLR 48, *I.E. Contractors Ltd. v. Lloyds Bank*, [1990] 2 Lloyd's Rep. 496.

cially under the conditions prevailing during the Iranian revolution, may increase the risk of the guarantee being called and possibly being called fraudulently. However, such an increase could also result from other changes, such as change of management or change in shareholding. A further reason is that if the argument of non-compliance were upheld, it would result in an undeserved windfall for the account party, for then the guarantee could not be called by anyone. While the successor of the original beneficiary is thus entitled to call the guarantee, it must show that the original beneficiary has ceased to exist and that it is indeed the genuine legal successor.[8]

The request for payment can be lodged by an agent, for example the beneficiary's attorney or bank, which has been instructed to call the guarantee on behalf of the beneficiary. If in doubt, the bank should verify the agent's authority, for example by asking for the power of attorney.[9] Although the agent's authority should exist on or before the expiry date, it need not be proven on or before that date. One should, however, bear in mind that the lodging of the demand for payment by an agent does not alter the fact that the decision to request payment and the statement of default, if required, must originate from the beneficiary. This could be apparent from the beneficiary's instructions whereby the power of attorney is given. On the other hand, a general (irrevocable) power of attorney to an agent (e.g. the bank of the beneficiary) under which, with a view to the agent's own interest, the decision whether or not and when to call the guarantee is left to the agent's discretion, is ineffective. As stated, that decision must be made by the beneficiary himself.[10]

Where the beneficiary has been declared insolvent and a receiver has been appointed, he is the proper person to call the guarantee.[11]

---

[8] Since the *CA Amsterdam, 13 January 1983*, No. 65/81 KG, not reported, was not satisfied in this respect, it affirmed a stop-payment order which had previously been granted by the court of first instance on other grounds.

[9] In *CA Brussels, 5 April 1990*, TBH 1992, p. 82, a call by the beneficiary's attorney, who did not possess a written and explicit power of attorney, was considered to be a valid call on the grounds that neither the account party nor the beneficiary had ever challenged the attorney's mandate. See also *Cass., 21 June 1988*, D. 1989 Somm. p. 148. In *Rb Arnhem, 20 October 1986*, KG 1986, 482, the authority of the agent was apparent from previous contacts concerning the guarantee. In *OLG München, 23 June 1999*, WM 1999, p. 2456, the call was held to be invalid, *inter alia*, because the demand failed to indicate that the entity which made the demand, but which was not the beneficiary, did so as agent of the beneficiary. See also *Cass., 24 March 1992*, D. 1993 Somm. p. 99, where a call by the beneficiary's attorney caused serious difficulties.

[10] See also Chapter 12.5.4, No. 12-71.

[11] See, for example, *Rb Amsterdam, 31 March 1988*, KG 1988, 179. The authority of the receiver had been confirmed by a legal opinion.

The Demand for Payment

If the proceeds of the guarantee have been assigned, the assignee is entitled to lodge the request for payment but, otherwise, the terms and conditions must be complied with.[12]

Addressee and place of the call

13-6 In the absence of provisions to the contrary, the request for payment as well as any documents which the beneficiary is to submit, must be lodged with the bank, more specifically with the office or branch which issued the guarantee.[13] Consequently, requests lodged with another branch are not valid and this holds true whether or not this other branch has a separate legal entity.[14] However, this does not necessarily mean that such a request is without consequence, since this other branch could be expected to forward the request and documents to the issuing bank. Moreover, circumstances could be such that the bank's complaints ought not to be upheld.[15]

The rule that the beneficiary should turn to the issuing bank (or the issuing branch of the bank) gains special importance in the case of direct guarantees, since the issuing bank and the beneficiary are often located in different countries. This could cause problems with a view to the timeliness of the call. Of course, the beneficiary may present the request for payment and the documents to a branch in his own country and this branch could be expected to forward them to the issuing bank or branch. However, should the request and documents reach the issuing bank or branch only after the expiry date of the guarantee, then the call must be considered too late. If, however, the

---

[12] See Chapter 12.5.3.

[13] Cf. art. 19 URDG, art. 15(2) UNCITRAL Convention and ISP98 Rule 3.04(b). See also von Westphalen, p. 161, Zahn/Ehrlich/Neumann, 9/115. In *OG Austria, 3 December 1986*, JIBL 1987, N-51, the Supreme Court observed that because of the independent nature of the bank guarantee it is necessary to examine carefully whether all requirements have been fulfilled, and that this rule is of particular importance where, as was the case, different legal entities and not branches of one legal entity are concerned.

[14] Cf. von Westphalen, p. 162, but see the observations of OG Austria, cited in the previous note.

[15] See, for example, *Paris, 29 January 1981*, D. 1981 J. p. 336. The guarantee had been issued by a branch office of a French bank in Oman in connection with a project to be executed in that country. The beneficiary, a French company, addressed the request for payment to the head office in France which refused payment for a number of reasons which are not relevant here. The head office did not object to the fact that the request for payment was directed to itself instead of to the Oman branch until some time during the proceedings. The Court of Appeal brushed this objection aside observing that the Oman office was merely a branch without corporate personality and that the bank had not been prejudiced. The court ordered the bank to pay.

local branch has forwarded the request and documents with considerable delay or by inefficient means of transmission, that branch may incur liability in tort.[16] This is a matter to be answered under local law and bank practice.

Direct guarantees are sometimes issued through a local bank or local branch of the issuing bank, acting as an advising bank or branch, in the beneficiary's country. This technique does not affect the issues examined above, unless the advising bank or branch has also been designated as the paying or nominated bank. The beneficiary is not required to make the demand for payment through the advising bank or branch and may directly turn to the issuing bank. The guarantee may, however, stipulate that the beneficiary must present the demand via the local advising bank or branch, so that this bank or branch may check the authenticity of the person making the call. In this event, the demand for payment is valid if it reaches the advising bank or branch on or prior to the expiry date, unless clearly stipulated otherwise.

Formal requirements

13-7 Most guarantees explicitly require the request for payment to be made in writing. In addition to letters, requests made by cable, telex, telefax or S.W.I.F.T (in relation to calls on the counter-guarantee by the foreign issuing bank) are considered valid provided that the source and the message itself can be authenticated.[17] In order to ensure the authenticity of the call, banks often only accept telex, telefax or S.W.I.F.T. messages which contain the test code. More generally, banks appear to be entitled to require written confirmation bearing the signature of the person calling the guarantee if there are any doubts concerning the authenticity or authority of the person requesting payment.[18] Even apart from requirements as to authentication it is uncertain whether, in the absence of specific provisions, a demand by email is permitted. Such a demand appears to be permitted under the URDG because of the definition of the term 'writing' and 'written' in art. 2(d) which includes an authenticated teletransmission or tested electronic data exchange ('EDI') message equivalent thereto,[19] while ISP98 Rule 3.06(b/c/d) only allows such a demand if so indicated.[20] If the URDG or ISP98 do not apply,

---

[16] Cf. von Westphalen, p. 163.

[17] Cf. art. 2(d) j. art. 20(a) URDG and art. 7(2) j. art. 15(1) UNCITRAL Convention. ISP98 Rule 3.06(b) provides that, where no medium is indicated, the demand must be presented as a paper document unless only a demand is required.

[18] See also No. 13-5.

[19] Affaki, No. 61.

[20] See for this subject in general S. Kröll, Rechtsfragen elektronischer Bankgarantien, WM 2001, pp. 1553-1360, and the same, Electronic Bank Guarantees and Stand-by Letters of Credit, in 'Legal Issues in Electronic Banking', pp. 288-306.

the question of whether a demand for payment by email is permitted is ultimately a matter of construing the formal requirements of the guarantee. In any event, it would appear that a requirement of a signature on the demand precludes the possibility of a presentation by email, unless an electronic signature has also been agreed upon.

The guarantee may require that a specific means of transmission is used, for example a letter or registered mail. Such requirements have to be strictly complied with, since these are not inserted without reason or meaning.[21] The guarantee may also require that the beneficiary's demand for payment must be routed via a bank in the beneficiary's country affirming the authenticity of the signature on the demand.[22,23]

Has a proper request for payment been made?

13-8 It is not always clear, for example because of its loose or vague wording, whether a particular communication from the beneficiary to the bank is to be considered as a proper request for payment or not. The issue becomes critical when it is not followed by an unequivocal call on or before the expiry date of the guarantee. It is for this reason that the matter is examined in more detail in Chapter 13.2.7, no. 13-24.

---

[21] The Supreme Court in *OG Austria, 24 March 1988*, JIBL 1988, N-154, held that a call by telex did not constitute a valid call where the guarantee prescribed the call to be made by registered mail. See further *HR, 9 June 1995*, NJ 1995, 639 (invalid demand for payment since the prescribed court decision had not been served by means of a formal writ by a bailiff), *Trib. com. Brussels, 26 May 1988*, JT 1988, p. 460 (restraining orders against instructing and issuing bank granted, one of the reasons being that the demand had not been made by registered mail).

[22] *Trib. com. Hasselt, 2 October 1998*, TBH 1999, p. 723, allowed a demand which was made directly by the beneficiary, but followed by a seperate confirmation by the beneficiary's bank as regards the authenticity of the signature.

[23] Pursuant to a directive of the Ministry of Finance, No. 17/2740 of 8 July 1985 and a SAMA Circular, No. 7204/M/A 153 of 9 February 1986 Saudi Arabian beneficiaries should not make demands for payment until a special administrative committee has reviewed and approved the reasons for the proposed call. A further SAMA Circular, No. 15493/M/A 362 of 1 September 1986, states that the previous announcements do not accord any rights to banks or account parties. Payment cannot be refused or delayed on the grounds that no approval has been given or that the review is still pending. These rules have been reaffirmed in the 1991 SAMA Circular.

13.2.2 The call must relate to the secured contract and/or obligation

General

13-9 The request for payment must relate to the contract and/ or obligation that has been secured by the guarantee. It is the contract or obligation which is referred to in the text of the guarantee and it is nearly always a contract or obligation between the account party and beneficiary. The guarantee cannot be called for another contract or obligation.[24] Depending on the terms of the guarantee, this may be different where the beneficiary is not the contracting partner of the account party in the underlying transaction but, for example, the bank of that contracting partner.[25]

Position of beneficiary, bank and account party

13-10 Although the call must relate to the secured contract and/or obligation, it is not a condition of payment which the beneficiary must show has been met. The reason is that such a requirement would otherwise virtually compel the beneficiary to adduce substantive proof of default, which would be incompatible with the independent nature of the guarantee. Accordingly, the beneficiary need not produce evidence that the request for payment indeed relates to the secured contract.[26] For example, if the guarantee prescribes the submission of a statement of default, the statement must merely refer to non-performance in respect of the secured contract concerned. No more is required.

The bank owes no duty to the account party to ascertain whether the request for

---

[24] *BGH, 25 February 1999*, WM 1999, p. 895 (beneficiary's claim against bank dismissed), *Paris, 14 November 1978*, D. 1979 J. p. 259, (beneficiary's claim for payment against the bank dismissed), *BGH, 14 December 1995*, WM 1996, p. 193 (beneficiary's claim rejected), *Trib. com. Brussels, 11 March 1981*, BRH 1981, p. 361 (general observation), *Trib. com. Brussels, 21 October 1986*, RDC 1987, p. 706 (general observation), *Trib. com. Brussels, 26 May 1988*, JT 1988, p. 460 (restraining orders granted, see also Chapter 14.5.6, No. 27), *Trib. com. Hasselt, 2 October 1999*, TBH 1999, p. 723 (restraining order partially granted), *Hall's Motor Transit Co. v. Chase Manhattan Bank*, N.Y. Supreme Court, 13 June 1983, IFLR October 1983, p. 42 (account party's application for stop-payment injunction against the bank granted), *Roman Ceramics Corp. v. Peoples Nat. Bank*, 714 F. 2d. 1207 (3d. Cir. 1983), IBL April 1984, p. 122 (beneficiary's claim for payment against bank dismissed). See also the case law cited in the following notes. See further Pabbruwe, rede p. 6, Mijnssen, p. 47, Schmitthoff, JBL 1984, p. 302, Staudinger/Horn, No. 245.

[25] See Chapter 8.4.

[26] For example, in *Cass., 20 November* 1985, D. 1986 J. p. 213, the primary guarantee was payable on demand 'provided that the call was made within the direct scope of the matter (principal contract)'. This formula does not require positive corroboration by the beneficiary.

payment does indeed relate to the secured contract. Not only would such a duty be impossible to fulfil,[27] it would also be incompatible with the absence of any right to require proof from the beneficiary. If, however, the account party presents the bank with facts which seriously cast doubts, the bank may ask for a confirmation from the beneficiary, but the bank cannot and need not do more.

The views expressed above are consistent with case law. In *Trib. com. Brussels, 11 March 1981*, the court made the general observation that the bank should summarily investigate the matter.[28] The case which most clearly illustrates the issues at hand is *Paris, 18 March 1986*.[29] Acting on the persistent requests from the account party, the bank did not proceed to payment until the beneficiary had confirmed twice that the call related to the secured contract referred to in the guarantee. After payment and the debiting of his account, the account party commenced proceedings for recovery against the bank and beneficiary. The Court of Appeal was satisfied with the evidence that the call did not relate to the secured contract and gave judgment against the beneficiary. The claim against the bank was dismissed, since the bank, having no knowledge of the true facts, was not responsible to the account party. In *Paris, 24 January 1984*, the account party challenged the debiting of his account by the instructing bank. The Court of Appeal gave judgment against the instructing bank because it had proceeded to pay under the counter-guarantee without having obtained, and without the issuing bank having furnished, corroboration that the request for payment by the beneficiary related to the secured contract.[30] This decision was quashed by *Cass., 20 November 1985*, on the grounds that guarantee and counter-guarantee are independent of each other. Although the final decision is correct, perhaps a more convincing argument would have been that the issuing bank had not breached its duty of examination.[31]

---

[27] See Chapter 10.8, No. 10-26.

[28] BRH 1981, p. 361.

[29] D. 1987 Somm. p. 173.

[30] D.1984 I.R. p. 203, see also note 26 *supra*.

[31] D. 1986 J. p. 213, see also Chapter 11.2.2, and in particular No. 11-13. Upon referral *Amiens, 6 June 1988*, D. 1989 Somm. p. 151, ordered the instructing bank to reimburse the issuing bank, and the account party to reimburse the instructing bank. A decision which is inconsistent with the views expressed above, but equally inconsistent with the 1986 decision of the Paris Court of Appeal and the 1985 decision of the Cour de Cassation, is *Trib. com. Paris, 1 August 1984*, D. 1986 I.R. p. 159. The court granted an injunction against the instructing bank restraining it from reimbursing the issuing bank upon clear evidence that the beneficiary of the primary guarantee had called the guarantee for a project not covered by the guarantee. The difficulty with this case is that there was no mention, let alone any evidence of the fact that the issuing bank had any knowledge of the true facts when it made payment. The decision rested, however, on other grounds as well, see note 34.

If the account party seeks a stop-payment order against the bank or a restraining order against the beneficiary, or if the bank refuses payment, it is for the account party, or as the case may be, for the bank, promptly to adduce clear evidence that the call relates to a transaction not covered by the guarantee.[32] After all, the account party or bank should not be allowed to delay immediate payment through protracted proceedings. In the event of an indirect guarantee, the account party or the instructing bank must also prove that the issuing bank was aware of the relevant facts when it proceeded to pay. The procedural aspects thus resemble those of fraud cases.[33]

13.2.3 Call on a first demand guarantee

Simple demand guarantees

13-11 Apart from such matters as those examined in Chapter 13.2.6 and the period of validity, the only condition for payment in the case of first demand guarantees which do not prescribe the submission of a statement of default or other statements, is a proper request for payment.

Statement of default and other statements by the beneficiary

13-12 If the guarantee calls for a statement of default or other statements by the beneficiary, the submission of such a statement is a condition of payment. A statement of default is also required if the guarantee is subject to the URDG, see art. 20(a) URDG. The bank owes a duty to the account party to verify that the correct statement as prescribed in the guarantee has been presented and it must refuse payment if the statement has not been tendered.[34] Depending on the particulars prescribed in the guarantee,

---

[32] Cf. *Trib. com. Paris, 1 August 1984*, D. 1986 I.R. p. 159, *Hall's Motor Transit Co. v. Chase Manhattan Bank*, N.Y. Supreme Court, 13 June 1983, IFLR October 1983, p. 42, *Roman Ceramics Corp. v. Peoples Nat. Bank*, 714 F.2d. 1207 (3d. Cir. 1983), IBL April 1984, p. 22, Vasseur, D. 1984 I.R. p. 204. In *BGH, 25 February 1999*, WM 1999, p. 895, the beneficiary called the guarantee because of non-payment of rent. However, the guarantee, upon construction of its terms, was held to only secure non-performance by the account party in connection with a construction contract. Under these circumstances it was for the beneficiary to show that the guarantee also covered the payment of rent.

[33] In fact, the decisions cited in the previous note were decided on the basis of fraud.

[34] See, for example, *CA Amsterdam, 27 February 1992*, NJ 1992, 735, *OLG Karlsruhe, 21 July 1992*, RIW 1992, p. 843, *OLG Frankfurt a.M., 18 March 1997*, RIW 1998, p. 477, *OLG München, 23 June 1999*, WM 1999, p. 2456, Trib. com. Brussels, 16 June 1989, TBH 1990, p. 1076. In *Trib. com. Paris, 1 August 1984*, D. 1986 I.R. p. 159, and *Trib. com. Brussels, 26 May 1988*, JT 1988, p. 460, Rev. Banque 1990, p. 167 involving indirect guarantees, the

The Demand for Payment   289

examination by the bank involves several aspects. As far as purely factual matters are concerned the examination is governed by the rule of strict compliance. Unless otherwise provided, the statement of default or other statement must originate from the beneficiary.[35] As far as the precise wording is concerned, the principle of strict compliance ought not to be applied too strictly.[36] It is sufficient that the wording of the statement is consistent with and conforms in substance to the formula prescribed in the guarantee, as was recognised in, e.g., *BGH, 23 January 1997*,[37] and *BGH, 10 October 2000*.[38]

---

    court granted a stop-payment order against the instructing bank because the issuing bank had failed to obtain the required statement of default.

[35] In *Trib. com. Brussels, 27 July 1984*, RDC 1984 p. 567, a stop-payment order against the bank was granted because the statement of default had been issued by another person. See Chapter 12.5.3 and 12.5.7 for cases involving the assignment and pledge of the guarantee.

[36] Cf. *Siporex Trade SA v. Banque Indosuez*, [1986] 2 Lloyd's Rep. 146, *I.E. Contractors Ltd. v. Lloyds Bank*, [1990] 2 Lloyd's Rep. 496, *OLG Bremen, 14 June 1990*, WM 1990, p. 1369, *First Bank v. Paris Savings & Loan Association*, 756 S.W.2d. 329 (Tex. Ct. App. 1988), *Trib. com. Brussels, 25 September 1987*, RDC 1988 p. 808. In *Trib. com. Liege, 7 April 1995*, RDC 1996, p. 1063, the guarantee required, *inter alia*, the beneficiary's specification of the sections in the underlying contract which had been breached. As there was no written contract between account party and beneficiary, the beneficiary presented a general description of the various items of breach of contract. This was considered sufficient. See also *Rb Haarlem, 9 January 1987*, KG 1987, 85, *CA Amsterdam, 8 June 1993*, KG 1993, 301, von Westphalen, p. 151, Nielsen, p. 82, and Dolan, § 6.04[5][b]. In *BGH, 24 November 1998*, WM 1999, p. 72, the discrepancies between the prescribed and submitted statements were considered to be too significant. See, however, *Frans Maas(UK) Ltd v. Habib Bank AG Zürich*, (5 August 2000, unreported, but mentioned in Jack, 12.66) for an unusually rigid application of the rule of strict compliance.

[37] WM 1997, p. 656. See also *OLG Köln, 30 October 1997*, WM 1998, p. 707, and *I.E. Contractors Ltd. V. Lloyds Bank Plc and Rafidain Bank*, (1990) 2 Lloyd's Rep. 496, see No. 13-13.

[38] WM 2000, p. 2334. In this case the guarantee required the beneficiary to make four seperate statements the wording of which was stated in the guarantee. Instead of making these four statements in an integral, full length manner, the beneficiary merely stated: 'we confirm that the facts mentioned under number 1-4 have occurred'. This statement was held to comply with the requirements of the relevant clause. The German Supreme Court in this case and in its 1997 decision, see previous footnote, and *OLG Frankfurt a.M., 8 February 2000*, WM 2001, p. 1108, only required strict or literal compliance if the guarantee contains an explicit clause to the effect that the beneficiary's statement must be strictly in accordance with the prescribed wording of the statement.

Moreover, the statement of default or other required statements need not contain other particulars or further specifications than those prescribed by the guarantee.[39]

First demand guarantees sometimes require the beneficiary to specify the nature of his complaints. This is also the case if the URDG apply, see art. 20(a). In these cases merely a formal statement that the account party is in default or that he has not fulfilled his obligations is insufficient.[40] There should be some description of the account party's default, but this can be expressed in general terms.[41]

By virtue of the independent nature of the guarantee the bank is not entitled and owes no duty to the account party to investigate the truthfulness of the statement of default or any other required statement.[42]

Ambiguous texts and statements; '*Effektivklauseln*'; guarantees payable on 'first justified demand'

13-13 The submission of a statement of default or any other statement by the beneficiary is only required if stipulated in the guarantee. However, the text of the guarantee is sometimes ambiguous in this respect.

In the case of *I.E. Contractors Ltd. v. Lloyds Bank Plc. and Rafidain Bank* the primary guarantee read: 'We undertake to pay to you, unconditionally, the said amount on demand, *being your claim for damages brought about by the above named principal*' [italics added]. The majority of the Court of Appeal held that the passage in italics was to be construed as requiring the submission of a statement by the beneficiary to the effect that the demand was 'a claim for damages brought about by the principal'. This is a matter of construction indeed, but it would appear that such a statement is required only if it is sufficiently apparent for the beneficiary and if it can be readily derived from

---

[39] See, for example, *BGH, 24 November 1983*, WM 1984, p. 44, *BGH, 28 October 1993*, WM 1994, p. 106, *OLG Köln, 30 October 1997*, WM 1998, p. 707, *Trib. com. Brussels, 21 October 1997*, RDC 1998, p. 850.

[40] *Trib. com Brussels, 15 December 1992*, RDC 1993, p. 1055, ruled that the bank correctly refused payment since the beneficiary had failed to indicate in what respect the account party had defaulted on his obligations, as was prescribed in the guarantee. See also *Trib. com. Brussels, 26 May 1988*, JT 1988, p. 460 (restraining orders granted). In this case the account party had particular reasons for insisting on a clause prescribing a specification of the complaints, see also Chapter 14.5.6, No. 14-27.

[41] See Affaki, No. 90 and the examples given, Goode, p. 93, Bertrams, TVVS 1993, p. 98.

[42] See Chapter 10, No. 10-20. See also *State Trading Corp. of India v. E.D. & F. Man*, [1981] Com LR 235, *BGH*, WM 1996, p. 770, *BGH, 17 October 1996*, WM 1996, p. 2228, von Westphalen, pp. 164-166, Zahn/Ehrlich/Neumann, 9/21, Dolan, § 6.04[5][b].

the text of the guarantee. One may question whether this was the case in respect of this particular text.[43]

Guarantees sometimes state that they are payable on first demand 'in the event of non-performance of the principal contract' or 'in the event that the contracting party fails to comply with its contractual obligations' or contain similar phrases. Such clauses, known as '*Effektivklauseln*', may give rise to difficulties regarding the nature of the 'guarantee'. If upon construction of the entire text the 'guarantee' is found to be an independent first demand guarantee, the bank cannot require any proof of non-performance or a statement of default, unless clearly stipulated, and the bank does not owe a duty to this effect to the account party.[44] Under German law, however, the submission of a formal statement appears to be required.[45]

Guarantees sometimes state that they are 'payable on first justified demand'. Case law construes this phrase to mean that the beneficiary must present a statement of default as discussed in no. 13-12, but no more.[46]

Documents from the account party

13-13a Guarantees, which are expressed to be payable on the beneficiary's first demand, sometimes call for a document to be signed by the account party, confirming, for example, that default has occurred. Alternatively, they may provide for payment on demand unless the account party submits a certain document, confirming, for example, that the secured contract has been fulfilled or that performance has been excused, which

---

[43] (1990) 2 Lloyd's Rep. 496. It should, however, be noted that the majority thought that substantial, rather than strict compliance with this requirement was sufficient. According to Buckley L.J. the passage merely expressed the purpose of the guarantee, with which view this study agrees. In a similar case *Cass., 20 November 1985*, D. 1986 J p. 213, it was held that the submission of this kind of statement was not required.

[44] See, for example, *Cass., 5 February 1985*, D. 1985 J. p. 269, *Paris, 29 January 1981*, D. 1981 J. p. 336, *Toulouse, 9 January 1992*, D. 1992 Somm. p. 236, *Brussels, 26 June 1992*, RDC 1994, p. 51. But see *Esal (Commodities) v. Oriental Credit*, [1985] 2 Lloyd's Rep. 546, where the court ruled that a statement of default was required. This rule was rejected by the Court of Appeal in *I.E. Contractors Ltd. v. Lloyds Bank Plc.*, [1990] 2 Lloyd's Rep. 496. See further for '*Effektivklauseln*' Chapter 10.8, No. 10-26, and Chapter 12.3, No. 12-21.

[45] In relation to a suretyship payable on first demand containing an '*Effektivklausel*', *BGH, 17 October 1996*, WM 1996, p. 2228, and *OLG München, 23 July 1997*, WM 1998, p. 342, referred to the submission of a statement of default, which the beneficiary had in fact presented. Staudinger/Horn, No. 27, 236, and Lienesch, pp. 127-128, take the view that, also in relation to an independent first demand guarantee with an '*Effektivklausel*', the beneficiary should submit a statement of default.

[46] See Chapter 12.3, No. 12-33.

may be a document issued by the account party itself, within a certain period of time. The bank should not pay in the first situation unless the beneficiary presents the required document signed by the account party, and, in the second situation, if the account party submits the stated document.[47]

Such conditions of payment clearly protect the interests of the account party in that they ensure that certain conditions are satisfied ('locking device') before the beneficiary is able to take advantage of the guarantee. On the other hand, these clauses render the beneficiary's position most vulnerable and in fact reverse the ordinary allocation of risks under first demand guarantees.

13.2.4 Call on a guarantee requiring submission of third-party documents

Documents to be tendered by the beneficiary

13-14 If the guarantee calls for the presentation of third-party documents certifying non-performance of the secured contract, the beneficiary must submit the documents containing the particulars as prescribed in the guarantee. The bank owes a duty to the account party to refuse payment if the beneficiary fails to tender these documents.[48]

---

[47] In *Ghent, 25 February 1988*, TBH 1989 p. 40, the guarantee was payable on demand unless the account party submitted a statement that the non-performance of the contract was caused by any of the reasons stated in Clause 9 of the secured contract. The account party did submit the statement and the bank refused payment. The Court of Appeal dismissed the beneficiary's claim for payment, affirming the rule stated in the text. See Dolan, § 2.05[3], for a review of similar American decisions.

[48] On these grounds stop-payment orders against the bank were granted in *Trib. com. Brussels, 14 August 1979*, Rev. Banque 1980, p. 101, and in *Trib. com. Brussels, 17 July 1984*, RDC 1985, p. 567. In *Gur Corporation v. Trust Bank of Africa*, IBL July 1986, p. 24, the court ordered the release of the security furnished by the account party on the same grounds, while it declined to adjudicate the beneficiary's claim for payment, for reasons of public international law. In *Brussels, 25 February 1982*, JCB 1982, p. 349, the account party's claim against the instructing bank was dismissed, because in the opinion of the court the documents tendered to the second issuing bank met the conditions of payment. Idem: *Trib. gr. inst. Paris, 26 January 1983*, D. 1983 I.R. p. 297. In *Rb Amsterdam, 27 January 1983*, KG 1983, 62 (interlocutory proceedings) and in *Rb Amsterdam, 26 February 1986*, NJ 1987, 398 (main proceedings), the payment guarantee required the submission of several documents, including a document to be drawn up by the bank itself confirming that the beneficiary had performed certain obligations pursuant to the secured contract. As the beneficiary had failed to do this, the bank refused to release the document and, consequently, to effect payment. The beneficiary's claim for payment was dismissed, since the bank's decisions were held to be correct.

The Demand for Payment 293

As regards the conformity of the documents, the principle of strict compliance applies to factual matters, such as, for example, the identity of the person who has issued the document and reference to the secured contract. As far as the contents of the certificates are concerned, this principle cannot always be applied, for instance where the guarantee does not specify the contents or does so in general terms only. But even if the text of the certificate has been specified, the circumstances of the case and the nature of the document may require that the principle of strict compliance be applied with restraint and moderation, lest substance is sacrified to form. To the extent that the principle of strict compliance has no application, the bank may have a certain degree of discretion in deciding whether the particular document satisfies the condition for payment. In addition, examination by the bank is to be carried out with reasonable care.[49]

In view of the principle of independence, the bank cannot and owes no duty to verify the truthfulness of the statements and findings contained in the documents. The bank is to decide on the basis of the documents only. On the other hand, if the beneficiary is unable to produce the required documents, he cannot be permitted to establish non-performance by the account party by other means.[50] Accordingly, the beneficiary bears the risk of not being able to obtain the prescribed documents, although the account party may have in fact breached his obligations.[51]

Documents to be tendered by the account party

13-15 Guarantees sometimes provide that they are payable on demand unless the account party tenders certain documents specified in the guarantee. The documents ordinarily confirm the performance of the secured contract by the account party. Such clauses are common in repayment guarantees. The guarantee usually states the period within which the account party must present the documents. The bank must refrain from payment if the account party submits the documents in accordance with the relevant clauses of the guarantee.[52] Should the account party be unable to produce the

---

[49] See further Chapter 10.8, Nos. 24-25.

[50] *Trib. com. Brussels, 27 July 1984*, RDC 1985, p. 567.

[51] See further Chapter 4, No. 4-10 last paragraph.

[52] See, for example, *OLG Hamburg, 4 November 1977*, RIW 1978, p. 615, and *BGH, 12 March 1984 (ll ZR 198/82)*, NJW 1984, p. 2030. In this case the account party had submitted the document, a certificate of the competent Teheran court, and the bank refused payment. The beneficiary then initiated summary proceedings against the bank arguing that the certificate had been obtained by fraudulent means with the connivance of the authority that had issued the certificate. This contention was rejected. In *Paris, 2 June 1982*, D. 1983 J. p. 437, upheld by *Cass., 5 February 1985*, D. 1985 J. p. 269, the Court of Appeal granted a stop-payment order against the instructing bank on the grounds that the primary guarantee and counter-guarantee had been called when the period during which the account party could submit the documents had not yet lapsed.

documents, then the bank must pay.[53] The observations in no. 13-14 concerning documents to be tendered by the beneficiary also apply here.

13.2.5 Call on guarantee requiring submission of an arbitral or court decision

General

13-16 If the guarantee requires the submission of a court judgment or an arbitral award, the bank should only pay if the beneficiary presents the decision. *Paris, 27 May 1991*,[54] and *Rb Rotterdam, 28 October 1993*,[55] ruled that a court decision in provisional proceedings (*procedure en réferé, kort geding*) satisfied this requirement.

There are certain criteria which the arbitral or judicial decision must always meet and which must be ascertained by the bank. It must be apparent from the decision that it relates to the dispute between account party and beneficiary concerning the underlying contract covered by the guarantee. It must also be apparent that judgment is given against the account party for a specified amount. A decision which merely contains general observations concerning breach of contract in the course of the judgment, will not do, not only because such observations are not conclusive of liability, but also because it would be impossible for the bank to evaluate such decisions.[56]

It has been suggested that the decision must clearly state that the beneficiary is entitled to demand payment under the guarantee.[57] Although such a statement would indeed be useful in view of the ultimate purpose of the decision, it is submitted that it is not a condition of payment, unless explicitly required under the terms of the guarantee. It should also be noted that the court or arbitrators are called upon to adjudicate the dispute between the parties to the underlying contract, and not the issue of whether the beneficiary is entitled to payment under the guarantee from the bank, which is not a party to the proceedings.

Under most insolvency laws it is not possible to initiate or pursue proceedings against a defendant who has been declared insolvent. This rule may cause difficulties if the

---

[53] See, for example, *Paris, 1 February 1984*, D. 1984 I.R. p. 265 (sequestration lifted) This case was the sequel to the French decisions cited in the previous note. In *Paris, 9 July 1986*, D. 1988 Somm. p. 243, and *Trib. com. Brussels, 15 November 1984*, RDC 1985, p. 569, restraining orders were granted, although the account party had not produced the documents, on the grounds that the '(counter-)guarantee' had to be construed as an accessory suretyship requiring proof of default.

[54] D. 1992 Somm. p. 239.

[55] Docket number 1066/93, not reported.

[56] Cf. Eisemann, Revue Arbitrage 1972, p. 395, and Dohm, No. 208.

[57] Dohm, No. 208, Eisemann, Revue Arbitrage 1972, pp. 395, 396.

guarantee requires a court judgment. However, the Dutch Supreme Court decision of *HR, 7 September 1990*, provides indirect authority for the proposition that in such a case recognition by the receiver of the claim against the insolvent account party is sufficient.[58]

Validity of the arbitral or court decision

13-17 Guarantees requiring the submission of an arbitral award or judicial decision can be particularly troublesome with respect to matters concerning the validity of the decision for the purpose of the guarantee. This holds true whether or not the guarantee imposes specific requirements. It is important to state at the outset that as a general rule the bank cannot be expected to investigate these matters. Any corroboration in this respect should come from the beneficiary or account party.

If the guarantee states that the decision should be rendered by a particular court or tribunal, a decision from another court or tribunal will not be acceptable, except in such special circumstances as was the case in *OLG Hamburg, 7 July 1977*, and *Paris, 10 November 1988*.[59] However, by no means all guarantees contain such specific provisions. In this situation the question could arise as to whether the court or tribunal was competent to adjudicate the dispute between account party and beneficiary for the purposes of the guarantee. Difficulties in this respect could perhaps best be resolved by applying the general rules for recognition of foreign judgements and arbitral awards *per analogiam*. The bank's duty in this respect extends no further than the exercise of reasonable care.

As far as the possibilities of challenging the judicial decision or arbitral award are concerned, the decision or award need not satisfy requirements which have not been stipulated in the guarantee. For instance, the fact that the account party has commenced appeal proceedings does not frustrate the beneficiary's right to immediate payment.[60] However, payment cannot be claimed should, in the meantime, the decision have been reversed on the merits of the case. If the guarantee provides for submission of a 'final' decision, the beneficiary must demonstrate that the decision can no longer be appealed

---

[58] Docket number 7523, not reported.

[59] See Chapter 10.8, No. 10-22.

[60] In *CA Amsterdam, 8 January 1987*, KG 1988, 300, the guarantee became payable upon submission of a judgment of the Dutch Supreme Court affirming the decision of the Court of Appeal concerning the underlying relationship. The decision of the Supreme Court had been submitted, but the bank refused payment on the grounds that in other, related proceedings a judge had granted an interlocutory order staying the execution of the judgment of the Court of Appeal. In the proceedings against the bank, the Amsterdam Court of Appeal held that the terms of the guarantee had been met and that the guarantee did not state that decisions such as the interlocutory order precluded a call on the guarantee.

against. Guarantees requiring the submission of a 'valid' arbitral award are apt to cause difficulties as regards the meaning of that term. Does it mean that the award should not be an absolute nullity, or that certain formal requirements under the applicable arbitration law, such as the signing and dating of the award by the arbitrators, the forwarding of a copy to parties and the lodging of the award with the court, have to be satisfied? Or does it mean that leave for enforcement must have been obtained, which is only refused in truly exceptional circumstances, or perhaps that the award must have withstood a challenge in full-scale proceedings for setting aside the award?[61] It is submitted that, in the absence of further qualifications which clearly point the other way, the term 'valid' award merely implies that the award is enforceable in accordance with the applicable arbitration law.

13.2.6 Other conditions and clauses

Conditions precedent

13-18 If the guarantee contains a condition precedent, the beneficiary must demonstrate that the condition has been fulfilled in accordance with its terms, or by other means should the relevant condition not mention the documentary evidence. The bank owes a duty to the account party to ascertain fulfilment and to refuse payment if the condition has not been met.[62] The various aspects of conditions precedent have been examined elsewhere.[63]

---

[61] Thus *Rb Utrecht, 7 August 1986*, KG 1986, 413. In his critical comment Hammerstein, NJB 1987, pp. 656-659, prefers a construction according to which leave for enforcement is sufficient. See also Eisemann, Revue Arbitrage 1972, p. 397.

[62] In *CA Brussels, 2 March 2001*, TBH 2002, p. 484, the condition precedent read as follows: 'This guarantee enters into effect only upon receipt of an irrevocable letter of credit in favour of ... (the account party) for an amount of USD 765.201. We shall inform you (the beneficiary) by fax message as soon as the guarantee is effective'. The letter of credit had been issued and received by the bank/guarantor. When the beneficiary called the guarantee, the bank refused to pay arguing, *inter alia*, that the guarantee had not entered into effect because the bank had not sent a fax message confirming the receipt of the letter of credit. *CA Brussels* rightly rejected this defence as untenable. In *BGH, 26 April 2001*, WM 2002, p. 1208, the guarantee required confirmation from the account party that certain works had been completed as a condition precedent to payment. There was no such confirmation. The German Supreme Court rejected the beneficiary's argument that the confirmation was not required in this particular case as the the account party's entry in the register of the Chamber of Commerce had been deleted because of its financial position. The court observed that it was still possible for the beneficiary to commence proceedings against the account party in order to obtain the required confirmation.

[63] Chapter 8.5 and Chapter 10.8, Nos. 10-19 and 10-26.

Clauses limiting or terminating the right to payment

13-19 The guarantee may contain clauses which limit or terminate the right to payment upon certain events. Ordinarily it is incumbent on the account party to show that these events have occurred in accordance with the terms of the relevant provisions, unless the events are quite apparent to the bank. If demonstrated in the appropriate manner, the bank should refrain from payment.[64]

Repayment guarantees and advance payment

13-20 Most repayment guarantees designate actual advance payment by the beneficiary as a condition precedent or as an ordinary condition of payment. Usually they also specify the manner in which the advance payment is to be effected, such as by transferring the amount to the account party's account with the issuing bank. Since this particular manner of payment serves the interests of the bank, it is entitled to refuse payment if the conditions have not been strictly complied with.[65] The beneficiary should, therefore, be most meticulous when effecting the down payment. It has been argued that on the grounds of good faith the bank may not be permitted to invoke the rule of strict compliance if the bank has not been prejudiced by the departure from the prescribed manner of payment.[66] This proposition may be accepted, albeit along a different line of reasoning. Provided that the interests of the bank have not been impaired and provided that the account party has actually received the down payment, the forfeiting of the beneficiary's right to payment would have the practical effect of bestowing an undeserved windfall on the account party. In such circumstances adherence to the principle of strict compliance may not serve the legitimate interests of the account party and bank. However, in such like circumstances *Paris, 17 December 1992*,[67] and *Trib. com. Brussels, 5 February 1996*,[68] abided by the principle of strict compliance.

---

[64] See further Chapter 10.8, Nos. 10-19, 10-26, 10-27.

[65] *Cass., 3 June 1986*, D. 1987 Somm. p. 174, *OLG Frankfurt a.M., 25 November 1977*, WM 1978, p. 1188, *OLG Stuttgart, 20 December 2000*, WM 2001, p. 1335. In all three cases the beneficiary's claim for payment against the bank was dismissed on the grounds of failure to comply with such specific terms as mentioned in the text. In *Paris, 26 February 1985*, D. 1985 I.R. p. 244, the bank had transferred the down payment to the principal contractor, who had gone bankrupt, instead of to the subcontractor/account party. The bank was ordered to pay damages of FF 1 million (€ 151,000) to the subcontractor/account party.

[66] Canaris, No. 1133b, Zahn/Ehrlich/Neumann, 9/119.

[67] D. 1993 Somm. p. 98, examined in Chapter 10.8, No. 10-22.

[68] RW 1996/1997, p. 1263. The beneficiary/buyer had agreed to make an advance payment of 30% of the purchase price. The guarantee required, as a condition precedent, the payment of '30%, i.e. DEM 140,220' (approx. € 70,000). In fact, the beneficiary/buyer made an advance

If the repayment guarantee fails to designate actual down payment by the beneficiary as a condition precedent or as an ordinary condition of payment, it could still be argued that the beneficiary is not entitled to payment under the repayment guarantee unless he shows that the down payment has been made. The essence of a repayment guarantee is to secure repayment of the advance payment. Actual transmission of the advance payment would, therefore, seem to be an implied condition in repayment guarantees.[69]

Reduction clauses

13-21 Clauses which reduce the maximum amount of the guarantee upon progressive performance of the secured contract by the account party are the most common type of clauses reducing or terminating the beneficiary's right to payment. It is for the account party to establish progressive performance and the bank owes no duty to investigate of its own accord whether and when the reduction clause is to be put into effect. Difficulties arise when the reduction clause does not contain an appropriate mechanism for its implementation, as is illustrated in *Cass. 16 June 1992*.[70] In this case the guarantee provided for a reduction in accordance with the deliveries by the seller/account party, but without specifying a particular documentary mechanism. The bank also acted as the issuer of a documentary credit in favour of the seller. Although the seller had presented all documents in accordance with the terms of the documentary credit to the bank, it paid the full amount under the guarantee to the buyer, who alleged that the goods had never arrived. The seller's claim against the bank and beneficiary was rejected on the grounds that he was unable to prove that the contract had been fully performed in accordance with its terms, the presentation of the documents under the documentary credit being insufficient evidence thereof.[71]

---

payment of DEM 123,000, being 30% of the purchase prices, exclusive of V.A.T. Because of non-performance by the seller the beneficiary made a demand for payment under the guarantee for the amount of DEM 123,000, which matched his advance payment. This claim was rejected because, according to the court, the condition precedent had not been fulfilled. See also Chapter 12.3.5, No. 12-37.

[69] Cf. Mattout, No. 212, Poullet, thesis No. 323, von Westphalen, p. 152-154, Canaris, No. 1131. See also Chapter 14.5.16.

[70] D. 1993 Somm. p. 97.

[71] See also: *Paris, 19 May 1988*, D. 1989 Somm. p. 146, where an application for a restraining order against the first instructing bank was dismissed because the account party had made none of the projected shipments. In *BGH, 21 April 1988*, WM 1988, p. 934, the bank was ordered to pay the full amount of the guarantee as the works had not been approved and because the contractor had discontinued the project. Contra: *Paris, 14 October 1983*, D. 1984 I.R. p. 202. In this case, the method of implementation of the reduction clause was

Reduction clauses usually specify the documents evidencing the progressive performance of the contract. In this event the reduction clause becomes operative only if the account party has produced these documents to the bank prior to payment in the manner specified in the relevant clause. If this has not been done, the bank is not liable for having paid the full amount of the guarantee and is entitled to reimbursement. And similarly, the beneficiary continues to be entitled to claim the full amount of the guarantee, unless the terms of the reduction clause have been met.[72] Should the reduction be linked to a particular event, for example delivery or provisional acceptance, without specification of any corroborating documents, it is for the account party to show that the event has occurred. If he succeeds, the reduction clause becomes operative and the beneficiary can no longer claim the full amount arguing that his actual loss exceeds the reduced amount, as is perfectly demonstrated in *CA Brussels 26 June 1992*.[73]

---

expressed in a general and, for the bank unascertainable, fashion (automatic reduction in accordance with the terms of the secured contract). The Court of Appeal ruled that the (issuing) bank owed a duty to ascertain whether the maximum amount had to be reduced. Its failure to do this rendered the (issuing) bank liable and the instructing bank was restrained from reimbursing the issuing bank. In a similar case, *Trib. com. Paris, 7 September 1983*, D. 1987 Somm. p. 174, also granted a restraining order against the instructing bank for the same reasons. This order was, however, set aside by *Trib. com. Paris, 6 January 1987*, D. 1987 Somm. p. 174, on other grounds, namely that the instructing bank must repay the issuing bank except in cases of fraudulent collusion by the issuing bank. In *Aix-en-Provence, 31 March 1978*, not reported, but mentioned by Poullet, JCB 1982, p. 653, the bank was held liable to the account party on the grounds that it was in possession of the shipping documents in its capacity as bank charged with the execution of the documentary credit relating to the same transaction. See also Chapter 10.8, Nos. 10-19, 10-26 and 10-27.

[72] *Trib. com. Paris, 7 February 1989*, D. 1990 Somm. p. 207 (restraining order against the instructing bank granted as the the terms of the reduction clause had been fulfilled, namely the presentation by the account party of the required statement from the beneficiary evidencing performance). *Brussels, 26 June 1992*, RDC 1994, p. 51 (injunctions granted against the beneficiary to cause the maximum amount to be reduced in accordance with the reduction clause and against the bank to act in accordance therewith, since the terms of the reduction clause were fulfilled). *Cass. 23 October 1990*, D. 1991 Somm. p. 197 (account party's claim against the bank rejected because the account party had not presented the required documents). *Trib. com. Nantes, 22 September 1983*, D. 1984 I.R. p. 202 (instructing bank's defence against the claim for reimbursement to the issuing bank rejected). In *Paris, 16 March 1988*, D. 1989 Somm. p. 146, affirmed by *Cass. 5 December 1989*, D. 1990 Somm. p. 146, the instructing bank was also ordered to reimburse the second issuing bank. The Court of Appeal reasoned that even if the appointed surveyor had issued documents evidencing proper execution of the shipments, these documents had not been presented to the issuing bank at the time of the call on the guarantee and the payment by the bank. *Trib. com. Brussels, 10 January 1992*, RDC 1993, p. 1052 (bank ordered to pay the full amount because the terms of the reduction clause were not fulfilled). See also von Westphalen, pp. 129, 130.

13.2.7 Period of validity

Call must be made on or before the expiry date or before the expiry event

13-22 As far as the countries covered in this study and most other countries are concerned, it is established law that the call must be made *on* or *before* the expiry date and that, if the expiry depends on a certain event, the call must be made *before* this event, cf. art. 19 URDG, Rule 3.05(a) j. Rule 3.01 ISP98 and art. 15(2) UNCITRAL Convention. If made after this date or event the bank is entitled to refuse payment to the beneficiary and it owes a duty to this effect to the account party.[74] It should be noted that the expiry date need not be the expiry date mentioned in the guarantee, since the period of validity may have been extended pursuant to an 'extend or pay' request. Such requests must also be made within the then existing period of validity.[75]

---

[73] RDC 1994 p. 51. In this case 50% was to be released upon completion of 90% of the project and the remainder upon the submission of certain documents. The court found that 90% of the project had indeed been completed and ordered the beneficiary to cause the maximum amount to be reduced by 50% and the bank to act in accordance therewith. The court also observed that the beneficiary continued to be allowed to call the guarantee for the remainder of the maximum amount, since the required documents for the release of the other half had not been produced.

[74] See, for example, *Rb Amsterdam, 5 September 1991*, KG 1991, 335, *BGH, 13 July 1989*, WM 1989, p. 1496, *OLG Hamburg, 4 November 1977*, RIW 1978, p. 615, *OLG Stuttgart, 25 January 1979*, RIW 1980, p. 729, *OLG Frankfurt a.M., 16 September 1982*, RIW 1983, p. 785, *Cass., 3 June 1986*, D. 1987 Somm. p. 174, *Cass., 24 January 1989*, D. 1989 Somm. p. 159, *Trib. com. Paris, 8 July 1983*, D. 1984 I.R. p. 92, *Brussels, 7 November 1988*, RDC 1990, p. 91, *Trib. com. Turnhout, 30 October 1995*, RW 1996/1997, p. 328, *Trib. com. Brussels, 15 December 1992*, RDC 1993, p. 1055, *Offshore Enterprises Inc. v. Nordic Bank PLC*, IBL November 1984, p. 86, *Gur Corporation v. Trust Bank of Africa*, IBL July 1986, p. 24, *Nat. Westminster Bank v. Hardman*, not reported, but reviewed by Goode, JBL 1988, pp. 264-266. In *Cass., 26 January 1993*, D. 1995 Somm. p. 13, the bank, which had honoured a demand for payment made after the expiry date, claimed reimbursement from the account party, alleging that the account party had not objected to the payment and had extended the period of validity of his counter-guarantee in favour of the bank (rejected). Equally, in *RB Rotterdam, 28 February 2002*, JOR 2002, 105, the bank, which had had honoured a demand for payment made after the expiry date, was ordered to undo the debiting of the account party's account. See also other case law cited in Chapter 13.2.7. See for legal writing, for example, von Westphalen, pp. 155, 161, Zahn/Ehrlich/Neumann, 9/33, Prüm. pp. 179-181, Dolan, § 5.03[3][b/e] with references to American case law. The same rule applies to calls on the counter-guarantee, see Chapter 13.3, No. 13-39.

[75] See also *Paris, 25 February 1988*, D. 1989 Somm. p. 150. As far as the laws of Saudi Arabia are concerned, this rule is laid down in Circular No. 17/2273 of the Ministry of Finance and National Economy.

The Demand for Payment 301

While the issue of the applicable, national law is normally of little importance, it is of particular significance in matters concerning expiry dates. The law governing the guarantee determines the question of whether or not expiry dates are enforceable.[76]

Regarding the timeliness of the call, the question may arise as to whether the time of dispatch of the request for payment or the time of receipt by the bank is to be considered as the proper yardstick. *Trib. com. Brussels, 21 November 1997*, ruled that, in the absence of a clause to the contrary, the date of despatch is the proper test.[77] Most guarantees resolve this problem by stating explicitly that the request must have been 'received by us (the bank)' on or before the expiry date, with the result that delays in transmission are a risk borne by the beneficiary. It has been suggested that this rule also prevails in the absence of such a specific provision.[78] Indeed, it can be argued that the question of whether the date of despatch or the date of receipt by the bank is the proper citerion should not be left to the general rules in this respect under the applicable law, and that there exists a special uniform rule for bank guarantees and standby letters of credit to the effect that the date of receipt is decisive.[79] A further question is whether the demand for payment must have been received by the bank, at the latest, on the expiry date during banking hours or that it suffices that the demand reaches the bank before 12.00 p.m. on the expiry date. Rule 3.05 (b) and 9.04 ISP98 provide for the former, while *CA Liège, 24 September 1999*, ruled in favour of the latter test.[80] Obviously, it is best if the guarantee also specifies the particular time of day on the expiry date before which the demand must have been received.

A timely call may be prevented by *force majeure*, but stringent requirements for a succesful plea ought to be set. *OLG Stuttgart, 25 January 1979*, provides a salient example.[81] The demand for payment from the Lebanese beneficiary was received four

---

[76] An overview of the countries concerned is given in Chapter 12.4.5, Nos. 12-53/54. In *Offshore Enterprises Inc. v. Nordic Bank PLC*, IBL November 1984, p. 86, the direct guarantee in favour of an Indian company was made subject to Indian law. Referring to the clause concerning the period of validity of the guarantee the court brushed aside the contention that such provisions are not enforceable under Indian law.

[77] RDC 1998, p. 850.

[78] Von Westphalen, p. 156, Zahn/Ehrlich/Neumann, 9/33-34, Boll, p. 113.

[79] This seems to be the case under the ISP98, see Rule 3.05(b) and 9.04, and under art. 15(2) UNCITRAL Convention.

[80] RDC 2000, p. 734. In relation to a guarantee which provided that the demand for payment should reach the bank on 30 December 1995, the Court of Appeal ruled that the call by SWIFT message sent on Friday 29 December 1995, 4.31 p.m. after banking hours had reached the bank on that day, although it had not been processed until 2 January 1996, 3.19 p.m.

[81] RIW 1980, p. 729.

days after the expiry date. The beneficiary argued that civil war conditions and the closing of banks, including the closing of the Lebanese advising bank through which the call had to be transmitted, prevented the call being made in time. The Court of Appeal emphasised the importance of strictly adhering to expiry dates and rejected the beneficiary's contention of bad faith on the part of the bank and the plea of *force majeure*.

The principles stated above are not affected by the fact that the request for payment has been transmitted through a local branch of the issuing bank or through the advising bank in the beneficiary's country, unless the local branch or the advising bank has been designated as the entity where the demand can be lodged.[82]

It often happens, especially if the period of validity has been extended, that the expiry date falls on a non-business day at the bank's place of business. In that event the expiry date shall be extended to the following business day.[83]

In the absence of explicit provisions to the contrary, the mere retention of the guarantee document does not prevent the guarantee from ceasing to be valid upon the expiry date.[84]

Significance and effect of expiry dates; independence and relationship with underlying contract; submission of statements and documents; discharge of restraining orders

13-23 A call on or before the expiry date or before the expiry event is just one of the conditions that have to be fulfilled. A call made after the expiry date/event is invalid even if the default of the account party has occurred within the validity period.[85] In this respect independent guarantees are markedly different from accessory guarantees.

Because of the principle of independence, the period of validity of the guarantee is determined by the terms of the guarantee and not by reference to the underlying contract. Thus, it may happen that the guarantee has expired in accordance with its terms, even though the secured contract has not yet been completed or terminated.[86] In such

---

[82] Cf. Chapter 13.2.1, No. 13-6.

[83] *BGH, 18 December 1986*, NJW 1987, p. 1760, art. 12(a) UNCITRAL Convention, Rule 3.13 ISP98. See also Mijnssen, and von Westphalen, p. 157.

[84] See also Chapter 12.4.6, No. 12-57.

[85] *BGH, 13 July 1989*, WM 1989, p. 1496, *OLG Stuttgart, 25 January 1979*, RIW 1980, p. 729, *OLG Frankfurt a.M., 16 September 1982*, RIW 1983, p. 785.

[86] Cf. *Cass., 3 June 1986*, D. 1987 Somm. p. 174, *Offshore Enterprises v. Nordic Bank PLC*, IBL November 1984, p. 86. See also the American case of *Exxon Co. U.S.A. v. Banque de Paris et des Pays-Bas*, 828 F2d 1121 (5th. Cir. 1987), IFLR December 1987, p. 41. In connection with a swap contract for the delivery of oil a guarantee had been issued payable upon

The Demand for Payment 303

circumstances the beneficiary should consider lodging an 'extend or pay' request. The reverse is also true: the period of validity of the guarantee does not depend on completion or termination of the secured contract in accordance with its terms or upon mutual agreement or on other clauses in the secured contract. Thus, for example, the Cour de Cassation in *Cass., 19 May 1992*, ruled that the primary guarantee and counter-guarantee, which stated that they expired upon final acceptance of the works, continued to be in force until that event, although the secured contract provided that the guarantee had to be called no later than 31 July 1987.[87] While, as stated above, clear evidence of completion of the secured contract does not terminate the guarantee, it might constitute a basis for the account party to obtain injunctions against the beneficiary or bank because of fraud, as was recognised in *Paris, 8 November 1988*.[88]

---

a statement that the account party had failed to deliver the oil 'between September and December 1981'. This guarantee also provided that it expired on 31 October 1981. The account party was unable to deliver the oil, but the beneficiary could not possibly issue the above-mentioned statement on 31 October. The US Court of Appeal decided that the bank was correct in refusing to honour the request for payment made after 31 October and that the bank did not act in bad faith in issuing the guarantee even though the beneficiary would not be able to use it; see further Dolan, § 4.08[5]. In a similar case *Cass., 3 June 1986*, D. 1987 Somm. p. 174, reached the same conclusion, see Chapter 13.3, No. 13-39.

[87] D. 1993 Somm. p. 103 (2e decision). See also, for example, *Paris, 8 November 1988*, D. 1990 Somm. p. 206, *BGH, 31 January 1985*, WM 1985, p. 511, *Paris, 22 November 1985*, D. 1986 I.R. p. 155, *Trib. com. Paris, 6 March 1987*, D. 1988 Somm. p. 249 and the annotations by Vasseur. *Harris Corp. v. Nat. Iranian Radio and Television*, 691 F2d. 1344 (11th. Cir. 1982) (account party's argument that the termination of the principal contract in accordance with its *force majeure* provisions terminates the guarantee rejected; stop-payment order granted on the grounds of fraud). See, however, *CA Amsterdam, 19 January 1989*, KG 1990, 74, where the guarantee provided for a calendar expiry date, which had been extended several times due to delays in the execution of the project, while art. 60.8.b of the secured contract stated that the guarantee was to be automatically released upon substantial completion as evidenced by certain documents. The Court of Appeal took the view that the certificates did satisfy the relevant requirements. It then ruled that the fact that the guarantee did not contain any references to art. 60.8.b. of the secured contract did not alter the fact that account party and beneficiary had agreed that the guarantee was to be considered as automatically released and that consequently *between account party and beneficiary* the guarantee had ceased to be valid. It is submitted that this ruling violates the principle of independence.

[88] D. 1990 Somm. p. 206. The Court of Appeal observed, however, that the release of certificates of completion was insufficient evidence because they were only provisional certificates and because the account party had agreed to an extension of the guarantee which suggested that the works had not been fully completed. See also Chapter 14.5.5.

If the guarantee requires the submission of a statement of default, third-party documents or any other documents, these have to be presented on or before the expiry date too. It is not sufficient that the request for payment has been made within the period of validity.[89] It could be argued, however, that minor defects in the documents, which have been submitted in time, can be remedied within a very short period after the expiry date.[90] One must bear in mind that these documents, unlike those in the case of documentary credits, do not have an intrinsic value and that, by their nature, they cannot be used for other purposes.

Once the request for payment and the fulfilment of the other conditions of payment have taken place within the period of validity, it does not, of course, matter that payment is effected after the expiry date.[91] Likewise, in the event of repeated demands for payment, for example because the bank delays payment, the call is valid if the first call is made within the validity period even though subsequent demands for payment are made after the expiry date.[92] In fact, a considerable delay between the call and actual payment is not uncommon. Delays could also occur as a result of a stop-payment or conservatory attachment orders (freezing orders) which are not discharged until some time later. A fresh demand for payment upon discharge but after the expiry date is clearly valid, since it is merely a restatement of the previous call. It may, however, happen that the beneficiary has been prevented from making a timely call by virtue of a restraining order. It is submitted that, if such an order is lifted after the expiry date, the beneficiary is entitled to call the guarantee notwithstanding the expiry thereof because otherwise the discharge of the previous restraining order would not achieve its intended effect. Should this exception not be recognised, courts should only grant orders restraining the beneficiary from calling the guarantee on condition that the period

---

[89] *CA Amsterdam, 2 February 1992*, NJ 1992, 735, *BGH, 12 March 1996*, WM 1996, p. 770, OLG *Karlsruhe, 21 July 1992*, RIW 1992, p. 843, *CA Amsterdam, 3 December 1981*, rolnr. 471/180, not reported, but mentioned by Boll, p. 115, *Gur Corporation v. Trust Bank of Africa*, IBL July 1986, p. 24, art. 19 URDG, von Westphalen, pp. 155, 167, Zahn/Ehrlich/Neumann, 9/33/113, Dolan, § 5.03[3][b], p. 5-47.

[90] Cf. Canaris, No. 1127. See also No. 13-24.

[91] *Cass., 13 December 1983*, D. 1984 J. p. 420, *Paris, 22 November 1985*, D. 1986 I.R. p. 155, *OG Austria, 18 December 1987*, IBL November 1988, p. 92. In all three cases the account party's complaint that the bank had proceeded to payment after the expiry date was rejected. In *CA 's-Hertogenbosch, 1 December 1993*, NJ 1994, 740, the Court of Appeal granted the account party's application for a judicial statement that the guarantee had expired. The correctness of this statement is unclear since the guarantee had been called prior to the expiry date. It should be noted, however, that this decision involved a case of established fraud.

[92] Cf. *Montpellier, 12 July 1995*, Banque November 1995, p. 90.

The Demand for Payment

of validity is extended or limit such orders against the beneficiary to a prohibition to receive payment.[93]

Special problems. 'Extend or pay' requests, ambiguous requirement as to statements by the beneficiary

13-24 The communications from the beneficiary to the bank must be such that it is clear he is seeking payment. General statements concerning difficulties with the account party or non-performance are not sufficient. In a number of cases it has indeed been held that the communication did not constitute a proper call, with the result that unambiguous requests for payment made after the expiry date were considered to be too late.[94] If the beneficiary calls the guarantee but omits to specify the amount, it is suggested that the call is validly made, unless the indication of the amount claimed is

---

[93] Cf. Zahn/Ehrlich/Neumann, 9/140.

[94] *Rb Amsterdam, 5 September 1991*, KG 1991, 335; Court of first instance in the case of *OLG Stuttgart, 11 February 1981*, WM 1981, p. 631, which granted a stop-payment order against the instructing bank, reversed by the Stuttgart Court of Appeal on other grounds, and *OLG Frankfurt a.M., 16 September 1982*, RIW 1983, p. 785. In this case the beneficiary claimed an amount of DM 20,000 (approx. € 10,000) within the period of validity, which had been paid out, and a further amount of DM 95,000 (approx. € 48,000) after the expiry date. The Court of Appeal rejected the second claim on the grounds that it had been made too late and because the beneficiary had failed to announce explicitly that the first call related to part of the claim only. In *Brussels, 17 November 1988*, RDC 1990, p. 91, the Court of Appeal ruled that the beneficiary's communications relating to the general state of affairs did not amount to a clear demand for payment. The bank was held liable to the account party for honouring a call made after the expiry date; *Brussels, 28 March 1991*, TBH 1992, p. 996 (the mere presentation of an invoice in relation to a payment guarantee does not constitute a proper demand for payment); Trib. *com. Brussels, 15 December 1992*, RDC 1993, p. 1055 (no clear demand before expiry, bank correctly refused to honour a clear demand after expiry); *LG Berlin, 13 April 2000*, WM 2000, p. 2378 (no clear demand before expiry, bank correctly refused payment upon a clear demand two years later and made after the expiry date while the second demand was also inconsistent with the previous demand). In *Cass., 13 December 1983*, D. 1984 J. p, 420, the communications from the issuing bank to the instructing bank, transmitted before the expiry date of the counter-guarantee, were interpreted as constituting a proper demand for payment. In *Trib. com. Lyon*, D. 1990 Somm. p. 206, a demand for payment unless the account party agreed to modifications in the underlying contract was held to be an invalid call and was in fact considered as fraudulent. In *CA Amsterdam, 20 January 1983*, docket number 62/82 KG, not reported, the Court of Appeal held that a communication whereby the beneficiary requested 'conditional' payment of the outstanding debts without specification of the amount and without the (timely) submission of the required statement of default did not constitute a proper and valid demand.

a specific condition of payment to be made before the expiry date.[95] The bank should not, however, proceed to payment until the beneficiary has specified the amount.[96]

'Extend or pay' requests made within the validity period of the guarantee constitute a proper demand for payment when extension has not been granted.[97] In order to be a valid demand the request must, according to art. 26 URDG, Rule 3.09 ISP98 and *BGH, 23 January* 1996,[98] comply with all conditions for payment, including the submission of the prescribed statements by the beneficiary prior to the non-extended expiry date. It has been pointed out that the propriety of this rule might be questioned.[99] Rigid enforcement of the principle of strict compliance in these circumstances may invite dubious delaying tactics on the part of the bank and account party where, as is often the case, the 'extend or pay' request is made shortly before the expiry date and there might be cause to allow the beneficiary to still submit the prescribed documents or to make the demand in the correct form shortly after the expiry date.[100]

---

[95] Cf. *OLG Frankfurt a. M., 16 September 1982*, RIW 1983, p. 785. This issue remained undecided in *Rb Utrecht, 24 February 2003*, JOR 2004, 21, with annotation by Bertrams. *CA Amsterdam, 27 February 1992*, NJ 1992, 735, ruled, however, that the beneficiary must specify the amount prior to the expiry of the guarantee. This decision has been criticised by Bertrams, V&O 1992, pp. 62-64, who observes that it would virtually force the beneficiary to always claim the full amount which is not in the bank's or account party's interest

[96] Cf. Canaris, No. 1126, Nielsen, p. 82, Zahn/Ehrlich/Neumann, 9/117, von Westphalen, pp. 150, 151, 155. Von Westphalen argues, however, that such a call should be deemed to relate to the full amount of the guarantee.

[97] Chapter 12.4.3, No. 12-41.

[98] WM 1996, p. 393.

[99] See Chapter 12.4.3, No. 12-41.

[100] In the above-mentioned case of *BGH, 23 January 1996*, WM 1996, p. 393, the validity period had been extended several times, lastly until 31 October 1992. The beneficiary made an 'extend or pay' request, without a certain statement, on 15 October 1992, with a reminder on 30 October 1992. Not until 2 November 1992 did the bank inform the beneficiary that it would revert to the matter and as late as 11 November 1992 did the bank reply that the validity period would not be extended. On 15 November 1992 the beneficiary lodged a demand for payment with the required statement. The court's decision that the bank was correct in refusing payment on the ground that a valid call, i.e. with the required statement, had been made after the unamended expiry date, seems rather harsh. This case should be contrasted with *CA Liège, 24 September 1999*, RDC 2000, p. 734, in which the court ruled that the bank could not refuse payment because of certain irregularities in a fourth 'extend or pay' request as it had not objected to three previous requests which suffered from the same defects.

The Demand for Payment 307

In the event of a 'hold for value' request made within the period of validity, the definite demand for cash payment could be made after the expiry date.[101]

It is sometimes not clear from the text of the guarantee whether or not the beneficiary is expected to submit certain statements.[102] Should it be determined that the submission of such documents is indeed a condition of payment and if the bank rejects the demand for payment on this account, it is suggested that the beneficiary is permitted to present these statements after the expiry date, provided that he acts without undue delay after receiving notice of refusal.[103]

Commencement date

13-25 The guarantee may state that it cannot be called before a certain date. Obviously, the bank should not honour requests for payment made before this date.

A hybrid form of such commencement clauses is the provision that the guarantee is payable on demand unless the account party submits certain documents before a certain date. These clauses are not uncommon in repayment guarantees. Such a clause enables the account party to show in accordance with the terms of the clause that he has performed (part of) the contract. In this event the bank should not proceed to payment before this date.[104]

Expiry event

13-26 Instead of or in addition to a calendar date, guarantees sometimes also contain an expiry event, for example 'the guarantee expires upon release of the certificates from the engineer confirming completion'. Such clauses could present difficulties for the bank because it may not be aware of the release of the documents and it may also

---

[101] *OG Austria, 18 December 1987*, IBL November 1988, p. 92, and see Chapter 12.4.4, No. 12-48.

[102] See Chapter 13.2.3, No. 13-13.

[103] If the guarantee is a so-called 'simple' demand guarantee but subject to the URDG, the beneficiary should certainly be allowed to present the statement of default shortly after the expiry date because the requirement concerning such a statement does not appear in the text of the guarantee and will, therefore, come as a surprise.

[104] In *Paris, 2 June 1982*, D. 1983 J. p. 437, in this respect upheld by *Cass., 5 February 1985*, D. 1985 J. p. 269, the Court of Appeal ordered the sequestration of the moneys of the counter-guarantee, because the repayment guarantee, and therefore also the counter-guarantee, had been called prematurely. In *Paris, 1 February 1984*, D. 1984 I.R. p. 265, the sequestration was lifted when the account party was unable to produce the required documents at the time stated in the guarantee.

be difficult for the bank to decide whether the documents tendered satisfy the requirements of the documents described in the guarantee.[105] Even more problematical are clauses which do not refer to documents which evidence the event but which refer to the event itself, for example 'the guarantee ceases to be valid one month after the maintenance period'[106] or 'the guarantee is valid until the last reception of the goods by the administration'.[107]

If the event described in the guarantee has occurred, the bank should refuse payment to the beneficiary, but this is only of practical relevance if the bank is aware of the occurrence. Events such as those mentioned above are not ascertainable by the bank. Therefore, it is for the account party to show the bank before payment that the event has occurred.[108] This he must do by presenting the required documents to the bank or, in the case of a non-documentary event, by adducing proof that the event has taken place. Especially in the case last mentioned, discharge of the burden of proof often turns out to be difficult, as is shown by case law. Should the account party fail to notify the bank in the appropriate manner that the event has occurred, then the bank incurs no liability if it has made payment to the beneficiary. Nor does the mere fact that the event

---

[105] In the case of *Paris, 24 April 1992*, D. 1993 Somm. p. 102, the guarantee expired upon submission by the account party of a certificate of provisional acceptance in respect of the entire works signed by the beneficiary. The Court of Appeal ruled that the certificate which the account party had submitted, did not amount to the prescribed certificate, since it contained qualifications which were considered significant by both parties and that the guarantee had, therefore, not expired. In *OLG Köln, 7 August 1986*, WM 1988, p. 21, the first demand guarantee stated that it expired upon delivery, which had to be evidenced by the relevant shipping documents. In an application for a restraining order against the bank the seller/account party produced some statements from a forwarding agency to the effect that it had received the goods for further dispatch, and argued that the guarantee had expired. The Court of Appeal ruled that these documents did not amount to the kind of documents mentioned in the expiry clause and held that the guarantee had not expired. The Court of Appeal rightly refused to investigate whether the seller had delivered the goods in accordance with the terms of the underlying sale contract for the purposes of the expiry date set out in the guarantee. See also the case of *CA Amsterdam, 19 January 1989*, KG 1990, 74, where the Court of Appeal took the view that the documents met the requirements, whereas the court of first instance considered them insufficient.

[106] This example is taken from *Rb Amsterdam, 10 January 1997*, KG 1997, 44. The court held that the account party had not shown that this expiry event had occurred prior to the demand for payment.

[107] The last example is taken from *Rb Amsterdam, 5 September 1991*, KG 1991, 335. The court construed the precise meaning of the event by reference to the relevant terms of the underlying contract (cf. Chapter 12.3.5, No. 12-37) and found that the call was made after this event.

[108] See also Chapter 10.8. Nos. 10-26 and 10-27.

has occurred prevent the bank from claiming reimbursement, because this fact by itself does not evidence breach of its duty of examination.[109] If the account party is unable to prove in the appropriate manner that the event has occurred, the guarantee continues to be in force.

The principles set out above equally apply to indirect guarantees, albeit that the issues described above will then apply to the counter-guarantee in favour of the issuing bank.[110] It sometimes happens that the counter-guarantee contains the same expiry event as the primary guarantee. In this event, the question arises as to whether the account party can obtain an injunction against the instructing bank restraining it from paying under the counter-guarantee, if the account party demonstrates that the event terminating the primary guarantee and counter-guarantee has occurred prior to payment by the instructing bank. It is submitted that such an injunction should not be granted, unless the account party had notified the issuing bank of the event in the appropriate manner before payment by the issuing bank to the beneficiary. As stated above, the mere fact that the event terminating the (counter-)guarantee has taken place does not prevent the issuing bank from claiming reimbursement.[111] Accordingly, in the absence of evidence that the issuing bank has breached its duty of examination, the instructing bank must repay the issuing bank regardless of the clause of the counter-guarantee and the account party must reimburse the instructing bank.

---

[109] See, for example, *CA Amsterdam, 5 February 1993*, KG 1993, 113, involving an indirect guarantee. The Court of Appeal dismissed the application for an injunction restraining the instructing bank from reimbursing the issuing bank, on the grounds that the account party had by no means proven the event which would terminate the primary guarantee, and that the issuing bank's decision that the primary guarantee was still in force was not incorrect. See also *Paris, 24 April 1992*, D. 1993 Somm. p. 102. In *Paris, 14 December 1987*, Banque 1988, p. 236, D. 1988 Somm. p. 248, the application for a stop-payment order against the instructing bank was denied on the sole ground that the account party could not discharge the burden of proving the event. The aspect of (in)sufficient examination by the issuing bank was not considered. In *Trib. com. Brussels, 21 October 1986*, RDC 1987, p. 706, stop-payment injunctions against both the instructing and issuing bank had been granted upon proof by the account party that the event terminating the guarantee had occurred. The decision rested, however, primarily on the grounds that the beneficiary evidently acted fraudulently and that the beneficiary had not yet called the guarantee.

[110] In fact, most cases cited in No. 13-26 involved indirect guarantees and counter-guarantees.

[111] Contra: Vasseur, note to *Trib. com. Paris, 8 July 1983*, D. 1984 I.R. p. 92, arguing that the counter-guarantee expires on its own terms. In this case, the court did indeed grant a stop-payment injunction against the instructing bank on the grounds that the prescribed certificates from the engineer had been released. The court failed, however, to address the question of whether the certificates had been brought to the attention of the issuing bank before payment to the beneficiary and whether the issuing bank had breached its duty of examination, see also Chapter 11.2.2, Nos. 13-20.

If the guarantee contains both a calendar expiry date and an expiry event, the guarantee ceases to be valid on whichever of the expiry date or expiry event occurs first, cf. art. 22 URDG and *Trib. com. Brussels, 15 December 1992*, which explicitly referred to this Rule, although the guarantee had not been made subject to the URDG.[112] On the other hand, if the guarantee is called before the expiry date, the demand for payment continues to be valid even though the expiry event, e.g. the submission of a protocol of acceptance, occurred shortly after the call, cf. *BGH, 24 September 1998*.[113]

13.2.8 Amount and currency

Amount, partial and successive drawings

13-27 Provided that all terms and conditions have been fulfilled the beneficiary is entitled to claim the full amount of the guarantee. Because of the principle of independence he need not show that the amount claimed accords with the actual loss he has suffered by reason of non-performance by the principal debtor. Nor does he have to produce a specification or account of the amount claimed.[114] An exception to the above is the situation where the guarantee is payable upon an arbitral award or judicial decision and when damages have been awarded for less than the maximum amount of the guarantee.

The beneficiary can never claim more than the maximum amount of the guarantee, even though his actual loss plus interest exceeds that amount. Some guarantees provide, however, that the amount of the guarantee increases with a certain percentage of interest. This applies especially to Syrian and Turkish repayment guarantees where the advance payment is viewed as a loan to the account party. Also repayment guarantees in favour of a bank which gives a credit facility to the account party, often provide that the maximum amount is to be increased with interest and costs.

The beneficiary may, of course, claim less than the maximum amount. It would appear that this does not preclude the possibility of subsequent calls up to the maxi-

---

[112] RDC 1993, p. 1055.

[113] WM 1998, p. 2363.

[114] *BGH, 17 October 1996*, WM 1996, p. 2228, *OLG Frankfurt a.M., 8 February 2000*, WM 2001, P. 1108, CA *Amsterdam, 8 January 1987*, KG 1988, 300, CA *Brussels, 4 January 1989*, TBH 1990, p. 1073, *Trib. com. Liege, 7 April 1994*, RDC 1996, p. 1063 (in the absence of a reduction clause the beneficiary can claim the full amount), Cargill *International v. Bangladesh Sugar & Food Industries*, [1998] 2 All ER 406, at 414, *Paris, 3 March 1990*, D. 1990 Somm. P. 209 (see also Chapter 10.8, No. 10-23), Affaki, No. 90. See further Chapter 14.5.11.

The Demand for Payment

mum amount and within the period of validity of the guarantee.[115] Successive drawings do not necessarily suggest fraud. It is quite possible that the beneficiary is still undecided as regards the total amount of loss, desiring some more time for further calculations. After all, he would have been perfectly entitled to claim the full amount at once.

It is submitted that, unless stipulated otherwise, a call without mention of the amount claimed is a valid call, but the bank should not proceed to payment until the beneficiary has specified the amount.[116]

Currency

13-28 The beneficiary is not entitled to claim payment in a currency other than the one mentioned in the (counter-)guarantee and a demand in a non-stipulated currency constitutes an invalid call.[117] However, if the guarantee or counter-guarantee provides for payment in a non-convertible currency, the beneficiary may obtain payment of the countervalue in another currency.[118] Counter-guarantees in particular sometimes provide explicitly that the issuing bank is entitled to demand payment in another currency for the countervalue of the amount expressed in the nominated currency.[119]

The beneficiary cannot claim for loss due to depreciation of the currency stated in the (counter-)guarantee.[120]

13.2.9 Period of examination. Time of payment

13-29 The bank has a reasonable time to examine whether the demand for payment complies with the terms and conditions of the guarantee, cf. art. 10(a) URDG. What is reasonable depends on the circumstances of the case and especially on the nature of the conditions of payment and the type of documents submitted by the beneficiary. As far as first demand guarantees are concerned, a period of up to three business days following the day of receipt is usually considered reasonable, taking into account the

---

[115] Cf. *OLG Frankfurt a.M., 16 September 1982*, RIW 1983, p. 785, Affaki, No. 104, Rule 3.08(b) ISP 98.
[116] See Chapter 13.2.7, No. 13-24.
[117] *Cass., 21 June 1988*, D. 1989 Somm. p. 148, *Trib. com. Paris, 3 October 1989*, D. 1990 Somm. p. 202, *Paris, 24 October 1989*, D. 1990 Somm. p. 203.
[118] *Cass., 4 July 1995*, D. 1996 J. p. 249.
[119] See Chapter 11.4, No. 11-28 and Chapter 13.3, No. 13-41.
[120] *Trib. com. Paris, 25 June 1985*, D. 1986 I.R. p. 156, *Cass., 21 June 1988*, D. 1989 Somm. p. 148, *Rb Haarlem, 9 January 1987*, KG 1987, 85.

time needed for the actual handling of the demand for payment by the appropriate department within the bank.[121] The period could be longer, for instance, when the documents tendered by the beneficiary are of a complex or problematical nature, or when the guarantee contains clauses limiting or terminating the right to payment. In this event the bank may have to turn first to the account party in order to enable him to show that these conditions have been fulfilled.[122]

ISP98 and the UNCITRAL Convention contain combined provisions for the total period of both examination and the period within which notice of dishonour has to be given if the bank decides not to pay because of non-compliance. According to Rule 5.01(a) ISP98 this total period should not be unreasonable, whereby a period of three business days following the business day of presentation is deemed to be not unreasonable and a period beyond seven business days is deemed to be unreasonable. These provisions provide a useful degree of guidance and avoid unnecessary disputes. Art. 16(2) UNCITRAL Convention also refers to a reasonable time, with a maximum of seven business days.[123]

Payment is due once the bank has ascertained compliance. Nonetheless, payment within three days after this point in time is considered acceptable.[124] Art. 17(1) UNCITRAL Convention provides that payment should be made promptly and Rule 2.01 ISP98 refers to the period mentioned above. Practice indicates, however, that considerable delays are by no means uncommon. Guarantees occasionally specify the period within which payment is to be effected, ranging from three to thirty days.

13.2.10 Interest and damages for late payment

13-30 Guarantees rarely contain provisions in respect of payment of interest in the case of late payment by the bank, but such clauses are occasionally inserted in repayment guarantees and counter-guarantees, often providing for payment at LIBOR (London Interbank Offered Rate). If inserted, they tend to provide for interest as from the date of the advance payment or, respectively, the date of the request for payment. In the absence of specific clauses the issue of interest is governed by the applicable

---

[121] ICC Banking Commission, Opinion 470/TA.467rev. of 1 December 2000; Rule 5.01(i) ISP98, Affaki, No. 41(5), Goode, p. 69, Boll, p. 16, 18, von Westphalen, p. 208, Zahn/Ehrlich/Neumann, 9/122, Dohm, No. 141, 210, Nielsen WM 1999, pp. 2057, 2058.

[122] See Chapter 10.8, No. 27.

[123] In the special circumstances of the case *Rb Utrecht, 25 February 2003*, JOR 2004, 21, with critical annotation by Bertrams, ruled that the bank should have completed its examination and should have given notice of dishonour the same day on which it had received the beneficiary's demand for payment.

[124] Von Westphalen, p. 171, 206, 358, Zahn/Ehrlich/Neumann, 9/122, Nielsen, p. 69.

The Demand for Payment 313

law.¹²⁵ The applicable law also determines whether a formal notice of default is required and the question of whether and to what extent the beneficiary or issuing bank in the case of an indirect guarantee is entitled to damages in addition to interest. In several French cases the bank has indeed been ordered to pay interest as well as damages on the grounds that it had refused or delayed payment for reasons that could only be described as frivolous, untenable or spurious.¹²⁶ These defences included contentions that the 'guarantee' was an accessory suretyship, that the terms of the guarantee had not been met or that the call was fraudulent, while in most of these cases the true reason for delaying payment was the fact that the account party had been declared insolvent.

If the bank has been prevented from paying on account of a conservatory attachment order (freezing order) obtained by the account party, it cannot be deemed to be in default and does not, therefore, owe statutory interest as long as the order remains in force.¹²⁷ The bank may, however, be under a duty to transfer the guarantee amount to a blocked interest bearing account in order to minimise the beneficiary's loss and in that event the bank is entitled to pass the interest on to the account party. The bank does not

---

¹²⁵ *Paris, 28 June 1989*, D. 1990 Somm. p. 212.

¹²⁶ *Cass., 20 December 1982*, D. 1983 J. p. 365 (FF 100,000, approx. € 15,000 for interest and damages), *Cass. 9 January 1990*, D. 1990 Somm. p. 191 (FF 10,000, approx. € 1,500 for damages), *Trib. com. Nantes, 22 September 1983*, D. 1984 I.R. p. 202 (FF 50,000, approx. € 7,750 for interest, FF 10,000, approx. € 1,500 for damages), *Trib. com. Paris, 6 January 1987*, D. 1987 Somm. p. 174 right column (interest plus FF 50,000, approx. € 7,750 for damages), *Paris, 13 December 1984*, D. 1985 I.R. p. 239, ordering the bank to pay interest at LIBOR plus 2%, observing that damages in respect of late payment are not confined to the rate of interest as provided by the general statutory provisions. *Paris, 11 February 1986*, upheld by *Cass., 8 December 1987*, D. 1988 Somm. p. 240. The Paris Court of Appeal ordered the bank to pay FF 500,000, approx. € 77,000 for interest and damages plus FF 20,000, approx. € 3,000 for initiating appeal proceedings on frivolous grounds, totalling FF 520,000, approx. € 80,000 which amounted to 28.7% of the sum of the guarantee. *Paris, 18 December 1991*, D. 1993 Somm. p. 106 (FF 450,000 damages against the bank), *Trib. com. Paris, 12 April 1991*, D. 1992 Somm. p. 239 (FF 10,000 damages plus interest against the bank). See also *Trib. com. Brussels, 16 May 1991*, JT 1991, p. 711. See Chapter 10.6, No. 10-11, for the question of whether and in which circumstances the bank could pass its loss incurred by reason of having to pay damages and interest on to the account party. *OLG Frankfurt a.M., 16 September 1982*, RIW 1983, p. 785, recognised the possibility of giving judgment for interest, but in the case at hand the beneficiary had not claimed interest. In *Rb Rotterdam, 9 June 1989*, KG 1989, 270, the claim for statutory interest was rejected on the grounds that the delay in payment could not be attributed to the bank.

¹²⁷ *Paris, 26 July 1985*, D. 1986 I.R. p. 157, *Rb Amsterdam, 2 June 1994*, KG 1994, 373 and Bb 1994, pp. 225-227.

incur liability for interest if the delay has been caused by the beneficiary's 'extend or pay' request, cf. art. 26 URDG.

13.2.11 Procedures on non-compliance. Notice of dishonour. Preclusion rule

13-31 If the bank decides that the demand for payment does not comply with the terms and conditions of the guarantee and therefore refuses the demand, it must give notice thereof to the beneficiary. Under art. 10(b) URDG the notice of dishonour should be given immediately by teletransmission or, if not possible, by other expeditious means. As mentioned in no. 13-29, ISP98 and the UNCITRAL Convention contain combined provisions for the total period of both examination and the period within which notice of dishonour has to be given if the bank decides not to pay because of non-compliance. According to Rule 5.01(a) ISP98 this total period should not be unreasonable, whereby a period of three business days following the business day of presentation is deemed to be not unreasonable and a period beyond seven business days is deemed to be unreasonable. Art. 16(2) UNCITRAL Convention also refers to a reasonable time, with a maximum of seven business days.[128] In both cases the notice should given by telecommunication or, if not available, by other expeditious means. Rule 5.02 ISP98 and art. 16(2) UNCITRAL Convention explicitly require the bank to state the discrepancies, while this appears to be implied in art. 15 URDG.[129] Apart from these sources of law, case law (see hereafter) has also recognised the bank's duty to forward a notice of dishonour to the beneficiary forthwith after the bank's decision not to pay. The reason for this procedure is to enable the beneficiary to cure the non-conformity and to make a fresh and conforming demand within the period of validity of the guarantee. Prompt

---

[128] While there is an advantage to providing for an aggregate period of time for both examination and the giving of notice of dishonour, it may also create a problem as Rule 5.01 ISP98 and art. 16(2) UNCITRAL Convention do not explicitly state that notice of dishonour is to be given promptly following the bank's decision not to pay. What is the situation if the bank decides not to pay on the same day it has received the demand? In particular, is the bank allowed to wait for three further days and then to give notice, taking advantage of Rule 5.01(a)(1) ISP98, which states that a period of three business days after the presentation is deemed to be not unreasonable. Such a conclusion is not warranted. This particular Rule is formulated as a presumption, which, by implication, is capable of rebuttal, and, more importantly, the general rule under both ISP98 and the UNCITRAL Convention is that the notice of dishonour should be given within a reasonable time. It may, therefore, be assumed that a notice of dishonour which is not given promptly after the decision not to pay, does not satisfy the 'reasonable period' test under ISP98 or the UNCITRAL Convention.

[129] Thus Affaki, No. 114. According to Zahn/Ehrlich/Neumann, 9/121, the bank need not specify the discrepancies as, according to these authors, this would endanger the bank's neutral position.

action is, therefore, especially important when, as is often the case, the request for payment is made shortly before the expiry date.[130]

The URDG and UNCITRAL Convention do not contain provisions as do Rule 5.03 ISP98, art. 14(e) UCP in relation to documentary credits and Article 5-108(c) of the Revised Article 5 U.C.C. in relation to documentary credits and standby letters of credit. According to these provisions, the bank is precluded from claiming that the terms of the (standby) credit have not been complied with if the bank has failed to give notice within the required period or if it has failed to state in what respect the terms and conditions have not been met.[131]

The above-mentioned rules in respect of the timely notice of dishonour and the preclusion rule have also been recognised in case law, see *HR, 9 June 1995, OLG Karlsruhe, 21 July 1992*,[132] and *CA Brussels, 2 March 2001*.[133] The practical effect of the preclusion rule is that the bank must pay as if the conditions had been fulfilled. While this sanction might be considered rigid and perhaps rather harsh, the preclusion rule is deemed to be crucial in the law of independent guarantees and standby letters of credit.[134] It provides clarity for all parties concerned, promotes discipline within the bank and discourages possible malpractices such as when the bank purposely keeps silent about purely formal defects in the demand for payment until after the expiry date, which might otherwise have been remedied by the beneficiary in time, if he had

---

[130] The imminence of the expiry date does not, however, obligate the bank to accelerate its examination and decision whether to pay or not, cf. *Banco Gen. Runinahui v. Citibank International*, 97 F.3d 480 (11th Cir. 1996) and Rule 5.01(a)(ii/iv) ISP98.

[131] Art. 17(4) of the Draft UNCITRAL Convention did contain a preclusion rule, but the provision was deleted in the final text since the majority felt that the sanction should be left to national law. This is also the case under the URDG, see Affaki, No. 115.

[132] *HR, 9 June 1995*, NJ 1995, 639. The Dutch supreme Court also ruled, however, that there might be situations in which a claim for damages might be the appropriate remedy. The German Court of Appeal in *OLG Karlsruhe, 21 July 1992*, RIW 1992, p. 843, ruled that the failure to immediately inform the beneficiary of a non-conforming demand rendered the bank liable for the loss suffered by the beneficiary, which loss, according to the court, is equal to the amount claimed by the beneficiary. It observed that it was not necessary to choose between the preclusion rule and the liability for damages rule because both remedies led to the same result. In effect, the same decision was reached in *Rb Amsterdam, 4 November 1998*, JOR 2003, 74.

[133] TBH 2002, p. 488. Idem: *Rb Utrecht, 25 February 2003*, JOR 2004, 21. Both courts applied the preclusion rule.

[134] Cf. Wunnicke/Wunnicke/Turner, § 6.06[A][B], § 18.05[B]. See Dolan, § 6.06 for an extensive analysis of the preclusion rule.

been immediately notified of the defect.[135] After payment in accordance with the preclusion rule, the bank is ordinarily not entitled to reimbursement by the account party on the basis of the mandate because the payment is the consequence of the bank's own fault. The bank is, however, subrogated in the beneficiary's claim against the account party in accordance with the secured contract.[136] Such subrogation may also avoid unjust enrichment on the part of the account party.

In the event that the guarantee has been called after the expiry date, the bank should, of course, also inform the beneficiary, but the above-mentioned sanction does not apply if the bank does not do so without delay, because it would have been impossible for the beneficiary to cure the defect, cf. Rule 5.04 ISP98.

13.2.12 Bank's defences

General. Judgment in summary proceedings and other procedural aspects

13-32 Obviously, if the terms and conditions of the guarantee have not been complied with, the bank is entitled to refuse payment. The bank may also reject payment if the guarantee does not secure the claim for which the beneficiary demands payment. It may also happen that the bank raises a defence derived from the general law of contract, such as invalidity, mistake, misrepresentation or deceit.[137]

In the case of a dispute between the bank and the beneficiary in relation to such defences by the bank, the question arises as to whether such a dispute must be litigated in ordinary main proceedings or whether the beneficiary may obtain judgment against the bank in summary proceedings.[138] Some guidance on this issue is given in *Solo Industries v. Canara Bank*.[139] In this case the bank refused payment, arguing that it had validly avoided the guarantee because it had been induced to issue the guarantee by fraudulent misrepresentations by the beneficiary. The beneficiary then sued the bank in

---

[135] See also von Westphalen, p. 172, Zahn/Ehrlich/Neumann, 9/121, Dohm, No. 213. In *BGH, 23 January 1996*, WM 1996, p. 393, the German Supreme Court ruled, however, that the bank need not inform the benefeciary of the non-compliance if the beneficiary is already aware of this. This decision undermines the clarity of the rule and may lead to unnecessary disputes as to whether the beneficiary was or was not aware of the defects.

[136] See Chapter 10.11.

[137] See several of the cases mentioned hereafter. See also von Westphalen, p. 175, Canaris, Nos. 1007, 1135.

[138] A similar question arises if the bank argues that it has issued a traditional suretyship as opposed to an independent (first demand) guarantee, see Chapter 12.3.3, No. 12-29, or if the bank rejects payment arguing that the demand for payment is fraudulent, see Chapter 14.6.

[139] [2001] 2 Lloyd's Rep. 578.

The Demand for Payment 317

summary proceedings. The Court of Appeal distinguished between a defence by the bank relating to fraud, which is subject to a stringent test of immediately available evidence of fraud, and a defence relating to the validity of the guarantee itself, which is subject to a general, less stringent test in such proceedings. As the bank had a reasonable or real prospect that the guarantee had been procured by, and had been validly avoided on account of a fraudulent misrepresentation, the court refused to give summary judgment against the bank. Accordingly, defences such as those with respect to the validity of the guarantee itself or with respect to compliance with the terms and conditions of the guarantee should ordinarily be determined in ordinary proceedings, unless they lack real substance or can readily be disproven. Indeed, several German decisions provide examples of cases where summary judgment against the bank was granted as the bank's defence was quite unconvincing.[140]

In relation to the so-called suretyship payable on first demand, which is peculiar to German law, the question has also arisen as to whether defences by the bank should be resolved first before judgment against the bank is given or whether such defences should be deferred to proceedings for recovery after payment. Bearing in mind that one of the purposes of both a first demand guarantee and a first demand suretyship is to enable the beneficiary to obtain payment quickly, the German Supreme Court in *BGH, 10 February 2000*, and in *BGH, 8 March 2001*, ruled that, if the soundness of the bank's defence is not immediately evident from the text and clauses in the guarantee or from established facts, judgment against the bank must be given first ('*im Erstprozess*'), but the bank may seek recovery after payment in subsequent proceedings ('*Rückforderungsprozess*').[141] These decisions indicate that, unless the bank's defence is very strong and

---

[140] *BGH, 28 October 1993*, WM 1994, p.106, *BGH, 17 October 1996*, WM 1996, p. 2228, *BGH, 2 April 1998*, WM 1998, p. 1062, *BGH, 10 February 2000*, WM 2000, p. 715, *BGH, 24 January 2002*, WM 2002, p. 555, *BGH, 5 March 2002*, WM 2002, p. 743, OLG *München, 23 July 1997*, WM 1998, p. 342, *OLG Frankfurt a.M., 8 February 2000*, WM 2001, p. 1108; *Trib. com. Liege, 7 April 1995*, RDC 1996, p. 1063. American courts have also often held that disputes under (standby) letters of credit are ripe for summary judgment, see Dolan, § 11.06[1] and Wunnicke/Wunnicke/Turner, § 7.03[I]. See Chapter 14.6 for the bank's defence on the basis of fraud and summary judgment.

[141] *BGH, 10 February 2000*, WM 2000, p. 715. In this case the bank had issued a suretyship payable on first demand, but refused payment arguing that the account party and beneficiary had only agreed on a traditional suretyship. The strength of this defence was considered insufficient and judgment was given against the bank. See also the German case law cited in the previous footnote. In *BGH, 8 March 2001*, NJW 2001, p. 1857, the invalidity of the suretyship payable on first demand was evident from the established and undisputed facts and judgment against the bank was refused. In *BGH, 14 December 1995*, WM 1996, p. 193, and in *BGH, 25 February 1999*, WM 1999, p. 895, judgment against the bank was also refused as the soundness of the bank's defence that the guarantee did not secure the claim for which the beneficiary demanded payment, was sufficiently evident from the clauses of the guarantee.

convincing, the principle of 'pay first, argue later' also applies between bank and beneficiary, but this might be explained by the fact that these cases involved a so-called suretyship payable on first demand. Under German law in respect of this type of security, payment by the bank is deemed to be provisional and the bank is always entitled to recover the amount paid if in subsequent proceedings it appears that the beneficiary had no right to payment.[142] A judgment against the bank in the case of a suretyship on first demand may, therefore, always be followed by a final resolution of the dispute in subsequent proceedings.

Set-off with bank's own counter-claims

13-33 One particular type of defence, namely set-off with a counter-claim against the beneficiary, requires specific attention as the views expressed in case law and legal writing are by no means unanimous.

If permissible at all, set-off as a defence against payment must relate to counter-claims against the beneficiary which are undisputed by the beneficiary, certain or liquidated.[143] If it were otherwise, these defences would give rise to protracted proceedings before judgment could be given. This would entirely defeat one of the main objects of guarantees, namely to assure immediate payment once the terms of the guarantee have been fulfilled.

Guarantees rarely contain explicit provisions concerning the permissibility of set-off. General phrases such as 'payment will be made on first demand without objections' merely emphasise the independent nature of the first demand guarantee. In general, such phrases are insufficient to warrant a construction which precludes set-off.[144] On the other hand, a clause stating that 'in the event of a demand for payment the amount will be put at your disposal' could possibly be construed this way. Surrounding circumstances will usually shed no more light on the matter.

The fact that the guarantee may be payable on first demand does not dispose of the issue. The independent nature of the guarantee and the first demand clause means that the beneficiary has a claim without having to prove default and irrespective of any disputes between the account party and beneficiary. As has been observed by *LG Frankfurt a.M., 21 September 1983*, it does not answer the question of whether the beneficiary

---

[142] See Chapter 4.5, No. 4-19.

[143] *BGH, 22 April 1985*, RIW 1985, p. 650, *The Hongkong and Shanghai Banking Corporation v. Kloeckner & Co*, [1989] 2 Lloyd's Rep. 323, *Continental Illinois Nat. Bank v. John Paul Papanicolaou*, IBL October 1986, p. 75, *RB Haarlem, 9 January 1987*, KG 1987, 85. See also *OLG Hamburg, 18 December 1981*, WM 1983, p. 188, *OLG Hamburg, 7 July 1977*, WM 1978, p. 260, *Rb Almelo, 15 August 1984*, KG 1984, 261.

[144] Cf. Rümker, ZGR 1986, p. 342, but see Dohm, No. 245.

The Demand for Payment 319

is entitled to actual cash payment from the bank or whether the bank is permitted to invoke set-off on the basis of its own counter-claim against the beneficiary.[145] Moreover, the fact that first demand guarantees originate from the previously existing practice of making cash deposits may be of historical interest, but it is not conclusive for the answer to the issue either.[146]

How then is the question of set-off with the bank's own counter-claims to be resolved? The issue has been exhaustively analysed in a case which went all the way up to the German Supreme Court and which deserves close attention. *LG Frankfurt a.M., 21 September 1983*, ruled against set-off.[147] The court founded its decision on the balance of interests of all parties concerned. It observed that the guarantee is not just a contract between bank and beneficiary. The bank is entrusted with the execution of a task assigned by the account party and, according to the court, when executing this task the bank should not be guided by its own interests. Moreover, the interests of the beneficiary, i.e. the advantages consisting in the security and liquidity function of first demand guarantees, require that the beneficiary receive actual payment. If the bank were to be permitted to invoke set-off, it would, according to the court, thwart the liquidity ('cash in hand') function of the guarantee. It is to be noted that in the case at hand both beneficiary and account party had been declared insolvent and that the rights pursuant to the guarantee had been assigned to the beneficiary's bank. It was this bank/assignee who had initiated proceedings against the bank/guarantor upon the latter's refusal to pay on a plea of set-off. The court of first instance did not consider these factors relevant. While recognising that as a matter of principle the bank cannot invoke set-off because of the liquidity function of guarantees, the Court of Appeal reversed the decision in view of the special facts which have just been mentioned.[148] It observed that the bank would not be able to realise its counter-claims against the beneficiary other than by means of set-off. The Court of Appeal also remarked that in this case the principle of 'pay first, argue later' could not be realised in view of the insolvency of both account party and beneficiary. Finally, the Court of Appeal observed that the dispute was in fact one between two banks, not between account party and beneficiary or between bank and beneficiary. For these reasons it ruled in favour of set-off. This decision was upheld in *BGH, 22 April 1985*, but on other grounds.[149] The German Supreme Court ruled that as far as payment guarantees are concerned the bank is not, as a matter of principle, precluded from claiming set-off with its counter-claims which

---

[145] WM 1984, p. 86.

[146] Cf. Rümker, ZGR 1986, p. 338. Contra: Dohm, No. 249.

[147] WM 1984, p. 86

[148] *OLG Frankfurt a.M., 26 June 1984*, RIW 1985, p. 407.

[149] RIW 1985, p. 650. See also *Rb Amsterdam, 7 March 1985*, KG 1985, 87, see No. 13-35.

are certain and liquid. Unlike the Court of Appeal, the Supreme Court did not found its decision on the special circumstances of the case. It relied primarily on the security function of the guarantee and observed that the guarantee does not create rights broader than the beneficiary would have had in the case of a normal execution of the beneficiary's claim for payment of the contract price. In this context it noted that the beneficiary has no right to receive actual cash payment as far as the underlying relationship is concerned. Furthermore, inasmuch as the guarantee also has a liquidity ('cash in hand') function, this function, according to the Supreme Court, could be accomplished by set-off as well, since it extinguishes a debt which is due and payable.

With due respect, one could feel ill at ease with both the arguments and the practical outcome of the *BGH* decision.[150] As far as the reasoning concerning the security function is concerned, the Supreme Court relies heavily on the underlying relationship between account party and beneficiary and it transposes this relationship to the relationship between bank and beneficiary. It is questionable whether this accords with the principle of independence. This reasoning is all the more surprising since in the very same decision the Supreme Court rejected the possibility of set-off against counterclaims which originate from the underlying relationship. The reasoning in respect of the liquidity function of the payment is highly legalistic and does not accord with commercial perceptions and expectations. Is not the entire idea of first demand guarantees based on the common wisdom that it is better to have cash in hand than to be entitled to a right of payment or to be released from a debt?[151]

In conclusion, this study agrees with the arguments in the decision of the court of first instance to the effect that the bank cannot claim set-off in respect of its own counter-claims against the beneficiary regardless of insolvency of the beneficiary or account party. On the other hand, the fact that the issue of set-off did not affect the relationship between bank/guarantor and beneficiary, but the relationship between the bank/guarantor and another bank to which the proceeds of the guarantee had been assigned, is a valid argument for allowing set-off in this particular case, as was observed by the Court of Appeal.

There are a few other cases relating to set-off. The case of *The Hongkong and Shanghai Banking Corporation v. Kloeckner & Co* involved a standby letter of credit and a series of interrelated financial facilities which all formed part of one overall trans-

---

[150] It has been criticised by Zahn/Ehrlich/Neumann, 9/124, in both respects, and by Rümker, ZGR 1986, pp. 334-336, who raises doctrinal objections to its reasoning only. Von Westphalen, p. 178, approves of the decision.

[151] The Supreme Court confined its decision to payment guarantees. It observed that in the case of a performance guarantee the possibility of set-off may be precluded on the grounds that the purpose of such guarantees could be to furnish the financial means to undo the consequences of non-performance immediately.

action. Hirst J. ruled that the bank was entitled to set off its liability under the standby credit against one of the other accounts it had with the beneficiary because of the peculiar facts of the case, namely that the claim and counter-claim arose from one and the same transaction.[152] *Trib. com. Paris, 29 November 1988*, dismissed the bank's defence of set-off.[153] Also in the well-reasoned decision of *Geneva, 27 April 1989*, the court firmly rejected the possibility of set-off for similar reasons as mentioned hereafter.[154] In *Trib. com. Brussels, 18 April 1985*, which involved a letter of credit case, the bank's defence was accepted because set-off was also believed to be permitted in respect of guarantees.[155]

Leaving aside peculiar facts such as those in some of the above-mentioned decisions, three general arguments could be advanced against allowing the bank to invoke set-off. With a view to the general objection of banks that stop-payment orders against a bank damage its international reputation and violate the unconditional nature of its undertaking, it would hardly seem appropriate to allow banks to escape payment by raising such defences as set-off when that suddenly suits them better. Secondly, set-off by the bank would have the effect of interfering with the relationship between beneficiary and account party. One can be certain that the beneficiary will not be satisfied with the fact that the guarantee has brought him no advantage other than being discharged from a debt to the bank. This may well cause him to resort to retaliatory measures against the account party. Thirdly, set-off would seem to come as an unfair surprise to the beneficiary. If permitted, it would force beneficiaries to accept guarantees only from banks with which they have no dealings and also to avoid having any business with the bank in the future, or to revert to the former practice of insisting on a cash deposit. This is all most unsettling.

Legal writing is divided.[156] Those in favour of set-off derive their arguments from the general principles of the law of contracts. Art. 18 UNCITRAL Convention allows

---

[152] [1989] 2 Lloyd's Rep. 323.See also *SAFA v. Banque du Caire*, [2000] 2 Lloyd's Rep. 600, in which the Court of Appeal refused an application for summary judgment against the bank on the grounds that the bank had a counter-claim arising from a related transaction.

[153] D. 1990 Somm. p. 205.

[154] D. 1990 Somm. p. 183.

[155] RDC 1985, p. 729.

[156] Against set-off: Horn, No. 533, Lienesch, pp. 142-144, Zahn/Ehrlich/Neumann, 9/124, Nielsen, p. 16, von Westphalen, p. 178 (except in the case of payment guarantees), Vasseur, No. 101, Dohm, Nos. 248, 250, Wymeersch/Dambre/Troch, TvP 1999, p. 1840. See also Staudinger/Horn, Nos. 248-249. In favour of set-off: Rümker, ZGR 1986, pp. 336-339, Canaris, No. 1135, Pleyer, WM Sonderbeilage 2/1973, p. 12, Tours, p. 189, Mülbert, p. 49 note 89, Kleiner, 21/36, Pabbruwe, WPNR 1979, p. 183, RMThemis 1994, p. 149, van Lier, J.T. 1980, p. 355, De Vroede and Flamee, TPR 1982, p. 374, RPDB, Nos. 161-162, Goode, 1992 LMCLQ, p. 193.

the bank to invoke set-off against its own counter-claim, while the URDG do not contain provisions in this respect.

Set-off with the bank's own counter-claims in the case of indirect guarantees

13-34 In the case of indirect guarantees, the issue of set-off by the issuing bank has other dimensions as the issuing bank will often be the house bank of the beneficiary. In this situation payment by the bank under the primary guarantee means crediting the beneficiary's current account with the bank, which may show a deficit. Set-off then occurs as a matter of course. Moreover, the relationship is likely to be governed by the bank's general terms and conditions, which no doubt provide for the bank's power to set off counter-claims against debts pursuant to the guarantee.

Set-off with counter-claims derived from the underlying relationship; assigned counter-claims

13-35 Legal writing[157] and the majority of case law[158] reject the possibility of set-off by the bank with counter-claims against the beneficiary which it has obtained through assignment from the account party. The reason is that such a set-off would violate the principle of independence and upset the reallocation of risks which the account party had agreed to. Art. 18 UNCITRAL Convention also disallows set-off in this situation.

Set-off between banks

13-36 It is submitted that, in the absence of specific contractual provisions in the counter-guarantee and/or international banking practice, the instructing bank should be permitted to set off any counter-claim *vis-à-vis* the issuing bank against the latter's

---

[157] Staudinger/Horn, No. 248, Von Westphalen, p. 180, Canaris, No. 1137, Dohm, No. 247, Nielsen, ZIP 1982, pp. 255, 259, Rümker, ZGR 1986, pp. 334, 337, 339, Wymeersch/Dambre/Troch, TvP 1999, p. 1840.

[158] *BGH, 22 April 1985*, RIW 1986, p. 650, *OLG Hamburg, 18 December 1981*, WM 1983, p. 188, upheld by *BGH, 14 October 1982*, WM 1982, p. 1324, *Continental Illinois Nat. Bank v. John Paul Papanicolaou*, IBL October 1986, p. 72, *Rb Haarlem, 9 January 1987*, KG 1987, 85. In *Trib. com. Charleroi, 8 September 1992*, JLMB 1993, p. 892 (with critical comment by Wymeersch/Dambre/Troch, TvP 1999, pp. 1840-1841), and Rb *Amsterdam, 7 March 1985*, KG 1985, 87, set-off was held to be permissible in the absence of contrary provisions in the guarantee. Although not recorded in the report of the last-mentioned case, the counter-claim originated from the underlying relationship. See also *OLG Hamburg, 7 July 1977*, WM 1978, p. 260, which rejected set-off since the account party's counter-claim against the beneficiary was not certain. The Court of Appeal observed that it might be different if the counter-claim were certain and beyond doubt.

The Demand for Payment 323

claim under the counter-guarantee. The reason is that the arguments against set-off by the bank in respect of counter-claims against the beneficiary, as discussed in no. 13-33, are less compelling and probably not even applicable at all in respect of the inter-bank relationship so that the general principles of set-off apply.[159] If, however, the instructing bank maintains accounts with the second issuing bank, the former will often not be in a position to effect a set-off because the issuing bank could simply debit these accounts.

13.3 CALL ON THE COUNTER-GUARANTEE

General

13-37 The rules and principles in respect of a call on the guarantee also apply to a call on the counter-guarantee in the case of an indirect guarantee. In fact, several decisions mentioned in Chapter 13.2 related to indirect guarantees and counter-guarantees. Thus, for example, a demand for payment must be made strictly in accordance with the terms and conditions of the counter-guarantee.[160] It is usually easy for the issuing bank to comply with these conditions since counter-guarantees often provide for payment on demand regardless of whether the primary guarantee is payable on demand or upon submission of third-party documents, and they rarely refer to clauses in the primary guarantee which limit, reduce or exclude the beneficiary's right to payment. On the other hand, in *Cauxell v. Lloyds Bank* the Court of Appeal refused to imply a term in the counter-guarantee which was not mentioned therein.[161]

---

[159] Cf. *OLG Frankfurt a.M., 26 June 1984*, RIW 1985, p. 407, see No. 33. Incidentally, the case of *Trib. com. Brussels, 18 April 1985*, RDC 1985, p. 729, see note 126, also involved litigation between issuing and advising bank, but this fact was not mentioned as grounds for allowing set-off. According to Rümker, ZGR 1986, p. 343, set-off between banks is permissible.

[160] *Cass. 24 March 1992*, D. 1993 Somm. p. 99, *I.E. Contractors Ltd. v. Lloyds Bank Plc.*, [1990] 2 Lloyd's Rep. 496.

[161] *The Times*, 26 December 1995. The counter-guarantee was subject to a condition precedent that the instructing bank had given confirmation to the issuing bank that the underlying contract had been signed and that a letter of credit had been issued in favour of the account party of the guarantee. No letter of credit had been issued. Therefore the confirmation had not been given and the condition precedent of the counter-guarantee had not been fulfilled. The court refused to imply a term that the instructing bank should have taken reasonable steps to ascertain the position with regard to the underlying contract and the letter of credit. See also Chapter 12.3.5, No. 12-37a.

Because of the principle of independence between the counter-guarantee and the mandate/instructions to the issuing bank and the independence between the counter-guarantee and primary guarantee, the right to repayment under the counter-guarantee does not depend on proper execution by the issuing bank of the instructions from the instructing bank and on discharge by the issuing bank of its duty to ascertain compliance with the terms and conditions of the primary guarantee, unless the counter-guarantee provides otherwise or unless the instructing bank and/or the account party can prove forthwith that the issuing bank was in breach of those duties. This issue has been extensively explored in Chapter 11.2.2 and Chapter 11.4, no. 26.

Nos. 38-41 of this Chapter deal with some specific topics relating to calls on counter-guarantees.

Statement from the issuing bank concerning the primary guarantee. Transmission of documents. Art. 20(b) and 21 URDG

13-38 The counter-guarantee sometimes requires the issuing bank, when requesting payment, to submit a statement regarding the beneficiary's exercise of his right under the primary guarantee. Thus the counter-guarantee may stipulate a written affirmation from the issuing bank to the effect, for example, that it was obliged to pay under the primary guarantee and/or that the beneficiary has called the primary guarantee (in accordance with its terms). If indeed required, the submission of such a statement is a condition of payment and the call is not valid if the statement has not been presented.[162] Such statements are also required if the counter-guarantee has been made subject to the URDG, see art. 20(b) URDG.

Moreover, the counter-guarantee may also stipulate that the issuing bank transmits the documents which the beneficiary of the primary guarantee was required to submit, including his demand for payment. Art. 21 URDG also requires the issuing bank to transmit these documents (without delay), but this is not expressed as a formal condition of payment which needs to be fulfilled simultaneously with the request for payment.

Period of validity

13-39 Like guarantees, counter-guarantees must also be called within their period of validity and a demand for payment after the expiry date or expiry event is invalid.[163]

---

[162] *Cass. 24 March* 1992, D. 1993 Somm. p. 99, *I.E. Contractors Ltd. v. Lloyds Bank Plc.*, [1990] 2 Lloyd's Rep. 496.

[163] *Cass., 18 March* 1986, D. 1986 Somm. p. 166, Paris, *28 May 1985*, D. 1986 I.R. p. 155, *Paris, 2 April 1987*, D. 1988 Somm. p. 248, *OLG Stuttgart, 11 February 1981*, WM 1981, p. 631. See also the case law cited in Chapter 13.2.7 and hereafter. Banks take the same view. *Paris, 19 May 1988*, D. 1989 Somm p. 146, is clearly at variance with established case law.

The Demand for Payment 325

The initial period of validity of the counter-guarantee is, however, frequently prolonged pursuant to 'extend or pay' requests. These requests should also be made within the then existing period of validity.

Should the enforceability of the expiry date in the primary guarantee be uncertain or if the primary guarantee does not contain an expiry date, the counter-guarantee will ordinarily provide that it remains in force until discharge.[164] As far as its duration is concerned, the only event terminating the counter-guarantee is then, of course, discharge by the issuing bank. If the counter-guarantee is stated to remain in force until discharge despite an expiry date in the primary guarantee and if the instructing bank and/or account party take the view that the issuing bank has wrongfully accepted claims by the beneficiary submitted after the expiry date of the primary guarantee, reimbursement cannot be refused on the grounds that the counter-guarantee has ceased to be valid.[165] A refusal could only be based, it is submitted, on a breach of the issuing bank's duty to ascertain compliance with the terms of the primary guarantee.[166]

It is essential that the period of validity of the counter-guarantee matches that of the primary guarantee, which is usually accomplished by a clause providing that the counter-guarantee expires some time after the expiry date or event of the primary guarantee. In no circumstances should the validity period of the counter-guarantee be shorter, as was made painfully clear in *Cass., 3 June 1986*[167] and in *Cass., 29 April 1986*.[168] In

---

The Court of Appeal ruled that the period during which the counter-guarantee can be called is determined by the statutory provisions on limitation of actions.

[164] See further Chapter 12.4.5 and Chapter 8, No. 8-16.

[165] Cf. *Paris, 11 November 1990*, D. 1991 Somm. p. 200.

[166] See Chapter 11.2, No. 11-13.

[167] D. 1987 Somm. p.174. A repayment guarantee had been issued on behalf of a consortium of building firms in favour of the leading firm, which itself had caused a first demand performance guarantee to be issued in favour of Libyan employers. The repayment guarantee operated as a counter-guarantee. This counter-guarantee was payable on demand provided that the beneficiary/leading firm submitted a statement prior to 31 March 1981 to the effect that the Libyan employers had called the performance guarantee. The beneficiary/leading firm was unable to submit the statement on time, because the Libyan guarantee had not been called until after 31 March 1981. The insertion of the aforementioned date in said statement was, of course, a gross mistake on the part of the beneficiary/leading firm. It should also be noted that, while the Libyan beneficiary of the first demand performance guarantee was in a position to exact a prolongation by means of an 'extend or pay' request, the leading firm/beneficiary of the counter- guarantee was not in such a position. In a similar case, *Exxon Com. U.S.A. v. Banque de Paris et des Pays-Bas*, 828 F2d 1121 (5th. Cir. 1987), the US Court of Appeal reached the same decision, see Chapter 13.2.7, No. 13-23.

[168] D. 1987 J. p. 17. See also *Paris, 25 February 1988*, D. 1989 Somm. p. 150, affirmed by *Cass. 3 April 1990*, D. 1991 Somm. p. 195, where the Court of Appeal held as a matter of

both cases the claims for reimbursement were dismissed on the grounds that the counter-guarantee had been called after its expiry date. The absence of a clause covering the effects of 'extend or pay' requests from the issuing bank may also give rise to serious difficulties.[169]

Problems with respect to the adjustment of the period of validity of counter-guarantee and primary guarantee cannot always be avoided and circumstances may justify an exception to the rule that counter-guarantees must be called within their period of validity. In *Esal (Commodities), Reltor v. Oriental Credit, Wells Fargo*, the Egyptian issuing bank had repeatedly asked for an extension of the counter-guarantee in view of 'extend or pay' requests from the Egyptian beneficiary, but the instructing bank did not respond.[170] Some time later the Egyptian bank was ordered to pay by an Egyptian court and claimed reimbursement from the instructing bank. Although the Court of Appeal took the view that the counter-guarantee had expired,[171] it gave judgment in favour of the issuing bank because of the Egyptian court order. One can only approve of this decision.[172] In just the same circumstances a totally different result was reached in a French case which went all the way up to the Cour de Cassation. An Egyptian issuing

---

construction that, as the counter-guarantee did not contain an expiry date, the date was deemed to be the same as that of the primary guarantee and that the counter-guarantee had been called too late. Such construction of the validity period of the counter- guarantee has been rightly criticised by Vasseur. This decision should be contrasted with *Paris, 3 April 1990*, D. 1990, Somm. p. 197, affirmed by *Cass. 28 January 1992*, D. 1992 Somm. p. 234. In this case the counter-security was called shortly after its expiry date, which was the same as that of the primary security. The Court of Appeal observed that it was impossible for the issuing bank to call the counter-security in time. This might have been the reason why both the primary security and the counter-security in favour of the issuing bank had been construed as suretyships, because such construction permitted the issuing bank to have recourse against the instructing bank as long as the account party's default had occurred within the period of validity of the primary security, see also Chapter 12.3, No. 37a.

[169] This is illustrated in a case mentioned by van Orden Gnichtel, Banking L.J. 1983, p. 359, which involved a syndicated bank guarantee. In view of a 'hold for value' request from the beneficiary the leading bank requested a matching extension of the counter-guarantees from the counter-guaranteeing banks. These refused the extension in the absence of any contractual obligation to do so. The leading bank then urged the beneficiary to change its 'hold for value' request to a demand for cash payment, but the beneficiary was not inclined to do so. The contractor/account party, thereupon, secured an injunction against the issuing bank. In Chapter 12.4.3, No. 12-44, it has been argued, however, that the counter-guaranteeing bank cannot refuse extensions following 'extend or pay' (or 'hold for value') requests from the beneficiary.

[170] [1985] 2 Lloyd's Rep. 546.

[171] See for this aspect Chapter 12.4.3, No. 12-41.

bank refused to honour a claim for payment, probably because it was of the opinion that the call was made after the expiry date of the primary guarantee. However, Egyptian arbitrators made an award in favour of the beneficiary on the grounds that the account party and beneficiary had agreed to the extension of the primary guarantee. The Court of Appeal dismissed the issuing bank's claim for reimbursement, because the demand was made after the expiry date of the counter-guarantee and further because the instructing bank was not a party to the arbitral proceedings and not privy to the agreement to extend the period of validity of the primary guarantee. This decision was upheld in *Cass., 18 March 1986*.[173] It is difficult to feel at ease with the decision. The issuing bank had fully discharged its duty of examination and had emphatically refused payment. One cannot even reproach the issuing bank for omitting to ask for an extension of the counter-guarantee, because the primary guarantee had probably been called after its expiry date and because the bank was unaware of the prolongation consented to by the account party. Even more disturbing is the practical effect of the decision, namely that the account party is permitted to escape payment while he was the one who had consented to the extension of the primary guarantee, which caused arbitrators to render an award against the issuing bank. Losses such as the one suffered by the Egyptian bank should be borne by the account party.[174]

Another possibility for resolving such difficulties as those described above is to allow the issuing bank to have recourse against the instructing bank on the basis of the mandate relationship, which is not limited in time.[175] It should be noted that the instructions from the instructing bank often contain phrases such as 'please issue under our *full responsibility* ...' or 'we shall hold you harmless and indemnify you for *all consequences* arising from your issuing the requested guarantee'. German authors, therefore, argue that the issuing bank is entitled to invoke these clauses regardless of the expiry of the counter-guarantee.[176] According to this view the expiry of the counter-guarantee only terminates the issuing bank's rights under the counter-guarantee, but it does not affect the issuing bank's rights under the mandate. In that event, the issuing bank does not have the advantages associated with an independent counter-guarantee and it must, therefore, show that it has carried out the instructing bank's instructions and its duty of examination regarding the conditions of payment in the

---

[172] See also Chapter 10.10.

[173] D. 1986 I.R. p. 166.

[174] See Chapter 10.10.

[175] See Chapter 11.1.2, No. 11-2 and Chapter 11.2.2, Nos. 11-11 and 11-13 for the mandate between instructing and issuing bank and its relation to the counter-guarantee.

[176] Cf. von Westphalen, p. 238, 239, Zahn/EhrlichNeumann, 9/106, Lienesch, p. 211, Nielsen, pp. 96, 97 and ZHR 1983, p. 158, Dohm, p. 273, Bark, ZIP 1982, p. 410.

primary guarantee. The better view, however, appears to be that the expiry date in the counter-guarantee is ordinarily also intended to terminate the issuing banks's rights pursuant to the mandate, unless such extraordinary events as those in the case law cited above have occurred and the issuing bank has performed its above-mentioned obligations under the mandate.

Counter-guarantees and primary guarantees which refer to the same expiry event may also give rise to difficulties when the account party informs the instructing bank of the occurrence of the event, but fails to do the same in respect of the issuing bank. This aspect has been examined elsewhere.[177]

Is a call or actual payment under the primary guarantee a prerequisite?

13-40 It is submitted that, whether or not expressly stated in the counter-guarantee, the issuing bank can only request payment under the counter-guarantee if the beneficiary has claimed payment from the issuing bank under the primary guarantee. The accuracy of this proposition is confirmed by art. 20(b) URDG, by the definition of the term 'counter-guaarntee' in art. 6(c) UNCITRAL Convention as well as by case law.[178] Un-

---

[177] Chapter 13.2.7, No. 13-26.

[178] *Versailles, 29 March 1985*, D. 1986 I.R. p. 156, *Paris, 2 March 1990*, D. 1990 Somm. p. 209, *Trib. com. Brussels, 21 October 1986*, RDC 1987, p. 706. See also: *American Nat. Bank & Trust of Chicago v. Hamilton Industries Int*, 583 F. Supp. 164 (ND Ill. 1984) (the court dismissed the issuing bank's claim for reimbursement because it had fraudulently submitted a statement that it had been called to pay, whereas in fact the beneficiary had not made a formal written demand for payment), *Geneva, 12 September 1985*, D. 1986 I.R. p. 165 (the account party had obtained a Syrian stop-payment order against the Syrian issuing bank and there were no indications that the beneficiary had called the guarantee), *Wyle v. Bank Melli*, 577 F. Supp. 1148 (N.D. Cal. 1983)(the account party had long ceased operations in Iran and there were no indications of a call by the beneficiary). *Cass. 17 November 1984*, D. 1985 J. p. 269, is only a seeming exception to the rule because the primary guarantee provided that it became automatically payable on the expiry date, see Chapter 11.2.2, No. 15. Legal writing: Von Westphalen, p. 241, Kleiner, 20.08/9, Nielsen, p. 99, Prüm, p. 151, Rives-Lange, Banque 1986, p. 712, Banque 1987, p. 14, Mattout, No. 224, Stoufflet, JCP 1985 ll No. 20436(14), Stoufflet, Garantie Bancaire Internationale, No. 80. According to Vasseur, RDAI 1992, pp. 279/280 and his annnotations to the case law cited, neither a call on the primary guarantee nor actual payment to the beneficiary are required unless stipulated in the counter-guarantee. Certain banks in the Middle East sometimes insist on a clause according to which the bank can claim payment of the full or partial amount of the counter-guarantee if it considers this to be appropriate, even though the primary guarantee has not been called. Such a clause must be seen as a security device which protects the issuing bank against the risk that the instructing bank may be insolvent or delay its obligation promptly to reimburse it by the time the primary guarantee is called.

less the URDG or UNCITRAL Convention apply or unless stipulated otherwise, the issuing bank's call on the counter-guarantee is, however, not invalid if it does not state that the primary guarantee has been called. It is submitted, however, that the instructing bank is entitled to ask for such a statement and to defer payment until it has received the confirmation from the issuing bank. Accordingly, the issuing bank may, if requested, submit the statement after the expiry date of the counter-guarantee, the reason being that the statement was not a stipulated document.

Unless stipulated otherwise, actual payment by the issuing bank under the primary guarantee is not a prerequisite for a valid call on the counter-guarantee.[179] As a matter of fact, many counter-guarantees provide so explicitly. The reason for such a stipulation is to avoid the problem of interest covering the period between payment by the issuing bank and reimbursement by the instructing bank.

Payment under the counter-guarantee cannot be claimed if the primary guarantee has merely been extended pursuant to an 'extend or pay' request from the beneficiary of the primary guarantee.

Date for determining the rate of exchange

13-41 The counter-guarantee may permit the issuing bank to claim reimbursement from the instructing bank in a currency other than the one stated in the primary guarantee or counter-guarantee. If there are fluctuations in the rate of exchange in the period between the demand for payment under the primary guarantee and/or counter-guarantee and the actual payment by the instructing bank to the issuing bank under the counter-guarantee, the date for determining the rate of exchange gains particular significance. This issue is governed by the law applicable to the counter-guarantee. It appears that most national laws consider the date of payment (i.e. under the counter-guarantee) as the proper criterion, without prejudice to the creditor's right to claim damages in the event of late payment.[180]

---

[179] *OLG Saarbrücken, 23 January 1981*, RIW 1981, p. 338, *Cass., 26 November* 1996, RJDA 1997/3, No. 397, p. 252, *Paris, 1 October 1986*, D. 1987 Somm. p. 171, *Paris, 21 January 1987*, D. 1987 Somm. p. 176, *Paris, 28 June 1989*, D. 1990 Somm. p. 212, *Paris, 2 March 1990*, D. 1990 Somm. p. 209, *Paris, 23 November 1990*, D. 1991 Somm. p. 199. This rule is implicit in art. 20(b) URDG and art. 6(c) UNCITRAL Convention.

[180] In *Paris, 27 January 1989*, D. 1990 Somm. p. 213, the Court of Appeal ordered, however, the instructing bank to pay the issuing bank the countervalue calculated on the basis of the rate of exchange on the date of payment by the issuing bank. In this case the issuing bank had paid in US dollars in 1985, while the reimbursement in French francs took place in 1989 when the value of the US dollar had dropped by 30%. An award for damages for late payment, as provided by national law, appears to be the better approach.

13.4 THE EFFECT OF UN EMBARGOES

13-42 Following Iraq's invasion of Kuwait, the UN Security Council issued resolution No. 661 of 6 August 1990 whereby an embargo was imposed against Iraq. This and related resolutions prohibited both commercial and financial operations with Iraq and Iraqi entities. A similar, but more limited embargo was imposed against Libya by the UN Security Council resolution No. 748 of 31 March 1992. These resolutions have been implemented on European Union and national levels. The effect of these resolutions and regulations is that banks are prohibited from making any payment under guarantees and counter-guarantees in favour of Iraqi and Libyan beneficiaries in relation to transactions covered by such resolutions and regulations. This is illustrated in *Wahda Bank v. Arab Bank Plc*, where the court rejected the claim from the Libyan issuing bank for reimbursement because guarantee and counter-guarantee were given in respect of a contract, the performance of which was unlawful by virtue of the relevant resolution, even though the non-performance had not been caused by the embargo but by the account party's insolvency.[181] In *LG Essen, 1 July 1998*, the court also rejected the claim by the Iraqi issuing bank for reimbursement by the instructing bank.[182] Similarly, *Trib. Padua, 1 October 1993*, granted the account party's application for the discharge of its counter-guarantee to the Italian instructing bank on the grounds that both the primary guarantee issued by a Iraqi bank and the counter-guarantee from the Italian instructing bank had terminated as a result of the UN resolution.[183, 184]

In anticipation of a possible lifting of the embargo against Iraq, measures have been taken in order to avoid the situation that, after the lifting, Iraqi beneficiaries might successfully call guarantees or counter-guarantees. Art. 29 of the UN Security Council resolution No. 687 of April 1991 provides that all States shall take measures to ensure that no claim shall be made at the instance of any Iraqi entity or person in connection with any contract or other transactions where its performance was affected by reason of the measures taken by the Security Council in resolution No. 661 and related resolutions. The European Union implemented this resolution in regulation No. 354/92 of 7 December 1992.[185] In *Shanning International and Others v. Rasheed Bank* the

---

[181] [1993] 2 Bank. L.J. 233.

[182] WM 1999, p. 178.

[183] D. 1995 Somm. p. 23. The decision has been commented upon by Affaki, Banque et Droit, janv.-févr. 1994.3, and Vasseur, D. 1995 Chronique, p. 43. See also *Paris, 23 June 1995*, JCP Éd. E ll, No. 735, although the Court of Appeal in this case incorrectly took the view that the effect of the EC Regulation was a suspension of the guarantee or counter-guarantee, rather than a prohibition of payment, see the critical note by Affaki.

[184] See Wunnicke/Wunnicke/Turner, § 7.03[C] for further American case law.

[185] The regulation has been published in EC Official Journal No. L 361, 10 December 1992.

British House of Lords has, meanwhile, recognised the permanent effect of the prohibition to pay.[186] Accordingly, any claim by an Iraqi beneficiary or an Iraqi issuing bank under a counter-guarantee has been effectively and permanently barred, even after the lifting of the embargo. As a consequence of the permanent nature of the prohibition, the account party's claim in the *Shanning* case against the U.K. instructing bank for restitution of the security was sustained.

13.5 NON-COMPLIANCE AND RESTRAINING ORDERS

13-43 While applications for restraining orders are typically made in connection with allegations of fraud, account parties sometimes also apply for preventive relief, arguing that the terms of the guarantee or counter-guarantee have not been met. Such applications are often founded on both counts. As case law, especially Dutch, French and Belgian case law, cited in Chapter 13 indicates, restraining orders on the grounds of non-compliance are possible if the court is satisfied in this respect, subject to local rules of procedure. As far as applications for preventive restraining orders against the bank are concerned, it could be argued that the account party lacks a proper interest in such measures because the bank cannot claim reimbursement from the account party if it has effected payment while the terms and conditions of the (counter-)guarantee have not been fulfilled. This fact does not, however, appear to preclude the possibility of preventive measures against the bank. In general, this policy is commendable, for similar reasons to those raised in favour of preventive stop-payment orders against the bank in the event of established fraud.[187]

13.6 RECOVERY AFTER PAYMENT. FINAL SETTLEMENT

13-44 Apart from cases of established fraud, once the bank has made payment made to the beneficiary in accordance with the terms of the guarantee, its part is played. This is not the case as far as the account party/principal debtor and the beneficiary/creditor are concerned. As between these parties, there will be a final settlement on the basis of the underlying contract. In *Cargill International v. Bangladesh Sugar & Food Industries* the court observed that 'there would at some stage in the future be an 'accounting' between the parties in the sense that their rights and obligations would be finally determined ... If the amount of the bond was not sufficient to satisfy the beneficiary's claim for damages he could bring proceedings for his loss ... If a performance bond does not

---

[186] [2001] All ER (D) 321 (Jun).

[187] Cf. *Brussels, 5 April 1990*, TBH 1992, p. 82, Kleiner, No. 21.51. See also Chapter 16.3 and especially No. 16-9.

exhaust one party's rights it ought not to exhaust the rights of the other party; if there had been a call on the bond which turned out to exceed the true loss sustained then the party who provided the bond was entitled to recover the overpayment'.[188] The claim for recovery after payment under the guarantee is directly founded on the parties' agreement 'to pay first and argue later' and is of a contractual nature.[189]

Thus, the account party debtor may try to recover the amount paid under the guarantee from the beneficiary and, if necessary, initiate proceedings before the court or arbitrators as provided in the secured contract, if he is of the opinion that he was not in default or that the loss sustained by the beneficiary was less than the amount paid under the guarantee. This dispute has to be settled by reference to the terms of the underlying contract. Because of the agreed allocation of risks the burden of proof lies with the account party/principal debtor. Should arbitrators or the court agree with him, the creditor/beneficiary will be ordered to refund the amount.

If the arbitrators or the court determine that no breach of contract has been committed or that the actual loss was less than the amount paid under the guarantee, the account party is entitled to interest as from the date of payment by the bank, but ordinarily no action will lie for damages, in addition to repayment and interest.[190] The fact that arbi-

---

[188] [1996] 2 Lloyd's Rep. 524, at 528-530. The Court of Appeal in this case ruled: 'In these circumstances the obligation to account later to the seller, in respect of what turns out to be an overpayment, is a necessary corrective if a a balance of commercial fairness is to be maintained', [1998] 2 All ER 406, at 413. The decision was approved in *Comdel Commodities v. Siporex Trade*, [1997] 1 Lloyd's Rep. 424, 431. See also *State Trading Corp. of India v. E.D. & F. Man*, [1981] Comm. L.R.235: 'If [the beneficiary] receives too much, that can be rectified later in arbitration'. See for other examples of recovery by the account party/ principal debtor from the beneficiary/creditor after payment by the bank *Paris, 18 March 1986*, D. 1987 Somm. p. 173, *Trib. com. Paris, 20 September 1991*, D. 1992 Somm. p. 243, *Trib. com. Marseille, 19 September 1991*, D. 1992 Somm. p. 243, *Cass., 7 June 1994*, D. 1995 Somm. p. 19, *BGH, 24 September 1998*, WM 1998, p. 2363, and *OLG München, 31 October 1984*, WM 1985, p. 189.

[189] See also the three English cases cited in the previous note, *Trib. com. Liege, 7 April 1995*, RDC 1996, p. 1063, and Staudinger/Horn, No. 352. Derains, JDI 1980, p. 977, Stoufflet, JCP 1985 ll No. 20436 (5), Vasseur, D 1987 Somm. p. 172 take the view that this claim is based on restitution for payment by mistake. This does not seem to be correct , since the creditor/beneficiary has a right to payment when the terms of the guarantee have been satisfied. German law regards the account party's claim for recovery as one based on unjust enrichment, see von Westphalen, pp. 74-78, 81-84, 215-223, Staudinger/Horn, No. 353, Zahn/ Ehrlich/Neumann, 9/121-124, Canaris, Nos. 1141-1147, Schlegelberger/Hefermehl, No. 299, Mülbert, pp. 36-38, Dohm, Nos. 251-253, Schinnerer/Avancini, pp. 322-324. See also *BGH, 24 November 1983*, WM 1984, p. 44, *BGH, 21 April 1988*, WM 1988, p. 934, *BGH, 9 March 1989*, NJW 1989, p. 1606.

[190] Ad hoc arbitral decision rendered in 1979, reported by Derains, JDI 1980, p. 977.

trators or a court may ultimately find that the creditor is not entitled to compensation for breach of contract and that it should not keep the amount received under the guarantee, does not imply that the call on the guarantee has been fraudulent.[191] The right to immediate compensation while default of the account party/ debtor is (still) in dispute is precisely what a first demand guarantee is intended to bring about.

Claims for recovery from the beneficiary will ordinarily be filed in main proceedings. In *Rb Amsterdam, 10 January 1997*,[192] and in *Rb Alkmaar, 3 December 1998*,[193] the account party claimed, however, repayment in summary proceedings. In both cases the court ruled that for such claims in summary proceedings to succeed there must be clear and immediate evidence that the beneficiary had no entitlement to payment under the guarantee in accordance with the same stringent test which applies in applications for restraining orders in the event of (alleged) fraud. In *BGH, 12 July 2001*, it was held that claims for recovery cannot be adjudicated in summary proceedings as being inconsistent with the nature of a first demand guarantee.[194]

Claims by the account party for recovery of the amount paid under the guarantee should be made against the contracting party in the underlying contract. Accordingly, *BGH, 10 November 1998*, dismissed the claim for recovery made against a third party to whom the beneficiary/contracting party had assigned the rights to the proceeds of the guarantee.[195]

If the conditions for payment under the guarantee have been complied with and the bank has effected payment to the beneficiary, it has paid what it owed to the beneficiary pursuant to the guarantee. The bank has no right to reclaim the amount paid from the beneficiary arguing that the beneficiary was not entitled to payment as measured by the underlying contract, since the bank is not a party to that contract, as was rightly observed by *BGH, 10 November 1998*.[196] It is also noted that the bank's willingness

---

[191] *Cass., 7 June 1994*, D. 1995 Somm. p. 19.

[192] KG 1997, 44.

[193] KG 1999, 2.

[194] WM 2001, p. 2078.

[195] WM 1998, p. 2522.

[196] WM 1998, p. 2522. See also Canaris, No. 1142, von Westphalen, pp. 218-222, Lienesch, p. 216. See also the Canadian Court of Appeal in *Royal Bank v. Gentra Canada Investments Inc.*, (2001) 15. B.L.R. (3d) 25 (rejecting the bank's argument for repayment that the beneficiary's statement that certain amounts were due and payable, was not true). Certain German authors take the view that the bank does have a claim for recovery in its own right, see Zahn/Ehrlich/Neumann, 9/130-133, with further references. See Chapter 4.5, No. 4-19, for the bank's right of recovery in the event of the German first demand suretyship.

whether or not to issue a guarantee depends on the creditworthiness of the account party and the provision of security by the account party and is not affected by the incidents pertaining to the underlying transaction from which it wants to stay clear.[197]

---

[197] It may be that in respect of commercial letters of credit the issuing bank could have a claim for repayment in its own right in the event of forged documents and if no recovery from the account party/buyer proves to be possible, as the bank has a security interest in the documents. This would be a claim under the law of fraud in general where a beneficiary attempts to swindle money from a bank.

CHAPTER 14
THE CONCEPT OF FRAUD

14.1 INTRODUCTION

Significance

14-1 Through the years, a huge volume of case law concerning the issue of fraud has grown up. Legal writing on this topic is no less voluminous. If this abundance were the proper yardstick, one would surely be inclined to believe that fraud is the most important issue in the field of guarantees. It would be unwarranted, however, to draw that conclusion. The wealth of case law can simply be explained by the fact that first demand guarantees are capable of being abused. It is only natural for the account party, when the risk of a call has materialised, to assert that the demand for payment in his case is indeed fraudulent. He may, therefore, initiate proceedings in order to attempt to prevent payment and, of course, it hardly matters whether he believes honestly or with some diffidence or even with little conviction, that the demand is totally unjustified. It must also be borne in mind that fraud is, in practice, virtually the only defence available when one seeks to escape payment under a demand guarantee. It is worth noting that, in all countries concerned, the very first decisions on the law of first demand guarantees dealt with both the recognition of the independent nature of guarantees with their extraordinary features, and with the recognition of the limits of independence in the case of fraud. However, in order to maintain a realistic perspective on the matter, it is only fitting to keep in mind that the defence of fraud has been pleaded successfully in only a very small minority of cases.

As has been observed elsewhere,[1] general estimates of the percentage of fraudulent demands for payment are utterly unreliable and futile. Nonetheless, in some specific instances, it might be possible to detect certain patterns of suspicious behaviour. The clearest example appears to be the massive calling of guarantees, especially those issued by American banks for the account of American exporters, during the Iranian revolution.[2] Some other countries continue to be mentioned as singularly risk-prone. Even if such generalisations are not devoid of some substance, one ought to be careful

---

[1] Chapter 6, Nos. 6-4 and 6-9.

[2] It is only fair to note that experiences since approximately 1984 have, generally speaking, not been unfavourable.

not to be unduly influenced by these impressions when directing one's mind to individual cases. One must also bear in mind that the complex nature of the projects, and the accompanying circumstances in some of those countries, are apt to cause difficulties of all kinds and they are, hence, liable to engender differences of opinion more frequently than elsewhere. On the other hand, sharp practices on the part of the beneficiary do not only manifest themselves in the form of actual demands for payment. They could also consist of the beneficiary's continually exacting extension of the validity period and/or additional works under the threat of a call.

The issue of fraud arises if a defence against payment is made which is founded on grounds derived from the underlying transaction. Case law and legal writing occasionally treat non-compliance with the terms and conditions of the guarantee as an exception to the bank's payment obligation on the same footing as fraud. This is confusing as well as incorrect since this defence is solely and directly founded on the terms of the guarantee itself with the result that the payment obligation does not materialise. Non-compliance with the terms of the guarantee has nothing to do with fraud.

Compared with documentary credits, fraud in the form of forged or fraudulent documents is of minor significance.

Procedural background

14-2 The issue of fraud can arise in two different settings. In the majority of cases the account party raises the defence in proceedings in which it applies for an injunction against the bank restraining it from effecting payment, and/or applies for an injunction against the beneficiary (and/or second issuing bank, in the case of indirect guarantees) restraining it (them) from calling the (counter-)guarantee. Both types of preventive actions will be referred to as applications for restraining or stop-payment orders. These applications are made in proceedings known as provisional, interim, preliminary or interlocutory proceedings (*kort geding, einstweilige Verfügung, procédure en référé*). Another means of preventing payment is the application for a conservatory attachment under the bank or for a freezing order, which is the English equivalent of the Continental conservatory attachment. Attempts to secure injunctions through full-length main proceedings are futile, since payment will already have been effected by the time a favourable judgment might be rendered.

The account party could also raise the defence of fraud after payment by the bank when the bank claims reimbursement or when the account party seeks to undo the debiting of his accounts by the bank. This strategy is rarely pursued because the account party has to demonstrate fraud by the beneficiary as well as knowledge thereof on the part of the bank,[3] whereas the latter is not required in preventive stop-payment

---

[3] See Chapter 15.

proceedings, except, so it seems, in England.[4]

In the minority of cases, it is the bank that refuses to pay on the grounds of fraud, which may trigger litigation initiated by the beneficiary. This situation especially occurs when the account party is insolvent.

14.2 PLAN OF DISCUSSION

14-3 Fraud is a broad subject. This discussion is, therefore, spread over three chapters. Chapter 14 is mainly concerned with the concept of fraud on the part of the beneficiary and, more particularly, with the substantive elements and the aspect of evidence of fraud. A brief overview of the relevant case law and legal writing from several countries is given in Chapter 14.3, while Chapter 14.4 contains some concluding observations. Proceeding from a working hypothesis, Chapter 14.5 describes the substantive aspects of fraud more clearly by examining a series of specific fact situations on the basis of case law. Chapter 14.6 deals with summary proceedings against the bank in relation to fraud. The position of the bank in its relationship with the account party is examined in Chapter 15. Chapter 16 deals with preventive restraining orders against the bank and beneficiary and Chapter 17 with conservatory attachment and freeazing orders. These chapters contain an analysis of the particular aspects relating to these judicial measures and they are sub-divided into two sections, whereby a distinction is made between direct and indirect guarantees.

14.3 COMPARATIVE OVERVIEW

14.3.1 Introduction

14-4 Chapter 14.3 presents a brief overview of the concept of fraud as it has emerged in case law and legal writing in the countries covered in this study. The survey focuses on three questions. First, does fraud require (evidence of) deceitful or malicious conduct on the part of the beneficiary? Secondly, is fraud to be determined by having regard to the underlying relationship (fraud in the transaction) or is it restricted to fraudulent acts within the confines of the contract of guarantee (fraud in the documents)? And finally, what is the standard of proof of fraud? Chapter 14.3 concludes with a summary of the actual application of the principles as they are found in the various jurisdictions.

---

[4] See Chapter 14.3.6 and Chapter 16.3, No. 16-4.

14.3.2 The Netherlands

Case law

14-5 In the very first decision dealing with independent guarantees, *CA Amsterdam, March 30 1972*, laid down the rule that the demand for payment by the beneficiary should not be honoured if the call is 'evidently arbitrary or deceitful'.[5] This has become the standard formula in Dutch case law, and it has been repeated in numerous subsequent cases.[6] The adverb 'evidently' relates to the standard of proof, while the adjectives 'arbitrary or deceitful' relate to the substantive element of fraud. Slightly different phrases, often in conjunction with the previous formula, have occasionally been employed too, such as 'evidently unjustified',[7] 'if it is established beyond reasonable doubt that the beneficiary has no claim against the account party/principal debtor',[8] 'bad faith',[9] 'the evidence of fraud must be crystal clear',[10] or 'beyond reasonable doubt',[11] 'the facts alleged by the account party must be established with a degree of likelihood close to certainty',[12] or 'it must be evident that no reasonable creditor in the particular circumstances of the case would have called the guarantee'.[13]

---

[5] NJ 1973, 188.

[6] See, for example, *Rb Amsterdam, 18 December 1980*, S&S 1981, 135, *Rb Zwolle, 26 November 1982*, KG 1982, 220, *Rb Arnhem, 14 March 1983*, NJ 1983, 750, *Rb Amsterdam, 7 April 1988*, KG 1988, 181, *Rb Rotterdam, 9 June 1989*, KG 1989, 270, *Rb Amsterdam, 5 September 1991*, KG 1991, 335, *CA Amsterdam, 4 February 1993*, KG 1993, 113, *CA The Hague, 16 March 1993*, KG 1993, 222, *Rb The Hague, 9 April 1997*, KGK 1997, 1431.

[7] *Rb Amsterdam, 22 June 1989*, KG 1989, 279

[8] *CA Amsterdam, 5 February 1987*, NJ 1988, 591.

[9] *Rb Zwolle, 26 November 1982*, KG 1982, 220.

[10] *Rb Haarlem, 21 November 1986*, KG 1987, 47, *Rb Leeuwarden, 10 January 2001*, KGK 2001, 1567.

[11] *CA Amsterdam, 5 February 1987*, NJ 1988, 591.

[12] *Rb Amsterdam, 7 April 1988*, KG 1988, 181. This decision was reversed by *CA Amsterdam, 19 January 1989*, KG 1990, 74 substituting the formula 'sufficiently plausible' for that of the court of first instance. However, while the court of first instance employed its formula in the context of fraud, the Court of Appeal appears to use its formula in the context of the expiry of the guarantee, without apparent reference to the issue of fraud. See Chapter 13.2.7, No. 13-23, for a critical comment. Should the Court of Appeal, however, have had in mind the issue of fraud when pronouncing its formula, it would have patently departed from established patterns in Dutch case law.

[13] *Rb Amsterdam, 10 January 1997*, KG 1997, 44, *Rb Alkmaar, December 12 1998*, KG 1999, 2.

The Concept of Fraud

Whatever formula in respect of the standard of proof may be employed, its stringency is well-established. As far as the substantive aspects are concerned, the meaning of the phrase 'arbitrary or deceitful' has not been elucidated or elaborated upon. The above-mentioned alternative formulas must not be assumed to carry any other connotation, but they might possibly shed some light on the meaning of the standard phrase 'arbitrary or deceitful'. In any event, the notion of fraud is not restricted to deceit or spitefulness and evidence of such a mental condition of the beneficiary is not required. It is conceivable that the word 'deceitful' in the standard phrase continues to be included just by force of habit without any real significance.[14] Incidentally, in most cases courts did not bother to pronounce any particular formula other than the term 'fraud', simply because the facts, which according to the account party justified a finding of fraud, had not been established. The emphasis in judicial reasoning plainly lies on the aspect of clear evidence relating to the facts which have been alleged by the account party and which, according to him, constitute fraud. This heavy burden of proof falls on the account party. It is also clear and well-established that the question of whether the call by the beneficiary is fraudulent can only be answered by looking into the underlying relationship. However, the courts will not permit a protracted and in-depth investigation into the underlying transaction and insist that the account party produces clear evidence of fraud immediately within the constraints of the provisional proceedings.

Legal writing

14-6 Dutch legal writing has mainly focused on the issue of fraud in connection with applications for stop-payment injunctions and conservatory attachment orders.[15] These applications can involve additional difficulties. Nonetheless, as far as the standard of proof and the substantive aspects of the notion of fraud are concerned, the views expressed in legal writing are virtually unanimous and in line with case law. As an alternative to the common phrase 'arbitrary or deceitful', some authors, like some case law, have suggested that the call is fraudulent 'if no honest beneficiary could (reasonably) take the position that he has a claim against the account party' or just 'if the beneficiary has no claim against the account party'.[16]

---

[14] The mixture of various formulas without any real difference is well illustrated in *Rb Utrecht, 6 July 2000*, S & S 2001, 3, where the court found that 'it was evidently beyond reasonable doubt that the call was in violation of the principle of reasonableness and fairness, deceitful, arbitrary or abusive'.

[15] Pabbruwe, pp. 45-59, Mijnssen, pp. 51-66, Boll, pp. 121-130, Ebbink, WPNR 1984, pp. 434-438, Grootenhuis, AA 1986, pp. 415-418, Bartman, NJB 1986, pp. 1088-1093, Croiset van Uchelen, WPNR 1989, pp. 271-275, Hardenberg, WPNR 1995, pp. 842-847.

[16] Mijnssen, pp. 25, 53, Grootenhuis, AA 1986, p. 416, Croiset van Uchelen, WPNR 1989, p. 271, Ebbink, WPNR 1984, p. 437. See also Schoordijk, WPNR 1976, p. 681 (with respect to documentary credit).

14.3.3 Germany

Legal writing

14-7 German legal writing on the concept of fraud is most prolific.[17] According to the unanimous view in doctrine, the contract of guarantee, like any other contract, is subject to the precept of good faith, which forbids the creditor (beneficiary) to use his formal rights against his debtor (the bank) in an abusive or fraudulent manner. This point of departure might possibly explain why German doctrine approaches the issue of fraud as something that primarily pertains to the relationship between beneficiary and bank. Fraud constitutes a defence for the bank and justifies a refusal to pay. Nonetheless, the question of what kind of conduct of the beneficiary constitutes fraud is ultimately answered by reference to the underlying relationship between beneficiary and account party. While much has been written on the concept of fraud, including the dogmatic aspects, no clarity exists as to what precise kind of conduct on the part of the beneficiary and/or what specific facts relating to the underlying relationship, render a call fraudulent.[18]

Several avenues to the notion of fraud can be discerned. Some authors basically substitute other abstract notions, such as arbitrariness, abuse and bad faith, for the notion of fraud. Others consider a call fraudulent if it is made without grounds or justification or in violation of the principal contract, or, more specifically, if the beneficiary has no right to payment whatsoever, as determined by reference to the underlying relationship. Another group of authors seeks to define the concept of fraud by having regard to the purpose and premises underlying the contract of guarantee (*Geschäftszweck* or *Garantiezweck* or *Geschäftsgrundlage*). According to a fourth and prevailing approach the demand for payment is fraudulent if the event giving rise to a right to payment in the underlying relationship (*materielles Garantiefall*) has not ma-

---

[17] See, for example, Mülbert, pp. 49-81, Lohmann, pp. 102-125, von Westphalen, pp. 185-206, and WM 1981, pp. 296-298, Staudinger/Horn, Nos. 309-319, Lienesch, pp. 149-156, Nielsen, pp. 105-117, and ZIP 1982, pp. 253-260, ZHR 1983, pp. 152-158, Zahn/Ehrlich/Neumann, 9/126, Schlegelberger/Hefermehl, No. 298, Canaris, Nos. 1138-1139, Heinsius, FS Werner, pp. 229-250, Heldrich, FS Kegel, pp. 175-195, Mettenheim, RIW 1981, pp. 581-584, Coing, ZHR 1983, pp. 129-144, Mühl, FS Imre Zajtay, pp. 396-400, 403-406, von Marschall, in Dokumentenakkreditive und Bankgarantien, pp. 39-40, Horn, NJW 1980, pp. 2157-2158, IPRax 1981, pp. 152-153, and in Transnational Law of International Commercial Transactions, pp. 289-302, Schütze, WM 1980, pp. 1438-1441, and RIW 1981, p. 85, Bark, ZIP 1982, pp. 412-416. Swiss legal writing is very much akin to German doctrine: Kleiner, 21.41-54, Dohm, Nos. 225-243.

[18] In accordance with its tradition, it is typical of German legal writing to refer more amply to other writers than to case law, and if case law is cited there is usually no mention of the facts of the case, but see von Westphalen, pp. 259-277.

terialised. It is doubtful, however, whether the several approaches reflect truly substantive differences of opinion yielding divergent results if applied to concrete cases. The test as regards fraud is an objective one and evidence of malevolence or ill intent on the part of the beneficiary is not required.[19]

Unanimity exists as regards the standard of evidence. The proof of the facts which constitute fraud must be clear, evident, beyond doubt and immediately available ('*liquid*'). This usually implies documentary evidence as opposed to oral allegations, preferably consisting of statements or certificates from third parties or communications from the beneficiary, and undisputed or established facts. The burden of proof rests on the account party or bank. However, those authors who take the view that fraud also implies malevolence do not seem to require evidence in this respect. Fraudulent intent appears to be assumed once the objective conditions of fraud have been established.[20]

Case law

14-8 As far as the substantive aspects of fraud are concerned, the prevailing view in German case law is that there is fraud if it is evident or if there is clear, *liquid* proof that the '*materielles Garantiefall*' has not materialised,[21] but other formulas also occur.[22]

---

[19] Mülbert, p. 67, Horn, No. 553, Lohmann, p. 104, Nielsen, WM 1999, p. 2014, Lienesch, pp. 153-154, and DZWIR 2000, p. 495. See also von Westphalen, p. 191, Mettenheim, RIW 1981, p. 583, and Horn and Wymeersch, p. 483, who refer to constructive knowledge on the part of the beneficiary.

[20] Cf. the American device of constructive fraud, see Chapter 14.3.7, No. 14-14.

[21] *BGH, 12 March 1984 (ll ZR 198/82)*, NJW 1984, p. 2030, *BGH, 31 January 1985*, WM 1985, p. 511, *BGH, 29 September 1986*, WM 1986, p. 1429, *BGH, 21 April 1988*, WM 1988, p. 934, *BGH, 28 October 1993*, WM 1994, p. 106, *BGH, 17 October 1996*, WM 1996, p. 2228, *BGH, 5 March 2002*, WM 2002, p. 743, OLG *Köln, 7 August 1986*, WM 1988, p. 21, *OLG Bremen, 14 June 1990*, WM 1990, p. 1369, *OLG Köln, 15 March 1991*, RIW 1992, p. 145, *OLG Oldenburg, 15 February 2000*, WM 2001, p. 732, *OLG Saarbrücken, 6 July 2001*, WM 2001, p. 2055.

[22] See, for example, *OLG Saarbrücken, 23 January 1981*, RIW 1981. p. 338 (if the call is abusive or deceitful; if the call is totally unfounded; if the 'Garantiefall' (see text No. 7) has not materialised), *LG Frankfurt a.M., 11 December 1979*, NJW 1981, p. 56 (if the claim is evidently unjustified and hence abusive or deceitful, it violates the principle of good faith to enforce the principle of independence), *OLG Hamburg, 18 December 1981*, WM 1983, p. 188 (if there is gross and evident abuse of rights; if the call evidently violates the main contract), *OLG Frankfurt a.M., 3 March 1983*, WM 1983, p. 575 (if there is *liquid* proof of abuse of right or deceit in calling the guarantee), *BGH, 19 September 1985*, NJW 1986, p. 310 (if there is clear and *liquid* proof that the beneficiary has no right to payment); idem: *BGH, 13 July 1989*, WM 1989, p. 1496, *OLG Hamm, 24 June 1986*, WM 1986, p. 1503, *OLG Frankfurt a.M., 27 April 1987*, WM 1988, p. 1480.

Insofar as a few decisions refer to malevolence or deceitfulness, it has always been in addition to phrases which do not require a fraudulent state of mind of the beneficiary and, in any event, a fraudulent intent need not be proven. Case law also endorses the doctrinal view that fraud should or could be determined by reference to the underlying transaction. With a few exceptions,[23] courts require clear and *liquid* evidence of fraud which the account party or bank must be able to produce immediately without in-depth investigation into the underlying transaction.

14.3.4 France

Case law

14-9 There exists an abundance of French case law dealing with the issue of fraud. In most cases the court did not need to elaborate on the precise meaning and scope of the notion of fraud, because the facts alleged by the account party or bank were not clearly established, or for other reasons. In other cases, courts have merely restated the well-established rule that no payment is to be made if the demand for payment is fraudulent or abusive. The adjective 'fraudulent' is believed to imply some kind of deceit or ill intention on the part of the beneficiary. Such a culpable state of mind is, however, not a prerequisite and need not be proven or, alternatively, is presumed to exist once the objective conditions of fraud have been established.[24] The Cour de Cassation defines fraud as the manifest absence of the right of the beneficiary, which could and should be determined by examining the underlying contract and its performance.[25] Fraud, according to the Cour de Cassation, does not require deceit or disloyal manoeuvres by the beneficiary outside the scope of the secured contract. Thus these, as well as many other decisions, show that (evidence of a) fraudulent intent is not required and that fraud is to be determined by having regard to the underlying transaction. It should also

---

[23] The notion of 'plausible' evidence has been mentioned in *LG Frankfurt a.M., 11 December 1979*, NJW 1981, p. 56, *OLG Saarbrücken, 23 January 1981*, RIW 1981, p. 338, *LG Köln, 11 December 1981*, WM 1982, p. 430, *LG Dortmund, 9 July 1980*, WM 1981, p. 280, *LG München, 30 January 1981*, WM 1981, p. 416. One may, however, doubt whether the courts in these cases did indeed envisage a less stringent yardstick. For instance, there was very strong evidence of fraud in the Dortmund case, while the München court considered that the evidence from a great number of employees of the account party was insufficient. In the Saarbrücken decision the terms 'plausible' and 'evident' have been used interchangeably. The use of the term 'plausible' originates no doubt from the general criteria for interim injunctions.

[24] See Prüm, No. 477, with reference to case law and legal writing.

[25] *Cass., 10 June 1986*, D. 1987 J. p. 17, Banque 1986, p. 711, *Cass., 20 January 1987*, D. 1987 Somm. p. 177, JCP 1987 ll No. 20764, *Cass., 12 January 1993*, D. 1995 J. p. 24, *Cass., 28 November 1995*, Rev. Droit Bancaire 1996, p. 58.

be noted that French courts, as do courts in other jurisdictions, employ the notions 'fraud' and 'abuse' interchangeably or side by side. It appears that evidence of abuse implies evidence of fraud, or at least of constructive fraud, and that the two concepts cannot and need not be distinguished for the purpose of independent guarantees.[26] In any event, either evidence of fraud or evidence of abuse is sufficient to debar the beneficiary from claiming payment.

On the whole, French courts have refrained from attempts to enunciate a general formula or approach which would clarify the substantive elements of the notion of fraud. In those cases where stop-payment injunctions have been granted, courts have tended to merely state that the established facts justified judicial intervention, with or without adding that the proven facts rendered the call fraudulent or abusive.

The emphasis in fraud cases is clearly on the aspect of evidence: fraud must be established 'beyond doubt' or must be 'evident', 'clear', 'manifest' or must 'strike the eye of the beholder' (*'crève les yeux'*). Such clear evidence requires unambiguous statements or documents from independent third parties such as surveyors or engineers, communications from the beneficiary or undisputed and/or established facts.[27] This standard of proof also implies that the evidence must be adduced forthwith, without the need for protracted investigation into the underlying relationship. Moreover, courts could draw a finding of fraud on the part of the beneficiary from 'the whole of the circumstances'.[28] The burden of proof is on the account party. [29]

---

[26] Prüm, Nos. 445-449, 473-477, Cabrillac/Mouly, No. 408, Stoufflet, Garantie Bancaire Internationale, No. 58, Contamine-Raynaud, Rev. Droit Bancaire 1996, p. 58, Hanna, JCP 1998 Éd. E, p. 1781. See also, for example, *Cass., 7 June* 1994 (2 decisions), D. 1995 Somm. pp. 20, 21, Cass., *12 December 1997*, JCP Éd E. 1998, p. 1781, and *Paris, 15 November 1996*, Banque et Droit 1997, No. 53, p. 51, which refer to fraud *or* abuse.

[27] See, for example, *Cass., 12 December 1984*, D. 1985 J. p. 269, *Cass., 21 May 1985*, D. 1986 J. p. 213, *Cass. 12 December 1985*, D. 1986 J. p. 213, *Cass., 10 June 1986*, D. 1987 J. p. 17, *Cass. 18 December 1990*, D. 1991 Somm. p. 198, *Cass., 7 June* 1994, D. 1995 Somm. p. 20, *Cass., 7 October 1997*, JCP Éd. E, p. 226, Paris, *23 November 1990*, D. 1991 Somm. p. 199, *Paris, 6 March 1991*, D. 1992 Somm. p. 241, *Versailles, 16 September 1992*, D. 1993 Somm. p. 102, *Paris, 15 November 1996*, Banque et Droit 1997, No. 53, p. 51.

[28] *Cass., 10 June 1986*, D. 1987 J. p. 17. See also *Cass., 12 January 1993*, D. 1995 J. p. 24 (established fraud as the event to which the secured contract related had been cancelled, and the beneficiary knew that the amounts to be paid under the guarantee would have to be repaid immediately while the beneficiary had failed to comply with its contractual obligation to provide security for such repayment).

[29] See especially *Cass. 23 October 1990*, D. 1991 Somm. p. 197.

Legal writing

14-10 French legal writing is in line with case law as described above.[30] The emphasis is focused on the aspect of evidence,[31] while few attempts have been made to develop a general formula elucidating the notion of fraud.[32]

14.3.5 Belgium

Case law

14-11 The rule that a right to payment is to be denied, despite formal compliance with the terms of the guarantee, in the event of fraud is firmly entrenched in Belgian case law.[33] In a number of cases the courts have attempted to be more specific in respect of the general notions as 'fraud', 'abuse', 'violation of the principle of good faith', 'bad

---

[30] Prüm, Nos. 429-491, Vasseur, Nos. 119-128, and his annotations to the decisions cited in Chapters 14, 15 and 16 as reported in Dalloz, Cabrillac/Mouly, Nos. 442-446, Stoufflet, JCP 1985 ll No. 20436, JCP 1986 ll No. 20593, J.D.I. 1987, pp. 277-285, Stoufflet, Garantie Bancaire Internationale, Nos. 55-65, Mattout, No. 240, Rives-Lange, Banque 1986, pp. 711-713, Moatti, Journal des Notaires et des Avocats 1989, pp. 663-672.

[31] The well-known and often repeated phrase that fraud must 'strike the eye of the beholder' (*'crève les yeux'*) was coined by Vasseur.

[32] But see Prüm, Nos. 430-483, and Stoufflet, JCP 1985 ll No. 20436 and JCP 1986 ll No. 20593: 'if it is certain and evident that the beneficiary's claim is devoid of any substance'; 'if it is indisputably established that the beneficiary has no right to payment'; 'an intention to inflict harm on the account party is not necessary'. It is quite likely that the Cour de Cassation, when promulgating its formulas in 1986 and 1987, drew on these statements.

[33] See, for example, *Trib. com. Brussels, 15 January 1980*, JCB 1980, p. 147, *Trib. com. Brussels, 23 December 1980*, Rev. Banque 1981, p. 627, *Brussels, 18 December 1981*, Rev. Banque 1982, p. 99, *Trib. com. Brussels, 6 April 1982*, Rev. Banque 1982, p. 683, *Trib. com. Brussels, 8 October 1985*, RDC 1986, p. 648, *Trib. com. Brussels, 26 November 1987*, RDC 1989, p. 97, *Trib. com. Brussels, 15 April 1991*, D. 1992 Somm. p. 242, *Trib. com. Brussels, 30 January 1990*, TBH 1992, p. 84, CA *Brussels, 15 December 1992*, RDC 1993, p. 1055, CA *Brussels, 26 June 1992*, RDC 1994, p. 51, *Trib. com. Brussels, 3 September 1993*, RDC 1994, p. 1126 (fraud or abuse does not necessarily imply a fraudulent intent or intent to inflict harm, but encompasses the situation whereby the exercise of the beneficiary's right clearly exceeds the ordinary exercise of a prudent person), *Trib. com. Kortrijk, 21 October 1996*, RW 1996/1997, p. 1447 (fraud must be 'as clear as day' and be proven by immediately available evidence without further investigation), *Trib. com. Brussels, 21 November 1997*, RDC 1998, p. 850 (there is fraud or abuse if there is clear and indisputable evidence, which must be immediately available without extensive investigation, that the beneficiary has no right of payment pursuant to the underlying contract), *Trib. com. Hasselt, 2 October 1998*, TBH 1998, p. 723, CA *Brussels, 2 March 2001*, TBH 2002, p. 484 (fraud must be 'evident, manifest, indisputable and as clear as day').

faith' and 'arbitrariness or deceit'. Case law clearly shows that a fraudulent design on the part of the beneficiary is not a prerequisite, that no distinction is made between 'fraud' and 'abuse', and that the abusive or fraudulent nature of the demand is to be determined by reference to the underlying relationship.[34] As regards evidence, the standard of proof is the same as elsewhere: fraud must be clear, manifest or evident and the evidence must be immediately available.[35]

Legal writing

14-12 Belgian authors have taken the same position as case law.[36] In general, they have refrained from attempting to elaborate on the substantive aspects of fraud in order to arrive at a more practicable formula.[37]

14.3.6 England

14-13 English courts have recognised as a matter of principle that the rule of independence ceases to apply where fraud is involved. As far as the substantive notion of fraud is concerned, it appears from the forbidding language and the way the principle has been applied in such leading cases as *Harbottle v. Nat. Westminster Bank*, *Edward*

---

[34] See the case law cited in the previous footnote. In *Trib. com. Brussels, 26 May 1988*, JT 1988, p. 460, the court described fraud in general as 'intentional disloyal conduct with the purpose of inflicting harm or to secure an advantage' and abuse as 'utilising a right with the sole purpose of inflicting harm or in a manner which clearly exceeds the limits of the normal utilisation of a right by a prudent and diligent person'. When applying these general notions specifically to guarantees, the court merely referred to a situation where the beneficiary has no rights as regards the account party. This decision provides an excellent illustration of references to evil designs, as are apparent in a few other decisions and legal writings in the various jurisdictions, originating from the general concept of fraud. However, when applied to guarantees this stringent general notion has clearly been adapted in Belgium and elsewhere to the specific particularities of guarantees.

[35] See the case law cited above.

[36] See Poullet, thesis Nos. 122-131, 163-170, 219-238, 291-296, 326-338, JCB 1982, pp. 645-662, Simont, Rev. Banque 1983, pp. 595-603, Wymeersch, Hague-Zagreb Colloquium 6, pp. 102-107, TPR, 1986, pp. 494-503, Horn and Wymeersch, p. 498-500, T'Kint, Nos. 850-852. These articles are mainly a review of Belgian and French case law. See also the comments to some of the decisions cited above and RPDB, Nos. 140-150. See further Sion, Rev. Banque 1984, pp. 10-16, and de Ly, TBH 1986, pp. 185-193, who primarily deal with American case law.

[37] According to Wymeersch, TPR 1986, pp. 499, 500, fraud encompasses the situation where the beneficiary has evidently no right to payment as measured by the underlying relationship.

Owen v. Barclays Bank Int, Howe Richardson v. Polimex, Intraco v. Notis Shipping Corp. and *Boliventer Oil v. Chase Manhattan Bank*, that English courts employ a very restricted notion of fraud, which is perhaps even more narrow than that in other jurisdictions.[38] From these and several subsequent cases it would almost appear that English courts are inclined to treat the fraud exception as a principle of a rather theoretical nature which ought not to be put in practice. The reason is that English courts are extremely reluctant to interfere with the bank's 'absolute and unconditional' undertaking and to allow an exception to the principle of independence if this would affect the position of the bank, for example in the case of an application by the account party for

---

[38] Kerr J., in *Harbottle v. Nat. Westminster Bank*, [1977] 2 All ER 862, 870: 'It is only in exceptional cases that the courts will interfere with the machinery of irrevocable obligations assumed by banks. They are the life-blood of international commerce ... Except possibly in clear cases of fraud of which the banks have notice, the courts will leave the merchants to settle their disputes under the contracts by litigation or arbitration as available to them or stipulated in the contracts ... The machinery and commitments of banks are on a different level. They must be allowed to be honoured, free from interference by courts. Otherwise, trust in international commerce could be irreparably damaged.' These statements have been cited with approval in *Edward Owen v. Barclays Bank Int.*, [1978] 1 All ER 976, which is perhaps the most striking case. Denning M.R. and Browne L.J. accepted that the account party had not been in default and that it was the beneficiary who had failed to comply with its contractual obligations. They, nevertheless, concluded that the account party was a long way from establishing fraud. Browne L.J. observed: 'But it is certainly not enough to allege fraud: it must be 'established' and in such circumstances I should say very clearly established'. Unusually, this decision has elicited some critical remarks from Schmitthoff, JBL 1977, p. 353. Roskill L.J., in *Howe Richardson v. Polimex*, [1978] 1 Lloyd's Rep. 161, 164: 'in my view it would be quite wrong for the Court to interfere with Polimex's apparent right under the guarantee to seek payment from the bank ...'. Donaldson L.J., in *Intraco v. Notis Shipping Corp.*, [1981] 2 Lloyd's Rep. 256, 257: 'Irrevocable letters of credit and bank guarantees ... have been said to be the life-blood of commerce. Thrombosis will occur if, unless fraud is involved, the Courts intervene and thereby disturb the mercantile practice of treating rights thereunder as being the equivalent of cash in hand.' Donaldson M.R., in *Boliventer Oil v. Chase Manhattan Bank*., [1984] 1 WLR 392: 'If, save in the most exceptional cases, he is to be allowed to derogate from the bank's personal and irrevocable undertaking ... by obtaining an injunction restraining the bank from honouring that undertaking, he will undermine what is the bank's greatest asset, ..., namely its reputation for financial and contractual probity. Furthermore, if this happens at all frequently, the value of all irrevocable letters of credit and performance bonds and guarantees will be undermined.' These statements in the above-mentioned cases have been cited with approval in subsequent cases, such as *Deutsche Ruckversicherung AG v. Walbrook Insurance*, [1994] 4 ALL ER 181, *Group Josi v. Walbrook Insurance*, [1996] 1 Lloyd's Rep. 345, *Turkiye Is Bankasi v. Bank of China*, [1996] 2 Lloyd's Rep. 611, CA [1998] 1 Lloyd's Rep. 250, *Czarnikow-Rionda Sugar Trading v. Standard Bank London*, [1999] 2 Lloyd's Rep. 187, *Kvaerner John Brown v. Midland Bank*, [1998] CLC 446 and *Balfour Beatty Civil Engineering v. Technical & General Guarantee*, [1999] 68 Con.L.R. 180.

a restraining order against the bank.³⁹ A second reason for this very strict approach regarding the notion of fraud is probably that independent bank guarantees are treated in the same way as documentary credits.⁴⁰ Whilst not departing from previous case law, a less rigid approach is illustrated in *United Trading Corp. v. Allied Arab Bank*,⁴¹ where Ackner L.J. took the opportunity to vent some misgivings about judicial statements made in previous cases: 'While accepting that letters of credit and performance bonds are part of the essential machinery of international commerce (and to delay payment under such documents strikes not only at the proper working of international commerce but also at the reputation and standing of the international banking community), the strength of this proposition can be over-emphasised.' And referring to the greater ease with which interlocutory relief could be obtained in America, Ackner L.J observed: 'There is no suggestion that this more liberal approach has resulted in the commercial dislocation which has, by implication at least, been suggested would result from rejecting the respondent's submissions as to the standard of proof required from plaintiffs. Moreover, we would find it an unsatisfactory position if, having established an important exception to what had previously been thought an absolute rule, the Courts in practice were to adopt so restrictive an approach to the evidence required as to prevent themselves from intervening. Were this to be the case, impressive and high-sounding phrases such as 'fraud unravels all' would become meaningless'.

Despite the numerous expressions regarding fraud in case law, the question as to what precise kind of fact situation, if proven, amounts to fraud has largely remained unexplored and the substantive notion of fraud, therefore, remains rather vague. In *State Trading Corp. of India v. ED & F Man (Sugar)* Lord Denning MR stated: 'The only term which is to be imported is that the buyer when giving notice of default, must honestly believe that there has been a default on the part of the seller. Honest belief is enough. If there is no honest belief, it may be evidence of fraud'.⁴² The notion of fraud as meaning 'dishonesty' can also be found in *Balfour Beatty Civil Engineering v. Technical & General Insurance*⁴³ and *Kvaerner John Brown v. Midland Bank*⁴⁴. In *Deutsche Ruckversicherung AG v. Walbrook Insurance* Phillips J. remarked that there is no fraud if the beneficiary 'has a bona fide claim to payment under the underlying contract' and that beneficiaries 'will be acting fraudulently in that they will be claiming payment to which they know they have no entitlement'.⁴⁵ There are, however, no indications that

---

39 See Chapter 16.3, No. 16-4.
40 See for this aspect Chapter 14.5.18, No. 54.
41 [1985] 2 Lloyd's Rep. 554.
42 [1981] Com LR 235.
43 [1999] 68 Con. LR 180.
44 [1998] CLC 446.
45 [1994] 4 ALL ER 181, at 196, 197. See also *GKN Contractors v. Lloyds Bank*, [1985] 30 BLR 48, at 63.

there must be actual proof of 'dishonest' or '*male fide*' intentions on the part of the beneficiary or evidence of the beneficiary's actual knowledge that he has no entitlement to payment.[46] The existence of such knowledge, dishonesty or *male fide* conduct on the part of the beneficiary is simply derived from the established facts, as is clearly demonstrated in *Themehelp Ltd. V. West and Others*[47] and *Kvaerner John Brown v. Midland Bank*,[48] which are among the rare examples in English case law where the fraud exception was actually applied. While, as mentioned, the substantive notion of fraud has only been described in general formulas which lack precision, as is the case in other jurisdictions, it is clear that whatever fraud may mean, it is to be determined by reference to the underlying transaction.

As regards the standard of proof of fraud, the general formulas are the same as those in other jurisdictions: the fraud must be 'very clearly established' or the fraud must be 'clear and obvious' and it must be immediately available without the need for lengthy and in-depth investigation into the underlying transaction.[49] Elaborating on these well established, but general formulas Ackner L.J. went on to provide more specific guidance as to the standard of evidence in *United Trading Corp. v. Allied Arab Bank*: 'The evidence of fraud must be clear, both as to the fact of fraud and as to the banks's knowledge. The mere assertion or allegation of fraud would not be sufficient. We would expect the Court to require strong corroborative evidence of the allegation, usually in the form of contemporary documents, particularly those emanating from the buyer. In general, for the evidence of fraud to be clear, we would also expect the buyer to have been given an opportunity to answer the allegation and to have failed to provide any, or adequate answer in circumstances where one could properly be expected. If the Court considers that on the material before it the only realistic inference to draw is that of fraud, then the seller would have made out a sufficient case of fraud'.[50] The standard

---

[46] The references to 'dishonesty', '*male fide*' intentions, etc., are no doubt derived form the general notion of fraud.

[47] [1996]QB 84.

[48] [1998] CLC 446. The reference to the beneficiary's 'knowledge' that he has no entitlement to payment is probably inspired by *United City Merchants v. Royal Bank of Canada*, [1982] 2 All ER 720. This case involved a letter of credit whereby a bill of lading was presented which contained false statements made by a broker. As the sellers and the bank to whom their interests were assigned, had not been privy to these misrepesentations and had no knowledge thereof, the House of Lords held that there was no fraud. This scenario is not likely to occur in guarantees as they rarely prescribe the presentation of third-party documents.

[49] See *especially Harbottle v. Nat. Westminster Bank*, [1977] 2 All E.R. 862, *Edward Owen v. Barclays Bank*, [1978] 1 All ER 976 and *Boliventer Oil v. Chase Manhattan Bank*, [1984] 1 WLR 392.

[50] [1985] 2 Lloyd's Rep. at 561. In the case at hand, Ackner L.J. found that the account party had failed to meet the test, 'although the plaintiffs have provided, *on the available material*

The Concept of Fraud

laid down in this last sentence, has become the generally accepted formula for the evidence which is required in order to establish fraud.[51]

In contrast with other countries, English case law has yielded only three examples where the court accepted that a sufficient case of fraud had been made out: *Elian and Rabbath v. Matsas and Matsas*,[52] *Themehelp Ltd v. West and Others*,[53] and *Kvaerner John Brown v. Midland Bank*.[54] Interestingly, in the last two mentioned cases both the nature of the fraud and the evidence thereof was rather doubtful.[55]

14.3.7 United States of America

14-14/16 Ever since the landmark case of *Sztejn v. J. Henry Schroder Banking Corp.*[56] fraud has been recognised as an exception to the rule that the bank must pay if the conditions of payment of the letter of credit or standby letter of credit have been complied with. It is also a ground for injunctive relief in the form of a restraining order.[57] In the course of the development of the notion of fraud there has been some talk in case

---

[italics in the original], a seriously arguable case that there is good reason to suspect, certainly in regard to some of these contracts, that the demands on the performance bonds have not been honestly made.'

51 See, e.g., *Turkiye Is Bankasi v. Bank of China*, [1996] 2 Lloyd's Rep. 611, CA [1998] 1 Lloyd's Rep. 250, *Group Josi Re v. Walbrook Insurance*, [1996] 1 Lloyd's Rep. 345, *Kvaerner John Brown v. Midland Bank*, [1998] CLC 446, *Csarnikow-Rionda v. Standard Bank of London*, [1999] 2 Lloyd's Rep. 187, *Balfour Beatty Civil Engineering v. Technical & General Guarantee*, [1998] 68 Con. LR 180, *Solo Industries v. Canara Bank*, [2001] 2 Lloyd's Rep. 578.

52 [1966] 2 Lloyd's Rep. 495. The injunction had been granted on the grounds that the beneficiary/shipowner had refused to release the goods, which he had promised to do in consideration of the account party/shipper putting up the guarantee.

53 [1996] QB 84.

54 [1998]CLC 446.

55 The decisions have been criticised in *Csarnikow-Rionda v. Standard Bank of London*, [1999] 2 Lloyd's Rep. 187, 190. See also Chapter 14.5.6, No. 14-36, Chapter 14.5.17, No. 14-53, and Chapter 16. 2, No. 16-2.

56 177 Misc. 719 (N.Y. Sup. Ct. 1941).

57 See for an extensive overview Dolan, § 7.04, Wunnicke/Wunnicke/Turner, § 8.04, and The Task Force on the Study of U.C.C. Article 5, An Examination of U.C.C. Article 5 (Letters of Credit), the Business Lawyer, Vol. 45, June 1990, pp. 1527, 1610-1625. In dealing with the concept of fraud, American courts, like English courts, do not distinguish between commercial (documentary) letters of credit and standby letters of credit (= independent guarantees). In fact, standby letters of credit are often referred to as just 'letters of credit'. Unless indicated otherwise, the decisions involve standby letters of credit.

law and legal writing about a 'narrow' or 'stringent' view on the one hand and a 'less stringent' or 'more flexible/broad' view of fraud on the other hand. The truth probably is that there is and has been been only one view, the 'narrow' or 'stringent' view, but that some courts, and especially lower courts and some commentators have occasionally applied the various tests in a more relaxed and lenient fashion.[58] That approach has been rightly criticised for insufficiently taking account of the agreed allocation of risks.[59]

Article 5 of the Uniform Commercial Code acknowledges that fraud may constitute grounds for refusing payment and the granting of restraining orders. The text was revised in 1995.[60] In order to avoid certain ambiguities which existed under the previous 1962 text, the new fraud provision, Section 5-109, clearly recognises that fraud may relate to the underlying transaction. The official Comment 1 explains that when there is an allegation of fraud, one must examine the underlying transaction 'for only by examining the transaction can one determine whether a document is fraudulent or the beneficiary has committed fraud and, if so, whether the fraud is material'. There was, however, general agreement in the drafting committees that in too many cases courts had granted restraining orders on insufficient grounds. The requirements for injunctive relief have, therefore, been tightened both in respect of the notion of fraud and in respect of the evidence thereof. First, the fraud must be 'material'. Commercial

---

[58] For example, in the early development a more flexible approach was advocated by Editorial Note, Minn. Law Review 1979, pp. 487, 491-516, Editorial Note, H.L.R. 1980, pp. 992-1015, Getz, Harvard Int. L.R. 1980, pp. 189-247, Symons, Tulane L.R. 1980, pp. 338-381, Weisz and Blackman, Univ. Illinois L.R. 1982, pp. 355, 360-384 and Verner, Memphis State University L.R. 1985, pp. 153-187. Their criteria are, however, so nebulous that it is not certain whether two different schools of thought have ever in fact existed.

[59] See, for example, Harfield, Banking L.J. 1978, pp. 596-615 (noted for his fear that 'the sacred cow of equity will trample the tender vines of letter of credit law'), Reed, Columbia Jo. Transn. Law. 1981, pp. 301-332, Stern, University Chicago L.R. 1985, p. 153-187, and in particular the treatises of Dolan, § 7.04 and Wunnicke/Wunnicke/Turner § 8.04.

[60] 'Uniform Commercial Code Revised Article 5. Letters of Credit', 1995 official text with comments, published by the American Law Institute and National Conference of Commissioners on Uniform State Laws. Section 5-109(b): 'If an applicant claims that a required document is forged or materially fraudulent or that honour of the presentation would facilitate a material fraud by the beneficiary on the issuer or applicant, a court of competent jurisdiction may temporarily or permanently enjoin the issuer from honouring a presentation or grant similar relief against the issuer or other persons only if the court finds that: (1) ...; (2) ...; (3) all of the conditions to entitle one to the relief under the law of this State have been met; and (4) on the basis of the information submitted to the court, the applicant is more likely than not to succeed under its claim of forgery or material fraud and ...'. Each Section is accompanied by an explanatory comment. See also the extensive report of The Task Force on the Study of UCC Article 5, An Examination of UCC Article 5 (Letters of Credit), published in The Business Lawyer, Vol. 45, June 1990, p. 1521-1643.

disputes in relation to the underlying transaction and even (certain) breaches of contract by the beneficiary do not amount to fraud. As the official Comment 1 puts it, material fraud only occurs when the beneficiary has no 'colourable' right to expect honour and where there is no basis in fact to support such a right to honour. Secondly, there must be a strong likelihood of success at the trial with the burden of proof remaining on the account party. In this respect, the evidence of fraud should be clear ('competent') and the examination of the underlying transaction should not amount to a wholesale inquiry, since that would defeat the agreed allocation of risks which is implicit in (first demand) standbys.

This stringent notion of fraud was already prevalent prior to the 1995 revision of Section 5-109 UCC. In *American Bell Int. v. Islamic Republic of Iran* the court observed: a demand for payment 'may, nevertheless, be considered fraudulent if made with the goal of *mulcting* [italics added] the party who caused the Letter of Credit to be issued ... Even if we accept the proposition that the evidence does show repudiation, the plaintiff is still far from demonstrating the kind of evil intent necessary to support a claim of fraud. Surely, the plaintiff cannot contend that every party who breaches or repudiates his contract is for that reason culpable of fraud ... The evidence is ambivalent as to whether the purported repudiation results from non-fraudulent economic calculation or from fraudulent intent to mulct Bell.'[61] Courts in some other decisions have opined that there must be '*egregious*' conduct on the part of the beneficiary[62] or 'active' and/or 'intentional' fraud.[63] The stringency of this test has, however, been tempered by the doctrine of constructive knowledge or constructive fraud. If it is shown that the beneficiary's claim has no conceivable basis, having regard to the underlying contract, and he, nevertheless, makes a demand for payment, a fraudulent intent will be imputed to him. A similar technique is applied in relation to 'egregious' conduct, which is taken to mean outrageous conduct of the beneficiary which shocks the conscience of the court. In any event, fraudulent intent does not play a part under the 1995 revised Section 5-109 UCC.

---

[61] 474 F. Supp. 420 (S.D.N.Y. 1979).

[62] See, for example, *First Arlington Nat. Bank v. Stathis*, 413 NE 2d. 1288 (1980) (documentary credit), *Offshore Trading Co. v. Citizens Nat. Bank of Fort Scott*, 650 F. Supp. 1487 (D. Kan. 1987), *United States v. Mercantile Nat. Bank of Dallas*, 795 F. 2d. 492 (5th. Cir. 1986), *Airline Reporting Corp. v. First National Bank of Holly Hill*, 832 F.2d 823 (4th Cir.1987).

[63] See, for example, *Wyle v. Bank Melli*, 577 F. Supp. 1148 (N.D. Cal. 1983) (injunction granted), *Rockwell Int. Systems v. Citibank*, 719 F. 2d. 583 (2d. Cir. 1983) (injunction granted), *Chiat/Day Inc. Advertising v. Kaliman*, 483 NYS 2d. 235 (1984), *NMC Enterprises Inc. v. Columbia Broadcasting Systems*, 14 UCC Rep. Serv. 1427 (N.Y. Sup. Ct. 1974) (injunction granted) (documentary credit), *KMW International v. Chase Manhattan Bank*, 606 F 2d. 10 (2d. Cir. 1979), *Shaffer v. Brooklyn Park Garden Apartments*, 250 NW 172 (Minn. 1977) (injunction granted).

A second illustrative case is *Intraworld Industries v. Girard Trust Bank*: 'In the light of the basic rule of independence ... the circumstances which will justify an injunction against honour must be narrowly limited to situations of fraud in which the wrongdoing of the beneficiary has *so vitiated the entire transaction that the legitimate purposes of the independence of the issuer's obligation would no longer be served*' [italics added], and 'An injunction would be proper only if the beneficiary had no bona fide claim to payment' or 'where the beneficiary's claim has no colourable or plausible basis under the underlying contract'.[64]

The current approach both in respect of a narrow definition of the notion of fraud and in respect of the evidence thereof is perhaps described most accurately in the more recent case of *Ground Air Transfer v. Westate's Airlines*: 'We have said throughout that courts may not 'normally' issue an injunction because of an important exception to the general 'no injunction' rule. The exception, as we also explained in *Itek*, ..., concerns fraud so serious as to make it obviously pointless and unjust to permit the beneficiary to obtain the money. Where the circumstances 'plainly' show that the underlying contract forbids the beneficiary to call a letter of credit, *Itek*, ...; where they show that the contract deprives the beneficiary of even a 'colourable' right to do so, *id.*; where the contract and circumstances reveal that the beneficiary's demand for payment has 'absolutely no basis in fact', *id.*; see *Dynamics Corp. of America*, ...; where the beneficiary's conduct has 'so vitiated the entire transaction that the legitimate purposes of the independence of the issuer's obligation would no longer be served', *Itek* (quoting *Roman Ceramics Corps* and *Intraworld*), *then* a court may enjoin payment'.[65] This exposition of the notion of fraud has been cited with approval in Comment 1 to the 1995 revised UCC Section 5-109.[66]

---

[64] 461 Pa. 343 (1975).

[65] 899 F.2d 1269, 1272 (1st Cir. 1990).

[66] See further *Philipp Brothers Inc. v. Oil Country Specialists Ltd.*, 9 UCC Rep. Serv. 2d. 201(Tex. 1989) ('Fraud claims should not become surrogates for breach of contract claims'), *Recon Opticals Inc. v. Government of Israel*, 816 F. 2d. 854 (2d. Cir. 1987), *SRS Prods. Co. v. LG Eng'g. Co.*, 994 SW2d 380 (Tex. Ct. Ap. 1999) ('To allow an [account party] to obtain an injunction based on a mere contractual dispute between the commercial parties would destroy the commercial viability of letters of credit and, in this case, would undermine the rationale for utilizing a letter of credit – to shift leverage back to the purchaser in demanding performance by the seller of the warranty obligations.'), *New Orleans Brass v. Whitney National Bank*, 2002 WL 1018964 (La. App. 4th Cir. May 15, 2002) ('[There is a] need to interpret the 'fraud' provision narrowly. The very object of a letter of credit is to provide a near foolproof method of placing money in its beneficiary's hands when he complies with the terms contained in the letter itself ... Material fraud by the beneficiary occurs when the beneficiary has no colourable right to expect honour and where there is no basis in fact to support such a right to honour.').

The Concept of Fraud

The perception and approach to the notion of fraud have also significantly been influenced by the general criteria for preliminary injunctions, namely 'irreparable harm' to the account party and 'the balance of convenience'.[67]

14.3.8. Summary of the comparative overview, UNCITRAL Convention

14-17 All jurisdictions acknowledge the principle that fraud by the beneficiary constitutes a defence against payment, despite formal compliance with the terms and conditions of the guarantee, and that it may be a basis for injunctive relief for the account party. The major issue is to define what kind of facts and what kind of conduct in which circumstances, render a demand for payment fraudulent such as to justify judicial intervention.

As far as the European Continent and England are concerned, clarity and unanimity exist in at least one respect. The evidence of fraud must be clear, 'liquid' or beyond reasonable doubt and must be produced immediately, without in-depth and thorough investigation into the underlying relationship in protracted court hearings. These aspects have been emphasised time and again in case law as well as in legal writing. It is also because of the stringent requirements with respect to the evidence of fraud that most applications for interlocutory injunctions have foundered. This fact probably explains why courts have had little occasion to elaborate on and clarify the substantive aspects of the notion of fraud, apart from enunciating most elusive and magic formulas such as fraud, abuse or bad faith. Case law and legal writing in the Netherlands, Germany and Belgium have occasionally suggested formulas which go beyond these non-committal phrases. These alternatives are, however, hardly more precise. It is, nonetheless, clear that Continental and English law share four common features. First, all jurisdictions agree that, whatever the notion of fraud might entail, it can be determined by reference to the underlying relationship. Secondly, evidence of actual, as opposed to constructive fraudulent intent on the part of the beneficiary to inflict harm is not required. This explains why the terms 'fraud' and 'abuse' are used interchangeably and why there is no real need to distinguish clearly between them. Thirdly, no distinction is made between 'simple' demand guarantees and demand guarantees which require the submission of a statement from the beneficiary concerning the account party's default. Lastly, no distinction is made between domestic and crossborder cases.

The general formulas for the standard of proof and the substantive aspects of fraud as employed in the various countries display, as stated, a striking similarity. However, if one is to make a reliable comparison, one ought to examine the actual application of those formulas. Making a comparison on this basis is somewhat precarious, since the denial or granting of injunctions does not only depend on the perceptions of fraud on the part of the beneficiary, but also on other criteria, especially in the case of stop-

---

[67] See further Chapter 16.3, No. 16-8.

payment orders against the bank in indirect guarantees.[68] Nonetheless, on the basis of a close reading of all relevant case law, it is possible to make some comparative observations on the actual application of the general formulas regarding fraud.

It appears that English courts have taken the most stringent view as regards the notion of fraud and the evidence thereof, at least in the context of applications for injunctive relief against the bank(s).[69] This stems from the extreme reluctance of English courts to interfere with what is perceived as the absolute and independent nature of the bank's obligations.[70] As observed by Ackner L.J. with some misgivings,[71] English courts seem predetermined to conclude that fraud has not been established.

Case law in the Netherlands[72], Germany[73] and Belgium[74] has been quite consistent throughout the period from approximately 1978 until the present. As regards the stand-

---

[68] See Chapters 15.2 and 16.4.

[69] See Chapter 16.3, No. 16-4.

[70] The only cases in which an injunction was granted are *Elian and Rabbath v. Matsas and Matsas*, [1966] 2 Lloyd's Rep. 495 (against the beneficiary and bank), *Themehelp Ltd v. West and Others*, [1996] QB 84 (against the beneficiary), *Kvaerner John Brown v. Midland Bank*, [1998] CLC 446 (against bank and beneficiary).

[71] In *United Trading v. Allied Arab Bank,* [1985] 2 Lloyd's Rep. 554, see Chapter 14.3.6, No. 14-13.

[72] Stop-payment orders have been granted or conservatory attachment orders remained in force on the grounds of established fraud in *Rb Amsterdam, 18 December 1980*, S&S 1981, 135 (indirect guarantee), *Rb Zwolle, 26 November 1982*, KG 1982, 220, *Rb Amsterdam, 5 September 1991*, KG 1991, 335, *CA 's-Hertogenbosch, 1 December 1993*, NJ 1994, 740, *Rb The Hague, 9 April 1997*, KGK 1997, 1431, *Rb Amsterdam, 5 June 1997* KG 1997, 203, affirmed by *CA Amsterdam, 3 September 1998*, JOR 1999, 128, *Rb Utrecht, 22 January 1998/ CA Amsterdam, 25 March 1999*, JOR 2000, 40, *Rb Utrecht, 7 July 2000*, S & S 2001, 3.

[73] Stop-payment orders have been granted or claims for payment have been dismissed on the grounds of established fraud in *BGH, 12 March 1984 (ll ZR 10/83)*, RIW 1985, p. 78 (principal contract held void), *BGH 12 March (ll ZR 198/82)*, NJW 1984, p. 2030, *BGH, 28 April 1988*, RIW 1988, p. 558 (suretyship plus cash deposit which the beneficiary attempted to seize), *LG Düsseldorf, 9 August 1984*, RIW 1985, p. 77 (indirect guarantee), *LG Dortmund, 9 July 1980*, WM 1981, p. 280 (indirect guarantee), *LG Frankfurt a. M., 11 December 1979*, NJW 1981, p. 56 (indirect guarantee), *OLG Oldenburg, 15 February 2000*, WM 2001, p. 732 (direct guarantee).

[74] Stop-payment orders have been granted, conservatory attachment orders remained in force or claims for payment have been rejected on the grounds of established fraud in *Trib. com. Brussels, 30 October 1984*, RDC 1985, p. 572, *Trib. com. Brussels, 23 March 1982*, not reported, but mentioned by Poullet, JCB 1982, p. 647, *Trib. com. Brussels, 25 June 1985*, TBH 1987, p. 803, *Trib. com. Brussels, 15 January 1980*, JCB 1980, p. 147, *Trib. com. Brussels, 6 April 1982*, Rev. Banque 1982, p. 683 (indirect guarantee), *Trib. com. Ghent, 27 December 1983*, TBH 1986, p. 298, *Trib. com. Brussels, 21 October 1986*, RDC 1987, p.

ard of proof, the criteria have been stringent, but they are not applied in such a way that the evidence is bound to be rejected as inadequate.[75] Courts in these jurisdictions do consider the evidence adduced by the account party carefully and without predisposition. As far as the substantive aspects of fraud are concerned, and ignoring the general and abstract formulas, certain patterns have evolved from which one can conclude what sets of facts, if proven forthwith, are likely to result in a finding of fraud.[76]

As far as French law is concerned, the number of cases in which injunctions or alternative measures, such as conservatory attachment and sequestration orders, have been granted in the period until, say, 1990 appears significantly higher than that in the Netherlands, Germany and Belgium, even taking into account that the volume of reported case law far exceeds that of these three other countries. Lower courts especially during that period often dealt somewhat loosely with the evidence of fraud and also exhibited some erratic patterns of reasoning. At present, however, French courts and, especially, appelate courts set equally stringent criteria in respect of evidence and have adopted a notion of fraud which is no broader than in the three other jurisdictions.[77]

---

706 (indirect guarantee, applications with respect to three principal contracts granted, with respect to a fourth contract denied), *Trib. com. Brussels, 26 May 1988*, JT 1988, p. 460 (indirect guarantee), *Trib. com. Brussels, 15 April 1991*, D. 1992 Somm. p. 242, *Trib. com. Brussels, 3 September* 1993, RDC 1994, p. 1126, Trib. *com. Hasselt, 2 October 1998*, TBH 1999, p. 723 (restraining order limited to the amount which had already been paid to the beneficiary).

[75] The fact that the number of Dutch, German and Belgian cases in which the court was satisfied with the evidence of fraud, far exceeds that of English cases, is no cause for any supposition that the courts in these jurisdictions display a relaxed attitude as regards the evidence of fraud. It can be explained by the fact that there is far more reported case law in these countries than in England. In any event, in the vast majority of reported cases, the allegations of fraud have been rejected on the grounds of insufficient evidence.

[76] See Chapter 14.5.

[77] Stop-payment, conservatory attachment or sequestration orders have been granted and remained in force and claims for payment have been dismissed on the grounds of established fraud in, for example, *Cass., 12 January* 1993, D. 1995 J. p. 24 (direct guarantee, beneficiary's claim for payment dismissed), *Bordeaux, 7 March 1991*, D. 1992 Somm. p. 235 (direct guarantee, beneficiary's claim for payment dismissed), *Trib. com. Nanterre, 14 March 1991*, D. 1992 Somm. p. 241 (direct guarantee), *Paris, 27 June 1988*, D. 1989 Somm. p. 151 (direct guarantee, bank correctly refused payment), *Paris, 17 June 1987*, D. 1988 Somm. p. 245 (direct guarantee), *Trib. com. Paris, 1 August 1984*, D. 1986 I.R. p. 159 (indirect guarantee), *Cass., 11 December 1985*, D. 1986 J. p. 213 (indirect guarantee), *Trib. com. Melun, 29 April 1985*, D. 1986 I.R. p. 159 (indirect guarantee), *Cass., 10 June 1986*, D. 1987 J. p. 17 (indirect guarantee), *Paris, 18 November 1986*, D. 1988 Somm. p. 247 (indirect guarantee), *Trib. com. Paris, 15 March 1985*, D. 1985 I.R. p. 224, *Trib. com. Paris, 7 September 1983*, D. 1987 Somm. p. 174 (indirect guarantee, in the main proceedings, *Trib. com. Paris, 6 January 1987*, D. 1987 Somm. p. 174, the instructing bank was ordered to pay the second,

As far as the United States are concerned, it would appear that the current perceptions of fraud as summarised in *Ground Air Transfer v. Westate's Airlines*[78] and in Sec. 5-109 UCC are, in essence, not materially different from those in Europe and that, like in Europe, fraud could be determined by reference to the underlying transaction. Some differences may, however, be discerned in respect of the actual application of the criteria and the emphasis on the general criteria of the law of equity for injunctive relief, namely the probable or likely success on the merits, the balance of convenience and, most importantly, the chance of irreparable harm. As far as the evidence of fraud is concerned, the patterns in case law are, or at least have sometimes been, somewhat erratic, with the lower courts tending to be satisfied in this respect more readily and the appelate courts taking a more stringent view. By comparison, on account of the rules of procedure for injunctive relief, American courts appear allow a more in-depth and protracted investigation into the underlying transaction, for example by further hearings with the attendant delays, whereas in Europe the party alleging fraud must produce the evidence immediately, without further hearings. Moreover, the criteria 'irreparable harm' and 'the balance of convenience' do not play a part in Continental proceedings for preliminary injunctions.

Art. 19 UNCITRAL Convention also recognises the exception to the absolute and independent nature of guarantees. It deliberately avoids the terms 'bad faith', 'abuse' and 'fraud' because they have confusing and inconsistent meanings in various legal systems and are often influenced by criminal law notions of malicious intent which are not suitable in relation to guarantees. Instead, art. 19 employs the general formula of a demand for payment which 'has no conceivable basis', while sec. 2 provides some specific examples thereof. Actual or constructive awareness on the part of the beneficiary that his demand for payment has no conceivable basis, plays no part in this respect. Art. 19 also shows that the impropriety of the demand may relate, or could be determined by reference, to the underlying transaction. As far as the degree of proof is

---

issuing bank), *Trib. gr. inst. Paris, 13 May 1980*, D. 1980 J. p. 488 (attachment), *Trib. com. Paris, 2 February 1983*, D. 1985 I.R. p. 243 (attachment), *Trib. com. Paris, 29 October 1982*, D. 1983 I.R. p. 301 (sequestration), *Paris, 29 November 1982*, D. 1983 I.R. p. 302 (sequestration), *Trib. com. Paris, 12 February 1982*, D. 1982 I.R. p. 504 (indirect guarantee). In a number of other cases it is not clear on the basis of what principle stop-payment orders were granted. There are several other first instance decisions granting restraining orders, which were discharged in appeal proceedings. For decisions where fraud was established in 'after-payment' cases and where the bank's claim for reimbursement was rejected, see: *Lyon, 17 May 1991*, D. 1993 Somm. p. 99 (indirect guarantee, fraud of both the beneficiary and the foreign issuing bank was established and this should have been immediately apparent to the paying instructing bank), *Trib. com. Lyon, 3 July 1991*, D. 1993 Somm. p. 100, *Paris, 15 November 1996*, Banque et Droit 1997, No. 53, p. 51.

[78] 899 F.2d 1269, 1273 (1st Cir. 1990), see No. 14-14/16.

concerned, fraud must be 'manifest and clear' and ' immediately available'.[79] Art. 20 of the UNCITRAL Convention deals with restraining orders.[80]

14.4 FRAUD AND EVIDENCE OF FRAUD. SOME REFLECTIONS

Fraud in relation to the nature and purpose of first demand guarantees

14-18 As allegations of fraud are nearly always made in respect of first demand guarantees, it is justified to confine our investigation to this type of guarantee. When trying to determine what the notion of fraud in relation to demand guarantees entails, one should not expect to derive safe guidance from concepts such as 'fraud', 'abuse', 'bad faith' or 'arbitrariness'.[81] They are inherently vague and general and have been developed along national patterns which may not be suitable for demand guarantees, being a product of international trade. More importantly, these concepts have generally been applied and developed in contexts which are quite different from demand guarantees. Instead, safer guidance could be obtained by having regard to the specific nature and purpose of demand guarantees.[82]

Such guarantees should be viewed as an allocation of risks between the parties to the underlying transaction.[83] The notion of fraud must, therefore, be assessed against this background and never applied in such a way that it virtually undoes this agreed allocation.[84] A fundamental feature is that it provides financial compensation to the beneficiary independent of the account party's defences from the underlying transaction. While it is established law that an exception to this principle is made in the event of fraud, it should indeed be limited to exceptional case. Accordingly, not every defence from the underlying transaction amounts to fraud, but only defences which are material and relate to the essence of the secured contract or obligation. Another main feature concerns the aspect of evidence. When agreeing to the furnishing of a first

---

[79] See arts. 19 and 20.

[80] See Chapter 16.2 and Chapter 16.3, No. 16-8a.

[81] Cf. the deliberate avoidance of these terms by the drafters of the UNCITRAL Convention, see No. 14-17 last paragraph.

[82] Cf. Stoufflet, Dickinson Law Review, 2001, pp. 21-28, who affirms that the notion of 'fraud' or 'abuse' should not be confused with the meaning given to these concepts in the law general. See also *Emory-Waterhouse Co. v. Rhode Island Hosp. Trust Nat'l Bank*, 757 F.2d 399 (1st. Cir. 1985) which held that the general (common law) concept of fraud is not the same as fraud for the purpose of injunctive relief in relation to standby letters of credit under Article 5 UCC.

[83] See Chapter 6 and Chapter 2.1 and 2.2.

[84] Cf. Dolan, § 7.04 j. § 3.07.

demand guarantee, the account party accepts that the beneficiary is entitled to financial compensation without having to prove the account party's default or his substantive right to compensation. A third characteristic of their allocation of risks is that the beneficiary is entitled to immediate payment once the terms and conditions of the guarantee have been fulfilled (liquidity function). These two features have been lucidly encapsulated in the time-honoured phrase 'pay first, argue later', meaning that payment to the beneficiary for the account of the account party should be made first and that the latter could try to recover the moneys in subsequent proceedings, if he proves that the beneficiary had no right to payment as measured by the underlying relationship.

However, what is the situation if the account party is able to produce clear evidence thereof immediately upon the demand for payment? One author observed that, while the beneficiary need not prove his substantive rights, he cannot claim payment if the account party establishes beyond doubt that the beneficiary has no right to payment.[85] A famous American judge observed that 'If payment might have been recovered the moment after it was made, the seller cannot coerce payment if the truth is earlier revealed.'[86] Another author pointed out that 'paying first' [and, hence, leaving the account party to retrieve the moneys in subsequent proceedings] would make no sense if the outcome of 'later arguments' is already evident.[87] These statements reveal a most important element: whatever the notion of fraud may exactly entail, the evidence in this respect must be clear and it should be produced immediately without extensive investigation. This element has indeed played a preponderant part in fraud litigation before European courts.

Evidence of fraud

14-19 Courts and legal writing have consistently required that fraud must be established clearly and beyond doubt, although, at times, American lower court case law has occasionally been somewhat diffuse and inconsistent in this respect. Mere allegations, testimony or documentation from the account party are considered insufficient. He must, at least, produce documents from independent third parties which clearly corroborate the facts alleged by the account party, or documents, statements or acknowledgements from the beneficiary, or undisputed facts. Because of its precision, the formula advanced by Ackner L.J in *United Trading v. Allied Arab Banks* appears commendable: the account party has made his case if, based on the material before the court, the only realistic inference is that of fraud.[88]

---

[85] Stoufflet, JCP 1985 ll No. 20436, JCP 1986 ll No. 20593, and especially JDI 1987, p. 285.

[86] Cardozo J. in his dissenting opinion in *Maurice O'Meara Co. v. Nat. Park Bank*, 146 N.E. 636 (1925).

[87] Schoordijk, Beschouwingen over Drie-Partijen-Verhoudingen, pp. 201-203.

[88] [1985] 2 Lloyd's Rep. 554.

The Concept of Fraud 359

Most fraud cases are litigated in preliminary proceedings for injunctive relief in order to prevent fraud. Such proceedings do not permit a lengthy and thorough inquiry by the court or further hearings. This agrees with the requirement that the evidence of fraud should be produced immediately. Accordingly, if the account party is unable to present clear evidence of fraud at once, his application for stop-payment orders are dismissed.[89] American practice appears to be different in this respect since preliminary proceedings in fraud cases sometimes seem to allow for more extensive and even multiple hearings which may cause considerable delay. The requirement of immediately available clear evidence of fraud also applies in situations where the bank refuses payment on the grounds of fraud and where the beneficiary sues for payment in summary proceedings.[90]

What must be proven? Obviously, the account party must establish the facts which he alleges. In addition, he must demonstrate the legal consequences from these facts. In many cases this aspect will not present serious difficulties. For example, the consequence of perfect completion of the contract or fundamental breach of contract by the beneficiary is clearly that the beneficiary is not entitled to damages. It becomes more problematical if, for example, the account party argues that *force majeure* prevented the completion of the contract. The question then is whether the facts which rendered performance impossible qualify as *force majeure* such that the account party cannot be held accountable. These and similar questions might be resolved by having regard to the provisions of the underlying contract[91] or perhaps by reference to generally accepted principles of transnational commercial law. However, if these matters cannot

---

[89] See further Chapter 16.

[90] See further Chapter 14.6.

[91] See, for example, *Rb Amsterdam, 12 December 1980*, S&S 1981, 135 (in respect of *force majeure*), *Rb Amsterdam, 7 April 1988*, KG 1988, 181 (in respect of perfect completion) and in appeal *CA Amsterdam, 19 January 1989*, KG 1990, 74, *LG Frankfurt a.M., 11 December 1979*, NJW 1981, p. 56 (in respect of perfect completion), *LG Dortmund, 9 July 1980*, WM 1980, p. 280 (in respect of perfect completion), *OLG Köln, 7 August 1986*, WM 1988, p. 21 (in respect of perfect completion and the beneficiary's right to repudiate the contract), *Trib. com. Melun, 29 April 1985*, D. 1986 I.R. p. 159 (in respect of perfect completion), *Trib. com. Brussels, 21 October 1986*, RDC 1987, p. 706 (in respect of perfect completion), *Trib. com. Ghent, 27 December 1983*, TBH 1986, p. 298 (in respect of liability for costs of unloading), *Siporex Trade v. Banque Indosuez*, [1986] 2 Lloyd's L.R. 146 (in respect of perfect issuance of documentary credit), *Harris Corp. v. National Iranian Radio and Television*, 691 F. 2d. 1344 (11th. Cir. 1982) (in respect of *force majeure*), *Touche Ross v. Manufacturers Hanover Trust*, 449 N.Y.S. 2d. 125 (NY App. Div. 1982) (in respect of *force majeure*), *Rockwell Int. Systems v. Citibank*, 719 F. 2d 583 (2d. Cir. 1983) (in respect of *force majeure*). See also *Cass., 10 June 1986*, D. 1987 J. p. 17, *LG Braunschweig, 22 May 1980*, RIW 1981, p. 789, *Geneva, 27 September 1984*, D. 1986 I.R. p. 163, *Geneva, 12 September 1985*, D. 1986 I.R. p. 165.

be readily resolved or, more generally, if complex and controversial legal issues are involved or if the legal position can only be determined by reference to foreign domestic law, it will be extremely difficult for the account party to establish his case forthwith within the constraints of preliminary proceedings.

The notion 'fraud'

14-20 Although the capability of general formulas to spawn ready and predictable solutions in concrete cases is doubtful,[92] they could serve some function, if only for the sake of convenience. Having regard to the first main feature of demand guarantees mentioned in No. 14-18 above, fraud could tentatively be described as the condition whereby the beneficiary's demand for payment has no conceivable basis under the underlying relationship. This formula finds support in numerous decisions, as well as in legal writing, at least when one examines how the notion of fraud has been applied in concrete cases. Moreover, it has the advantage of being more specific and more comprehensible than other formulas which are marked by abstruseness. As evidence of malicious intent on the part of the beneficiary is not required, there is no need to clearly distinguish between the notion of 'fraud' and the notion of 'abuse'. In this study fraud, therefore, comprises abuse.

Bearing in mind that the above-mentioned formula or any other formula constitutes no more than a guiding principle, the difficulty being the application thereof to concrete facts in concrete cases, one will not be surprised to find that in the end courts might be predominantly prompted by their experience, common sense and the smell of a case. As observed by *Cass., 10 June 1986*, and a number of subsequent French decisions, a finding of fraud could be derived from 'the whole of the circumstances of a case'.[93] An instructive example thereof can be found in *Trib. com. Brussels, 26 May 1988*, where the court's finding of fraud was evidently founded on a chain of most suspicious conduct.[94]

14.5 OVERVIEW OF POSSIBLE TYPES OF FRAUD

14.5.1 Introduction

14-21 In this chapter an attempt will be made to define the notion of fraud more clearly by examining a number of specific factual situations concerning the underlying rela-

---

[92] Cf. Cabrillac/Mouly, Nos. 412, 429.

[93] D. 1987 J. p. 17.

[94] JT 1988, p. 460 (indirect guarantee, restraining orders against the instructing and issuing bank and beneficiary granted).

tionship. The general formula that the beneficiary's demand for payment is fraudulent if it has no conceivable basis under the underlying transaction[95] will serve as a guideline for this survey. By reviewing specific situations and the responses of the courts a reasonable degree of predictability could be attained in respect of the question which circumstances, if proven, are likely or unlikely to result in a finding of fraud, see the conclusions in Chapter 14.5.18. However, fraud can take many forms and, as noted in the last paragraph of Chapter 14.4, No. 14-20, an inference of fraud can be drawn from the whole of the circumstances of a case. The series of factual situations examined in Chapter 14.5 is, therefore, not meant to be exhaustive. Allegations of fraud are usually made by the account party, but occasionally also by the bank. This makes no difference.

This chapter concerns the substantive aspects of fraud and deals neither with the element of evidence,[96] nor with the position of the bank, nor with the specific aspects of counter-guarantees and legal procedures to prevent payment on the grounds of fraud.[97]

14.5.2 Lack of authority

14-22 The account party might argue that the beneficiary has no right to payment because the secured contract was concluded by an officer who had no authority to bind the account party.

This line of argument will rarely, if ever, succeed. Apart from the evidence as to the facts, the contention involves complex legal issues which are not suitable for adjudication in preliminary proceedings, especially if the issue is to be decided in accordance with foreign law. But even in the unlikely situation that the account party were able to establish beyond doubt and forthwith that he is not bound, a strong argument could be made for the proposition that the beneficiary is nonetheless entitled to claim under the guarantee. It is submitted that guarantees also provide protection against risks such as lack of authority.[98] The explanation is that, especially in the case of crossborder transactions, it may be difficult or impracticable for the beneficiary/creditor to ascertain the officer's authority and that he therefore seeks to avoid the attendant risks by insisting on a guarantee. It could also be argued that the furnishing of a guarantee in favour of the creditor/beneficiary can be viewed as a ratification of the officer's authority or, alternatively, as an affirmation of his apparent authority on which the beneficiary may rely.

---

[95] See Chapter 14.4, No. 14-20.
[96] See Chapter 14 and the summaries in Chapter 14.3.8 and 14.4.
[97] See Chapters 15-17.
[98] Similar exceptions to the co-extensiveness rule are also recognised in respect of the accessory suretyship.

14.5.3 Mistake, misrepresentation, economic duress, undue influence

14-23 Defences such as mistake, misrepresentation, economic duress and undue influence, which would entitle the account party to avoid or rescind the secured contract, are unlikely to amount to fraud. Within the constraints of preliminary proceedings, it will be extremely difficult for the account party to prove these allegations and that, if established, these facts clearly justify avoidance of the contract. This is borne out by case law.[99] Moreover, the nature of such defences is not sufficiently material as to deprive the beneficiary's demand for payment under the guarantee from any conceivable basis.

14.5.4 Conditions precedent

General

14-24 Under the general law of contract, the account party/principal debtor is, in principle, not liable for non-performance of the contract and the beneficiary/creditor cannot claim damages if a condition which the secured contract designates as a condition precedent has not been fulfilled. The non-fulfilment of a condition precedent does not, however, necessarily render the beneficiary's demand for payment under the guarantee fraudulent. This is certainly not the case if the account party has been responsible for the non-fulfilment or if the risk thereof should be attributed to him. It should also be noted that the account party could protect himself against the risk of a call by inserting a matching condition precedent in the guarantee. Moreover, the condition precedent must be truly essential for the operation of the contract and relate to a material aspect of the contract.[100]

---

[99] All applications for injunctive relief on these grounds have been dismissed: *Group Josi v. Walbrook Insurance*, [1996] 1 Lloyd's Rep. 345, *Csarnikow-Rionda v. Standard Bank London*, [1999] 2 Lloyd's Rep. 187, *Deutsche Rückversicherung v. Walbrook Insurance*, [1994] 4 All ER 181. In this case Philips, J. at 197, observed that avoidance on the grounds of fraudulent misrepresentation and/or non-disclosure involved difficult questions of fact and law which could not be determined in interlocutory proceedings; *Rb Amsterdam, 20 December 1984*, KG 1985, 21, *Rb Haarlem, 21 November 1986*, KG 1987, 57, *Rb Arnhem, 20 October 1986*, KG 1986, 482, *DTH Construction v. Steel Authority of India*, IBL May 1986, p. 175, *Cromwell v. Commercial & Energy Bank*, 40 UCC Rep. Serv. 1814 (La. 1985), *Brown v. United States Nat. Bank*, 41 UCC Rep. Serv. 1765 (Neb. 1985). In *Rb Amsterdam, March 19 1981*, KG 1981, 30, the court also observed that the beneficiary's insistence on a first demand guarantee did not amount to economic duress.

[100] In *Paris, 17 January 1983*, D. 1983 I.R. p. 303, the bank and account party argued that the beneficiary had failed to designate the vessel for the shipment of the equipment which, according to them, was a condition precedent and which also constituted breach of contract. This argument found favour with the Paris Court of Appeal, but the decision was quashed by

Condition precedent and breach of contract by the beneficiary

14-25 The beneficiary's failure to procure a documentary credit in favour of the account party of the guarantee, if required under the secured contract, has especially given rise to defences founded on fundamental breach of contract by the beneficiary and/or non-fulfilment of a condition precedent. This particular defence is further examined in Chapter 14.5.6, No. 14-37.

14.5.5 Completion of the secured contract or obligation

General

14-26 Legal writing[101] and case law unanimously and unequivocally recognise that the beneficiary's demand for payment is fraudulent if completion by the account party of the secured contract or obligation is established. This is also confirmed in art. 19 (2)(c) UNCITRAL Convention. The appropriateness of this defence is self-evident and it does not raise any particular legal problem which could not be resolved in interlocutory proceedings.

The greatest obstacle for the account party is, of course, to adduce clear and convincing evidence of proper performance. Case law indicates that corroborating statements from the beneficiary in the form of correspondence or certificates, or certificates from independent surveyors, especially from those nominated by the beneficiary, or from the engineer in the case of construction contracts, must be presented to the court in order to justify a finding of established fraud. Undisputed or established facts also qualify as appropriate evidence. Other factors which bear on the matter of evidence concern the existence of genuine differences of opinion between account party and beneficiary, and the conduct of the beneficiary. In general, if the court is satisfied that the beneficiary's complaints are genuine or plausible or have at least some basis, it is not likely to arrive at a finding of established fraud.[102] On the other hand, the absence

---

Cass., 17 October 1984, D. 1985 J. p. 269 (Vasseur), JCP 1985 ll No. 20436 (Stoufflet). Vasseur and Stoufflet suggest that the alleged obligation and condition precedent were mere contrivances of the bank and account party. See also von Westphalen, p. 114.

[101] See, for example, von Westphalen, p. 197, 198, Pabbruwe, p. 37, Dohm, No. 238, Kleiner, No. 21.48, Prüm, Nos. 464-466, Vasseur, No. 121. German legal writing generally refers to clear evidence concerning the absence of the '*materieller Garantiefall*', of which completion of the secured contract or obligation is the most typical manifestation.

[102] A call during consultation between account party and beneficiary in an attempt to resolve differences of opinion or pending litigation is, in itself, not an indication of fraud, see, for example, *LG Köln, 11 December 1981*, WM 1982, p. 438, *Cass., 17 October 1984*, D. 1985 J. p. 269, *Trib. com. Paris, 25 June 1985*, D. 1986 I.R. p. 156, *Antwerp, 13 October 1982*, BRH 1982, p. 642. In *LG Düsseldorf, 9 August 1984*, RIW 1985, p. 77, a temporary stop-

of (serious) complaints on the part of the beneficiary prior to his call and/or evidently spurious or trivial complaints are not favourable to the beneficiary's case. The survey of case law in Nos. 14-27 and 14-28 provides an illustration of the kind of evidence which is considered adequate or inadequate.

Assessment of the weight and significance of statements from the beneficiary or third parties in terms of evidence of completion continues to prove a difficult task for the courts. In several cases the precise implications of the various certificates were not straightforward and possibly liable to divergent interpretations.[103] While it is quite true that the account party bears the burden of proving completion, it would only be perilous to proffer the general proposition that, in such circumstances, the decision should always go against the account party. The issue under review does not permit generalisations and each case has to be decided on the merits of all of the specific facts.

Completion of the secured contract or obligation established

14-27 In *LG Frankfurt a.M., 11 December 1979*, the finding of completion of the contract was based on correspondence between account party and beneficiary with a view to the stipulations in the secured contract.[104] The court also observed that the complaints from the beneficiary were made not until some considerable time after delivery, that they were vague and that they related to aspects for which the account party was not responsible. In *LG Dortmund, 9 July 1980*, the beneficiary had released a protocol of acceptance confirming proper performance.[105] This protocol also referred to some minor transport damage to the amount of DM 650 (approximately € 325). The account party offered to pay this amount, but the beneficiary never responded to this offer. At the end of the contractual warranty period, the beneficiary had proceeded to payment of the remaining 10 per cent of the purchase price. The beneficiary did not complain until four years after the release of the protocol and three years after the

---

payment order was issued in view of the fact that arbitrators were about to deliver judgment. Three weeks later, arbitrators gave judgment against the beneficiary. The court declined to issue a permanent injunction because the bank intimated that it did not intend to pay.

[103] See, for example, *Paris, 6 March 1991*, D 1992 Somm. p. 241, *Trib. com. Brussels, 21 October 1986*, RDC 1987, p. 706 (indirect guarantee; injunctions granted in respect of three contracts, denied in respect of a fourth contract), *United Trading v. Allied Arab Bank*, [1985] 2 Lloyd's L.R. 554 (indirect guarantee, injunctions denied), *Rb Amsterdam, 7 April 1988*, KG 1988, 181 (direct guarantee; injunction denied, decision reversed by *CA Amsterdam, 19 January 1989*, KG 1990, 74, see also No. 14-27).

[104] NJW 1981, p. 56 (indirect guarantee in favour of Iranian Government agency, stop-payment order against instructing bank granted).

[105] WM 1981, p. 280 (indirect guarantee in favour of Iranian Government agency, stop-payment order against instructing bank granted)

expiration of the warranty period. In *Trib. com. Brussels, 6 April 1982*, a stop-payment order against the instructing bank was granted, one of the grounds being completion of the contract which was attested by engineers nominated by the beneficiary.[106] The evidence of proper performance in *Trib. com. Ghent, 27 December 1983*, consisted of a number of certificates issued by several independent and reputable agencies.[107] In *Trib. com. Melun, 29 April 1985*, the finding of completion was based on a certificate issued in the port of destination by an agent of the beneficiary.[108] In *Cass., 10 June 1986*, completion of the project was proven by certificates from the beneficiary and engineer and by certificates providing for payment in view of completion.[109] It was also observed that the beneficiary's complaints were vague and formalistic, and not in the least specified or substantiated. In the case of *Geneva, 12 September 1985*, proper performance was confirmed by a legal expert appointed by a Syrian court in accordance with the provisions of the secured contract.[110] The court also noted that, if there was a short delivery, it remained within the margin permitted by the contract. In *Trib. com. Brussels, 21 October 1986*, the beneficiary had issued a protocol of provisional acceptance in respect of three of the four contracts.[111] Moreover, he had indicated that the three performance guarantees had 'lost their function' because of completion of the three contracts and that he would release those three guarantees. The court also mentioned that the period of validity as provided for in the guarantee had expired (one year plus thirty days after provisional acceptance). The application in respect of the fourth guarantee was dismissed. In *Rb Amsterdam, 7 April 1988*, the court took the view that the various certificates issued by the engineer did not sufficiently evidence final completion of the entire project.[112] Moreover, the engineer had announced that a 'punch list of snag items' was being prepared. From the report of the case, it also transpires that

---

[106] Rev. Banque 1982, p. 683 (indirect guarantee in favour of Iranian Government agency, stop-payment order against instructing bank granted). The other grounds included non-performance by the beneficiary of its obligations, *force majeure* (Iranian revolution) and the fact that the demand was politically motivated.

[107] TBH 1986, p. 298 (direct guarantee in favour of Iranian authorities, stop-payment order against bank granted). The court was also convinced that the beneficiary just wanted a discount, which the seller had explicitly refused to agree to, as well as reimbursement of charges for taking delivery from the vessel while the sale was made on C & F terms.

[108] D. 1986 I.R. p. 159 (indirect guarantee, stop-payment order against instructing bank granted).

[109] D. 1987 J. p. 17 (indirect guarantee in favour of Iranian Government agency, stop-payment orders against instructing and issuing bank granted), confirming *Paris, 20 June 1984*, D. 1985 I.R. p. 241.

[110] D. 1986 I.R. p. 165 (indirect guarantee, stop-payment order against instructing bank granted).

[111] RDC 1987, p. 706 (indirect guarantee, stop-payment order against instructing and issuing bank granted).

[112] KG 1988, 181 (direct guarantee).

there had been considerable delays and several complaints from the beneficiary. The Court of Appeal, however, ruled that the certificates met the requirements of the stipulations of the secured contract concerning the release of the guarantee.[113] *Trib. com. Brussels, 26 May 1988*, also ruled in favour of proper performance, although there was no specific evidence which clearly supported this conclusion. The court was, however, persuaded by a clear and persistent pattern of suspicious behaviour on the part of the beneficiary.[114] In the case of *Rb Amsterdam, 5 September 1991*, the beneficiary had accepted the goods and confirmed this to the bank, which was considered clear evidence of the fraudulent nature of the beneficiary's demand for payment.[115] In *CA 's-Hertogenbosch, 1 December 1993*, the evidence of proper performance consisted of a certificate of completion issued by an independent surveyor nominated in the guarantee and co-signed by the beneficiary and written confirmation from the beneficiary that the contract had been wholly performed.[116] *Rb Utrecht, 22 January 1998*, involved a guarantee securing the payment of invoices by the employer to the contractor. As all invoices had been paid and such payment had not been disputed by the contractor, the court could readily conclude that the contractor's demand for payment was fraudulent.[117] In *Rb Amsterdam, 5 June 1997*, the court was satisfied with the evidence of completion of the underlying contract on a number of counts and found that the de-

---

[113] *CA Amsterdam, 19 January 1989*, KG 1990, 74. See also Chapter 13.2.7, No. 13-23, for more details concerning the facts and some critical observations concerning the Court of Appeal's line of reasoning.

[114] JT 1988, p. 460 (indirect guarantee, restraining orders against instructing and issuing bank granted). In view of unfavourable experiences with previous transactions whereby the beneficiary/buyer had called the guarantee, the seller/account party insisted that the demand for payment under the second guarantee was to be made by registered mail, specifying the reasons for the call. Delivery and payment under a documentary credit was made, and the buyer did not complain. The buyer, then, repeatedly lodged 'extend or pay' demands to which the seller was forced to give in. At no time did the buyer specify the nature of his complaints although he was repeatedly asked and also obliged to do this under the terms of the guarantee. At some time the foreign issuing bank produced a merely formal statement of default which bore a date of six months before and which had not previously been forwarded. The court was also convinced that the buyer sought to call the guarantee with a view to the previous transaction.

[115] KG 1991, 335 (direct guarantee, stop-payment order against the bank granted; a second reason was the expiry of the period of validity).

[116] NJ 1994, 740 (direct guarantee, conservatory attachment under the bank remained in force).See also *Rb Utrecht, 6 July 2000*, S & S 2001, 3, and No. 14-45 for the facts of this case.

[117] JOR 2000, 40, affirmed by *CA Amsterdam, 25 March 1999*, JOR 2000, 40. See also *Trib. com. Brussels, 3 September 1993*, RDC 1994, p. 1126 (evidence of full payment of purchase price).

The Concept of Fraud

mand for payment had been inspired by improper motives.[118] A similar decision was given in *Rb The Hague, 9 April 1997*.[119] *OLG Oldenburg, 15 February 2000*, upheld the bank's decision not to pay on account of fraud as, following an arbitral decision, it was certain that the secured event had not materialised.[120]

There are also two cases, *Bordeaux, 7 March 1991*, and *Trib. com. Nanterre, 14 March 1991*, where the evidence of proper performance was rather weak and where the court, nonetheless, granted a restraining order or dismissed the beneficiary's claim for payment.[121]

---

[118] KG 1997, 203, affirmed by *CA Amsterdam, 3 September 1998*, JOR 1999, 128. The completion of the works had been approved by the designated engineer who had also released a completion certificate; all invoices by the account party had been approved by the engineer and the beneficiary, and the beneficiary had paid all invoices; the call on the guarantee was made ten years after the approval of the works and invoices; from the beneficiary's demand it appeared that the call was inspired by the fact that a certain governmental agency in the beneficiary's country had objected to certain invoices.

[119] KGK 1997, 1431. The guarantee was payable upon submission of a written certificate by a certain independent agency confirming that the account party had failed to perform the contract. The beneficiary had submitted the required confirmation, but the court was, nonetheless, satisfied with the evidence of the fraudulent nature of the call for the following reasons: (i) the certificate had been issued at a time the equipment had not yet been delivered and the account party had not yet been enabled to complete the contract and to carry out performance tests, (ii) another report from another independent agency confirmed that, after certain problems had been resolved, the equipment operated properly and in accordance with the specifications, (iii) the beneficiary used the equipment and (iv) the beneficiary did not dispute the foregoing.

[120] WM 2001, p. 732. The guarantee had been issued in favour of the buyer in connection with an acquisition of a company. Upon construction of the guarantee the court determined that the purpose of the guarantee was limited to providing security against possible claims by certain third parties against the company. The guarantee provided that it would lapse upon confirmation by the third parties that they did not have a claim against the company. The fact that this confirmation had been given after the demand for payment was considered irrelevant, as the arbitrators had rejected the claim before the demand for payment.

[121] *Bordeaux, 7 March 1991*, D. 1992 Somm. p. 235 (direct guarantee, beneficiary's claim for payment dismissed). Due to insolvency, the account party was unable to complete the project whereupon the size of the works was reduced. The beneficiary, then, called the guarantee to recover its loss as a result of having to find and employ another contractor in order to complete the works. *Trib. com. Nanterre, 14 March 1991*, D. 1992 Somm. p. 241 (direct guarantee, stop-payment order granted). According to the court, completion was established by virtue of a certificate from a surveyance agency appointed by the beneficiary who had examined the equipment upon despatch. This agency found, however, some defects upon installation of the equipment while the court also referred to differences of opinion between account party and beneficiary.

Completion of the secured contract or obligation not established

14-28 In the majority of cases the courts found that the account party had not been able clearly to establish completion of the contract.[122] In none of these cases was there documentation or surrounding facts of the kind as mentioned in No. 14-27. Sometimes the account party could only produce evidence emanating from its own personnel or from self-appointed third parties, or communications from the beneficiary which did not clearly indicate approval. In other cases the court found that the differences of opinion and the complaints from the beneficiary were genuine. Sometimes the court could point to positive indications that the contract had not been completed.[123]

---

[122] See, for example, *CA Amsterdam, 30 March 1972*, NJ 1973, 188, *Rb Amsterdam, 19 March 1981*, KG 1981, 30, *Rb Arnhem, 14 March 1983*, KG 1983, 115, *Rb Amsterdam, 31 March 1988*, KG 1988, 179, *Rb Rotterdam, 9 June 1989*, KG 1989, 270, *Rb Leeuwarden, 4 July 1997* KGK 1998, 1454, *OLG Saarbrücken, 23 January 1981*, RIW 1981, p. 338, *LG München, 30 January 1981*, WM 1981, p. 416, (in main proceedings – after payment – the account party succeeded in establishing proper performance and obtained judgment for recovery, *OLG München, 31 October 1984*, WM 1985, p. 189), *OLG Hamm, 24 June 1986*, WM 1986, p. 1503, *OLG Köln, 7 August 1986*, WM 1988, p. 21, *BGH, 21 April 1988*, WM 1988, p. 934 (bank refused to pay the full amount, arguing that a substantial amount of work had been completed; bank ordered to pay as the work had not been approved and because the contractor had discontinued the project because of insolvency), *BGH, 17 January 1989*, NJW 1989, p. 1480, *OLG Bremen, 14 June 1990*, WM 1990, p. 1369, *Cass., 4 June 1994*, D. 1995 Somm. p. 20 (although independent surveyors, who had been nominated by the beneficiary, had approved the equipment before shipment, defects appeared when the equipment was installed and put into operation), *Cass., 21 May 1985*, D. 1986 J. p. 213, *Paris, 15 February 1989*, D. 1989 Somm. p. 158 (confirmed by *Cass., 5 February 1991*, D. 1991 Somm. p. 199), *Paris, 19 May 1988*, D. 1989 Somm. p. 146, *Paris, 8 July 1986* (confirmed by *Cass., 10 January 1989*, D. 1989 Somm. p. 153) (completion not evident despite strong proof, namely a certificate from an independent agency confirming perfect performance; the true reason for rejection of the application for a restraining order was the fact that there was no evidence of collusion by the second issuing bank), *Trib. com. Paris, 7 February 1989*, D. 1990 Somm. p. 207 (beneficiary had refused to sign the certificate of completion), *Paris, 6 March 1991*, D. 1992 Somm. p. 241 (genuine differences of opinion regarding proper performance), *Paris, 24 April 1992*, D. 1993 Somm. p. 102 (protocol of provisional acceptance with qualifications which were specified in the protocol and described by both parties as significant), *Versailles, 16 September 1992*, D. 1993 Somm. p. 102, *Trib. com. Brussels, 26 November 1987*, RDC 1989, p. 97, *Brussels, 4 January 1989*, TBH 1990, p. 1073, *Brussels, 26 June 1992*, RDC 1994, p. 51, *United Trading v. Allied Arab Bank*, [1985] 2 Lloyd's Rep. 554, *Siporex Trade v. Banque Indosuez*, [1986] 2 Lloyd's Rep. 146.

[123] The case of *Ghent, 25 February 1988*, TBH 1989, p. 40, involved a repayment guarantee with some remarkable stipulations. It was payable on demand, but no payment was to be made if the account party/seller submitted a statement that non-performance of the contract was caused by one of the reasons stated in art. 9 of the contract. The account party submitted the statement and the bank refused to pay. The Court of Appeal recognised the possibility of

Account party not liable for defects

14-29 What is the position if the beneficiary complains of defects for which the account party alleges not to be liable? One cannot generalise about these situations and it would be wrong to suggest that it is always incumbent on the account party to discharge the burden of disproving liability for any defect brought about by whatever cause the beneficiary might wish to complain of. There might be cases where, on the face of the general nature of the contract and its terms, the account party's liability is apparent, which could not be refuted within the constraints of interim proceedings. On the other hand, there could also be cases where the account party's liability for the particular defect is quite unlikely.[124]

Lapse of contractual warranty period

14-30 It is submitted that the lapse of the contractual warranty period within which the beneficiary/creditor must lodge his complaints or after which the account party/debtor's liability is stated to cease, does not in itself constitute evidence of proper performance of the contract for the purpose of establishing fraud.[125] It is for the account party to prove that he has properly completed the contract and this does not follow from the fact that the beneficiary/creditor has forfeited his right to hold the account party/debtor liable because of certain provisions in the secured contract. It must also be repeated that the lapse of the contractual warranty period does not terminate the guarantee, except inasmuch as, and to the extent that, this is expressly provided for in the guarantee.[126] On the other hand, protracted silence on the part of the beneficiary could suggest that his complaints are spurious.[127]

---

the account party fraudulently submitting the statement, but found that there was not the slightest indication of fraud.

[124] In *Rb Amsterdam, 19 March 1981*, KG 1981, 30, a survey report made in the port of destination indicated all kinds of defects. The account party argued that he was not responsible for these defects since the contract involved a C & F sale and that the goods were loaded in good order. This unsubstantiated contention was rejected. However, in *LG Frankfürt a.M., 11 December 1979*, NJW 1981, p. 56, and in *LG Dortmund, 9 July 1980*, WM 1981, p. 280, the account party was not held liable for the alleged defects, see also No. 14-27.

[125] Cf. *CA The Hague, 21 September 1994*, KG 1994, 381, *Rb Arnhem, 7 July 1993*, KG 1993, 312, *Rb Rotterdam, 9 June 1989*, KG 1989, 270, *OLG Saarbrücken, 23 January 1981*, RIW 1981, p. 338.

[126] See Chapter 13.2.7, No. 13-23.

[127] Cf. *LG Dortmund, 9 July 1980*, WM 1981, p. 280, see No. 14-27.

Account party complies with the terms of a documentary credit

14-31 Presentation by the account party of the correct documents under a documentary credit does not evidence proper performance of the contract of sale, as was decided quite rightly in *CA Amsterdam, 30 March 1972*.[128] The possibility of imperfect performance is precisely the kind of risk against which the buyer/beneficiary seeks cover by means of a performance guarantee.

Non-payment by the beneficiary

14-32 What is the position if the account party discontinues or suspends performance of the underlying contract arguing that the beneficiary has failed to pay advance or interim instalments of the contract price? It would appear that if this defence is to be honoured, stringent requirements have to be met. Obviously, the account party must prove that amounts were due and payable under the contract. This would at least require evidence that the account party has completed the phases of the project to which the instalments relate. It is quite possible that the beneficiary's dissatisfaction with regard to the phase concerned or any subsequent phase prompted him to withhold payment and to call the guarantee on account of malperformance and/or discontinuation of the project. A call on the guarantee under such circumstances is certainly not fraudulent. Moreover, regard must be had to the relevant provisions of the contract. These might provide for certain procedures to be followed or they could indicate which legal consequences occur when and under which circumstances. In general, the account party must convincingly establish that the beneficiary's failure to pay advance or interim instalments entitled him immediately to rescind the contract or to suspend performance. It will be quite difficult for the account party to adduce forthwith clear evidence thereof, especially if complex factual or legal issues are at stake which could not be readily resolved by reference to the provisions of the contract.[129]

---

[128] NJ 1973, 188. See also *Cass., 16 June 1992*, D. 1993, Somm. p. 97. However, tender of the correct documents appears to have been the sole piece of evidence of completion upon which *Paris, 18 November 1986*, D. 1988 Somm. p. 247, was prepared to grant a stop-payment order. The report does not mention any other grounds apart from the Court of Appeal's assumption that the beneficiary sought to exact a rebate on the purchase price. Tender of the documents could, however, result in a reduction of the maximum amount of the guarantee in the case of repayment guarantees if so stipulated, see also Chapter 14.5.16.

[129] The account party's argument was rejected in *Trib. com. Brussels, 21 October 1986*, RDC 1987, p. 706 in respect of one of the four contracts, in *Trib. com. Paris, 12 April 1991*, D. 1992 Somm. p. 239, and in *CA Amsterdam, 4 February 1993*, KG 1993, 113. In *Penn. State Const. Inc. v. Cambria Savings & Loan Ass'n.*, 2 UCC Rep. Serv. 2d. 1638 (Pa. 1987), a stop-payment order was, however, granted on the grounds that the account party had substantially completed the project and that the beneficiary's failure to make timely payments was responsible for whatever delays had occurred. See also Chapter 14.5.13.

Completion not yet due

14-33 In the absence of certain conditions precedent or commencement date clauses, guarantees can, in principle, be called immediately upon issuance, thus even before the contractually agreed date of completion. It is submitted that a temporary injunction could be an appropriate remedy if the account party could show, for example by reference to the terms of the contract, that completion was not yet due.[130] An exception would be cases of anticipatory breach of contract.

14.5.6 Material breach of contract by the beneficiary

General

14-34 Even in situations where the account party has not (entirely) completed the contract or only after considerable delay, case law recognises the possibility of fraud in cases where the beneficiary has breached his own contractual obligations or where he has severely impeded performance by the account party. From the general guideline that the beneficiary's demand for payment is fraudulent if it has no conceivable basis it follows that, in general, the beneficiary's breach of contract must be such as to entitle the account party immediately to rescind the contract without incurring any liability. In other words, the beneficiary's malfeasance must be serious and fundamental.[131] Demonstrating the legal consequences of such kind of breach of contract does not appear to pose grave difficulties. They are either self-evident or they can be readily derived from the provisions of the main contract. If the matter gives rise to complex legal or factual issues, it is likely that the breach was not sufficiently grave or evident. It should be noted that the fact that the underlying contract designates certain obliga-

---

[130] Cf. *Paris, 2 June 1982*, D. 1983 J. p. 437, see also Chapter 13.2.7., No. 13-25. See also Mülbert, p. 78.

[131] Thus explicitly *Rb Almelo, 15 August 1984*, KG 1984, 261, and *Rb Rotterdam, 16 March 1993*, KG 1993, 222. See also the observations of Stoufflet, JCP 1985 ll No. 20436, Vasseur, D. 1985 J. p. 269, and Wymeersch, TPR 1986, p. 495. They suggest that the decision of *Cass., 17 October 1984*, D. 1985 J. p. 269, rested on the grounds that the alleged obligation of the beneficiary, namely to designate the carrying vessel, did not in fact exist or that breach of this obligation was insufficiently serious to justify non-performance by the account party. This requirement tallies with several authoritative decisions concerning documentary credits, holding that there is only fraud if the merchandise is totally defective, see, for example, *BGH, 16 March 1987*, RIW 1987, p. 705, *BGH, 27 June 1988*, RIW 1988, p. 814, *OLG Frankfurt a.M., 6 October 1987*, RIW 1988, p. 905, *Discount Records Ltd. v. Barclays Bank*, [1975] 1 WLR 315, and the cases of *Sztejn v. Henry Schroder Banking Corp.* 177 Misc. 719 (N.Y. Sup. Ct. 1941), *United Bank v. Cambridge Sporting Goods*, 392 N.Y.S. 2d. 265 (1976), and *NMC Enterprises Inc. v. Columbia Broadcasting Systems Inc.*, 14 UCC Rep. 1427 (N.Y. Sup. Ct. 1974) in which three cases the defence of fraud was honoured.

tions of the beneficiary as fundamental or, in the case of non-performance, as grounds for termination by the account party is not in itself sufficient.

A second variant is the situation where the beneficiary renders performance impossible, see No. 14-38. The effect of non-payment by the beneficiary of the full contract price or instalments has been discussed in No. 14-32.

Material breach of contract not established

14-35 Case law provides several examples of decisions in which the application for stop-payment orders was dismissed because the beneficiary's breach of contract was not established or because the breach, if established, was not sufficiently material.[132]

Material breach of contract established

14-36 There are also examples of successful applications for interlocutory restraining orders on the grounds that material breach of contract by the beneficiary has been established. The injunctions in the so-called Iranian cases rested on other grounds too.[133]

---

[132] *Cass., 17 October 1984*, D. 1985 J. p. 269, see previous note, *Turkiye Is Bankasi v. Bank of China*, [1996] 2 Lloyd's Rep. 611, [1998] 1 Lloyd's Rep. 250 (no (clear) evidence of beneficiary's fraud), *BGH, 13 July 1989*, WM 1989, p. 1496 (bank alleged non-performance by beneficiary/seller), *CA Amsterdam, 4 February 1993*, KG 1993, 113 (no clear evidence of (material) breach of contract by beneficiary), *Rb Rotterdam, 16 March 1993*, KG 1993, 222 (payment guarantee in favour of seller, no clear evidence of breach of contract by seller), *Rb Almelo, 15 August 1984*, KG 1984, 261 (alleged late delivery of a few weeks does not render the call fraudulent), *Trib. com. Brussels, 25 September 1987*, RDC 1988, p. 808 (payment guarantee in favour of seller, alleged defectiveness of equipment not established), *Philipp Brothers, Inc. v. Oil Country Specialists*, 787 SW2d 38 (Tex. 1990) ('Fraud claims should not become surrogates for breach of contract claims'), *New Orleans Brass v. Whitney National Bank*, 2002 WL 1018964 (La. App. 4th Cir. 15 May 2002) (alleged breach of contract by beneficiary did not justify a finding of material fraud). In *LG Stuttgart, 8 August 1980*, WM 1981, p. 633, the account party argued that completion of the project had been made impossible because the beneficiary had failed to carry out certain ground works. The application for a stop-payment order against the first instructing bank was dismissed because the second issuing bank's knowledge of the beneficiary's fraud had not been proven.

[133] *Rb Zwolle, 26 November 1982*, KG 1982, 220 (exclusive distribution agreement whereby the distributor (buyer/account party) had undertaken to purchase a minimum number of goods per annum; in violation of the agreed exclusivity, the seller/ beneficiary sold the goods directly to end-buyers, which made performance of the above-mentioned obligation of the account party impossible), *Cass., 12 January 1993*, D. 1995 J. p. 24 (beneficiary's claim against bank dismissed; beneficiary had defaulted on its contractual obligation to provide security to the account party, see also Chapter 14.3.4, No. 14-9), *Paris, 27 June 1988*, D. 1989 Somm. p. 151 (unilateral repudiation, bank correctly refused payment), *Trib. com.*

Beneficiary's failure to furnish a documentary credit

14-37 A contractual obligation of the buyer to furnish a documentary credit assuring payment to the seller is generally regarded as a fundamental obligation. Breach of this obligation entitles the seller to rescind the contract or to suspend performance of his own obligations. Based on the principles explained in No. 14-34 and those underlying the decisions referred to in No. 14-36 it would appear that a call by the beneficiary/ buyer in these circumstances may be considered fraudulent. This was, indeed, the conclusion reached in *Trib. com. Paris, 14 December 1990*,[134] but a number of other decisions went the other way and applications for restraining orders were dismissed. It is worth noting that these decisions educed some critical comments.[135]

Paris, 15 March 1985, D. 1985 I.R. p. 244 (payment guarantee; seller unilaterally repudiated the contract and did not deliver), *Trib. com. Brussels, 15 January 1980*, JCB 1980, p. 147 (beneficiary ousted the account party and unilaterally repudiated the agreement in order to contract directly with the account party's subcontractors), *Themehelp Ltd. v. West and Others*, [1996] Q.B. 84 (the payment guarantee furnished by the account party/buyer in favour of the beneficiary/ seller related to the sale of a company; the buyer produced (weak) evidence that the seller had made fraudulent misrepresentations about the value and profitability of the business), *Elian and Rabbath v. Matsas and Matsas*, [1966] 2 Lloyd's Rep. 495 (beneficiary refused to release the goods which he had promised to release and which constituted the consideration for the account party to furnish a guarantee). *ICC arbitration, No. 5721/1990*, J.D.I. 1990, p. 1020, involved a repayment and performance guarantee in relation to a construction contract in favour of the main contractor on behalf of the subcontractor. The arbitrators ruled that the main contractor/beneficiary had failed to perform its obligations under the contract which made it impossible for the subcontractor to carry out the subcontracted work. The arbitrators terminated the contract and ruled that the main contractor/beneficiary's demand for payment under the guarantees was fraudulent. The following three cases involved indirect guarantees in favour of Iranian Government agencies: *LG Frankfurt a.M., 11 December 1979*, NJW 1981, p. 56 (refusal to take delivery, see also Chapter 14.5.5., No. 14-27), *Trib. com. Brussels, April 6 1982*, Rev. Banque 1982, p. 683 (beneficiary was unable to carry out certain construction works which he had contractually undertaken to perform, see also Chapter 14.5.5, No. 14-27), *Cass., 11 December 1985*, D. 1986 J. p. 213 (the account party was ousted and its personnel was expelled; works had been transferred to a new Iranian company which was substituted for the account party). In *Paris, 27 June 1988*, D. 1989 Somm. p. 151, a French bank, which had issued a direct guarantee in favour of an Iranian company, refused payment because of the beneficiary's fraud. This decision was approved by the Court of Appeal since the beneficiary had unilaterally repudiated the secured contract and had, therefore, no right to payment. This was evidenced, *inter alia*, by the fact that the beneficiary did not persist in his demand for payment, which the court understood to be an admission by the beneficiary that no compensation was due.

[134] D. 1991 Somm. p. 201. The decision involved an after-payment case whereby the account party's claim against the beneficiary for repayment succeeded.

[135] The most striking case is *Edward Owen Engineering v. Barclays Bank Int.*, [1978] 2 All E.R. 976, Schmitthoff, JBL 1988. p. 353. The Court of Appeal accepted that it was the beneficiary

374   Chapter 14

Beneficiary makes performance by the account party impossible

14-38 The beneficiary's demand for payment may also be fraudulent if he has made performance by the account party impossible or if his acts or ommissions are the sole cause of the delay in performance. Although formulated in a restrictive manner, this type of fraud is also recognised in art. 19 (2)(d) UNCITRAL Convention.[136] In general, there are two main variants. First, it could be that performance has been made physically impossible, as occurred in several Iranian cases.[137] Secondly, the impossibility or delay was the inevitable result of breach of certain obligations by the beneficiary, whether or not such breach was so fundamental as to entitle the account party to immediately rescind the contract. This may be the case, for example, where the beneficiary failed to carry out certain groundworks on the site, to supply energy and/or skilled labour or to procure the required import licences for building equipment as he was contractually obliged to do, or if there is no properly functioning plant where the equipment is to be installed and put into operation. This defence should, however, only be accepted in clear and exceptional cases. Accordingly, the account party must produce clear evidence that he has performed all his obligations except those which were prevented or delayed solely by causes for which the beneficiary was responsible and where the account party could not reasonably remedy the consequences of the beneficiary's acts or omissions. Case law provides a number of examples where the beneficiary's call was considered fraudulent for reasons as mentioned above.[138]

---

who was in default much rather than the account party and that the latter was (probably) entitled to repudiate the contract. See also *KMW International v. Chase Manhattan Bank*, 606 F.2d. 10 (2d. Cir. 1979), *American Bell Int. v. Islamic Republic of Iran*, 474 F. Supp. 420 (S.D.N.Y. 1979), comments from Getz, Harvard Int. L.R. 1980, p. 213, Note, HLR 1980, p. 1009, Ebbink, WPNR 1984, p. 457, Sion, Rev. Banque 1984, p. 19. These two decisions date from before the seizure of U.S. citizens.

[136] A demand for payment is improper if 'fulfillment of the underlying obligation has clearly been prevented by wilful misconduct of the beneficiary'.

[137] *Trib. com. Brussels, 6 April 1982*, Rev. Banque 1982, p. 683, *Cass., 11 December 1985*, D. 1986 J. p. 213, *Rockwell Internat. Systems v. Citibank*, 719 F.2d. 583 (2d. Cir. 1983).

[138] *Rb Zwolle, 26 November 1982*, KG 1982, 220, see No. 14-36, *Cass. 23 October 1990*, D. 1991 Somm. p. 197 (beneficiary had made performance impossible by unilaterally changing the nature of the contract; injunction against instructing bank, however, denied because of insufficient evidence concerning the issuing bank's knowledge of the beneficiary's fraud), *Trib. com. Brussels, 15 January 1980*, JCB 1980, p. 147, see No. 14-36, *Trib. com. Brussels, 25 June 1985*, TBH 1987, p. 803 (excessive interference with the account party's affairs), *ICC arbitration, No. 5721/1990*, J.D.I. 1990, p. 1020 see No. 14-36. See also *Ghent, 25 February 1988*, TBH 1989, p. 40 (beneficiary failed to forward the necessary documents required for the shipment of the goods despite repeated requests from the account party/seller). In the case of *CA Bordeaux, 14 June 1990*, a construction firm had procured an indirect customs guarantee in favour of the Algerian tax authorities in order to ensure re-

14.5.7 *Force majeure*

Force majeure not established

14-39 The account party's plea that he could not be held liable for non-completion of the contract because of *force majeure* and that the beneficiary's demand for payment was therefore fraudulent has been rejected in two Swiss decisions. In *Geneva, September 27 1984*, the court observed that the account party had neither presented sufficient evidence regarding the facts nor explained why these facts should render performance of the contract impossible, such that he would not be liable.[139] In the second case the Swiss *Federal Court, January 9 1985*, held that a bad harvest, which allegedly prevented delivery of beans from Turkey, did not constitute *force majeure* such that it would make the call on the guarantee fraudulent.[140] It should be noted that the dismissals of the applications were not founded on the grounds that *force majeure* could never constitute a proper defence.

In three American pre-hostage cases involving construction projects to be carried out in Iran, applications for interim stop-payment orders were dismissed too. The courts observed that powerful and knowledgeable U.S. companies must have anticipated the political risks which are inherent in major international transactions with Iranian state agencies and that they had therefore accepted those risks. The Iranian revolution and the ensuing turmoil did not, according to the courts, render the call fraudulent.[141]

Force majeure established

14-40 The Iranian revolution has also given rise to a number of cases in which the court did accept that completion of the contract had been made impossible because of

---

exportation of the equipment. In connection with another tax claim, the Algerian authorities seized and sold the equipment and also called the customs guarantee. The Court of Appeal granted an injunction against the instructing and issuing bank on the grounds of fraud because the authorities had made re-exportation impossible, but this decision was reversed by *Cass., 19 May 1992* (2e. decision), D. 1993 Somm. p. 103, because of insufficient reasoning by the Court of Appeal. See also the case law cited in No. 14-36.

[139] D. 1986 I.R. p. 163.

[140] D. 1986 I.R. p. 163. See also *LG Braunschweig, 22 May 1980*, RIW 1981, p. 789, see note 48.

[141] *KMW International v. Chase Manhattan Bank*, 606 F.2d. 10 (2d. cir. 1979), *American Bell Int. v. Islamic Republic of Iran*, 474 F. Supp. 420 (S.D.N.Y. 1979), *United Technologies Corp. v. Citibank*, 469 F. Supp. 473 (S.D.N.Y. 1979). The denial of the motions rested, however, primarily on the general criteria for interlocutory orders, see Chapter 14.3.7, No. 14. As far as the test of irreparable harm was concerned, the courts took the view that it had not been established that recovery of the loss was absolutely impossible and/or that the U.S. exporters had accepted jurisdiction of Iranian courts. The potential damage to the credibility of U.S. banks caused the balance of convenience to tip decidedly against the account party.

force majeure, that the account party was not in default and that the call was fraudulent.[142] In the American and Amsterdam decisions, the court observed that the secured contract contained specific *force majeure* clauses which the account party, upon the occurrence of the supervening events, had strictly observed and which entitled the account party to eventually terminate the contract. Moreover, the account party's liability for non-completion had not been seriously argued on the part of the beneficiary in the period before the litigation.

Government measures, embargoes

14-41 Government measures and embargoes are a particular form of *force majeure* which may render performance impossible. In *State Trading Corp. of India v. E. D. & F. Man,* the supply contract contained a *force majeure* clause allowing the seller/account party to extend the period of delivery by thirty days in the event of, *inter alia,* government intervention, and permitting the buyer/beneficiary to terminate the contract after that period.[143] Owing to a ban by the Indian Government, the contract was not fully performed. The application for an order enjoining the buyer/beneficiary to demand payment was dismissed. The Court of Appeal ruled that the beneficiary was entitled to call the guarantee as long as he honestly believed that there was default.

---

[142] *Itek v. First National Bank,* 511 F. Supp. 1341 (D. Mass. 1981), 730 F.2d. 19 (1st. Cir. 1984), *Touche Ross v. Manufacturers Hanover,* 449 N.Y.S. 2d. 125 (N.Y. App. Div. 1982), *Harris Corp. v. Nat. Iranian Radio and Television,* 691 F.2d. 1344 (11th. Cir. 1982), *Rockwell Int. Systems v. Citibank,* 719 F.2d. 583 (2d. Cir. 1983). These were post-hostage cases. American commentators also point out that it took some time for the courts to fully appreciate the true conditions prevailing in Iran. *Rb Amsterdam, 18 December 1980,* S & S 1981, 135, *Trib. com. Brussels, 6 April 1982,* Rev. Banque 1982, p. 683, *Supreme Court of Finland, 25 October 1992,* D. 1995 Somm. p. 22. The aforementioned cases involved indirect guarantees. In *BGH, 12 March 1984 (ll 198/82),* NJW 1984, p. 2030, a direct payment guarantee had been issued in favour of an Iranian lessor to secure payment of a penalty in the event that the account party/lessee failed to surrender the land free of occupation. The land was expropriated and allocated to a third party, which was confirmed in a protocol from a Teheran court. The guarantee was payable on demand unless the account party tendered certain documents, *inter alia* a protocol from a Teheran court. The account party presented the protocol to the bank and the bank refused to honour the beneficiary's demand for payment. His claim for payment filed in summary proceedings was rejected on the grounds that *force majeure* was sufficiently evidenced by the above-mentioned protocol. The beneficiary's argument that the account party had aided and abetted the expropriation was dismissed because these assertions could not be investigated in summary proceedings. However, the court declined to qualify the demand for payment as fraudulent. The impact of the 'unless' clause in the guarantee and the nature of the proceedings have been overlooked by the commentators on the decision.

[143] [1981] Com. L.R. 235. See also JBL 1981, p. 383 (Schmitthoff) and JBL 1982, p. 65.

This was the case since the sugar had not been delivered. The court refused to interfere with the beneficiary's rights and ruled that the question of whether or not there was a proper defence of *force majeure* was a matter for arbitration. No reference was made to the *force majeure* clauses in the main contract.

Similar facts occurred in *Dynamics Corp. v. Citizen & Southern Nat. Bank*. In this case, the court did grant an injunction restraining the bank from paying on the grounds that the beneficiary's statement of default had no basis in fact whatsoever and was, therefore, fraudulent.[144]

The effect of the UN embargoes against Iraq has been reviewed in Chapter 13.4.

Evaluation

14-42/43 The allegation of fraud on the basis of *force majeure* carries particular difficulties. The account party must at least prove that the supervening events have occurred and that these events rendered performance impossible. Apart from situations which are a matter of common knowledge, such as the conditions prevailing at the time of the Iranian revolution, discharge of this burden of proof may not be as easy as one might think. For example, there is, in general, no impossibility if the contract could have been completed by taking alternative measures or by modifying the manner of performance, even though these are more costly, or if the supervening events have a temporary character only.[145] Apart from impossibility, the general law on *force majeure* poses other requirements too, such as evidence that the supervening events had not been contemplated by the parties to the contract, that they were beyond the control of the debtor and that they exceeded the range of risks which are to be attributed to the debtor. The nature of the contract must be considered too. In short, the mere fact that performance has been made impossible does not mean that the account party is exculpated from all liability. It would appear that if the defence of *force majeure* involves complex legal issues concerning the general law on *force majeure*, it is unlikely that, within the confines of interlocutory proceedings, the account party will be able to establish that he cannot possibly be held liable for non-performance.

It might be different if the secured contract contains explicit and detailed clauses dealing with *force majeure* and the consequences thereof. Such clauses may provide for certain periods during which performance is suspended, for termination after a certain period and the financial implications thereof, and for procedures for consultation or intermediation aimed at adaptation of the contract with a view to continuation of the project.[146] However, even detailed clauses which appear to exculpate the ex-

---

[144] 356 F. Supp. 991 (N.D. Ga. 1973).

[145] This might have played a part in the two Swiss decisions mentioned in No. 14-39.

[146] These aspects played a part in *LG Braunschweig, May 22 1980*, RIW 1981, p. 789. The court observed that the account party had chosen not to bring the differences of opinion

porter from liability cannot always avert genuine differences of opinion regarding the particular facts of the case and their legal implications. It should be borne in mind that it remains for the account party to remove any reasonable doubts as regards the absence of liability. As long as the beneficiary's rights to damages continue to be plausible and if the absence of liability could only be determined in main proceedings, applications for interlocutory injunctions ought to be denied. It is also conceivable that a performance guarantee is intended to shift the risk of certain events onto the account party in derogation from the *force majeure* provisions in the main contract, notwithstanding the possibility of final adjudication in main proceedings.[147]

By way of a general conclusion, it is submitted that, apart from the requirements and difficulties described above, defences founded on *force majeure* should be restricted to clear and very exceptional cases, and to situations in which the contract could not be completed solely because of circumstances which clearly lie beyond the range of risks which international commerce or the contract attributes to the account party and if, for those reasons, the beneficiary's claim for payment has no plausible basis. An exception to this restrictive concept of fraud in the case of *force majeure* appears justified when the beneficiary calls the guarantee immediately upon discontinuation, without allowing for the possible short-term nature of the supervening events or without enabling the account party to consider alternative means of performance. In such cases, the nature of the contract and its *force majeure* clauses are also to be taken into account. On the other hand, it is submitted that *force majeure* is never a proper defence in the case of repayment guarantees. Such guarantees do not secure payment of damages, but repayment of advance payments in the event of non-performance, regardless of liability. Otherwise, stop-payment orders would have the practical effect of burdening the beneficiary with the consequences of *force majeure*.

14.5.8 Violation of public order; illegality

14-44 It is generally accepted that the beneficiary cannot claim payment if the underlying contract violates (international) public order.[148] In that event, under the laws of most jurisdictions the guarantee itself will probably be invalid or unenforceable, re-

---

before arbitrators in accordance with a clause in the contract. The account party argued that war between Iraq and Iran had delayed performance. After some time the deliveries were resumed and the beneficiary had not called the guarantee during the interval. This suggests that his complaints did not relate to late delivery, but to the defectiveness of the equipment.

[147] Cf. the *E. D. & F. Man* decision discussed in No. 14-41.

[148] See, for example, *Brussels, 18 December 1981*, Rev. Banque 1982, p. 99, *Trib. com. Brussels, 8 October 1985*, RDC 1986, p. 648, von Westphalen, p. 175, Zahn/Neumann/Ehrlich, 9/125, Boll, p. 122, Wymeersch, TPR 1986, p. 498, Vasseur, No. 116, Stoufflet, JDI 1987, p. 278.

gardless of its independent nature. The virtual absence of relevant case law suggests that these cases must be extremely rare.[149]

The notion of (international) public order ought to be construed narrowly. It is probably confined to contracts such as the sale of arms in violation of embargoes pursuant to international public law and the sale of narcotics. It does not encompass situations in which the underlying contract is a nullity, illegal, unlawful, void or unenforceable on the grounds that it contravenes, for example, statutory provisions of a technical nature, export or import regulations in the account party's or beneficiary's country, exchange control regulations or other regulations or statutory provisions which declare certain dealings unlawful if no licence has been obtained.[150] Since the beneficiary

---

[149] But see *BGH, April 28 1988*, RIW 1988, p. 558. The shareholder (X) of an Iranian company, who had fled from his country, agreed to act as surety and lodged a deposit with a bank situated in Germany and incorporated under German law. The State of Iran owned 85 per cent of the bank's shares. Iran expropriated X's shares without compensation and took over the company. The bank refused to release the deposit and set this amount off against the debts of X arising from the suretyship. The German Supreme Court affirmed the decision of the Court of Appeal, which had ordered the release of the deposit because the expropriation violated German public order and had no effect, observing that the proceeds of the deposit would flow to the State of Iran as 85 per cent shareholder.

[150] See especially *Trib. com. Namur, 12 September 1994*, RDC 1995, p. 68. The Belgian court ordered the bank to pay, which had refused payment on the grounds that the underlying contract was void because of art. 1855 of the Belgian Civil Code. The court observed that defences of this kind are limited to situations where the underlying contract violates public order, which was not the case. It also pointed out that the bank was fully aware of the fact that the contract was void, but that it tried to escape payment only when the account party became insolvent. In *Group Josi v. Walbrook Insurance*, [1996] 1 Lloyd's Rep. 345, 362, the sale of arms to Iraq at a time when such a sale was illegal, was mentioned as an example of a contract which might render a call for payment fraudulent. In the case at hand the (alleged) illegality consisted in the fact that the account party did not possess a licence to conduct the business of reinsurance. The Court of Appeal ruled that this type of illegality did not render the call on the guarantee fraudulent. In *Cass., 13 December 1983*, D. 1984 J. p. 420, the account party applied for an order restraining the instructing bank from reimbursing the second issuing bank arguing that the underlying trade in securities was illegal because the required licence was lacking. This application was dismissed on the grounds that any possible nullity of the secured contract would not render the counter-guarantee null and void. A divergent trend is conveyed in *Paris, 14 January 1993*, JCP 1993 Ed. G. No. 22069. A guarantee had been issued in favour of a main contractor which was payable on first demand provided that the main contractor submitted a statement to the effect that the subcontractor had breached its obligations pursuant to the subcontracting agreement. This agreement was voidable as the main contractor had not procured an accessory guarantee in favour of the subcontractor as required under certain French legislative provisions. When the main contractor/beneficiary called the first demand guarantee, the subcontractor avoided the underlying subcontracting agreement. While the Court of Appeal observed that the ensuing nullity of

might not be familiar with these regulations or statutory provisions, these are precisely the kinds of risk which he legitimately seeks to guard against.[151] Accordingly, such incidents do not affect the validity of the guarantee and do not render a call on the guarantee fraudulent. Guarantees sometimes expressly provide that the guarantor's liability remains unaffected by the fact that the secured contract might be void, invalid or unenforceable.

It has been argued, however, that no payment is to be made if the law governing the guarantee condemns the transaction as illegal or unenforceable too.[152] This proposition can only be approved of if applied restrictively. The suggested rule should not apply in a case in which, for example, a Dutch exporter/account party has not obtained the required export licence and the guarantee was issued by a Dutch bank, while both the export contract and guarantee are governed by Dutch law.[153] Again, the failure to obtain the required licence is the type of risk which the beneficiary seeks to avoid. Moreover, these regulations pertain to exports, not to payment of damages. It would also be inappropriate to allow the account party to escape liability on account of his own inability to procure the licence. Accordingly, violation of mere domestic economic laws does not render a call fraudulent, irrespective of the laws governing secured contract and guarantee. It is submitted that the claim for payment should be dismissed only if the secured contract is illegal under the applicable law and if the law governing the guarantee considers the kind of transaction manifestly illegal as measured by inter-

---

the underlying agreement did not affect as such the validity of the first demand guarantee, it ruled that the main contractor could not justifiably confirm that the subcontractor had defaulted on its obligations since the underlying contract was invalid, and concluded that the terms and conditions of the guarantee had not been fulfilled. It should be noted that this decision involved a domestic case.

[151] Cf. Vasseur, No. 45, 125, Mattout, No. 229.

[152] Simont, Rev. Banque 1983, pp. 595-596. See also von Westphalen, p. 182, who addresses the situation where the forum gives effect to foreign mandatory law.

[153] Facts of a similar kind occurred in *Cass., 13 December 1983*, D. 1984 J. p. 420, involving an indirect guarantee in a domestic case whereby both the secured illegal contract, the guarantee and counter-guarantee were governed by French law, see footnote 58. In *BGH, 12 March 1984 (ll ZR 10/83)*, RIW 1985, p. 78, the German Supreme Court honoured, however, the account party's application for an order restraining the beneficiary, an English broker, from calling the guarantee. The secured contract involved transactions in futures on the commodity exchanges in London and the U.S.A. The contract was governed by English law and was valid under that law. The guarantee had been issued by a German bank. The German account party argued that the contract was not enforceable because he lacked the capacity for such transactions pursuant to the German Commodity Exchange Act. This argument was accepted. The German Supreme Court ruled that the guarantee was not enforceable because the secured contract was not enforceable, observing that the choice of English law did not set aside German mandatory law.

national standards.[154] In such situations it could also be said that the beneficiary must have been aware of the illegality.

14.5.9 Termination, cancellation and avoidance of the secured contract

14-45 Termination, cancellation or dissolution of the secured contract by either party is not in itself conclusive as to the question of whether or not the demand for payment is fraudulent.[155]

Termination of the contract by the beneficiary and a subsequent call on the guarantee could be fraudulent if the account party establishes that the termination amounts to a material breach of contract and that he has given the beneficiary no cause to cancel the contract.[156]

In the event that the account party has terminated the contract, the defence of fraud should, in principle, be restricted to cases in which the account party proves that the sole cause for rescission was breach of a fundamental obligation or some kind of mis-

---

[154] As was the case in *United City Merchants Ltd. v. Royal Bank of Canada*, (HL), [1982] 2 All E.R. 720. It was found that the amount payable under the letter of credit was doubled by agreement between buyer and seller in order to secure the transfer of funds by the Peruvian buyer out of Peru in contravention of the Peruvian exchange control regulations. The House of Lords held that, with a view to the Bretton Woods Agreement, it was obliged under English law to refuse to enforce that portion of the agreement which contained the illegal exchange commitment.

[155] The effect of these occurrences and illegality, as examined in No. 14-44, on the guarantee was at one time a major issue in Belgium and France. The question was whether these occurrences deprived the guarantee of its *causa*, which would render the guarantee itself invalid. The protracted discussion was finally put to an end by *Cass., December 13 1983*, D. 1984 J. p. 420, see above. Mattout, Nos. 229-230, correctly observes that such occurrences never render the guarantee itself invalid because of its independent nature, but they may render the demand for payment by the beneficiary fraudulent.

[156] Injunctions were granted in *Trib. com. Brussels, 15 January 1980*, J.C.B. 1980, p. 147, *Cass., 11 December 1985*, D. 1986 J. p. 213, *Trib. com. Paris, 15 March 1985*, D. 1985 I.R. p. 244, *Paris, 27 June 1988, D. 1989 Somm.* p. 151, *confirmed by Cass., 6 February 1990*, D. 1990 Somm. p. 213 (bank correctly refused payment). In *Rb Utrecht, 6 July 2000*, S & S 2001, 3, a conservatory attachment order remained in force in a case where the beneficiary had unilaterally cancelled the contract, while it had been established that the beneficiary had agreed to price increases, had accepted and paid the account party's invoices and that the account party had fully performed his obligations. The application for an injunction was dismissed in *Paris, 7 January 1983*, D. 1983 I.R. p. 304, on the grounds that the beneficiary had terminated the contract for proper reasons. Also in *BGH, 28 October 1993*, WM 1994, p. 106, there was no clear evidence that the termination by the benificiary rendered the call fraudulent. See further *State Trading Corp. of India v. E. D. & F. Man*, [1981] Com. L.R. 235, see Chapter 14.5.7, No. 14-41. See also Mattout, No. 230(b).

conduct by the beneficiary,[157] or that the contract was correctly terminated because of *force majeure* and in accordance with the relevant provisions in the secured contract without liability on the part of the account party.[158] Termination by the account party on other grounds cannot, in principle, constitute a proper defence. The reason is that, even if, for example, the secured contract appears to entitle the account party to unilaterally cancel the contract, the beneficiary might still be entitled to damages. A demand for payment in these and similar circumstances cannot be considered fraudulent.[159]

If the secured contract was terminated upon mutual consent and if such termination entails release of the account party's liability to the beneficiary, a subsequent call on the guarantee is obviously fraudulent.[160]

The question whether avoidance by the account party of the underlying contract on such grounds as mistake, misrepresentation, economic duress or undue influence, may render a call on the guarantee fraudulent has been examined in Chapter 14.5.3.

14.5.10 Beneficiary's cause of action is time-barred

14-46 It is submitted that even proper evidence that the beneficiary/creditor's cause of action against the account party/debtor in respect of the secured contract is time-barred on account of the statutory provisions on limitations of actions does not constitute a defence against payment under the guarantee on the basis of fraud.[161] The matter is

---

[157] Cf. Chapter 14.5.6. In *Trib. gr. inst. Montlucon, 9 January 1981*, D. 1981 J. p. 390, involving an indirect guarantee to an Iranian Government state agency, the application for an order against the beneficiary was granted, while the application for an injunction against the first instructing bank was dismissed. The validity of the termination was affirmed by a court decision ordering the beneficiary to pay damages.

[158] See Chapter 14.5.7.

[159] Cf. *CA Amsterdam, 4 February 1993*, KG 1993, 113, *Trib. com. Paris, 12 April 1991*, D. 1992 Somm. p. 239. In *Trib.com. Brussels, 25 September 1987*, RDC 1988, p. 808, the account party's argument that he had cancelled the contract prior to execution was rejected. Idem: *Paris, 19 May 1988*, D. 1989 Somm. p. 146.

[160] This argument was raised against the issuing bank after payment in *Paris, 13 February 1987*, D. 1987 Somm. p. 172. The Court of Appeal rightly dismissed the claim for recovery because the existence of a final settlement as described in the text was not established and because, even if it were established, the paying bank had no knowledge thereof. In *Boliventer Oil v. Chase Manhattan Bank*, [1984] 1 WLR 392, a similar contention was dismissed on the same grounds.

[161] Cf. *BGH, 31 January 1985*, WM 1985, p. 511, *OLG Düsseldorf, 9 August 2001*, WM 2001, p. 2294. The decision of *Kammergericht, 20 November 1986*, NJW 1987, p. 1774, involving a suretyship payable on first demand, contains some observations which seem to suggest that clear and liquid evidence of the limitation of the cause of action would entitle the bank to refuse payment. The rule stated in the text does not apply to the traditional accessory suretyship, cf. *BGH, 19 September 1985*, NJW 1986, p. 310.

comparable to the lapse of the contractual warranty period.[162] Moreover, the fact that the beneficiary/creditor's remedy is time-barred does not mean that he has forfeited his substantive rights while the period during which he is entitled to claim payment under the guarantee is solely determined by the provisions of the guarantee.

14.5.11 The amount claimed is excessive; damages already assessed and/or paid; payment already made

14-47 The beneficiary is entitled to claim the full amount of the guarantee. Since he is entitled to payment without proof, he need not adduce evidence that the amount he demands corresponds with his actual loss.[163] On the other hand, the account party ought to be permitted to adduce evidence that the amount claimed is clearly excessive to the extent that it has no conceivable basis, with the result that the demand for the full amount must be considered fraudulent.[164] A similar situation arises where there is evidence that, in relation to a payment guarantee, the beneficiary has already received (full or partial) payment, or, in relation to a performance guarantee, has already obtained (full or partial) damages and also calls for (full) payment under the guarantee.[165]

---

[162] Chapter 14.5.5, No. 14-30.

[163] Cf. *CA Amsterdam, 8 January 1987*, KG 1988, 300, *Paris, 3 March 1990*, D 1990 Somm. p. 209, *Brussels, 4 January 1989*, TBH 1990, p. 1073, *Cargill International v. Bangladesh Sugar & Food Industries*, [1998] 2 All ER 406, at 414, *BGH, 28 October 1993*, WM 1994, p. 106, *OLG Frankfurt a.M., 8 February 2000*, WM 2001, p. 1108 and Chapter 13.2.8.

[164] In *LG Dortmund, 9 July 1980*, WM 1981, p. 280, a stop-payment order was granted, one of the reasons being that, even if the account party was liable for the transport damage of DM 650, a call for the entire amount of DM 82,000 was excessive. In *Shiv Ispatudyog v. Indus Valley*, IBL October 1986, p. 79, the buyer/beneficiary had agreed to an extension of the delivery date 'without prejudice to the rights to encash the bank guarantee'. Delivery was made within the extended period and was accepted by the buyer/beneficiary. The Delhi High Court ruled that, because the contract of sale contained explicit provisions for the computation of penalties in case of late delivery, the beneficiary could not claim the full amount. The contention was rejected due to lack of evidence in *CA Amsterdam, 8 January 1987*, KG 1988, 300, *Rb Haarlem, 21 November 1986*, KG 1987, 57, *Rb Almelo, 15 August 1984*, KG 1984, 261, *BGH, 21 April 1988*, WM 1988, p. 934 (reduction clause not operative, see further Chapter 14.5.6, No. 14-28), *Paris, 2 March 1990*, D. 1990 Somm. p. 209 (indirect guarantee, foreign issuing bank was not aware of the allegedly excessive nature of the beneficiary's demand for payment), *Trib. com. Paris, 7 October 1988*, D. 1989 Somm. p. 145, *Paris, 19 May 1988*, D. 1989 Somm. p. 146 (reduction clause not operative), *Brussels, 15 October 1987*, Rev. Banque 1988/2, p. 29. It is submitted that a call on both the performance and maintenance guarantees might in certain circumstances be considered fraudulent if the complaints concern the maintenance period only.

[165] *Rb. Utrecht, 22 January 1998*, affirmed by *CA Amsterdam, 25 March 1999*, JOR 2000, 40, *Trib. com. Hasselt, 2 October 1998*, TBH 1999, p. 723 (restraining order limited to the

What is the situation if, for example, € 1 million is payable under the guarantee and arbitrators or a court have given judgment in favour of the creditor/beneficiary of, say, € 500,000, which amount he has been able to obtain, for example by seizing the debtor/account party's assets? Could the beneficiary then claim € 500,000, or even the full amount, under the guarantee asserting that his real loss exceeds € 500,000, but without adducing evidence thereof? It can be argued that the right to claim under the guarantee without producing evidence ought to be reduced by the amount he has already received, since a first demand guarantee assures payment of damages without proof, but it does not assure double payment.[166] The fact that arbitrators or a court have given judgment for € 500,000 could be considered as a strong indication that the beneficiary is entitled to no more than that, with the result that any claim under the guarantee would be fraudulent. However, this need not necessarily be the case. It might be possible that the arbitral or judicial decision was based on one count of loss only, for example on losses owing to late delivery and not also on losses owing to defective performance, or that the total loss later turns out to be greater.

14.5.12 The call does not relate to the secured contract or obligation, or is inspired by improper motives

14-48 The beneficiary is only entitled to call the guarantee in respect of losses in connection with the contract or obligation secured by the guarantee. A demand for payment in view of losses originating from other contracts or obligations, or the attempt to call all outstanding guarantees for a loss arising from just one of a series of contracts, is considered fraudulent.[167] As always, the account party must produce clear evidence of these facts. This matter has been examined in Chapter 13.2.2. There is also a risk that liquidators entrusted with the winding-up of the beneficiary indiscriminately call all outstanding guarantees.

---

partial amount which had already been paid). In *Trib. com. Paris, 20 September 1991*, D. 1992 Somm. p. 243, the beneficiary was ordered to refund the amount of the guarantee which the bank had paid at a stage where the beneficiary's fraud was not yet apparent.

[166] Cf. *Baytur SA v. Moona Silk Mills*, JBL 1985, p. 324.

[167] *Paris, 15 November 1996*, Banque et Droit 1997, No. 53, p. 51 (restraining order granted), *Trib. com. Hasselt, 2 October 1998*, TBH 1999, p. 723 (partial restraining order granted, see also No. 14-47), *Trib. com. Brussels, 26 May 1988*, JT 1988, p. 460 (restraining orders granted, see also No. 27 above). In *Trib. com. Brussels, 21 October 1986*, RDC 1987, p. 706, the beneficiary called all four performance guarantees covering four different, although related, transactions. Stop-payment orders were granted in respect of three guarantees because of clear evidence that three of the four contracts had been fully performed. Similar facts occurred in *United Trading v. Allied Arab Bank*, [1985] 2 Lloyd's Rep. 554. The Court of Appeal rejected the argument that at least three of the four transactions had been completed since there were genuine differences of opinion in respect of all four contracts.

The Concept of Fraud 385

A call is also fraudulent if it is clearly inspired by improper motives. This is illustrated in *Lyon, 17 May 1991*, where the beneficiary lodged a demand for payment which should be deemed revoked if the account party accepted modifications in the terms of the underlying contract.[168] In *Rb Amsterdam, 5 June 1997*, the call had been prompted by a high-level government agency which was further up the hierarchy than the beneficiary and which had an internal dispute with the beneficiary.[169]

14.5.13 Liquid counterclaims against beneficiary, set-off

14-49 It could be argued that it would be improper for the beneficiary to receive the full amount of the guarantee while the account party has a clear, liquid and indisputable counterclaim against the beneficiary originating from the same secured contract. If such a counterclaim is equal to or exceeds the amount of the guarantee, the case for set-off could be made with the result that the beneficiary has no right to actual payment. A few decisions appear to affirm this line of argument.[170] In most cases the plea of set-off was, however, rejected on the grounds that the counterclaim was not certain or disputed.[171] In most of these cases, there was evidence that the secured contract had

---

[168] D. 1993 Somm. p. 99. The court considered that the beneficiary's fraud was so obvious from the demand itself that both the issuing and the instructing bank should have refused payment and ruled that they were liable to the account party.

[169] KG 1997, 203. See for the facts No. 14-27.

[170] *Trib. com. Brussels, 15 April 1991*, D. 1992 Somm. p. 242 (main proceedings between account party and beneficiary had resulted in a settlement according to which the beneficiary of the guarantee was the debtor of the account party), *Cass., 10 June 1986*, D. 1987 J. p. 17 (stop-payment order against first instructing and second issuing bank granted in view of certificates of completion from the beneficiary and engineer and certificates for full payment), *Paris, 17 June 1987*, D. 1988 Somm. p. 245 (stop-payment order against the bank granted; as observed by Vasseur the evidence that no compensation was due to the beneficiary and that the beneficiary owed large amounts to the account party was rather feeble or is, at any rate, not recorded in the report of the case). In *OLG Hamburg, 7 July 1977*, WM 1978, p. 260, the defence of set-off was rejected because the counterclaim was not certain. The Court of Appeal observed that it might be different if the counterclaim was certain and beyond doubt. Canaris, No. 1151a, von Westphalen, p. 397, and Nielsen, p. 117 also recognise that the existence of a clear and liquidated counterclaim may render the demand for payment fraudulent.

[171] See, for example, *Rb Rotterdam, 11 November 1990*, KG 1990, 405, *RB Amsterdam, 7 April 1988*, KG 1988, 181, reversed on other grounds by *CA Amsterdam, 19 January 1989*, KG 1990, 74, *Rb Haarlem, 21 November 1986*, KG 1987, 57, *RB Almelo, 15 August 1984*, KG 1984, 261, *OLG Hamburg, 18 December 1981*, WM 1983, p. 188, *OLG Hamburg, 7 July 1977*, WM 1978, p. 260, *Trib. com. Paris, 12 April 1991*, D. 1992 Somm. p. 239, *Paris, 19 May 1988*, D. 1989 Somm. p. 146, *Trib. com. Brussels, 8 October 1985*, RDC 1986, p. 648, *Trib. com. Brussels, 26 November 1987*, RDC 1989, p. 97, *Trib. com. Brussels, 21 October*

not or not satisfactorily been completed. Such facts justify a demand for payment under the guarantee, while in many cases these facts also suggest that any possible counterclaim could not be certain or beyond doubt.

However, it could also be argued that the agreed reallocation of risk between account party and beneficiary, and the liquidity function of demand guarantees are frustrated if counterclaims could deprive the beneficiary from his right to receive actual payment and that the account party cannot resort to set-off as a means of remedying his omission to obtain security for payment of his counterclaim.[172] On balance, it would appear that even the existence of clear, liquid and indisputable counterclaims does not render the beneficiary's call on the guarantee fraudulent.

The beneficiary's demand for payment can certainly not be regarded as fraudulent if the account party's counterclaims, even if they are certain and liquid, originate from another contract between account party and beneficiary. This is the counterpart of the rule that the beneficiary cannot call the guarantee in respect of a contract not covered by the guarantee.

The question of whether the account party could secure a conservatory attachment or freezing order because of counterclaims against the beneficiary is discussed in Chapter 17, Nos. 17-4/5.

14.5.14 Court or arbitral decision

14-50 If a court or arbitrator, in main proceedings, pronounces the dissolution or the avoidance of the secured contract without any liability on the part of the account party or if the beneficiary's claim against the account party has been dismissed on the merits of the case, a subsequent call on the guarantee is evidently fraudulent.[173]

1986, RDC 1987, p. 706, *Trib. com. Hasselt, 2 October 1998*, TBH 1999, p. 723. See also *Continental Illinois Bank v. John Paul Papanicolaou*, IBL October 1986, p. 72.

[172] See especially *Temtex Products v. Capital Bank & Trust*, 623 F. Supp. 816 (MD La. 1985).

[173] Cf. *Trib. com. Brussels, 15 April 1991*, D. 1992 Somm. p. 242, *Trib. gr. inst. Montlucon, 9 January 1981*, D. 1981 J. p. 390, *LG Düsseldorf, 9 August 1984*, RIW 1985, p. 77, *ICC Arbitration, No. 5721/1990*, J.D.I. 1990, p. 1020, (see also Chapter 14.5.6, No. 14-36). See also *OLG Brandenburg, 15 February 2000*, WM 2001, p. 732. See further Vasseur, No. 125, Mattout, No. 230(b) and art. 19(2)(b) UNCITRAL Convention. In *BGH, 10 October 2000*, WM 2000, p. 2334, the account party obtained a temporary court order restraining the beneficiary from calling the guarantee after it had demanded payment. The beneficiary had not been summoned and was not a party in the proceedings. The court order was solely based on the statements and evidence given by the account party. In its reasoning the court, which had given the order, did not pronounce on the merits of the case, nor did it decide that the beneficiary had no right to payment or that the demand for payment under the guarantee was fraudulent. Under these circumstances the German Supreme Court held that the beneficiary's demand for payment under the guarantee was not fraudulent and that the

14.5.15 Tender guarantees

14-51 With a view to the purpose of tender guarantees the beneficiary/employer is entitled to call the guarantee if the account party/contractor withdraws his tender or if the beneficiary/employer has awarded the contract to the account party/contractor and the latter refuses to sign the contract[174] or fails to furnish a performance guarantee as stipulated in the invitation for tenders.[175] On the other hand, the beneficiary's call must be considered fraudulent if he has not awarded the contract to the account party.[176]

A problematic situation arises when the beneficiary/employer intends, in principle, to accept the contractor's tender, but with modifications. Does the beneficiary act fraudulently when he demands payment, if the account party refuses to sign a contract upon terms which deviate from his tender? According to one view, the question should be answered in the affirmative since a tender guarantee only provides protection if the contractor fails to sign a contract upon the original tender.[177] According to another view, tender guarantees also protect the employer against any kind of abusive conduct on the part of the account party/contractor during further negotiations aimed at reaching agreement on the final text of the contract. During these negotiations, the beneficiary is permitted, according to this view, to utilise the guarantee as a means of putting pressure on the contractor.[178]

It would appear that the solution lies midway between these two views: the beneficiary is entitled to call the guarantee if the account party's refusal to agree to the requested modifications is unreasonable. That would be the case if the amendments are of a minor nature, and if they do not materially prejudice the account party's position and interests. It should be noted that, given the present market conditions, contractors generally appear willing to accept rather unfavourable and harsh conditions in order to win contracts. A refusal to agree to the propositions from the beneficiary/contractor could, therefore, ordinarily be presumed not to be unreasonable. In *Cass., 2 December*

---

beneficiary did not act wrongfully by not revoking its demand for payment. In the case at hand, this issue arose in proceedings for payment initiated by the issuing bank against the instructing bank which had refused to pay under its counter-guarantee, see Chapter 16.4.2, Nos. 16-13, 16-14.

[174] See, for example, *Paris, 6 May 1986*, D. 1987 Somm. p. 175 (application for stop-payment order dismissed; the report does not mention the reasons for the account party's refusal).

[175] See, for example, *Paris, 13 December 1984*, D. 1985 I.R. p. 239, upheld by *Cass., 10 March 1987*, D. 1987 Somm. p. 172 (application for stop-payment order dismissed).

[176] *Trib. com. Lyon, 3 July 1991*, D. 1993 Somm. p. 100. See also art. 19(1)(c) and (2)(a) UNCITRAL Convention.

[177] Dubisson, Tours, p. 116, DPCI 1977, p. 429, Cabrillac/Mouly, No. 439, Schütze, RIW 1981, p. 83.

[178] Poullet, thesis Nos. 46, 47, 94, Tours, p. 32.

1997, the demand for payment by the employer was held to be fraudulent as the amendments to the contract demanded by the employer, significantly deviated from the contractor's tender and the latter refused to accept those changes.[179] *Trib. com. Paris, 29 October 1982*, chose a different, rather practical solution which, according to the court, did justice to the purpose of a tender guarantee and to the legitimate interests of both account party and beneficiary: it ordered that the guarantee sum be paid into a blocked account and that the final determination concerning the account party's liability be left to the main proceedings.[180]

14.5.16 Repayment, retention and maintenance guarantees

14-52 The general purpose of repayment guarantees is to secure repayment of advance payments, made by the beneficiary/importer, in case of non-performance. These guarantees often contain a mechanism pursuant to which the maximum amount is reduced in accordance with the progressive execution of the guarantee. The mechanism often provides for a reduction to zero when works in excess of the advance payment have been carried out. This must ordinarily be evidenced by third-party documents or by statements of approval from the beneficiary. Completion of the entire contract may then be secured by a performance guarantee.

What is the situation if the repayment guarantee does not contain such a mechanism? In particular, does the beneficiary act fraudulently if he demands payment of the full amount when works in excess of the advance payment have been carried out?[181]

---

[179] JCP 1998 Éd. E, p. 1781.

[180] D. 1983 I.R. p. 301, involving an indirect guarantee. The court ruled that the evidence of the beneficiary's fraud and the issuing bank's knowledge thereof was insufficient to justify a stop-payment order against the instructing bank, but ordered the sequestration of the counter-guarantee funds. In an unreported decision from a Belgian court of 23 March 1982, cited by Poullet, JCB 1982, p. 647, and De Smedt, IFLR December 1983, p. 20, a stop-payment order was granted on the grounds that the beneficiary/employer called the guarantee after the expiry date of the tender and because the employer's letter of intent clearly departed from the tender. See also *Lyon, 17 May 1991*, D. 1993 Somm. p. 99, discussed in No. 48.

[181] This question is answered in the affirmative by Poullet, thesis, Nos. 329, 332, Vasseur, note to *Cass., 23 October 1990*, D. 1991 Somm. p. 197 (call beyond the terms of the guarantee and the guarantee was no longer operative). See also von Westphalen, pp. 130-131. In *Rb Utrecht, 6 July 2000*, S & S 2001, 3, the call on the repayment guarantee was indeed held to be fraudulent; see No. 14-45 for the facts of this case. In *Paris, 25 May 1983*, D. 1983 I.R. p. 484, affirmed by *Cass., 11 December 1985*, D. 1986 J. 213, involving an indirect guarantee to an Iranian Government agency, a stop-payment order against the instructing and the issuing bank was granted upon evidence that goods in excess of the value of the advance payment had been shipped. This order was, however, primarily founded on other grounds, see Chapter 14.5.6, No. 14-36; *Trib. com. Paris, 7 September 1983*, D. 1987 Somm. p. 174, with a critical comment from Vasseur, granted a restraining order against the first instructing bank

First of all, the account party must establish that such partial performance up to the amount of the advance payment was perfect. The production of shipping documents, such as those tendered under a documentary credit, is not sufficient. However, even clear evidence of perfect performance up to the value of the advance payment does not necessarily establish fraud when the contract has not been fully completed.[182] The explanation is that such a partial performance does not mitigate the loss which the beneficiary suffers as a result of non-completion of the entire contract and that the repayment guarantee may also serve as a performance guarantee. In this situation a demand for payment of the full amount of the repayment guarantee could possibly be fraudulent only if the same loss is also covered by a performance guarantee.

A demand for payment in the event that the underlying contract could not be carried out because of *force majeure*, illegality, avoidance or cancellation is not fraudulent since one of the purposes of a repayment guarantee is to entitle the beneficiary to retrieve his advance payment in situations like these.[183]

Most repayment guarantees state explicitly that actual transfer of the down payment is a condition precedent. With a view to the purpose of such guarantees it would appear that a demand for (re)payment is fraudulent if the advance payment has not been effected, with or without such an explicit provision.[184]

The purpose of retention and maintenance guarantees is also to secure repayment of amounts which have been released by the beneficiary and which, without such a guarantee, would have been withheld.[185] Accordingly, these guarantees presuppose that the corresponding amounts have indeed been released and, if this has not been done, a demand for payment under the guarantee is deemed to be fraudulent.[186]

---

for similar reasons. This order was discharged in *Trib. com. Paris, January 6 1987*, D. 1987 Somm. p. 174, on the grounds that an injunction against the instructing bank could only be issued upon evidence of collusion between issuing bank and beneficiary.

[182] *BGH, 21 April 1988*, WM 1988, p. 934, *OLG Frankfurt a.M., 8 February 2000*, WM 2001, p. 1108. See also Mülbert, p. 18.

[183] See Chapter 3.5, No. 3-5. See also *Gulf Bank v. Mitsubishi Heavy Industries*, [1994] 2 Lloyd's Rep. 145 (account party's application for discharge from his liability towards the issuing bank dismissed).

[184] Bergsten, 1993 Int. Lawyer vol. 27, p. 872 note 64, in relation to art. 19 UNCITRAL Convention, Mattout, No. 212, Poullet, thesis No. 323, von Westphalen, pp. 152-154. See also *Elian and Rabbath v. Matsas and Matsas*, [1996] 2 Lloyd's Rep. 495.

[185] See Chapter 3.4 and 3.6.

[186] *Kammergericht, 3 February 1982*, BauR 1982, p. 386; *OLG Köln, 30 October 1997*, WM 1998, p. 707. In this case fraud was, however, not established in view of a dispute regarding amounts owed and owing.

14.5.17 Beneficiary's statement is false. Third-party document is forged

14-53 *Kvaerner John Brown v. Midland Bank* raises the question of whether false representations in a statement from the beneficiary, which he is required to submit as a condition of payment, renders the demand for payment fraudulent.[187] This issue is hardly relevant for general statements by the beneficiary to the effect that the account party has defaulted on his obligations under the contract. The reason is that a call on the guarantee while the account party has fully performed his obligations under the contract and, therefore, is not in default, is already a recognized type of fraud.[188] A false statement of default does not, therefore, constitute a seperate instance of fraud. In the *Kvaerner* case, however, the beneficiary had to confirm to the bank that he had given the notice as required in accordance with Article 8.3 of the secured contract, which provided that the beneficiary had to give written notice to the account party of his intent to call the guarantee 14 days prior to any call. The beneficiary had made the prescribed statement to the bank, but in fact there had been no written, but several oral notices to the account party. The court ruled that the statement was false and that the demand for payment was therefore fraudulent. It would seem, however, that, while the statement could be said to be false or, rather, incorrect, it does not by itself necessarily render the call fraudulent.[189] On the basis of the guiding principle as formulated in Chapter 14.4 this is only the case if it is established that the demand for payment has no conceivable basis under the underlying contract. The incorrect representation in the beneficiary's statement in the *Kvaerner* case was not even an indication thereof and there was no evidence that the beneficiary was not entitled to payment under the underlying contract, on the contrary. It must also be borne in mind that, unlike the documents presented under a documentary credit, the statements which a beneficiary may be required to submit in the case of a first demand guarantee, do not have an intrinsic value.

The issue of an (allegedly) false statement by the benefciairy also arose in *Balfour Beatty Civil Engineering v. Technical & General Guarantee*.[190] The beneficiary in that case had submitted a prescribed statement to the effect that the account party had defaulted on its contractual obligations and that the sum demanded was due and payable, but indicated in an accompanying letter that he called the guarantee because the account party was in liquidation. The guarantor refused payment arguing that the

---

[187] [1998] CLC 446.

[188] See Chapter 14.5.5. See, however, *Paris, 14 January 1993*, JCP 1993 Ed. G. No. 22069, mentioned in No. 14-44.

[189] Cf., for example, *Airline Reporting Corp. v. First National Bank of Holly Hill*, 832 F.2d 823 (4th Cir. 1987), *Andy Marine Inc. v. Zidell Inc.*, 812 F2d 534 (9th Cir. 1987), *First Nat'l Bank v. Carmouche*, 504 So. 2d 1153 (La. Ct. App.).

[190] [1999] 68 Con LR 180.

beneficiary's statement was fraudulent because the fact that the account party was in liquidation does not mean that it was in breach of contract or that the beneficiary had suffered a loss. The Court of Appeal rejected this defence and held that the beneficiary's statement of default was not false, liquidation being an event of default under the terms of the underlying contract, and that the demand for payment was not fraudulent.

In relation to documentary credits it is established law that the presentation of documents which have been forged by the beneficiary constitutes fraud. No doubt the same applies in respect of third-party documents of the kind discussed in Chapter 4.3 and 4.5, which the beneficiary may have to submit under an independent guarantee.[191]

14.5.18 Conclusion

14-54 Proceeding on the basis of the guiding principle as formulated in Chapter 14.4 that the beneficiary's demand for payment is fraudulent if it is clearly established that it has no conceivable basis under the underlying relationship, several instances have been examined in which the beneficiary's (apparent) right to claim payment under the guarantee might be negated. The survey of case law and legal writing suggests that a call could be fraudulent, in particular, a) in the event of completion of the contract by the account party, b) in the event of breach of fundamental obligations or serious misconduct on the part of the beneficiary, c) in the event that the guarantee has been called in relation to contracts which are not covered by the guarantee, d) in the case of a clear judgment of a competent judicial or arbitral court on the merits against the beneficiary and e) in respect of tender guarantees where the contract has not been awarded to the account party. Other situations which have been examined in Chapter 14.5 do not ordinarily amount to fraud, even apart from the aspect of clear evidence. These other situations also give rise to complex legal issues which often could not be resolved in interlocutory or summary proceedings, while in view of the liquidity function of guarantees, payment should not be delayed when its terms have been fulfilled. Moreover, a demand for payment in such other circumstances lacks the opprobrious elements which the notion of fraud seems to imply.

14.5.19 Fraud: distinction between guarantees and documentary credits?

14-55 The issue of fraud could also arise and has arisen in connection with documentary credits. English and American law, but not Continental law, deal with this issue in the same way regardless of whether the case involves a guarantee or a documentary credit. One may question whether this equation is always conducive and commendable.[192]

---

[191] See also Section 19(1)(a) UNCITRAL Convention.

[192] Cf. Eveleigh L.J. in *Potton Homes Ltd. v. Coleman Contractors*, [1984] 28 Build. L.R. 19, Schmitthoff, JBL 1977, p. 353, De Ly, TBH 1986, p. 177.

There are some important differences in the way fraud manifests itself. Fraud in documentary credits ordinarily consists of forged third-party documents or in documents with false data or other false particulars. Although fraud in the underlying transaction has been accepted as a recognised form of fraud, at least as a matter of principle, fraud in the documents is and continues to be the more typical and established manifestation of fraud. In the case of first demand guarantees, however, fraud could only exist in relation to the underlying transaction. Fraud in respect of the documents does not conflict with the principle of independence and it does not raise any particular juristic difficulties or problems concerning the commercial utility of documentary credits. The equation of documentary credits and guarantees might conceivably have induced English courts to adhere, more steadfastly than Continental courts have done, to the principle of independence in fraud cases concerning guarantees.

Courts have shown a much greater reluctance to grant interim relief on account of fraud in relation to the underlying transaction in the case of documentary credits than in the case of guarantees. On the whole, Continental law does not differ from English law in this respect. With documentary credits, fraud appears to be restricted to cases of unscrupulous and delinquent conduct of the seller and to cases where fraud in the underlying contract of sale, in fact, also constitutes fraud in the documents, as is the case when the merchandise is utterly defective.[193] There are several sound reasons why the notion of fraud in respect of documentary credits should be more rigid than in respect of guarantees. A demand for payment under a documentary credit is normal, whereas it is the exception in the case of guarantees, while the amounts at stake are usually larger. Series of financial transactions and credit facilities often depend on the normal execution of the documentary credit. If courts were more susceptible to the defence of fraud and if they were more readily inclined to intervene than they are at present, it would have a considerably more unsettling effect on the viability of documentary credits than it would have on the viability of guarantees. Moreover, the possibility of fraud with respect to first demand guarantees is much greater than the possibility of fraud in the underlying contract of sale, which does not also constitute fraud in the documents in the case of documentary credits. The above-mentioned aspects also explain why there are sound reasons not to mechanically transpose the

---

[193] *Sztejn v. Henry Schroder Banking Corp.*, 177 Misc. 719 (N.Y. Sup. Ct. 1941) (cow hair instead of expensive bristles; injunction granted), *United Bank v. Cambridge Sporting Goods*, 392 N.Y.S. 2d. 265 (1976) (old, unpadded, ripped and mildewed gloves instead of new boxing gloves; injunction granted), *NMC Enterprises Inc. v. Columbia Broadcasting Systems*, 14 UCC Rep. Serv. 1427 (N.Y. Sup. Ct. 1974) (totally worthless equipment; injunction granted). See further *BGH, 16 March 1987*, RIW 1987, p. 705, *BGH, 27 June 1988*, RIW 1988, p. 814, *OLG Frankfurt a.M., 6 October 1987*, RIW 1988, p. 905. In these three cases the courts affirmed the principle that fraud must be narrowly defined. The applications for injunctions were dismissed on the grounds that there was no clear evidence that the merchandise was totally defective.

principles developed in the context of documentary credits to independent (first demand) guarantees.

14.6 FRAUD AND SUMMARY JUDGMENT. DIRECT AND INDIRECT GUARANTEES

14-56 One of the conclusions of the comparative overview in Chapter 14.3.8 was that, with respect to applications by the account party for injunctive relief, the evidence of fraud must not only be clear or beyond reasonable doubt, but it must also be produced immediately, without in-depth and thorough investigation in protracted proceedings. This requirement of immediately available evidence of fraud also applies in situations where the bank refuses payment on the grounds of fraud and where the beneficiary sues for payment. The liquidity function of guarantees requires that once the conditions of payment have been met, judgment in favour of the beneficiary should be given forthwith, unless clear evidence of fraud is immediately available. The possibility for speedy judgments depends, however, on national rules of procedure. For example, English and German law provide for summary judgments and Dutch law for judgments in preliminary proceedings if the defendant has no arguable case.

Indeed, in *Balfour Beatty Engineering v. Technical & General Guarantee* the court observed that in summary proceedings initiated by the beneficiary against the guarantor, which refuses payment on the grounds of fraud, the same test applies as in applications for restraining orders by the account party against the guarantor and/or beneficiary. Accordingly, summary judgment against the guarantor will be given unless, based on the material available to the court within the confines of such proceedings, the only realistic inference to draw is that of fraud. As there was no such evidence, summary judgment was given against the guarantor.[194] Similar decisions in a number of cases have been given by the German Supreme Court.[195] The same rule applies in case of indirect guarantees when the issuing bank sues the instructing bank for payment in summary proceedings, as is shown in *Turkiye Is Bankasi v. Bank of China*.[196]

---

[194] [1999] 68 Con. LR 180.

[195] See, e.g., *BGH, 28 October 1993*, WM 1994, p. 106, *BGH, 17 October 1996*, WM 1996, p. 2228, *BGH, 2 April 1998*, WM 1998, p. 1062, *BGH, 24 January 2002*, WM 2002, p. 555, *BGH, 5 March 2002*, WM 2002, p. 743. In all these case summary judgment was given against the bank as there was no immediately available clear evidence of fraud. See also *Continental Illinois Nat. Bank v. John Paul Papanicolaou*, IBL October 1986, p. 72, where the court expressly noted that protracted proceedings would defeat the object of first demand guarantees. See also *Solo Industries v. Canara Bank*, [2001] 2 Lloyd's Rep. 578, where the court distinguished between a defence by the bank which related to the validity of the guarantee itself and a defence on the grounds of fraud, which is subject to the strict test of immediately available evidence of fraud, see further Chapter 13.2.12, No. 13-32.

[196] [1996] 2 Lloyd's Rep. 611, CA [1998] 1 Lloyd's Rep. 250 (summary judgment against instructing bank).See further Chapter 16.4.2 for the notion of fraud by the issuing bank.

CHAPTER 15
FRAUD AND THE POSITION OF THE BANK. BANK'S LIABILITY IN 'AFTER-PAYMENT' CASES

15.1 DIRECT GUARANTEE

If fraud is evident to the bank, it is liable to the account party when it pays under the guarantee

15-1 Case law[1] and legal writing[2] in all jurisdictions concerned confirm the principle that *if* fraud by the beneficiary is evident to the bank it owes a duty to the account party to refrain from payment. If the bank disregards this duty, it incurs liability towards the account party, which for all practical purposes means that it forfeits its right of

---

[1] See, for example, *CA Amsterdam, 30 March 1972*, NJ 1973, 188, *Rb Amsterdam, 18 December 1980*, S & S 1981, 135, *CA Amsterdam, 5 February 1987*, NJ 1988, 591, *CA Amsterdam, 4 February 1993*, KG 1993, 113, *CA The Hague, 8 June 1993*, KG 1993, 301, *LG Frankfurt a.M., 11 December 1979*, NJW 1981, p. 56, *LG Dortmund, 9 July 1980*, WM 1981, p. 280, *LG Stuttgart, 8 August 1980*, WM 1981, p. 633, *OLG Stuttgart, 11 February 1981*, WM 1981, p. 631, *OLG Saarbrücken, 23 January 1981*, RIW 1981, p. 338, *Kammergericht, 20 November 1986*, NJW 1987, p. 1774, *OLG München, 6 May 1987*, WM 1988, p. 1554, *OLG Bremen, 14 June 1990*, WM 1990, p. 1369, *OlG Köln, 15 March 1991*, RIW 1992, p. 145, *Trib. com. Brussels, 11 March 1981*, BRH 1981, p. 361, *CA Brussels, 4 January 1989*, TBH 1990, p. 1073, *Cass., 12 December 1997*, JCP 1998 Éd. E, p. 1781, *Trib. com. Nanterre, 14 March 1991*, D. 1992 Somm. p. 241, *Lyon, 17 May 1991*, D. 1993 Somm. p. 99, *Trib. com. Lyon, 3 July 1991*, D. 1993 Somm. p. 100, *Harbottle v. Nat. Westminster Bank*, [1977] 2 All ER 862, *Edward Owen v. Barclays Bank Int.*, [1978] 1 All ER 976, *United Trading v. Allied Arab Bank*, [1985] 2 Lloyd's Rep. 554, *Tukan Timber v. Barclays Bank*, [1987] 1 Lloyd's Rep. 171, 177, *Deutsche Ruckversicherung AG v. Walbrook Insurance Co*, [1994] 4 All ER 181, *Csarnikow-Rionda v. Standard Bank* London, [1999] 2 Lloyd's Rep. 187, 202, *Grenoble, November 12 1987*, D 1988 Somm. p. 247. See No. 15-2 last paragraph for the position in the United States.

[2] See, for example, Mijnssen, pp. 54-58, Croiset van Uchelen, WPNR 1989, p. 272, Prüm, No. 441, Vasseur, No. 119, von Westphalen, pp. 358-360, 389, Zahn/Ehrlich/Neumann, 9/84, 9/125-126, Staudinger/Horn, No. 35, 333, Nielsen, pp. 113-115, Canaris, No. 1140, Mülbert, pp. 94-95, 98-103, Zahn/Ehrlich/Neumann, 9/125-126, Coing, ZHR 1983, pp. 134-139, Kleiner, Nos. 21.41-21.53, Dohm, Nos. 226, 241-243, Wymeersch, TPR 1986, p. 500, Simont, Rev. Banque 1983, pp. 597-598.

reimbursement and that the bank is not allowed to debit the customer's accounts. The banks's knowledge of fraud must exist at the time of payment.[3]

The aforementioned liability arises from the bank's ancillary duty to carry out the contract of mandate in good faith and with due care. Discharge of this duty does not conflict with the bank's obligations towards the beneficiary. If fraud has been established, the beneficiary has no right to demand payment and the bank is entitled to refuse payment. Moreover, no one is entitled or obliged to assist in fraudulent practices by third parties.[4]

Distinction between 'before-' and 'after-payment' cases. Extent of the bank's duty and potential liability

15-2 Proper assessment of the practical significance and impact of the principle stated in No. 15-1 is promoted by making a clear distinction between the two elements which the principle encompasses: on the one hand, the rule which merely states that *if* fraud is evident to the bank it must refrain from payment, and, on the other hand, the rule that the bank is liable when it has proceeded to payment while the beneficiary's fraud was or must have been evident to the bank.

The second element has no function in applications for interlocutory restraining orders against the bank since the object of such proceedings is not to determine liability of the bank but to prevent payment by the bank in cases of established fraud. The first element might possibly perform a meaningful function in such proceedings, namely in order to establish a cause of action against the bank. This aspect will be explored in Chapter 16.3.1. The second element, namely the liability rule, only becomes relevant if the bank has actually proceeded to payment and seeks recourse from the account party. Thus, the significance of the principle stated in No. 15-1 in preventive stop-payment proceedings is different from that in proceedings between bank and account party after payment by the bank in which the account party argues that the bank should not have paid.

---

[3] *Trib. com. Marseille, 19 September 1991*, D. 1992 Somm. p. 243, *Paris, 18 March 1986*, D. 1987 Somm. p. 173, *United Trading v. Allied Arab Bank*, [1985] 2 Lloyd's Rep. 554, *Group Josi v. Walbrook* Insurance, [1996] 1 WLR 1152, 1161, Turkiye *Is Bankasi v. Bank of China*, [1996] 2 Lloyd's Rep. 611, [1998] 1 Lloyd's Rep. 250, *Csarnikow-Rionda v. Standard Bank London*, [1999] 2 Lloyd's Rep. 187, 202, Bank *of Nova Scotia v. Angelica Whitewear*, Supreme Court of Canada, March 11 1987, JIBL 1987, N-52. See also *Trib. gr. inst. Paris, January 26 1983*, D. 1983 I.R. p. 297.

[4] Thus, explicitly, *LG Frankfurt a.M., 11 December 1979*, NJW 1981, p. 56, and *LG Dortmund, 9 July 1980*, WM 1981, p. 280. See also Schoordijk, WPNR 1976, p. 680, Mülbert, pp. 94-95, p. 101.

In the proceedings last-mentioned, so-called 'after-payment' cases, liability of the bank has repeatedly been rejected on the grounds that the beneficiary's call was not fraudulent or, if so, that the bank had no actual or constructive knowledge thereof.[5] *Trib. com. Marseille, 19 September 1991*, is a most illustrative example. The beneficiary of an indirect guarantee obtained payment, whereafter the issuing bank received reimbursement from the instructing bank which debited the accounts of the account party. The account party subsequently obtained a court judgment in main proceedings in which the beneficiary's call was held to be fraudulent and the beneficiary was ordered to repay the amount collected under the guarantee. The account party sought, however, to recover it from his (the instructing) bank. This claim was rejected because there was no evidence that, at the time of payment, the issuing bank was aware of the beneficiary's fraud and even less evidence that the instructing bank had clear knowledge of the beneficiary's fraud and the issuing bank's awareness thereof.[6] The point is that the significance of the principle relating to the bank's liability is thoroughly – and quite correctly – eroded by the premise that the beneficiary's fraud must have been evident to the bank prior to payment. Courts are extremely reluctant to accept that such a situation has occurred, and this reserve is understandable and fitting.

The principle that the bank should not pay *if* fraud is evident does not imply a duty which obliges the bank to pursue any particular active course of action in cases of (alleged) fraud. In fact, the only and recurrent observations that can be found in case law and legal writing negate the existence of obligations of this nature. Thus, there are countless statements to the effect that the bank is not concerned with the underlying relationship or with disputes and differences of opinion between account party and beneficiary, that the bank owes no duty to enquire or to decide on the (im)propriety of the beneficiary's demand for payment and that it is for the account party to adduce clear and convincing evidence of fraud and to dispel any doubts in this respect.[7] In

---

5   See, for example, *CA Amsterdam, 30 March 1972*, NJ 1973, 188, *Kammergericht, 20 November 1986,** NJW 1987, p. 1774, *OLG München, 6 May 1987*, WM 1988. p. 1554, *Cass., 13 December 1983,** D. 1984 J. p. 420, *Trib. gr. inst. Paris, 26 January 1983*, D. 1983 I.R. p. 297, *Paris, 13 February 1987,** D. 1987 Somm. p. 172, *Paris, 10 July 1992*, D. 1993 Somm. p. 100, *Brussels, 18 December 1981,** Rev. Banque 1982, p. 99, *Grenoble 12 November 1987*, D. 1988 Somm. p. 247, and other decisions cited in Chapter 15. In the cases marked with an asterisk the dismissal of the account party's claim was primarily based on lack of evidence of the beneficiary's fraud.

6   D. 1992 Somm. p. 243. The same decision on similar facts was reached in *Cass., 25 March 1991*, D. 1991 Somm. p. 202, and *Paris, 18 March 1986*, D. 1987 Somm. p. 173 (see also Chapter 13.2.2, No. 13-10).

7   See, for example, *CA Amsterdam, 30 March 1972*, NJ 1973, 188, *CA Amsterdam, 5 February 1987*, NJ 1988, 591, *CA Amsterdam, 4 February 1993*, KG 1993, 113, *CA The Hague, 8 June 1993*, KG 1993, 301, *BGH, 17 October 1996*, WM 1996, p. 2228, *OLG Schleswig, 6 December 1983*, WM 1984, p. 651, *OLG Saarbrücken, 23 January 1981*, RIW 1981, p. 338,

Turkiye Is Bankasi v. Bank of China this basic principle was put this way: 'It is simply not for the bank to make enquiries about the allegations that are being made one side against the other. If one side wishes to establish that a demand is fraudulent it must put the irrefutable evidence in front of the bank. It must not simply make allegations and expect the bank to check whether those allegations are founded or not', and 'It is not the role of a bank to examine the merits of allegations and counter allegations of breach of contract. To hold otherwise would place banks in a position where they would in effect have to act as courts in deciding whether to make payment or not'.[8]

In short, fraud and the clear evidence of it is the account party's, not the bank's concern and risk. Moreover, the account party must adduce clear evidence of fraud within a short period of time, since the bank cannot be expected to unduly delay payment in view of its obligations to proceed to payment forthwith once the terms of the guarantee have been met.[9]

The above expositions are consistent with Section 5-109 paragraph 2 of the American UCC. In substance it states that, in the event of material fraud, the issuer, acting in good faith, may honour or dishonour a request for payment. Accordingly, the bank has a discretionary power. Official Comment 2 explains that, merely because the issuer has a right to dishonour, it does not mean that it has a duty to the account party to

---

OLG Stuttgart, 25 January 1979, RIW 1980, p. 729, *LG Braunschweig, 22 May 1980*, RIW 1981, p. 789, *OLG Köln, 7 August 1986*, WM 1988, p. 21, *Kammergericht, 20 November 1986*, NJW 1987, p. 1774, *OLG München, 6 May 1987*, WM 1988, p. 1554, *Brussels, 25 February 1982*, JCB 1982, p. 349, *Trib. com. Brussels, 26 May 1988*, JT 1988, p. 460, *Brussels, 26 June 1992, 1994, p. 51, Cass., 18 December 1990*, D. 1991 Somm. p. 197, *Paris, 18 March 1986*, D. 1987 Somm. p. 173, *Paris, 13 February 1987*, D. Somm. p. 172, *Aix-en-Provence, 19 January 1995*, Banque et Droit 1995, No. 43, p. 30, *Harbottle v. Nat. Westminster Bank*, [1977] 2 All ER 862, *Edward Owen v. Barclays Bank Int.*, [1978] 1 All ER 976, *Howe Richardson Scale v. Polimex-Cekop*, [1978] 1 Lloyd's Rep. 161, *United Trading v. Allied Arab Bank*, [1985] 2 Lloyd's Rep. 554, *Royal Bank v. Darlington*, [1995] O.J. No. 1044 ('there was no duty on the [issuer] to embark upon inquiries beyond a careful examination of the ... materials provided [by the account party], acting honestly and in good faith in their capacity as bankers in doing so'). See also, for example, Bertrams, WPNR 1999, pp. 706-711, Mijnssen, pp. 25, 54-58, Croiset van Uchelen, WPNR 1989, p. 272, von Westphalen, pp. 196-203, 247-248, 359, Zahn/Ehrlich/Neumann, 9/84, 9/126, Mülbert, pp. 99-100, Dohm, Nos. 241-243, Kleiner, No. 21.53, Bark, ZIP 1982, p. 413, Wymeersch, Hague-Zagreb Essays 6, p. 105, Mattout, No. 240, Stoufflet, Garantie Bancaire Internationale, No. 65, Simont, Rev. Banque 1983, pp. 597, 598, Jeffery, [2002] 18 B.F.L.R. p. 94. With a view to the legitimate interests of the bank Coing, ZHR 1983, p. 139, Nielsen, ZIP 1982, p. 260, and von Mettenheim, RIW 1981, p. 586, allow the bank a certain degree of discretion when deciding whether or not the account party has adduced clear evidence of fraud.

[8] [1999] 2 Lloyd's Rep. 611, 617.

[9] Cf. Von Westphalen, pp. 206, 248. See also Chapter 13.2.9.

dishonour. The reason for this and the bank's discretion in this respect is that a bank is ordinarily unable to determine whether or not the account party has adduced clear evidence of material fraud and that it, therefore, needs protection. The account party's normal recourse is, as the Official Comment notes, to procure an injunction. The bank's only duty is to act in good faith, which is a subjective test. Accordingly, if the bank determines in good faith that the evidence of fraud is insufficient, it is entitled to pay in its relationship with the account party. On the other hand, if the bank considers the evidence adequate, it would not act in good faith if it were to honour a demand for payment.[10]

Bank's knowledge of the beneficiary's fraud. The test

15-3 Since knowledge of the beneficiary's fraud is a mental condition, evidence in this respect can only be inferred and courts can only decide on the basis of constructive knowledge. However, one should not arrive too readily at a finding that the bank must have been aware of the beneficiary's fraud, quite the contrary. At any rate, it is commendable that judgments relate the facts upon which the inference of knowledge is based.

The bank cannot, ordinarily, possess knowledge of fraud unless the account party produces convincing evidence thereof before payment. It is, therefore, vital that the account party makes his complaints and supporting documents known to the bank (see No. 15-2). The evidence must be clear and unambiguous such that the ordinary, prudent and diligent bank ought to have appreciated, on the strength of the material before it, that the beneficiary's call was fraudulent, or, which is basically the same test, such that the only realistic inference for the bank to draw was that of fraud.[11] In other words, the account party might not have left the bank with any doubts in respect of the impropriety of the beneficiary's call. This is a very severe test, and there is no room for laxness in favour of the account party.

Courts are most reluctant to give judgment in favour of the account party and against the bank (see No. 15-2) and examples of decisions in which the bank has been held liable are extremely rare. *Trib. com. Lyon, 3 July 1991*, is such an instance. In relation to a tender guarantee, the account party had presented the bank with clear evidence that the beneficiary had not awarded the contract to him and nonetheless called the guarantee, while the bank ignored the evidence and chose to proceed to payment with

---

[10] Cf. Dolan, § 7.05[1].

[11] Cf. *Trib. com. Brussels, 26 May 1988*, JT 1988, p. 460, *Paris, 14 December 1987*, D. 1988 Somm. p. 248, Banque 1988, p. 236, *United Trading v. Allied Arab Bank*, [1985] 2 Lloyd's Rep. 554, *Turkiye Is Bankasi v. Bank of China*, [1996] 2 Lloyd's Rep. 611, [1998] 1 Lloyd's Rep. 250. See also von Westphalen, pp. 247-248.

a view to its reputation.[12] *Cass., 2 December 1997*, provides another example.[13] In this case the bank was fully aware of the fact that the employer/beneficiary of a tender guarantee had demanded from the contractor amendments to the contract which significantly deviated from the contractor's tender and which the contractor refused to accept.

Appraisal and suggestions for an alternative set of rules

15-4 The difficulty with the rule that the bank is liable to the account party *if* it has paid while the beneficiary's fraud was, or must have been, evident is not that it is possibly incorrect – it is correct – but that it leaves the bank with a certain risk which it should not be responsible for. An unavoidable consequence of the principle is that the bank is forced to make a decision on the question of whether a case of established fraud has presented itself. An affirmative answer might subsequently be found to be wrong and may render the bank liable to the beneficiary while a decision in the negative might also subsequently be overturned in its relationship with the account party. It is true that case law and legal writing clearly indicate that this risk is not likely to materialise, but the possibility of actual liability can never be discarded.[14] This is an awkward prospect. Moreover, as is apparent from Chapter 14 the concept of fraud remains complex while the difficulties concerning evidence do not so much relate to the content of the rule (the evidence must be clear and unambiguous) but to the actual application thereof to concrete cases. How, then, and in which circumstances, can it be said that the bank was or must have been aware of the beneficiary's fraud? The crux of the matter is that it is unfair to burden the bank with this kind of decision and the inherent risks in matters which are not its concern while, at the same time, it is inappropriate to allow the account party to leave the prevention of fraud in the hands of the bank.[15]

There is an alternative set of rules which accommodates the legitimate interests of the bank and customer more evenhandedly. It is submitted that the bank can never be liable to the account party in cases of (alleged) fraud if it notifies the account party of the demand for payment and if it postpones payment for a few days, should the account party furnish plausible evidence of fraud. This interval allows the account party to initiate interlocutory proceedings in order to prevent payment on the basis of a

---

[12] D. 1993 Somm. p. 100, see also Chapter 16.5, No. 16-24. See also *Lyon, May 17 1991*, D. 1993 Somm. p. 99, involving an indirect guarantee, see Chapter 15.2, No. 15-6.

[13] JCP 1998 Éd. E, p. 1781.

[14] In fact, certain German decisions and authors emphasise the bank's (potential) liability which is put forward as an argument against injunctions against the bank, see Chapter 16.3.1.

[15] Cf. *Turkiye Is Bankasi v. Bank of China*, as quoted in No. 15-2, and Bertrams, WPNR 1999, pp. 706-711.

court judgment. If the account party does not apply for a restraining order within this short period of time, the bank is entitled to proceed to payment because, in that situation, fraud can never be said to be evident and because further delays would conflict with the bank's obligations to the beneficiary. This procedure has several advantages. The right person, namely the account party, is to take the initiative to prevent fraudulent practices and the right body, namely the court, will decide whether fraud has been established. The bank knows exactly how it is supposed to act and it is relieved from the necessity to make decisions which it should not be expected to make. Moreover, the bank can maintain its neutral position. The recommended procedure has the further advantage that it is aimed at the prevention of fraud. The liability aspect of the principle becomes relevant only after payment by the bank, i.e. when the fraud has materialised. It then merely transfers the loss from the account party to the bank while the beneficiary is still in possession of the proceeds he should not have received.

These suggestions are not revolutionary at all. They accord very well with what happens in actual practice. They are akin to the 1995 Revised Section 5-109 (a)(2) UCC: 'the issuer, acting in good faith, may honor or dishonor the presentation in any other case' (in the event of (alleged) fraud other than in the situations mentioned in (a)(1)), to which the Official Comment adds that it is the normal course for the account party to apply for an injunction. Accordingly, the Revised Section 5-109(b) allows the account party to obtain a restraining order against the bank in the event of established fraud. Similarly, art. 19 UNCITRAL Convention entitles the bank, as against the beneficiary, to withhold payment, while art. 20 permits the account party to obtain restraining orders against the beneficiary and/or bank if fraud is evident. Several decisions in which the account party's complaint against the bank was rejected can very well be explained in the light of the observations and suggestions outlined above. It seems that the dismissals are founded not only on the test relating to the bank's knowledge but also on an assessment of the propriety of the bank's conduct in the light of the circumstances and its duties towards both account party and beneficiary, and the account party's conduct.[16]

---

[16] In the case of *CA Amsterdam, 30 March 1972*, NJ 1973, 188 (indirect guarantee), the first instructing bank had not proceeded voluntarily to reimbursement of the issuing bank but its accounts had been debited. In *Trib. gr. inst. Paris, 26 January 1983*, D. 1983 I.R. p. 297, the bank had postponed payment but eventually proceeded to payment since the beneficiary had tendered the correct third-party documents, while the account party did not commence interlocutory proceedings. The court considered it irrelevant that subsequently an arbitral award was rendered against the beneficiary and was in favour of the account party. In *Grenoble, 12 November 1987*, D. 1988 Somm. p. 247, (indirect guarantee), the first instructing bank notified the account party of the request for payment and postponed payment upon the complaints of the account party who announced that he intended to initiate interlocutory proceedings. As he did not do so, at least not within a reasonable period, and as he failed to substantiate his allegations, the instructing bank then proceeded to payment. See Chapter 13.2.2, No. 13-10, for the facts of *Paris, 18 March 1986*, D. 1987 Somm. p. 173.

15.2 INDIRECT GUARANTEE

Issuing bank's liability

15-5 The principles relating to the bank's liability in 'after-payment' cases, outlined in Chapter 15.1, also apply to the issuing bank in the case of an indirect guarantee. The issuing bank's duty to the account party to refrain from payment and its liability when it proceeds to payment *if* the beneficiary's fraud was, or should have been, evident to the issuing bank at the time of payment, is founded on the general duty of care towards the account party, and not on a contractual duty since there is no contractual relationship between the issuing bank and the account party.[17] Questions relating to the foreign issuing bank's knowledge in respect of the beneficiary's fraud usually arise in the context of applications for restraining orders against the first instructing bank in respect of the counter-guarantee in favour of the issuing bank. These aspects will, therefore be examined in Chapter 16.4.2.

Instructing bank's liability

15-6 If the foreign issuing bank has honoured the beneficiary's demand for payment and the instructing bank has reimbursed the issuing bank, and if the account party takes the view that the instructing bank should not have paid because of fraud, he must establish not only the beneficiary's fraud and the issuing bank's awareness thereof at the time of payment, but also the instructing bank's knowledge concerning the foregoing at the time of honouring the counter-guarantee, i.e. knowledge that the call on the counter-guarantee by the issuing bank was also fraudulent. Discharge of this burden of proof is virtually impossible, see, for example, *CA Amsterdam, 30 March 1972*,[18] *Cass., 7 June 1994*,[19] *Cass., 3 March 1991*,[20] and *Trib. com. Marseille, 19 September*

---

[17] Cf. *United Trading v. Allied Arab Bank*, [1985] 2 Lloyd's Rep. 554, *Paris, 26 February 1985*, D. 1985 I.R., p. 244, *Paris, 3 April 2002*, D. Affaires 2002, p. 1750, Canaris, No. 1119a, Mülbert, p. 142. The dogmatic foundation of the issuing bank's liability in the case of an indirect guarantee has been thoroughly analysed in German legal writing, see Chapter 16.4.2, No. 16-13. In *GKN Contractors v. Lloyds Bank*, [1985] 30 BLR 48, and especially in *Csarnikow-Rionda v. Standard Bank london*, [1999] 2 Lloyd's Rep. 187, it was doubted whether the account party has a cause of action against the issuing bank in the case of an indirect guarantee.

[18] NJ 1973, 188.

[19] D. 1995 Somm. p. 21.

[20] D. 1992 Somm. p. 202. Although the instructing bank had expressed its doubts regarding the appropriateness of the call on the primary guarantee and the counter-guarantee, there was insufficient evidence at the time of payment that the issuing bank had knowledge of the beneficiary's fraud and that the instructing bank had certainty in this respect.

1991.[21] However, *Lyon, May 17 1991*, provides a rare example of a case where the court gave judgment in favour of the account party and against the instructing bank. The court ruled that the beneficiary's fraud and the issuing bank's knowledge thereof should have been evident to the instructing bank without any investigation into the underlying transaction, as it was immediately apparent from the issuing bank's request for payment. This stated that it should be deemed revoked if the account party agreed to modifications in the terms of the underlying contract, which was considered a kind of blackmail.[22]

15.3 BANKING PRACTICE

15-7 Although case law and legal writing correctly define the bank's responsibilities in cases of (alleged) fraud in a restrictive manner (see No. 15-2), it must not be assumed that banks always adopt an aloof and uncooperative attitude. They consider their customer's interests to be their concern too. If presented with plausible evidence of fraud, banks are often willing to postpone payment, to act as an intermediary between account party and beneficiary and to assist in attempts to sort out misunderstandings or differences of opinion. However, they are in general not inclined to take a position as far as the merits of the complaints from either side are concerned. If the beneficiary persists in his demand for payment, they will usually take the view, against their customer, that they must proceed to payment. On the other hand, practice shows that banks, when confronted with strong evidence of fraud, sometimes overtly allude to the possibility of the customer applying for stop-payment injunctions. Towards the beneficiary they could, then, plead the court's decision as a shield and excuse for non-payment. It should also be noted that, in such situations, the bank's attitude is guided not only by the general reputation of customer and beneficiary, but also by its interests in not straining its relationship with those who are of vital importance to the bank's business. Thus, for example, banks tend to respond to situations involving a direct guarantee in favour of a beneficiary in country X in a different way than to situations involving an indirect guarantee and counter-guarantee in favour of a beneficiary and correspondent bank in country Y. At any rate, cases are known involving direct and indirect guarantees in which the (instructing) bank refused payment because it was convinced of the fraudulent nature of the demand.

---

[21] D. 1992 Somm. p. 243, see No. 15-2.
[22] D. 1993 Somm. p. 99.

CHAPTER 16
FRAUD AND RESTRAINING ORDERS

16.1 INTRODUCTION

General

16-1 Chapter 16 focuses on several aspects of applications for restraining (or stop-payment) orders against the beneficiary and bank(s) on the grounds of fraud. The purpose of these applications is to prevent payment. They are made in proceedings known as provisional, interim, preliminary or interlocutory proceedings (*kort geding, einstweilige Verfügung, procédure en référé*). Injunctions granted in such proceedings are provisional in the sense that they can be set aside in main proceedings. However, the party which feels aggrieved by the decision will ordinarily prefer to initiate interlocutory appeal proceedings in order to have the decision in the first instance reversed. Unlike applications for conservatory attachment orders, see Chapter 17, applications for restraining orders in the Netherlands and Germany cannot be made without the defendant having been summoned and given an opportunity to defend himself. Temporary *ex parte* injunctions are, however, possible under English and American law of procedure, but they are always followed within a short period of time by an *inter partes* hearing in which the initial *ex parte* injunction is reviewed in the light of the defendant's arguments.[1] In Belgium and France temporary *ex parte* injunctions are only permitted in very exceptional circumstances.

Questions concerning the concept of fraud and the issue of evidence thereof will not be considered, since they have been dealt with in Chapter 14. It is sufficient to repeat that a restraining order may be issued only if the account party produces clear and convincing evidence of fraud and he must be able to do so immediately for two reasons: first, interlocutory proceedings do not allow for lengthy and protracted hearings and, secondly, the purpose of independent (demand) guarantees is to give the beneficiary a right to immediate payment once the conditions for payment have been fulfilled, unless fraud can be established forthwith. It is also for these two reasons that a court in interlocutory proceedings will not investigate the underlying transaction in depth and detail. If this were necessary, a court would be more inclined to conclude

---

[1] In *Boliventer Oil v. Chase Manhattan Bank*, [1984] 1 WLR 392, Sir John Donaldson MR issued a special warning against *ex parte* injunctions.

that the evidence of fraud is not clear and liquid and that the application must be dismissed.[2]

Restraining orders against the bank and especially restraining orders against the instructing and/or issuing bank in the case of indirect guarantees raise additional problems. These will be examined in Chapter 16.3 and 16.4.

16.2 APPLICATIONS FOR RESTRAINING ORDERS AGAINST THE BENEFICIARY, DIRECT GUARANTEE

16-2 Applications for orders to restrain the beneficiary from demanding or receiving payment on the grounds of fraud do not give rise to special objections or difficulties, apart from, of course, the basic rule that the account party must immediately adduce clear and convincing evidence of the beneficiary's fraud.[3]

In the past, several authors have suggested that, compared to applications for stop-payment orders against the bank, the chances of securing restraining orders against the beneficiary are more promising. With respect to the latter proceedings, they argue, first, that the position of the bank need not be considered and, secondly, that the incursion on the principle of independence is less problematic and that the test with respect to evidence of fraud could be less stringent.[4] The same approach is voiced in *Themehelp Ltd. v. West and Others*,[5] and in *Potton Homes v. Coleman Contractors*.[6] While the first argument is correct, the second one is liable to foster misunderstandings. Any suggestion that the principles of independence and of the test for the evidence of fraud in the

---

[2] See the summary in Chapter 14.3.8. It is noted that, in contrast to European procedures, interlocutory proceedings in the U.S.A. could last for a period of days and involve a series of hearings.

[3] See Chapter 13.2.7, No. 13-23 last paragraph, for the effect of a discharge of a previous restraining order after the expiry date of the guarantee.

[4] Bartman, WPNR 1989, p. 601, NJB 1987, p. 1090, Mijnssen, pp. 26-27, Betalingsverkeer, pp. 71-72, Blomkwist, WPNR 1986, pp. 552-553, Croiset van Uchelen, WPNR 1989, pp. 271-272. See also *CA Amsterdam, 19 January 1989*, KG 1990, 74, where the court observed that '*as between account party and beneficiary* [italics added] the guarantee had ceased to be valid and that the beneficiary was, therefore, no longer entitled to payment under the guarantee.' See for this decision also Chapter 13.2.7, No. 13-23.

[5] [1996] QB 84. The Court of Appeal granted an interlocutory injunction against the beneficiary since, according to the majority judgment, the account party had an *arguable* case at trial that fraud was the only realistic inference. The evidence of fraud was, in fact, rather weak. In his strong dissenting opinion, Evans L.J. noted that the fraud exception would not be available if an injunction against the bank had been requested. See for a comment Goodliffe, [1995] 9 JIBL, p. 405.

[6] [1984] 28 Build. L.R. 19.

relationship between account party and beneficiary have a meaning and effect different from the principles of independence and evidence of fraud in the relationship between bank and beneficiary or between account party and bank is erroneous. One must not forget that the idea of 'pay first, argue later' and all other conditions of payment – and especially the absence thereof – as contained in the contract of guarantee between bank and beneficiary represent the agreement between the account party and beneficiary concerning the allocation of risks between them.[7] Accordingly, apart from the fact that in proceedings against the bank other aspects might have to be considered too, the circumstances which render a call fraudulent, as well as the stringent requirements in respect of the evidence of fraud, are the same in both procedures. This is explicitly confirmed in a number of German decisions,[8] by Phillips J. in *Deutsche Ruckversicherung AG v. Walbrook Insurance Co*,[9] and by Staughton LJ in *Group Josi v. Walbrook Insurance* who obeserved that 'the effect on the life blood of commerce will be precisely the same whether the bank is restrained from paying or the beneficiary is restrained from asking payment.[10] This is also the case under art. 20 UNCITRAL Convention which does not distinguish between applications for restraining orders against the bank or beneficiary.

16.3 APPLICATIONS FOR RESTRAINING ORDERS AGAINST THE BANK, DIRECT GUARANTEE.

Must the beneficiary's fraud be evident to the bank? Cause of action. Are restraining orders against the bank permissible?

Introduction

16-3 Pursuant to the general principles of law, applications for restraining orders are based on the existence of a cause of action against the defendant. In the case of applications by the account party for stop-payment orders against the bank, the plaintiff's cause of action could only be the bank's (imminent) breach of its duty to desist from

---

[7] See Chapter 6.
[8] *OLG Köln, 30 October 1997*, WM 1998, p. 707, OLG *Düsseldorff, 9 August 2001*, WM 2001, p. 2294.
[9] [1994] 4 All ER 181, 196-197.
[10] [1996] 1 Lloyd's Rep. 345, at 361. Idem: Rix J. in *Csarnikow-Rionda v. Standard Bank London*, [1999] 2 Lloyd's Rep. 187, at 202, *Kvaerner John Brown v. Midland Bank*, [1998] CLC 446. Recent case law in the Netherlands, Belgium and France does not distinguish either between applications for restraining orders against the bank and beneficiary. The same applies to the United States of America, see Dolan, § 7.04[4][f].

payment if the beneficiary's fraud is evident to the bank.[11] The question then arises of whether knowledge on the part of the bank of the beneficiary's fraud is a crucial issue and whether evidence of such knowledge is required in applications for a restraining order against the bank for preventive relief in 'before-payment' cases.[12] A second question relates to the permissibility of restraining orders against the bank. It could, and has been argued, that such orders are never permitted because the account party's loss in the event of established fraud does not result from payment by the bank itself but from the debiting of his accounts. The approach to these two issues is different in various jurisdictions.

For clarity's sake, it is repeated that it is for the account party to adduce clear evidence of fraud and that the bank is not expected to investigate the (im)propriety of the demand for payment.[13]

England

16-4 With respect to applications for restraining orders against the bank, English courts have consistently required some proof that the beneficiary's fraud is or must be deemed to be evident to the bank, this constituting the cause of action against the bank.[14] In several cases the focus of the court's attention was directed rather at evidence in this respect than at evidence of the beneficiary's fraud itself. This was especially the case in *Edward Owen v. Barclays Bank Int.*[15] and in *Boliventer Oil v. Chase Manhattan Bank*,[16] where the court accepted that fraud of the beneficiary was clearly arguable, but concluded that it was not evident to the bank. In his judgment in *United Trading v. Allied Arab Bank*, Ackner L.J., however, mainly addressed the question of whether clear evidence of the beneficiary's fraud was available.[17] As he answered this question in the negative, Ackner L.J. could confine himself to the observation that there was no hint of dishonesty on the part of the bank. In *Group Josi Re v. Walbrook Insurance* it was also suggested that, by way of exception to the general rule, a substantive cause of action

---

[11] See Chapter 15.1.

[12] See Chapter 15.1, No. 15-2 for the distinction between 'before-payment' and 'after-payment' cases. Knowledge of the beneficiary's fraud on the part of the second issuing bank in the case of indirect guarantees will be examined in Chapter 16.4. For the sake of convenience, the issue concerning the first instructing bank's knowledge of the beneficiary's fraud and of the involvement of the second issuing bank is also dealt with in Chapter 16.3.1.

[13] See Chapter 15, No. 15-2.

[14] See Chapter 14.3.6 for references and citations.

[15] [1978] 1 All ER 976.

[16] [1984] 1 WLR 392.

[17] [1985] 2 Lloyd's Rep. 554, see further Chapter 14.3.6.

against the bank may not be necessary in applications for restraining orders for the purpose of preventive relief.[18] However, the requirement that the beneficiary's fraud is known to the bank was strongly reaffirmed in the recent case of *Csarnikow-Rionda v. Standard Bank* by Rix J. who rejected the suggested wider principle that 'the source of the power to injunct (the bank, R.B.) is the law's interest in preventing the beneficiary from benefiting from his own fraud'. He observed that if that view were correct, there would indeed be no need for 'the added requirement that the fraud be patent to the bank'.[19] While the requirement of the bank's knowledge of the beneficiary's fraud is firmly established in English case law, there is an interesting observation by Phillips J. in *Deutsche Ruckversicherung v. Walbrook Insurance Co:* 'Evidence of the bank's knowledge of fraud is academic once the proceedings have reached the *inter partes* stage. At this point, the evidence of fraud will be placed simultaneously before the court and before the bank which is party to the proceedings. If the court concludes that there is clear evidence of fraud, it will necessarily conclude that the bank has acquired knowledge of the fraud.'[20] According to this view, evidence regarding the bank's knowledge does not pose an additional threshold and is, in fact, irrelevant in applications for preventive restraining orders. Interestingly, this is precisely the approach in case law in other jurisdictions. The observation by Phillips J. has, however, attracted little attention in subsequent English cases.

With respect to applications for restraining orders against the instructing bank in the case of indirect guarantees, courts seem to require evidence that the beneficiary's fraud is evident to the second issuing bank as well as to the first instructing bank.[21]

Even if the account party has succeeded to provide clear proof of the beneficiary's fraud and the bank's awareness thereof, there is a further test for the grant of a restraining order against the bank: the balance of convenience. While in general this test entails various considerations depending on the circumstances, two of them are particularly important. If damages would be a sufficient remedy for the account party, no injunction against the bank would ordinarily be granted. Apart from this, it must be considered whether the grant of a restraining order would do more harm than refusing it. In *Harbottle v. Nat. Westminster Bank*, Kerr. J. observed that, if the bank were indeed to breach its duty to refrain from payment in a case where it was aware of the beneficiary's fraud, restraining orders against the bank would still be inappropriate because such orders

---

[18] [1996] 1 WLR 1152, at 1160.

[19] [1999] 2 Lloyd's Rep. 187, 197, 203 *et seq.*

[20] [1994] 4 All ER 181, 195.

[21] See, for example, *Harbottle Ltd. v. Nat. Westminster Bank*, [1977] 2 All ER 862, [1978] QB 146, *Edward Owen v. Barclays Bank Int.*, [1978] 1 All ER 976, *Boliventer Oil v. Chase Manhattan Bank*, [1984] 1 WLR 392, *Csarnikow-Rionda v. Standard Bank*, [1999] 2 Lloyd's Rep. 187.

interfere with the bank's unconditional obligations and especially because the account party would then have an adequate remedy against the bank in damages.[22] This has become known as the 'insuperable difficulty' in the way of the granting of an injunction against the bank. In *Tukan Timber v. Barclays Bank*, which involved a documentary credit, Hirst J. was prepared to accept that this was one of those very rare cases of established fraud, namely the presentation of forged documents, but nevertheless rejected the application for a restraining order against the bank for the same reasons as those advanced by Kerr. J. in the *Harbottle* case.[23] Kerr. J. also expected that the bank, who had already refused payment on two previous occasions, would scritinise the documents with the utmost care, should the seller attempt to obtain payment again, observing that if the bank were to pay on documents which the bank knew were forged, the account party would have a 'cast-iron' claim against the bank. The application of the balance of convenience test was again as a matter of principle thoroughly considered by Rix J. in *Csarnikow-Rionda v. Standard Bank*.[24] He left no doubts that the availability of an ordinary claim for damages against the bank militates against the granting of a restraining order against the bank, but he also referred to the strong policy of not interfering with the bank's unconditional obligations to pay, this being the lifeblood of international commerce. He, therefore, rejected the view that the source of the power to injunct the bank is the law's interest in preventing fraud by the beneficiary. Nonetheless, Rix. J. did not entirely rule out the possibility of an injunction against the bank.[25]

The conclusion with respect to English law should be that even if the account party were to succeed in clearly establishing fraud by the beneficiary, thus bringing him within the fraud exception, and even if such fraud were known to the bank, applications for a stop-payment order against the bank would fail on the balance of convenience test. It should be noted, however, that, with the possible exception of the *Tukan Timber* case, in none of the cases had the courts to deal with a case of established fraud. They

---

[22] [1977] 2 All ER 862, [1978] QB 146 at 155. This second argument also troubled Ackner L.J. in the *United Trading* case.

[23] [1987] 1 Lloyd's Rep. 171.

[24] [1999] 2 Lloyd's Rep. 187 at 197 *et seq.* and 202-206.

[25] 'I do not know that it can be affirmatively stated that a Court would never, as a matter of balance of convenience, injunct a bank from making payment under its letter of credit or performance guarantee obligations in circumstances where a good claim within the fraud exception was accepted by the Court at a pre-trial stage. I do not regard Mr. Justice Kerr and the other Courts which have approved or applied the logic of his 'insuperable difficulty' as necessarily saying that it could *never* be done. It is perhaps wise to expect the unexpected, even the presently unforeseeable', [1999] Lloyd's Rep. at 204. Other reasons for the refusal to grant an injunction in this case on the balance of convenience was the grant of a freezing order against the beneficiary, see further Chapter 17, No. 17-9.

either found that there was no evidence of the beneficiary's fraud or they considered a decision on this point unnecessary because the granting of an injunction against the bank would be refused anyway because of the absence of proof of the bank's knowledge of fraud or, if there were such proof, because of the balance of convenience. The only exception to this clear pattern in case law is *Kvaerner John Brown v. Midland Bank*. In this case an injunction against the bank was granted without attention being given to the bank's knowledge of the beneficiary's fraud and the test of the balance of convenience.[26]

Germany

16-5 A substantial part of German legal writing takes the view that the account party, even in the event of established fraud, could never successfully apply for orders restraining the bank from effecting payment to the beneficiary.[27] They argue that the account party lacks a proper interest in such measures because his interests are not impaired by the bank effecting payment to the beneficiary, but by the bank seeking reimbursement from the account party. If, however, the bank were to pay while the beneficiary's fraud was evident to the bank, the account party has a cause of action against the bank in damages which prevents the latter from claiming reimbursement. This approach is, therefore, the same as expounded in English case law, see No. 16-4. Some of them also point out that, while the bank is entitled to refuse payment in the event of established fraud, it cannot be prohibited from proceeding to payment, since that would conflict with the independent nature of its undertaking, its international standing and its discretionary power to decide whether or not to pay, notwithstanding its liability to the account party.

A major part of German legal writing does accept the possibility of preventive restraining orders against the bank on the grounds that, in the event of established fraud, the bank is obliged to refrain from payment in view of its ancillary duty to the account party to act in good faith and with due care.[28] Preventive relief against the bank is

---

[26] Q.B. [1998] 446. Moreover, the evidence and the nature of the beneficiary's fraud was rather doubtful, see Chapter 14.5.17.

[27] Zahn/Ehrlich/Neumann, 9/143, Goerke, p. 135, Jedzig, WM 1988, p. 1471, Heinsius, FS Werner, pp. 239-248, Aden, RIW 1981, p. 441, von Mettenheim, RIW 1981, pp. 585, 587, Coing, ZHR 1983, pp. 135-139, Trost, ZIP 1981, pp. 1307-1308.

[28] Von Westphalen, pp. 286-296, Nielsen, pp. 122-128, Canaris, Nos. 1140, 1025, Mülbert, pp. 93-146, Lohmann, pp. 125-130, Hein, NJW 1981, p. 58, Horn, NJW 1980, p. 2152, Schütze, RIW 1981, p. 85, Schwericke and Regel, WM 1991, p. 1753, Dohm, Nos. 355-373, Horn and Wymeersch, p. 512. And see especially because of its more recent date: Lienesch, p. 174-175, Lienesch, DZWIR 2000, pp. 492, 496-497, Edelmann, DB 1998, pp. 2453-2458, Horn, Nos. 583-586, Staudinger/Horn, Nos. 336-337, Heymann/Horn, Handelsgesetzbuch, Kommentar, Bd. LV, Anh. Zu 372, Bankgeschäfte V, Rdn. 70.

viewed as the necessary corollary of the bank's duty to refrain from payment in the event of established fraud. They also argue that, in the event of established fraud, it is inexpedient to condone payment to the beneficiary and they point to the practical difficulties for the account party to challenge the bank's right to reimbursement because the bank is usually in a position to debit the customer's accounts.

The question of whether, in applications for preventive relief against the bank, the account party is required to show that the bank is aware of the beneficiary's fraud has not been answered unequivocally. One author refers to clear evidence of the beneficiary's fraud only, and there is no suggestion that the bank's awareness of fraud has any particular bearing on applications for restraining orders against the bank.[29] Three other authors who extensively analyse the prerequisites for such preventive injunctions reiterate the well-established principle that *if* fraud is evident to the bank it is entitled, as well as obliged, to refuse payment, which constitutes the cause of action, and that it is for the account party to adduce evidence of the beneficiary's fraud.[30] Their references to the bank's knowledge of fraud have to be appreciated in this context. It is clearly their view and that of other German writers that applications for preventive restraining orders against the bank are, in effect, to be decided on the basis of clear evidence of the beneficiary's fraud to the satisfaction of the court, irrespective of the question of whether or not the account party succeeds in establishing that the beneficiary's fraud is also evident to the bank.[31]

Until 1987, the predominant view of German case law favoured the possibility of preventive restraining orders against the bank.[32] The approach to the issues under review is the same as that of the authors mentioned in the two previous paragraphs. Evidence of knowledge on the part of the bank of the beneficiary's fraud appears to be immaterial for the purposes of preventive relief.[33]

---

[29] Dohm, cited above.

[30] Von Westphalen, Nielsen and Mülbert, cited above.

[31] See especially Mülbert, pp. 136-138, p. 146, Lienesch and Horn, both cited above. See also von Westphalen, pp. 294, 315 (the account party must present the bank, and thereby the court, with clear evidence of fraud).

[32] See, for example, *OLG Saarbrücken, 23 January 1981*, RIW 1981, p. 338, *OLG Frankfurt a.M., 3 March 1983*, WM 1983, p. 575, *LG Frankfurt a.M., 11 December 1979*, NJW 1981, p. 56, *LG Dortmund, 9 July 1980*, WM 1981, p. 280, *LG Stuttgart, 8 August 1980*, WM 1981, p. 633, *LG Braunschweig, 22 May 1980*, RIW 1981, p. 789, *LG Köln, 11 December 1981*, WM 1982, p. 438, *OLG Franfurt a.M., 3 March 1983*, WM 1983, p. 575, LG *Düsseldorf, 9 August 1984*, RIW 1985, p. 77. In *OLG Köln, 7 August 1986*, WM 1988, p. 21, the Court of Appeal declined to take a position since a ruling in this respect was not necessary for the decision. Contra: *OLG Stuttgart, 11 February 1981*, WM 1981, p. 631, *LG München, 30 January 1981*, WM 1981, p. 416.

[33] Only *OLG Saarbrücken, 23 January 1981*, RIW 1981, p. 338 (application dismissed because fraud had not been established), and *LG Frankfurt a.M., 11 December 1979*, NJW

There appears to be a change of attitude in case law as from 1987. In 1987 *OLG Frankfurt a.M.*, in 1991 *OLG Köln,* and in 1999 *OLG Düsseldorf* ruled against the possibility of preventive injunctions against the bank on the grounds mentioned in the first paragraph of No. 16-5.[34] Accordingly, payment in the face of established fraud results in a cause of action which is limited to the bank forfeiting its right of repayment from the account party, but the bank cannot be enjoined from proceeding to payment. These decisions are significant because of their recent date and because they were issued by appelate courts. In view of the criticisms of these decisions,[35] it is still uncertain whether they have finally settled the law to the extent that preventive restraining orders against the bank are impossible. It should also be noted that in none of these cases had the court determined that fraud had been sufficiently established.

1981, p. 56 (application granted) contain a seemingly casual reference to knowledge of the instructing bank in the case of an indirect guarantee. This, however, played no significant part in the court's reasoning and decision. Moreover, in the Frankfurt case the bank had stated that it did not doubt the account party's contention regarding the beneficiary's fraud.

[34] *OLG Frankfurt, 27 April 1987,* WM 1988, p. 1480, *OLG Köln, 15 March 1991,* RIW 1992, p. 145, *OLG Düsseldorf, 14 April 1999,* ZIP 1999, p. 1518. The *OLG Frankfurt* decision was also based on the fact that the beneficiary had not been summoned although, as the court observed, the requested restraining order against the bank primarily affected the position of the beneficiary. The question of whether there was established fraud remained undecided. In the *OLG Köln* decision it was certain that the bank could not pay because of the UN resolution against Iraq, as was confirmed by the bank. In the *OLG Düsseldorf* case the allegations of fraud had been rejected and in concurrent proceedings judgment was given in favour of the beneficiary. While the issue did not need to be decided because there was no established fraud *OLG Bremen, 14 June 1990,* WM 1991, p. 1751, observed that, although the bank is obliged to refuse payment, it is doubtful whether the account party has the right to enjoin the bank to pay. See also *LG Dortmund, 5 April 1988,* WM 1988, p. 1695, although the court in this case recognised the possibility of interlocutory restraining orders against the bank, provided that the beneficiary is joined as co-defendant.

[35] Von Westphalen, pp. 291-292, Schwericke and Regel, WM 1991, p. 1753, Lienesch DZWIR 2000, pp. 492, 496-497. See also Mankowski, EwiR 1998, pp. 833-832, and Edelmann, DB, 1998, pp. 2454-2456 (who suggests, as an alternative, that an application for an order restraining the bank from debiting the account party's account should certainly succeed). In some recent text books, such as Lienesch (1999), Staudinger/Horn (1997) and Horn (2001), the view that restraining orders against the bank are allowed, is still presented as the prevailing one. Moreover, Horn, No. 586, mentions several appelate decisions in the period 1991-1994 (OLG Frankfurt a.M., NJW-RR 1991, p. 174, OLG Frankfurt a.M., BB 1993, p. 96, OLG Stuttgart, NJW-RR 1994, p. 1204) in relation to the traditional suretyship, in which the possibility of restraining orders against the bank was recognised.

The Netherlands

16-6 The possibility of preventive stop-payment orders against the bank in the event that the account party succeeds in producing clear evidence of fraud has never been doubted in Dutch case law or legal writing.

While in the past certain authors might possibly have taken the view that, in applications for preventive restraining orders against the bank, the account party must also demonstrate that the beneficiary's fraud is evident to the bank,[36] the curent view is that such evidence is not required in 'before-payment 'cases.[37] This approach is in line with Dutch case law. Dutch courts merely refer to the rule that the bank must refrain from payment in the event of established fraud and, then, proceed to examine whether the account party has indeed succeeded in furnishing clear evidence of the beneficiary's fraud or, in the case of indirect guarantees, clear evidence of the beneficiary's fraud and the second issuing bank's involvement therein. Applications for restraining orders against the bank do not turn on the question of whether the beneficiary's fraud is also evident to the (instructing) bank.[38]

France and Belgium

16-7 French and Belgian case law, as well as legal writing, recognise the possibility of stop-payment orders against the bank in the event of established fraud. Interestingly, the Court of Appeal in *Brussels, 5 April 1990*, explicitly rejected the arguments levelled against such measures.[39]

As regards the question of whether the beneficiary's fraud or, in the case of indirect guarantees, the beneficiary's fraud and the second issuing bank's involvement therein should be evident to the (instructing) bank, French and Belgian case law follow the same patterns as Dutch case law and that part of German legal writing which allows preventive restraining orders against the bank. In short, evidence of the (instructing) bank's awareness of fraud is not required in 'before-payment' applications for injunctive relief.[40] As a matter of fact, French and Belgian courts do not refer to the cause of

---

[36] Croiset van Uchelen, WPNR 1989, p. 272, Blomkwist, WPNR 1986, p. 552, Bartman, NJB 1987, pp. 1089-1090.

[37] Bertrams, WPNR 1999, pp. 706-711.

[38] Exceptionally, *CA Amsterdam, 4 February 1993*, KG 1993, 113, did, however, refer to the issue of the (instructing) bank's knowledge of fraud, but the Court of Appeal did not need to elaborate on this aspect since there was no established fraud on the part of the beneficiary.

[39] TBH 1992, p. 82. See also Cabrillac/Mouly, No. 444.

[40] In *Trib. com. Brussels, 26 May 1988*, JT 1988, p. 460, the court, when granting a stop-payment order against the instructing bank, did pay attention to this bank's awareness of fraud. However, the court was evidently content with a kind of imputed awareness. *Trib. com. Brussels, 30 January 1990*, TBH 1992, p. 84, is the only other example in which the

action against the bank when hearing applications for restraining orders against the bank. This issue has not attracted attention in French and Belgian legal writing either.

United States of America

16-8 The possibility of restraining orders against the bank in the event of established fraud has always been recognised in American case law and legal writing.[41] This is also confirmed in Section 5-109(b) of the 1995 Revised Article 5 UCC. Apart from satisfying the criteria for material fraud and the evidence thereof,[42] two additional requirements for injunctive relief must be met. The first requirement for injunctive relief concerns 'irreparable harm' to the account party, i.e. the injury the account party would suffer if a preliminary injunction is denied on account of the fact that he would be unable to effectively recover his loss from the beneficiary. The second test involves 'the balance of convenience', i.e. would the injury to the account party, if the application for preliminary relief were dismissed, outweigh the harm which granting the injunction would inflict on the defendants? These criteria are rather flexible and elusive and could, therefore, be applied by the courts with quite divergent results. This is illustrated in the Iranian cases. While the principles for preliminary relief continued to be the same, a marked contrast in the actual application of these criteria could be seen in the decisions dating from before and after the taking hostage of U.S. citizens in November 1979. In three pre-hostage cases, *American Bell Int. v. Islamic Republic of Iran*,[43] *KMW International v. Islamic Republic of Iran*[44] and *United Technologies Corp. v. Citibank*[45] the applications were denied on all criteria.[46] After the seizure of American citizens, at least fifteen applications for preliminary relief were filed. Two of them

---

court alluded to the (instructing) bank's knowledge of fraud as a requirement for a stop-payment order against the (instructing) bank.

41   See extensively Dolan, § 7.04, and Wunnicke/Wunnicke/Turner, § 8.04[C].
42   See Chapter 143.7, Nos. 14-14/16.
43   474 F. Supp. 420 (S.D.N.Y. 1979).
44   606 F. 2d. 10 (2d. Cir. 1979)
45   469 F. Supp. 473 (S.D.N.Y. 1979)
46   As far as the notion of fraud is concerned, the courts adopted a narrow view while setting high standards for the degree of evidence. The contention of irreparable harm was rejected for the reason that the account party had more or less accepted this risk and/or because litigation for recovery of the loss before Iranian courts had been agreed to and was not considered to be totally impracticable. In respect of the second criterion, the courts opined that the hardship to the banks, consisting in the impairment of their credibility in the international banking community and in possible measures of retaliation, clearly outweighed the hardship to the account party who, as between two innocent parties, must bear the consequences of the contract he has chosen to undertake.

were denied,[47] at least thirteen were granted.[48] It is worth noting that the surrounding facts of the cases and the conduct of the Iranian beneficiaries and U.S. exporters were quite the same as those of earlier cases.[49] These 'less strict' cases are not, however, representative of current case law,[50] and can only be explained with a view to the political turmoil at that particular period of time.

In respect of applications for restraining orders against the bank, the question of whether the bank is aware of the beneficiary's fraud has never been regarded as a relevant issue.

UNCITRAL Convention

16-8a Art. 20 UNCITRAL Convention recognises the possibility of restraining orders against the beneficiary and/or bank on the basis of immediately available strong evidence that the beneficiary's demand for payment has no conceivable basis, as further described in art. 19. In addition, the court should take into account whether in the absence of such order the account party would be likely to suffer serious harm. The bank's knowledge of the beneficiary's fraud is not a relevant issue.

Summary and evaluation

16-9 Dutch, French, Belgian and American courts have always accepted the possibility of restraining orders against the bank in the event of established fraud and, what is

---

[47] One of them, *Werner Lehara Int . v. Harris Trust & Sav. Bank*, 484 F. Supp. 65 (W.D. Mich. 1980) on the grounds that no demand for payment had been made.

[48] *Itek Corp. First Nat. Bank*, 730 F. 2d. 19 (1st. Cir. 1984), *Harris Corp. v. Nat. Iranian Radio and Television*, 691 F. 2d. 1344 (11th. Cir. 1982), *Rockwell Int. Systems v. Citibank*, 719 F. 2d. 583 (2d. Cir. 1983), *Touche Ross & Co. v. Manufacturers Hanover Trust*, 449 N.Y.S. 2d. 125 (N.Y. App. Div. 1982), *Wyle v. Bank Melli*, 577 F. Supp. 1148 (N.D. Cal. 1983). Eight restraining orders were delivered without a written opinion, which is an indication of the comparative ease with which these orders were granted. These cases are listed by Zimmett, Law & Policy Int. Business 1984, p. 944, note 81.

[49] The courts either adopted a less stringent view of fraud or did not bother to pronounce on the precise meaning thereof. This attitude is also revealing for the standard of proof, since the evidence adduced was no more compelling than it had been in the pre-hostage cases. In fact, the courts made no utterances in respect of the standard of proof and confined themselves to perfunctory remarks that the evidence was sufficient to support a conclusion that there was a substantial likelihood of prevailing on the merits. The account parties also succeeded on each of the two other criteria. Moreover, in the *Itek* and *Harris* cases the court also observed that public interest and the utility of (standby) letters of credit would not be disserved by granting preliminary restraining orders under the circumstances of the case.

[50] See the overview in Wunnicke/Wunnicke/Turner, § 8.04[c].

more, are prepared to put this principle into practice if an appropriate case presents itself (which is rare). This possibility is also recognised in the 1995 Revised Section 5-109(b) UCC and in art. 20 UNCITRAL Convention. While the possibility of restraining orders against the bank has not been definitely rejected, English courts and, in the most recent decisions, German courts have for all practical purposes eliminated the actual application of such a possibility, partly for the same reasons. This significant difference in approach can be explained on the grounds that Dutch, French, Belgian and American courts, but also courts in most other jurisdictions, have recognised that a restraining order against the bank in the event of established fraud is the most effective means of preventing fraud by the beneficiary, while English and German courts have not adopted this broader policy. This difference has a bearing on two other aspects, namely the question of the cause of action and the possibility of an alternative adequate remedy against the bank on the basis of the balance of convenience.

As a general rule all jurisdictions require a cause of action against the party to be injuncted. With respect to applications for restraining orders against the bank the cause of action would be the bank's (imminent) breach of duty to desist from payment if the beneficiary's fraud is evident to the bank. However, the courts in most jurisdictions consider it pointless to require the account party to also adduce evidence of the bank's knowledge of the beneficiary's fraud. First, such evidence is only relevant in 'after-payment' cases where the liability of the bank towards the account party is at issue.[51] In contrast, proceedings for preventive stop-payment orders against the bank are not meant to have the bank's liability to the account party determined but aim at the prevention of wrongdoing, i.e. by the beneficiary. Dutch, French, Belgian and American courts, but also the courts in most other jurisdictions, except English courts, therefore direct their attention to the question of whether the account party has succeeded in producing clear evidence of the beneficiary's fraud to *their* satisfaction, instead of to the bank's satisfaction. This is also the case in Germany. Secondly, once the court is satisfied in this respect, it would be odd to expect it then to dwell on the question of whether the beneficiary's fraud is also evident to the bank, which is a party to the proceedings.[52] As Phillips J. in *Deutsche Ruckversicherung AG v. Walbrook Insurance Co* aptly put it, (evidence of) the bank's knowledge of the beneficiary's fraud is an academic issue in applications for preventive restraining orders once that fraud has been established to the satisfaction of the court.[53]

Unlike the courts in most other jurisdictions, English and, in the most recent cases, German courts reject restraining orders against the bank on the grounds that, if the

---

[51] See Chapter 15, No. 15-2.

[52] In *Bank of Nova Scotia v. Angelica Whitewear*, [1987] 1 S.C.R. 59 (S.C.C.), the Supreme Court of Canada explicitly distinguished between preventive orders against the bank and 'after-payment' claims against the bank, in the same way as expressed in the text.

[53] [1994] 4 All ER 181, 195. See also Bertrams, WPNR 1999, pp. 706-711.

beneficiary's fraud were known to the bank at the time of payment, the account party has an ordinary remedy against the bank for damages which is considered to be adequate. This approach is most unfortunate and highly impracticable, while the argument that the account party's interests are not prejudiced by the bank's payment to the beneficiary is unconvincing. Upon payment, the bank will debit the accounts of its customer and the latter occupies an inferior, and needlessly uncomfortable, position during the often protracted proceedings for recovery from the bank. This may severely damage his liquidity position. Should the account party succeed in establishing the beneficiary's fraud but fail to demonstrate the bank's awareness thereof at the time of payment, which is required in 'after-payment' cases,[54] he loses the case. The result is that, even in cases of established fraud on the part of the beneficiary, the account party is left with a loss which could have been avoided. Should the account party succeed on both counts, the loss will merely be shifted from the account party to the bank while the true perpetrator of the fraud, namely the beneficiary, is still in possession of the proceeds which he should not have received in the first place.[55]

One may also doubt whether the impossibility of restraining orders against the bank on the basis of the balance of convenience and the policy of not interfering with the bank's independent obligations, does indeed enhance the position of the bank. In this approach, it is for all practical purposes the bank which is left with the decision to decide whether the account party has produced clear evidence of fraud. Remarkably, this is precisely what Waller J. in *Turkiye Is Bankasi v. Bank of China* warned against.[56] Moreover, if the bank were to proceed to payment, there remains the risk that it might subsequently be found liable to the account party on the grounds that the fraud should have been obvious to the bank. On the other hand, if the bank were inclined to refuse payment, it might feel, rightly or wrongly, that such a decision would jeopardise its reputation. There would, however, be no cause for embarrassment if the bank's refusal flowed from a court injunction on the basis of the court's determination with respect to established fraud by the beneficiary.

Lastly, the great reluctance of English courts to allow injunctions against the bank because it would interfere with the bank's *independent* obligation towards the beneficiary, does not seem to be very convincing. It is a well established rule, also in English case law, that the principle of independence allows for an exception in the case of established fraud.

---

[54] See Chapter 15, No. 2.

[55] This situation has occasioned a needless discussion among German writers on whether the bank is entitled to recover its loss from the beneficiary.

[56] [1996] 2 Lloyd's Rep. 611, at 617: 'It is not the role of a bank to examine the merits of allegations and counter allegations of breach of contract. To hold otherwise would place banks in a position where they would in effect have to act as courts in deciding whether to make payment or not'. See also Chapter 15.1, No. 15-2.

Applications for restraining orders against beneficiary and bank is the better procedure

16-10 It is only natural that account parties seek to secure restraining orders against the bank since such orders are a most effectual means of preventing fraud by the beneficiary. However, a cogent argument against applications for restraining orders against the bank alone is that they are addressed to the wrong party.[57] What the account party is complaining of is not so much the bank's imminent breach of duty, but the fraud which the beneficiary is about to commit. This is also recognised by the courts, judging from their emphasis on evidence concerning the beneficiary's conduct. Consequently, why should the bank be implicated in proceedings in a matter which is not its concern, but the concern of the account party and the beneficiary? Moreover, the account party's application against the bank is, in fact, aimed at the beneficiary. Banks are, therefore, fully justified in challenging the propriety of these applications.

A second difficulty is that proceedings against the bank concentrate predominantly on the beneficiary's conduct and that any ruling in favour of the account party, and against the bank, affects primarily the position of the beneficiary, while he is not a party to the proceedings and not given an opportunity to defend himself. It is true that the beneficiary is not bound by a restraining order against the bank but the practical effect of such an order is much the same, since it constitutes a valid defence for the bank to refuse payment.[58] The absence of the beneficiary also poses problems for the courts. They are asked to pronounce on the beneficiary's allegedly improper conduct, without being able to hear his views. Under these circumstances, courts might be even more reluctant to be persuaded by the evidence presented by the account party alone. Accordingly, the account party may well jeopardise his own chances when omitting to summon the beneficiary as well.[59] On the other hand, if the beneficiary were properly summoned and given a fair chance to argue his case, a court might be more favourably disposed should the beneficiary choose not to appear or if his arguments lack any substance.[60]

---

[57] *LG Dortmund, April 5 1988*, WM 1988, p. 1695, Bertrams, WPNR 1999, pp. 706-711, Pabbruwe, p. 53, Nielsen, p. 119, Kleiner, No. 22.05. See also von Westphalen, pp. 366-367.

[58] Cf. *Paris, 26 July 1985*, D. 1986 I.R. p. 157, *OG Austria, 24 March 1988*, JIBL 1988 N-154. Under English law, payment by the bank in the face of a restraining order constitutes contempt of court.

[59] The fact that the beneficiary had not been summoned was one of the reasons why *OLG Frankfurt, 27 April 1987*, WM 1988, p. 1480, *LG Dortmund, 5 April 1988*, WM 1988, p. 1695 and *Paris, 2 March 1990*, D. 1990 somm. p. 209, dismissed the application for a restraining order against the bank.

[60] See the statements of Denning M.R. in *Etablissement Esefka Int. Anstalt v. Central Bank of Nigeria*, [1979] 1 Lloyd's Rep. 445, and the statements of Ackner L.J. in *United Trading v. Allied Arab Bank*, [1985] 2 Lloyd's Rep. 554, with respect to the inference of guilt to be

In conclusion, applications for restraining orders against both the beneficiary and bank are unquestionably the better procedure.[61] Indeed, in the case of *Rb Amsterdam, 5 June 1997*, where the account party applied for a restraining order against the bank only on the grounds of fraud by the beneficiary, the court ordered the account party in an interlocutory judgment to also summon the foreign beneficiary in order to enable that party to present its view.[62] If, upon clear evidence of fraud, a restraining order against the beneficiary is granted, a stop-payment order against the bank could then be added as a logical sequel, in order to confer full efficacy on the first measure and in order to clarify the position of the bank. A further advantage of this procedure is that, if the beneficiary does appear, the bank could defer to the court's judgment and, thereby, maintain its neutral position. This often happens. Banks might also feel more at ease if they could refuse payment on the strength of a court order.

16.4 APPLICATIONS FOR RESTRAINING ORDERS IN RESPECT OF INDIRECT GUARANTEES AND COUNTER-GUARANTEES

16.4.1 General

Restraining orders against instructing and/or issuing bank and/or beneficiary. Cause of action

16-11 In the case of indirect guarantees, it is advisable for reasons mentioned in No. 16-10 not only to apply for injunctions against the instructing bank, but also against the foreign issuing bank and the beneficiary of the primary guarantee. As regards the foreign issuing bank, the account party could apply for an order restraining that bank from demanding or receiving payment under the counter-guarantee and/or for an order to restrain payment under the primary guarantee. With respect to the beneficiary, the account party could request an order to restrain the beneficiary from demanding or receiving payment under the primary guarantee.

Courts have, ordinarily, jurisdiction to hear cases against the foreign issuing bank and beneficiary, especially if the local instructing bank has been made co-defendant.[63]

---

drawn from the beneficiary's failure to outline his defence without any justification. However, as has also been observed by Ackner L.J., a beneficiary (and also the second foreign bank) of an indirect guarantee may decline to submit to the jurisdiction of foreign courts for quite understandable and valid reasons. See also *OLG Saarbrücken, 23 January 1981*, RIW 1981, p. 338.

[61] Cf. *LG Dortmund, 5 April 1988*, cited above, *OLG Franfurt, 27 April 1987*, cited above. See further Bertrams, WPNR 1999, pp. 706-711.

[62] KG 1997, 203.

[63] See Chapter 18.1, No. 18-4.

Fraud and Restraining Orders 421

There is, however, the difficulty of whether a court has jurisdiction *ratione materiae* to issue injunctions which only take effect abroad, as is the case with respect to orders restraining the foreign issuing bank from paying under the primary guarantee and orders restraining the foreign beneficiary from demanding or receiving payment under the primary guarantee.[64] Nonetheless, the advantage of summoning the foreign beneficiary is that he is enabled to present his views. This is also important in relation to applications for restraining orders concerning the counter-guarantee.

Certain English cases suggest that the foreign issuing bank owes no duty of care towards the account party and that the account party has, therefore, no cause of action against the issuing bank.[65] This would preclude any possibility of obtaining a restraining order against the issuing bank, even apart from all other severe obstacles to be examined hereafter. This is not the position in other jurisdictions.

Beneficiary's fraud and foreign applicable law

16-12 German doctrine in particular expresses the view that the issue of the beneficiary's fraud, in the case of indirect guarantees, must be determined in accordance with foreign law, namely the local law governing the relationship between the foreign issuing bank and the foreign beneficiary.[66] This view seems sound and logical. However, the actual significance of private international law and of foreign applicable law should not be overestimated.[67] As far as reported case law dealing with (alleged) fraud in cases involving indirect guarantees – which totals at least ninety decisions – is concerned, courts very rarely bother to raise the issue of applicable law. It is even more significant that those courts which perfunctorily noted that the primary guarantee was governed by foreign law, evidently applied their own, but not necessarily provincial, notions of fraud.[68] The explanation is, no doubt, that the law with respect to independ-

---

64 See Chapter 16.4.3, No. 16-17.

65 *Csarnikow-Rionda v. Standard Bank London*, [1999] 2 Lloyd's Rep. 187, *GKN Contractors v. Lloyds Bank*, [1985] 30 BLR 48, but see *United Trading v. Allied Arab Bank*, [1985] 2 Lloyd's Rep. 554.

66 Von Westphalen, pp. 245-247, 252-255, 297, 360-364, Lienesch, pp. 154-156, Nielsen, p. 130, Zahn/Ehrlich/Neumann, 9/127-129, Canaris, No. 1139a, Mülbert, pp. 87-91, Heinsius, FS Werner, pp. 248-249, Heldrich, FS Kegel, pp. 187-194, ZHR 1983, p. 155, Bark, ZIP 1982, pp. 412-413, von Mettenheim, RIW 1981, pp. 584-586. Idem: Dohm, Nos. 285, 288, Kleiner, No. 21.70, Prüm, No. 479, De Ly, Rev. Banque 1990, p. 172.

67 See also Chapter 18.2, No. 5.

68 This is especially obvious in German, English and American (but also in some Dutch and Belgian) decisions which are scattered with references to national case law, legal writing and (German) statutory provisions. Vasseur, RDAI 1992, No. 31, p. 265, also observes that courts apply their own notions of fraud. But see *OG Austria, 10 July 1986*, JIBL 1986 N-140, where the Austrian Supreme Court upheld a ruling that the application for preventive

ent (demand) guarantees is very much characterised by its transnational nature and that the principles of fraud in relation to such guarantees are strikingly similar.[69] The application of foreign law in respect of fraud may also be dispelled on the grounds of public policy.[70] Moreover, litigation in cases of (alleged) fraud predominantly turns on evidence, and the standards in this respect also display a striking uniformity.

It would also be unrealistic to require the account party to adduce reliable and unambiguous evidence with respect to the contents of the foreign domestic law in relation to the specific facts of the case, or to expect the court to pass judgment on that basis. While most jurisdictions have developed general principles with respect to fraud and perhaps even some more specific rules – which are most likely to be similar – it would be too much to expect that each jurisdiction disposes of a comprehensive, detailed and unambiguous set of rules which is capable of resolving each and every situation. Moreover, the law in certain regions tends to be customary law, without proper records of decisional law. This renders the law highly inaccessible. One must simply ask oneself what would be likely to happen if, for example, a Dutch court were to endeavour to apply, for example, Sudanese law on fraud in the context of guarantees.[71] In conclusion, in the absence of reliable and unambiguous information on the foreign domestic law concerning fraud in the context of guarantees, the more realistic and workable approach is to presume that the law in respect of fraud is uniform. A clear example of this approach is *CA Leeuwarden, 12 September 1990*.[72] This presumption is, however, counterbalanced by the stringent requirements concerning evidence of fraud. Thus, positive indications to the effect that the foreign applicable law takes a more restrictive

---

restraining orders in interlocutory proceedings was to be dismissed since the court could not determine the issue of fraud without knowledge of Iraqi law.

[69] See Chapter 14.3.8. See also Coing, ZHR 1983, pp. 133, 139-144, who argues that in view of the transnational nature of bank guarantees the specific notion of fraud in the context of guarantees should not be derived from the general notion of fraud as it exists in domestic law, but from an autonomous and transnational appraisal. This view is absolutely correct and this is precisely what courts have done.

[70] *LG Frankfurt a.M., December 11 1979*, NJW 1981, p. 56, *LG Dortmund, July 9 1980*, WM 1981, p. 280, expressly rejected the application of foreign law if divergent from the law of the forum on the grounds of public policy. See also BGHZ 104, 240, ZIP 1988, p. 765, and Staudinger/Horn, No. 307. *OG Austria, July 10 1986*, JIBL 1986 N-140, ruled that foreign law should not be applied if it is incompatible with the basic tenets of the Austrian legal system.

[71] It is also noted that affidavits from local experts drawn up upon the request of each of the litigants are sometimes unreliable and/or contradictory. See also von Westphalen, p. 298.

[72] KG 1990, 316. The Court of Appeal observed that, while the primary guarantee was governed by Egyptian law, it nonetheless applied Dutch law since there were no indications that Egyptian law deviates from Dutch law. (This part of the decision does not appear in the law report as published in KG).

view of fraud should have an impact on the court's assessment regarding the evidence of fraud. In situations like these, the court may well conclude that it has not been presented with a case of established fraud. In other words, in the event of indirect guarantees, a court in the account party's country is likely to display even greater restraint in finding established fraud. This is another way of taking foreign law into account.

16.4.2 Restraining orders against the instructing and/or issuing bank in 'after-payment' cases

Fraud by the issuing bank. Issuing bank's knowledge of beneficiary's fraud

16-13 Chapter 16.4.2 deals with applications for orders restraining the instructing bank from paying under the counter-guarantee and/or orders restraining the foreign issuing bank from demanding payment under the counter-guarantee where the issuing bank has already paid under the primary guarantee ('after-payment' cases).[73] German writers were the first to recognise that such applications do not only turn on clear evidence of the beneficiary's fraud in respect of the primary guarantee, but additionally on the involvement of the foreign issuing bank.[74] Such applications require evidence that the foreign bank had, or must have had, knowledge of the beneficiary's fraud when effecting payment to the beneficiary under the primary guarantee. This view has subsequently been adopted in legal writing in other countries.[75] Outside Germany, it was some time before this rule was also fully recognised in case law. At present, however, it is established case law in all jurisdictions,[76] and it is also recognised in art. 19(1)(e) UNCITRAL

---

[73] The principles examined hereafter also apply in cases whereby the issuing bank, after payment under the primary guarantee, seeks reimbursement from the instructing bank and that bank challenges that right.

[74] Von Westphalen, pp. 249-252, 297-301, 360-364, Canaris, No. 1139a, Nielsen, pp. 129-133, Zahn/Ehrlich/Neumann, 9/127-129, Mülbert, pp. 87-88, Coing, ZHR 1983, pp. 136-137, Bark, ZIP 1982, pp. 412-413, von Mettenheim, RIW 1981, pp. 584-585.

[75] See, for example, Croiset van Uchelen, WPNR 1989, p. 272, Prüm, No. 480, Vasseur, No. 152, D. 1987 J. p. 19, Rives-Langes, Banque 1986, p. 711, Poullet, JCB 1982, p. 606, Wymeersch, Hague-Zagreb Essays 6, p. 106, Dohm, Nos. 293-297, Kleiner, Nos. 21.69-21.70.

[76] See for example *The Netherlands*: *Rb Amsterdam, 19 March 1981*, KG 1981, 30, *CA Leeuwarden, 12 September 1990*, KG 1990, 316, *CA Amsterdam, 4 February 1993*, KG 1993, 113, *CA The Hague, 8 June 1993*, KG 1993, 301; *Germany: LG Stuttgart, 8 August 1980*, WM 1981, p. 633, *OLG Saarbrücken, 23 January 1981*, RIW 1981, p. 338, *LG Braunschweig, 22 May 1980*, RIW 1981, p. 789, *BGH, 10 October 2000*, WM 2000, p. 2334; *France: Cass., 12 December 1984*, D. 1985 J. p. 269, *Cass., 11 December 1985*, D. 1986 J. p. 213, *Cass., 23 October 1990*, D. 1991 Somm. p. 197, *Cass., 19 February 1991*,

Convention. It is not surprising that because of the fact that the account party must adduce clear evidence of both the beneficiary's fraud and the issuing bank's knowledge thereof at the time of payment, the vast majority of applications for restraining orders against the instructing and/or issuing bank has been rejected and that successful applications are extremely rare.[77]

The reason why the position of the foreign issuing bank should be considered is the fact that a fraudulent call on the primary guarantee by the beneficiary does not in itself necessarily render the issuing bank's call on the counter-guarantee fraudulent too. The demand for reimbursement under the counter-guarantee is fraudulent only if the issuing bank was involved in the beneficiary's fraud or if it was aware of the fraudulent practices by the beneficiary at the time of payment.[78] The issuing bank´s general duty

---

D. 1991 Somm. p. 199, *Cass., 19 May 1992*, D. 1993 Somm. p. 103 (first decision), *Cass., 17 June 1992*, D. 1995 Somm. p. 19, *Cass., 29 March 1994*, D, 1995 Somm. p. 20, *Cass., 6 April 1993*, D. 1995 Somm. p. 20; *Belgium: Trib. com. Brussels, May 26 1988*, JT 1988, p. 460, *Brussels, 4 January 1989*, TBH 1990, p. 1073, *Trib. com. Brussels, 30 January 1990*, RDC 1992, p. 84; *United Kingdom: Harbottle (Mercantile) v. Nat. Westminster Bank*, [1977] 2 All E.R. 862, *Edward Owen Engineering v. Barclay's Bank*, [1978] 1 All. E.R. 976, *Boliventer Oil v. Chase Manhattan Bank*, [1984] 1 WLR 392, *United Trading v. Allied Arab Bank*, [1985] 2 Lloyd's Rep. 554, *Csarnikow-Rionda v. Standard Bank London*, [1999] 2 Lloyd's Rep. 187, *Turkiye Is Bankasi v. Bank of China*, [1996] 2 Lloyd's Rep. 611, [1998] 1 Lloyd's Rep. 250 (in relation to summary proceedings initiated by the issuing bank against the instructing bank); *Switzerland: Zürich, 9 May 1985*, JIBL 1986, N-153/D. 1987 Somm. p. 177, *Geneva, September 12 1985*, D. 1986 I.R. p. 165.

[77] Restraining orders have been granted and remained in force in: *Rb Amsterdam, 18 December 1980*, S&S 1981, 135 (Iran), *LG Düsseldorf, 9 August 1984*, RIW 1985, p. 77 (Syria), *Cass., 17 June 1992*, D. 1995 Somm. p. 19, *Cass., 11 December 1985*, D. 1986 J. p. 213 (Iran), *Paris, 17 June 1992*, D. 1995 Somm. p. 19 (Spain), *Trib. com. Melun, 29 April 1985*, D. 1986 I.R. p. 159 (Syria), *Trib. com. Brussels, 6 April 1982*, Rev. Banque 1982, p. 683 (Iran), *Trib. com. Brussels, 26 May 1988*, JT 1988, p. 460 (Egypt), *Geneva, 12 September 1985*, D. 1986 I.R. p. 165 (Syria). The *Supreme Court of Finland, 25 October 1992*, D. 1995 Somm. p. 22, endorsed the instructing bank's refusal to pay under the counter-guarantee in favour of the Iranian issuing bank during the 1979 Iranian revolution.

[78] The decisive moment for the issuing bank's knowledge of the beneficiary's fraud is the time of payment under the primary guarantee, cf. *Turkiye Is Bankasi v. Bank of China*, [1996] 2 Lloyd's Rep. 611,[1998] 1 Lloyd's Rep. 250, *Paris, 23 November 1990*, D. 1991 Somm. p. 199, *Paris, 27 November 1990*, D. 1991 Somm. p. 200, Prüm, No. 483, Rives-Lange, Banque 1986, p. 713, Mattout, No. 240, and the case law cited in Chapter 15.1 note 3 for the similar rule in relation to direct guarantees. See also art. 19(1)(e) UNCITRAL Convention which refers to bad faith in relation to payment under the primary guarantee, von Westphalen, pp. 251, 252, 297, Nielsen, p. 130. However, according to *Cass., 29 March 1994*, D. 1995 Somm. p. 20 and Vasseur, RDAI 1990, pp. 374, 375 and D. 1991 Somm. p. 198, the decisive moment is the time of the issuing bank's call under the counter-guarantee. This view might stem from an erroneous perception of the independence between counter-guarantee and primary guarantee.

Fraud and Restraining Orders 425

of care owed to the instructing bank, and the account party in particular, to refrain from payment to the beneficiary is only breached in these circumstances and such a breach also renders the issuing bank's call on the counter-guarantee fraudulent. If the bank did not possess this knowledge at the time of payment under the primary guarantee, it was not at fault and it is consequently entitled to reimbursement. This precludes the possibility of restraining orders against the instructing and/or issuing bank. The legal position is, in fact, much the same as in the case of a direct guarantee where the account party challenges the bank's right to reimbursement after payment because of fraud.[79]

Certain German authors express the view that applications for restraining orders against the instructing and/or issuing bank concern the fraudulent nature of the issuing bank's call under the counter-guarantee only. However, focusing on the issuing bank's fraud in relation to the counter-guarantee is unduly rigid and misleading. It ignores the natural interdependence between counter-guarantee and primary guarantee and the fact that the issuing bank's fraud is ordinarily premised on the beneficiary's fraud, as is quite clear from case law. Situations whereby the issuing bank's call on the counter-guarantee must be considered fraudulent without fraud on the part of the beneficiary in relation to the primary guarantee must be extremely rare and are probably limited to cases where the issuing bank calls the counter-guarantee although the beneficiary of the primary guarantee has not demanded payment.[80]

Certain writers and some French decisions refer to 'collusion' between the issuing bank and the beneficiary.[81] Ordinarily, the term 'collusion' appears to imply an active participation by the issuing bank in the beneficiary's fraud. This is, however, not the case: there is collusion if the issuing bank is fully aware of the beneficiary's fraud at the time of payment and if that bank nonetheless calls the counter-guarantee. Accordingly, to the extent that the notion of 'collusion' has been used, it does not add anything to the usual criterion of the issuing bank's knowledge concerning the beneficiary's fraud.[82] Art. 19(1)(e) UNCITRAL Convention refers to 'bad faith' on the part of the issuing bank in relation to payment under its primary guarantee.

---

[79] See Chapter 15.1.

[80] Cases whereby the issuing bank's right to payment under the counter-guarantee is challenged on the grounds that it has failed to verify compliance with the terms and conditions of the primary guarantee should not be treated as 'fraud' cases. See Chapter 11.2.2, No. 11-13 (Limits of independence. The exception).

[81] *Cass., 29 March 1994*, D. 1994 Somm. p. 20 ('fraudulent collusion') and *Cass., 6 April 1993*, D. 1995 Somm. p. 20 ('fraudulent concert').

[82] In most cases French courts merely refer to the issuing bank's knowledge of the beneficiary's fraud, see in particular *Cass., 10 June 1986*, D. 1987 J. p. 17, *Cass., 19 May 1992*, D. 1993, Somm. p. 103 (1e decision), *Cass., 17 June 1992*, D. 1995 Somm. p. 19, *Cass., 12 December 1995*, No. 93-14.756, Bull Civ. IV No. 289, p. 266, *Paris, 14 December 1987*, D. 1988 Somm. p. 248, *Paris, 27 November 1990*, D. 1991 Somm. p. 2000, *Paris, 23 November*

Issuing bank's knowledge of the beneficiary's fraud. The test

16-14 The test with respect to the evidence concerning the issuing bank's knowledge of the beneficiary's fraud at the time of payment under the primary guarantee is the same stringent test as the one which applies to the bank's liability in the case of direct guarantees in 'after-payment' cases, see Chapter 15.1, No. 15-3.

As far as case law involving calls on guarantees and counter-guarantees at the time of the Iranian revolution is concerned, courts in all but one case[83] opined that the Iranian issuing bank was, or must have been, aware of the beneficiary's fraud. It is important to note that no particular facts are mentioned which convincingly explain and support these findings. It appears that the courts generously utilised the device of constructive knowledge. In the light of the conditions prevailing at the time in Iran, this lenient attitude need not, perhaps, cause surprise.[84] What will cause surprise indeed is the fact that, at some time, some courts in other cases displayed a similar attitude.[85] There are two decisions in which the court's finding in respect of the issuing bank's knowledge of fraud was founded on solid evidence. In *LG Düsseldorf, 9 August 1984*, the account party had obtained an ICC arbitral award ordering the Syrian beneficiary to return the guarantee and a copy of the award was forwarded to the Syrian bank.[86] In *Geneva, 12*

1990, D. 1991 Somm. p. 199, Lyon, *23 March 1992*, RTD Com. 1992, No. 12, p. 658, Paris, *17 June 1992*, D. 1995 Somm. p. 19, *Trib. com. Brussels, 26 May 1988*, JT 1988 p. 460, von Westphalen, p. 252, Mattout, No. 240, Stoufflet, Garantie Bancaire Internationale, Nos. 82-83, Prüm, No. 482, Cabrillac/Mouly, No. 412, Rives-Lange, Banque 1986, p. 713. See also RPDB, Nos. 170-171.

[83] *Trib. gr. inst. Montlucon, 9 January 1981*, D. 1981 J. p. 390. The application against the Iranian beneficiary was, however, granted.

[84] For example, in a circular letter dated 12 November 1981, the Iranian Central Bank urged all Iranian beneficiaries to call guarantees or standby letters of credit issued by U.S. banks. This fact was, however, mentioned in one decision only.

[85] In *Trib. com. Melun, 29 April 1985*, D. 1986 I.R. p. 159, the court stated that the Syrian issuing bank had acted in collusion without mention of one single fact which could support the finding. The decision of *Versailles, 1 December 1988*, D. 1989 Somm. p. 155, abounds with observations such as 'the issuing bank could not have been ignorant' and 'it cannot have escaped the attention of the issuing bank', without reference to specific facts which convincingly corroborate these findings (the decision has been quashed in *Cass., 18 December 1990*, D. 1991 Somm. p. 198, because of insufficient reasoning by the Court of Appeal). The same is true of *Trib. com. Brussels, 26 May 1988*, JT 1988, p. 460, albeit that the foreign issuing bank had ignored persistent allegations of fraud and requests for clarification from the beneficiary and that the issuing bank did not produce the beneficiary's statement indicating the nature of his complaints as stipulated in the guarantee. After repeated requests, the bank only surrendered a formal statement of default which bore a date of 6 months before, see also Chapter 13.2.3, No. 13-12.

[86] RIW 1985, p. 77.

September 1985, the account party had secured a stop-payment order against the Syrian bank from a Syrian court, while the bank, nonetheless, called the counter-guarantee.[87] In another case, *Lyon, 17 May 1991*, the fraudulent nature of the beneficiary's call should have been clear to the issuing bank from the demand itself.[88] In *BGH, 10 October 2000*, the German Supreme Court determined that the issuing bank did not have knowledge of the beneficiary's fraud although the account party had obtained a temporary restraining order against the beneficiary which had been forwarded to the issuing bank after the beneficiary's demand for payment, but before actual payment. The reason was that the issuing bank could not have concluded on the basis of this particular court order that the beneficiary's demand for payment was fraudulent.[89]

Identification

16-15 In a series of Iranian cases following the Iranian revolution in 1979, the device of identification of foreign issuing bank and beneficiary was resorted to in order to sidestep the issue of the foreign bank's knowledge of fraud, or in order to impute this knowledge to the foreign bank.[90] Apart from these cases, courts have ruled that the mere fact that both issuing bank and beneficiary are government agencies or state controlled is insufficient to apply the doctrine of identification for the purpose mentioned.[91] This is the correct view.[92]

---

[87] D. 1986 I.R. p. 165. The report of the case suggests that the beneficiary had not called the guarantee.

[88] D. 1993 Somm. p. 99, see Chapter 15.2, No. 15-6.

[89] WM 2000, p. 2334. See Chapter 14.5.14, No. 14-50, for the facts of the case.

[90] See especially *Itek Corp. v. First Nat. Bank of Boston*, 730 F2d. 19 (1st. Cir. 1984), *Rockwell Systems Int. v. Citibank*, 719 F. 2d. 583 (2d. Civ. 1983), *Harris Corp. v. National Iranian Radio and Television*, 691 F2d. 1344 (11th. Cir. 1982), *Collins v. Citibank*, 82 Civ. 613 (VLB)(S.D.N.Y. 1982), *Cass., December 11 1985*, D.1986, J. p. 213, *Trib. com. Brussels, 6 April 1982*, Rev. Banque 1982, p. 683. See also *BGH, 28 April 1988*, RIW 1988, p. 558

[91] *Rb Amsterdam, May 23 1985*, KG 1985, 165 (Iraq), *LG Stuttgart, 8 August 1980*, WM 1981, p. 633 (Iraq), *OLG Saarbrücken, 23 January 1981*, RIW 1981, p. 338 (Egypt), *Cass., 29 March 1994*, D. 1995 Somm. p. 20 (Libya), *Cass., 6 April 1993*, D. 1995 Somm. p. 20, *Paris, 15 February 1989*, D. 1989 Somm. p. 158 (Algeria), *Zürich, 9 May 1985*, JIBL 1986 N-153, D. 1987 Somm. p. 177 (Egypt).

[92] Idem: Nielsen, p. 133, Mülbert, p. 89, and von Westphalen, p. 255. See also Horn and Wymeersch, p. 513, and Heldrich, FS Kegel, p. 193. Canaris, No. 1139a, and Dohm, No. 291, are more readily inclined to apply the doctrine of identification.

16.4.3 Restraining orders against the instructing and/or issuing bank and/or beneficiary in 'before-payment' cases

Introduction

16-16 Chapter 16.4.3 deals with situations whereby the foreign issuing bank has not yet proceeded to payment under the primary guarantee when it calls the counter-guarantee. It is important to consider the implications thereof since issuing banks ordinarily turn to the instructing bank for payment before they themselves effect payment to the beneficiary. One of the issues is whether in 'before-payment' cases the account party also needs to produce evidence of the issuing bank's knowledge of the beneficiary's fraud, as is the case in 'after-payment' situations. An important decision on this point is *Cass., 10 June 1986*.[93] In this case, the French Cour de Cassation affirmed the judgment of *Paris, 20 June 1984*, which granted orders against the instructing bank restraining it from paying under the counter-guarantee, and against the issuing bank restraining that bank from paying under the primary guarantee. The Court of Appeal observed that the foreign issuing bank had not proceeded to payment and that it could not have been ignorant of the beneficiary's fraud. This second observation was not repeated in the decision of the Cour de Cassation. This omission, especially when contrasted with previous judgments from the Cour de Cassation, indicates, according to commentators, that the Cour de Cassation dispenses with the need to demonstrate to the court's satisfaction that the foreign issuing bank was, or must have been, aware of fraud in the event that the foreign bank has not (yet) proceeded to pay the beneficiary under the primary guarantee.

Before examining the implications of 'before-payment' cases, one preliminary remark should be made. While, as mentioned above, issuing banks ordinarily await reimbursement from the instructing bank before paying the beneficiary under the primary guarantee, it seems incorrect to derive from this general practice any presumptions to this effect in specific instances. Moreover, it is possible that the foreign bank feels that it can no longer resist the beneficiary's demand for payment and it cannot be expected to delay payment for the sake of the account party's attempts to prevent (alleged) fraud. In any event, it is for the account party to convince the court that payment by the foreign bank has not yet been made.

---

[93] D. 1987 J. p. 17 (note Vasseur), Banque 1986, p. 711 (note Rives-Lange). See further Prüm, DPCI 1987, pp. 121-127.

Applications for orders restraining the issuing bank from paying under the primary guarantee and for orders restraining the beneficiary from demanding or receiving payment under the primary guarantee

16-17 With respect to applications for restraining orders against the bank in 'before-payment' cases in direct guarantees, the conclusion made in Chapter 16.3, No. 16-9, was that Dutch, French, Belgian and American case law does not require evidence of the bank's knowledge of the beneficiary's fraud.[94] The explanation is that such applications are not meant to determine the bank's liability but to prevent fraud by the beneficiary. It is arguable that this approach may also be adopted in respect of applications for restraining orders against the foreign issuing bank to pay under the primary guarantee in the case of indirect guarantees, cf. *Cass., 10 June 1986*, see No. 16-16, a decision which has been approved of by several writers.[95] Evidence of the issuing bank's knowledge of the beneficiary's fraud is, obviously, not required with respect to applications for orders restraining the beneficiary from demanding or receiving payment under the primary guarantee.

The true difficulties with respect to restraining orders against the foreign issuing bank and beneficiary concern the jurisdiction of the courts in the account party's country and the recognition of judgments in the beneficiary's country. While courts in the account party's country ordinarily have jurisdiction *ratione personae* over the foreign issuing bank and beneficiary,[96] one might seriously question whether these courts have also jurisdiction *ratione materiae*, since these orders are intended to take effect in the foreign country only.[97] It should also be noted that, by insisting on and procuring an indirect guarantee provided by a bank in his own country, the beneficiary may justifiably expect that any proceedings in respect of such a guarantee will take place in his own country. This is precisely why the foreign beneficiary wishes to obtain an indirect guarantee and the account party has agreed to this. Similar considerations apply from the perspective of the foreign issuing bank. Nonetheless, in several instances, courts have ignored or disregarded these aspects.[98]

---

[94] This is also the case in German law, albeit that according to more recent German case law such orders against the bank are never possible, see Chapter 16.3, No. 16-5.

[95] Prüm, No. 483, Rives-Lange, Banque 1986, p. 711, Contamine-Raynaud, Rev. Droit Banc. 1987, p. 19. See also Poullet, No. 367, and JCB 1982, p. 656 and De Ly, Rev. Banque 1990, p. 172. The decision has been questioned by Vasseur, note, D. 1987 J. p. 17. Nos. 9-12.

[96] See also Chapter 18.1, No. 18-4.

[97] In *OG Austria, 10 July 1986*, JIBL 1986 N-140, jurisdiction in respect of an application restraining the beneficiary from calling the primary guarantee was rejected but accepted in respect of an application for a stop-payment order against the foreign issuing bank (not granted).

[98] See, for example, *Trib. com. Brussels, 26 May 1988*, JT 1988, p. 460 (restraining order against beneficiary and stop-payment order against foreign issuing bank granted), *Trib. com. Brussels, 21 October 1986*, RDC 1987, p. 706 (stop-payment order against foreign issuing

Apart from the implications concerning jurisdiction, courts in the account party's country should bear in mind that it is unlikely that stop-payment orders against the foreign issuing bank and restraining orders against the foreign beneficiary will be recognised abroad. The practical result is that the foreign bank is exposed to the considerable risk that it will not be able to invoke such judicial orders as a valid defence against the beneficiary. This effect is unacceptable since this risk should not be borne by the foreign issuing bank but by the account party. These implications call for great judicial restraint with respect to such orders, even if there is established fraud on the part of the beneficiary as was clearly recognised in *United Trading v. Allied Arab Bank* and *CA Leeuwarden, 12 September 1990*.[99]

Applications for orders restraining the instructing bank from paying under the counter-guarantee and for orders restraining the issuing bank from demanding or receiving payment under the counter-guarantee

16-18 The particular difficulties concerning the jurisdiction *ratione materiae* of courts in the account party's country, as discussed in No. 16-17, do not arise in respect of applications for restraining orders in relation to the counter-guarantee, since they take effect in or, at least, relate to that jurisdiction.

The true issue in these 'before-payment' cases is whether the account party must also produce evidence of the issuing bank's knowledge of the beneficiary's fraud or whether this additional requirement can be dispensed with, as was apparently decided in *Cass., June 10 1986*,[100] and advocated by several writers.[101] The answer to this ques-

---

bank granted), *Trib. com. Brussels, 6 April 1982*, Rev. Banque 1982, p. 633 (restraining order against beneficiary granted), *Cass., 10 June 1986*, D. 1987 J. p. 17 (stop-payment order against foreign issuing bank granted), *Trib. gr. inst. Montlucon, 9 January 1981*, D. 1981 J. p. 390 (restraining order against foreign beneficiary granted, application against instructing bank denied), *Trib. com. Paris, 1 August 1984*, D. 1984 I.R. p. 159 (stop-payment order against foreign issuing bank granted). In these cases restraining orders in respect of the counter-guarantee were also issued. In *United Trading v. Allied Arab Bank*, [1985] 2 Lloyd's Rep 554, jurisdiction in respect of an application for a stop-payment order against the foreign issuing bank was accepted (application not granted), see also the following note. It is noted that applications for stop-payment orders against the foreign issuing bank and for restraining orders against the beneficiary are comparatively rare, especially in Germany.

[99] *United Trading v. Allied Arab Bank*, [1985] 2 Lloyd's Rep. 554 (applications denied), *CA Leeuwarden, 12 September 1990*, KG 1990, 316 (applications denied). See also *Harbottle (Mercantile) v. Nat. Westminster Bank*, [1977] 2 All ER 862. See also No. 16-19.

[100] D. 1987 J. p. 17, see No. 16-16.

[101] Prüm, No. 483, Rives-Lange, Banque 1986, p. 711, Contamine-Raynaud, Rev. Droit Banc. 1987, p. 19. See also Poullet, No. 367, and JCB 1982, p. 656 and De Ly, Rev. Banque 1990, p. 172. The decision has been questioned by Vasseur, note, D. 1987 J. p. 17. Nos. 9-12.

tion is most difficult and cannot be unequivocal. One of the possible approaches to this matter is that once the court has accepted jurisdiction over the foreign issuing bank and once the court has ruled that the beneficiary's call under the primary guarantee is fraudulent, the foreign bank might be deemed to have notice of the fraud. If the bank were then to proceed to payment, it cannot claim reimbursement under the counter-guarantee since the time of payment to the beneficiary is the proper yardstick when determining the bank's knowledge. In this approach the question of evidence concerning the issuing bank's knowledge of fraud becomes academic.[102]

It is doubtful, however, whether this approach is sound and convincing. The juridical basis of restraining orders in respect of the counter-guarantee remains unclear if they are not founded on wrongful conduct on the part of the issuing bank. However, in 'before-payment' cases there can be no such wrongful conduct, apart from situations where the issuing bank calls the counter-guarantee even though no demand for payment has been made under the primary guarantee. It must also be embarrassing for the instructing bank if it is enjoined from honouring its counter-guarantee in favour of the issuing bank without a showing of (imminent) improper conduct by the latter. The greatest objection to the approach described in the previous paragraph is that the court's ruling that the beneficiary's demand for payment under the primary guarantee is fraudulent is not likely to be recognised in the issuing bank's country. This exposes that bank to the risk that it may be forced in its own country to pay under the primary guarantee while it cannnot claim reimbursement under the counter-guarantee. This is unacceptable, cf. the last paragraph of No. 16-17.

In conclusion, if courts in 'before-payment' cases were indeed to dispense with the need for evidence of the issuing bank's wrongdoing, they should at least require that the evidence concerning the beneficiary's fraud is of such a nature that the issuing bank has a valid defence in its own jurisdiction against payment under the primary guarantee. Anyhow, whether or not evidence of the issuing bank's knowledge concerning the beneficiary's fraud in 'before payment' cases is required, the effect of restraining orders in respect of the counter-guarantee is limited, see No. 16-19.

The limited effect of restraining orders. Non-recognition and contrary decisions by the foreign court

16-19 If a court in the account party's country grants a restraining order in relation to the counter-guarantee, the issuing bank is likely to refuse or, at least, to delay payment under the primary guarantee because it cannot claim reimbursement under the counter-guarantee. The same may happen if that court also issues restraining orders in respect of the primary guarantee. In these events, the beneficiary will probably start proceedings against the issuing bank. These proceedings will take place abroad, namely in the

---

[102] Cf. Chapter 16.3, No. 16-9.

country of their mutual place of business. In most situations it is unlikely that the foreign court will recognise interlocutory restraining orders granted by a court in the account party's country.[103] If the foreign court rules that the beneficiary's call is not fraudulent and, consequently, orders the foreign issuing bank to make payment to the beneficiary, the question arises as to the effect of that foreign court's ruling in the account party's jurisdiction. Although courts in the account party's country are in their turn likely to refuse recognition of the foreign court's decision as such, they ought to recognise as a matter of fact that the foreign issuing bank's conduct is governed by local law and practice and that it must obey orders from local courts.[104] Consequently, if the foreign issuing bank is forced to pay pursuant to an order from a local court, it does not commit a wrong towards the instructing bank or account party. The foreign issuing bank is, therefore, entitled to reimbursement from the instructing bank, which can recover the amount from the account party. This is a typical loss which should be allocated to the account party, not to either the issuing or instructing bank.[105] In order to accomplish such a recovery, courts in the account party's jurisdiction should honour an application by the instructing and/or issuing bank to lift previous restraining orders in respect of the counter-guarantee.[106] Moreover, because of the foreign court's ruling described above the foreign issuing bank can never be said to possess knowledge of the beneficiary's fraud.

16.4.4 The limited effect of restraining orders. Inter-bank relationship. Recourse against account party

16-20 The effect of restraining orders by a court in the account party's country in relation to the counter-guarantee in both 'before-' and 'after-payment' cases is often

---

[103] See also *Power Curber Int. v. National Bank of Kuwait*, [1981] 1 WLR 1233: Parker J. refused to give effect to an attachment order in respect of a documentary credit granted by a Kuwaiti court, and *OLG Frankfurt a.M., 8 February 2000*, WM 2001, p. 1108: The German Court of Appeal ruled that a Turkish provisional restraining order against the bank and beneficiary in relation to a direct guarantee did not prevent it from giving its own judgment in respect of the claim by the beneficiary against the German bank for payment in summary proceedings. In fact, it gave judgment in favour of the beneficiary. See, however, for a contrary decision *Rb Amsterdam, 17 January 2002*, JOR 2002, 71. In this case the account party obtained a provisional restraining order against the beneficiary of a direct guarantee issued by a Dutch bank in Turkey, where the beneficiary had his place of business. In summary proceedings in the Netherlands initiated by the beneficiary against the bank the court recognised the Turkish order and gave judgment against the beneficiary.

[104] German doctrine refers to this phenomenon as 'Tatbestandswirkung'.

[105] Cf. Chapter 10.10.

[106] See Chapter 13.2.7, No. 13-23 last paragraph for the effect of a discharge of a previous restraining order after the expiry date of the (counter-)guarantee.

limited not only for the reasons explained in No. 16-19, but also because of the interbank relationship. It often happens that the instructing and issuing bank do regular business with one another and maintain a current account with each other. If this is the case, the issuing bank will usually be in a position to debit that account for the amount it claims from the instructing bank under the counter-guarantee and no restraining order is capable of stopping the issuing bank from so doing. Again, this is a risk which should be allocated to the account party, not to the instructing bank. Accordingly, in the situation described above, the instructing bank is entitled to have recourse against the account party despite the restraining orders, as was clearly recognised in *LG Düsseldorf, 9 August 1984*.[107]

16.5 OTHER ASPECTS CONCERNING RESTRAINING ORDERS

Restraining orders and the commercial viability of guarantees

16-21 It has been suggested that judicial intervention in the form of restraining orders on the grounds of fraud might endanger the utility of guarantees, since beneficiaries might lose faith in this instrument and revert to the former practice of demanding cash deposits. These assertions have found no favour with the courts. For example, in *Dynamics Corp. v. Citizens & Southern National Bank* the court observed: 'There is as much public interest in discouraging fraud as in encouraging the use of letters of credit.'[108] In *Itek Corp. v. First National Bank of Boston* it was said: '... the failure to issue an injunction where otherwise appropriate would send a clear signal to those inclined to engage in fraudulent activities that they are likely to be rewarded. Such a result would have an even greater adverse impact upon issuing banks and ultimately discourage the use of letters of credit.'[109] Neil J. in *United Trading v. Allied Arab Bank* put it this way: 'It cannot be in the interest of international commerce or of the banking community as a whole that this important machinery ... should be misused for the purposes of fraud.'[110]

Indeed, fraud by the beneficiary, just as much as too great a willingness of courts to interfere in the ordinary execution of guarantees, would imperil their commercial viability. However, there are in fact no indications that courts are slack in applying the guiding principle of 'pay first, argue later'. They have, in general, adopted a restrictive

---

[107] RIW 1985, p. 77. See also Nielsen, p. 136.
[108] 356 F.Supp. 991 (N.D. Ga. 1973).
[109] 730 F.2d. 19 (1st. Cir. 1984).
[110] [1985] 2 Lloyd's Rep. 554. The statement of Neil J. in first instance was approved of by Ackner L.J. Similar observations can be found in *Cromwell v. Commerce & Energy Bank*, 464 So. 2d. (La. 1985) and in *LG Dortmund, 9 July 1980*, WM 1981, p. 280.

view of what kinds of facts constitute fraud and they have set stringent requirements as regards evidence. The instances in which restraining orders have been issued are, therefore, rare.

Hardship for the account party to litigate in the beneficiary's country

16-22 Account parties have occasionally argued that the difficulties in recovering the amounts, which are about to be paid under the guarantee, before courts in the beneficiary's country justify a preventive stop-payment order. Courts have rejected this argument.[111] This is an ordinary risk which the account party has accepted by agreeing to a first demand guarantee and, in respect of the underlying transaction, by agreeing to a choice of foreign jurisdiction clause or by failing to stipulate that disputes are to be settled before courts or arbitrators elsewhere. An exception to this rule might only be appropriate if the administration of justice in the beneficiary's country were to collapse suddenly and unexpectedly. American case law is illustrative in this respect. While this argument was ignored in the ligation before the seizure of U.S. citizens during the Iranian revolution in 1979, it was accepted for some time thereafter in some cases as one of the grounds which justified restraining orders.[112]

Restraining orders and the reputation of the bank

16-23 Banks repeatedly argue that stop-payment orders damage their reputation. This argument is voiced in several, especially English, court decisions and in legal writing too. Courts and doctrine have, however, equally challenged the soundness of this assertion.[113]

---

[111] See explicitly *Riom, 14 May 1980*, D. 1981 J. p. 336 (Iran), *LG Köln, 11 December 1981*, WM 1982, p. 438 (Saudi Arabia), *Geneva, 24 June 1983*, D.1983 I.R. p. 486 (Iran), *Southern Energy Homes v. Amsouth Bank*, 35 UCC Rep. Serv. 2d (Callaghan) 250 (Ala. 1998), *Fluor Daniel Argentine Inc. v. ANZ Bank*, 13 F. Supp 2d 562 (S.D.N.Y. 1998). See also Nielsen, ZIP 1982, p. 258, and Dolan, § 3.07[5].

[112] See especially *Wyle v. Bank Melli*, 577 F. 1148 (ND Cal. 1983)and No. 16-8.

[113] See, for example, *LG Frankfurt a.M., 11 December 1979*, NJW 1981, p. 56, *LG Dortmund, 9 July 1980*, WM 1981, p. 280, *LG Stuttgart, 8 August 1980*, WM 1981, p. 633, *Versailles, 29 March 1985*, D. 1986 I.R. p. 156, *Trib. com. Lyon, 3 July 1991*, D. 1993 Somm. p. 100, *Trib. com. Brussels, 26 May 1988*, JT 1988, p. 460, *Brussels, 5 April 1990*, TBH 1992, p. 82, *United Trading v. Allied Arab Bank*, [1985] 2 Lloyd's Rep. 554, per Ackner L.J., *Itek Corp. v. First National Bank of Boston*, 730 F2d. 19 (1st. Cir. 1984), *Harris Corp. v. National Iranian Radio and Television*, 691 F2d. 1344 (11th. Cir. 1982), *Collins Systems Int. v. Citibank*, 82 Civ. 613 (V.L.B.) (S.N.N.Y. 1982), *Rockwell Systems Int. v. Citibank*, 719 F2d. 583 (2d. Civ. 1983). See also von Westphalen, p. 287, and Edelmann, DB 1998, pp. 2456-2458.

Fraud and Restraining Orders 435

The bank's argument is indeed fallacious for the same reasons as those which refute the idea that judicial intervention imperils the commercial viability of guarantees.[114] As has been observed in several court decisions, the denial of adequate remedies in the event of established fraud would ultimately have an adverse impact on the banking community as a whole. Moreover, in the light of the fact that in at least forty reported cases it was the bank which refused, delayed or frustrated payment, although the terms and conditions of the guarantee were met, there is good reason why courts should not be unduly impressed by this argument. It is quite revealing that their credibility appears to play a less preponderant part especially when the chances of recovery from the account party are in danger because of the latter's insolvency.[115]

Bank's duty to defer payment if the account party applies for restraining orders?

16-24 In Chapter 10.9 we examined the issue of the bank's duty to notify the account party of the beneficiary's request for payment. To the extent that such a duty exists, it would appear appropriate for it to be reinforced by a waiting period not exceeding a few days to allow the account party to seek interim relief, should that prove to be his intention and provided that he immediately informs the bank thereof.[116] If the account party does not commence legal proceedings immediately, the bank cannot be expected

---

[114] See No. 21.

[115] As occurred in at least forty reported cases, see, for example, the trilogy of *Rb. Haarlem, 9 January 1987*, KG 1987, 85, *22 January 1987*, KG 1987, 86 and *6 February 1987*, KG 1987, 104, *CA The Hague, 20 April 1993*, NJ 1995, 542, *Turkiye Is Bankasi v. Bank of China*, [1996] 2 Lloyd's Rep. 611, *Balfour Beatty Civil Engineering v. Technical & General Guarantee*, [1999] 68 Con.L.R. 180, *Csarnikow-Rionda v. Standard Bank London*, [1999] 2 Lloyd's Rep. 187, *BGH, 12 March 1984 (11 ZR 10/83)*, RIW 1985, p. 78, *Paris, 8 December 1977*, D. 1979 J. p. 259, *Trib. com. La Roche-sur-Yon, 14 September 1981*, D. 1982 I.R. p. 199, *Cass., 20 December 1982*, D. 1983 J. p. 365, *Trib. com. Nantes, 22 September 1983*, D. 1984 I.R. p. 202, *Cass., 8 December 1987*, D 1988 Somm. p. 240, *Paris, 18 December 1991*, D. 1993 Somm. p. 106, *Cass., 30 January 2001*, D. Affaires 2001, p. 1024, *Trib. com. Brussels, 11 March 1981*, BRH 1981, p. 361, *Trib. com. Brussels, 16 May 1991*, JT 1991, p. 701, *Trib. com. Brussels, 10 January 1992*, RDC 1993, p. 1052, *Trib. com. Namur, 12 September 1994*, RDC 1995, p. 68, *Trib. com. Brussels, 21 November 1997*, RDC 1998, p. 850, *Trib. com. Brussels, 11 February 1999*, RDC 2000, p. 725, *Trib. com. Charleroi, 23 April 1997*, JLMB 1998, p. 1073, CA *Brussels, 2 March 2001*, TBH 2002, p. 484, *Chase Manhattan Bank v. Equibank*, 394 F. Supp. 352 (1977), 21 UCCRS 247 (1977), *Wahda Bank v. Arab Bank*, [1993] 2 Bank L.J. 233. See also Chapter 7, No. 7-2, Chapter 12.3.3, No. 12-27 for cases where the bank argued that it had issued a traditional suretyship, and Chapter 13.2.10, No. 13-30.

[116] Thus *Geneva, 14 March 1985*, D. 1986 I.R. p. 164. See also Dohm, No. 141. Art. 17 URDG does not contain such a duty. See also Vasseur, No. 102.

to delay payment.[117] On the other hand, if the account party starts legal proceedings within this short period of time, it is submitted that because of its duty of care the bank should, in general, await the court's judgment before proceeding to payment.[118] In several French decisions such duty has, however, been denied.[119] In any event, banks in most countries often postpone payment when notified of applications by the account party for restraining orders. Their motive is not so much any perceived legal obligation in this respect but the wish not to impair its relationship with its customer unnecessarily. Difficulties may arise if judgment in interim proceedings cannot be obtained speedily and also when the account party's evidence concerning the beneficiary's fraud is not very strong, while the beneficiary insists on immediate payment. Under circumstances such as these, it is doubtful whether the bank could be expected to delay payment in view of its conflicting duties towards the beneficiary and its reputation, unless, of course, it is aware of the beneficiary's fraud. In order to gain time, the account party may then try to obtain an order for conservatory attachment under the bank or a freezing order, which can ordinarily be obtained, at least provisionally, within a very short time.[120]

The foreign issuing bank, in the case of an indirect guarantee, never owes a duty to defer payment in the event that the account party applies for restraining orders in his own jurisdiction against that foreign bank.

---

[117] Cf. von Westphalen, p. 358, Kleiner, No. 21.15.

[118] See further Bertrams, Bb 1994, pp. 225-227.

[119] In *Cass., 7 June 1994*, D. 1995 Somm. p. 21, *Cass., 10 June 1997*, Banque 1997, p. 90, *Aix-en-Provence, 19 January 1995*, Banque et Droit 1995, No. 43, p. 30, and *Paris, 26 January 1995*, Banque et Droit 1995, No. 43, p. 31, the bank was not held liable when it paid under the counter-guarantee, although the account party had applied for a restraining order. It should be noted that in none of these cases had fraud been established. Moreover, in the 1997 decision of the Cour de Cassation the bank was not a party to the proceedings and it had paid before the temporary restraining order had been served on it. In the case of *Trib. com. Lyon, 3 July 1991*, D. 1993 Somm. p. 100, the account party applied for a restraining order against the bank on the grounds of fraud, but prior to the hearing the bank proceeded to payment with a view to its international reputation. At the hearing, the account party was able to produce clear evidence of the beneficiary's fraud. The court dismissed the bank's plea and rejected its claim for reimbursement from the account party.

[120] See also No. 16-3 last paragraph.

CHAPTER 17
CONSERVATORY ATTACHMENT AND THE U.K. FREEZING (MAREVA) INJUNCTION

Introduction

17-1 Conservatory attachment, as regulated in the statutory provisions on procedural law in the European Continent, is aimed at the preservation of the debtor/defendant's assets in order to avoid the risk that the debtor/defendant has disposed of his assets by the time that the creditor/plaintiff obtains judgment, which is often rendered only after protracted proceedings. Conservatory attachment may involve the debtor's real property as well as his accounts with, or rights to payment from the bank, such as the right to payment pursuant to a guarantee. The effect of conservatory attachment is that the debtor cannot dispose of his assets or, as the case may be, that the bank is not to proceed to actual payment of the debtor/beneficiary.[1] Once the creditor has obtained judgment in main proceedings, he can seize the assets (guarantee funds) and recoup his claims.

One of the prerequisites for conservatory attachment is that the plaintiff/creditor's claim against the defendant/debtor must, depending on the rules of procedure in each jurisdiction, be plausible, certain or liquidated. The orders are often readily granted in an *ex parte* hearing. They can, however, be discharged in *inter partes* proceedings upon application of the debtor (beneficiary of the guarantee) or a third party (the bank).

Conservatory attachment is incompatible with the agreement between account party and beneficiary in the event of non-established fraud

17-2 On several occasions, especially in the Netherlands, account parties have attempted to obtain leave for conservatory attachment in respect of the guarantee funds with the bank alleging that the beneficiary's demand for payment is fraudulent. As regards situations where the account party's case consists in allegations only, as opposed to clear evidence of fraud, it is well established, both in case law[2] and in legal

---

[1] The bank is accountable to the creditor if, despite these orders, it proceeds to payment.

[2] See, for example, *Rb Amsterdam, 14 May 1981*, KG 1981, 71, *Rb Arnhem, 14 March 1983*, KG 1983, 115, *Rb Amsterdam, 9 August 1984*, KG 1984, 254, *Rb Haarlem, 21 November 1986*, KG 1987, 57, *Rb Haarlem, 22 January 1987*, KG 1987, 86, *Rb Rotterdam, 9 June 1989*, KG 1989, 270, *Rb Breda, 22 July 1992*, KG 1992, 301, *Rb Rotterdam, 16 March 1993*, KG 1993, 222, *Rb Leeuwarden, 4 July 1997*, KGK 1998, 1454, *Paris, 25 March 1982*,

writing,[3] that conservatory attachment is incompatible with the nature of (first) demand guarantees, and that, when the attachment is initially permitted in an *ex parte* hearing, it will subsequently be discharged in *inter partes* proceedings. The reason is that conservatory attachment frustrates the agreement between account party and beneficiary to the effect that the beneficiary is entitled to immediate payment once the terms of the guarantee are met, without the need to prove his substantive rights in any further manner and, despite the account party's allegations that the beneficiary has no right to payment. Conservatory attachment prevents the beneficiary from receiving the proceeds of the guarantee forthwith, and, if granted on the basis of alleged, but not established, fraud, it is, therefore, incompatible with the agreed allocation of risks. Thus, the general rule that conservatory attachment can be obtained, and remains in force, in the event of plausible claims, is inapplicable to guarantees. Moreover, it is well-known that account parties often apply for conservatory attachment for no purpose other than to delay or prevent payment and courts appear to be conscious of this strategy.

Especially in Dutch decisions, the possibility of conservatory attachment is also rejected for technical reasons. It would appear that these objections are of secondary significance only, but they may become relevant in the event of established fraud, see No. 17-3.

The objections to conservatory attachment do not, of course, apply to creditors of the beneficiary other than the account party. They are entitled to attach the guarantee funds in accordance with the ordinary rules of procedures in this respect.[4]

D. 1982 I.R. p. 497, *Paris, 3 December 1984*, D. 1985 I.R. p. 240, *Paris, 6 May 1986*, D. 1987 Somm. p. 175. See also *LG Duisburg, 27 November 1987*, WM 1988, p. 1483. See Dolan, § 7.03[5] for American case law. As far as documentary credits are concerned the French Cour de Cassation ruled on several occasions that conservatory attachment orders are not permissible: October 14 1981, D. 1982 J. p. 301 (note Vasseur), Banque 1982, p. 524 (note Martin), Banque 1982, p. 595 (note Boudinot), JCP 1982 11 No. 19815 (note Gavalda and Stoufflet); March 14 1984, D. 1985 I.R. p. 245; June 24 1986, D. 1987 Somm. p. 218; March 18 1986, D. 1986 J. p. 374; October 18 1988, D. 1989 Somm. p. 195. The Belgian Supreme Court has also ruled against conservatory attachment: *HC, 23 June 1994*, RW 1994/1995, p. 564. Contrary to the prevailing view in Switzerland, the *Federal Swiss Court, 20 August 1991*, D. 1992 Somm. p. 233, ruled that, in general, conservatory attachment is permissible.

[3] See, for example, Mijnssen, pp. 62-66, Pabbruwe, p. 53, Bartman, WPNR 1989, p. 601, von Westphalen, pp. 312-317, Mülbert, p. 181, Canaris, Nos. 1152, 1065, Dohm, No. 340, Prüm, Nos. 527-539, T'Kint, No. 856. See further Blau, WM 1988-1477, and legal writing cited in No. 17-3.

[4] *Cass., 5 July 1983*, Banque 1984, p. 245, *Rb Zwolle, 24 September 2003*, JOR 2004, 23.

Conservatory attachment in the event of established fraud

17-3 On several occasions Dutch courts have ruled that conservatory attachment orders are ordinarily lifted upon application of the beneficiary or bank for reasons mentioned in No. 17-2, unless there is established fraud.[5] This exception has been put into practice in a number of cases. In *CA 's-Hertogenbosch, 1 December 1993*,[6] *Rb Zwolle, 26 November 1982*,[7] *Rb The Hague, April 9 1997*,[8] *Rb Utrecht, 23 January 1998*[9] and *Rb Utrecht, 6 July 2000*,[10] but also in a Belgian case, *Trib. com. Brussels, 15 January 1980*,[11] the court refused to lift the attachment on the grounds that the beneficiary's fraud was clearly established. Several authors take the same view.[12]

It has been argued that, even in the event of established fraud, conservatory attachment is not possible or should be lifted for both technical and functional reasons.[13] First, in the case of established fraud, conservatory attachment is impossible because of lack of object since, in that event, the beneficiary has, according to the account

---

5 *Rb Arnhem, 14 March 1983*, KG 1983, 115, *Rb Amsterdam, 23 May 1985*, KG 1985, 165, *Rb Haarlem, 11 November 1986*, KG 1987, 57, *Rb Rotterdam, 9 June 1989*, KG 1989, 270, *CA Leeuwarden, 12 September 1990*, KG 1990, 316, *Rb Utrecht, 7 February 1995*, KG 1995, 163.

6 NJ 1994, 740. See Chapter 14.5.5, No. 14-27 for the facts.

7 KG 1982, 220. See Chapter 14.5.6, No. 14-36 for the facts.

8 KGK 1997, 1431.

9 JOR 2000, 40. This decision was affirmed by *CA Amsterdam, March 25 1999*, JOR 2000, 40, however without reference to established fraud, see the critical comment by Bertrams, WPNR 2000, pp. 225-226.

10 S & S 2001, 3. See Chaper 14.5.9, No. 14-45 for the facts.

11 JCB 1980, p. 147.

12 Hardenberg, WPNR 1995, pp. 842, 845, Pabbruwe, p. 53, Canaris, Nos. 1152, 1065, Edelmann, DB 1998, p. 2457, Croiset van Uchelen, WPNR 1989, pp. 273-275, Schütze, WM 1980, pp. 1438-1442, DB 1981, p. 779, Vasseur, D. 1986 J. p. 374, Stoufflet, JCP 1985 11 No. 20436, Schoordijk, RMThemis 1985, p. 391, Staudinger/Horn, Nos. 321-322. See further Aden, RIW 1981, pp. 441-442, Pilger, RIW 1979, pp. 588-590.

13 See especially *Rb Amsterdam, 5 September 1991*, KG 1991, 335, where the court discharged the conservatory attachment order, but allowed a restraining order because of established fraud, and further *Rb Amsterdam, 14 May 1981*, KG 1981, 71, *Rb Amsterdam, 9 August 1984*, KG 1984, 254. Bertrams, WPNR 2000, pp. 225-226, Blomkwist, WPNR 1986, p. 552-553, von Westphalen, pp. 314-317, Zahn/Ehrlich/Neumann, 9/146, Mülbert, pp. 186-193, Pleyer, WM Sonderbeilage 2/1973, pp. 24-26, Dohm, No. 341-343, Prüm, No. 523, Poullet, Banca Borsa 1984, p. 72, JCB 1982, p. 660, Simont, Rev. Banque 1983, p. 604, Moatti, Journal des Notaires et des Avocats 1989, p. 667. See also Nielsen, p. 120, Bertrams, Bb 1994, pp. 225, 226, Mattout, No. 237 and RPDB, Nos. 151-160. German case law is divided, see Edelmann, DB 1998, p. 2457, footnotes 45 and 46.

party, no right to payment and the bank owes no moneys which can be subject to attachment. The application is, therefore, self-contradictory. Secondly, conservatory attachment precludes the account party's claim against the beneficiary for repayment or damages from coming into existence, because these orders prevent the beneficiary from receiving the guarantee funds, with the consequence that the account party suffers no loss. These technical objections might possibly be viewed as artificial. This is particularly the case if the bank honours the beneficiary's call but, because of the attachment, pays the amount into a blocked account with the bank. In that event, the attachment does not relate to the guarantee funds but to the beneficiary's blocked accounts with the bank, and the bank will also be entitled to debit the account party's accounts, with the result that the latter suffers a loss, see No. 17-8.

The above-mentioned technical difficulties do not arise either if the account party applies for conservatory attachment in respect of the beneficiary's general accounts with the bank and not in respect of the funds payable under the guarantee. However, this possibility only presents itself in domestic cases as far as direct guarantees are concerned, and, in the case of indirect guarantees, only when the beneficiary happens to maintain accounts with the issuing bank. In that event, however, the account party must apply for leave for conservatory attachment in the foreign issuing bank's jurisdiction. An example of a successful application for conservatory attachment on the general accounts of the beneficiary with the foreign issuing bank is provided in *Trib. com. Paris, 2 February 1983*.[14]

It remains a fact, however, that even in the case of established fraud, the technique of conservatory attachment is utilised for inappropriate purposes, namely the prevention of actual payment to the beneficiary,[15] instead of the preservation of assets to be seized if the plaintiff's claim against the defendant/beneficiary is affirmed in main proceedings. If the account party seeks to prevent payment on the grounds of fraud, he should apply for interlocutory restraining orders, not for for conservatory attachment.[16] The main objection is that, in *ex parte* conservatory attachment proceedings, the court has no opportunity to determine whether there is established fraud. That issue has to be dealt with in main proceedings but these tend to be protracted. This is incompatible with the basic principle of 'pay first, argue later' and the rule that the beneficiary is entitled to immediate payment unless fraud can be established forthwith.[17]

---

[14] D. 1985 I.R. p. 243. It is noted that this order was granted because of the *appearance* of a counterclaim against the beneficiary. It is not clear on what grounds the court accepted jurisdiction to grant attachment orders in respect of funds located abroad.

[15] Cf. *Rb. Rotterdam, 7 July 2002*, KG 2002, 195.

[16] Cf. Bertrams, WPNR 2000, pp. 225-226, Kleiner, 22.22, Prüm, No. 532, Poullet, Banca Borsa 1984, p. 73.

[17] What happens in actual (Dutch) practice is that the beneficiary applies in interlocutory proceedings for discharge of the conservatory attachment and that, in the same proceedings, the

Applications for conservatory attachment only appear to be an acceptable technique as an *ultimum remedium*, for example where the account party has applied for interlocutory restraining orders on the grounds of established fraud, but where judgment cannot be obtained soon and the bank is under acute pressure from the beneficiary to proceed to payment.[18]

Conservatory attachment and counterclaims ex secured contract. Set-off

17-4 In the case of *Trib. gr. inst. Paris, 13 May 1980*, the account party, a construction firm, obtained leave for conservatory attachment to secure payment of certain amounts which the employer/beneficiary of a performance guarantee owed under the secured contract for works completed. The court refused to discharge the attachment, observing that the account party did not seek to challenge the beneficiary's right to payment under the guarantee, which would have been incompatible with the nature of first demand guarantees. On the contrary, the account party, according to the court, proceeded on the assumption that the beneficiary was entitled to payment. The court ruled that the account party's promise to renounce defences against the beneficiary's right to payment under the guarantee did not imply that the account party was prohibited from attaching the guarantee funds, which was a practicable means of securing a counterclaim which was certain, liquid and due.[19] The decision, as well as its reasoning, has been approved of by some authors,[20] and disapproved of by others.[21] A contrary deci-

---

account party files a counterclaim whereby he requests the court to issue a restraining order because of fraud. The court will, then, have the opportunity to determine this issue. If the court is not convinced of the beneficiary's fraud, it will discharge the attachment and refuse the restraining order. Should, however, the court be satisfied with the evidence of fraud, it will grant the restraining order. Curiously, in *RB The Hague, 9 April 1997*, KGK 1997, 1431, the court declined to lift the conservatory attachment and yet also granted a restraining order against the beneficiary because of established fraud. In both situations, the account party gained the advantage of delaying actual payment to the beneficiary. Although in the above-mentioned scenario, the court has the opportunity to determine the issue of (established) fraud within a comparatively short period of time, there is still the objection that payment is delayed and that, instead of the account party, it is the beneficiary who is compelled to initiate proceedings with the attendant expenditures and inconvenience, particularly if he is a foreign resident.

[18] See Chapter 16.5, No. 16-24, end of first paragraph.

[19] D. 1980 J. p. 488.

[20] Gavalda and Stoufflet, D. 1980 J. p. 490, Dubisson, DPCI 1980, p. 580, Poullet, Banca Borsa 1984, pp. 75-77, JCB 1982, pp. 658-659.

[21] Cabrillac and Rives-Lange (hesitantly), RTDC 1981, p. 124, Vasseur, JCP 1981 11 No. 19550, D. 1983 I.R. p. 301.

sion was rendered in *Rb Breda, 22 July 1992*, where the court observed that the attachment frustrated the envisaged purpose and effect of the guarantee and that it was incompatable with the agreement between the account party and beneficiary that the guarantee '[but otherwise] shall be and remain in full force and effect'.[22]

Applications for conservatory attachment in relation to the account party's counterclaims for payment against the beneficiary which are not certain and liquid, are clearly inappropriate for the same reasons as stop-payment orders in the event of non-established fraud are incompatible with the nature of first demand guarantees. Even in the event of certain and liquidated counterclaims, however, conservatory attachment should be regarded as irreconcilable with the reallocation of risk between account party and beneficiary and the principle of independence, pursuant to which defences and other factors relating to the underlying contract do not affect the ordinary execution of the guarantee. It should also be noted that conservatory attachment on the basis of counterclaims has eventually the effect of accomplishing set-off with the beneficiary's claim for payment under the guarantee.[23] Such a set-off appears to be incompatible with the liquidity function of (demand) guarantees which assures actual payment. Moreover, the account party is in fact utilising the guarantee in favour of the beneficiary as a means of securing payment of his own counterclaim which also appears to frustrate the purpose of a guarantee.[24]

Conservatory attachment and counterclaims ex other contracts. Set-off

17-5 In an *obiter dictum*, *Trib. Arrond. Luxembourg, 17 June 1982*, ruled that conservatory attachment must be discharged not only in the event that the counterclaim relates to the underlying transaction but also in the case that it arises from another contract which was not the one covered by the guarantee.[25] A reverse decision was reached in *Paris, 5 May 1982*, which accepted the possibility of conservatory attach-

---

[22] KG 1992, 301. See also *Trib. Arrond. Luxembourg, 17 June 1982*, mentioned in No. 17-5.

[23] For example, if the beneficiary's claim for payment under the guarantee amounts to € 2 million and if, in respect of the account party's counterclaim, judgment is given in the amount of € 1 million, the bank will pay € 1 million to the beneficiary, while the account party's counterclaim is then satisfied and extinguished.

[24] Cf. von Westphalen, who recognises the admissibility of set-off between account party and beneficiary (p. 397), but rejects the possibility of conservatory attachment (p. 319), Prüm, Nos. 541-542, and *Potton Homes v. Coleman Contractors*, see No. 9. below. See also Chapter 14.5.13. Poullet, Banca Borsa 1984, pp. 75-76, however, recognises the possibility of set-off to be accomplished by means of conservatory attachment.

[25] D. 1983 I.R. p. 301.

ment in the event previously mentioned.[26] Several authors take the same view.[27] It is doubtful, however, whether this decision is still good law in France since, with respect to documentary credits, *Cass., 18 March 1986*, and *Cass., 18 October 1988*, ruled that conservatory attachment is not permitted in the event of counterclaims relating to other contracts either.[28]

The question of whether conservatory attachment on the guarantee funds in relation to counterclaims from other contracts is permissible is more difficult to answer than in relation to counterclaims from the underlying contract. The crucial issue is whether the agreed reallocation of risk, the purpose of the principle of independence and the liquidity function of (demand) guarantees, as mentioned in No. 17-4, are limited to the underlying transaction which is covered by the guarantee, or whether they also extend to other contracts between the account party and beneficiary. Although with some reserve, this study answers this question in the sense mentioned above, with the result that conservatory attachment is also not permissible in relation to counterclaims from other contracts.[29]

Conservatory attachment in respect of the beneficiary's accounts after payment

17-6 Is the account party entitled to obtain conservatory attachment orders after payment of the guarantee funds by the bank/guarantor, if arguing – but not establishing – that the beneficiary's claim for payment under the guarantee was fraudulent, and that he has therefore a claim for recovery?

This question was answered in the negative in *Rb Rotterdam, 16 March 1993*, where the bank effected payment through transfer to the beneficiary's account with the bank. The court ruled that such a transfer does not amount to payment proper.[30] The same issue arose in *Rb Haarlem, 6 February 1987*, where the bank effected payment by remitting the amount to the bailiff and, simultaneously, secured leave for conservatory attachment in respect of the beneficiary's entitlement to collect the amount from the bailiff. This was the fourth attempt by the bank and the account party to thwart the beneficiary's right to actually receive the guarantee funds, and it proved unsuccessful,

---

[26] D. 1982 I.R. p. 497. The reasoning was the same as in *Trib. gr. inst. Paris, May 13 1980*, examined in No. 17-4. The order was, however, lifted for the sole reason that the court was not convinced of the existence of the counterclaim.

[27] Von Westphalen, p. 319, Poullet, Banca Borsa 1984, pp. 77-78, JCB 1982, p. 658, Mouly, JCP 1981 éd. C.I. No. 10109, Bontoux, Banque 1982, p. 172, Dohm, Nos. 331, 335, 343. See further Mijnssen, p. 66, Pabbruwe, p. 59, note 5, Mülbert, p. 193.

[28] D. 1986 J. p. 374, and D. 1989 Somm. p. 195.

[29] Idem Vasseur, D. 1986 J. pp. 376, 379, and also Prüm, Nos. 541-542. See for this subject also RPDB, Nos. 156-158.

[30] KG 1993, 222.

as had the previous three attempts. With increasing impatience, the court took into account that the fourth application was founded on the same grounds as those advanced in vain in the three previous instances, that a conservatory attachment in respect of the funds held by the bailiff had the practical effect of preventing the beneficiary from gaining free disposition of the guarantee funds, which ran counter to the purpose of first demand guarantees, and ruled that the present application amounted to an abuse of the law on conservatory attachment. The court discharged the order which was previously granted in an *ex parte* hearing.[31]

Does the impermissibility of conservatory attachment in non-established fraud cases extend to situations where the beneficiary has actually received the funds, which is ordinarily accomplished by remission to the beneficiary's accounts with his own bank, and where the account party applies for a conservatory attachment order in respect of his general accounts? The difficulty is that the contract of guarantee has been fully executed and that, under the general principles, the creditor (account party) is entitled to seize, by means of conservatory attachment, all assets of the debtor (beneficiary), while on the other hand conservatory attachment in such circumstances may, to a large extent, have the same effect as attachment of the guarantee funds before payment.[32] *CA The Hague, 21 September 1994*, ruled that attachment immediately after payment into the beneficary's accounts with a financial institution, which merely acted as an intermediary, was impermissible since it frustrates the beneficiary's right to freely dispose of the guarantee funds.[33] Nonetheless, it would appear that the impermissibility of conservatory attachment in respect of the beneficiary's accounts or other assets must cease once the beneficiary has received actual payment, which occurs as soon as the account designated by the beneficiary has been credited, as was correctly decided in *CA Amsterdam, 16 October 2003*.[34] At any rate, applications for conservatory attachment after payment must be made in the jurisdiction where the accounts or property

---

[31] KG 1987, 104. In *Rb Haarlem, 21 November 1986*, KG 1987, 57, the court discharged a conservatory attachment order in respect of the guarantee funds with the bank on the grounds that the beneficiary's fraud was not established. When, subsequently, the bank refused payment because of (alleged) fraud, it was ordered to pay by *Rb Haarlem, 9 January 1987*, KG 1987, 85. The bank then obtained a conservatory attachment order in respect of the guarantee funds held by the bank itself, which was lifted in *Rb Haarlem, 22 January 1987*, KG 1987, 86. It is to be noted that the account party was declared insolvent and that he had assigned his (asserted) claim against the beneficiary to his bank.

[32] It is noted that remission of the guarantee funds to the beneficiary's accounts with his own bank often results in reducing his deficit, rather than in increasing his credit balance. Conservatory attachment orders are futile in the event of a (reduced) debit balance.

[33] KG 1994, 381. But see *Intraco v. Notis Shipping Corp. (The Bhoja Trader)*, [1981] 2 Lloyd's Rep. 256, see No. 17-9. See also Bartman, NJB 1987, p. 1093.

[34] JOR 2004, 291. Critical: Janssen/Slegers, Advocatenblad 2004, p. 60.

are located. If the beneficiary is not situated in the same country as the bank, this will often be abroad.

Conservatory attachment and indirect guarantees

17-7 It is established law that conservatory attachment under the first instructing bank founded on the account party's (counter)claim against the beneficiary is not possible, or, at least, ineffectual.[35] The reason is that the instructing bank does not stand in a contractual relationship with the beneficiary and that it does not owe anything to the beneficiary. In the case of indirect guarantees, applications for conservatory attachment founded on claims against the beneficiary must be directed at the funds with the foreign issuing bank. Such applications are to be submitted in the jurisdiction of the foreign bank.

Conservatory attachment in respect of the counter-guarantee funds with the instructing bank is only – theoretically – possible in the event that the second issuing bank participated in, or was aware of, the beneficiary's fraud, apart from the objections discussed in No. 17-3.[36]

Conservatory attachment does not prohibit the bank from paying into a blocked account and from debiting the account party's accounts

17-8 As stated in No. 17-1 above, conservatory attachment is meant to preserve assets which can be seized when judgment in main proceedings against the defendant (beneficiary) has been obtained. These Continental measures do not prohibit the bank from paying the amount of the guarantee into a blocked account in the beneficiary's name and to debit the accounts of the account party.[37] Accordingly, while in the event of a successful attachment, the account party is able to prevent actual payment to the beneficiary, he cannot avoid the debiting of his accounts. This is another reason why, in appropriate cases, it is in the account party's interest to apply for stop-payment orders instead of conservatory attachment, although the latter technique has the advan-

---

[35] See, for example, *Rb Amsterdam, 23 May 1985*, KG 1985, 165, *CA Amsterdam, 15 January 1987*, NJ 1988, 268, *Rb Amsterdam, 31 March 1988*, KG 1988, 179, *CA Leeuwarden, 12 September 1990*, KG 1990, 316 (the attachment was, however, not lifted because it was ineffectual for reasons as stated in the text), *CA The Hague, 8 June 1993*, KG 1993, 301, *Paris, 25 March 1982*, D. 1982 I.R. p. 497, *Trib. com. Montlucon, 9 January 1981*, D. 1981 J. p. 390, *Trib. com. Paris, 2 February 1983*, D. 1985 I.R. p. 243. See also the following note. See further von Westphalen, p. 320, Zahn/Ehrlich/Neumann, 9/147, Prüm, No. 533, Vasseur, No. 132, Mattout, No. 237, Poullet, Banca Borsa 1984, p. 77, Dohm, Nos. 344-347.

[36] Cf. *Cass., 12 December 1984*, D. 1985 J. p. 269, and *Paris, 3 December 1984*, D. 1985 I.R. p. 240 (orders discharged).

[37] Cf. *CA Leeuwarden, 12 September 1990*, KG 1990, 316.

tage of gaining time. It is recommended practice that the bank puts the amount into an interest-bearing blocked account in order to reduce the beneficiary's loss of interest during the period that the attachment remains in force.[38]

In *Cass., 7 October 1987*, and in *CA Amsterdam, 5 February 1987*, it was held that actual payment by the bank to the beneficiary did not constitute a breach of contract or wrongful conduct, despite the attachment.[39] This strategy is, however, not to be recommended since it exposes the bank to an avoidable risk. If the account party were able to obtain judgment, the bank would be accountable to its customer. A safer procedure for the bank is to apply for discharge of the order, a request which is virtually always honoured.

The U.K. freezing (Mareva) injunction

17-9 The English technique of a freezing (Mareva) injunction serves the same purpose as the Continental conservatory attachment, namely the preservation of the debtor's assets pending litigation.[40] When granted, a freezing injunction enjoins the debtor from removing his assets from the court's jurisdiction. Like their Continental counterparts, a freezing injunction can be issued in respect of the debtor's real property or bank accounts and other receivables. When the bank has been given notice of the injunction, it is prohibited from allowing the debtor to withdraw the frozen funds, on pain of being in contempt of court. A technical difference is that the freezing injunction is an action *in personam* whereas the Continental conservatory attachment is an action *in rem*.

In the event that the bank has not yet proceeded to payment under the guarantee, freezing injunctions have the same effect as restraining orders against the bank and/or beneficiary. Indeed, in this situation, applications for freezing injunctions have been treated in the same way and were dismissed or discharged for virtually the same reasons. However, Donaldson L.J. in *Intraco v. Notis Shipping Corp. (The Bhoja Trader)* stressed that there is a crucial difference between the situation whereby the bank has not yet effected payment and the case whereby the bank has paid by transferring the guarantee amount to the beneficiary's account ('before-' and 'after-payment' situations): 'It is the natural corollary of the proposition that a letter of credit or bank guarantee is to be treated as cash that when the bank pays and cash is received by the beneficiary, it should be subject to the same restraints as any other of his cash assets. Enjoining the

---

[38] See Bertrams, Bb 1994, pp. 225-227.

[39] Banque 1988, p. 234 (in respect of documentary credit), and NJ 1988, 591, respectively. See, however, *CA Amsterdam, 15 January 1987*, NJ 1988, 268, and *CA Leeuarden, 12 September 1990*, KG 1990, 316, where the Court of Appeal observed that the bank should not pay as long as the attachment remains in force.

[40] See, for freezing (Mareva) injunctions in the context of bank guarantees, especially O'Driscoll, Northwestern Jo. of Intern. Law & Business, 1985, pp. 398-407.

beneficiary from removing the cash assets from the jurisdiction is not the same as taking action, whether by injunction or an order staying execution, which will prevent him obtaining the cash.'[41] Thus, a freezing injunction will not be granted in order to prevent payment under the guarantee but 'it may apply to the proceeds as and when received by or for the defendant.'[42] Accordingly, the possibility of a freezing injunction under English law is limited to 'after-payment' cases and should be compared with the Continental conservatory attachment examined in No. 17-6. The distinction between 'before-' and 'after-payment' cases for the purpose of freezing injunctions underlines the fact that the preponderant motive for dismissing applications for freezing orders before payment by the bank and restraining orders against the bank stems from the great reluctance of English courts to interfere with the bank's absolute and independent undertaking under a bank guarantee.[43]

While Donaldson L.J., in the *Intraco* case, discharged the freezing order on the grounds that the guarantee provided for payment in Greece, thus outside the court's jurisdiction, he intimated that he would have been prepared to affirm the order in appropriate cases, if the guarantee were payable in London. In view of subsequent cases, it remains to be seen whether and under which conditions freezing injunctions will indeed be allowed if the guarantee is payable in the court's jurisdiction. In *Potton Homes v. Coleman Contractors* the account party had a liquidated counterclaim against the beneficiary for moneys under the secured contract. Hawser J. refused to grant a restraining order against the beneficiary but ordered a freeze of the guarantee funds and directed these funds to be paid into a joint account until all issues between account party and beneficiary could be tried. The Court of Appeal ruled, however, that such a freeze violated the beneficiary's right to receive payment and discharged the order.[44] However, in the recent case of *Csarnikow-Rionda v. Standard Bank London* a freezing order had been granted and remained unchallenged, and Rix J. pointed out that the availability of the protection of a freezing order is an important factor in persuading the court not to grant a restraining order against the bank.[45]

---

[41] [1981] 2 Lloyd's Rep. 256, 258. The same difference was emphasized by Rix J. in *Csarnikow-Rionda v. Standard Bank London*, [1999] 2 Lloyd's Rep. 187, 203.

[42] Per Denning MR in *Z Ltd. v. A*, [1982] 1 All E.R. 556, 563, who affirmed the *Intraco* decision.

[43] Cf. Chapter 14.3.6 and Chapter 16.3, No. 16-4.

[44] [1984] 28 Build. L.R. 19.

[45] [1999] 2 Lloyd's Rep. 187. In *Themehelp Ltd v. West and Others*, [1996] QB 84, Evans L.J., in his dissenting opinion, believed that the case 'cried out for *Mareva* relief' (as opposed to an interlocutory injunction against the beneficiary), see Chapter 16.2, No. 16-2.

CHAPTER 18
JURISDICTION AND APPLICABLE LAW

18.1 JURISDICTION

Introduction

18-1 In respect of the member states of the European Union, jurisdiction is determined by EU Regulation No. 44/2001 of 22 December 2000 on Jurisdiction and the Enforcement of Judgments in Civil and Commercial Matters. This EU Regulation applies if the defendant has his place of business in one of the EU member states.[1] In that event, jurisdiction must be founded on one of the grounds mentioned in the Regulation, in derogation of the domestic rules for jurisdiction of the forum. However, as far as provisional and protective measures are concerned, art. 31 of the EU Regulation permits the court to found its jurisdiction on its domestic rules. This is of great significance, since a great many cases concern applications for interlocutory restraining orders or for conservatory attachment and freezing injunctions.

A choice of jurisdiction or arbitration clause in the secured contract does not affect the jurisdiction in matters concerning the guarantee.[2]

Proceedings between the parties to the (counter-)guarantee

18-2 For obvious reasons, proceedings between the parties to the (counter-)guarantee are nearly always initiated by the beneficiary against the bank and, in the case of an indirect guarantee, by the issuing bank against the instructing bank. As far as reported case law is concerned, beneficiaries and foreign issuing banks have invariably brought proceedings for payment in the (instructing) bank's place of business, which is universally recognised as a proper forum, cf. art. 2(1) EU Regulation and art. 28 URDG.[3]

---

[1] The EU Regulation does not apply to Denmark which remains subject to the 1968 EU (Brussels) Convention on Jurisdiction and the Enforcement of Judgments in Civil and Commercial Matters, as amended. The Lugano Convention of 16 September 1988 applies, at present, in the relationship with Iceland, Norway, Switzerland and Poland.

[2] Cf. *BGH, 12 March 1984 (11 ZR 10/83)*, RIW 1985, p. 78, *LG Duisburg, 27 November 1987*, WM 1988, p. 1483, *Trib. com. Liege, 20 June 1983*, Jur. Liege 1984, p. 512, *Antwerp, 13 October 1982*, BRH 1982, p. 642, *Paris, 25 May 1983*, D. 1983 I.R. p. 484, *Paris, 14 December 1987*, D. 1988 Somm. p. 248, *Paris, 25 February 1988*, D. 1989 Somm. p. 150.

[3] The only exception appears to be *Attock Cement Co. v. Romanian Bank for Foreign Trade*,

Art. 5(1) EU Regulation also allows for jurisdiction at the place of payment pursuant to the guarantee. This is particularly relevant if the (counter-)guarantee has been issued by a foreign branch of the (instructing) bank. In that event art. 28 URDG also allows proceedings to take place at the place of business of the issuing branch.

In accordance with the general rules for jurisdiction and art. 28 URDG, first sentence, a choice of jurisdiction by the parties takes priority over the rules mentioned in the previous paragraphs. Direct guarantees sometimes provide for exclusive jurisdiction in the bank's country. If the beneficiary with a dominant bargaining power is desirous of being able to sue the bank in his own country, he is likely to insist on an indirect guarantee. In this event, the issuing bank and the beneficiary are ordinarily domiciled in the same (foreign) country. Counter-guarantees in favour of issuing banks in the Middle East and North Africa often stipulate that disputes are to be settled in the country of the issuing bank.

Proceedings initiated by the account party. Direct guarantee

18-3 Litigation, whether interlocutory or in main proceedings, against the bank does not present any jurisdictional problems since both parties are ordinarily domiciled in the same country.[4] If the account party applies for a stop-payment order against the bank, he often also applies for a restraining order against the foreign beneficiary. Depending on the domestic law of the forum, including the EU Regulation, jurisdiction over the beneficiary might be founded on the place where the order takes effect or on the ground of multiple defendants. The ground last-mentioned is also provided for in art. 6(1) EU Regulation. In any event, courts have never declined jurisdiction in interlocutory proceedings over foreign beneficiaries. The URDG do not contain rules of jurisdiction for proceedings brought by the account party.

In *BGH, 16 October 1984*, the German Supreme Court ruled on the applicability of art. 5(1) and 5(3) of the EU Brussels Convention (currently the EU Regulation), when a German account party sued the Belgian beneficiary in main proceedings for recovery of the amounts paid under the guarantee, alleging that the demand for payment was fraudulent.[5] Proceedings were brought in München, being the place of business of the German bank. The Supreme Court ruled that there was jurisdiction because the loss

---

[1989] 1 All ER 1189. The beneficiary applied for leave to serve the writ abroad on the grounds that the guarantee, issued by the Romanian bank, was governed by English law (RSC Order 11 Rule 1 (1)(d)(iii)). The Court of Appeal held that the guarantee was not governed by English law and refused leave, see also No. 18-5.

4   In *Muduroglu Ltd. v. T.C. Ziraat Bankasi*, [1986] 1 Q.B. 1225, the Court of Appeal declined to accept jurisdiction on the grounds of *forum non conveniens*, since neither of the litigants had any real connections with England.

5   RIW 1985, p. 72.

was suffered in Munich, art. 5(3), and because the beneficiary's ancillary contractual duty to refrain from fraudulently demanding payment was also to be performed in Munich, art. 5(1). The German court thus viewed the (allegedly) fraudulent call both as a tort and as a breach of a contractual obligation. As far as applications for preventive restraining orders against the beneficiary are concerned, the applicability of art. 5(3) EU Regulation, in respect of the place where the loss occurs, is questionable when the damage has not yet materialised.[6]

Proceedings initiated by the account party. Indirect guarantee

18-4 In addition to applications for stop-payment orders against the instructing bank, account parties in the Netherlands, France, Belgium and the United Kingdom sometimes also apply for restraining orders against the foreign issuing bank and beneficiary. Jurisdiction over those defendants can be based on grounds mentioned in No. 18-3. Courts have usually accepted jurisdiction over the foreign issuing bank and the foreign beneficiary. One may, however, doubt whether courts in the account party's country have jurisdiction *ratione materiae* in relation to applications for orders restraining the foreign issuing bank from paying under the primary guarantee and for restraining orders against the foreign beneficiary in respect of the primary guarantee.[7] The applicability of art. 5(1) and art. 5(3) EU Regulation and their domestic counterparts must also be doubted as far as the foreign beneficiary is concerned.

It appears that a clause in the counter-guarantee providing for exclusive jurisdiction in the foreign issuing bank's country does not prevent the account party from suing that bank as co-defendant in the instructing bank's domicile, since such a clause relates to disputes between the two banks and does not ordinarily bind the account party. This proposition seems to be supported by the dearth of litigation in this respect, although many counter-guarantees contain such a clause.[8]

18.2 APPLICABLE LAW

(In)significance of private international law

18-5 Although the majority of the huge body of case law deals with guarantees and counter-guarantees containing crossborder elements, private international law as a tech-

---

[6] See also *EC Court of Justice, 27 September 1988, 189/87* (Kalfelis). The European Court ruled that the obligations arising from tort, as envisaged in art. 5(3) 1968 EU (Brussels) Convention (replaced by the EU Regulation), must be unconnected with contractual obligations.

[7] See Chapter 16.4.3, No. 16-17.

[8] But see *Paris, 23 June 1995*, JCP Éd. E II, No. 735, where jurisdiction over the foreign issuing bank was explicitly accepted.

nique for selecting the applicable law has not played a significant role.[9] In only a very small number of cases did the court touch, albeit perfunctorily, on the issue of applicable law. In none of these cases was it made clear why this issue was broached, as no mention was made of any speculations concerning possible differences between the various national laws. Nor did the fact that the (counter-)guarantee was governed by a particular system of foreign law have any impact on the outcome of the litigation.[10] In those cases where the (counter-)guarantee was evidently governed by foreign law, such as in the case of a choice of law clause or an indirect (primary) guarantee, courts either ignored this fact or referred to the applicability of foreign law, and then proceeded to apply the notions prevailing in the court's own jurisdiction. The predominance of the concepts and rules originating from domestic sources is especially apparent in German, French, Belgian and English case law which contains frequent references to domestic statutory provisions, case law and legal writing. It must be emphasised, however, that the attitude and perceptions of courts, when evidently applying their own notions, can by no means be described as provincial.

The tendency to disregard the issue of private international law is especially manifest in the following cases. In *Attock Cement Co. v. Romanian Bank for Foreign Trade*, the Court of Appeal referred to the oddity of the situation that the issue of the applicable law was only relevant for the purpose of jurisdiction, while it was unlikely that the matter would be raised at the trial.[11] In *Brussels, 25 February 1982*, involving an indirect guarantee issued by an Indian bank in favour of an Indian beneficiary – which was unquestionably governed by Indian law – the court tersely observed that the selection of Indian or Belgian law was indifferent because they are the same.[12] Similar observa-

---

[9] Cf. Mattout, No. 209.

[10] The only exception appears to be *OG Austria, 10 July 1986*, JIBL 1986 N-140, see Chapter 16.4.1, No. 16-12. In certain situations the applicable law might be relevant for the purpose of determining jurisdiction.

[11] [1989] 1 All ER 1189, see also note 3. The Court of Appeal also pointed to an affidavit submitted on behalf of the Romanian bank to the effect that Romanian and English law were believed to be the same. A subsequent attempt to preserve the possibility of their being different was discarded as being motivated by tactical reasons only. See also *ICC arbitration* (Geneva), No. 3316 (1979), JDI 1980, p. 970, where the Mexican beneficiary did not object to the application of Belgian law, stating that all countries apply the same rule. The application of Belgian law consisted of a reference to one Belgian article, which in its turn referred to French sources, and of a few statutory provisions of a most general and uninformative nature. In *OLG Hamburg, 4 November 1977*, RIW 1978, p. 615, the Court of Appeal applied German rules of private international law when answering the question of which law would have been applied by an Egyptian court. It is also worth noting that German legal writing frequently refers to German statutory provisions in relation to indirect guarantees, which are governed by foreign law.

[12] JCB 1982, p. 349.

tions were made in *I.E. Contractors Ltd. v. Lloyds Bank Plc.* and in *CA Leeuwarden, 12 September 1990*, where the court applied the law of the forum because there were no indications that the applicable foreign (Iraqi and Egyptian, respectively) law was different from the law of the forum.[13] In *Offshore Enterprises v. Nordic Bank PLC*, the guarantee was governed by Indian law, and expert evidence was adduced to the effect that, under Indian law, guarantees can be called after the expiry date. This argument was brushed aside, which reveals that the Court of Appeal, in fact, applied English law, which, for that matter, is the same as the law in most countries.[14]

In conclusion, case law shows that the issue of private international law and the possible applicability of foreign law is of little significance in matters concerning guarantees and counter-guarantees. This finding tallies with the view of this study that the technique of independent guarantees and counter-guarantees, as well as the relevant rules of law, have developed on a transnational level, away from domestic concepts and structures, and that it is a fallacy to think in terms of significant divergence of national laws. The transnational character of the law of independent guarantees is especially reflected in *CA The Hague, 8 June 1993*, where the Court of Appeal observed that the meaning of an 'extend or pay' request had to be determined in accordance with internationally accepted notions and that the applicable law of Yemen was assumed to adhere to these notions.[15]

The issue of applicable law is, however, relevant in respect of the (non-)enforceability of expiry dates and, possibly, in respect of some other specific matters, such as interest and damages in the event of late payment, requirements of a formal notice of default, formation of the contract of guarantee, the place of payment, set-off, assignment and pledge, limitation of actions and the bank's duty of notification before payment.

General rules of private international law. 1980 Rome Convention

18-6 The EU Convention on the Law Applicable to Contractual Obligations, Rome 1980, came into force in 1991 in The Netherlands, United Kingdom, Germany, France, and Belgium and also in other countries of the European Community in that same or subsequent years. Under the Convention, the contract is governed by the law chosen by the parties, either explicitly or tacitly, see art. 3. In the absence of a choice of law, the contract is governed by the law of the country with which the contract is most closely connected, art. 4(1). This is presumed to be the country in which the party that renders the characteristic performance has his place of business, art. 4(2).

---

[13] [1990] 2 Lloyd's Rep. 496; KG 1990, 316, r.o. 5 which is not published in the KG reports.

[14] IBL November 1984, p. 86. See Chapter 12.4.5. for the (non-)enforceability of expiry dates.

[15] KG 1993, 301. See also *CA Zürich, 9 May 1985*, D. 1987, Somm. p. 177, which referred to the supranational '*lex mercatoria*' and Staudinger/Horn, No. 305, who refers to the diminishing importance of the applicable law because of the increasing transnational uniform law.

Relationship account party/bank

18-7 The place of business of the account party and bank is nearly always situated in the same country. In these situations, the issue of private international law does not arise. Should they have their place of business in different countries, their relationship is governed by the law of the bank's place of business, either because of a choice of law clause or because of the criterion of the characteristic performance.

Relationship bank/beneficiary

18-8 In the case of indirect guarantees, the issuing bank and the beneficiary have ordinarily their place of business in the same, foreign country. If not, the issue of applicable law is resolved in the same way as with direct guarantees.

Direct guarantees in favour of foreign beneficiaries occasionally contain a choice of law clause. If they do, they usually provide for the applicability of the law of the issuing bank's country. This is, however, not always the case, especially in respect of guarantees in favour of Saudi Arabian beneficiaries. Selected banks from a number of countries are authorised to directly issue guarantees, provided that the guarantee is made subject to the laws and regulations of Saudi Arabia. In other situations, beneficiaries who insist on the applicability of their own law usually require an indirect guarantee issued by a local bank.

In the absence of a choice of law clause, the guarantee is governed by the law of the country in which the issuing bank or issuing branch has its place of business, both in the case of direct and indirect guarantees, cf. art. 4(2) Rome Convention.[16] Art. 27 URDG and art. 21/22 UNCITRAL Convention contain the same conflict rule. This rule is not affected by the interposition of an advising, but not paying, bank. On account of the equation of independent guarantees and documentary credits, English courts sometimes consider the law of the country where the guarantee is payable as the applicable law.[17] This usually coincides with the country in which the issuing bank or branch has its place of business.

---

[16] See, e.g., *BGH, 16 October 1984*, RIW 1985, p. 72, *OLG Hamburg, 4 November 1977*, RIW 1978, p. 615, *LG Frankfurt a.M., 11 December 1979*, NJW 1981, p. 56 (indirect guarantee), *LG Dortmund, 9 July 1980*, WM 1981, p. 280 (indirect guarantee), *OLG Saarbrücken, 6 July 2001*, WM 2001, p. 2055, Rb *Rotterdam, 22 June 1984*, NIPR 1984, No. 327. See also von Westphalen, pp. 324, 329, Staudinger/Horn, No. 302, Zahn/Ehrlich/Neumann, 9/36. In *OLG Frankfurt a.M., 16 September 1982*, RIW 1983, p. 785, involving a direct guarantee issued by a Swedish bank in favour of a German beneficiary, the Court of Appeal held, however, that the guarantee was governed by German law, invoking the device of the 'presumed' choice of law.

[17] *Attock Cement & Co v. Romanian Bank for Foreign Trade*, [1989] 1 All ER 1189. The Court of Appeal cited *Power Curber Int. v. Nat. Bank of Kuwait*, [1981] WLR 1233, which involved a documentary credit case.

Relationship instructing bank/issuing bank in the case of indirect guarantees

18-9 Counter-guarantees occasionally specify the applicable law. Counter-guarantees in favour of issuing banks in the Middle East and North Africa often contain explicit clauses providing for the applicability of the issuing bank's law. In their absence, a choice of jurisdiction in favour of settlement in those countries is likely, in effect, to dispose of the issue of private international law.

The determination of the applicable law in the absence of a choice of law clause very much depends on the way one perceives the relationship between instructing and issuing bank. As discussed elsewhere,[18] German doctrine splits this relationship into two distinct segments: the mandate and the counter-guarantee, which is viewed as an ordinary guarantee. In the absence of a choice of law, the conflict rules result in the applicability of the law of the issuing bank as far as the mandate relationship is concerned,[19] whereas the counter-guarantee is governed by the law of the country in which the instructing bank has its place of business.[20] On three occasions, German courts declared the (German) law of the instructing bank to be applicable without distinguishing between mandate and counter-guarantee. Insofar as the courts particularised the relevant rule of private international law, they exhibited a marked keenness for finding in favour of the law of the forum, the more so as the counter-guarantees in favour of the Iranian bank almost certainly, and the one in favour of the Egyptian bank probably, contained a clause providing for the applicability of the foreign bank's law.[21]

The approach in French case law regarding the inter-bank relationship is uncertain. All one could say is that, without paying specific attention to the issue of the applicable law, French courts appear to favour French law whenever a French instructing bank is

---

[18] Chapter 11.2.2, No. 11-11.

[19] Von Westphalen, pp. 250, 328, Staudinger/Horn, No. 306, Goerke, p. 101-102, Zahn/Ehrlich/Neumann, 9/36, Mülbert, pp. 28, 29, von Mettenheim, RIW 191, p. 584, Bark, ZIP 1982, p. 408, Schütze, WM 1982, p. 1398, Dohm, Nos. 270, 318, Kleiner, No. 26.04.

[20] Von Westphalen, pp. 250, 328, Staudinger/Horn, No. 306, Goerke, pp. 101-102, Zahn/Ehrlich/Neumann, 9/36, Mülbert, pp. 28, 29, 81, Pleyer, WM Sonderbeilage 2/1973, p. 15, Horn, IPRax 1981, p. 153, Bark, ZIP 1982, p. 410, Schütze, WM 1982, p. 1398, Rümker, ZGR 1986, p. 341, Dohm, Nos. 319-322, Kleiner, No. 26.04. See also Pabbruwe, p. 69.

[21] *LG Frankfurt a.M., 11 December 1979*, NJW 1981, p. 56 (referring to the presumed intention of the parties and the characteristic performance), *LG Dortmund, 9 July 1980*, WM 1981, p. 280 (the court laconically stated that the inter-bank relationship was governed by German law and sought secondary support in the presumed intention of the parties and the balance of interests taking all (unrevealed) factors into consideration). It might be noted, by way of comment, that the Iranian bank cannot conceivably have had any intention of subjecting itself to German law. *OLG Saarbrücken, 23 January 1981*, RIW 1981, p. 338 (no mention of the relevant rules of private international law; the court referred to the inter-bank relationship as mandate; foreign issuing bank situated in Egypt).

involved.[22] In *Paris June 28 1989* the Court of Appeal explicitly ruled, however, that a counter-guarantee is governed by the law of the country where the bank issuing the counter-guarantee has its place of business on the grounds that counter-guarantee and primary guarantee are seperate transactions.[23]

Under the UNCITRAL Convention and URDG, the counter-guarantee is governed by the law of the country where the instructing bank has its place of business in the absence of a contrary choice of law, see art. 21/22 UNCITRAL Convention and art. 27 URDG. This is the consequence of the principle enshrined in the Convention and the URDG that a counter-guarantee is independent of the primary guarantee and that it is to be treated as an ordinary guarantee.

English law takes a contrary view. In *Turkiye Is Bankasi v. Bank of China* and *Wahda Bank v. Arab Bank* the court observed that counter-guarantee and primary guarantee are intimately connected because the issue of the primary guarantee provides the consideration for the counter-guarantee, and that it is important for the issuing bank that its right of reimbursement is back to back to its liability under the primary guarantee. The court in both cases, therefore, ruled that the counter-guarantee was governed by the law applicable to the primary guarantee.[24] Staughton L.J. in *Wahda Bank v. Arab Bank PLC* also thought that the rule in art. 27 URDG would be not very attractive to bankers and he expected that bankers would adopt something which is more suitable to their needs.[25]

This study views the inter-bank relationship as being one and indivisible. The relationship consists of the instructions by the instructing bank to the issuing bank with an explicit or implicit undertaking to reimburse the issuing bank, i.e. the mandate, and the counter-guarantee which qualifies the terms for reimbursement.[26] It is totally unrealistic to split this relationship into two distinct segments, as German doctrine does, the more so as the mandate and counter-guarantee are ordinarily contained in one and the same document. It is, therefore, submitted that this entire relationship is governed by the law of the country in which the foreign issuing bank has its place of business, since

---

[22] See, e.g., *Paris, July 26 1985*, D. 1986 I.R. p. 157 (counter-guarantee governed by the law of the instructing bank. The Court of Appeal saw fit to enumerate no less than five creative arguments for applying French law and none in favour of the law of Rwanda). In several other French cases, the courts referred to French statutory provisions without observations concerning private international law. See further *Luxembourg, March 16 1983*, D. 1983 I.R. p. 299 (counter-guarantee is governed by the law of the instructing bank).

[23] D. 1990 Somm. p. 212 (resulting in the applicability of French law in respect of the computation of interest). See also Prüm, No. 86.

[24] *Turkiye Bankasi AS v. Bank of China*, [1993] 1 Lloyd's Rep. 132, *Wahda Bank v. Arab Bank PLC*, [1996] 1 Lloyd's Rep. 470.

[25] [1996] 1 Lloyd's Rep. 470, 474.

[26] See Chapter 11.2.2, No. 11-13.

that bank is entrusted with the characteristic performance, namely the issuance of the primary guarantee and the examination in respect of compliance with the terms of the guarantee, whereas the first instructing bank is merely to pay charges and to reimburse the issuing bank. This conflict rule has the added advantage that the issuing bank's conduct, and its rights and obligations as regards the beneficiary pursuant to the primary guarantee and as regards the instructing bank on account of the counter-guarantee are governed by the same law, so that it will not be caught in between (conceivably) divergent systems. References to the supposed independence between primary guarantee and counter-guarantee totally ignore the functional interdependence between the two, as so convincingly emphasised in English case law. Moreover, it is quite revealing that if the counter-guarantee contains an explicit choice of law, it invariably refers to the issuing bank's law and instructing banks do not object to such choice. A conflict of laws rule, which applies in the absence of an explicit choice, should not be at odds with established practice and clear expectations.

Several other authors also take the view that, in the absence of a choice of law, the counter-guarantee should be governed by the law of the issuing bank.[27]

Public mandatory law

18-10 Irrespective of the law governing the guarantee or counter-guarantee, courts must apply the public mandatory law of the forum, such as regulations concerning the licence to issue guarantees and currency exchange regulations. Some foreign banks require the instructing bank to confirm that the necessary approvals have been obtained.

---

[27] Davenport and Smith, JIBFL Jan. 1994 pp. 3, 5, Chatterjee, JIBL 1994 pp. 20, 23, Nielsen, pp. 44, 98, Poullet, Tours, p. 142, Pelichet, RDAI 1990 pp. 345-347 (who argues that the applicability of one and the same law to the counter-guarantee and primary guarantee can be derived from subsection 5 of art. 4 of the 1980 EC Convention), Looyens, TBH 1966, p. 881, RPDB, No. 177. The disadvantages of applying the instructing bank's law to the counter-guarantee have also been recognised by Vasseur, RDAI 1992 p. 264, D. 1990 Somm. p. 212, and D. 1989 Somm. p. 146, Stoufflet, JDI 1987 p. 276, Mattout, No. 209.

CHAPTER 19
BANK GUARANTEES AND CONSTRUCTION CONTRACTS

First demand guarantees as financing instruments

19-1 Major transactions carried out over a period of time, such as construction contracts, face the problem of financing the project. In a hypothetical situation, the arrangements may be such that the construction firm or exporter of capital goods does not receive payment until after completion of the plant or the setting-up of the equipment. Such a scheme is not necessarily unreasonable, since plant or equipment only begin to generate revenues for the employer or importer if and when they are capable of use. An additional advantage is that, if the employer or importer is dissatisfied, they can refuse payment. Accordingly, payment after completion also serves as a means of security. The obvious disadvantage for the contractor is that he must then finance the entire project with the attendant costs, diminishing liquidity and the risk of not being paid. The situation described is, of course, unlikely to occur. Construction firms and exporters of capital goods will usually negotiate with the employer or importer for participation by the latter in the financing of the transaction.

Bank guarantees, and especially first demand guarantees, are useful instruments in order to accomplish such a mutually agreeable re-allocation of the burden of financing projects. In fact, construction firms and employers tend to view bank guarantees as a financing instrument no less than as a security instrument. This tallies with the fact that guarantees are only called in a small number of cases, while the financing aspect is nearly always present. For example, an employer or importer of capital goods might be prepared to make an advance payment against a first demand repayment guarantee. Certain interim payments, as the work progresses, can be made by the employer if a first demand performance guarantee is furnished. The full percentage of interim instalments and/or the last instalment can be released if a retention and/or a maintenance guarantee is made available. First demand guarantees can function as financing instruments because the employer or importer is assured that he will be able to retrieve the payments immediately and without court proceedings, once he is of the opinion that the contractor or exporter is in default. Thus, as far as his security for defective performance is concerned, the position of the employer or importer has not changed, while the contractor or exporter's position, in respect of the financing of the transaction, has improved.

The technique of utilising guarantees as financing instruments can be used in every phase and in respect of every part of the works. For example, in a contract for the construction of harbour facilities, it might initially have been agreed that fifty per cent of the contract price will be paid once the ground works have been completed. If it turns out that the springing of rock formations accounts for seventy per cent of the expenditures and that it can be accomplished in a short period of time, whereas the removal of the debris is a time-consuming chore, parties may reconsider the payment scheme. They may opt for a release of the fifty per cent instalment upon completion of the springing against a first demand guarantee. In all these and other situations, the financing of the project and more particularly, the alleviation of the difficulties on the part of the contractor depend on the availability of first demand guarantees. On the other hand, if payment will not be made until after completion, the need for a performance guarantee will be severely reduced, while the other types of guarantees are in that event irrelevant.

First demand guarantees as financing instruments can also be used in run-of-the mill letter of credit transactions. Take, for example, a buyer who only wants to agree to payment by means of a commercial letter of credit for 90% of the contract value, withholding the remaining 10% as security for defective delivery. He may, however, be persuaded to agree to a letter of credit for the full contract price against a first demand performance guarantee for 10% of the contract price. In this scenario the seller will receive the full contract price at once while the buyer retains the same degree of security.

Disputes revolve on the payment scheme. Call as *ultimum remedium*

19-2 Construction contracts usually provide for interim payments as certain quantities or certain phases of the project have been carried out. Dissatisfaction on the part of the engineer and/or employer/beneficiary with respect to the progress of the works ordinarily results in a refusal to release the certificates so that the contractor cannot obtain payment. This withholding of the certificates is usually an adequate response to the contractor's failure to carry out the works according to plan and it is the common way of putting pressure on the contractor. Accordingly, disputes between the contractor and employer tend to revolve around the question of interim payments, while the role of a performance guarantee is limited. In many situations, a threat or an actual call on the guarantee would not only be disproportionate, but it might also be ineffectual and perilous. A response of this nature puts a severe strain on the relationship, with the risk that the contractor might abandon the project. The consequences of a final breakdown are often more disastrous for the employer than for the contractor, since an uncompleted project is of little value while completion of the works by another contractor proves to be very difficult and pushes up the costs dramatically. Moreover, the amounts which have, meanwhile, been invested by the employer might have to be considered, at least partially, written off. Consequently, performance guarantees will ordinarily not be called as long as there is a reasonable prospect that the contract will be performed. The situation changes when the contractor has received the larger part of the contract price. He may then choose not to remedy remaining defects, while taking the forfeiture of the last instalments for granted. A threat to call the guarantee(s) could, then, be the only means of putting pressure on the contractor. Accordingly, guarantees tend to be called as *ultimum remedium* and also towards the completion of the project.

Joint ventures

19-3 For a number of reasons, construction projects are often carried out by a joint venture in which the chief contractors participate for the duration of the project. These joint ventures do not ordinarily possess a significant amount of capital and they are, therefore, not in a position to procure bank guarantees on the strength of a counter-guarantee issued by the joint venture. On the other hand, the employer is likely to insist on the issuance of one guarantee covering the entire project, instead of a number of guarantees issued by the banks of the participants. The technique which is often used to resolve this problem, is that a leading bank furnishes a guarantee for the full amount and that this bank – the issuing bank – can take recourse against the banks of the participants in the joint venture, in accordance with their participation. The recourse arrangement is contained in a written instrument which is often labelled as a counter-guarantee. It operates in the same way as a counter-guarantee in the event of an indirect guarantee. The only difference is that recourse against each of the banks is limited to a particular percentage. This technique is shown in diagram 1 below, where A participates for 60% and B for 40% in the joint venture.

Diagram 1

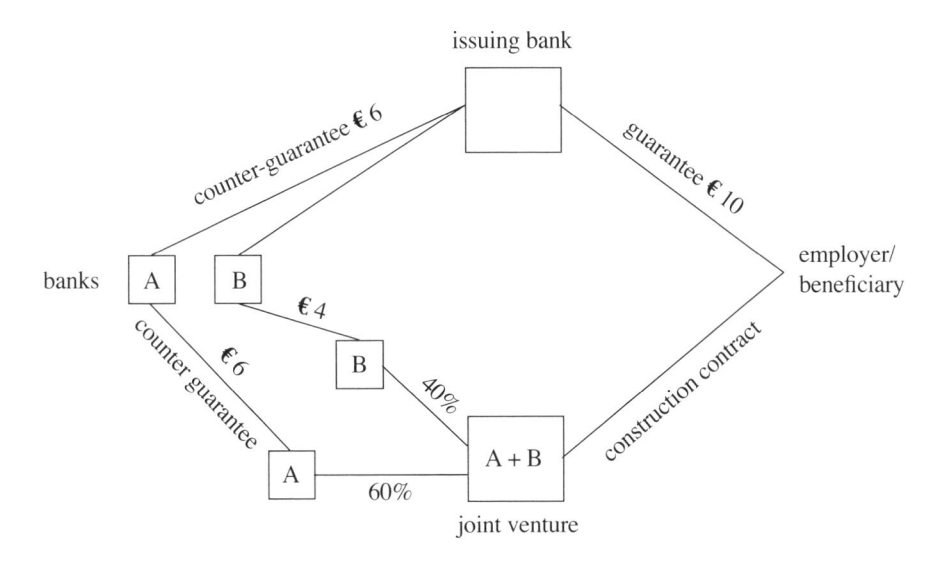

If the leading, issuing bank has effected payment to the employer/beneficiary it will take recourse against bank A and bank B for € 6 million and € 4 million, respectively. The banks will then seek reimbursement from A and B. The situation then is that A and B have contributed € 6 million and € 4 million respectively towards damages paid to the employer/beneficiary, irrespective of the question of which party is responsible, or to what extent, for the breach of contract. The joint venture agreement may provide that a final settlement between A and B is to be made in accordance with the percentage of fault, but this entirely depends on the intensity of their cooperation and the degree of risk-sharing in particular.

It should be noted that this technique can also be used in the absence of a joint venture, for example, when the chief contractor is only prepared to have substantial parts of the works carried out by those subcontractors which are willing to share in the funding and risks of the guarantee in the manner described above. This is shown in diagram 2, where the subcontractors A and B participate for € 2 million each in the guarantee.

Diagram 2

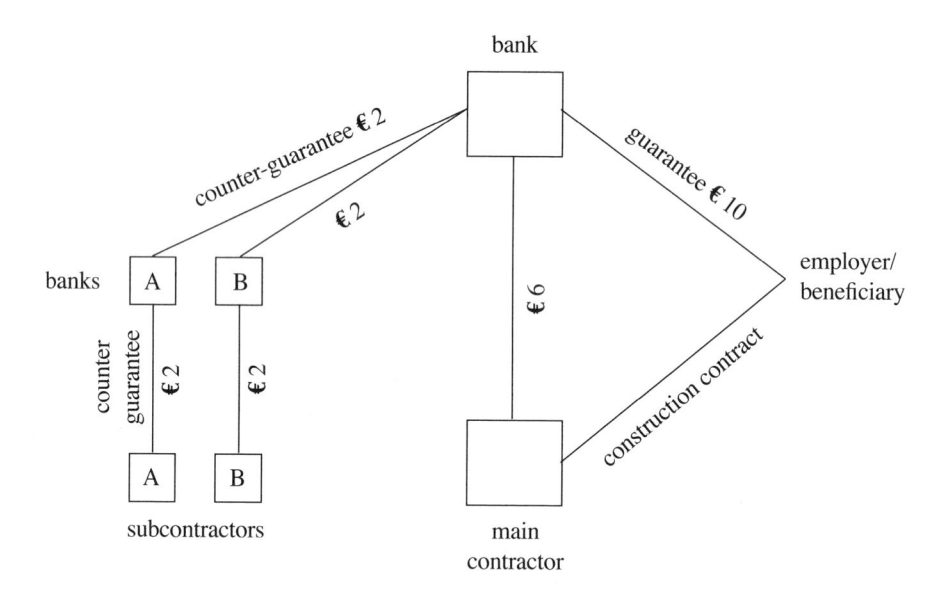

After payment the bank will take recourse against the main contractor for € 6 million, and against the banks of the subcontractors for € 2 million each.

Subguarantees from subcontractors. Subguarantees distinguished from counter-guarantees

Diagram 3

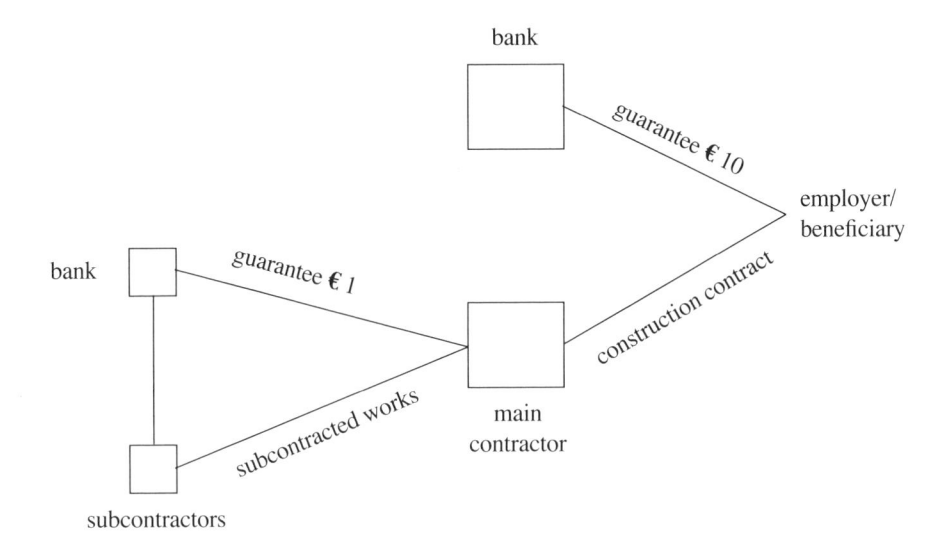

```
                          bank
                          ┌──┐
                          └──┘
                              \  guarantee €10
                               \
                                \
                                 employer/
                                 beneficiary
                                /
           guarantee €1        / construction contract
 bank  ┌──┐                   /
       └──┘─────────────┐   ┌──┐
        │                \  │  │
        │   subcontracted works└──┘
       ┌──┐                   main
       └──┘                   contractor
  subcontractors
```

19-4 The main contractor usually employs subcontractors for parts of the works, or for the supply of goods, materials or services. Depending on the circumstances of the case, the main contractor, who will often have to furnish guarantees covering the entire project, may also require guarantees from the subcontractors in order to assure proper performance by the subcontractors. They are often also payable on demand. For the sake of convenience, these guarantees issued on behalf of subcontractors may be referred to as subguarantees. Such subguarantees are proper and ordinary guarantees, assuring payment in the event of default by the subcontractor, see diagram 3. They should not be confused with counter-guarantees in the case of indirect guarantees or with those discussed in No. 19-3 above. Counter-guarantees issued on behalf of subcontractors, as examined in No. 19-3, become payable once the bank has paid under its own guarantee and irrespective of default by the subcontractor, while subguarantees can be called by the main contractor only in relation to default of the subcontractor, although in the event of a first demand subguarantee the main contractor need not prove default by the subcontractor. The two following decisions are most instructive in this respect.

In *OLG München, 31 October 1984*, a Belgian bank had issued a counter-guarantee in favour of an issuing bank on behalf of the Belgian main contractor, while a German subcontractor had furnished two 'subguarantees' which, in this instance, were made available not in favour of the main contractor, but in favour of his bank, namely the Belgian counter-guaranteeing bank. When the counter-guarantee was called by the issuing bank, the Belgian bank called the two 'subguarantees'. The main contractor was insolvent and in the process of liquidation. After payment pursuant to the two 'subguarantees', the subcontractor sought recovery from the Belgian bank in main proceedings. The Court of Appeal rejected the view of the Belgian bank that the two 'subguarantees' were counter-guarantees which the Belgian bank could call immediately without restrictions, if it was made to pay under its own counter-guarantee in favour of the issuing bank, and regardless of default in respect of the subcontracted works. The Court of Appeal ruled that the two guarantees in question were subguarantees, which could only be called in the event of default by the subcontractor, although no evidence thereof needed to be presented at the time of the call. Recovery was allowed upon evidence that the subcontractor had fully discharged his obligations.[1]

In *BGH, 29 September 1986*, the P bank had issued a first demand guarantee on behalf of the main contractor, while the D bank had issued three first demand subguarantees in favour of the main contractor as security for works to be carried out by three subcontractors. The P bank required a cash deposit from the main contractor in view of his financial situation. In order to have the cash deposit released, the main contractor offered to assign his rights from the subguarantees, but the P bank was only prepared to do so if the D bank issued directly a counter-guarantee in its favour, payable on first demand upon a statement that it had been called to pay under its own guarantee. Such a counter-guarantee was issued indeed, and this dramatically changed the position of all parties concerned, as will appear hereafter. When the P bank was requested to effect payment under its own guarantee, it turned to the D bank for reimbursement under the counter-guarantee. The latter, however, refused to pay, alleging that, upon construction of the full text of the 'counter-guarantee', it only contemplated the provision of security for non-performance by the subcontractors, who had fully performed their contracts. The P bank argued that the 'counter-guarantee' was a proper counter-guarantee, which could be called irrespective of perfect completion by the subcontractors, and that the subcontractors had participated in the risk of a call on the

---

[1] WM 1985, p. 189. It is noted that a previous attempt to prevent payment to the Belgian bank through interlocutory proceedings failed on the grounds that preventive restraining orders against the bank are never possible and because full performance had not been established (*LG München, 30 January 1981*, WM 1981, p. 416). See further: *Paris, 17 June 1987*, D. 1988 Somm. p. 245 (restraining order granted although the evidence concerning the main contractor's fraud was weak), *Cass., 8 December 1987*, D. 1988 Somm. p. 240 (bank ordered to pay), *Trib. com. Brussels, 8 October 1985*, RDC 1986, p. 648 (application for restraining order dismissed).

principal guarantee. The German Supreme Court ordered the D bank to reimburse the P bank, observing that the terms of the counter-guarantee were fulfilled, and that the view of the P bank was quite plausible and that the call on the counter-guarantee was, therefore, not evidently fraudulent.[2] In short, the subguarantees, as initially envisaged, had been converted into counter-guarantees as discussed in No. 19-3.

Subguarantees and clauses; special risks

19-5 It is in the interest of the subcontractor that the subguarantee is not linked to the principal guarantee issued on behalf of the main contractor in favour of the employer. The amount and the period of validity of the subguarantee should be adjusted to the size of the subcontracted works and to the period of completion, irrespective of the validity period of the principal guarantee. Once the subguarantee has expired, it can no longer be called, not even when, at a later stage, the employer complains about defects concerning the subcontracted works. This is not unduly onerous for the main contractor since he should inspect proper performance for himself and because he effectively controls the validity period of the subguarantee if it is payable on demand or if it terminates, for example, X days after approval. Clauses which state that the subguarantee is payable if and when the principal guarantee is called must be avoided at all costs, since they effectively turn the subguarantee into a counter-guarantee as examined in No. 19-3.

A call on the principal guarantee poses additional risks for those subguarantees which are still in force at that time, since the main contractor might be tempted to call indiscriminately all outstanding subguarantees in order to recoup his own loss. When the subguarantee is payable on demand, the subcontractor can only prevent payment if he is able clearly to establish that the call on the subguarantee is fraudulent, for example because he has fully performed the subcontracted works. Evidence that the call on the principal guarantee was unconnected with the subcontracted works is ordinarily not sufficient.

---

[2] WM 1986, p. 1429.

UNIFORM RULES FOR DEMAND GUARANTEES (URDG)
ICC Publication No. 458

A. SCOPE AND APPLICATION OF THE RULES

Article 1

These Rules apply to any demand guarantee and amendment thereto which a Guarantor (as hereinafter described) has been instructed to issue and which states that it is subject to the Uniform Rules for Demand Guarantees of the International Chamber of Commerce (Publication No. 458) and are binding on all parties thereto except as otherwise expressly stated in the Guarantee or any amendment thereto.

B. DEFINITIONS AND GENERAL PROVISIONS

Article 2

a) For the purpose of these Rules, a demand guarantee (hereinafter referred to as "Guarantee") means any guarantee, bond or other payment undertaking, however named or described, by a bank, insurance company or other body or person (hereinafter called "the Guarantor") given in writing for the payment of money on presentation in conformity with the terms of the undertaking of a written demand for payment and such other document(s) (for example, a certificate by an architect or engineer, a judgment or an arbitral award) as may be specified in the Guarantee, such undertaking being give

  i) at the request or on the instructions and under the liability of a party (hereinafter called "the Principal"); or

  ii) at the request or on the instructions and under the liability of a bank, insurance company or any other body or person (hereinafter "the instructing Party") acting on the instructions of a Principal to another party (hereinafter the "Beneficiary").

b) Guarantees by their nature are separate transactions from the contract(s) or tender conditions on which they may be based, and Guarantors are in no way concerned with or bound by such contract(s), or tender conditions, despite the inclusion of a

---

© International Chamber of Commerce, Paris, France

reference to them in the Guarantee. The duty of a Guarantor under a Guarantee is to pay the sum or sums therein stated on the presentation of a written demand for payment and other documents specified in the Guarantee which appear on their face to be in accordance with the terms of the Guarantee

c) For the purpose of these Rules, "Counter-Guarantee" means any guarantee, bond or other payment undertaking of the Instructing Party, however named or described, given in writing for the payment of money to the Guarantor on presentation in conformity with the terms of the undertaking of a written demand for payment and other documents specified in the Counter-Guarantee which appear on their face to be in accordance with the terms of the Counter-Guarantee. Counter-Guarantees are by their nature separate transactions from the Guarantees to which they relate and from any underlying contract(s) or tender conditions, and Instructing Parties are in no way concerned with or bound by such Guarantees, contract(s) or tender conditions, despite the inclusion of a reference to them in the Counter-Guarantee

d) The expressions "writing" and "written" shall include an authenticated teletransmission or tested electronic date interchange ("EDI") message equivalent thereto.

Article 3

All instructions for the issue of Guarantees and amendments thereto and Guarantees and amendments themselves should be clear and precise and should avoid excessive detail. Accordingly, all Guarantees should stipulate:

a) the Principal;

b) the Beneficiary;

c) the Guarantor;

d) the underlying transaction requiring the issue of the Guarantee;

e) the maximum amount payable and the currency in which it is payable;

f) the Expiry Date and/or Expiry Event of the Guarantee;

g) the terms for demanding payment;

h) any provision for reduction of the guarantee amount.

Article 4

The Beneficiary's right to make a demand under a Guarantee is not assignable unless expressly stated in the Guarantee or in an amendment thereto.

This Article shall not, however, affect the Beneficiary's right to assign any proceeds to which he may be, or may become, entitled under the Guarantee.

Article 5

All Guarantees and Counter-Guarantees are irrevocable unless otherwise indicated.

Article 6

A Guarantee enters into effect as from the date of its issue unless its terms expressly provide that such entry into effect is to be at a later date or is to be subject to conditions specified in the Guarantee and determinable by the Guarantor on the basis of any documents therein specified.

Article 7

a) Where a Guarantor has been given instructions for the issue of a Guarantee but the instructions are such that, if they were to be carried out, the Guarantor would by reason of law or regulation in the country of issue be unable to fulfil the terms of the Guarantee, the instructions shall not be executed and the Guarantor shall immediately inform the party who gave the Guarantor his instructions by telecommunication, or, if that is not possible, by other expeditious means, of the reasons for such inability and request appropriate instructions from that party.

b) Nothing in this Article shall oblige the Guarantor to issue a Guarantee where the Guarantor has not agreed to do so.

A Guarantee may contain express provision for reduction by a specified or determinable amount or amounts on a specified date or dates or upon presentation to the Guarantor of the document(s) specified for this purpose in the Guarantee.

C. LIABILITIES AND RESPONSIBILITIES

Article 9

All documents specified and presented under a Guarantee, including the demand, shall be examined by the Guarantor with reasonable care to ascertain whether or not they appear on their face to conform with the terms of the Guarantee. Where such documents do not appear so to conform or appear on their face to be inconsistent with one another, they shall be refused.

Article 10

a) A Guarantor shall have a reasonable time within which to examine a demand under a Guarantee and to decide whether to pay or to refuse the demand.

b) If the Guarantor decides to refuse a demand, he shall immediately give notice thereof to the Beneficiary by teletransmission, or, if that is not possible, by other expeditious means. Any documents presented under the Guarantee shall be held at the disposal of the Beneficiary.

Article 11

Guarantors and Instructing Parties assume no liability or responsibility for the form, sufficiency, accuracy, genuineness, falsification, or legal effect of any document presented to them or for the general and/or particular statements made therein, nor for the good faith or acts or omissions of any person whomsoever.

Guarantors and Instructing Parties assume no liability or responsibility for the consequences arising out of the delay and/or loss in transit of any messages, letters, demands or documents, or for delay, mutilation or other errors arising in the transmission of any telecommunication. Guarantors and Instructing Parties assume no liability for errors in translation or interpretation of technical terms and reserve the right to transmit Guarantee texts or any parts thereof without translating them.

Article 13

Guarantors and Instructing Parties assume no liability or responsibility for consequences arising out of the interruption of their business by acts of God, riots, civil commotions, insurrections, wars or any other causes beyond their control or by strikes, lock-outs or industrial actions of whatever nature.

Article 14

a) Guarantors and Instructing Parties utilising the services of another party for the purpose of giving effect to the instructions of a Principal do so for the account and at the risk of that Principal.

b) Guarantors and Instructing Parties assume no liability or responsibility should the instructions they transmit not be carried out even if they have themselves taken the initiative in the choice of such other party.

c) The Principal shall be liable to indemnify the Guarantor or the Instructing Party, as the case may be, against all obligations and responsibilities imposed by foreign laws and usages.

Article 15

Guarantors and Instructing Parties shall not be excluded from liability or responsibility under the terms of Articles 11, 12 and 14 above for their failure to act in good faith and with reasonable care.

A Guarantor is liable to the Beneficiary only in accordance with the terms specified in the Guarantee and any amendment(s) thereto and in these Rules, and up to an amount not exceeding that stated in the Guarantee and any amendment(s) thereto.

D. DEMANDS

Article 17

Without prejudice to the terms of Article 10, in the event of a demand the Guarantor shall without delay so inform the Principal or, where applicable, his Instructing Party, and in that case the Instructing Party shall so inform the Principal.

Article 18

The amount payable under a Guarantee shall be reduced by the amount of any payment made by the Guarantor in satisfaction of a demand in respect thereof and, where the maximum amount payable under a Guarantee has been satisfied by payment and/or reduction, the Guarantee shall thereupon terminate whether or not the Guarantee and any amendment(s) thereto are returned.

Article 19

A demand shall be made in accordance with the terms of the Guarantee before its expiry, that is, on or before its Expiry Date and before any Expiry Event as defined in Article 22. In particular, all documents specified in the Guarantee for the purpose of the demand, and any statement required by Article 20, shall be presented to the Guarantor before its expiry at its place of issue; otherwise the demand shall be refused by the Guarantor.

Article 20

a) Any demand for payment under the Guarantee shall be in writing and shall (in addition to such other documents as may be specified in the Guarantee) be supported by a written statement (whether in the demand itself or in a separate document or documents accompanying the demand and referred to in it) stating:
   i) that the Principal is in breach of this obligation(s) under the underlying contract(s) or, in the case of a tender guarantee, the tender conditions; and
   ii) the respect in which the Principal is in breach.
b) Any demand under the Counter-Guarantee shall be supported by a written statement that the Guarantor has received a demand for payment under the Guarantee in accordance with its terms and with this Article.

c) Paragraph a) of this Article applies except to the extent that it is expressly excluded by the terms of the Guarantee. Paragraph b) of this Article applies except to the extent that it is expressly excluded by the terms of the Counter-Guarantee.

d) Nothing in this Article affects the application of Articles 2b) and 2c), 9 and 11.

Article 21

The Guarantor shall without delay transmit the Benefici-ary's demand and any related documents to the Principal or, where applicable, to the Instructing Party for transmission to the Principal.

E. EXPIRY PROVISIONS

Article 22

Expiry of the time specified in a Guarantee for the presentation of demands shall be upon a specified calendar date ("Expiry Date") or upon presentation to the Guarantor of the document(s) specified for the purpose of expiry ("Expiry Event"). If both an Expiry Date and an Expiry Event are specified in a Guarantee, the Guarantee shall expire on whichever of the Expiry Date or Expiry Event occurs first, whether or not the Guarantee and any amendment(s) thereto are returned.

Article 23

Irrespective of any expiry provision contained therein, a Guarantee shall be cancelled on presentation to the Guarantor of the Guarantee itself or the Beneficiary's written statement of release from liability under the Guarantee, whether or not, in the latter case, the Guarantee or any amendments thereto are returned.

Article 24

Where a Guarantee has terminated by payment, expiry, cancellation or otherwise, retention of the Guarantee or of any amendments thereto shall not preserve any rights of the Beneficiary under the Guarantee.

Article 25

Where to the knowledge of the Guarantor the Guarantee has terminated by payment, expiry, cancellation or otherwise, or there has been a reduction of the total amount payable thereunder, the Guarantor shall without delay so notify the Principal or, where applicable, the X2structing Party and, in that case, the Instructing Party shall so notify the Principal.

Article 26

If the Beneficiary requests an extension of the validity of the Guarantee as an alternative to a demand for payment submitted in accordance with the terms and conditions of the Guarantee and these Rules, the Guarantor shall without delay so inform the party who gave the Guarantor his instructions. The Guarantor shall then suspend payment of the demand for such time as is reasonable to permit the Principal and the Beneficiary to reach agreement on the granting of such extension and for the Principal to arrange for such extension to be issued.

Unless an extension is granted within the time provided by the preceding paragraph, the Guarantor is obliged to pay the Beneficiary's conforming demand without requiring any further action on the Beneficiary's part. The Guarantor shall incur no liability (for interest or otherwise) should any payment to the Beneficiary be delayed as a result of the above-mentioned procedure.

Even if the Principal agrees to or requests such extension, it shall not be granted unless the Guarantor and the Instructing Party or Parties also agree thereto.

F. GOVERNING LAW AND JURISDICTION

Article 27

Unless otherwise provided in the Guarantee or Counter-Guarantee, its governing law shall be that of the place of business of the Guarantor or Instructing Party (as the case may be), or, if the Guarantor or Instructing Party has more than one place of business, that of the branch that issued the Guarantee or Counter-Guarantee.

Article 28

Unless otherwise provided in the Guarantee or Counter-Guarantee, any dispute between the Guarantor and the Beneficiary relating to the Guarantee or between the Instructing Party and the Guarantor relating to the Counter-Guarantee shall be settled exclusively by the competent court of the country of the place of business of the Guarantor or Instructing Party (as the case may be), or, if the Guarantor or Instructing Party has more than one place of business, by the competent court of the country of the branch which issued the Guarantee or Counter-Guarantee.

INTERNATIONAL STANDBY PRACTICES (ISP98)
ICC Publication No. 590

RULE 1. GENERAL PROVISIONS

Scope, Application, Definitions, and Interpretation of These Rules

1.01 Scope and Application
a. These Rules are intended to be applied to standby letters of credit (including performance, financial, and direct pay standby letters of credit).
b. A standby letter of credit or other similar undertaking, however named or described, whether for domestic or international use, may be made subject to these Rules by express reference to them.
c. An undertaking subject to these Rules may expressly modify or exclude their application.
d. An undertaking subject to these Rules is hereinafter referred to as a "standby".

1.02 Relationship to Law and Other Rules
a. These Rules supplement the applicable law to the extent not prohibited by that law.
b. These Rules supersede conflicting provisions in any other rules of practice to which a standby letter of credit is also made subject.

1.03 Interpretative Principles
These Rules shall be interpreted as mercantile usage with regard for:
a. integrity of standbys as reliable and efficient undertakings to pay;
b. practice and terminology of banks and businesses in day-to-day transactions;
c. consistency within the worldwide system of banking operations and commerce; and
d. worldwide uniformity in their interpretation and application.

© International Chamber of Commerce, Paris, France

1.04 Effect of the Rules

Unless the context otherwise requires, or unless expressly modified or excluded, these Rules apply as terms and conditions incorporated into a standby, confirmation, advice, nomination, amendment, transfer, request for issuance, or other agreement of:

i. the issuer;

ii. the beneficiary to the extent it uses the standby;

iii. any advisor;

iv. any confirmer;

v. any person nominated in the standby who acts or agrees to act; and

vi. the applicant who authorises issuance of the standby or otherwise agrees to the application of these Rules.

1.05 Exclusion of Matters Related to Due Issuance and Fraudulent or Abusive Drawing

These Rules do not define or otherwise provide for:

a. power or authority to issue a standby;

b. formal requirements for execution of a standby (e.g. a signed writing); or

c. defenses to honour based on fraud, abuse, or similar matters.

These matters are left to applicable law.

General Principles

1.06 Nature of Standbys

a. A standby is an irrevocable, independent, documentary, and binding undertaking when issued and need not so state.

b. Because a standby is irrevocable, an issuer's obligations under a standby cannot be amended or cancelled by the issuer except as provided in the standby or as consented to by the person against whom the amendment or cancellation is asserted.

c. Because a standby is independent, the enforceability of an issuer's obligations under a standby does not depend on:

   i. the issuer's right or ability to obtain reimbursement from the applicant;

   ii. the beneficiary's right to obtain payment from the applicant;

   iii. a reference in the standby to any reimbursement agreement or underlying transaction; or

   iv. the issuer's knowledge of performance or breach of any reimbursement agreement or underlying transaction.

International Standby Practices 477

d. Because a standby is documentary, an issuer's obligations depend on the presentation of documents and an examination of required documents on their face.
e. Because a standby or amendment is binding when issued, it is enforceable against an issuer whether or not the applicant authorised its issuance, the issuer received a fee, or the beneficiary received or relied on the standby or the amendment.

1.07 Independence of the Issuer-Beneficiary Relationship

An issuer's obligations toward the beneficiary are not affected by the issuer's rights and obligations toward the applicant under any applicable agreement, practice, or law.

1.08 Limits to Responsibilities

An issuer is not responsible for:
a. performance or breach of any underlying transaction;
b. accuracy, genuineness, or effect of any document presented under the standby;
c. action or omission of others even if the other person is chosen by the issuer or nominated person; or
d. observance of law or practice other than that chosen in the standby or applicable at the place of issuance.

Terminology

1.09 Defined Terms

In addition to the meanings given in standard banking practice and applicable law, the following terms have or include the meanings indicated below:
a. Definitions

"Applicant" is a person who applies for issuance of a standby or for whose account it is issued, and includes (i) a person applying in its own name but for the account of another person or (ii) an issuer acting for its own account.

"Beneficiary" is a named person who is entitled to draw under a standby. See Rule 1.11(c)(ii).

"Business Day" means a day on which the place of business at which the relevant act is to be performed is regularly open; and "Banking Day" means a day on which the relevant bank is regularly open at the place at which the relevant act is to be performed.

"Confirmer" is a person who, upon an issuer's nomination to do so, adds to the issuer's undertaking its own undertaking to honour a standby. See Rule 1.11(c)(i).

"Demand" means, depending on the context, either a request to honour a standby or a document that makes such request.

"Document" means a draft, demand, document of title, investment security, invoice, certificate of default, or any other representation of fact, law, right, or opinion, that upon presentation (whether in a paper or electronic medium), is capable of being examined for compliance with the terms and conditions of a standby.

"Drawing" means, depending on the context, either a demand presented or a demand honoured.

"Expiration Date" means the latest day for a complying presentation provided in a standby.

"Person" includes a natural person, partnership, corporation, limited liability company, government agency, bank, trustee, and any other legal or commercial association or entity.

"Presentation" means, depending on the context, either the act of delivering documents for examination under a standby or the documents so delivered.

"Presenter" is a person who makes a presentation as or on behalf of a beneficiary or nominated person.

"Signature" includes any symbol executed or adopted by a person with a present intent to authenticate a document.

b. Cross References

"Amendment" – Rule 2.06

"Advice" – Rule 2.05

"Approximately" ("About" or "Circa") – Rule 3.08(f)

"Assignment of Proceeds" – Rule 6.06

"Automatic Amendment" – Rule 2.06(a)

"Copy" – Rule 4.15(d)

"Cover Instructions" – Rule 5.08

"Honour" – Rule 2.01

"Issuer" – Rule 2.01

"Multiple Presentations" – Rule 3.08(b)

"Nominated Person" – Rule 2.04

"Non-documentary Conditions" – Rule 4.11

"Original" – Rule 4.15(b) & (c)

"Partial Drawing" – Rule 3.08(a)

"Standby" – Rule 1.01(d)

"Transfer" – Rule 6.01

International Standby Practices 479

"Transferee Beneficiary" – Rule 1.11(c)(ii)

"Transfer by Operation of Law" – Rule 6.11

c. Electronic Presentations

The following terms in a standby providing for or permitting electronic presentation shall have the following meanings unless the context otherwise requires:

"Electronic Record" means:

i. a record (information that is inscribed on a tangible medium or that is stored in an electronic or other medium and is retrievable in perceivable form);

ii. communicated by electronic means to a system for receiving, storing, re-transmitting, or otherwise processing information (data, text, images, sounds, codes, computer programs, software, databases, and the like); and

iii. capable of being authenticated and then examined for compliance with the terms and conditions of the standby.

"Authenticate" means to verify an electronic record by generally accepted procedure or methodology in commercial practice:

i. the identity of a sender or source, and

ii. the integrity of or errors in the transmission of information content.

The criteria for assessing the integrity of information in an electronic record is whether the information has remained complete and unaltered, apart from the addition of any endorsement and any change which arises in the normal course of communication, storage, and display.

"Electronic signature" means letters, characters, numbers, or other symbols in electronic form, attached to or logically associated with an electronic record that are executed or adopted by a party with present intent to authenticate an electronic record.

"Receipt" occurs when:

i. an electronic record enters in a form capable of being processed by the information system designated in the standby, or

ii. an issuer retrieves an electronic record sent to an information system other than that designated by the issuer.

1.10 Redundant or Otherwise Undesirable Terms

a. A standby should not or need not state that it is:

i. unconditional or abstract (if it does, it signifies merely that payment under it is conditioned solely on presentation of specified documents);

ii. absolute (if it does, it signifies merely that it is irrevocable);

iii. primary (if it does, it signifies merely that it is the independent obligation of the issuer);
iv. payable from the issuer's own funds (if it does, it signifies merely that payment under it does not depend on the availability of applicant funds and is made to satisfy the issuer's own independent obligation);
v. clean or payable on demand (if it does, it signifies merely that it is payable upon presentation of a written demand or other documents specified in the standby).
b. A standby should not use the term "and/or" (if it does it means either or both).
c. The following terms have no single accepted meaning:
   i. and shall be disregarded:
   "callable",
   "divisible",
   "fractionable",
   "indivisible", and
   "transmissible",
   ii. and shall be disregarded unless their context gives them meaning:
   "assignable",
   "evergreen",
   "reinstate", and
   "revolving".

1.11 Interpretation of These Rules
a. These Rules, are to be interpreted in the context of applicable standard practice.
b. In these Rules, "standby letter of credit" refers to the type of independent undertaking for which these Rules were intended, whereas "standby" refers to an undertaking subjected to these Rules.
c. Unless the context otherwise requires:
   i. "Issuer" includes a "confirmer" as if the confirmer were a separate issuer and its confirmation were a separate standby issued for the account of the issuer;
   ii. "Beneficiary" includes a person to whom the named beneficiary has effectively transferred drawing rights ("transferee beneficiary");
   iii. "Including" means "including but not limited to";
   iv. "A or B" means "A or B or both"; "either A or B" means "A or B, but not both"; and "A and B" means "both A and B";
   v. Words in the singular number include the plural, and in the plural include the singular; and

International Standby Practices 481

      vi. Words of the neuter gender include any gender.

d. i. Use of the phrase "unless a standby otherwise states" or the like in a rule emphasizes that the text of the standby controls over the rule;

    ii. Absence of such a phrase in other rules does not imply that other rules have priority over the text of the standby;

    iii. Addition of the term "expressly" or "clearly" to the phrase "unless a standby otherwise states" or the like emphasizes that the rule should be excluded or modified only by wording in the standby that is specific and unambiguous; and

    iv. While the effect of all of these Rules may be varied by the text of the standby, variations of the effect of some of these Rules may disqualify the standby as an independent undertaking under applicable law.

e. The phrase "stated in the standby" or the like refers to the actual text of a standby (whether as issued or effectively amended) whereas the phrase "provided in the standby" or the like refers to both the text of the standby and these Rules as incorporated.

RULE 2. OBLIGATIONS

2.01 Undertaking to Honour by Issuer and Any Confirmer to Beneficiary

a. An issuer undertakes to the beneficiary to honour a presentation that appears on its face to comply with the terms and conditions of the standby in accordance with these Rules supplemented by standard standby practice.

b. An issuer honours a complying presentation made to it by paying the amount demanded of it at sight, unless the standby provides for honour:

    i. by acceptance of a draft drawn by the beneficiary on the issuer, in which case the issuer honours by:

      (a) timely accepting the draft; and

      (b) thereafter paying the holder of the draft on presentation of the accepted draft on or after its maturity.

    ii. by deferred payment of a demand made by the beneficiary on the issuer, in which case the issuer honours by:

      (a) timely incurring a deferred payment obligation; and

      (b) thereafter paying at maturity.

    iii. by negotiation, in which case the issuer honours by paying the amount demanded at sight without recourse.

c. An issuer acts in a timely manner if it pays at sight, accepts a draft, or undertakes a deferred payment obligation (or if it gives notice of dishonour) within the time permitted for examining the presentation and giving notice of dishonour.

d. i. A confirmer undertakes to honour a complying presentation made to it by paying the amount demanded of it at sight or, if the standby so states, by another method of honour consistent with the issuer's undertaking.
   ii. If the confirmation permits presentation to the issuer, then the confirmer undertakes also to honour upon the issuer's wrongful dishonour by performing as if the presentation had been made to the confirmer.
   iii. If the standby permits presentation to the confirmer, then the issuer undertakes also to honour upon the confirmer's wrongful dishonour by performing as if the presentation had been made to the issuer.
e. An issuer honours by paying in immediately available funds in the currency designated in the standby unless the standby states it is payable by:
   i. payment of a monetary unit of account, in which case the undertaking is to pay in that unit of account; or
   ii. delivery of other items of value, in which case the undertaking is to deliver those items.

2.02 Obligation of Different Branches, Agencies, or Other Offices

For the purposes of these Rules, an issuer's branch, agency, or other office acting or undertaking to act under a standby in a capacity other than as issuer is obligated in that capacity only and shall be treated as a different person.

2.03 Conditions to Issuance

A standby is issued when it leaves an issuer's control unless it clearly specifies that it is not then "issued" or "enforceable". Statements that a standby is not "available", "operative", "effective", or the like do not affect its irrevocable and binding nature at the time it leaves the issuer's control.

2.04 Nomination

a. A standby may nominate a person to advise, receive a presentation, effect a transfer, confirm, pay, negotiate, incur a deferred payment obligation, or accept a draft.
b. Nomination does not obligate the nominated person to act except to the extent that the nominated person undertakes to act.
c. A nominated person is not authorised to bind the person making the nomination.

2.05 Advice of Standby or Amendment

a. Unless an advice states otherwise, it signifies that:

International Standby Practices 483

   i. the advisor has checked the apparent authenticity of the advised message in accordance with standard letter of credit practice; and
   ii. the advice accurately reflects what has been received.
b. A person who is requested to advise a standby and decides not to do so should notify the requesting party.

2.06 When an Amendment is Authorised and Binding

a. If a standby expressly states that it is subject to "automatic amendment" by an increase or decrease in the amount available, an extension of the expiration date, or the like, the amendment is effective automatically without any further notification or consent beyond that expressly provided for in the standby. (Such an amendment may also be referred to as becoming effective "without amendment".)
b. If there is no provision for automatic amendment, an amendment binds:
   i. the issuer when it leaves the issuer's control; and
   ii. the confirmer when it leaves the confirmer's control, unless the confirmer indicates that it does not confirm the amendment.
c. If there is no provision for automatic amendment:
   i. the beneficiary must consent to the amendment for it to be binding;
   ii. the beneficiary's consent must be made by an express communication to the person advising the amendment unless the beneficiary presents documents which comply with the standby as amended and which would not comply with the standby prior to such amendment; and
   iii. an amendment does not require the appli-cant's consent to be binding on the issuer, the confirmer, or the beneficiary.
d. Consent to only part of an amendment is a rejection of the entire amendment.

2.07 Routing of Amendments

a. An issuer using another person to advise a standby must advise all amendments to that person.
b. An amendment or cancellation of a standby does not affect the issuer's obligation to a nominated person that has acted within the scope of its nomination before receipt of notice of the amendment or cancellation.
c. Non-extension of an automatically extendable (renewable) standby does not affect an issuer's obligation to a nominated person who has acted within the scope of its nomination before receipt of a notice of non-extension.

RULE 3. PRESENTATION

3.01 Complying Presentation Under a Standby

A standby should indicate the time, place and location within that place, person to whom, and medium in which presentation should be made. If so, presentation must be so made in order to comply. To the extent that a standby does not so indicate, presentation must be made in accordance with these Rules in order to be complying.

3.02 What Constitutes a Presentation

The receipt of a document required by and presented under a standby constitutes a presentation requiring examination for compliance with the terms and conditions of the standby even if not all of the required documents have been presented.

3.03 Identification of Standby

a. A presentation must identify the standby under which the presentation is made.
b. A presentation may identify the standby by stating the complete reference number of the standby and the name and location of the issuer or by attaching the original or a copy of the standby.
c. If the issuer cannot determine from the face of a document received that it should be processed under a standby or cannot identify the standby to which it relates, presentation is deemed to have been made on the date of identification.

3.04 Where and to Whom Complying Presentation Made

a. To comply, a presentation must be made at the place and any location at that place indicated in the standby or provided in these Rules.
b. If no place of presentation to the issuer is indicated in the standby, presentation to the issuer must be made at the place of business from which the standby was issued.
c. If a standby is confirmed, but no place for presentation is indicated in the confirmation, presentation for the purpose of obligating the confirmer (and the issuer) must be made at the place of business of the confirmer from which the confirmation was issued or to the issuer.
d. If no location at a place of presentation is indicated (such as department, floor, room, station, mail stop, post office box, or other location), presentation may be made to:
   i. the general postal address indicated in the standby;
   ii. any location at the place designated to receive deliveries of mail or documents; or

International Standby Practices

iii. any person at the place of presentation actually or apparently authorised to receive it.

3.05 When Timely Presentation Made

a. A presentation is timely if made at any time after issuance and before expiry on the expiration date.
b. A presentation made after the close of business at the place of presentation is deemed to have been made on the next business day.

3.06 Complying Medium of Presentation

a. To comply, a document must be presented in the medium indicated in the standby.
b. Where no medium is indicated, to comply a document must be presented as a paper document, unless only a demand is required, in which case:
   i. a demand that is presented via S.W.I.F.T., tested telex, or other similar authenticated means by a beneficiary that is a S.W.I.F.T. participant or a bank complies; otherwise
   ii. a demand that is not presented as a paper document does not comply unless the issuer permits, in its sole discretion, the use of that medium.
c. A document is not presented as a paper document if it is communicated by electronic means even if the issuer or nominated person receiving it generates a paper document from it.
d. Where presentation in an electronic medium is indicated, to comply a document must be presented as an electronic record capable of being authenticated by the issuer or nominated person to whom it is presented.

3.07 Separateness of Each Presentation

a. Making a non-complying presentation, withdrawing a presentation, or failing to make any one of a number of scheduled or permitted presentations does not waive or otherwise prejudice the right to make another timely presentation or a timely re-presentation whether or not the standby prohibits partial or multiple drawings or presentations.
b. Wrongful dishonour of a complying presentation does not constitute dishonour of any other presentation under a standby or repudiation of the standby.
c. Honour of a non-complying presentation, with or without notice of its non-compliance, does not waive requirements of a standby for other presentations.

3.08 Partial Drawing and Multiple Presentations; Amount of Drawings

a. A presentation may be made for less than the full amount available ("partial drawing").
b. More than one presentation ("multiple presentations") may be made.
c. The statement "partial drawings prohibited" or a similar expression means that a presentation must be for the full amount available.
d. The statement "multiple drawings prohibited" or a similar expression means that only one presentation may be made and honoured but that it may be for less than the full amount available.
e. If a demand exceeds the amount available under the standby, the drawing is discrepant. Any document other than the demand stating an amount in excess of the amount demanded is not discrepant for that reason.
f. Use of "approximately", "about", "circa", or a similar word permits a tolerance not to exceed 10% more or 10% less of the amount to which such word refers.

3.09 Extend or Pay

A beneficiary's request to extend the expiration date of the standby or, alternatively, to pay the amount available under it:

a. is a presentation demanding payment under the standby, to be examined as such in accordance with these Rules; and
b. implies that the beneficiary:
   i. consents to the amendment to extend the expiry date to the date requested;
   ii. requests the issuer to exercise its discretion to seek the approval of the applicant and to issue that amendment;
   iii. upon issuance of that amendment, retracts its demand for payment; and
   iv. consents to the maximum time available under these Rules for examination and notice of dishonour.

3.10 No Notice of Receipt of Presentation

An issuer is not required to notify the applicant of receipt of a presentation under the standby.

3.11 Issuer Waiver and Applicant Consent to Waiver of Presentation Rules

In addition to other discretionary provisions in a standby or these Rules, an issuer may, in its sole discretion, without notice to or consent of the applicant and without effect on the applicant's obligations to the issuer, waive

a. the following Rules and any similar terms stated in the standby which are primarily for the issuer's benefit or operational convenience:
   i. treatment of documents received, at the request of the presenter, as having been presented at a later date (Rule 3.02);
   ii. identification of a presentation to the standby under which it is presented (Rule 3.03(a));
   iii. where and to whom presentation is made (Rule 3.04(b), (c), and (d)), except the country of presentation stated in the standby; or
   iv. treatment of a presentation made after the close of business as if it were made on the next business day (Rule 3.05(b)).
b. the following Rule but not similar terms stated in the standby:
   i. a required document dated after the date of its stated presentation (Rule 4.06); or
   ii. the requirement that a document issued by the beneficiary be in the language of the standby (Rule 4.04).
c. the following Rule relating to the operational integrity of the standby only in so far as the bank is in fact dealing with the true beneficiary:
   acceptance of a demand in an electronic medium (Rule 3.06(b)).

Waiver by the confirmer requires the consent of the issuer with respect to paragraphs (b) and (c) of this Rule.

3.12 Original Standby Lost, Stolen, Mutilated, or Destroyed

a. If an original standby is lost, stolen, mutilated, or destroyed, the issuer need not replace it or waive any requirement that the original be presented under the standby.
b. If the issuer agrees to replace an original standby or to waive a requirement for its presentation, it may provide a replacement or copy to the beneficiary without affecting the applicant's obligations to the issuer to reimburse, but, if it does so, the issuer must mark the replacement or copy as such. The issuer may, in its sole discretion, require indemnities satisfactory to it from the beneficiary and assurances from nominated persons that no payment has been made.

Closure on Expiry Date

3.13 Expiration Date on a Non-Business Day

a. If the last day for presentation stated in a standby (whether stated to be the expiration date or the date by which documents must be received) is not a business day of the issuer or nominated person where presentation is to be made, then presentation made there on the first following business day shall be deemed timely.

b. A nominated person to whom such a presentation is made must so notify the issuer.

3.14 Closure on a Business Day and Authorization of Another Reasonable Place for Presentation

a. If on the last business day for presentation the place for presentation stated in a standby is for any reason closed and presentation is not timely made because of the closure, then the last day for presentation is automatically extended to the day occurring thirty calendar days after the place for presentation re-opens for business, unless the standby otherwise provides.

b. Upon or in anticipation of closure of the place of presentation, an issuer may authorise another reasonable place for presentation in the standby or in a communication received by the beneficiary. If it does so, then

   i. presentation must be made at that reasonable place; and

   ii. if the communication is received fewer than thirty calendar days before the last day for presentation and for that reason presentation is not timely made, the last day for presentation is automatically extended to the day occurring thirty calendar days after the last day for presentation.

RULE 4. EXAMINATION

4.01 Examination for Compliance

a. Demands for honour of a standby must comply with the terms and conditions of the standby.

b. Whether a presentation appears to comply is determined by examining the presentation on its face against the terms and conditions stated in the standby as interpreted and supplemented by these Rules which are to be read in the context of standard standby practice.

4.02 Non-Examination of Extraneous Documents

Documents presented which are not required by the standby need not be examined and, in any event, shall be disregarded for purposes of determining compliance of the presentation. They may without responsibility be returned to the presenter or passed on with the other documents presented.

4.03 Examination for Inconsistency

An issuer or nominated person is required to examine documents for inconsistency with each other only to the extent provided in the standby.

4.04 Language of Documents

The language of all documents issued by the beneficiary is to be that of the standby.

4.05 Issuer of Documents

Any required document must be issued by the beneficiary unless the standby indicates that the document is to be issued by a third person or the document is of a type that standard standby practice requires to be issued by a third person.

4.06 Date of Documents

The issuance date of a required document may be earlier but not later than the date of its presentation.

4.07 Required Signature on a Document

a. A required document need not be signed unless the standby indicates that the document must be signed or the document is of a type that standard standby practice requires be signed.
b. A required signature may be made in any manner that corresponds to the medium in which the signed document is presented.
c. Unless a standby specifies:
   i. the name of a person who must sign a document, any signature or authentication will be regarded as a complying signature.
   ii. the status of a person who must sign, no indication of status is necessary.
d. If a standby specifies that a signature must be made by:
   i. a named natural person without requiring that the signer's status be identified, a signature complies that appears to be that of the named person;
   ii. a named legal person or government agency without identifying who is to sign on its behalf or its status, any signature complies that appears to have been made on behalf of the named legal person or government agency; or
   iii. a named natural person, legal person, or government agency requiring the status of the signer be indicated, a signature complies which appears to be that of the named natural person, legal person, or government agency and indicates its status.

4.08 Demand Document Implied

If a standby does not specify any required document, it will still be deemed to require a documentary demand for payment.

4.09 Identical Wording and Quotation Marks

If a standby requires:

a. a statement without specifying precise wording, then the wording in the document presented must appear to convey the same meaning as that required by the standby;

b. specified wording by the use of quotation marks, blocked wording, or an attached exhibit or form, then typographical errors in spelling, punctuation, spacing, or the like that are apparent when read in context are not required to be duplicated and blank lines or spaces for data may be completed in any manner not inconsistent with the standby; or

c. specified wording by the use of quotation marks, blocked wording, or an attached exhibit or form, and also provides that the specified wording be "exact" or "identical", then the wording in the documents presented, including typographical errors in spelling, punctuation, spacing and the like, as well as blank lines and spaces for data, must be exactly reproduced.

4.10 Applicant Approval

A standby should not specify that a required document be issued, signed, or countersigned by the applicant. However, if the standby includes such a requirement, the issuer may not waive the requirement and is not responsible for the appli-cant's withholding of the document or signature.

4.11 Non-Documentary Terms or Conditions

a. A standby term or condition which is non-docu-mentary must be disregarded whether or not it affects the issuer's obligation to treat a presentation as complying or to treat the standby as issued, amended, or terminated.

b. Terms or conditions are non-documentary if the standby does not require presentation of a document in which they are to be evidenced and if their fulfillment cannot be determined by the issuer from the issuer's own records or within the issuer's normal operations.

c. Determinations from the issuer's own records or within the issuer's normal operations include determinations of:

  i. when, where, and how documents are presented or otherwise delivered to the issuer;

  ii. when, where, and how communications affecting the standby are sent or received by the issuer, beneficiary, or any nominated person;

  iii. amounts transferred into or out of accounts with the issuer; and

  iv. amounts determinable from a published index (e.g., if a standby provides for determining amounts of interest accruing according to published interest rates).

International Standby Practices 491

d. An issuer need not re-compute a beneficiary's computations under a formula stated or referenced in a standby except to the extent that the standby so provides.

4.12 Formality of Statements in Documents

a. A required statement need not be accompanied by a solemnity, officialization, or any other formality.
b. If a standby provides for the addition of a formality to a required statement by the person making it without specifying form or content, the statement complies if it indicates that it was declared, averred, warranted, attested, sworn under oath, affirmed, certified, or the like.
c. If a standby provides for a statement to be witnessed by another person without specifying form or content, the witnessed statement complies if it appears to contain a signature of a person other than the beneficiary with an indication that the person is acting as a witness.
d. If a standby provides for a statement to be counter-signed, legalized, visaed, or the like by a person other than the beneficiary acting in a governmental, judicial, corporate, or other representative capacity without specifying form or content, the statement complies if it contains the signature of a person other than the beneficiary and includes an indication of that person's representative capacity and the organization on whose behalf the person has acted.

4.13 No Responsibility to Identify Beneficiary

Except to the extent that a standby requires presentation of an electronic record:

a. a person honouring a presentation has no obligation to the applicant to ascertain the identity of any person making a presentation or any assignee of proceeds;
b. payment to a named beneficiary, transferee, an acknowledged assignee, successor by operation of law, to an account or account number stated in the standby or in a cover instruction from the beneficiary or nominated person fulfills the obligation under the standby to effect payment.

4.14 Name of Acquired or Merged Issuer or Confirmer

If the issuer or confirmer is reorganized, merged, or changes its name, any required reference by name to the issuer or confirmer in the documents presented may be to it or its successor.

4.15 Original, Copy, and Multiple Documents

a. A presented document must be an original.

b. Presentation of an electronic record, where an electronic presentation is permitted or required is deemed to be an "original".

c. i. A presented document is deemed to be an "original" unless it appears on its face to have been reproduced from an original.

   ii. A document which appears to have been reproduced from an original is deemed to be an original if the signature or authentication appears to be original.

d. A standby that requires presentation of a "copy" permits presentation of either an original or copy unless the standby states that only a copy be presented or otherwise addresses the disposition of all originals.

e. If multiples of the same document are requested, only one must be an original unless:

   i. "duplicate originals" or "multiple originals" are requested in which case all must be originals; or

   ii. "two copies", "two-fold", or the like are requested in which case either originals or copies may be presented.

Standby Document Types

4.16 Demand for Payment

a. A demand for payment need not be separate from the beneficiary's statement or other required document.

b. If a separate demand is required, it must contain:

   i. a demand for payment from the beneficiary directed to the issuer or nominated person;

   ii. a date indicating when the demand was issued;

   iii. the amount demanded; and

   iv. the beneficiary's signature.

c. A demand may be in the form of a draft or other instruction, order, or request to pay. If a standby requires presentation of a "draft" or "bill of exchange", that draft or bill of exchange need not be in negotiable form unless the standby so states.

4.17 Statement of Default or Other Drawing Event

If a standby requires a statement, certificate, or other recital of a default or other drawing event and does not specify content, the document complies if it contains:

a. a representation to the effect that payment is due because a drawing event described in the standby has occurred;

b. a date indicating when it was issued; and

c. the beneficiary's signature.

4.18 Negotiable Documents

If a standby requires presentation of a document that is transferable by endorsement and delivery without stating whether, how, or to whom endorsement must be made, then the document may be presented without endorsement, or, if endorsed, the endorsement may be in blank and, in any event, the document may be issued or negotiated with or without recourse.

4.19 Legal or Judicial Documents

If a standby requires presentation of a govern-ment-issued document, a court order, an arbitration award, or the like, a document or a copy is deemed to comply if it appears to be:

i. issued by a government agency, court, tribunal, or the like;
ii. suitably titled or named;
iii. signed;
iv. dated; and
v. originally certified or authenticated by an official of a government agency, court, tribunal, or the like.

4.20 Other Documents

a. If a standby requires a document other than one whose content is specified in these Rules without specifying the issuer, data content, or wording, a document complies if it appears to be appropriately titled or to serve the function of that type of document under standard standby practice.
b. A document presented under a standby is to be examined in the context of standby practice under these Rules even if the document is of a type (such as a commercial invoice, transport documents, insurance documents or the like) for which the Uniform Customs and Practice for Documentary Credits contains detailed rules.

4.21 Request to Issue Separate Undertaking

If a standby requests that the beneficiary of the standby issue its own separate undertaking to another (whether or not the standby recites the text of that undertaking):

a. the beneficiary receives no rights other than its rights to draw under the standby even if the issuer pays a fee to the beneficiary for issuing the separate undertaking;
b. neither the separate undertaking nor any documents presented under it need be presented to the issuer; and

c. if originals or copies of the separate undertaking or documents presented under it are received by the issuer although not required to be presented as a condition to honour of the standby:

   i. the issuer need not examine, and, in any event, shall disregard their compliance or consistency with the standby, with the beneficiary's demand under the standby, or with the beneficiary's separate undertaking; and

   ii. the issuer may without responsibility return them to the presenter or forward them to the applicant with the presentation.

RULE 5. NOTICE, PRECLUSION, AND DISPOSITION OF DOCUMENTS

5.01 Timely Notice of Dishonour

a. Notice of dishonour must be given within a time after presentation of documents which is not unreasonable.

   i. Notice given within three business days is deemed to be not unreasonable and beyond seven business days is deemed to be unreasonable.

   ii. Whether the time within which notice is given is unreasonable does not depend upon an imminent deadline for presentation.

   iii. The time for calculating when notice of dishonour must be given begins on the business day following the business day of presentation.

   iv. Unless a standby otherwise expressly states a shortened time within which notice of dishonour must be given, the issuer has no obligation to accelerate its examination of a presentation.

b. i. The means by which a notice of dishonour is to be given is by telecommunication, if available, and, if not, by another available means which allows for prompt notice.

   ii. If notice of dishonour is received within the time permitted for giving the notice, then it is deemed to have been given by prompt means.

c. Notice of dishonour must be given to the person from whom the documents were received (whether the beneficiary, nominated person, or person other than a delivery person) except as otherwise requested by the presenter.

5.02 Statement of Grounds for Dishonour

A notice of dishonour shall state all discrepancies upon which dishonour is based.

International Standby Practices 495

5.03 Failure to Give Timely Notice of Dishonour

a. Failure to give notice of a discrepancy in a notice of dishonour within the time and by the means specified in the standby or these rules precludes assertion of that discrepancy in any document containing the discrepancy that is retained or re-presented, but does not preclude assertion of that discrepancy in any different presentation under the same or a separate standby.

b. Failure to give notice of dishonour or acceptance or acknowledgment that a deferred payment undertaking has been incurred obligates the issuer to pay at maturity.

5.04 Notice of Expiry

Failure to give notice that a presentation was made after the expiration date does not preclude dishonour for that reason.

5.05 Issuer Request for Applicant Waiver without Request by Presenter

If the issuer decides that a presentation does not comply and if the presenter does not otherwise instruct, the issuer may, in its sole discretion, request the applicant to waive non-compliance or otherwise to authorise honour within the time available for giving notice of dishonour but without extending it. Obtaining the applicant's waiver does not obligate the issuer to waive noncompliance.

5.06 Issuer Request for Applicant Waiver upon Request of Presenter

If, after receipt of notice of dishonour, a presenter requests that the presented documents be forwarded to the issuer or that the issuer seek the applicant's waiver:

a. no person is obligated to forward the discrepant documents or seek the applicant's waiver;

b. the presentation to the issuer remains subject to these Rules unless departure from them is expressly consented to by the presenter; and

c. if the documents are forwarded or if a waiver is sought:

   i. the presenter is precluded from objecting to the discrepancies notified to it by the issuer;

   ii. the issuer is not relieved from examining the presentation under these Rules;

   iii. the issuer is not obligated to waive the discrepancy even if the applicant waives it; and

   iv. the issuer must hold the documents until it receives a response from the applicant or is requested by the presenter to return the documents, and if the issuer receives no such response or request within ten business days of its notice of dishonour, it may return the documents to the presenter.

5.07 Disposition of Documents

Dishonoured documents must be returned, held, or disposed of as reasonably instructed by the presenter. Failure to give notice of the disposition of documents in the notice of dishonour does not preclude the issuer from asserting any defense otherwise available to it against honour.

5.08 Cover Instructions/Transmittal Letter

a. Instructions accompanying a presentation made under a standby may be relied on to the extent that they are not contrary to the terms or conditions of the standby, the demand, or these Rules.

b. Representations made by a nominated person accompanying a presentation may be relied upon to the extent that they are not contrary to the terms or conditions of a standby or these Rules.

c. Notwithstanding receipt of instructions, an issuer or nominated person may pay, give notice, return the documents, or otherwise deal directly with the presenter.

d. A statement in the cover letter that the documents are discrepant does not relieve the issuer from examining the presentation for compliance.

5.09 Applicant Notice of Objection

a. An applicant must timely object to an issuer's honour of a noncomplying presentation by giving timely notice by prompt means.

b. An applicant acts timely if it objects to discrepancies by sending a notice to the issuer stating the discrepancies on which the objection is based within a time after the applicant's receipt of the documents which is not unreasonable.

c. Failure to give a timely notice of objection by prompt means precludes assertion by the applicant against the issuer of any discrepancy or other matter apparent on the face of the documents received by the applicant, but does not preclude assertion of that objection to any different presentation under the same or a different standby.

RULE 6. TRANSFER, ASSIGNMENT, AND TRANSFER BY OPERATION OF LAW

Transfer of Drawing Rights

6.01 Request to Transfer Drawing Rights

Where a beneficiary requests that an issuer or nominated person honour a drawing from another person as if that person were the beneficiary, these Rules on transfer of drawing rights ("transfer") apply.

6.02 When Drawing Rights are Transferable

a. A standby is not transferable unless it so states.
b. A standby that states that it is transferable without further provision means that drawing rights:
   i. may be transferred in their entirety more than once;
   ii. may not be partially transferred; and
   iii. may not be transferred unless the issuer (including the confirmer) or another person specifically nominated in the standby agrees to and effects the transfer requested by the beneficiary.

6.03 Conditions to Transfer

An issuer of a transferable standby or a nominated person need not effect a transfer unless:

a. it is satisfied as to the existence and authenticity of the original standby; and
b. the beneficiary submits or fulfills:
   i. a request in a form acceptable to the issuer or nominated person including the effective date of the transfer and the name and address of the transferee;
   ii. the original standby;
   iii. verification of the signature of the person signing for the beneficiary;
   iv. verification of the authority of the person signing for the beneficiary;
   v. payment of the transfer fee; and
   vi. any other reasonable requirements.

6.04 Effect of Transfer on Required Documents

Where there has been a transfer of drawing rights in their entirety:

a. a draft or demand must be signed by the transferee beneficiary; and
b. the name of the transferee beneficiary may be used in place of the name of the transferor beneficiary in any other required document.

6.05 Reimbursement for Payment Based on a Transfer

An issuer or nominated person paying under a transfer pursuant to Rule 6.03(a), (b)(i), and (b)(ii) is entitled to reimbursement as if it had made payment to the beneficiary.

Acknowledgment of Assignment of Proceeds

6.06 Assignment of Proceeds

Where an issuer or nominated person is asked to acknowledge a beneficiary's request to pay an assignee all or part of any proceeds of the beneficiary's drawing under the standby, these Rules on acknowledgment of an assignment of proceeds apply except where applicable law otherwise requires.

6.07 Request for Acknowledgment

a. Unless applicable law otherwise requires, an issuer or nominated person
   i. is not obligated to give effect to an assignment of proceeds which it has not acknowledged; and
   ii. is not obligated to acknowledge the assignment.
b. If an assignment is acknowledged:
   i. the acknowledgment confers no rights with respect to the standby to the assignee who is only entitled to the proceeds assigned, if any, and whose rights may be affected by amendment or cancellation; and
   ii. the rights of the assignee are subject to:
      (a) the existence of any net proceeds payable to the beneficiary by the person making the acknowledgment;
      (b) rights of nominated persons and transferee beneficiaries;
      (c) rights of other acknowledged assignees; and
      (d) any other rights or interests that may have priority under applicable law.

6.08 Conditions to Acknowledgment of Assignment of Proceeds

An issuer or nominated person may condition its acknowledgment on receipt of:
a. the original standby for examination or notation;
b. verification of the signature of the person signing for the beneficiary;
c. verification of the authority of the person signing for the beneficiary;
d. an irrevocable request signed by the beneficiary for acknowledgment of the assignment that includes statements, covenants, indemnities, and other provisions which may be contained in the issuer's or nominated person's required form requesting acknowledgment of assignment, such as:
   i. the identity of the affected drawings if the standby permits multiple drawings;
   ii. the full name, legal form, location, and mailing address of the beneficiary and the assignee;

iii. details of any request affecting the method of payment or delivery of the standby proceeds;
  iv. limitation on partial assignments and prohibition of successive assignments;
  v. statements regarding the legality and relative priority of the assignment; or
  vi. right of recovery by the issuer or nominated person of any proceeds received by the assignee that are recoverable from the beneficiary;
e. payment of a fee for the acknowledgment; and
f. fulfillment of other reasonable requirements.

6.09 Conflicting Claims to Proceeds

If there are conflicting claims to proceeds, then payment to an acknowledged assignee may be suspended pending resolution of the conflict.

6.10 Reimbursement for Payment Based on an Assignment

An issuer or nominated person paying under an acknowledged assignment pursuant to Rule 6.08(a) and (b) is entitled to reimbursement as if it had made payment to the beneficiary. If the beneficiary is a bank, the acknowledgment may be based solely upon an authenticated communication.

Transfer by Operation of Law

6.11 Transferee by Operation of Law

Where an heir, personal representative, liquidator, trustee, receiver, successor corporation, or similar person who claims to be designated by law to succeed to the interests of a beneficiary presents documents in its own name as if it were the authorised transferee of the beneficiary, these Rules on transfer by operation of law apply.

6.12 Additional Document in Event of Drawing in Successor's Name

A claimed successor may be treated as if it were an authorised transferee of a beneficiary's drawing rights in their entirety if it presents an additional document or documents which appear to be issued by a public official or representative (including a judicial officer) and indicate:
a. that the claimed successor is the survivor of a merger, consolidation, or similar action of a corporation, limited liability company, or other similar organization;
b. that the claimed successor is authorised or appointed to act on behalf of the named beneficiary or its estate because of an insolvency proceeding;

c. that the claimed successor is authorised or appointed to act on behalf of the named beneficiary because of death or incapacity; or
d. that the name of the named beneficiary has been changed to that of the claimed successor.

6.13 Suspension of Obligations upon Presentation by Successor

An issuer or nominated person which receives a presentation from a claimed successor which complies in all respects except for the name of the beneficiary:
a. may request in a manner satisfactory as to form and substance:
   i. a legal opinion;
   ii. an additional document referred to in Rule 6.12 (Additional Document in Event of Drawing in Successor's Name) from a public official;
   iii. statements, covenants, and indemnities regarding the status of the claimed successor as successor by operation of law;
   iv. payment of fees reasonably related to these determinations; and
   v. anything which may be required for a transfer under Rule 6.03 (Conditions to Transfer) or an acknowledgment of assignment of proceeds under Rule 6.08 (Conditions to Acknowledgment of Assignment of Proceeds);
   but such documentation shall not constitute a required document for purposes of expiry of the standby.
b. Until the issuer or nominated person receives the requested documentation, its obligation to honour or give notice of dishonour is suspended, but any deadline for presentation of required documents is not thereby extended.

6.14 Reimbursement for Payment Based on a Transfer by Operation of Law

An issuer or nominated person paying under a transfer by operation of law pursuant to Rule 6.12 (Additional Document in Event of Drawing in Successor's Name) is entitled to reimbursement as if it had made payment to the beneficiary.

RULE 7. CANCELLATION

7.01 When an Irrevocable Standby is Cancelled or Terminated

A beneficiary's rights under a standby may not be cancelled without its consent. Consent may be evidenced in writing or by an action such as return of the original standby in a manner which implies that the beneficiary consents to cancellation. A beneficiary's consent to cancellation is irrevocable when communicated to the issuer.

7.02 Issuer's Discretion Regarding a Decision to Cancel

Before acceding to a beneficiary's authorization to cancel and treating the standby as cancelled for all purposes, an issuer may require in a manner satisfactory as to form and substance:

a. the original standby;

b. verification of the signature of the person signing for the beneficiary;

c. verification of the authorization of the person signing for the beneficiary;

d. a legal opinion;

e. an irrevocable authority signed by the beneficiary for cancellation that includes statements, covenants, indemnities, and similar provisions contained in a required form;

f. satisfaction that the obligation of any confirmer has been cancelled;

g. satisfaction that there has not been a transfer or payment by any nominated person; and

h. any other reasonable measure.

RULE 8. REIMBURSEMENT OBLIGATIONS

8.01 Right to Reimbursement

a. Where payment is made against a complying presentation in accordance with these Rules, reimbursement must be made by:

   i. an applicant to an issuer requested to issue a standby; and

   ii. an issuer to a person nominated to honour or otherwise give value.

b. An applicant must indemnify the issuer against all claims, obligations, and responsibilities (including attorney's fees) arising out of:

   i. the imposition of law or practice other than that chosen in the standby or applicable at the place of issuance;

   ii. the fraud, forgery, or illegal action of others; or

   iii. the issuer's performance of the obligations of a confirmer that wrongfully dishonours a confirmation.

c. This Rule supplements any applicable agreement, course of dealing, practice, custom or usage providing for reimbursement or indemnification on lesser or other grounds.

8.02 Charges for Fees and Costs

a. An applicant must pay the issuer's charges and reimburse the issuer for any charges that the issuer is obligated to pay to persons nominated with the applicant's consent to advise, confirm, honour, negotiate, transfer, or to issue a separate undertaking.
b. An issuer is obligated to pay the charges of other persons:
    i. if they are payable in accordance with the terms of the standby; or
    ii. if they are the reasonable and customary fees and expenses of a person requested by the issuer to advise, honour, negotiate, transfer, or to issue a separate undertaking, and they are unrecovered and unrecoverable from the beneficiary or other presenter because no demand is made under the standby.

8.03 Refund of Reimbursement

A nominated person that obtains reimbursement before the issuer timely dishonours the presentation must refund the reimbursement with interest if the issuer dishonours. The refund does not preclude the nominated person's wrongful dishonour claims.

8.04 Bank-to-Bank Reimbursement

Any instruction or authorization to obtain reimbursement from another bank is subject to the International Chamber of Commerce standard rules for bank-to-bank reimbursements.

RULE 9. TIMING

9.01 Duration of Standby

A standby must:
a. contain an expiry date; or
b. permit the issuer to terminate the standby upon reasonable prior notice or payment.

9.02 Effect of Expiration on Nominated Person

The rights of a nominated person that acts within the scope of its nomination are not affected by the subsequent expiry of the standby.

9.03 Calculation of Time

a. A period of time within which an action must be taken under these Rules begins to run on the first business day following the business day when the action could have been undertaken at the place where the action should have been undertaken.

b. An extension period starts on the calendar day following the stated expiry date even if either day falls on a day when the issuer is closed.

9.04 Time of Day of Expiration

If no time of day is stated for expiration, it occurs at the close of business at the place of presentation.

9.05 Retention of Standby

Retention of the original standby does not preserve any rights under the standby after the right to demand payment ceases.

RULE 10. SYNDICATION / PARTICIPATION

10.01 Syndication

If a standby with more than one issuer does not state to whom presentation may be made, presentation may be made to any issuer with binding effect on all issuers.

10.02 Participation

a. Unless otherwise agreed between an applicant and an issuer, the issuer may sell participations in the issuer's rights against the applicant and any presenter and may disclose relevant applicant information in confidence to potential participants.

b. An issuer's sale of participations does not affect the obligations of the issuer under the standby or create any rights or obligations between the beneficiary and any participant.

UNCITRAL CONVENTION ON INDEPENDENT GUARANTEES AND STAND-BY LETTERS OF CREDIT

CHAPTER I. SCOPE OF APPLICATION

Article 1. Scope of application

(1) This Convention applies to an international undertaking referred to in article 2:
   (a) If the place of business of the guarantor/issuer at which the undertaking is issued is in a Contracting State, or
   (b) If the rules of private international law lead to the application of the law of a Contracting State,
   unless the undertaking excludes the application of the Convention.
(2) This Convention applies also to an international letter of credit not falling within article 2 if it expressly states that it is subject to this Convention.
(3) The provisions of articles 21 and 22 apply to international undertakings referred to in article 2 independently of paragraph (1) of this article.

Article 2. Undertaking

(1) For the purposes of this Convention, an undertaking is an independent commitment, known in international practice as an independent guarantee or as a stand-by letter of credit, given by a bank or other institution or person ("guarantor/issuer") to pay to the beneficiary a certain or determinable amount upon simple demand or upon demand accompanied by other documents, in conformity with the terms and any documentary conditions of the undertaking, indicating, or from which it is to be inferred, that payment is due because of a default in the performance of an obligation, or because of another contingency, or for money borrowed or advanced, or on account of any mature indebtedness undertaken by the principal/applicant or another person.
(2) The undertaking may be given:
   (a) At the request or on the instruction of the customer ("principal/applicant") of the guarantor/issuer;
   (b) On the instruction of another bank, institution or person ("instructing party") that acts at the request of the customer ("principal/applicant") of that instructing party; or

(c) On behalf of the guarantor/issuer itself.

(3) Payment may be stipulated in the undertaking to be made in any form, including:

(a) Payment in a specified currency or unit of account;

(b) Acceptance of a bill of exchange (draft);

(c) Payment on a deferred basis;

(d) Supply of a specified item of value.

(4) The undertaking may stipulate that the guarantor/issuer itself is the beneficiary when acting in favour of another person.

Article 3. Independence of undertaking

For the purposes of this Convention, an undertaking is independent where the guarantor/issuer's obligation to the beneficiary is not:

(a) Dependent upon the existence or validity of any underlying transaction, or upon any other undertaking (including stand-by letters of credit or independent guarantees to which confirmations or counter-guarantees relate); or

(b) Subject to any term or condition not appearing in the undertaking, or to any future, uncertain act or event except presentation of documents or another such act or event within a guarantor/issuer's sphere of operations.

Article 4. Internationality of undertaking

(1) An undertaking is international if the places of business, as specified in the undertaking, of any two of the following persons are in different States: guarantor/issuer, beneficiary, principal/applicant, instructing party, confirmer.

(2) For the purposes of the preceding paragraph:

(a) If the undertaking lists more than one place of business for a given person, the relevant place of business is that which has the closest relationship to the undertaking;

(b) If the undertaking does not specify a place of business for a given person but specifies its habitual residence, that residence is relevant for determining the international character of the undertaking.

CHAPTER II. INTERPRETATION

Article 5. Principles of interpretation

In the interpretation of this Convention, regard is to be had to its international character and to the need to promote uniformity in its application and the observance of good faith in the international practice of independent guarantees and stand-by letters of credit.

Article 6. Definitions

For the purposes of this Convention and unless otherwise indicated in a provision of this Convention or required by the context:

(a) "Undertaking" includes "counter-guarantee" and "confirmation of an undertaking";

(b) "Guarantor/issuer" includes "counter-guarantor" and "confirmer";

(c) "Counter-guarantee" means an undertaking given to the guarantor/issuer of another undertaking by its instructing party and providing for payment upon simple demand or upon demand accompanied by other documents, in conformity with the terms and any documentary conditions of the undertaking, indicating, or from which it is to be inferred, that payment under that other undertaking has been demanded from, or made by, the person issuing that other undertaking;

(d) "Counter-guarantor" means the person issuing a counter-guarantee;

(e) "Confirmation" of an undertaking means an undertaking added to that of the guarantor/issuer, and authorized by the guarantor/issuer, providing the beneficiary with the option of demanding payment from the confirmer instead of from the guarantor/issuer, upon simple demand or upon demand accompanied by other documents, in conformity with the terms and any documentary conditions of the confirmed undertaking, without prejudice to the beneficiary's right to demand payment from the guarantor/issuer;

(f) "Confirmer" means the person adding a confirmation to an undertaking;

(g) "Document" means a communication made in a form that provides a complete record thereof.

CHAPTER III. FORM AND CONTENT OF UNDERTAKING

Article 7. Issuance, form and irrevocability of undertaking

(1) Issuance of an undertaking occurs when and where the undertaking leaves the sphere of control of the guarantor/issuer concerned.

(2) An undertaking may be issued in any form which preserves a complete record of the text of the undertaking and provides authentication of its source by generally accepted means or by a procedure agreed upon by the guarantor/issuer and the beneficiary.

(3) From the time of issuance of an undertaking, a demand for payment may be made in accordance with the terms and conditions of the undertaking, unless the undertaking stipulates a different time.

(4) An undertaking is irrevocable upon issuance, unless it stipulates that it is revocable.

Article 8. Amendment

(1) An undertaking may not be amended except in the form stipulated in the undertaking or, failing such stipulation, in a form referred to in paragraph (2) of article 7.

(2) Unless otherwise stipulated in the undertaking or elsewhere agreed by the guarantor/issuer and the beneficiary, an undertaking is amended upon issuance of the amendment if the amendment has previously been authorized by the beneficiary.

(3) Unless otherwise stipulated in the undertaking or elsewhere agreed by the guarantor/issuer and the beneficiary, where any amendment has not previously been authorized by the beneficiary, the undertaking is amended only when the guarantor/issuer receives a notice of acceptance of the amendment by the beneficiary in a form referred to in paragraph (2) of article 7.

(4) An amendment of an undertaking has no effect on the rights and obligations of the principal/applicant (or an instructing party) or of a confirmer of the undertaking unless such person consents to the amendment.

Article 9. Transfer of beneficiary's right to demand payment

(1) The beneficiary's right to demand payment may be transferred only if authorized in the undertaking, and only to the extent and in the manner authorized in the undertaking.

(2) If an undertaking is designated as transferable without specifying whether or not the consent of the guarantor/issuer or another authorized person is required for the actual transfer, neither the guarantor/issuer nor any other authorized person is obliged to effect the transfer except to the extent and in the manner expressly consented to by it.

Article 10. Assignment of proceeds

(1) Unless otherwise stipulated in the undertaking or elsewhere agreed by the guarantor/issuer and the beneficiary, the beneficiary may assign to another person any proceeds to which it may be, or may become, entitled under the undertaking.

(2) If the guarantor/issuer or another person obliged to effect payment has received a notice originating from the beneficiary, in a form referred to in paragraph (2) of article 7, of the beneficiary's irrevocable assignment, payment to the assignee discharges the obligor, to the extent of its payment, from its liability under the undertaking.

Article 11. Cessation of right to demand payment

(1) The right of the beneficiary to demand payment under the undertaking ceases when:
   (a) The guarantor/issuer has received a statement by the beneficiary of release from liability in a form referred to in paragraph (2) of article 7;
   (b) The beneficiary and the guarantor/issuer have agreed on the termination of the undertaking in the form stipulated in the undertaking or, failing such stipulation, in a form referred to in paragraph (2) of article 7;
   (c) The amount available under the undertaking has been paid, unless the undertaking provides for the automatic renewal or for an automatic increase of the amount available or otherwise provides for continuation of the undertaking;
   (d) The validity period of the undertaking expires in accordance with the provisions of article 12.
(2) The undertaking may stipulate, or the guarantor/issuer and the beneficiary may agree elsewhere, that return of the document embodying the undertaking to the guarantor/issuer, or a procedure functionally equivalent to the return of the document in the case of the issuance of the undertaking in non-paper form, is required for the cessation of the right to demand payment, either alone or in conjunction with one of the events referred to in subparagraphs (a) and (b) of paragraph (1) of this article. However, in no case shall retention of any such document by the beneficiary after the right to demand payment ceases in accordance with subparagraph (c) or (d) of paragraph (1) of this article preserve any rights of the beneficiary under the undertaking.

Article 12. Expiry

The validity period of the undertaking expires:
   (a) At the expiry date, which may be a specified calendar date or the last day of a fixed period of time stipulated in the undertaking, provided that, if the expiry date is not a business day at the place of business of the guarantor/issuer at which the undertaking is issued, or of another person or at another place stipulated in the undertaking for presentation of the demand for payment, expiry occurs on the first business day which follows;
   (b) If expiry depends according to the undertaking on the occurrence of an act or event not within the guarantor/issuer's sphere of operations, when the guarantor/issuer is advised that the act or event has occurred by presentation of the document specified for that purpose in the undertaking or, if no such document is specified, of a certification by the beneficiary of the occurrence of the act or event;
   (c) If the undertaking does not state an expiry date, or if the act or event on which expiry is stated to depend has not yet been established by presentation of the

required document and an expiry date has not been stated in addition, when six years have elapsed from the date of issuance of the undertaking.

CHAPTER IV. RIGHTS, OBLIGATIONS AND DEFENCES

Article 13. Determination of rights and obligations

(1) The rights and obligations of the guarantor/issuer and the beneficiary arising from the undertaking are determined by the terms and conditions set forth in the undertaking, including any rules, general conditions or usages specifically referred to therein, and by the provisions of this Convention.

(2) In interpreting terms and conditions of the undertaking and in settling questions that are not addressed by the terms and conditions of the undertaking or by the provisions of this Convention, regard shall be had to generally accepted international rules and usages of independent guarantee or stand-by letter of credit practice.

Article 14. Standard of conduct and liability of guarantor/issuer

(1) In discharging its obligations under the undertaking and this Convention, the guarantor/issuer shall act in good faith and exercise reasonable care having due regard to generally accepted standards of international practice of independent guarantees or stand-by letters of credit.

(2) A guarantor/issuer may not be exempted from liability for its failure to act in good faith or for any grossly negligent conduct.

Article 15. Demand

(1) Any demand for payment under the undertaking shall be made in a form referred to in paragraph (2) of article 7 and in conformity with the terms and conditions of the undertaking.

(2) Unless otherwise stipulated in the undertaking, the demand and any certification or other document required by the undertaking shall be presented, within the time that a demand for payment may be made, to the guarantor/issuer at the place where the undertaking was issued.

(3) The beneficiary, when demanding payment, is deemed to certify that the demand is not in bad faith and that none of the elements referred to in subparagraphs (a), (b) and (c) of paragraph (1) of article 19 are present.

Article 16. Examination of demand and accompanying documents

(1) The guarantor/issuer shall examine the demand and any accompanying documents in accordance with the standard of conduct referred to in paragraph (1) of article 14. In determining whether documents are in facial conformity with the terms and conditions of the undertaking, and are consistent with one another, the guarantor/issuer shall have due regard to the applicable international standard of independent guarantee or stand-by letter of credit practice.

(2) Unless otherwise stipulated in the undertaking or elsewhere agreed by the guarantor/issuer and the beneficiary, the guarantor/issuer shall have reasonable time, but not more than seven business days following the day of receipt of the demand and any accompanying documents, in which to:

(a) Examine the demand and any accompanying documents;

(b) Decide whether or not to pay;

(c) If the decision is not to pay, issue notice thereof to the beneficiary.

The notice referred to in subparagraph (c) above shall, unless otherwise stipulated in the undertaking or elsewhere agreed by the guarantor/issuer and the beneficiary, be made by teletransmission or, if that is not possible, by other expeditious means and indicate the reason for the decision not to pay.

Article 17. Payment

(1) Subject to article 19, the guarantor/issuer shall pay against a demand made in accordance with the provisions of article 15. Following a determination that a demand for payment so conforms, payment shall be made promptly, unless the undertaking stipulates payment on a deferred basis, in which case payment shall be made at the stipulated time.

(2) Any payment against a demand that is not in accordance with the provisions of article 15 does not prejudice the rights of the principal/applicant.

Article 18. Set-off

Unless otherwise stipulated in the undertaking or elsewhere agreed by the guarantor/issuer and the beneficiary, the guarantor/issuer may discharge the payment obligation under the undertaking by availing itself of a right of set-off, except with any claim assigned to it by the principal/applicant or the instructing party.

Article 19. Exception to payment obligation

(1) If it is manifest and clear that:

(a) Any document is not genuine or has been falsified;

(b) No payment is due on the basis asserted in the demand and the supporting documents; or

(c) Judging by the type and purpose of the undertaking, the demand has no conceivable basis, the guarantor/issuer, acting in good faith, has a right, as against the beneficiary, to withhold payment.

(2) For the purposes of subparagraph (c) of paragraph (1) of this article, the following are types of situations in which a demand has no conceivable basis:

(a) The contingency or risk against which the undertaking was designed to secure the beneficiary has undoubtedly not materialized;

(b) The underlying obligation of the principal/applicant has been declared invalid by a court or arbitral tribunal, unless the undertaking indicates that such contingency falls within the risk to be covered by the undertaking;

(c) The underlying obligation has undoubtedly been fulfilled to the satisfaction of the beneficiary;

(d) Fulfilment of the underlying obligation has clearly been prevented by wilful misconduct of the beneficiary;

(e) In the case of a demand under a counter-guarantee, the beneficiary of the counter-guarantee has made payment in bad faith as guarantor/issuer of the undertaking to which the counter-guarantee relates.

(3) In the circumstances set out in subparagraphs (a), (b) and (c) of paragraph (1) of this article, the principal/applicant is entitled to provisional court measures in accordance with article 20.

CHAPTER V. PROVISIONAL COURT MEASURES

Article 20. Provisional court measures

(1) Where, on an application by the principal/applicant or the instructing party, it is shown that there is a high probability that, with regard to a demand made, or expected to be made, by the beneficiary, one of the circumstances referred to in subparagraphs (a), (b) and (c) of paragraph (1) of article 19 is present, the court, on the basis of immediately available strong evidence, may:

(a) Issue a provisional order to the effect that the beneficiary does not receive payment, including an order that the guarantor/issuer hold the amount of the undertaking, or

(b) Issue a provisional order to the effect that the proceeds of the undertaking paid to the beneficiary are blocked, taking into account whether in the absence of such an order the principal/applicant would be likely to suffer serious harm.

(2) The court, when issuing a provisional order referred to in paragraph (1) of this article, may require the person applying therefor to furnish such form of security as the court deems appropriate.

(3) The court may not issue a provisional order of the kind referred to in paragraph (1) of this article based on any objection to payment other than those referred to in subparagraphs (a), (b) and (c) of paragraph (1) of article 19, or use of the undertaking for a criminal purpose.

CHAPTER VI. CONFLICT OF LAWS

Article 21. Choice of applicable law

The undertaking is governed by the law the choice of which is:
    (a) Stipulated in the undertaking or demonstrated by the terms and conditions of the undertaking; or
    (b) Agreed elsewhere by the guarantor/issuer and the beneficiary.

Article 22. Determination of applicable law

Failing a choice of law in accordance with article 21, the undertaking is governed by the law of the State where the guarantor/issuer has that place of business at which the undertaking was issued.

CHAPTER VII. FINAL CLAUSES

Article 23. Depositary

The Secretary-General of the United Nations is the depositary of this Convention.

Article 24. Signature, ratification, acceptance, approval, accession

(1) This Convention is open for signature by all States at the Headquarters of the United Nations, New York, until 11 December 1997.

(2) This Convention is subject to ratification, acceptance or approval by the signatory States.

(3) This Convention is open to accession by all States which are not signatory States as from the date it is open for signature.

(4) Instruments of ratification, acceptance, approval and accession are to be deposited with the Secretary-General of the United Nations.

Article 25. Application to territorial units

(1) If a State has two or more territorial units in which different systems of law are applicable in relation to the matters dealt with in this Convention, it may, at the time of signature, ratification, acceptance, approval or accession, declare that this Convention is to extend to all its territorial units or only one or more of them, and may at any time substitute another declaration for its earlier declaration.

(2) These declarations are to state expressly the territorial units to which the Convention extends.

(3) If, by virtue of a declaration under this article, this Convention does not extend to all territorial units of a State and the place of business of the guarantor/issuer or of the beneficiary is located in a territorial unit to which the Convention does not extend, this place of business is considered not to be in a Contracting State.

(4) If a State makes no declaration under paragraph (1) of this article, the Convention is to extend to all territorial units of that State.

Article 26. Effect of declaration

(1) Declarations made under article 25 at the time of signature are subject to confirmation upon ratification, acceptance or approval.

(2) Declarations and confirmations of declarations are to be in writing and to be formally notified to the depositary.

(3) A declaration takes effect simultaneously with the entry into force of this Convention in respect of the State concerned. However, a declaration of which the depositary receives formal notification after such entry into force takes effect on the first day of the month following the expiration of six months after the date of its receipt by the depositary.

(4) Any State which makes a declaration under article 25 may withdraw it at any time by a formal notification in writing addressed to the depositary. Such withdrawal takes effect on the first day of the month following the expiration of six months after the date of the receipt of the notification of the depositary.

Article 27. Reservations

No reservations may be made to this Convention.

Article 28. Entry into force

(1) This Convention enters into force on the first day of the month following the expiration of one year from the date of the deposit of the fifth instrument of ratification, acceptance, approval or accession.

(2) For each State which becomes a Contracting State to this Convention after the date of the deposit of the fifth instrument of ratification, acceptance, approval or accession, this Convention enters into force on the first day of the month following the expiration of one year after the date of the deposit of the appropriate instrument on behalf of that State.

(3) This Convention applies only to undertakings issued on or after the date when the Convention enters into force in respect of the Contracting State referred to in subparagraph (a) or the Contracting State referred to in subparagraph (b) of paragraph (1) of article 1.

Article 29. Denunciation

(1) A Contracting State may denounce this Convention at any time by means of a notification in writing addressed to the depositary.

(2) The denunciation takes effect on the first day of the month following the expiration of one year after the notification is received by the depositary. Where a longer period is specified in the notification, the denunciation takes effect upon the expiration of such longer period after the notification is received by the depositary.

TABLE OF CASES

THE NETHERLANDS
(last figure of the citation refers to the number of the year concerned, not to the page number)

HOGE RAAD (Supreme Court)

HR, 12 March 1982, NJ 1982, 267	12-24,12-34
HR, 9 June 1995, NJ 1995, 639	10-21,13-7,13-31
HR, 25 September 1998, NJ 1998, 892	12-20,12-27,12-31
HR, 15 January 1999, NJ 1999, 241	12-54
HR, 26 March 2004, JOR 2004, 153	10-22

HOF (Court of Appeal)

CA Amsterdam, 30 March 1972, NJ 1973, 188	2-1,10-20,14-5,14-28,14-31, 15-1/2,15-4,15-6
CA The Hague, 13 June 1980, NJ 1982, 267	7-1,10-20,12-34
CA Amsterdam, 3 December 1981, rolnr. 471/180, not reported	13-23
CA Amsterdam, 4 June 1982, rolnr. 903/81 KG, not reported	12-23,12-28,12-34
CA Amsterdam, 13 January 1983, rolnr. 65/81 KG, not reported	13-5
CA Amsterdam, 20 January 1983, rolnr. 62/82 KG, not reported	13-24
CA Amsterdam, 8 January 1987, KG 1988, 300	13-5,13-17,13-27,14-47
CA Amsterdam, 15 January 1987, NJ 1988, 268	17-7/8
CA Amsterdam, 5 February 1987, NJ 1988, 591	14-5,15-1/2,17-8
CA Amsterdam, 21 April 1988, unreported	12-73
CA Amsterdam, 19 January 1989, KG 1990, 74	12-71,13-23,13-26,14-5, 14-19,14-26/277, 14-49,16-2
CA Leeuwarden, 12 September 1990, KG 1990, 316	16-12/13,16-17,17-3, 17-7,18-5
CA Amsterdam, 21 February 1991, NJ 1992, 141	12-71
CA Amsterdam, 27 February 1992, NJ 1992, 735	10-21,13-12,13-24
CA Amsterdam, 4 February 1993, 1993, 113	11-16,11-22,14-5,14-32, 4-35,14-45,15-1/2,16-6,16-13
CA The Hague, 4 April 1993, NJ 1995,542	7-2,10-22
CA The Hague, 8 June 1993, KG 1993, 301	11-22,12-41,15-1,16-13,17-7,18-5
CA 's-Hertogenbosch, 1 December 1993, NJ 1994, 740	13-23,14-17,14-27,17-3

CA The Hague, 21 September 1994, KG 1994, 381   14-30,17-6
CA Amsterdam, 3 September 1998, JOR 1999, 128   10-20,14-17,14-27,14-48
CA Amsterdam, 25 March 1999, JOR 2000, 40   17-3
CA Amsterdam, 10 August 2000, JOR 2000, 205   10-33
CA 's-Hertogenbosch, 17 September 2002, JOR 2003, 19   12-37
CA Amsterdam, 16 October 2003, JOR 2003, 291   17-6

RECHTBANK (court of first instance)

Rb Amsterdam, 18 December 1980, S & S 1981, 135   2-1,14-5,14-17,14-40, 15-1,16-13
Rb Amsterdam, 19 March 1981, KG 1981, 30   2-1,6-9,14-23,14-28/29,16-13
Rb Amsterdam, 14 May 1981, KG 1981, 71   2-1,17-2/3
Rb Zwolle, 26 November 1982, KG 1982, 220, NJ 1985, 575   14-5,14-17,14-36, 14-38,17-3
Rb Amsterdam, 27 January 1983, KG 1983, 62   13-14
Rb Arnhem, 14 March 1983, KG 1983, 115, NJ 1983, 750   14-5,14-28,17-2/3
Rb Arnhem, 27 October 1983, NJ 1986, 79   12-12
Rb Amsterdam, 5 April 1984, KG 1984, 122   12-20,12-27,12-31
Rb Rotterdam, 22 June 1984, NIPR 1984, No. 327   18-8
Rb Amsterdam, 9 August 1984, KG 1984, 254, NJ 1985, 242   17-2
Rb Almelo, 15 August 1984, KG 1984, 261   13-33,14-34,14-47,14-49
Rb Amsterdam, 20 December 1984, KG 1985, 21   14-23
Rb Amsterdam, 7 March 1985, KG 1985, 87   5-5,13-33,13-35
Rb Amsterdam, 23 May 1985, KG 1985, 165   16-15, 17-3,17-7
Rb Amsterdam, 26 February 1986, NJ 1987, 398   13-14
Rb Utrecht, 7 August 1986, KG 1986, 413   13-17
Rb Arnhem, 20 October 1986, KG 1986, 482   12-70,13-5,14-23
Rb Haarlem, 21 November 1986, KG 1987, 57   5-5,14-5,14-23,14-47, 14-49,17-2,17-6
Rb Haarlem, 9 January 1987, KG 1987, 85   13-12,13-28,13-33,13-35,17-6
Rb Haarlem, 22 January 1987, KG 1987, 86   17-2,17-6
Rb Haarlem, 6 February 1987, KG 1987, 104   17-6
Rb Amsterdam, 31 March 1988, KG 1988, 179   13-5,14-28,17-7
Rb Amsterdam, 7 April 1988, KG 1988, 181   12-40,12-70,14-5,14-19, 14-26/27,14-48
Rb Rotterdam, 9 June 1989, KG 1989, 270   13-5,13-30,14-5,14-28,14-30,17-2/3
Rb Amsterdam, 22 June 1989, KG 1989, 279   14-5
Rb Rotterdam, 20 November 1990, KG 1990, 405   13-5
Rb Amsterdam, 5 September 1991, KG 1991, 335   13-22,13-24,13-26,14-5, 14-17,14-27,17-3
Rb Haarlem, 12 January 1993, NJ 1995, 53   12-70
Rb Rotterdam, 16 March 1993, KG 1993, 222   6-1,14-34,17-2,17-6

Table of cases 519

Rb Arnhem, 7 July 1993, KG 1993, 312	14-30
Rb Amsterdam, 2 June 1994, KG 1994, 373	13-30
Rb Utrecht, 7 February 1995, KG 1995, 163	17-3
Rb Amsterdam, 10 January 1997, KG 1997,	445-5,13-26,13-44, 14-5
Rb The Hague, 9 April 1977, KGK 1997, 1431	14-5,14-17,14-27,17-3
Rb Leeuwarden, 4 July 1997, KGK 1998, 1454	6-2,14-28,17-2
Rb Amsterdam, 5 June 1997, KG 1997, 203	14-17,14-27,14-48,16-10
Rb Utrecht, 10 September 1997, JOR 1998, 34	12-72
Rb Amsterdam, 4 November 1998, JOR 1999, 74	13-31
Rb Alkmaar, 3 December 1998, KG 1999, 2	5-5,13-44,14-5
Rb Utrecht, 22 January 1998, JOR 2000, 40	5-5,12-28, 12-37,14-17,14-27, 14-47,17-3
Rb Amsterdam, 28 June 2000, JOR 2000, 249	12-37
Rb Utrecht, 6 July 2000, S & S 2001, 3	14-5,14-17,14-27,14-45,14-52,17-3
Rb Leeuwarden, 10 January 2001, KGK 2001, 1567	5-5,6-2,14-5
Rb Amsterdam, 17January 2002, JOR 2002, 71	16-19
Rb Rotterdam, 28 February 2002, JOR 2002,	10513-22
Rb Rotterdam, 7 July 2002, KG 2002, 195	17-3
Rb Utrecht, 25 february 2003, JOR 2004, 21	13-24,13-29,13-31
Rb Zwolle, 24 September 2003, JOR 2004, 23	17-2

FEDERAL REPUBLIC of GERMANY

BUNDESGERICHTSHOF (Supreme Court)

BGH, 28 October 1954, WM 1955, p. 265	3-11
BGH, 5 May 1960, NJW 1960, p. 1567	3-11
BGH, 21February 1968, WM 1968, p. 680	3-11
BGH, 2 May 1979, NJW 1979, p. 1500 (= WM 1979, p. 691)	4-18,12-35
BGH, 14 October 1982, WM 1982, p. 1324	12-19,12-24,12-27,12-32, 12-34,13-35
BGH, 24 November 1983, WM 1984, p. 44 (=RIW 1984, p. 917)	4-18,6-9,9-4, 10-20,12-24,12-35, 13-37a,13-12,13-44
BGH, 23 February 1984, WM 1984, p. 633	12-35
BGH, 12 March 1984 (ll ZR 198/82), NJW 1984, p. 2030 (=WM 1984, p. 689)	1-2,6-1,13-15,14-8
BGH, 12 March 1984 (ll ZR 10/83), RIW 1985, p. 78 (= WM 1984, p. 1245)	14-17,14-44
BGH, 3 May 1984, WM 1984, p. 768	12-8,12-12
BGH, 16 October 1984, RIW 1985, p. 72 (= WM 1984, p. 1563)	18-3,18-8

BGH, 31 January 1985, WM 1985, p. 511
  (= NJW 1985, p. 1694)   4-18,10-20,12-35,13-23,14-8,14-46
BGH, 22 April 1985, RIW 1985, p. 650
  (= WM 1985, p. 685)   12-32,12-34, 12-72,13-33,13-35
BGH, 19 September 1985, NJW 1986, p. 310
  (= WM 1985, p. 1387)   7-2,10-5,10-29,10-30,12-8,12-19,12-23,
                                                12-27,12-36,14-8,14-46
BGH, 29 September 1986, WM 1986, p. 1429   14-9,19-4
BGH, 11 December 1986, WM 1987, p. 367   4-18, 12-35
BGH, 18ecember 1986, NJW 1987, p. 1760   13-22
BGH, 26 February 1987, NJW 1987, p. 2075
  (= WM 1987, p. 553)   4-18,12-35,12-70,12-71,12-72
BGH, 16 March 1987, RIW 1987, p. 705   14-34,14-54
BGH, 21 April 1988, WM 1988, p. 934
  (= NJW 1988, p. 2610)   12-35,13-21,13-44,14-8,14-28,14-47
BGH, 28 April 1988, RIW 1988, p. 558   14-17,14-44,16-15
BGH, 27 June 1988, RIW 1988, p. 814   14-34,14-54
BGH, 17 January 1989, NJW 1989, p. 1480
  (= WM 1989, p. 433)   4-19,12-35,14-28
BGH, 9 March 1989, NJW 1989, p. 1606
  (= WM 1989, p. 709)   4-18,4-19, 12-35,13-44
BGH, 13 July 1989, WM 1989, p. 1496   4-18,12-35,13-22,13-23,14-9,14-35
BGH, 5 July 1990, WM 1990, p. 1410   12-15
BGH, 12 March 1992, WM 1992, p. 854   12-15,12-28
BGH, 28 October 1993, WM 1994, p. 106   4-18,6-2,13-12, 13-32,
                                                14-8,14-45,14—56
BGH, 26 April 1994, WM 1994, p. 1063   12-37
BGH, 14 December 1995, WM 1996, p. 193   4-18,12-37,13-9,13-32
BGH, 23 January 1996, WM 1996, p. 393   12-41,13-24,13-31
BGH, 12 March 1996, WM 1997, p. 770   13-23
BGH, 17 October 1996, WM 1996, p. 2228   4-18,10-26,13-13, 13-27,
                                                13-32,14-8,14-56,15-2
BGH, 25 September 1996, WM 1997, p. 13   8-6
BGH, 23 January 1997, WM 1997, p. 656   4-18,12-15,13-12
BHG, 6 May 997, WM 1997, p. 1242   12-8
BGH, 5 June 1997, WM 1997, p. 1675   12-15a
BGH, 2 April 1998, WM 1998, p. 1062   4-19,12-15, 12-28,12-29,13-32,14-56
BGH, 24 September 1998, WM 1998, p. 2363   12-37,13-26,13-44
BGH, 10 November 1998, WM 1998, p. 2522   4-19,5-5,13-44
BGH, 24 November 1998, WM, 1999, p. 72   12-70,13-5,13-12
BGH, 25 February 1999, WM 1999, p. 895   4-19,12-37,13-9,13-10,13-32
BGH, 10 February 2000, WM 2000, p. 715   10-12,10-16,10-17,12-8,13-32
BGH, 2 March 2000, WM 2000, p. 1299   12-15a

Table of cases 521

BGH, 10 October 2000, WM 2000, p. 2334   5-5,11-11,11-16,13-12,
                                          14-50,16-13,16-14
BGH, 8 March 2001, NJW 2001, p. 1857   12-15a,13-32
BGH, 26 April 2001, WM 2001, p. 1208   12-37,13-18
BGH, 12 July 2001, WM 2001, p. 2078   4-19,6-2,13-44
BGH, 24 January 2002, WM 2002, p. 555   13-32,14-56
BGH, 5 March 2002, WM 2002, p. 743   12-15a,13-32,14-8,14-56
BGH, 18 April 2002, WM 2002, p. 1415   12-15a

OBERLANDESGERICHT (Court of Appeal)

OLG Stuttgart, 8 September 1976, WM 1977, p. 881   12-31
OLG Hamburg, 7 July 1977, WM 1978, p. 260   10-18,10-22,13-17,13-33,
                                                      13-35,14-49
OLG Hamburg, 4 November 1977, RIW 1978, p. 615   10-4,10-20,12-12-61,
                                                      12-62,13-15,13-22,18-5,18-8
OLG Frankfurt a.M., 25 November 1977, WM 1978, p. 1188   12-25,13-20
OLG Stuttgart, 25 January 1979, RIW 1980, p. 729   7-1,10-12,10-21,
                                                      13-22/24,15-2
OLG Saarbrücken, 23 January 1981, RIW 1981, p. 338   2-1,11-2,13-40,14-8,
                                                      14-28,14-30,15-1/2,16-5,
                                                      16-10,16-13,16-15,18-9
OLG Stuttgart, 11 February 1981, WM 1981, p. 631   13-24,13-39,15-1,16-5
OLG Hamburg, 18 December 1981, WM 1983, p. 188   12-19,12-23/24,
                                                      12-27,12-32,12-34,13-33,
                                                      13-35,14-8,14-49
Kammergericht, 3 February 1982, BauR 1982, p. 386   14-52
OLG Frankfurt a.M., 16 September 1982, RIW 1983, p. 785   13-22/23/24,
                                                      13-30,18-15
OLG Frankfurt a.M., 3 March 1983, WM 1983, p. 575   6-2,12-40,14-8,16-5
OLG Schleswig, 6 December 1983, WM 1984, p. 651   10-20,12-8,15-2
OLG Frankfurt a.M., 26 June 1984, RIW 1985, p. 407   6-2,12-32,12-34,
                                                      12-72,13-33,13-36
OLG München, 31 October 1984, WM 1985, p. 189   13-44, 14-28,19-4
OLG Hamburg, 10 October 1985, NJW 1986, p. 1691   10-20,12-28,12-35,12-55
OLG Hamm, 24 June 1986, WM 1986, p. 1503   6-5,14-8,14-28
OLG Köln, 7 August 1986, WM 1988, p. 21   13-26,14-8,14-19,
                                                      14-28,15-2,16-5
Kammergericht, 20 November 1986, NJW 1987, p. 1774   4-19,10-20,10-29,
                                                      10-30,12-35,14-46,15-1/2
OLG Frankfurt a.M., 27 April 1987, WM 1988, p. 1480   6-1,14-8,16-5
OLG München, 6 May 1987, WM 1988, p. 1554   10-26,10-29,12-8,15-1/2
OLG Frankfurt a.M., 6 October 1987, RIW 1988, p. 905 14-34,14-55

OLG Bremen, 14 June 1990, WM 1990, p. 1369	13-12, 14-8,14- 28,15-1,16-5
OLG Köln, 15 March 1991, RIW 1992, p. 145	10-2,14-8,15-1,16-5
OLG Karlsruhe, 21 July 1992, RIW 1992, p. 843	2-13,10-20/21,13-12, 13-23,13-31
OLG Frankfurt a.M., 18 March 1997, RIW 1998, p. 477	1-4,12-26,12-37,13-12
OLG München, 23 July 1997, WM 1998, p. 342	10-26,12-26,12-27, 12-35,13-13,13-32
OLG Köln, 24 October 1997, WM 1998, p. 1443	12-23,12-26,12-27,12-33,12-35
OLG Köln, 30 October 1997, WM 1998, p. 707	12-70,12-72,13-12,14-52,16-2
OLG Düsseldorf, 14 April 1999, ZIP 1999, p. 1518	16-5,16-9
OLG München, 23 June 1999, WM 1999, p. 2456	13-5,13-12
OLG Frankfurt a.M., 8 February 2000, WM 2001, p. 1108	13-12,13-27,13-32, 14-47,14-52,16-19
OLG Oldenburg, 15 February 2000, WM 2001, p. 732	14-8,14-17,14-27,14-50
OLG Stuttgart, 20 December 2000, WM 2001, p. 1335	13-20
OLG Saarbrücken, 6 July 001, WM 2001, p. 2055	14-8,18-8
OLG Düsseldorff, 9 August 2001, WM 2001, p. 2294	4-8,12-15a,12-72,14-46,16-2

LANDESGERICHT (court of first instance)

LG Frankfurt a.M., 16 October 1962, NJW 1963, p. 450	4-2,12-34
LG Frankfurt a.M., 30 November 1977, WM 1978, p. 442	12-70
LG Frankfurt a.M., 11 December 1979, NJW 1981, p. 56	2-1,14-8,14-17,14-19, 14-27,14-29,14-36,15-1, 16-5,16-12,16-16-23,18-8/9
LG Braunschweig, 22 May 1980, RIW 1981, p. 789	2-1,10-26,12-34,12-40, 14-19,14-39,14-42, 15-2,16-5,16-13
LG Dortmund, 9 July 1980, WM 1981, p. 280	11-4,11-18,13-5,14-8, 14-17,14-19,14-29,14-47, 15-1,16-5,16-12,16-23,18-8/9
LG Stuttgart, 8 August 1980, WM 1981, p. 633	10-5,10-29,14-35,15-1,16-5, 16-13,16-15,16-23
LG München, 30 January 1981, WM 1981, p. 416	14-8,14-28,16-5,19-4
LG Köln, 11 December 1981, WM 1982, p. 438	10-32,12-40,14-8, 14-26,16-5,16-22
LG Frankfurt a.M., 21 September 1983, WM 1984, p. 86	13-33
LG Düsseldorf, 9 August 1984, RIW 1985, p. 77	10-32,14-17,14-26,16-5, 16-13,14,16-20
LG Duisburg, 27 November 1987, WM 1988, p. 1483	17-2,18-1
LG Dortmund, 5 April 1988, WM 1988, p. 1695	16-5,16-10
LG Hamburg, 4 April 1995, RIW 1996, p. 686	12-77
LG Essen, 1 July 1998, WM 1998, p. 178	13-42

Table of cases 523

LG Hamburg, 15 March 1999, WM 1999, p. 1713	11-4
LG Berlin, 13 April 2000, WM 2000, p. 2378	13-24

FRANCE

COUR DE CASSATION (Supreme Court)

Cass., 20 December 1982, D. 1983 J. p. 365	5-5,7-5,12-27/28,12-34,13-30
Cass., 5 July 1983, Banque 1984, p. 245	17-2
Cass., 13 December 1983, D. 1984 J. p. 420	13-23,14-44/45,15-2
Cass., 17 October 1984, D. 1985 J. p. 269	14-24,14-26,14-35
Cass., 27 November 1984, D. 1985 J. p. 269	11-15
Cass., 12 December 1984, D. 1985 J. p. 269	5-2,11-15,14-9,16-13,17-7
Cass., 5 February 1985, D. 1985 J. p. 269	10-26/27,11-15,11-19,12-34, 13-13,13-15,13-25
Cass., 20 February 1985, D. 1986 I.R. p. 153	12-22,12-32, 12-34,13-10
Cass., 21 May 1985, D. 1986 J. p. 213	14-9,14-28
Cass., 20 November 1985, D. 1986 J. p. 213	11-15,13-10,13-13
Cass., 11 December 1985, D. 1986 J. p. 213	14-17,14-36,14-38,14-45, 14-52,16-13,16-15
Cass., 18 March 1986, D. 1986 I.R. p. 166, D. 1986 J. p. 374	10-32,11-15, 13-39,13-39,17-5
Cass., 29 April 1986, D. 1987 J. p. 17	11-16,12-37a,13-39
Cass., 3 June 1986, D. 1987 Somm. p. 17	12-8,12-37,13-20, 13-23,13-39
Cass., 10 June 1986, D. 1987 J. p. 17	14-9,14-17,14-19/20,14-27, 14-49,16-13,16-16/17/18
Cass., 20 January 1987, D. 1987 Somm. p. 177	14-9
Cass., 10 March 1987, D. 1987 Somm. p. 172	3-2,11-18,14-51
Cass., 7 October 1987, Banque 1988, p. 234	17-8
Cass., 8 December 1987, D. 1988 Somm. p. 240	7-2,12-27/28,12-34,13-30,19-4
Cass., 2 February 1988, D. 1988 Somm. p. 239	12-8,12-26/27,12-32, 12-34
Cass., 23 February 1988, D. 1988 I.R. p. 69	10-33
Cass., 21 June 1988, D. 1989 Somm. p. 148	13-5,13-28
Cass., 18 October 1988, D. 1989 Somm. p. 195	17-5
Cass., 10 January 1989, D. 1989 Somm. p. 153	10-16,14-28
Cass., 24 January 1989, D. 1989 Somm. p. 159	12-41,13-22
Cass., 5 December 1989, D. 1990 Somm. p. 207	12-37a
Cass., 9 January 1990, D. 1991 Somm. p. 191	12-34
Cass., 6 February 1990, D. 1990 Somm. p. 213	14-45
Cass., 27 February 1990, D. 1990 Somm. p. 213, D. 1991 Somm. p. 197	11-15,11-22

Cass., 3 April 1990, D. 1991 Somm. p. 195	13-39
Cass., 9 May 1990, RTD civ. 1990, p. 662	10-33
Cass., 23 October 1990, D. 1991 Somm. p. 197	14-52
Cass., 18 December 1990, D. 1991 Somm. p. 198	10-16,15-2,16-14
Cass., 5 February 1991, D. 1991 Somm. p. 199	14-28
Cass., 19 February 1991, D. 1991 Somm. p. 199	16-13
Cass., 25 March 1991, D. 1991 Somm. p. 202	15-2
Cass., 22 May 1991, D. 1992 Somm. p. 233	10-16,12-34
Cass., 28 January 1992, D. 1992 Somm. p. 234 .	12-37a,13-39
Cass., 24 March 1992, D. 1993 Somm. p. 99	13-5
Cass., 19 May 1992 (1e. decision), D. 1993 Somm. p. 103	16-13
Cass., 19 May 1992 (2e. decision), D. 1993 Somm. p. 103	13-23,14-38
Cass., 19 May 1992 (3e. decision), D. 1993 Somm. p. 104	12-23,12-33
Cass., 16 June 1992, D. 1993 Somm. p. 97	14-31
Cass., 3 November 1992, D. 1993 Somm. p. 96	12-33/34
Cass., 12 January 1993, D. 1995 J. p. 24	12-69,14-9,14-17,14-36
Cass., 26 January 1993, D. 1995 Somm. p. 13	10-4,13-22
Cass., 26 January 1993, D. 1995 Somm. p. 14	10-16
Cass., 6 April 1993, D. 1995 Somm. p. 20	16-13,16-15
Cass., 1 February 1994, D. 1995 Somm. p. 11	12-27,12-34
Cass., 29 March 1994, D. 1995 Somm. p. 20	11-11-15,16-13
Cass., 10 May 1994, D. 1995 Somm. p. 12	12-27,12-31,12-34
Cass., 7 June 1994, D. 1995 Somm. p. 19	13-44
Cass., 7 June 1994, D. 1995 Somm. p. 20	14-9
Cass., 7 June 1994, D. 1995 Somm. p. 21	15-6,16-24
Cass., 13 December 1994, D. 1995 J. p. 209	12-31
Cass., 7 February 1995, RJDA 1995/6, No. 754, p. 600	10-22
Cass., 4 July 1995, D. 1996 J. p. 249	13-28
Cass., 28 November 1995, Rev. Droit Bancaire 1996, p. 58	14-9
Cass., 12 December 1995, No. 93-14.756, Bull Civ. IV No. 289, p. 266	16-13
Cass., 13 March 1996, JCP 1997 Éd E, No. 633, p. 102	12-31
Cass., 26 November 1996, RJDA 1997/3, No. 397, p. 252	11-10,13-40
Cass., 11 March 1997, Bull. Civ. 1997, No. 67, p. 60	12-31
Cass., 10 June 1997, Banque 1997, p. 90	16-24
Cass., 7 October 1997, JCP 1998 Éd. E, No. 6, p. 226	5-5,12-22,12-28,12-34,14-9
Cass., 2 December 1997, JCP 1998 Éd. E, p. 1781	14-9,14-51,15-1,15-3
Cass., 9 December 1997, Rev. Droit Bancaire 1998, p. 66	12-20,12-34,12-36
Cass., 12 January 1999, Revue Droit Bancaire 1999, p. 76	12-31
Cass., 23 February 1999, JCP Éd. G ll, No. 10 189, p. 1940	12-31
Cass., 18 May 1999, JCP Éd G ll, No. 10199, p. 2044	12-23
Cass., 15 June 1999, D. Affaires 2000, p. 112	12-34,12-37a
Cass., 25 January 2000, Banque&Droit 2000, p. 44	12-64
Cass., 3 May 2000, Droit&Patrimoine, novembre 2000, p. 98	10-16

Table of cases 525

Cass., 14 June 2000, Revue Droit Bancaire et Financier 2000, p. 355   12-31
Cass., 27 June 2000, Revue Droit Bancaire et Financier 2000, p. 355   12-31
Cass., 30 January 2001, D. Affaires 2001, p. 1024   7-2,12-23,12-27,
12-34,16-23
Cass., 25 June 2002, D. Affaires 2002 p. 3333   12-31,12-34

COUR D'APPEL (Court of Appeal)

Paris, 8 December 1977, D. 1979 J. p. 259	4-17,7-2
Paris, 14 November 1978, D. 1979 J. p. 259	13-9
Aix-en-Provence, 13 March 1980, D. 1981 I.R. p. 505	12-22,12-25,12-28,12-34
Riom, 14 May 1980, D. 1981 J. p. 336	2-1,12-6,16-22
Paris, 29 January 1981, D. 1981 J. p. 336	10-11,10-26,13-6,13-13
Paris, 24 November 1981, D. 1982 J. p. 296	7-1,12-33
Paris, 25 March 1982, D. 1982 I.R. p. 497	17-2,17-7
Paris, 5 May 1982, D. 1982 I.R. p. 497	339
Paris, 2 June 1982, D. 1983 J. p. 437	10-27,11-15,11-19,12-34, 13-5,13-15,13-25,14-33
Paris, 29 November 1982, D. 1983 I.R. p. 302	14-17
Paris, 7 January 1983, D. 1983 I.R. p. 304	14-45
Paris, 17 January 1983, D. 1983 I.R. p. 303	14-24
Paris, 26 April 1983, D. 1983 I.R. p. 485	11-15
Paris, 25 May 1983, D. 1983 I.R. p. 484	14-52,18-1
Paris, 14 October 1983, D. 1984 I.R. p. 202	12-34,13-21
Paris, 24 January 1984, D. 1984 I.R. p. 203	11-15
Paris,1 February 1984, D. 1984 J. p. 265	13-15,13-25
Paris, 20 June 1984, D. 1985 I.R. p. 241	14-26,16-16
Paris, 3 December 1984, D. 1985 I.R. p. 240	17-2,17-7
Paris, 13 December 1984, D. 1985 I.R. p. 239	3-2,11-18,13-30,14-51
Paris, 26 February 1985, D. 1985 I.R. p. 244	9-3,10-4,13-20,15-5
Poitiers, 13 March 1985, D. 1988 Somm. p. 241	4-17,12-34
Versailles, 29 March 1985, D. 1986 I.R. p. 156	11-17,13-4,13-40,16-23
Paris, 28 May 1985, D. 1986 I.R. p. 155	12-41,13-39
Paris, 26 July 1985, D. 1986 I.R. p. 157	9-3,13-30,16-10,18-9
Paris, 22 November 1985, D. 1986 I.R. p. 155	12-41,12-43,13-23
Paris, 10 January 1986, D. 1986 I.R. p. 154	12-29
Paris, 18 March 1986, D. 1987 Somm. p. 173	13-44, 13-10,15-1/2/3
Paris, 10 April 1986, D. 1988 Somm. p. 244	12-29
Paris, 6 May 1986, D. 1987 Somm. p. 175	12-32,12-34,14-51,17-2
Paris, 1 July 1986, D. 1987 Somm. p. 171	12-27,12-34
Paris, 9 July 1986, D. 1988 Somm. p. 243	10-16,12-22,12-36,13-15
Paris, 1 October 1986, D. 1987 Somm. p. 171	8-20,12-40,12-73,13-40
Paris, 18 November 1986, D. 1988 Somm. p. 247	12-37a,14-17,14-31

Paris, 21 January 1987, D. 1987 Somm. p. 176   12-48,13-40
Paris, 13 February 1987, D. 1987 Somm. p. 172   14-45,15-2
Paris, 2 April 1987, D. 1988 Somm. p. 248   12-41,13-39
Paris, 17 June 1987, D. 1988 Somm. p. 245   14-17,14-49,19-4
Paris, 22 September 1987, D. 1988 Somm. p. 248   9-5
Grenoble, 12 November 1987, D. 1988 Somm. p. 247   15-1,15-4
Paris, 14 December 1987, D. 1988 Somm. p. 248   10-5,11-15, 13-26,15-3,18-1
Paris, 25 February 1988, D. 1989 Somm. p. 150   11-17,13-22, 13-39,18-1
Paris, 14 March 1988, D. 1989 Somm. p. 152   9-3,11-15,11-22
Paris, 19 May 1988, D. 1989 Somm. p. 146   13-21,13-39, 14-28, 14-45,14-47,14-49

Amiens, 6 June 1988, D. 1989 Somm. p. 151   11-15,11-22,13-10
Paris, 27 June 1988, D. 1989 Somm. p. 151   10-32,14-17,14-36,14-45
Paris, 23 September 1988, D. 1989 Somm. p. 156   12-71
Paris, 12 October 988, D. 1990 Somm. p. 205   12-43
Paris, 8 November 1988, D. 1990 Somm. p. 206   11-16,13-5,13-23
Paris, 10 November 1988, D. 1990 Somm. p. 201   10-22,13-17
Versailles, 1 December 1988, D. 1989 Somm. p. 155   16-14
Paris, 27 January 1989, D. 1990 Somm. p. 213/214   13-41
Paris, 15 February 1989, D. 1989 Somm. p. 158   14-28,16-15
Paris, 1 March 1989, D. 1990 Somm. p. 196   12-26/27,13-5
Paris, 28 June 1989, D. 1990 Somm. p. 212   13-30,13-40,18-9
Nimes, 27 September 1989, D. 1990 Somm. p. 200   10-15/16
Paris, 24 October 1989, D. 1990 Somm. p. 203   13-28
Paris, 2 March 1990, D. 1990 Somm. p. 209   1-1,14-47,16-10
Paris, 3 April 1990, D. 1990, Somm. p. 197   13-39
Versailles, 13 June 1990, D. 1991 Somm. p. 191   12-23,12-26/27,12-34
Paris, 27 June 1990, D. 1991 Somm. p. 193   12-15
Paris, 29 June 1990, D. 1993 Somm. p. 98   12-12
Paris, 23 November 1990, D. 1991 Somm. p. 199   11-15,13-40,14-9,16-13
Paris, 27 November 1990, D. 1991 Somm.p. 200   12-6,16-13
Paris, 9 January 1991, D. 1991 Somm. p. 196   12-33,12-41
Paris, 22 January 1991, D. 1991 Somm. p. 200   11-19
Paris, 14 February 1991, D. 1993 Somm. p. 109   12-28
Paris, 6 March 1991, D. 1992 Somm. p. 241   14-9,14-26,14-28
Bordeaux, 7 March 1991, D. 1992 Somm. p. 235   12-20,12-27,12-31,14-17,14-27
Lyon, 17 May 1991, D. 1993 Somm. p. 99   14-17,14-48,14-52, 15-1,15-3,15-6,16-14

Paris, 27 May 1991, D. 1992 Somm. p. 239   13-16
Paris, 18 December 1991, D. 1993 Somm. p. 106   7-2,12-34,13-30
Paris, 7 January 1992, D. 1993 Somm. p. 96   12-20,12-27,12-31
Toulouse, 9 January 1992, D. 1992 Somm. p. 236   12-34, 13-13
Paris, 5 February 1992, D. 1993 Somm. p. 107   12-15,12-28

Table of cases 527

Rouen, 19 February 1992, D. 1993 Somm. p. 108	12-8,12-15
Paris, 21 February 1992, D. 1993 Somm. p. 108	12-28
Lyon, 23 March 1992, RTD com. 1992, No. 12, p. 658	16-13
Paris, 24 April 1992, D. 1993 Somm. p. 102	13-26,14-28
Paris, 17 June 1992, D. 1995 Somm. p. 19	16-13
Paris, 10 July 1992, D. 1993 Somm. p. 100	15-2
Versailles, 16 September 1992, D. 1993 Somm. p. 102	14-9,14-28
Paris, 17 December 1992, D. 1993 Somm. p. 98	10-22,13-20
Paris, 14 January 1993, JCP 1993 Ed. G. No. 22069	14-44,14-53
Paris, 20 March 1993, D. 1993 Somm. p. 96	12-25,12-27,12-34
Versailles, 9 June 1994, D. 1995 Somm. p. 15	12-12
Aix-en-Provence, 19 January 1995, Banque et Droit 1995, No. 43, p. 30	11-15,15-2,16-24
Paris, 26 January 1995, Banque et Droit 1995, No. 43, p. 31	16-24
Paris, 23 June 1995, JCP 1995 Éd. E ll, No. 735, p. 209	12-41,12-63,13-42,18-4
Montpellier, 12 July 1995, Banque November 1995, p. 90	13-23
Paris, 16 April 1996, JCP 1997 Éd. E l, No. 633, p. 102	12-15
Paris, 15 November 1996, Banque et Droit 1997, No. 53, p. 51	14-9,14-17,14-48
Paris, 6 July 2001, D.Affaires 2001, p. 2820	12-34
Paris, 3 April 2002, D.Affaires 2002, p. 1750	9-3,11-19,12-34, 12-36,12-37a,15-5

TRIBUNAL DE COMMERCE/TRIBUNAL DE GRANDE INSTANCE (court of first instance)

Trib. gr. inst. Paris, 13 May 1980, D. 1980 J. p. 488	14-17,17-4/5
Trib. gr. inst. Montlucon, 9 January 1981, D. 1981 J. p. 390	12-6,14-45,14-50,16-14,16-17
Trib. com. Paris, 24 March 1981, D. 1981 J. p. 482	2-1,12-6,12-33
Trib. com. La Roche-sur-Yon, 14 September 1981, D. 1982 I.R. p. 199	7-2,9-5
Trib. com. Versailles, 17 September 1981, D. 1982 I.R. p. 496	10-13,10-15,11-5
Trib. com. Paris, 12 February 1982, D. 1982 J. p. 504	2-1,14-17
Trib. com. Paris, 29 October 1982, D. 1983 I.R. p. 301	14-17
Trib. gr. inst. Paris, 26 January 1983, D. 1983 I.R. p. 297	12-22,12-25, 13-14,15-2,15-4
Trib. com. Paris, 2 February 1983, D. 1985 I.R. p. 243	14-17,17-3,17-7
Trib. com. Paris, 8 July 1983, D. 1984 I.R. p. 92	10-2,13-22,13-26
Trib. com. Paris, 7 September 1983, D. 1987 Somm. p. 174	13-21, 14-17,14-52
Trib. com. Nantes, 22 September 1983, D. 1984 I.R. p. 202	7-2,12-19,12-27, 12-34,37a,13-21,13-30
Trib. com. Paris, 1 August 1984, D. 1986 I.R. p. 159	11-19,13-10,14-17,16-17
Trib. com. Paris, 15 March 1985, D. 1985 I.R. p. 244	14-17,14-36,14-45

Trib. com. Melun, 29 April 1985, D. 1986 I.R. p. 159	10-29,14-17,14-19, 14-27,16-13/14
Trib. com. Paris, 25 June 1985, D. 1986 I.R. p. 156	13-28,14-26
Trib. com. Paris, 6 January 1987, D. 1987 Somm. p. 174 (right column)	13-21,13-30,14-17,14-52
Trib. com. Paris, 6 March 1987, D. 1988 Somm. p.249	12-59,12-65,13-23
Trib. com. Paris, 7 October 1988, D. 1989 Somm. p. 145	3-8,4-17,12-34,14-47
Trib. com. Paris, 29 November 1988, D. 1990 Somm. p. 205	13-33
Trib. com. Paris, 7 February 1989, D. 1990 Somm. p. 207	11-19,13-21,14-28
Trib. com. Paris, 22 February 1989, D. 1990 Somm. p. 204	12-68
Trib. com. Paris, 26 May 1989, D. 1990 Somm. p. 206	12-8
Trib. com. Lyon, 27 June 1989, D. 1990 Somm. p. 206	12-36,12-37a
Trib. com. Paris, 3 October 1989, D. 1990 Somm. p. 202	12-33,13-28
Trib. com. Toulouse, 26 September 1990, D. 1992 Somm. p. 238	10-17
Trib. com. Toulouse, 26 September 1990, D. 1993 Somm. p. 97	11-31
Trib. com. Paris, 14 December 1990, D. 1991 Somm. p. 201	2-11,12-76, 13-5,14-37
Trib. com. Nanterre, 14 March 1991, D. 1992 Somm. p. 241	14-17,14-27,15-1
Trib. com. Paris, 12 April 1991, D. 1992 Somm. p. 239	13-30,14-32,14-45,14-49
Trib. com. Lyon, 3 July 1991, D. 1993 Somm. p. 100	14-17,14-51,15-1, 15-3,16-23/24
Trib. com. Marseille, 19 September 1991, D. 1992 Somm. p. 243	13-44, 15-1/2,15-6
Trib. com. Paris, 20 September 1991, D. 1992 Somm. p. 243	13-44,14-47

BELGIUM

COUR DE CASSATION (CC)/HOF VAN CASSATIE (HC) (Supreme Court)

HC, 23 June 1994, RW 1994/1995, p. 564	17-2
HC, 16 December 1994, RW 1995/1996, p. 323	4-19

COURT D'APPEL/HOF VAN BEROEP (Court of Appeal)

CA Brussels, 18 December 1981, Rev. Banque 1982, p. 99	2-1,10-5,10-16, 12-6,12-23,12-34,13-5, 14-11,14-44,15-2
CA Brussels, 25 February 1982, JCB 1982, p. 349	6-2,10-18,10-20,10-25, 11-18,12-22,12-25, 12-34,13-14,15-2,18-5
CA Antwerp, 13 October 1982, BRH 1982, p. 642	12-34,14-26,18-1

Table of cases

CA Antwerp, 15 October 1985, TBH 1986, p. 646	5-5,12-27,12-28,12-34
CA Brussels, 3 April 1987, RGDC 1989, p. 475	12-18,12-20,12-34
CA Brussels, 15 October 1987, Rev. Banque 1988, p. 29	12-8,12-10,14-47
CA Ghent, 25 February 1988, TBH 1989, p. 40	6-2,10-20,14-28,14-38
CA Brussels, 17 November 1988, RDC 1990, p. 91 (D. 1989 Somm. p. 147)	12-19,12-34,13-24
CA Brussels, 4 January 1989, TBH 1990, p. 1073	10-20/21,10-23,11-19, 13-27,14-28,14-47, 15-1,16-13
CA Brussels, 5 April 1990, TBH 1992, p. 82	13-5,13-43,16-7,16-23
CA Brussels, 28 March 1991, TBH 1992, p. 996	13-24
CA Brussels, 26 June 1992, RDC 1994, p. 51	6-2,10-20/21,12-34,13-13, 13-21,14-11,14-28,15-2
CA Liege, 8 June 1999, RDC 2000, p. 731	11-4,12-23,12-24, 12-37a
CA Liege, 24 September 1999, RDC 2000, p. 734	12-41,13-22,13-24
CA Brussels, 14 February 2000, R.N.B. 2000, p. 403	13-37
CA Brussels, 2 March 2001, TBH 2002, p. 484	12-8,13-18,13-31,14-11,16-23

TRIBUNAL DE COMMERCE/RECHTBANK VAN KOOPHANDEL (court of first instance)

Trib. com. Brussels, 14 August 1979, Rev. Banque 1980, p. 101	13-14
Trib. com. Brussels, 21 November 1979, JCB 1980, p. 140	10-18,12-22
Trib. com. Brussels, 15 January 1980, JCB 1980, p. 147	2-1,6-2,14-11,14-17, 14-36,38,14-45,17-3
Trib. com. Brussels, 23 December 1980, Rev. Banque 1981, p. 627	2-1,12-34,12-40,14-11
Trib. com. Brussels, 11 March 1981, BRH 1981, p. 361	6-2,7-2,12-23/24, 12-27,1234,12-37a, 13-910,15-1
Trib. com. Brussels, 6 April 1982, Rev. Banque 1982, p. 683	12-6,14-11,14-17,14-27,14-36,14-38,14-40,16-13,16-15,16-17
Trib. com. Brussels, 28 April 1983, RDC 1984, p. 57	12-18,12-20,12-27
Trib. com. Ghent, 27 December 1983, TBH 1986, p. 298	14-17,14-19,14-27
Trib. com. Brussels, 15 March 1984/July 27 1984, RDC 1984, p. 567	10-20
Trib. com. Antwerp, 5 July 1984, TBH 1985, p. 571	12-18,12-20,12-31
Trib. com. Brussels, 17 July 1984, RDC, 1985 p. 567	13-14
Trib. com. Brussels, 30 October 1984, RDC 1985, p. 572	10-17,12-43,14-17
Trib. com. Brussels, 15 November 1984, RDC 1985, p. 569	10-27,12-6,12-18, 12-20,12-22,12-31,13-14
Trib. com. Brussels, 18 April 1985, RDC 1985, p. 729	13-33,13-36
Trib. com. Brussels, 25 June 1985, TBH 1987, p. 803	14-17,14-38

Trib. com. Brussels, 8 October 1985, RDC 1986, p. 648   14-44,14-49,19-4
Trib. com. Brussels, 21 October 1986, RDC 1987, p. 706   13-9,13-26,13-40,
14-17,14-19,14-26/27,
14-32,14-48/49,16-17
Trib. com. Brussels, 25 September 1987, RDC 1988, p. 808   10-21,13-12,14-35
Trib. com. Brussels, 26 November 1987, RDC 1989, p. 97   14-11,14-28,14-49
Trib. com. Antwerp, 25 September 1987, TBH 1989, p. 100   2-5,12-12
Trib. com. Brussels, 26 May 1988, JT 1988, p. 460,
   Rev. Banque 1990, p. 167   11-17,13-9,13-12,14-17,
14-20,14-27,14-48,15-23,16-7,
16-13/14,16-17,16-23
Trib. com. Brussels, 16 June 1989, TBH 1990, p. 1076   13-12
Trib. com. Brussels, 30 January 1990, RDC 1992, p. 84   16-13
Trib. com. Brussels, 15 April 1991, D. 1992 Somm. p. 242   14-11,14-17,14-49/50
Trib. com. Brussels, 16 May 1991, JT 1991, p. 711   7-2,13-30,16-23
Trib. com. Brussels, 10 January 1992, RDC 1993, p. 1052   7-2,13-21
Trib. com. Brussels, 15 December 1992, RDC 1993, p. 1055   2-13,10-21,
13-24,13-26
Trib. Brussels, 3 September 1993, RDC 1994, p. 1126   12-6,14-11,14-17,14-27
Trib. com. Namur, 12 September 1994, RDC 1995, p. 68   2-13,7-2,14-44
Trib. com Turnhout, 30 October 1995, RW 1996/1997, p. 328   12-37,13-22
Trio. com. Brussels, 5 February 1996, RW 1996/1997, p. 1263   10-21,12-37,13-20
Trib. com . Liege, 7 April 1995, RDC 1996, p. 1063   6-2,13-12, 13-27,
13-32,13-44
Trib. com. Kortrijk, 21 October 1996, RW 1996/1997, p. 1447   6-2,14-11
Trib. civ. Antwerp, 16 January 1997, RW 1998/1999, p. 679   12-15,12-28,12-32
Trib. com Charleroi, 23 April 1997, JLMB 1998, p. 1073   4-19,7-2,12-26,
12-27,12-28,12-31,16-23
Trib. com. Brussels, 21 November 1997, RDC 1998, p. 850   7-2,12-6,12-43,
13-12,13-22,14-11,16-23
Trib. com. Hasselt, 2 October 1998, TBH 1999, p. 723   13-7,13-9,14-11,14-17,
14-47,14-48,14-49
Trib. com. Ghent, 12 February 1999, TBH 1999, p. 727   10-33
Trib. com Brussels, 11 February 1999, RDC 2000, p. 725   4-19,7-2,12-26,
12-27,12-28,12-31, 16-23

UNITED KINGDOM

Attock Cement Co. v. Romanian Bank of Foreign Trade (CA),
   [1989] 1 All. ER 1189   18-2,18-5

Table of cases 531

Bache & Co. v. Banque Vernes et Commerciale de Paris S.A. (CA),
  [1973] 2 Lloyd's Rep 437. 4-20
Balfour Beatty Civil Engineering v. Technical & General
  Guarantee (CA), [1999] 68 Con. L.R. 180 1-2,4-20,5-5,7-2,
   12-34,14-13,14-53,14-56
Baytur S.A. v. Moona Silk Mills, reported in JBL 1985, p. 324 12-6
Boliventer Oil SA v. Chase Manhattan Bank (CA),
  [1984] 1 WLR 392 14-13,14-45,16-1,16-4,16-13
Cargill International v. Bangladesh Sugar & Food Industries,
  [1996] 2 Lloyd's Rep. 524, CA, [1998] 2 All ER 406 13-27,13-44,14-47
Cauxell Ltd v. Lloyds Bank, The Times 26 December 1995 12-37a, 13-37
Comdel Commodities v. Siporex Trade, [1997] 1 Lloyd's Rep. 424 13-44
Csarnikow-Rionda Sugar Trading v. Standard Bank London,
  [1999] 2 Lloyd's Rep. 187 1-3,7-2,9-3,14-13,14-23,
   15-1,15-5-16-2,16-4,16-11,
   16-13,16-23,17-9
Continental Illinois National Bank v. John Paul
  Papanicolaou (CA), [1986] 2 Lloyd's Rep. 441 13-33,13-35,14-56
Deutsche Ruckversicherung v. Walbrook Insurance,
  [1994] 4 All ER 181 14-13,14-23,15-1,15-5,
   16-2,16-4,16-9,16-11
Discount Records Ltd. v. Barclays Bank Ltd., [1975] 1 WLR 315 14-34
Edward Owen Engineering Ltd. v. Barclays Bank Int. Ltd. (CA),
  [1978] 1 All ER 976, [1978] Q.B 976 2-1,6-9,8-8,16-4
Elian and Rabbath v. Matsas and Matsas (CA),
  [1966] 2 Lloyd's Rep. 495 14-13,14-17,14-36
Esal (Commodities) Ltd. and Reltor Ltd. v. Oriental
  Credit Ltd. (CA), [1985] 2 Lloyd's Rep. 546 7-1,10-29,11-18,
   12-18,12-34,13-13
Etablissement Esefka Int. Anstalt v. Central Bank of Nigeria,
  [1979] 1 Lloyd's Rep. 445 16-10
Frans Maas (UK) Ltd v. Habib Bank AG Zürich,
  5 August 2000, unreported 13-12
GKN Contractors v. Lloyds Bank (CA), [1985]
  30 BLR 48 9-3,13-5,14-13, 15-5,16-11
Group Josi Re v. Walbrook Insurance Co. Ltd., CA,
  [1996] 1 Lloyd's Rep. 345, [1996] 1 WLR 1152 14-44,14-23, 15-1,16-2
Gulf Bank v. Mitsubishi Heavy Industries (CA),
  [1994] Lloyd's Rep. 145 1-1,10-5,14-52
Gur Corporation v. Trust Bank of Africa, [1986] 3 WLR 583,
  IBL, July 1986, 12-61,13-14,13-22/23
Gyllenhammar & Partners Int. Ltd. v. Sour Brodogradevna Industrya,
  [1989] 2 Lloyd's Rep. 403 6-8

Harbottle (Mercantile) Ltd. v. National Westminster Bank Ltd.,
  [1977] 2 All ER 862, [1978] Q.B. 146   2-1,4-2,6-9,7-1,10-20,
                                                          12-24,16-4,16-13,16-17
Hong Kong and Shanghai Banking Corp. v. Kloeckner & Co.,
  [1989] 2 Lloyd's Rep. 323   13-33
Howe Richardson Scale Co. v. Polimex-Cekop (CA),
  [1978] 1 Lloyd's Rep. 161   8-8
Hyundai Heavy Industries v. Papadopoulos, [1980] 2 All ER 29   12-25
I.E. Contractors Ltd. v. Lloyds Bank PLC and Rafidain Bank (CA),
  [1990] 2 Lloyd's Rep. 496   10-21,10-22,11-18,
                                                          11-23,12-22,12-34,13-5,
                                                          13-12/13,13-37/38,18-5
Intraco Ltd. v. Notis Shipping Corporation (CA),
  [1981] 2 Lloyd's Rep. 256   5-3
Kvaerner John Brown v. Midland Bank, [1998] CLC 446   14-13, 14-53,16-2,16-4
Muduroglu Ltd. v. T.C. Ziraat Bankasi, [1986] 1 Q.B. 1225   18-3
Offshore Enterprises Inc v. Nordic Bank PLC (CA),
  reported in IBL, November 1984, p. 86   12-25,13-22/23,18-5
Potton Homes Ltd. v. Coleman Contractors (Overseas) Ltd.
  (CA), [1984] 28 Build. L.R. 19   5-5,10-18,12-28,
                                                              12-34,14-54,16-2
Power Curber Int. Ltd. v. National Bank of Kuwait (CA),
  [1981] 1 WLR 1233   16-19
SAFA v. Banque du Caire, [2000] 2 Lloyd's Rep. 600   13-33
Siporex Trade SA v. Banque Indosuez, [1986]
  2 Lloyd's Rep. 146   10-20,12-22,13-12
Shanning International and Others v. Rasheed Bank,
  [2001] All ER (D) 321 (Jun)   10-8,13-42
Solo Industries v. Canara Bank, [2001] 2 Lloyd's Rep. 578   13-32,14-56
State Trading Corp. of India v. E. D. & F. Man (CA),
  [1981] Com LR 235   4-20,13-44,14-13,14-41,14-45
Themehelp Ltd. v. West and Others, [1996] QB 84   14-13, 14-36,16-2,17-9
Trafalgar House Construction (Regions) v. General Surety
  and Guarantee Co., [1995] 3 All ER 737   1-2
Tukan Timber Ltd. v. Barclays Bank PLC, [1987] 1 Lloyd's Rep. 171   16-4
Turkiye Bankasi AS v. Bank of China, [1993] Lloyd's Rep. 132   18-9
Turkiye Is Bankasi v. Bank of China, [1996]
  2 Lloyd's Rep. 611; CA [1998] 1 Lloyd's Rep. 250   7-2,14-13, 14-35, 14-56,
                                                          15-1,15-2,15-3,15-4,
                                                          16-9,16-13,16-23
United City Merchants Ltd. v. Royal Bank of Canada, (HL),
  [1982] 2 All E.R. 720   14-44

Table of cases 533

United Trading Corp. S.A. v. Allied Arab Bank Ltd. (CA),
　[1985] 2 Lloyd's Rep. 554　　　　　　　　　　　　　5-3,14-13, 16-4
Wahda Bank v. Arab Bank Plc, [1993] 2 Bank. L.J. 233,
　(CA) [1996] 1 Lloyd's Rep. 470　　　　7-2,11-10,13-42, 16-23,18-9
Z Ltd. v. A (CA), [1982] 1 ALL ER 556　　　　　　　　　　　　17-9

UNITED STATES OF AMERICA
(selected table of cases)

Airline Reporting Corp. v. First national bank of Holly Hill,
　832 f.2d 823 (4th. Cir. 1987)　　　　　　　　　　　　　　14-14/16
American National Bank & Trust v. Hamilton Industries International,
　583 F. Supp. 164 (N.D. Ill. 1984)　　　　　　　　　　　　　　　1-4
American Bell Int. v. Islamic Republic of Iran, 474 F. Supp. 420
　(S.D.N.Y. 1979)　　　　　　　　　　　　　　　1-1,14-14/16,16-8
Amoco Oil v. First Bank & Trust, 759 SW2d 877 (Mo. Ct. App. 1988)　12-10
Banco Gen. Runinahui v. Citibank International, 97 F.3d 480
　(11th. Cir. 1996)　　　　　　　　　　　　　　　　　　　　　13-31
Brenntag International Chemicals v. Norddeutsche Landesbank GZ,
　70 F. Supp. 2d 399 (SDNY 1999)　　　　　　　　　　　　　　12-72
Collins Systems Int. v. Citibank, 82 Civ. 613 (V.L.B.)
　(S.D.N.Y. 1982)　　　　　　　　　　　　　　　　　　10-32,16-23
Continental Illinois Nat. Bank v. John Paul Papanicolaou,
　IBL October 1986, p. 72　　　　　　　　　　　　　　　　　　14-56
Dynamics Corp. v. Citizens S. Nat'l Bank, 356 F. Supp. 991
　(N.D. Ga. 1973)　　　　　　　　　　　　　　　　　　　13-5,16-21
Exxon Co. U.S.A. v. Banque de Paris et des Pays-Bas,
　828 F2d 1121 (5th. Cir. 1987)　　　　　　　　　12-8,12-37,13-39
Ground Air Transfer v. Westate's Airlines, 899 F.2d 1269
　(1st Cir. 1990)　　　　　　　　　　　　　　　　　　14-14/16, 14-17
GTE international Inc. v. Manufacturers Hanover Trust,
　case No. 3525/79 (Sup. Ct., March 29,1979)　　　　　　　　　　1-1
Hall's Motor Transit Co. v. Chase Manhattan Bank
　N.Y. Supreme Court, June 13 1983, IFLR October 1983, p.42　　13-9/10
Harris Corp. v. National Iranian Radio and Television,
　691 F.2d. 1344 (11th. Cir. 1982)　　　　　　14-40,16-8,16-15,16-23
Intraworld Industries v. Girard Trust Bank, 461 Pa. 343 (1975)　14-14/16
Itek Corporation v. First National Bank, 511 F. Supp. 1341
　(D. Mass. 1981), 730 F. 2d. 19 (1st. Cir. 1984)　　　　　　　　6-2,16-8
KMW International v. Chase Manhattan Bank, 606 F. 2d. 10
　(2d. Cir. 1979)　　　　　　　　　　　　　8-8,14-14/16,16-8,14-37,39

New Orleans Brass v. Whitney National Bank,
  2002 WL 1018964 (La. App. 4th Cir. May 15, 2002)   14-14/16,14-35
Pan American World Airways v. Bank Melli, No 79 Civ. 1190
  (S.D.N.Y. 1979)   13-5
Philipp Brothers, Inc v. Oil Country Specialists, 9 UCC Rep.
  Serv. 2d. 201 (Tex. 1989)   14-14/16
Philipp Brothers, Inc v. Oil Country Specialists, 787 SW2d 38 (Tex. 1990)   14-35
Recon Optical Inc. v. Government of Israel, 816 F. 2d. 854
  (2d. Cir. 1987)   14-14/16
Rockwell International Systems v. Citibank, 719 F. 2d. 583
  (2d. Civ. 1983)   10-32,14-14/16,14-20,14-40,
  14-38,16-8,16-15,16-23
Roman Ceramics Corp. v. Peoples & National Bank,
  714 F. 2d. 1207 (3d. Cir. 1983)   13-9/10
SRS Prods. Co. v. LG Eng'g Co., 994 S.W.2d. 380 (Tex. Ct. Ap. 1999)   14-14/16
Sztejn v. Henry Schroder Banking Corp., 177 Misc 719
  (N.Y. Sup. Ct 1941)   14-14/16,14-34,14-54
Temtex Products v. Capital Bank & Trust, 623
  F. Supp. 816 (MD La. 1985)   14-49
Touche Ross & Co. v. Manufacturers Hanover Trust,
  434 N.Y.S. 2d. 575 (N.Y. Sup. Ct.   16-8
United Technologies Corp. v. Citibank, 469 F. Supp. 473
  (S.D.N.Y. 1979)   16-8,14-39
Wyle v. Bank Melli, 577 F. Supp. 1148 (N.D. Cal. 1983)   13-40, 14-14/6,16-8

AUSTRIA

OG Austria, 7 Ob 653/85, JIBL 1986 N-50   12-17,12-19
OG Austria, 10 July 1986, JIBL 1986 N-140   16-12,16-17,18-5
OG Austria, 3 December 1986, JIBL 1987, N-51   13-6
OG Austria, 18 December 1987, IBL November 1988, p. 92   12-28,12-32,12-34,
  12-43,12-47,13-23/24
OG Austria, 24 March 1988, JIBL 1988 N-154,
  D. 1992 Somm. p. 233   10-21,13-7,16-10

CANADA

Angelica-Whitewear Ltd. v. Bank of Nova Scotia, [1987] 1.
  S.C.R. 59 (S.C.C.)   16-9
Royal Bank v. Gentra Canada Investments Inc., (2001) 15 B.L.R. (3d) 25   13-44

Table of cases 535

Royal Bank v. Darlington, [1995] O.J. No. 1044 15-2

SWITZERLAND

Federal Court, 9 January 1985, D. 1986 I.R. p.163 14-39
Geneva, 24 June 1983, D. 1983 I.R. p. 486 16-22
Geneva, 27 September 1984, D. 1986 I.R. p.163 14-19,14-39
Geneva, 14 March 1985, D. 1986 I.R. p. 164 10-29,16-24
Geneva, 12 September 1985, D. 1986 I.R. p. 165 6-2,12-6,13-40,14-19,14-27,16-13,16-14
Zürich, 9 May 1985, D. 1987 Somm. p. 177, BLZürich
 Rspr. 85 (1986, No. 23) 12-24,12-34, 16-13,16-15
Federal Court, 25 July 1988, D. 1990 Somm. p. 195 12-26
Federal Court, 20 August 1991, D. 1992 Somm. p. 233 12-26,17-2
Federal Court, 13 April 1993, D. 1995 Somm. p. 12 12-26,12-28

ITALY

Trib. Padua, 1 October 1993, D. 1995 Somm. p. 23 13-42

FINLAND

Supreme Court, 25 October 1992, D. 1995 Somm. p. 22 14-40,16-13

ARBITRATION

ICC Arbitration, No. 3316 (1979), J.D.I. 1980, p. 970 6-2,12-23,12-24,
 12-27,12-34
ICC Arbitration, No. 5639 (1987), D. 1988 Somm. p. 242 12-22, 12-27, 12-34
ICC Arbitration, No. 5721 (1990), J.D.I. 1990, p. 1020 12-6,14-36,14-38,14-50

BIBLIOGRAPHY

MONOGRAPHS on BANK GUARANTEES and STANDBY LETTERS OF CREDIT

Affaki Georges, ICC Uniform Rules on Demand Guarantees; A User's Handbook to the URDG, ICC Publication No. 631, 2001 (cited: Affaki)

Byrne James E, The Official Commentary on the International Standby Practices, The Institute of International Banking & Law Practice, 1998 (cited: ISP98 Commentary)

Colloque de Tours, June 1980, Les Garanties Bancaires dans les Contrats internationaux, Paris (cited: Tours)

De Bankgarantie, Preadviezen van de Vereeniging 'Handelsrecht', 1984 (F.H.J. Mijnssen, J.M. Boll)

Dohm J., Bankgarantien im internationalen Handel, Bern 1985

Dolan, John F., The Law of Letters of Credit (Commercial and standby Credits), (1996) (update 2002 No 1) Boston (cited: Dolan)

Goerke E., Kollisionsrechtliche Probleme internationaler Garantien, Konstanz 1982

Goode, R., Guide to the ICC Uniform Rules for Demand Guarantees, ICC Publication, no. 510 (cited: Goode)

Horn, Norbert, Bürgschaften und Garantien: aktuelle Rechtsfragen der Bank-, Unternehmens- und Aussenwirtschaftspraxis, 8 ed. , 2001, Köln (cited: Horn)

Kleiner B., Bankgarantie, 4th ed., Zürich 1990

Lienesch, Irmtraud, Internationale Bankgarantien und die UN-Konvention über unabhangige Garantien und Stand-by Letters of Credit, Berlin-New York, 1999 (cited: Lienesch)

Lohmann U., Einwendungen gegen den Zahlungsanspruch aus einer Bankgarantie und ihre Durchsetzung in rechtsvergleichender Sicht, Köln 1984

Mülbert P.O., Missbrauch von Bankgarantien und einstweiliger Rechtsschutz, Tübingen 1985

Nielsen, J., Bankgarantien bei Aussenhandelsgeschäften, Köln, 1986 (cited: Nielsen)

Pabbruwe H.J., Bankgarantie, 4th ed., Deventer 2000 (cited: Pabbruwe)

Poullet Y., L'abstraction de la garantie bancaire automatique, thesis, Louvain 1982-1982 (cited: thesis)

Prüm, A., Les garanties à première demande, Paris 1994 (cited: Prüm)

Rowe M., Guarantees, standby letters of credit and other securities, London 1987
Westphalen F. Graf von, Die Bankgarantie im internationalen Handelsverkehr, 2nd ed., Heidelberg 1990 (cited: von Westphalen)
Wunnicke B., Wunnicke D.B and Turner P., Standby and commercial letters of credit, New York, 3d edition , 2003 Supplement (cited: Wunnicke/Wunnicke/Turner)

OTHER BOOKS

Association Nationale des Juristers de Banque, Suretes et Garanties, Colloque January 2001, La Lettres des Juristes d'Affaires
Bärmann J. (Hrsg.), Recht der Kreditsicherheiten in europäischen Ländern, Band Xl, Teil L, Berlin 1976
Benjamin's Sale of Goods (Ellinger E.P.), 3rd ed., London 1987
Bergström/Schultz/Käser, Garantieverträge im Handelsverkehr, Frankfurt a.M. 1972 (cited: Handelsverkehr)
Boon M.N., Het Documentaire Accreditief, NIBE, Amsterdam 1988
Cabrillac, Mouly, Droit des suretes, 5th. ed. 1999 (cited:Cabrillac/Mouly)
Canaris C.W., Bankvertragsrecht, Erster Teil, 3rd ed., Berlin 1988
Croiset van Uchelen A.R.J., Documentaire kredieten en bankgaranties: een onderzoek naar het 'abstracte' karakter van deze rechtsfiguren en naar de rechtsmiddelen van de opdrachtgever bij misbruik, Deventer 1989
Delden R. van, et. al., Hoofdstukken Handelsrecht, 2nd. ed. Deventer 1993 (cited: HH)
Delden R. van, Betalingsverkeer (documentair krediet/documenten), Deventer 1990 (cited: Betalingsverkeer)
Gutteridge H.C. and Megrah M., The Law of Bankers' Commercial Credits, 7th ed., London 1984
Harfield H., Bank Credits and Acceptances, 5th ed., New York 1974
Horn/von Marschall/Rosenberg/Pavicevic, Dokumentenakkreditive und Bankgarantien im internationalen Zahlungsverkehr, Frankfurt 1977
Horn, Norbert, Bürgschaften und Garantien: aktuelle Rechtsfragen der Bank-, Unternehmens-, und Aussenwirtschaftspraxis, 8th ed., 2001 (cited: Horn)
Kurkela M., Letters of Credit under International Trade Law, New York 1985
Mattout J.P., Droit Bancaire International, Paris , 2d ed. 1996 (cited: Mattout)
Répertoire Pratique du Droit Belge, Complément Vll Les garanties bancaires autonomes (1990) (Martin/Delierneux) (cited: RPDB)
Sarna L., Letters of Credit, Toronto 1984

Schinnerer E. and Avancini P., Bankverträge Teil l, Vienna 1978

Scott and Reynolds on Surety Bonds, Toronto, Carswell, looseleaf

Staudinger J. von (Horn), Kommentar zum Bürgerlichen Gesetzbuch, Recht der Schuldverhältnisse, Achtzehnter Titel. Bürgschaft, Vorbemerkungen zu 765-778, 13th ed., Berlin 1997 (cited: Staudinger/Horn)

Schlegelberger/Hefermehl, Handelsgesetzbuch Band lV 343-372, 5th ed., München 1976

Schmitthoff C.M., Export Trade, 9th ed., London 1990

Schoordijk H.C.F., Beschouwingen over drie-partijen-verhoudingen van obligatoire aard, Zwolle 1958

Stoufflet, Jean, Garantie Bancaire Internationale, in Banque et Credit, 1988, Supplement 1991, 1999

T'Kint, Francois, Suretés et principes généraux du droit de poursuite des créanciers, 3rd. ed. 2000

Travaux de l'Association Henri Capitant, La Responsabilité du Banquier: aspects nouveaux, Tome XXXV, 1984, Economica

Vasseur M., VE Garantie indépendante, in Rép. Com. Dalloz, loose-leaf (cited: Vasseur)

Ventris F.M., Bankers' Documentary Credits, 2nd ed., London 1983

Wattiez J.P., Le cautionnement bancaire, Paris 1964

Wessely W., Die Unabhängigkeit der Akkreditiv-Verplichtungen von Deckungsbezeichnung und Kaufvertrag, München 1975

White J.T. and Summers R.S., Uniform Commercial Code, 2nd ed., St. Paul 1980

Zahn/Ehrlich/Neumann, Zahlung und Zahlungssicherung im Aussenhandel, 7th ed., Berlin 2001

ARTICLES, *etc*. (selected readings)

Aden M., Der Arrest in den Auszahlungsanspruch des Garantie-Begünstigten durch den Garantie-Auftraggeber, RIW 1981, p. 439-442

Affaki, M.B.G., Les garanties indépendantes sont-elles encore indépendantes? Lecons de la crise du Golfe, Banque et Droit, janv.-févr. 1994.3

Arnold H.J., and Bransilver E., The Standby Letter of Credit - The Controversy continues, UCCLJ 1978, p. 272-288

Bannier, F.W., Bankguarantees and Documentary Credit, in Hague- Zagreb Essays 6, p. 65-90, Dordrecht 1987

Bark C., Rechtsfragen und Praxis der indirekten Garantie im Aussenwirtschaftsverkehr, ZIP 1982, p. 405-416

Bark C., Bestätigung von Garantien im Aussenwirtschaftsverkehr, ZIP 1982, p. 655-660

Bartman S.M., De kracht van de bankgarantie, NJB 1987, p. 1088-1093

Battaille lll J.F., Guaranty Letters of Credit: Problems and Possibilities, Arizona L.R. 1974, p. 822-859

Beckers L., Bank policies on guarantee calls, IFLR October 1982, p. 32-34

Ben Slimane M., De quelques aspects des lettres de garanties bancaires émises au profit d'entités publiques en Arabie Saoudite, DPCI 1986, p. 285-305

Ben Slimane M., Guarantee bonds issued in favour of Saudi public entities, IFLR September 1986, p. 27-31

Bergsten E.E., A new regime for international independent guarantees and stand-by letters of credit: the UNCITRAL Draft Convention on Guaranty Letters, 27 Int. Lawyer, p. 859-879 (1993)

Bertrams R.I.V.F., Geldigheidsduur van bankgaranties en andere kwesties, Bb 1990, p. 45-47

Bertrams R.I.V.F., Omtrent de waarschuwingsplicht van de bank bij de bankgarantie, WPNR 1987, p. 515-519

Bertrams R.I.V.F., Formele toetsing bij het inroepen van een onafhankelijke bankgarantie, V & O 1992, p. 62-64

Bertrams R.I.V.F., Uniforme regels voor bankgaranties van de Internationale Kamer van Koophandel, TVVS 1993, p. 95-100

Bertrams R.I.V.F., De bankgarantie als zekerheidsinstrument bij internationaal contracteren, in Contracteren in de internationale praktijk, Deventer (1994), p. 123-147 (cited: International Contracts)

Bertrams R.I.V.F., Bankgaranties. Verschuldigdheid van rente in verband met te late betaling en wachttijd bij uitbetaling, Bb 1994, p. 225-227

Bertrams R.I.V.F., Bankgaranties. Een niet-conform betalingsverzoek en de mededelingsplicht van de bank, NTBR 1996, p. 27-30

Bertrams R.oeland., Counter-Guarantees in an indirect, independent (first demand) guarantee structure, JIBFL 1997, p. 373-380

Bertrams R.I.V.F, Hoe ver reikt de onderzoeksplicht van de bank en hoe is de procesorde bij een vordering tot een betalingsverbod?, WPNR 1999, p. 706-711

Bertrams R. I.V.F., Conservatoir beslag en bankgaranties, WPNR 2000, p. 225-226

Bertrams, Roeland, The New Forms of Security in FIDIC's 1999 Conditions of Contract, ICLR 2000, p. 369-383

Blau W. and Jedzig J., Bank Guarantees to Pay upon First Written Demand in German Courts, International Lawyer 1989, p. 725-735

Blau W., Blockierung der Auszahlung einer Bankgarantie auf erstes Anfordern durch Arrest und Hinterlegung?, WM 1988, p. 1474-1477

Blomkwist J.W.H., De Bankgarantie, WPNR 1986, p. 551-556

Boll J.M., De Afroep(bank)garantie, in Betalingsverkeer, p. 102-119, Zwolle 1987

Boll J.M., De Bankgarantie, Preadviezen van de Vereeniging 'Handelsrecht', 1984

Bontoux C., Les garanties bancaires dans le commerce international, Banque 1982, p. 171-174

Bydlinski P., Die Bürgschaft auf erstes Anfordern: Darlegungs- und Beweislast bei Rückforderung durch den Bürgen, WM 1990, p. 1401-1405

Bydlinski P., Personaler numerus clausus bei der Bürgschaft auf erstes Anfordern?, WM 1991, p. 257- 262

Bydlinski P., Die aktuelle höchstgerichtliche Judikatur zum Bürgschaftsrecht in der Kritik, WM 1992, p. 1301-1310

Byrne J.E., Standby Letter of Credit Rules: An Exercise in Drafting a Commercial Statute, Arizona Jo. Int. & Comp. Law, vol. 9 (1992), p. 366-485

Caemmerer E. von, Bankgarantien im Aussenhandel, in Festschrift Otto Riese, p. 295-307, Karlsruhe 1964

Castelvvi M.B., Zum Übergang der gesicherten Forderung auf den zahlenden Garanten, WM 1995, p. 868-872.

Chatterjee S.K., The Method of Determining the Governing law of Performance Bonds and Counter- Guarantees: A Commercial Approach, [1994] 1 JIBL p. 20-24

Coing H., Probleme der internationalen Bankgarantie, ZHR 1983, p. 125-144

Collins L. and Livingstone D.K., Aspects of Conclusive Evidence Clauses, JBL 1974, p. 212-219

Croiset van Uchelen A.R.J., Rechtsmiddelen tegen misbruik van bankgaranties en documentaire kredieten, WPNR 1989, p. 269-276

De Ly F., Garanties en standby letters of credit, TBH 1986, p. 172-194

Dolan J.F., Weakening the letter of credit product: the new Uniform Customs and Practice for Documentary Credits, IBLJ 1994, p. 149-177

Dolan J.F., Standby letters of credit and fraud (is the standby only another invention of the goldsmiths in Lombard street?), Cardozo Law Review 1985, p. 1-45

Dolan, J.F., Efforts at International Standardization of Bank Guarantees, 4 Banking & Finance L.R. (1992), p. 238-266

Dolan, J.F., The UN Convention on International Idependent Undertakings: Do States with Mature Letter-of-Credit Law Regimes need it?, in: The 1999 Annual Survey of Letter of Credit Law & Practice, p. 97

Dohm J., Mesures provisionelles et séquestre pour empêcher l'appel abusif d'une garantie bancaire sur demande, RDAI 1992, p. 887-914

Driscoll R.J., The Role of Standby Letters of Credit in International Commerce: Reflections After Iran, Virginia Journal Int. Law 1980, p. 459-504

Dubisson M., Le droit de saisir les cautions de soumission et les garanties de bonne execution, DPCI 1977, p. 423-456

Ebbink R.E., Uitzonderingen op de betalingsplicht van de bank onder het documentaire crediet, WPNR 1984, p. 433-438, 453-458

Edelmann H, Blockierung der Inaspruchname einer direkten Auslandgarantie, DB 1998, p. 2453-2458

Eberth R., Der Standby Letter of Credit im Recht der Vereinigten Staaten von Amerika, ZVglRWiss. 1981, p. 29-58

Eisemann M.F., Arbitrage et Garanties contractuelles, Rev. Arbitrage 1972, p. 379-405

El Hakim J., National report (Middle East), in Colloque de Tours, p. 383-406

Elland-Goldsmith M., Performance Bonds in the English Courts, DPCI 1978, p. 151-156

Elland-Goldsmith M., Garantie bancaire: L'évolution de la jurisprudence en Angleterre, RDAI 1990, p. 421-436

Ellinger E.P., Letters of Credit, in The Transnational Law of International Commercial Transactions, p. 241-273, Deventer 1982

Gable C.I., Standby Letters of Credit: Nomenclature has confounded analysis, Law & Policy Int. Business 1980, p. 903-945

Gavalda C. and Stoufflet J., La lettre de garantie internationale, RTDC 1980, p. 1-13

Getz H.A., Enjoining the International Standby Letter of Credit: the Iranian Letter of Credit Cases, Harv. Int. L.J. 1980, p. 189-247

Goode, Roy, Surety and On-Demand Performance Bonds, JBL 1988, p. 87-91

Goode, Roy, Abstract Payment Undertakings, in Essays for Patrick Atiyah (1991), p. 209-235

Goode, Roy, The new I.C.C. Uniform Rules for Demand Guarantees, Lloyd's Mar. & Com. L.Q. 1992, p. 190-206

Grootenhuis I., Misbruik van het documentaire krediet en de bankgarantie, AA 1986, p. 413-418

Hammerstein E., Het Rotterdams Garantieformulier, NJB 1987, p. 656-659

Hardenberg L., De nakomingsgarantie na veertig jaar rechtspraak, WPNR 1995, p. 842-847

Harfield H., The increasing domestic use of the letter of credit, 4 U.C.C. L.J., p. 251 (1972)

Harfield H., The standby letter of credit debate, Banking L.J. 1977, p. 293-303

Harfield H., Enjoining letters of credit transactions, Banking L.J. 1978, p. 596-615

Harfield H., Guaranties, Standby Letters of credit, and Ugly Ducklings, 26 U.C.C. L.J. 1994, p. 195-203

Hasse A., Die einheitlichen Richtlinien für auf Anfordern zahlbare Garantien der Internationalen Handelskammer, WM 1993, p. 1985-1993.

Heinsius Th., Zur Frage des Nachweises der rechtsmissbräuchlichen Inanspruchnahme einer Bankgarantie auf ertes Anfordern mit liquiden Beweismitteln, in Festschrift für Werner, 1984, p. 229-250

Heinsius Th., Bürgschaft auf erstes Anfordern, Festschrift F. Merz, p. 177-196

Heldrich A., Kollisionsrechtliche Aspekte des Missbrauchs von Bankgarantien, in Festschrift für Gerhard Kegel, 1987, p. 175-195

Herbots H.J., Een Antwerpse borgbrief is geen borgtocht, RW 1983-1984, p. 1183-1193

Horn N. and Wymeersch E., Bank-Guarantees, Standby Letters of Credit, And Performance Bonds in International Trade, in The Law of International Trade Finance, p. 455-529, Deventer 1989 (cited: Horn and Wymeersch)

Horn N., Bürgschaften und Garantien zur Zahlung auf erstes Anfordern, NJW 1980, p. 2153-2158

Jedzig J., Aktuelle Rechtsfragen der Bankgarantie auf erstes Anfordern, WM 1988, p. 1469-1474

Jeffery, Steven P., Standby Letters of Credit and the Fraud Exception, [2002] 18 BFLR , p. 69-109

Käser J., Garantieversprechen als Sicherheit im Handelsverkehr, RabelsZ. 1971, p. 601-631

Katskee M.R., Standby letter of credit debate - the case for congressional resolution , Banking L.J. 1975, p. 697-714

Kimball G. and Sanders B.A., Preventing Wrongful Payment of Guaranty Letters of Credit - Lessons from Iran, Business Lawyer 1984, p. 417-440

Kozolchyk B., The Emerging Law of Standby Letters of Credit and Bank Guarantees, Arizona L.R. 1982, p. 319-369

Kozolchyk B., Bank guarantees and letters of credit: time for a return to the fold, 1989 Univ. Pennsylv. Jo. Intern. Business Law, p. 7-70

Krimm J.J., U.C.C. - Letters of Credit and 'Fraud In The Transaction', Tulane L.R. 1986, p. 1088-1103

Kröll, S, Rechtsfragen elektronischer Bankgarantien, WM 2001, p. 1553-1560

Kröll Stefan, Electronic Bank Guarantees and Stand-by Letters of Credit, in 'Legal Issues in Electronic Banking', Studies in Transnational Economic Law, vol. 17, 2002, p. 287-305

Kronfol Z.A., Legal Theory and Practice of guarantee bonds in the Arabian Gulf, ICLR 1984, p. 218-240

Kronfol Z.A., The Syndication of Risk in Unconditional Bonds, JBL 1984, p. 13-20

Lawson M., Performance Bonds - Irrevocable Obligations, JBL 1987, p. 259-268

Lier H. van, Les garanties dites 'à première demande' ou abstraites, JT 1980, p. 345-357

Lienesch, Irmtraud, Rechtsmissbrauch und einstweiliger Rechtsschutz im internationalen Garantiegeschäft, DZWIR 2000, p. 492-501

Lipton J., Uniform regulation of standby letters of credit and other first demand security instruments in international transactions, JIBL 1993, p. 402-409

Looyens, Michel, Toepasselijke wet(ten) bij grensoverschrijdende borgtocht- en garantieovereenkomsten, TBH 1996, p. 867-882

MacDonald G.P., Construction Guarantees in Saudi Arabia, IFLR July 1982, p. 22-25

Mankowski, Peter, annotation LG Kleve June 15 1998, EWIR, 1998, p. 831-832

Marschall W. Graf von, Bankgarantien, Bonds und Standby Letters of Credit als Sicherheiten im Aussenhandel, in Kolloquium aus Anlass des 75 Geburtstages von Ernst von Caemmerer 1983, p. 66-73

Martin C. and Delierneux M., Les nouvelles Regles uniformes de la C.C.I. relatives aux garanties sur demande, RDC 1993, p. 288-328

Matray L., L'Arbitrage et le problème des garanties contractuelles, Rev. Banque 1974, p. 280-288

MvLaughlin Gerald T., Exploring Boundaries: A Legal and Structural Analysis of the Independence Principle of Letter of credit Law, [2002] 119 BLJ p. 501-565

Mettenheim H. von, Die missbräuchliche Inanspruchnahme bedingungsloser Bankgarantien, RIW 1981, p. 581-588

Mijnssen, F.H.J., Documentair Krediet, in Betalingsverkeer, p.64-78, Zwolle 1987

Mijnssen, F.H.J., De Bankgarantie, Preadviezen van de Vereeniging 'Handelsrecht', 1984

Moatti L., La garantie bancaire à première demande dans les opérations de commerce international, Journal des Notaires et des Avocats, 1989, p. 649-604

Molenaar F., Rapport Général, Traveaux de l'Association Henri Capitant, La responsabilité de banquier: aspects nouveaux, p. 217-228

Moschner M., Bemerkungen zur Gestaltung von Bankgarantien, O. Bank-Archiv 1983, p. 128-144

Mühl O., Materiellrechtliche und verfahrensrechtliche Fragen bei der Bankgarantie Zahlung auf erstes Anfordern, in Festschrift Imre Zajtay, p. 389-407

Nada Nassar Chaoul, La garantie Bancaire en Droit Libanais, Proche-Orient études juridiques 1984-1985, p. 107-179

Nielsen J., Ausgestaltung internationaler Bankgarantien unter dem Gesichtspunkt etwaigen Rechtsmissbrauchs, ZHR 1983, p. 145-161

Nielsen J., Rechtsmissbrauch bei der Inanspruchnahme von Bankgarantien als typisches Problem der Liquiditätsfunktion abstrakter Zahlungsverscprechen, ZIP 1982, p. 253-266

Nielsen J., Internationale Bankgarantie, Akkreditiv und anglo-amerikanisches Standby nach Inkrafttreten der ISP 98, WM 1999, p. 2005-2020, 2049-2063

Note, Recent extensions in the use of commercial letters of credit, 66 Yale L.J., p. 902-917 (1957)

Note: 'Fraud In The Transaction': Enjoining Letters Of Credit During The Iranian Revolution, HLR 1980, p. 992-1015

Note: Letters of Credit: Injunction As A Remedy For Fraud In UCC Section 5-114, Minn. Law Review 1979, p. 487-516

O'Driscoll P.S., Performance Bonds, Banker's Guarantees, and the Mareva Injunction, Northwestern Journal of Int. Law & Business 1985, p. 381-412

Orden Gnichtel W. van, The Intricacies of Performance Guarantees in Saudi Arabia, Banking L.J. 1983, p. 354-363

Pabbruwe H.J., De betekenis van de onafhankelijke bankgarantie, inaugurale rede, Deventer 1984

Pabbruwe H.J., Een Bijzondere Bankgarantie, WPNR 1979, p. 181-185

Pabbruwe H.J., Overdracht van de Rechten uit Abstrakte Bankgaranties, WPNR 1983, p. 429-432

Pabbruwe H.J., Uniforme regels voor bankgaranties van de Internationale Kamer van Koophandel, WPNR 1993, p. 921-925

Pabbruwe H.J., Nogmaals: overdracht van de rechten uit een abstracte bankgarantie, WPNR 1995, p. 605-606

Pelichet M., Garanties bancaires et conflits de lois, RDAI 1990, p. 335-356

Penn G., On-demand Bonds - Primary or secondary Obligations? JIBL 1986, p. 224-230

Pilger G., Einstweiliger Rechtsschutz des Käufers und Akkreditivstellers wegen Gewährleistung durch Arrest in den Auszahlungsanspruch des Akkreditivbegünstigten? RIW 1979, p. 588-590

Pleyer K., National report (Federal Republic of Germany), in Colloque de Tours, p. 185-196

Pleyer K., Die Bankgarantie im zwischenstaatlichen Handel, WM Sonderbeilage Nr. 2/1973, July 7 1973

Poullet Y., Présentation et définition des garanties pratiquées en Europe, in Colloque de Tours, p. 13-47

Poullet Y., Les garanties contractuelles dans le commerce international, DPCI 1979, p. 387-442

Poullet Y., Le contrat de garantie, examen de quelques problèmes juridiques particuliers, in Colloque de Tours, p. 127-142

Poullet Y., La garantie bancaire automatique: présentation de quelques décisions récentes, JCB 1982, p. 645-662

Poullet Y., La saisie arrêt par le donneur d'ordre de la créance née d'un crédit documentaire ou d'une garantie à première demande, Banca Borsa 1984, p. 47-79

Poullet Y., La jurisprudence récente en matière de garantie bancaire dans les contrats internationaux, Banca Borsa 1982, p. 397-440

Prüm A., Application de l'adage 'fraus omnia corrumpit' à propos des garanties à première demande, DPCI 1987, p. 121-127

Pugh-Thomas, Anthony, Letters of Credit-Injunctions-The Purist and the Pragmatist: Can a Buyer Bypass the Guarantor and Stop the Seller from Demanding Payment from the Guarantor?, [1996] 5 JIBL p. 210-213

Quickenborne Van, Marc, Ondoeltreffende subrogatie en verval van borgtocht, TvP 1996, p. 361-

Ransbeeck Van, R, De borgtocht op eerste verzoek. Een geldige rechtsfiguur?, TBBR 1998, p. 173-194

Reed P.C., A Reconsideration of American Bell International Inc. v. Islamic Republic of Iran, Columbia Journal Transnational Law 1981, p. 301-332

Rives-Lange J.L., Rapport Francais, in Travaux de l'Association Henri Capitant, La responsabilité du banquier: aspects nouveaux, 1984, p. 301-318

Rives-Lange J.L., Chronique de jurisprudence bancaire, Banque 1986, p. 711-713

Robinson J.M., Choice of security in construction contracts, IFLR September 1982, p. 33-37

Romain J.F., Principes d'interprétation et de qualification des garanties indépendantes 'à première demande', RGDC 1989, p. 429-448

Rosenblith R.M., What Happens When Operations Go Wrong: Enjoining the Letter-of-Credit Transaction and Other Legal Stratagems, UCC LJ 1985, p. 307-342

Rümker D., Garantie 'auf erstes Anfordern' und Aufrechnungsbefugnis der Garantiebank, ZGR 1986, p. 332-344

Schoordijk H.C.F., Bespreking inaugurale rede H.J. Pabbruwe, RMThemis 1985, p. 387-391

Schmidt, Jörg, Die Effektivklausel in der Bürgschaft auf ertses Anfordern, WM 1999, p. 308-313

Schütze R.A., Einstweilige Verfügungen und Arreste im internationalen Rechtsverkehr, insbesondere im Zusammenhang mit der Inanspruchnahme von Bankgarantien, WM 1980, p. 1438-1442

Schütze R.A., Zur Nichtrückgabe von Garantieurkunden nach Erlöschen der Garantieverplichtung, WM 1982, p. 1398-1402

Schütze R.A., Zur Geltendmachung einer Bankgarantie 'auf erstes Anfordern', RIW 1981, p. 83-85

Seung Chong W., The Abusive Calling of Performance Bonds, JBL 1990, p. 414-427

Simont L., Les garanties indépendantes, Rev. Banque 1983, p. 579-611

Simont L., De abstracte verbintenissen van de bankier naar Belgisch recht, TPR 1985, p. 691-711

Simont L., Misbruik bij Dokumentair Krediet, TPR 1986, p. 71-102

Simont L. and Bruyneel A., Chronique de droit bancaire privé; Les opérations de banque: garanties indépendantes (1979-1988), Rev. Banque 1989, p. 519-531

Sion G., La garantie bancaire internationale et les enseignements du droit américain, Rev. Banque 1984, p. 5-26

Stern M., The Independence Rule in Standby Letters of Credit, University Chicago L.R. 1985, p. 218-246

Stoufflet J., La garantie bancaire à première demande, JDI 1987, p. 265-287

Stoufflet, J., Fraud in documentary credit, letter of credit and demand guaranty, Dickinson Law Review, 2001, p. 21-28

Stumpf H. and Ullrich C., Die missbräuchliche Inanspruchnahme von Bankgarantien im internationalen Geschäftsverkehr, RIW 1984, p. 843-845

Symons E.L., Letters of Credit: Fraud, Good faith and the Basis for Injunctive Relief, Tulane L.R. 1980, p. 338-381

Task Force on the Study of U.C.C. Article 5, An Examination of U.C.C. Article 5 (Letters of Credit), The Business Lawyer, vol. 45, June 1990, p. 1521-1643

Thorup A.R., Injunctions against Payment of Standby Letters of Credit: How Can Banks Best Protect themselves?, Banking L.J. 1984, p. 6-30

Tiedtke K., Kurzkommentar BGH 12.3.1992, EWiR 1992, p. 865-866

Trost U. Der Aufwendungsersatzanspruch der Garantiebank bei Garantien 'auf erstes Anfordern', ZIP 1981, p. 1307-1308

Trost U., Problemlösung beim Bankgarantiegeschäft durch Umstrukturierung des Geschäftstypus?, RIW 1981, p. 659-663

UNCITRAL, Report of the Secretary General, Stand-by Letters of Credit and Guarantees, JIBFL 1988, p. 458-461, 508-513

Vasseur M., Rapport de synthèse, in Colloque de Tours, p. 319-364

Vasseur M., Dix ans de jurisprudence francaises relative aux garanties independantes, présentation des projets de la C.C.I. et de la C.N.U.D.C.I., RDAI 1990, p. 357-392

Vasseur M., Les nouvelles Regles de la Chambre de Commerce internationale pour les 'guaranties sur demande', RDAI 1992, p. 239-294

Vasseur M., Les conséquences de règlement communautaire du 7 décembre 1992 sur les garanties indépendantes consenties á l'Irak avant la crise du Golfe, D. 1995 Chronique p. 43-45

Velu S., National report (Belgium), in Colloque de Tours, p. 211-249

Verkuil P.R., Bank solvency and guaranty letters of credit, 25 Stanf. L. Rev. p. 716 (1973)

Verner J.L., 'Fraud in the Transaction': Intraworld Comes of Age in Itek, Memphis State University L.R. 1984, p. 153-187

Villerey A., National report (France), in Colloque de Tours, p. 259-278

Vroede de, and Flamee, De Garantie op eerste Verzoek, TPR 1982, p. 365-386

Vuyst B.M. de, Het documentair krediet als loutere waarborg: de standby letter of credit, TPR 1984, p. 1017-1038

Ward Allan and Gerry McCormack, A New Applicationfor the Doctrine of Subrogation?, [1999] J.I.B.L., p. 39-44

Weisz G. and Blackman J.I., Standby Letters of Credit After Iran: Remedies of the Account Party, University Illinois L.R. 1982. p. 355-384

Westphalen F., Ausgewählte Fragen zur Interpretation der Einheitlichen Richtlinien für auf Anfordern zahlbare Garantien, RIW 1992, p. 961-965

Westphalen F., Die neuen einheitlichen Richtlinien für 'Demand Guarantees', DB 1992, p. 2017-2021

Wheble B.S., 'Problem Children' - Standby Letters of Credit and Simple First Demand Guarantees, Arizona L.R. 1982, p. 301-317

Williams K., On demand and conditional performance bonds, JBL 1981, p. 8-16

Wiley, How to use letters of credit in financing the sale of goods, 20 Bus. Law. p. 495 (1965)

Wymeersch E., Garanties op eerste verzoek, TPR 1986, p. 471-503

Wymeersch E., Bank Guarantees on First Demand under Belgian Law, in Hague-Zagreb Essays 6, p. 91-116, Dordrecht 1987

Wymeersch/Dambre/Troch, Overzicht van rechtspraak privaat bankrecht 1992-1998, TvP 1999, p. 1779, 1835-1842.

Wymeersch E. and Horn, see Horn and Wymeersch

Zahn J., Auswirkungen eines politischen Umsturzes auf schwebende Akkreditive und Bankgarantien, die zugunsten von staatlichen Stellen oder in deren Auftrag eröffnet sind, ZIP 1984, p. 1303-1313

Zimmett M.P., Standby Letters of Credit in the Iran Litigation: Two Hundred Problems in Search of a Solution, Law & Policy Int. Business 1984, p. 927-962

INDEX

(The table of contents serves a similar purpose; the figures refer to the margin numbers)

Abstraktes Schuldversprechen	5-1
Abuse (s. Fraud)	
Accessory guarantee (s. Suretyship)	
Account party	2-3,2-4,2-5,9-1
Advance payment guarantee (s. Repayment guarantee)	
Advance payment	3-5,8-11,13-20,14-52,19-1
Advising bank	2-5,9-2,13-6
'After-payment' cases	15-2,16-13
Agent/Agency	13-5
Allocation of risks	2-2,4-4,6-1,6-2,7-1,14-18,16-2
Amendments to secured contract	8-19
Amendments to guarantee	10-12,12-14,12-73
Anweisung	5-1
Amount (maximum)	8-17,241
— reduction (s. Reduction clause)	
— increase	8-18
Applicable law	8-25,16-12,18-5/10
Assignment	8-22,12-67/72,13-5
Authority (lack of)	12-12,13-6,14-22
Autonomous guarantee	3-11
Avoidance of secured contract (s. Termination)	
Back-to-back guarantee	2-11,12-76
Bank	7-1/4
— as beneficiary	8-6,8-16
— (credit) risk	7-1,7-4,10-4
— discretion	47,10-24/26,119
— duty to advise account party	10-16,11-7
— duty of care	10-4,10-14,10-24/26
— duty of examination	10-18/27,11-21/23
— - by second issuing bank	11-7,11-9,11-13,11-20
— duty to inform beneficiary of non-compliance	13-31
— duty to defer payment	16-24

— duty of prior notification of demand for payment	10-28/31
— duty to refuse payment, non-compliance	10-18,13-2
— duty to refuse payment, fraud	15-1,15-5
— and fraud	15-1/7
— reasonable care	10-24/26
Bank charges (s. Commission)	
Bank guarantee	
— and accessory guarantee (s. Suretyship)	
— and autonomous guarantee	3-11
— consensual contract	12-8/9
— and documentary credit	1-1,5-3,14-55
— and domestic market	1-1,2-14,5-4
— as financing instrument	2-2,3-4/5,6-9,19-1
— and independence	1-1,2-1, 12-1/7
— and international trade	1-1,1-7,5-2
— legal nature	5-1/4
— meaning	1-2,5-1,12-1
— as multi-party relationship	2-3,12-5
— payable on arbitral/court decision	4-13/16,6-1,13-16/17
— payable on first demand	1-1,4-2/8,13-11/13a
— payable on third party documents	4-9/12,6-1,13-14/15
— simple demand	4-3,13-11
— state regulations	2-17,6-5
— statement of default	4-3/3a,13-12
— and suretyship (s. Suretyship)	
— terminology (s. meaning)	
— unilateral engagement	12-8/9
'Before-payment' cases	15-2
Beneficiary	2-1,2-3/4,6-18-4,13-5
Bonds (s. Performance bonds)	
Call on the guarantee (s. Demand for payment)	
Cash deposit	4-6
Causa	5-1,12-6
Cause of action and restraining orders	16-3/9
Choice of law	8-25,11-29,18-6,18-9
Clauses in the (counter-)guarantee	
— and bank	7-3
— counter-guarantee	11-26/30
— documentary nature	2-14,4-1,7-3,8-1
— guarantee	8-1/15
Commencement date	8-14,12-13,23913-25
Commission	10-9,12-60/65

Index 551

Completion of secured contract	14-26/33
Compliance with conditions of payment	10-18/27,13-2
— by beneficiary	10-18,13-2
— and counter-guarantee	13-37
— and examination by bank	10-18/27,13-2
— inconsistencies	10-23
— non-compliance (s. Non-compliance)	
— and primary guarantee	11-3,11-7
— and verification by instructing bank	11-21/25
— (s. also Strict/Formal compliance)	
Conclusive evidence clause	4-3,4-5,4-20,12-22
Conditional guarantee	1-2,4-9
Conditions of payment	4-1/20
— compliance (s. Strict/Formal compliance)	
— documentary nature	2-14,4-1,7-3,8-1
— examination by bank (s. Bank)	
— payment on arbitral or court decision	4-13/16,13-16/17
— payment on first demand	4-2/8,13-11/13a
— payment on third-party documents	4-9/12,13-14/15
Condition precedent	
— and principal contract	6-8,14-24/25
— term of guarantee	8-7/10,12-13
— and fraud	14-24/25
Confirmed guarantee	2-8
Conservatory attachment	17-1/8
— after payment	17-6
— counterclaim	17-4/5
— established fraud	17-3
— incompatibility	17-2
— indirect guarantee	17-7
— judicial guarantee	3-9
— set-off	17-4/5
Consideration	8-5,12-11
Construction contracts and guarantees	19-1/5
Construction of the guarantee	12-16/37a
— counter-guarantee	12-37a
— first demand guarantee	4-5,12-34
— independent guarantee or suretyship	12-16/36
— suretyship	112-31,12-36
— terms of independent guarantee	12-37
Costs (of litigation)	1010-10/11
Counter-claim	
— by account party against beneficiary	13-35,17-4/5

— by bank against beneficiary 13-33/35
— conservatory attachment 17-4/5
— and fraud 14-49
— by instructing bank against issuing bank 13-36
Counter-guarantee (indirect guarantee) 11-8/20
— amount 11-28
— applicable law 18-9
— clauses 11-26/30
— compliance with terms and conditions 13-37/40
— demand for payment 13-37/40
— 'extend or pay' 12-44/45,13-39
— garnishment clause 11-30
— independence 11-9/20
— independence from primary guarantee 11-9/20
— independence from secured contract 11-12
— legal nature 11-9/20
— and mandate between instructing and issuing bank 11-11,11-13
— payable on first demand 11-13,11-20
— restraining order 16-11/18
— valid until discharge (s. Validity period)
— validity period 11-27,13-39
Counter-guarantee from account party 10-5/6
Counter-guarantee from parent company 2-9,10-6
Currency 8-17,11-28,13-28,13-41
Customs guarantees 3-8

Damages for late payment 13-30
Demand for payment
— addressee 13-6
— amount 13-24,13-27
— arbitral or court decision 13-16/17
— bank's defences
— from contract of guarantee 13-32
— fraud 15-1
— from mandate 12-1,9-5,12-2
— from secured contract 2-1,12-2
— set-off 13-33/36
— call 13-4/8
— by agent 13-5
— by assignee 12-69/70,13-5
— by beneficiary 13-5
— by legal successor 13-5
— formal requirements 13-7

Index

— compliance with terms and conditions (s. Compliance)	
— counter-guarantee	13-37/41
— currency	13-28,13-41
— damages for late payment	13-30
— examination by the bank (s. Bank)	
— expiry	13-22/26
— first demand guarantee	13-11/13a
— inconsistencies	10-23
— interest for late payment	13-30
— must relate to secured contract	13-9/10
— period of examination	13-29
— place	13-6
— procedures on non-compliance	13-31
— set-off	13-33/36
— statement of default	13-12
— third party documents	13-14/15
— time of payment	13-29
— validity period	13-22/26
Direct guarantee	2-4,6-6,9-1
Discharge (statement of)	12-54,12-58,12-64/65
— counter-guarantee	12-58/59,12-64/65
— liability account party	12-66
— (s. also Validity period)	
Documentary credit	1-1,3-7,5-3,14-55
Documents	
— examination by bank	2-14,7-3,10-18/27,13-2
— tendered by account party	4-11,13-15
— tendered by beneficiary	4-10,12-22,13-12
Domestic (first demand) guarantee	1-1,2-15,5-4,12-26,12-28
Down payment (s. Advance payment)	
Drafting	7-3,8-2/3,12-21
Effektivklauseln	4-8,10-19,10-26,12-21,13-13
Embargoes	13-42,14-41
Expiry date (s. Validity period)	
Expiry event (s. Validity period)	
Export credit insurance	7-4
'Extend or pay'	8-12,11-27,12-38,12-40/45,13-24
'Extend or withdraw'	12-42
Extension clause	8-13,11-27,12-39
Extension validity period (s. Validity period)	
First bank (s. Instructing bank)	

First demand guarantee	1-1,4-2/8,13-11/13a
— allocation of risks	4-4,6-1/4,6-9,14-18,16-2
— creation of international trade	1-1,1-7,5-2
— as financing instrument (s. Bank guarantee)	
— first demand suretyship	4-18/19
— and general terms and conditions	12-15a
— origins	1-1,4-6
— payable on simple demand	4-3,13-11
— payable on statement of default	4-3/3a,13-12
First justified demand	4-7,12-33,13-13
Force majeure	14-39/43
Formal compliance	2-14,10-20,13-2
Formation of the guarantee	12-8/15a
Fraud	14-1/56
— applicable law	16-12
— bank's duty to refuse payment	15-1/6
— bank's position and liability	15-1/6
— instructing bank's position and liability	15-6
— Belgium	14-11/12
— comparative overview	14-17
— counter-guarantee	16-11/18
— documentary credit	14-55
— England	14-13
— evidence to be adduced by account party	14-19,15-2,16-3
— evidence	14-17,14-19
— France	14-9/10
— Germany	14-7/8
— hardship	16-22
— independence	1-2,2-1/2,12-1/7,14-17/18
— Netherlands	14-5/6
— restraining orders (s. Fraud and restraining orders)	
— summary judgment	14-56
— Uncitral Convention	14-17,14-38,16-8a
— United States of America	14-14/16
Fraud and conservatory attachment	17-8
Fraud and freezing (Mareva) injunction	17-9
Fraud and restraining orders	16-1/24
— against bank, direct guarantee	16-3/10
— against bank(s), indirect guarantee	16-11/20
— against beneficiary, direct guarantee	16-2
— against beneficiary, indirect guarantee	16-11,16-17
— applicable law, indirect guarantee	16-12
— bank's duty to defer payment	16-24

Index 555

— bank's knowledge of fraud, direct guarantee 15-1/3,16-3/8a
— bank's knowledge of fraud, indirect guarantee 15-5,16-13/15
— Belgium 16-7
— cause of action against bank 16-3/9
— collusion 16-13/14
— commercial viability of guarantees 16-21
— England 16-4
— France 16-7
— Germany 16-5
— hardship 16-22
— identification 16-15
— jurisdiction, indirect guarantee 16-11,16-18
— Netherlands 16-6
— non-recognition 16-19
— reputation of the bank 16-23
— restraining orders against bank permissible? 16-3/9
— Uncitral Convention 16-8a
— United States 16-8
Fraud and summary proceedings 14-56
Fraud and (possible) types of fraud 14-21/54
Fraudulent trading in bank guarantees 12-77
Freezing orders 17-9
Functions of (first demand) bank guarantee 10-12,60-61

Garantievertrag 3-11,5-1,12-6
Garnishment clauses 11-30
General terms and conditions and first demand guarantee (or suretyship) 12-15a
Grace Period 4-3,8-20/1

'Hold for value' 12-46/48,13-24

ICC 2-13
Identification 16-15
Illegality 14-44
Incidental expenses and costs 10-10/11
Inconsistencies 10-23
Independence 1-2,2-1,12-1/7
— and bank 2-2,7-2
— and conditions of payment 2-1,4-1
— counter-guarantee (s. Counter-guarantee)
— fraud 2-1,14-17,14-18
— from mandate 2-1,9-5,12-3
— parties to secured contract 6-1/2,12-5

Independent guarantee (s. Bank guarantee)	
Indirect guarantee	2-6,6-6,9-3,11-1/30
— disadvantages for account party	6-6
— advantages for beneficiary	6-6
Injunctions (s. Fraud and restraining orders)	
Instructing bank	2-6,9-3,11-1/2
Instructions to the bank	
— acceptance/refusal	10-17
— direct guarantee	10-4,10-12/17
— imprecise/incomplete	10-15
— indirect guarantee	10-13,11-2,11-4/6
— strict compliance	10-12,11-4
— from third party	2-9,10-6
Interdependence	2-3,12-5
Interest	8-21,12-48,13-27,13-30
Interlocutory restraining orders (s. Fraud and restraining orders)	
Interpretation (s. Construction)	
Irrevocability	12-9,12-14
ISP98	2-13/14
Issuance of the guarantee	12-8,12-13
Issuers of guarantees	
— banks	1-5
— Germany	12-15a
— other financial institutions	1-5
— parent companies	1-5,12-15
— private individuals	1-5,12-15,12-28
Judicial guarantee	3-9
Jurisdiction	8-25,11-29,18-1/4
— restraining orders	16-11,16-17/20
Lease contracts	12-73
Letter of commitment	3-2,10-17
Letter of credit (s. Documentary credit)	
Liquidity function	2-2,13-33,14-18/19,14-55/56,17-2
Maintenance guarantee	3-4
Mandate	
— direct guarantee	10-2
— indirect guarantee	9-3,11-2
Mandatory law (s. Public mandatory law)	
Mareva injunction	17-9
Maximum amount	8-17,11-28,13-27

Index

— reduction	8-18,13-21
— increase	8-18
Misrepresentation	14-23
Mistake	12-55,14-23
National law and regulations	2-17,6-6,10-12
Negotiations	6-5/9
Non-compliance	
— with conditions of payment	10-18,13-2,13-31
— bank's duty to inform beneficiary	13-31
— restraining orders	13-43
Non-documentary conditions of payment	2-14,10-26
Notice of dishonour/refusal of payment	13-31
Offer and acceptance	12-8/11
OHADA	2-17
Operative instrument	12-12
'Pay first, argue later'	6-2,14-18/20,16-2,16-21
'Pay or extend' (s. 'Extend or pay')	
Payment guarantee	3-7
— and documentary credit	3-7
— and standby letter of credit	3-7
Payment mechanism (see Conditions of payment)	
Performance bond	1-2
Performance guarantee	3-3
Period for examination of compliance	13-29
'Perpetual' guarantees	12-38
Pledge	8-22,1274
Power of attorney	12-71,13-5
Preclusion rule	13-31
Primary guarantee	2-6,11-1
Private individuals as guarantors	1-5,12-15,12-28
Private international law (s. Applicable law)	
Public mandatory law	18-10
Public order	14-44
Rate of exchange	13-41
Recognition of foreign judgments	16-19
Recovery after payment	6-3,13-44
Reduction (clause)	8-18,11-26,13-21,14-52
Reference to the secured contract	
— and construction	12-23,12-37

557

558   *Index*

— and text of the guarantee   8-4
Reimbursement
— by account party   2-4,7-1,10-4
— by instructing bank   11-2/3
Repayment guarantee   3-5,14-52
Reputation of the bank   6-1,16-23
Restraining orders (s. Fraud and restraining orders)
Retention guarantee   3-6
Return of the guarantee document   8-15,12-54/57
Risk (evaluation)   1-1,4-4,6-4,10-11,10-32,16-20

SAMA   2-17
Second bank (s. Issuing bank)
Security for reimbursement   2-9,7-4,10-7,11-3
— release of security   12-60/64
Set-off
— account party and beneficiary   13-35,14-49,17-4/5
— by bank   8-23,13-33/36
— conservatory attachment   17-4/5
— and fraud   14-49
Simple demand guarantee   4-3,13-11
Standby letter of credit   1-3/4
— and UCP,URDG,UCC   2-15,3-7
— and Uncitral Convention   2-12
— as counter-guarantee   2-7,9-4
— as independent guarantee   1-1,1-4,3-7
— as payment guarantee   3-7
Statement of default   4-3/3a,10-19/20,12-22,13-12, 13-23
Statute of limitation   12-50
Stop-payment orders (s. Fraud and restraining orders)
Strict compliance   10-21/22,13-2,13-12,13-14
Subguarantee   19-4
Subrogation   10-33,13-31
Summary proceedings   13-32,14-56
Suretyship
— distinguished from independent guararantee   1-2,4-1,5-3
— on first demand   4-17/19,12-35
Syndicated guarantee   2-10

Tender guarantee   3-2,14-51
Termination of secured contract   14-45
Terminology   3-4
Time of payment   8-21,13-29

Index 559

Transfer of guarantee	8-22,12-75/76
Transfer of lease	12-73
Transfer of secured contract	12-73
U.C.C. Article 5 (1995)	2-16,14-14/16,16-8
UCP (ICC)	2-15
U.N. embargoes	13-44
Uncitral Convention	2-12
URCB 1993 (ICC)	2-16
URCG 1978 (ICC)	2-13
URDG 1992 (ICC)	2-13/15
Validity period and expiry date	8-11/16,12-38/53,13-22/26,13-39
— absence of expiry date	8-16
— applicable law	13-22
— clauses	8-12/13,11-27
— commencement date	8-14,13-25
— and commission charges	12-60,12-65
— compliance, counter-guarantee	13-39
— compliance, guarantee	13-22/24,13-26
— condition of payment	13-22/23
— counter-guarantee	11-27,13-39
— enforceable/ not enforceable	12-49/53
— expiry event	8-12,13-26
— 'extend or pay' (s. 'Extend or pay')	
— extension clause	8-13,12-39
— non-business day	13-22
— and secured contract	13-23
— release of security	12-60/65
— statute of limitation	12-50
— submission of documents	13-23/24

Warranty guarantee (s. Maintenance guarantee)

ABOUT THIS BOOK AND ITS AUTHOR

At present, major, especially crossborder, transactions do not take off without some kind of guarantee support, while the frequency in smaller deals depends on a number of factors. Bank guarantees are increasingly used in domestic contracts too. In this book the term 'bank guarantee' means the independent (first demand) guarantee, including the American standby letter of credit, as opposed to the traditional accessory guarantee or suretyship. Several factors have contributed to their growth. One reason is that bank guarantees can be employed to back up all kinds of transactions, both non-financial, such as contracts of sale, leases and construction contracts, and financial transactions, such as loans and overdraft facilities, participation in joint ventures, bond issues and other financial commitments. Accordingly, a bank guarantee could serve as a security device for both non-financial and financial obligations. A predominant factor is that in international trade especially, risk is becoming an aspect of increasing significance and concern. Transactions tend to grow bigger and investments in projects are becoming larger. A particular feature of trade today is its global expansion. As a result of their size and complexity the execution of many transactions often takes a considerable period of time and a wide range of events could impede completion. The element of risk is, however, no less important in smaller and short-term transactions, even in a domestic context. One particular type which has attracted the greatest attention and which is prevalent in many branches of trade and geographic regions is the bank guarantee 'payable on first demand'. These first demand guarantees represent a reallocation of risks, to the advantage of the creditor and to the detriment of the principal debtor, for whose account bank guarantees are issued and who bears the grave risks which attend their issuance. Bank guarantees have given rise to new and major difficulties, both legal and practical.

This book contains a comprehensive study of the legal and practical aspects of bank guarantees and standby letters of credit The table of contents provides an overview of the subjects which are examined. It is based on case law and legal writing from the Netherlands, Germany, France, Belgium and the United Kingdom. In order to ensure reliability, all case law in the area of guarantees as from 1977 has been reviewed on the basis of the original reports as cited. As far as the United States is concerned a major part of the prolific legal writing and case law has been taken into account. In addition, some Swiss, Austrian and ICC arbitral decisions have been included. Throughout this book the effect and significance of the 1992 Uniform Rules for Demand Guarantees (URDG) of the International Chamber of Commerce, the 1998 International Standby Practices (ISP98) and the 1995 UNCITRAL Convention on Independent Guarantees and Stand-by letters of credit are examined too. Considerable attention is also paid to the way guarantees function in actual practice and to the numerous practical aspects and issues to which they give rise. Since guarantees are nothing but a creation of practice in international trade and business the law must start from the grass roots. To this end intensive contacts over a number of years have been maintained with the banking community, construction firms and their organisations, and export credit insurance companies. Much energy has been spent on researching a huge number of files, which provided insight into 'the daily life' of the world of independent (first demand) guarantees and the practices, difficulties and peculiarities in a great number of countries and regions. Legal opinions from local lawyers and circular letters from foreign banks have especially been an invaluable source of information, which is particularly relevant in relation to countries in the Middle East and North Africa.

Since independent (first demand) guarantees and standby letters of credit are relatively recent phenomena and as they are born and bred in a crossborder setting, the law on this subject, as developed in and applied by national courts and as treated in legal writing in different jurisdictions, shows a remarkable degree of uniformity. This book has, therefore, been written on that basis and no particular system of national law has been taken as a point of reference. It can, therefore, and is used in both Civil Law and Common Law jurisdictions.

In 1972 Roeland F. Bertrams graduated from the Faculty of Law, State University of Utrecht. A Leverhulme fellowship enabled him to continue his studies at the University of London (London School of Economics), where he took an LL.M degree in 1973. In 1974 he obtained an LL.M degree from Harvard Law School, Cambridge Mass. In the period 1974-1978 Roeland F. Bertrams was an associate of an Amsterdam law firm and in 1978 he joined the Faculty of Law at the Free University, Amsterdam. In 1991 he also joined the Amsterdam office of Clifford Chance, solicitors, as senior associate, practicing banking and financial law, security interests and (international) insolvency, commercial and private international law. The author has published several books and many articles in these fields and he is a frequent speaker in seminars.